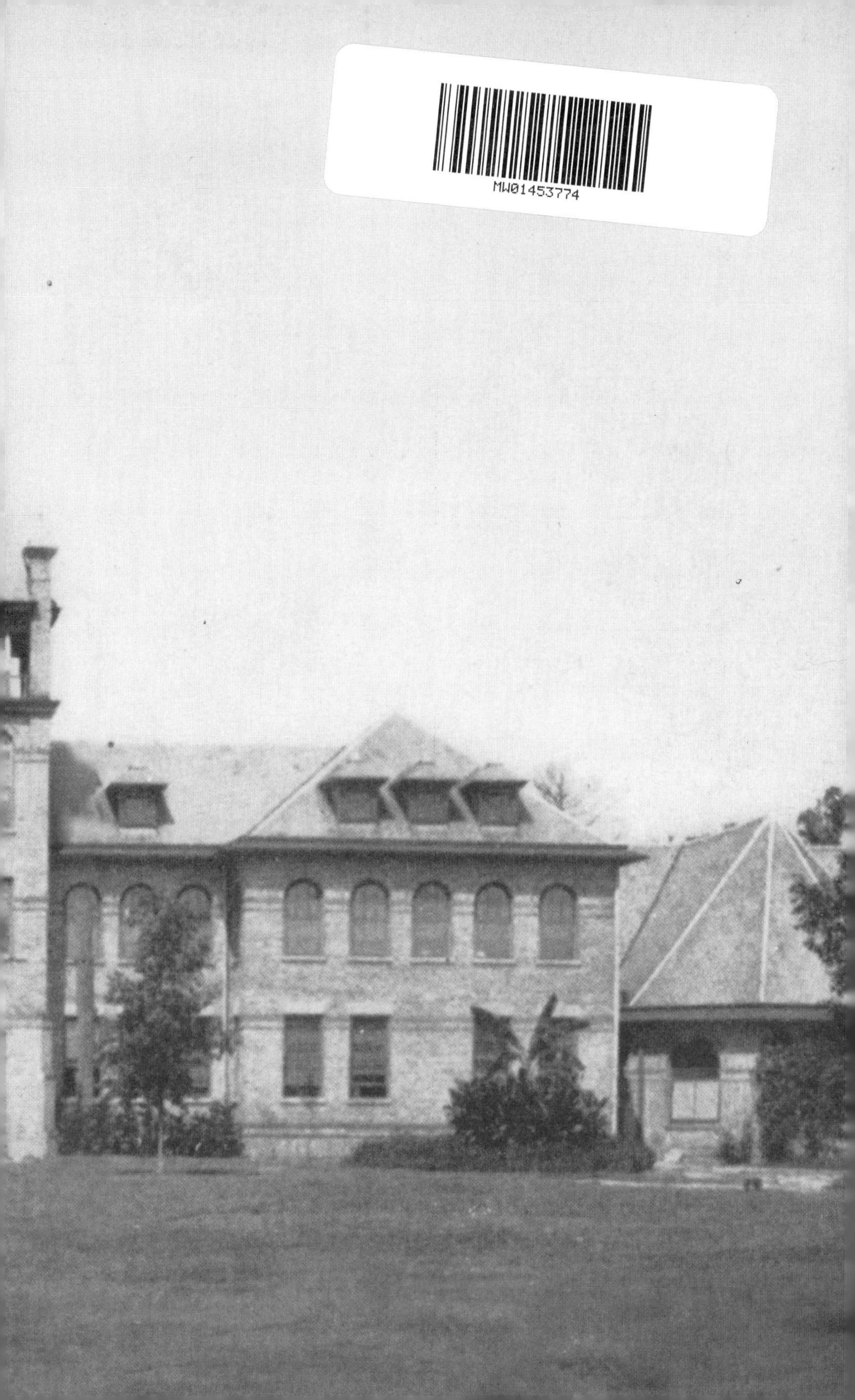

Barton College

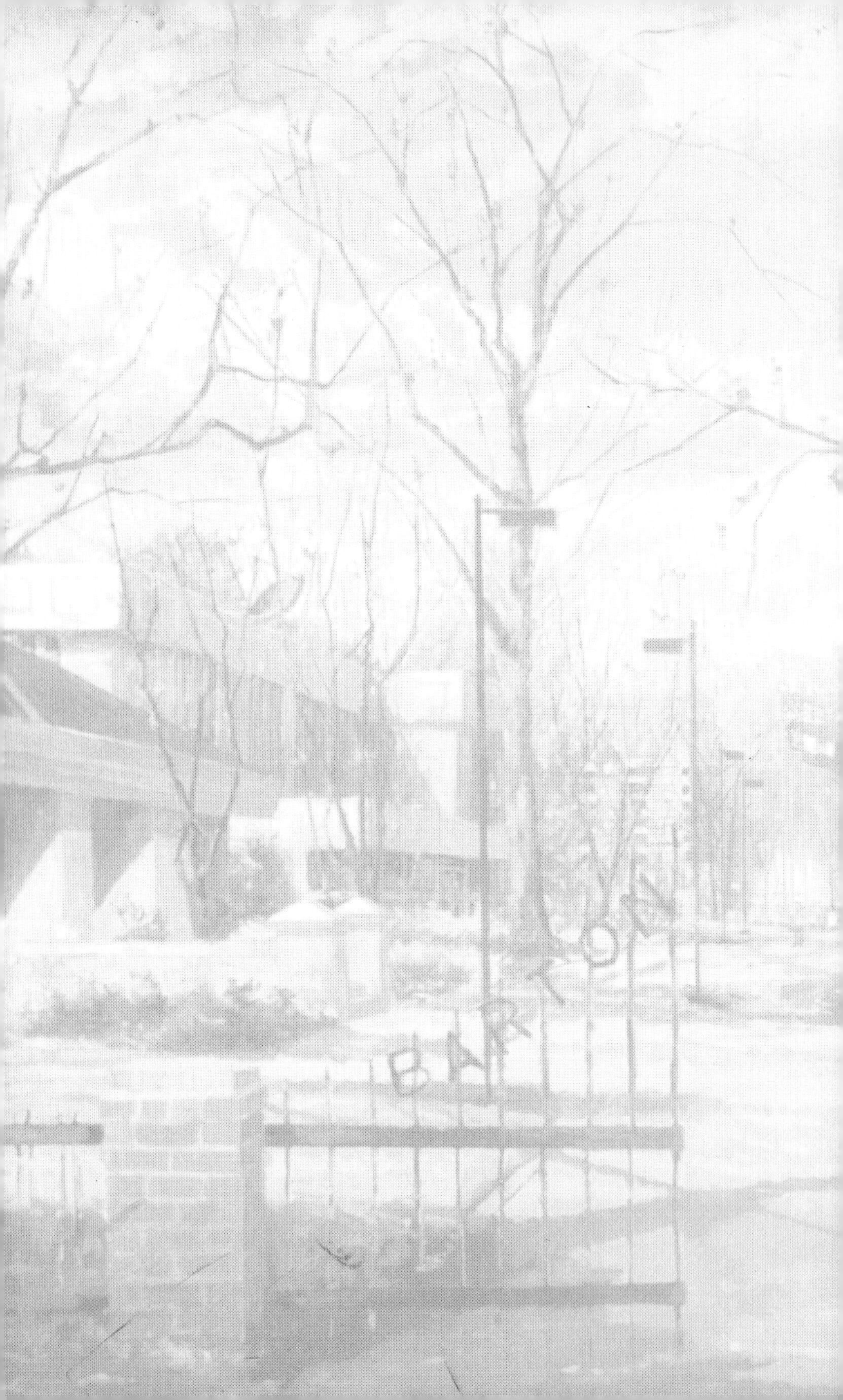

Barton College

Our Century

WILLIAM JERRY MACLEAN

Copyright © 2002 by Barton College
All rights reserved
The following artists have allowed the use of their work in this volume:
J. Keith Tew, J. Christian Wilson
Design and production by B. Williams & Associates
Manufactured in the United States of America
ISBN 0-9718842-0-X
Library of Congress Control Number 2002102843

*This centennial history is
dedicated to all who have ever loved
Atlantic Christian-Barton College
and to
Betty, Mark, Laura, and Ralph.*

Contents

Foreword ix

Preface xi

1 An Admirable Place for a College 1

2 The Father of Atlantic Christian College 17

3 A Bold Stand in Support of Academic Freedom 31

4 He Won't Let Us Dance but He Wants Us to Walk 45

5 Greet Us with Beauty and Fragrance When We Return in September 62

6 Here's to Next Year's Team 82

7 The Professor Who Cannot Walk Slow 103

8 The Very Sweetest Way I Ever Heard of Getting Through College 123

9 Some of Our Friends, Relatives, and Brothers May Be Leaving 145

10 The Dawn of a New Day 163

11 Come, and Trip It as Ye Go, On the Light Fantastic Toe 184

12 The Cotton Still Grows 205

13 A Display of Fire and Flower Power   226

14 At the Still Point of the Turning World   249

15 A Rich Lode in Our Own Backyard   272

16 An Elegant Presence on Stately West Nash Street   294

17 A Touch of Class for Barton   316

   Epilogue   335

   Appendices   339

   Notes   373

   Bibliography   409

   Index   414

Foreword

PRIVATE HIGHER EDUCATION, in all of its manifestations, underwent major change in the past century. Barton College marked streams of excellence during that one hundred years, serving students from eastern North Carolina in the beginning to a vastly more inclusive audience recently.

This work chronicles those years with anecdotal precision and global perspective. From the opening chapter through the epilogue, people's stories measure Barton's roses and thorns with a spicy accuracy that energizes the early years and grows full blown memories of more recent days.

Chronologically delineated, this second history of Barton (Atlantic Christian) speaks of the College's role in local, regional and world events. The two world wars, the great depression, Korea, Vietnam, gubernatorial races, racial strife, economic down turns, bull markets and bear markets all found some expression, reaction, influence on this small eastern North Carolina campus.

Students, faculty, and staff mirrored the social events of the century with sometimes eccentric, sometimes humorous, sometimes sad clarity. None escapes the microscopic and telescopic pen of the writer.

As the excitement of the Barton experience unfolds, the readers crawl into the very psyches of those characters who lived the history. Veterans returning as older, more experienced learners, rebels (both students and faculty) championing a cause, athletes, old and young, imaging the College in new ways, musicians, artists, scholars, all populate the landscape of our College's century. Each brings unique flavor, sound, and sight to our alma mater.

Eclectic faculty join soon to be internationally recognized students to create the special fabric that we know as Barton College. From the indelible memories relived on these pages Barton colors her story. At those outer limits, which stretch beyond living memory, we, the alumni, find new threads with which to sew our particular patches.

People who care shape traditions, breathe life into a heritage, and celebrate the peaks and valleys of colleges and universities. Dr. Jerry MacLean leaves nothing to chance in bringing ACC/Barton to life on these pages.

When the next century's historian labors with the memories we create may his or her readers pick up the gauntlet of Barton's heritage and run headlong into its promising future. At that point we can accept our roles in this continuing saga. At that time in history we will merge with future generations to make the fabric whole.

—James B. Hemby, Jr.
President of Barton College

Preface

Barton College: Our Century, the first history of the college in nearly fifty years, is intended to be a readable and accurate description of Barton's past that complements the school's centennial celebration. The impracticality of including everyone who appeared in Barton's first one hundred years led me to attempt to capture the spirit of the institution by focusing upon individuals who represent significant periods of the college's past. The use of such an approach means that some deserving individuals—alumni, students, benefactors, trustees, faculty, administrators, and staff—are excluded.

The task of researching and writing the centennial history of Atlantic Christian/Barton College has been encouraged and generously supported by many alumni and friends. Personal interviews and conversations with individuals who lived, studied, worked, and played on the campus provided insights that helped to enrich the story of the school's first century. Recollections of Annie Harper Chamblee, who played on the campus as a child between 1904–08, and of Mamie Jennings Lucas, who arrived as a young teacher in 1913, are part of Barton's archives and legends. B. B. Plyler Jr., whose mother was Harriet Settle Plyler, sister-in-law of Barton president James C. Caldwell, generously shared her scrapbooks containing memorabilia of life at the college and in the town of Wilson during the early twentieth century. Three decades of living and teaching in Wilson provided opportunities to know and work with C. H. Hamlin, Mildred Hartsock, Sarah Bain Ward, Arthur D. Wenger, J. P. Tyndall, Milton Adams, Bethany Rose Joyner, Phil Witherington, and many other individuals whose contributions determined the nature and success of ACC/Barton.

I owe a special debt to James B. Hemby Jr. and Edward B. Holloway who read the manuscript, provided suggestions and corrections, and continually offered support and encouragement. President Hemby initiated the project and arranged release time from college responsibilities to permit my research and writing. Holloway, the college archivist and former professor of history, shared his own research and vast knowledge while assisting with interviews and appendices. Milton and Sarah Adams, Kathy Daughety, and Vernon Lindquist read the manuscript and made helpful suggestions. Keith Tew provided photography and suggested the title. J. Chris Wilson contributed the painting of the Barton campus. Other contributors included Tyson Aldridge, Clint Bowen, Richard Fulling, Carrie Lowe, Lynne Medlin, Laura Miller, Sheila Milne, Darla Raper, and Russell Rawlings.

The greatest debt is owed to my wife and best friend, Betty Spruill MacLean, who provided encouragement and helpful suggestions while serving as editor of the project.

William Jerry MacLean
Wilson, North Carolina
MAY 23, 2001

ONE

An Admirable Place for a College

BARTON COLLEGE was born as Atlantic Christian College in 1902, a year in which two Ohio bicycle mechanics soared high above the wind-swept sand dunes of North Carolina's Outer Banks, testing a glider and pursuing their dream of powered flight. In the nation's capital, Theodore Roosevelt neared the end of his first year as president, while in communities across America, the fledgling automobile began to compete with horse-drawn carriages and the railroad. Americans became more world-conscious as they adjusted to their country's newly acquired status as a global empire and read more about foreign lands acquired during the Spanish-American War. Clearly, the newly arrived twentieth century promised to bring experiences unlike any in man's history.

In the little town of Wilson, perched upon the western fringe of North Carolina's central coastal plain, church and civic leaders pursued an exciting dream of their own—the opening of a new college that could provide quality educational programs within a Christian framework. Wilson was already known as a significant regional educational center. Accomplished school leaders Charles Force Deems and Sylvester Hassell had enhanced the town's reputation for good schools during the late nineteenth century. Charles Brantley Aycock, a governor noted for his interest in education, and Josephus Daniels, a respected newspaper editor and future Secretary of the Navy, were renowned Tarheels who praised the quality of education they had received in Wilson. Accordingly, when the highly regarded Wilson Collegiate Institute closed in 1895 after years of distinguished service, area citizens immediately began to search for a suitable new school for their community.[1]

Barton College traces its beginning to the closing of two earlier institutions created by the Disciples of Christ in eastern North Carolina during the late nineteenth century—Carolina Christian College and Kinsey Seminary. When the former opened in Ayden on 18 September 1893, the institution apparently was intended to become the leading Disciples of Christ school in North Carolina. Offering three separate programs of courses (primary, intermediate, and collegiate), Carolina Christian realized some degree of success, and, by 1897, the college boasted an impressive faculty and an enrollment of 129 students.[2]

Despite early success and continued strong support from the Ayden community, the college closed in 1903, apparently because of its inability to communicate its accomplishments beyond the coastal plain of North Carolina. In addition, church leaders may have considered its avowed commitment to provide educational programs to young people of all ages proof that the school was primarily a preparatory institution rather than a true college. This factor may also account for the lack of recognition accorded Carolina Christian College by the national office of the Christian Church. As historian Charles C. Ware has noted, although the *Disciples Yearbook* for 1897 listed universities, colleges, institutes, and schools, it made no mention of a denominational school in North Carolina. Records proving that the college was a growing institution in the 1890s render that omission especially difficult to understand. Carolina Christian College had more enrolled students and possessed a larger endowment than over half of the Disciples schools listed in the yearbook. Church historian Walter Anderson argues that Carolina Christian College closed because of a loss of public funding. In 1903, the North Carolina General Assembly stopped permitting the use of state school funds to support "sectarian or denominational" schools.[3]

Kinsey Seminary, Atlantic Christian College's other forerunner, was at least as important to the creation of the new school in Wilson as the college in Ayden was. In 1896, as Carolina Christian College continued to grow, Wilson church and civic leaders asked Lenoir County educator Joseph Kinsey, renowned for establishing successful Disciples schools in Kinston and LaGrange, to open a school in their community. Kinsey agreed and immediately began forming a board of directors for Kinsey Seminary. Joining him on the board were ten of Wilson's most prominent citizens: Jonathan Applewhite, J. F. Bruton, Henry Groves Connor, Haywood Edmundson, Pleasant D. Gold, George D. Green, Silas Lucas, Jonas Oettinger, Frederick A. Woodard, and George Hackney, who served as president. Following the purchase of a prime building plot of approximately five acres, a large school building was completed during the summer of 1897.[4]

When Kinsey Seminary opened as a young ladies' boarding school on 15 September 1897, offering both a four-year course of study and a preparatory program, prospects for success appeared good. Classes were available in art,

George Hackney of Wilson, a founder of the college and chairman of the board of trustees, 1907–31. 1913 Pine Knot.

chapel management, elocution, English, history, Latin, mathematics, piano, science, violin, and voice. The board decided to require students to wear uniforms because, it contended, the measure "obviates the difficulty of invidious distinction in dress, saves expense, time, [and] thought." Tuition and board for the entire school year, from September to June, cost only $150.[5]

While the seminary received strong support from the Wilson community, the school failed to realize its initial promise. Monetary inflation, lack of adequate endowment funds, and the failing health of principal Joseph Kinsey, caused the seminary to flounder, and the school closed its doors in 1901. As Kinsey prepared to close his seminary, leaders of the North Carolina Christian Church reached a decision to create yet another Disciples college in the state. While meeting in Kinston, 31 October 1901, the North Carolina Christian Missionary Convention approved a resolution to purchase Kinsey Seminary as an initial step toward establishing a college in Wilson. Fortunately, Kinsey's health recovered sufficiently to permit his continued educational leadership, and Old Kinsey Hall, as his seminary building was later called, became the centerpiece of a bold new venture. John J. Harper, a Johnston County Disciple preacher and chairman of the newly formed executive board, recommended that the new school be called Atlantic Christian College.[6]

The initial *College Catalog* listed the features which attracted Christian church leaders to Wilson as a suitable location for a Disciples college:

a beautiful little city of six thousand inhabitants. . . . Wilson is the business center of Eastern North Carolina and is bottomed on a strong belief in education. Electric lights, water works, paved streets and other modern conveniences make it an admirable place for a college. Wilson's superior educational advantages, pure climate and varied business interests attract large numbers of people to the city every year. Her homes are beautiful, her churches are handsome and commodious and her citizens are aggressive, cultured and hospitable.[7]

After purchasing Kinsey Seminary, trustees joined Harper in developing plans to open the new college. Other officers of the first board of trustees were B. H. Melton, Wilson Disciples minister, as secretary, and George Hackney, Wilson businessman and local Christian Church leader, as treasurer. Additional board members were D. W. Arnold of Farmville, J. S. Basnight of New Bern, J. W. Hines of Rocky Mount, Joseph Kinsey of Wilson, E. A. Moye of Farmville, and K. R. Tunstall of Kinston.[8]

Intent on hiring a capable president to lead the college, the trustees initially offered the post to Daniel Motley, a respected Christian evangelist who had served churches in Virginia and North Carolina. A brilliant man with a Ph.D. from prestigious Johns Hopkins University, Motley had called repeatedly for the Disciples to establish a college of high quality in North Carolina. Unfortunately, he refused the offer because he had a commitment to serve another new Disciples college then in the planning stages. After considering several candidates, the board offered the post to James C. Coggins, minister of a large Disciples church in Decatur, Illinois. Born at Bee Tree near Asheville, North Carolina, in 1865, James Caswell Coggins attended Newton Academy in Asheville and graduated from Milligan College in 1894. Coggins's graduate degrees included an M.A. from Bethany College, an LL.D. from Nashville College, and a Ph.D. from American University in Tennessee. *The Watch Tower*, a church newspaper published by North Carolina Disciples, described Dr. Coggins as a "thoroughly educated man."[9]

Coggins promptly accepted the call and became an ex-officio member of the board of trustees. Earlier in 1902, while visiting Wilson to inquire about the position of college president, the Illinois preacher had been a guest in the home of trustee B. H. Melton. Melton had seized the opportunity to literally take full measure of the man. The Wilson preacher actually measured the height and weight of his house guest. He reported that the thirty-six-year-old Coggins stood an even six feet tall and weighed 185 pounds. Melton added

President James C. Coggins, 1902–04. College archives.

that he had also found the man to be an eminent Bible scholar, fluent in several languages, and "a preacher of unusual power." With Coggins' acceptance of the presidency, trustees believed they had hired a man who would fit well within the community and lead the new school toward a promising future.[10]

Although many supporters of Atlantic Christian College (ACC or AC College as the school was quickly dubbed) appeared optimistic as 1902 began, Melton was concerned that few local church members had pledged financial support. He warned that a fledgling college would require significant monetary support from large numbers of people in order to succeed. However, most parishioners, he wrote caustically, had given nothing. W. G. Johnston, a Disciples preacher in Kinston, agreed, predicting that unless funding increased greatly, the college would never reach its potential. Johnston was convinced that most North Carolina Disciples failed to understand the cost and sacrifice required to sustain a good college.[11]

A principal reason for the creation of Barton College was to improve the intellectual level of the Disciples of Christ in North Carolina. As historian Charles C. Ware has noted, local preachers had been reminded by outsiders about the importance of an educated ministry. Visiting preacher Claris Yeuell, after visiting Disciples churches across the South in 1903, immediately realized the problem. Voicing disdain for the lack of education which he had noticed among Disciples preachers, Yeuell labeled their sermons "pitiful" and filled with "pious platitude, [and] senseless superstition." He charged that "Nothing but the schoolmaster can remove such conditions." While preaching in northeastern North Carolina pulpits, Yeuell warned that the Disciples were then either on the verge of "collapse or a revolution. . . . Ignorance and selfishness are at the bottom of the situation in North Carolina." It is unlikely that members of Atlantic Christian College's initial board of trustees or concerned North Carolina Disciples could have stated the situation with greater clarity.[12]

Coggins' acceptance of the presidency convinced ACC trustees that they had found a leader who would inspire North Carolina Disciples to raise the educational level of preachers and help reduce widespread apathy within the state's Christian churches. In accepting the leadership of Atlantic Christian College, the newly hired president had agreed to a reduction in salary from that offered by his former church. Intrigued by the challenges presented by the new college, Coggins promptly moved his family to Wilson, announcing that he would devote the time prior to the opening of school in September to promote the college and visit Christian churches in the state. Significantly, the president-elect also launched an immediate campaign to recruit students for Atlantic Christian College.[13]

Eastern North Carolina Disciples joined the founding fathers of AC College in eagerly anticipating the opening of fall term. Reverend Johnston of the Kinston Christian Church wrote that Dr. Coggins' promise that the new college would be judged an institution of high quality had produced excitement in his community and other areas of eastern North Carolina. Local preachers also hoped that the college would help generate additional financial support for Disciples churches within the area. Writing in *The Watch Tower* of July 1902, New Bern trustee J. S. Basnight proudly proclaimed that the new college was virtually ready for fall semester to begin. He voiced his conviction that the board had hired a faculty that was "second to none in the state." Early publications echoed the prevailing optimism, referring to the college's facilities as outstanding and boasting that everything had been designed to provide young ladies with the finest living conditions available. Kinsey Hall offered electricity, steam heat, modern plumbing, and an auditorium that could accommodate over 500 people. Other appealing features included a large dining hall, attractive classrooms, and a total of thirty-five "well ventilated" dormitory rooms. The interior had been completely repainted and furnished with modern and attractive furniture throughout the building. The initial *College Catalog* proclaimed that the facilities would make Kinsey Hall "one of the best equipped college buildings in the South."[14]

Disciples leaders had challenged churches and individuals throughout North Carolina to assume the cost of furnishing thirty-two dormitory rooms prior to the beginning of fall semester. For the sum of $30, each bedroom could be furnished with an iron bedstead, mattress and springs, bed coverings, washstand, bureau, chair, carpet, and window shades. By late March, generous supporters from as far away as Asheville had pledged adequate funds to furnish over half of the dorm rooms. Kinston Disciples had agreed to furnish four bedrooms and announced that they planned to send several students to the college in September. As midsummer approached, church leaders noted that, in addition to raising most of the requested funds, local Disciples expressed excitement about the opening of the college. Enthusiastic reports continued to arrive from several communities, some promising to send their young ladies to ACC.[15]

Officially incorporated 1 May 1902, Atlantic Christian College formally opened its doors to students on 3 September when President Coggins and the newly appointed faculty members welcomed and registered 107 students for fall classes. Within that first student body, the eighty-seven females far outnumbered the twenty males (81 percent to 19 percent). Total enrollment for the 1902–03 academic year was 218 students representing ten states, including one from distant Montana. The success of the college's first year exceeded the most optimistic expectations.[16]

The college offered courses of study in ten schools and departments leading to B.A., B.S., or B.D. degrees. Early catalogs and advertisements listed a wide variety of available courses and programs, including ancient languages and literature, Bible, business and pedagogy, English language and literature, ethics and logic, expression and physical culture, fine arts, history, mathematics, modern languages, natural sciences, oratory, Oriental languages, philosophy, piano, political economy, sociology, and voice. In addition to courses within degree programs, the college offered preparatory classes and a limited number of postgraduate courses.[17]

Early publications also indicated that music, art, spiritual development, and a solid grounding in the liberal arts would be principal elements of the academic and cultural environment provided at the college. Students would have opportunities to participate in chorus, glee club, orchestra, painting, drawing, and public speaking. A Young People's Society of Christian Endeavor would assist in providing activities and religious training. While heavily emphasizing the strong moral and religious environment which young ladies and gentlemen should find attractive at the college, the administration assured prospective students that life on campus would feature a stimulating mixture of work and recreation. Listed under "Life at A.C. College," the initial *College Catalog* described the type of environment which students could expect to find:

> Life at the college will not be humdrum and monotonous, but full of interest, overflowing with good cheer, and crowded with honest work. Ample opportunity will be afforded for recreation necessary for health and comfort. The home-life will be maintained as far as possible. It will not be an 'all play and no work,' nor 'all work and no play,' but work will be the rule. 'Diligence' will be our watch-word and our motto, 'onward by effort.' The government will be kind and gentle, but firm and unwavering. We want 300 honest, industrious boys and girls, with high aims, and noble purposes, and we are not looking for any other kind.[18]

Roberta Worthington, a member of the Rountree Christian Church near Ayden and an honors graduate of Carolina Christian College, expressed excitement as she anticipated joining the college's first student body for the fall semester in 1902. Her unpublished journal completed in the 1980s reveals concerns about leaving home and furnishes insights about the early college:

> I am really a little nervous and excited as it is my first trip away from home on my own. The train pulls into Wilson station and I am soon out of the car standing on the depot platform with several other students who have just arrived when a big conveyance, with a horse and driver from the college, drives up and yells 'all aboard.' In about fifteen minutes we are on the campus, in the registration office and all signed up. . . .
>
> I was a junior in music, with a selective course—Literature, English, French and Art. Someone took me to my room. The college was in a very large building. On one side were the dormitory rooms and large auditorium. On the other side of the hall were offices and classrooms, etc.—all under one roof. My roommate was already in and unpacked. She seemed very nice and [was] . . . from Washington, N.C. . . .
>
> I soon had my study schedule all worked out—there was a lot of piano

practice every day and I liked Miss Zackery, my teacher, who was an old maid, with a wrinkled face. I was her highest grade pupil. I was lucky to get Miss Anderson for English teacher. I was in her class at C.C.C., also she taught me dramatics there. I was in one short amateur stage play, but somehow my 'stage-struck' ardor had cooled off.[19]

Like Roberta Worthington, most of Barton College's early students came from homes located within a seventy-five-mile radius of Wilson. Many arrived with limited cultural experiences and likely had not traveled far beyond the coastal plain region. Consequently, when students enrolled in college, both they and their parents ventured into unfamiliar territory. Certainly, many residents of eastern North Carolina in 1902 would have been enthralled by impressive-sounding credentials and tales of worldly travels reportedly brought to the Wilson campus by faculty members. Publicists of the college were well aware of the effect that impressive and exotic-sounding titles and academic degrees created. Abdullah Ben Kori, a newly hired professor of linguistics and a native of Syria, had been educated in both America and Italy. He was claimed to be fluent in ten languages and one of the country's finest linguists. Professor Ruth Alderman, who taught English, French, and German, was promoted as "easily one of the ablest scholars in Kansas." College publications proclaimed newly hired professor Adele Martin to be one of the most popular soloists of the entire Chicago area. Clearly, such an array of scholars promised to bring a host of exciting experiences and opportunities to a region that, at the beginning of the twentieth century, remained primarily a rural, provincial area of the country.[20]

Professor Luther Reic Shockey, who had moved to Wilson from Illinois, was reported to be the most talented, demanding, and eccentric of the recently arrived scholars. Shockey was described as "a young master who sees music in everything. His soul is one great ocean of music whose waves beat the keys of a piano with sublime masterpieces of eloquence." Clyde Watson of Wilson, reportedly the first student to enroll at Atlantic Christian College, remembered Professor Shockey's eccentric nature as well as his attractiveness to the ladies in a letter given to the college archives in 1955:

One outstanding recollection I have of the college is of the piano teacher, Professor L. R. Shockey. He seemed to make the greatest impression on the school and the town, for not only the college students wanted to take lessons from him but many ladies from in town. He wore his hair long, was very tall and handsome, and apparently thought so well of himself that he seldom spoke to any of us if he could avoid it. He announced that he would not give any of the piano students a piece until certain finger exercises were learned perfectly. All practiced diligently, and finally in late November he gave me my first piece, 'The Flower Song,' by Lange.

Another teacher I remember as liking so much was my expression teacher, Miss Christine Arnberg. She impressed me as being very charming. By the way, she seemed to be the only person that Professor Shockey had time for.

Clyde Watson was even less charitable in describing her Greek class, which, to her dismay, she had discovered to be a dismal experience during which virtually no one learned anything. In addition, she added, none of the students seemed to know why they were taking the course "unless we were out for the unusual."[21]

The collegiate environment which Clyde Watson and her schoolmates experienced in the early twentieth century appears quaint upon examination a hundred years later. Required daily chapel attendance and faculty-staff intrusion into the students' private lives would likely offend modern students. There would have been little or no audio-visual equipment available for early classrooms and few adequate textbooks or other aids considered essential by educators today. The college woman of the twenty-first century would also be shocked by the school restrictions presented at registration day on the ACC campus in the late summer of 1902. Arriving promptly at 9:00 AM on 3 September she would have been required to present "testimonials of good character" prior to being permitted to register and expected to sign a pledge to "live a pure and honorable life and conform faithfully to the rules and regulations of Atlantic Christian College." However, the twenty-first century campus, featuring an absence of social restrictions and such amenities as fast food, voice mail, personal computers, e-mail, and co-ed dormitories, would seem equally bizarre to Watson and her friends.[22]

Because of social mores of the time, early female students at ACC were subjected to rules that did not permit them to socialize with male students on the campus. In fact during the formative years of the college, the administration made no effort to treat male students equitably. Early catalogs indicate clearly that the college admitted both males and females. However, the same publications specifically indicate that young men on the campus were treated like "second class citizens" by twenty-first century standards: "Notwithstand-

Snack time in old Kinsey Hall. 1910 Pine Knot.

ing the fact that this institution is coeducational we want it clearly understood that the young men will not room in the College. They will simply attend the various class sessions, going to their boarding places when through with their recitations. The college building will be the young ladies home, and the campus will be their recreation grounds."[23]

The policy made it very clear that male students did not have the right to live on campus or use the grounds for "recreation." Many gray areas existed, however. What, for example, were the young men to do about purchasing textbooks on campus? What rights did they have to use the college library? Today, with the exception of institutions which focus upon the education of future military officers, few, if any, colleges or universities, including Barton, would attempt to mandate where students go after classes are over. In the early twentieth century, however, the intervention of state and national governments into the affairs of private education to correct sexual or racial discrimination was virtually unthinkable. Government regulatory measures, such as those included in Title IX, remained a part of the distant future. When the government did become increasingly intrusive in the affairs of American private colleges in the second half of the twentieth century, concern with protection of the rights of white males was hardly a primary focus.

Despite early discriminatory treatment according to gender, the favorable impact that young men had upon the college certainly did not go unnoticed. Clyde Watson remarked that men and women enjoyed each other's company during the limited opportunities for social contact afforded on the early ACC campus. Leaders of the administration and the board of trustees also were paying attention. President Coggins recognized very early the need to provide suitable accommodations for male students. His column appearing in *The Watch Tower* of April 1902, some months prior to the opening of ACC, urged an immediate drive to raise funds for construction of a dormitory for men. Coggins had already selected an appropriate location on the northwest corner of the campus. The new president suggested that the first person to donate $500 toward the project would receive the right to name the dormitory. Before the completion of the first academic year, trustees had become convinced of the merit of the president's suggestion. In an executive meeting of the board in May 1903, the trustees voted to build a dormitory for men, at a projected cost of $10,000.[24]

Except for the reappointment of President Coggins at the May 1903 meeting, trustees were not pleased with conditions at the college. An issue of particular concern was reappointment of continuing faculty for the fall term. Coggins informed the board that a high faculty attrition rate would cause the college to need to fill a number of academic positions for 1903–04. In fact, only three members of the original faculty had indicated plans to return in the fall. Apparently, Atlantic Christian College's highly touted initial faculty suffered even greater culture shock than students did. The problem actually turned out to be an omen of things to come, as retention of competent teachers would prove to be among Atlantic Christian College's most vexing and continuing challenges.[25]

The campus of 1903 where administrators and trustees gathered to plan the college's future bears little resemblance to Barton College today. The early ACC campus occupied slightly less than six acres and might be described as a relatively barren landscape. Located on the northern edge of Wilson, the land was covered mostly by a green and brown carpet of grass and weeds interrupted by intermittent patches of bare ground. A scattering of slender pines and young hardwood trees towered over the land. Dominating the landscape was Kinsey Hall, also called Old Kinsey and the College Building, a large and solitary structure that housed the entire school. Kinsey Hall faced Whitehead

Kinsey Hall, west or dormitory entrance. 1916 Pine Knot.

Avenue to the south and was bordered by Lee Street on the west. Measuring 126 feet long by 121 feet wide, Kinsey Hall crowned a modest hilltop, which sloped away from the north side of the building toward a small stream.[26]

Photographs and written descriptions of Kinsey Hall reveal a large, rambling structure that might accurately be described as both engineering marvel and architectural monstrosity. Architecturally, the structure reflected a hybrid style somewhat typical of late nineteenth and early twentieth-century structures, which borrowed freely from both Romanesque and medieval styles. The three-story brick structure featured a symmetrical facade dominated by a large squared central tower, which was capped by four squared turrets. The gable roof contained clipped dormers with arched windows. The first floor had large rectangular windows whereas the second floor featured smaller, more numerous rounded windows. The rear of the building, facing north, reflected asymmetrical massing as did the sides of the structure. The western side of Kinsey Hall contained a large porch, which sheltered the entrance to the dormitory part of the building. The eastern side housed a large chapel, which also served as an auditorium and featured large, leaded, stained glass windows.[27]

Old Kinsey Hall was an impressive building in many respects and seemed perfect for a small college, especially a rural eastern North Carolina college struggling with indebtedness and tight budgets. The college's early catalogs boasted of the modern, comfortable amenities afforded by Kinsey Hall, including steam heat, electric lights, and sewer connection. During the college's first decade, a drawing or photograph of the College Building was a prominent feature in publications that went out to the public.[28]

Those who studied, worked, and lived in Kinsey Hall were quickly dismayed to learn that the impressive-looking building, upon which the future of the college depended, revealed serious problems during severe weather. A building that was airy and comfortable during warm months proved almost impossible to heat adequately during cold months. The first extended period of cold weather showed that the heating plant was incapable of warming the building. As students, faculty, and staff added warmer clothing and huddled around radiators, trustees and administrators searched for emergency funds to purchase a larger furnace.[29]

Warm spring weather gradually replaced cold winter days as the college's initial year neared completion. The president and trustees continued to assess the health of the institution and survey prospects for the next academic year. Clearly, Atlantic Christian College had made important gains during the first year. Enrollment had exceeded expectations, and numerous congregations and individuals had responded with enthusiasm and generosity to support the college. They had sent their daughters and sons to be educated and had opened their purses to furnish financial support. Unfortunately, most early monetary gifts were nominal sums contributed by an eastern North Carolina citizenry with limited income. As the college's first historian has noted, some of those who gave token amounts early followed later with more significant contributions. These included Mrs. Heber Coward of Greenville, Mrs. Orpah Hackney of Wilson, J. W. Hines of Rocky Mount, Mrs. J. O. Proctor of Grimesland, and Charles Nurney of Wilson. Mrs. Hackney's gift was of particular importance. The widow of Wilson businessman Willis Napoleon Hackney and mother of college founder and trustee George Hackney, she donated real estate valued at $3,000 in 1901. This notable early gift marked the beginning of the school's endowment. Of even greater significance, the "Willis N. and Orpah Hackney Memorial Fund" strengthened a relationship that ultimately became one of the most significant and enduring associations in the college's history.[30]

In the spring of 1903, the magnitude of Atlantic Christian College's financial problem was not clearly recognized. Almost certainly, none foresaw that the school then stood at the brink of a period of "epic struggle." A substantial part of the debt incurred by purchasing the Kinsey property remained unpaid. Unfortunately, the cost of refurbishing Kinsey Hall for the opening semester absorbed most of the early gift money received. Two additional factors that combined to render the little college impoverished for the immediate future were too few contributors and the establishment of tuition and fees at levels that proved too low to cover expenses. Several months before the college opened its doors, trustee B. H. Melton correctly identified the problem when he wrote in the Disciples newspaper that although a few people had given money to support the school willingly and generously, "The majority have so far done nothing. God have mercy upon them!" John J. Harper, president of the board of trustees, had also voiced deep concern. Writing in *The Watch Tower* in January 1902, Harper urged church leaders to move rapidly to secure funds to retire the college's debt and warned his fellow Disciples that "there must not be any flinching, dodging, or hesitating on the part of our generous people."[31]

Among the group of Christian Church leaders who had called boldly for the creation of a new Disciples college, none had been more vocal than state evangelist Daniel E. Motley. Motley's superb education and years of effective service had raised him to an influential position within the denomination. While insisting that the Disciples' new college be of exceptional quality, the evangelist also emphasized that tuition and fees must be realistic. Experience had shown Motley that church colleges often made the mistake of charging inadequate fees. In June of 1901, Motley wrote prophetically, "Colleges gain in no way by putting tuition down at starvation wages.... Put tuition at living rates." The founding fathers of ACC would have done well to listen.[32]

While the severe problem of inadequate funds continued, a leadership crisis also developed. Within a brief period, several church leaders who had provided valuable support for ACC moved away from the area. Daniel Motley, as mentioned previously, left the state to serve the church in Washington, D.C. Joseph Kinsey moved to LaGrange to go into business. B. H. Melton of Wilson and W. G. Johnston of Kinston, leading area preachers and devoted friends of the college, also left the area. President Coggins worked hard to accentuate positive aspects of the college and to attract monetary support. The graduation of the first student was an obvious achievement and a historic event. Ada Tyson, a Farmville native, graduated from AC College in the spring of 1903. Tyson had studied previously at Farmville Academy, at Woman's College in Greensboro, and at Claremont College in Hickory, where she graduated with the degree of Bachelor of Didactics. She taught several years in the state's public schools prior to coming to ACC in the fall of 1902 to teach secretarial courses.

While serving on the faculty, she also enrolled as a senior student and completed her B.S. degree.[33]

Writing in July of 1903, Coggins optimistically predicted that the college's second year would also prove successful. He expected a large enrollment and promised that the Bible department would be considered first-rate. The president also announced that he had received a commitment from a well-known author to lecture on the campus and had hired an excellent scholar-teacher from Texas to teach ancient languages. Unfortunately, bold forecasts and lofty words could not solve ACC's fiscal problems. Coggins' comment that the necessity of hiring numerous new faculty members had delayed publication of the new college catalog appeared to substantiate rumors that all was not well at the college. Friends and supporters joined the president and trustees in anxiously anticipating September and the opening of fall term.[34]

TWO

The Father of Atlantic Christian College

TRAVELING TO BARTON COLLEGE in the early years could be difficult for students and faculty members because of inconvenient and unpredictable transportation. Eastern North Carolina roads remained mostly unpaved, and automobiles were largely a curiosity in the area until after World War I. Residents of the rural South and other agrarian regions depended upon travel by horseback or horse and carriage. Livery stables where horses could be boarded and hired at the going rate were readily available in Wilson County communities. In March of 1902, *The Elm City Elevator* advertised the services of A.W. Pippen's combined livery stable, blacksmith shop, and wood shop. In addition to listing the boarding and renting of horses, ads offered the availability of buggy repair and proclaimed "horseshoeing a specialty."[1]

Traveling preachers were among those most dependent upon the horse or horse and carriage to reach their destinations. Virtually from the time that its doors first opened, Atlantic Christian College supplied ministers from the faculty and student body to fill pulpits of churches scattered across the coastal plain region. Factors such as distance from the college and the lateness of the hour would have determined whether visiting preachers remained overnight in communities where they conducted church services.

For millions of Americans in towns and cities of the late nineteenth and early twentieth centuries, bicycles were available to those who could afford them. Interestingly, a few weeks before ACC officially opened its doors, President Theodore Roosevelt became the nation's first chief executive to ride a bicycle. Wilson County newspaper ads in the spring of 1902 listed bicycles for sale by the American Cycle Company of New York City. Monarch brands were available at prices ranging from $25 to $60, while Columbia models sold for $40 to $80. Photographs in the *College Catalog* of 1906–07 show bicycles and horse-drawn carriages on an unpaved Nash Street. A picture in the college's first yearbook, *The Pine Knot* of 1910, reveals a parked bicycle in an alcove of Kinsey Hall. A cartoon in the same issue features a sporty automobile enveloped by a cloud of dust as a uniformed chauffeur speedily drives a baseball player to Durham. Since few Wilsonians actually owned automobiles at the time, the cartoon may represent a case of anticipating the future on the part of *The Pine Knot* staff.[2]

People walked frequently during the early twentieth century, sometimes covering many miles, and commuting students living within a few miles of the campus typically walked to school. Since the college was located a mile and a half from the Wilson railroad station, early presidents dispatched a driver and horse-drawn wagon or carriage to transport passengers between the campus and the depot. At certain times of the year—including the opening and closing of semesters, holidays, and other significant occasions—providing transportation to and from the train station became a necessity for the college.

While individuals experienced difficulty in reaching ACC for the opening of the second year, bad news had no such problem. From the beginning of the fall semester of 1903, the difficult financial conditions, which some had predicted, descended heavily upon the school. The first blow came in the form of decreasing enrollments. Unhappy students had abandoned the institution as readily as disgruntled faculty after the first year. On opening day, 12 September, only thirty-six students registered for classes. As compared to registration day the previous year, the figure represented a decline of over 66 percent. Although the number of registrants gradually increased, only 113 students enrolled during the entire year. The 1903–04 student body contained eighty-two females and thirty-one males, nearly 73 percent female.[3]

The decrease in revenues from tuition and fees, the large debt that had lingered since the purchase of the Kinsey property, and mounting personnel expenses created an especially difficult problem. The increased expense caused by a larger faculty, up three from the previous year and now numbering fourteen members, threatened to drive the operating budget even higher than that of the previous year. The college soon faced another obstacle that had not been fully anticipated in the early autumn of 1903. Clement Manly Morton, editor of the first college yearbook and a first-hand observer of the crisis, stated that Atlantic Christian College very nearly went under during the 1903–04 academic year. Morton described both the magnitude and source of the financial problem in *The Pine Knot*: "At the close of the second year it seemed that failure was inevitable. The people had lost confidence in the school, and it looked like the doors would never be opened again." Since the people's confidence in the future of the institution was virtually as critical as the issue of adequate funding, the situation of the college could hardly have been worse.[4]

President Coggins and the trustees worked diligently to solve the crisis, but their efforts were not successful. They were unable to recruit new friends to replace the departed supporters who had contributed both guidance and financial support for the college from the outset. The absence of Daniel Motley and B. H. Melton alone represented a major loss for the college. Historian Charles C. Ware argues that the departure of so many key supporters within such a short period provides a reasonable explanation for the serious loss of confidence which developed during this time.[5]

Finally, although school leaders appeared reluctant to admit it, problems with facilities also caused Atlantic Christian College to lose students. Simply put, Kinsey Hall had always been ill suited to severe weather. The school's first winter was especially cold, causing great discomfort for occupants of the College Building. In January of the second academic year, a visitor to the campus wrote that the furnace in Kinsey would not heat the building adequately during extremely cold weather. College officials were forced to turn off radiators in the auditorium so that classrooms and dormitory rooms would receive additional heat. The newly appointed business manager displayed relief when the cold spell finally broke in March 1904, bringing warmer weather and an end to "the cold, sleety winter, which has caused much anxiety."[6]

President Coggins exerted great effort to make the college a success. At another time and under different circumstances, he might have realized his goal. During the summer of 1903, Coggins temporarily returned to the area near his home in the Blue Ridge Mountains where he directed a summer school. In all likelihood, his understanding of the severity of the problems faced by the college caused him to begin looking for a new position. As conditions continued to grow worse during the following year, Coggins submitted his resignation, effective upon the end of the spring semester.[7]

The spring and summer of 1904 witnessed the worst of times for the struggling Disciples college. Church leaders, trustees, and the entire college community worked with concerted effort to save the school. Glen G. Cole, math, sciences, and pedagogy professor and one of the few remaining members of the original faculty, publicly urged friends of the college to rally to the aid of the institution. Stating the problem with simplicity and accuracy, Cole wrote that nothing was wrong with Atlantic Christian College that a gift of $100,000 could not fix. Although of little consolation to those struggling to save the institution, many American colleges and universities experienced serious economic difficulties during the early twentieth century.[8]

Assets needed almost as desperately as adequate funds at the Wilson college were fresh leadership and a new furnace. J. Boyd Jones, the new chairman of the board of trustees and a resident of Wilson, listed priorities for securing the college's future. He urged trustees to move immediately "to put the heating plant in first-class condition . . . [and] hire the president and teachers and pay them a salary—not a commission." While openly admitting that ACC faced a crisis, he admonished churches and individuals whom he considered obligated to support the school to "Remember Atlantic Christian College is not dead nor dying but fully alive."[9]

Fortunately, the trustees realized that the capable leader they sought was a member of their own group but were not certain that he would accept the position. The man they wanted to approach, John James Harper, had acquired an enviable record as preacher and leader within the Christian Church, served in the state legislature, and gained friends and respect throughout North Carolina. As the first chairman of the board of trustees, his hand had helped guide the school from the start. In fact Harper had literally named the new college. In 1903–04, he had served the college as chancellor and teacher, while continuing as a member of the board of trustees. Finally, President Coggins placed such high value upon Harper as chancellor and trustee that he had arranged for the college to award him one of its first honorary degrees. Harper seemed to be a perfect fit for the presidency. The only problem was that, having recently observed his sixty-third birthday, he really did not want the job. Although he loved the college dearly and had served it faithfully, Harper remained anxious to pursue his great passion of preaching the gospel as a pulpit minister. An additional dream was to write a history of the Disciples of Christ Church in North Carolina. Acceptance of the presidency of Atlantic Christian College would certainly delay the realization of such dreams.[10]

Fortunately, Harper considered the call to duty too important and too urgent to decline. Insistence from trustees and the chancellor's strong belief that the continued success of the Christian Church and the future well-being of the college were intertwined brought him to agree to become the school's second president in May 1904. Although acceptance came at great personal sacrifice, Harper responded as he had always done, pledging to devote all of his attention to the needs of "this sacred trust. . . . I hesitated long, and pon-

President John J. Harper, 1904–08. 1910 Pine Knot.

dered over it well, and prayed over it much, before I could consent to undertake the work. The duties of the office will require and shall receive my closest personal attention in all their details. My daughters and I will reside in the college building, and I shall have no other work but that which pertains to the institution, and I shall give to its interests the best thought and effort of which I am capable."[11]

Harper's appointment was met with widespread praise. The Raleigh *News and Observer* lauded his intelligence, leadership, and commitment, and predicted that his acceptance of the presidency virtually assured the future of Atlantic Christian College. The newspaper praised Harper for his hard labor and sound judgment and called him the "wisest leader of his church" in the state.[12]

The newly selected president was born in Johnston County, North Carolina, on 10 April 1841. His forebears had settled in a beautiful valley in the mountains of western Virginia in the eighteenth century and had given the community the family name, calling it Harper's Ferry. Harper's parents were a religious, hardworking farm couple who impressed their strong belief in the value of education upon their five children. John's early education came mostly from enrollment at a private school in Beaufort County, North Carolina, operated by Thomas and Josephus Latham. Instruction from private tutors encouraged him to read great classical works. Harper was baptized in the Christian Church at age nineteen. He married Arrita Anderson Daniel of Pitt County on 1 May 1862, the same year that he was ordained.[13]

Today, the two-story, frame farmhouse in Johnston County where John J. Harper grew up is one of North Carolina's most famous buildings. Located on the Bentonville Battleground, scene of the last major battle of the Civil War, the structure is the central attraction of a popular state historic site. General William Tecumseh Sherman's huge Union army had left a wide path of twisted rails, solitary chimneys, and smoldering ruins between Atlanta and Columbia when they invaded North Carolina in the early spring of 1865. On 19 March, Sherman's troops met strong resistance from General Joseph E. Johnston's army of the Carolinas in a deadly conflict fought across barren sandy fields and pine-dotted woodlands near a little crossroads called Bentonville. The Harper home served as a hospital as the family provided humanitarian assistance to wounded soldiers of both the Union and Confederate armies. Their story, often repeated today, has been woven into the history and legend of the Tarheel state.

During the difficult years of military and political reconstruction that followed the Civil War, John Harper taught school and began his career as a Disciples minister. Over the next quarter century, he served as a pastor in the eastern North Carolina communities of Wilson, Wilson Mills, Kinston, Washington, and Dunn. The clergyman's talent and increasing popularity prompted area citizens to elect him to the state senate and caused him to attain statewide leadership in the Christian Church during the 1880s. The first edition of *The Radiant*, a literary magazine published in 1908 by the students of Atlantic Christian College, credited Harper with playing an important role in the creation of the North Carolina Christian Missionary Convention. He was also praised for helping prevent "tricky preachers from other States" from moving into North Carolina and splitting the mainstream churches.[14]

Charles C. Ware, Disciples' state secretary, praised Harper's contributions as presiding officer over state conventions and described his role in guarding the integrity and mission of the church. Ware called Harper "a faithful sentinel . . . against the marauders of the night . . . a living scourge of the ecclesiastical cheat . . . who would . . . make a carnival in Carolina for fleecing of the flock." Ware also commended Harper for laying the foundations of the Carolina Discipliana archives and could just as accurately have lauded his role in

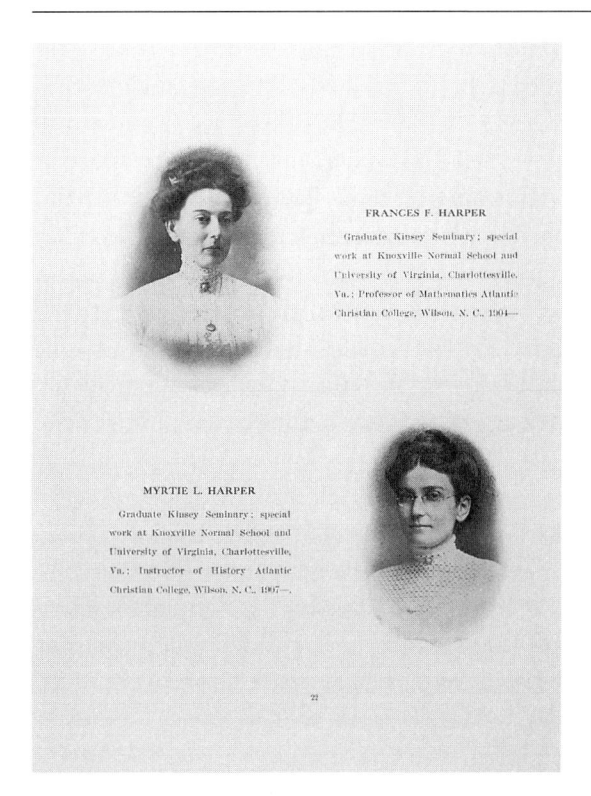

Frances and Myrtle Harper, "Miss Fannie" and "Miss Myrtie." 1910 Pine Knot.

establishing the archival collection of Barton College. Wilson Disciples were especially excited to learn that their former pastor and friend, who had preached in the local Christian Church nearly a quarter of a century earlier, would rejoin their community on a full-time basis. In the 1880s, Harper had found the congregation, which then claimed only twenty-five members, to be genuine, hospitable, and hardworking. He singled out Peter E. Hines and Moses T. Moye as members who had been particularly dedicated and helpful in supporting the Wilson church.[15]

The new president would find his new challenge among the greatest of his life. The task required recruiting people who would embrace the mission and meet the needs of the institution, including helping to restore confidence and pay the bills. Fortunately, two family members whom he brought to live with him in Kinsey Hall, daughters Frances and Myrtle, proved to be helpmates to their father and assets to the institution for many years. Both "Miss Fannie" and "Miss Myrtie" are remembered as campus characters and as significant figures in the folklore of the school.[16]

Dr. Harper, whom Disciples educators and church leaders called a "prudent, Godly man," demonstrated a shrewd business mind and an air of confidence as he shouldered the responsibilities of the college. His first year was characterized by fiscal restraint, careful planning, and hard work aimed at restoring confidence and strengthening academic programs. When the college opened in September, only thirty-two students enrolled. The *College Catalog* for 1904–05 listed eight "Officers and Faculty" members, including Dr. Harper and Miss Frances F. Harper, who assisted in teaching preparatory classes and served as bookkeeper. By late January 1905, the president wrote that support for ACC was increasing and called on assistance from the Disciples to help build an excellent college that would become a source of pride to the denomination.[17]

Despite a sense of gloom created by the small fall enrollment, the academic year progressed better than the slow start seemed to predict. A relieved board of trustees, meeting in March 1905, reported favorably upon several accomplishments. The heating plant in Kinsey Hall had been fixed during the previous summer and was now capable of keeping the large building warm during the coldest weather. The trustees voiced particular praise for the work of the new president. Chairman Jones declared that Harper had resolved the problems facing the college more rapidly than anticipated. Jones added that the board had unanimously reelected the president and that Harper had accepted "which means that the school is safe. He has the confidence of the Wilson people and his credit is good anywhere." Jones revealed that Raymond Abner Smith, a Yale graduate, had been hired by the church as state evangelist and that his duties would include teaching at the college.[18]

By commencement in May 1905, a total of 103 students had attended the college during the year, seventy-eight females and twenty-five males. President Harper's brief analysis of the school year in June included words of gratitude for support rendered and an assessment of the college's current progress as "normal and substantial." Unwilling to claim credit for the accomplishments himself, Harper acknowledged the aid of a higher power: "The Lord has raised up friends whom we knew not of a year ago. Viewing the year's work from every standpoint, we can but thank God and take courage."[19]

While supporters of the college were understandably relieved to learn that progress was being made to resolve problems that threatened the future of the college, they also realized that such improvements might best be described as modest. Writing in January 1905, the chairman of the board reminded fellow Disciples that building a high-quality institution would require even greater cooperation from a larger group of supporters over a period of several years. Unless the "brethren" cooperated, J. Boyd Jones warned, the result would be mediocrity. The college needed to attract 300 young men and women of good character who also demonstrated a strong work ethic. Hoping to attract more high caliber students, Harper appealed to Disciples to start a fund-raising campaign to establish a student loan fund to help poor, but worthy, young people attend the college. He noted that "one good brother" had offered assistance and challenged others to join the effort.[20]

In 1905, George Hackney, new chairman of the board of trustees, challenged Disciples to support a bond drive to raise $20,000 to liquidate the college's indebtedness. Writing in *The Watch Tower* the following April, Abram J. Moye, a Bethany College graduate and Farmville trustee, urged area Disciples to purchase the bonds. Arguing that the future of the college and the church were closely connected, he pointedly questioned whether the Lord would continue to bless "brethren . . . so short-sighted, and so lost to all self-respect as to fail" the college.[21]

During Harper's second year as president, the college continued its slow growth. Enrollment for the year reached 114, but the number of male students declined to only 16. The *College Catalog* for 1906–07 extolled the faculty and urged parents to send their sons and daughters to be "inspired by vital contact with a body of teachers of high purpose, noble inspiration, and godly character. . . . [which] ought to be the final test in selecting an institution of learning." For entertainment and recreation, the college offered basketball, croquet, tennis, and "other open-air amusements." In addition, parents and prospective students were assured that all "lamentable conditions as ripen into the brutalities of foot-ball and the abomination of hazing, are unknown at Atlantic Christian College."[22]

The lengthy list of rules and regulations that the college embraced may have impeded enrollment by convincing potential students, particularly males, that they should look elsewhere. Daily chapel attendance was required of all students, and young ladies were responsible for keeping their rooms in order. Women students were not allowed "to spend the night out of the college without written consent of parents or guardians" mailed directly to the president. The college also proclaimed that too much time was being wasted by students upon such distractions as "dressmaking, dentistry, and photography [which] should be attended to at home." The administration had determined that a more serious, academic-oriented atmosphere should prevail on the campus.[23]

A baseball game behind Kinsey Hall. 1916 Pine Knot.

On a more positive note to potential students, the *College Catalog* for the 1906–07 academic year announced the establishment of three new literary societies, which would affect almost every student enrolling at AC College during the next four decades. The Alethian and Hesperian Societies were coeducational organizations that encouraged literary endeavors and cultural growth. The societies met twice each month to support such exercises as group discussions, recitations, vocal and instrumental musical presentations, essay writing, and debates. The third group, the Demosthenian Society, was reserved for young men only. The Demosthenian focus was upon the writing of essays and newspaper reviews, public speaking, and debating.[24]

Prior to the appearance of Greek letter fraternities and sororities, literary societies helped to enhance a sense of community and served a variety of purposes upon college campuses across America. In addition to improving literary skills, the societies encouraged refinement of social graces and the development of poise. The associations also provided academic enrichment and entertainment opportunities within the college and the Wilson community through presentations of carefully planned and highly publicized oratorical contests. Members of the faculty were frequently recruited to judge these events, which could be lengthy and tedious. Contest winners, in addition to receiving much coveted acclaim, were awarded prizes that included trophies, books, and scholarships. Prior to their demise in the 1940s, the Alethian, Hesperian, and Demosthenian Societies were central to the academic and cultural life of the college.[25]

President Harper believed that Christianity should be ecumenical and was always ready to welcome quality students of all denominations. In January 1906, he wrote "the school has many warm friends and supporters 'which are not of this fold,' and whose encouragement is always highly appreciated." After classes began the following fall, Harper noted that fully half of the ninety-six students who had enrolled were not Disciples. The dormitory was filled to capacity, and room and board in local residencies were offered to young men at a rate not to exceed $10 per month.[26]

The state secretary of the Christian Church, W. Graham Walker, was instructed at the fall convention of 1906 to lead a fund-raising campaign to retire the school's bonded debt. *The Carolina Evangel*, a new weekly bulletin, was created in March 1907 to aid Walker in carrying out his new duties. During the same month, he also organized a large rally in the college chapel to build enthusiastic support for ACC. President Harper delivered a strong opening speech, which was followed by remarks from the chairman of the board of trustees and members of the faculty and staff. An impressive number of Disciples ministers, attending from locations throughout the state, also spoke, as did Jesse C. Caldwell, a visitor from Alabama. Large numbers of students, who readily welcomed rare opportunities to miss class, gave the session an enthusiastic and festive air. Their "orderly yells and songs" demonstrated a vibrant college spirit. The lengthy and dynamic session culminated with a successful dollar crusade led by the Disciples' Women's Board of Missions.[27]

Convinced that financial and enrollment crises had been weathered and the college's economic status had greatly improved, Harper asked the trustees to bring in a new leader and free him to return to the pulpit. Although reluctant to see their effective and popular president leave, the board acquiesced and began the search for a replacement in the early spring of 1907. Jesse Cobb Caldwell, minister of the Selma, Alabama, Christian church, came to Wilson to interview for the position. After conferring with trustees and other officials, Caldwell agreed to join the college. He would not move to Wilson as the president of Atlantic Christian College, however. The board persuaded Harper to remain as president for one additional year. Caldwell would be brought in as dean of the faculty and given the additional challenge of filling the pulpit of the Wilson Christian Church.[28]

A native of Missouri, Jesse Caldwell had a grandfather who had served central Kentucky as a distinguished Disciples minister. His mother, a devout Christian and a schoolteacher, contributed significantly to Jesse's early education and, reportedly, inspired her son's decision to become a preacher. After graduating from the University of Kentucky and the College of the Bible in Lexington, Caldwell served his first congregation in Owenton, Kentucky. He was ordained by the Christian Church in 1897 and, the following year, married Mary Settle of Owenton, eldest daughter of Congressman E. E. Settle, the most prominent politician in the state. After receiving the B.D. degree from Yale in 1903, Caldwell served four years as pastor of the First Christian Church of Selma, Alabama, leaving in 1907 to accept the call to Wilson.[29]

In the spring of 1908, the editor of *The Radiant*, the newly created student magazine of ACC, praised Caldwell as "a man of wonderful tact, of boundless energy, of fine judgement, of rare executive ability . . . [who] won the confidence and admiration of the entire student body." The students were also captivated by Caldwell's family—especially by the charm and youthful beauty of his four-year-old daughter. Elizabeth Settle Caldwell was described as "a sparkling, vivacious little fairy who rules her College Court" through a pleasant disposition and childish laughter. Having won the hearts of the students, Elizabeth was featured in the first yearbook in 1910 as sponsor of the senior class and was easily the most photographed nonstudent on campus.[30]

With Harper and Caldwell sharing the burden of leadership, the future of the college appeared especially promising. The new dean assisted in preparing a public relations brochure, which the college distributed widely. Harper was quite pleased that increased publicity regarding ACC brought more requests for the *College Catalog* from states other than North Carolina. He wrote in August 1907 that people were now convinced that "the college has come to stay." Later that fall, speaking at the annual church convention in Belhaven, the president optimistically predicted that the school "was destined to become . . . a great center of knowledge, secular and religious." Dean Caldwell followed Harper's lead with a stirring speech of his own. The results were electrifying. Those attending the convention proclaimed the event as a major achievement for Disciples in North Carolina that had created attention in other states. Delegate J. A. Lord, a veteran newspaper editor from Cincinnati, Ohio, joined in the spirit of the convention, praising the event as one of the greatest church assemblies that he had attended.[31]

A young but perceptive observer of Disciples activities during this time was student leader C. Manly Morton. As preacher, religion major, and one of the most active students at the college, Morton knew both Harper and Caldwell quite well. Writing in the initial issue of *The Pine Knot*, Morton evaluated the efforts made by the two men on behalf of the school as a perfect union of "'two giants' who skillfully blended their unique talents to move the college forward." Unfortunately, in early January 1908, a time when the future of the college appeared much brighter, tragedy stunned the campus. President Harper caught a cold that quickly developed into pneumonia. Before most people even knew that he was ill, the most vibrant force in the brief life of Atlantic Christian College had died. Memorial services for Dr. Harper attracted huge crowds to the college campus and to the site of his burial in Smithfield. People of all classes had found much to admire in the saintly preacher, Disciples leader, teacher, college president, and devoted father. Harper's family and members of the college community were joined in paying their respects by numerous church and government leaders, residents of Wilson and Smithfield, and mourners from distant places.[32]

In February 1908, the initial publication of *The Radiant* provided a vehicle through which students could express their emotions regarding the loss of their president. An editorial by C. Manly Morton referred to Harper as "the father of Atlantic Christian College" and revealed that he had encouraged publication of a student magazine, provided financial support, and even suggested the name. The staff dedicated the first volume of *The Radiant* to the memory of their mentor, leader, and friend. One verse of a poem, "The Broken Cord," written by Morton, expressed sentiments likely felt by the student body upon learning of Dr. Harper's death:

> A cedar by the river growing;
> Has bowed its head below decay:
> A light along the desert throwing
> Through the night a golden ray
> Has a moment glowed and flickered
> Then has died and passed away.

The editors challenged friends of the college to help make the new publication one of the best literary magazines available. Their intent was to proceed toward the goal of "spreading light and knowledge."[33]

Unfolding events of early 1908 brought momentous and far-reaching change to Atlantic Christian College, prompting a quick move by trustees to name Chancellor Jesse C. Caldwell as the institution's third president. Their action brought an end to the formative years in the life of the college, a period dominated by John J. Harper and Disciples from eastern North Carolina. For the first time, the school turned to leadership from outside the state, as Atlantic Christian College entered a period that might be termed the "Caldwell chapter" of the institution's history.

THREE

A Bold Stand in Support of Academic Freedom

JESSE COBB CALDWELL, officially appointed president 24 January 1908, inherited a college of 126 students, 74 percent of whom were female. An overwhelming majority of the student body came from Wilson (46 percent) and surrounding counties (38 percent). Only nine students were from other states, including Kentucky, Virginia, Alabama, New York, and Georgia. Most were listed as majors in the literary department (85) and the department of instrumental music (55). Others were in art, commercial studies, elocution, and vocal music. Forty-one students listed two majors. The college also featured a preparatory department, which accepted students who had successfully completed at least six grades at "the best graded schools of the State."[1]

Beginning with the 1910 academic year, the college required that students entering the preparatory program must have completed "work equivalent to seven grades of the graded school." Requirements for enrollment in college programs were more specific, demanding a minimum of fourteen units in six specified areas: English, three units; Latin, three units; Greek or modern language, one unit; mathematics, three units; history, two units; and science, two units. A unit was based upon academic work done five periods per week for thirty-six weeks.[2]

In 1900, North Carolina's elementary and secondary schools ranked at or near the bottom among the Southern states regarding both average annual school days and educational expenditures based upon total population. The state's annual average of seventy-one school days amounted to only 49 percent of the national norm. North Carolina's per capita figure of fifty cents spent on education amounted to less than 18 percent of the national average. Obviously, the state's poor record in addressing the educational needs of its young people had a negative impact on colleges in the state. Although educational reforms had improved North Carolina's comparative rank among

Southern states by 1920, the state remained far below the national average. Thus, ACC's teaching faculty, beginning with the preparatory department, encountered serious challenges because of earlier inadequate elementary and secondary schooling and because of the wide variety of skill levels possessed by incoming students. The small size of the college's early senior classes indicates that many who enrolled in the preparatory department failed to survive academic demands, transferred to other institutions, or dropped out for other reasons.[3]

On a more positive note, the college frequently succeeded in educating students who initially appeared unlikely to advance. An early defining characteristic of Barton College was its ability to take students with average academic abilities and mold them into successful seniors. Over the years, the college's success in producing graduating classes with proven academic skills and accomplishments became a source of institutional pride. Apparently, the school was in the process of developing this characteristic as early as President Caldwell's administration.[4]

Although Caldwell had spent but half a year as academic dean and understudy to President Harper, the arrangement proved highly successful. Observers of the fall term of 1907 noted that combined efforts by the president and new dean had begun to move the college forward. Caldwell's youth, vigor, and enthusiasm complemented Harper's experience, wisdom, and knowledge of the school, community, and state. Both were Disciples preachers with reputations as strong leaders and forceful public speakers. As college administrators, they shared a commitment to creating an environment that encouraged development of strong moral character within a Christian framework. Both men also supported high academic standards and placed heavy emphasis on literary skills.[5]

Caldwell and Harper's shared pride in literary accomplishments was demonstrated by students whose efforts both men encouraged. Led by irrepressible editor-in-chief C. Manly Morton, *The Radiant* became a triumph from the start. Within the second full year of Caldwell's presidency, the school's first yearbook, *The Pine Knot*, made its appearance. The two student publications provided an impressive array of opportunities for ACC students to develop and display writing skills and strengthen organizational talents. The publications served as an open form of communication between ACC and editors of student magazines on other campuses. *The Radiant* and *The Pine Knot* also prompted significant interaction between students and residents of the Wilson community through such ventures as selling advertise-

The Radiant *staff of 1908; the 1910* Pine Knot.

ments and magazines and sponsoring cultural events. The yearly subscription rate for *The Radiant*, which listed itself as a bimonthly magazine, was one dollar, while single copies sold for fifteen cents.[6]

AC students readily joined in to create and circulate the new literary publications. Most of the students who graduated with academic honors participated, and some classes listed 100 percent involvement by graduating seniors. Fortunately, for friends of the college and historians, the magazines serve as windows to the past through which to learn their stories. That legacy sheds light upon a broad and interesting array of ideas, concerns, and experiences during Barton's formative years. Much of the writing which appeared in early editions of *The Radiant* and *The Pine Knot* were essays and poems addressing mankind's principal intellectual and aesthetic concerns, including beauty, love, the wisdom and power of God, and man's struggle against the forces of nature. Like many young women and men of the Western world of the early twentieth century, ACC students had been reared by parents whose values were heavily influenced by Victorian customs. Strong emphasis on forthrightness, honesty, character, enterprise, and success was reflected by a high-minded, self-righteous society, which also drew clear distinctions between the sexes.[7]

Few students in the college's history have exerted as much impact upon the institution as the initial editor-in-chief of both *The Radiant* and *The Pine*

Knot. Upon arrival, C. Manly Morton became a presence on campus, and he stayed long enough to become the school's first "professional student." As a driving force behind the creation and continued development of Barton's first two student publications, Morton left his most significant and lasting legacy. In addition to editing and organizing, Morton was neither bashful nor hesitant about sharing his thoughts and talents in print. A religion major, his poetry, editorials, and articles abound throughout early editions of both publications. Morton's writing typically reflects a highly romanticized Victorian style. Examples include two poems, which appeared in the second edition of *The Radiant*. The style and theme of these verses from "The Mountain Flower" are typical of Morton's poetry:

>I wandered up the mountain side
>Alone one winter day
>While all around the wild wind blew,
>And thick the soft snow lay.
>
>And if our hands will clear away
>The snow that lies so deep,
>A blessed flower of peace we'll see,
>And hope again will leap.
>
>For all the good can ne'er be killed,
>Although but death we see;
>Then up poor heart, still on, still on,
>Discouraged never be.[8]

Carrie Bowen, college editor of *The Radiant*, secretary-treasurer of the Hesperian Literary Society, and secretary of the Girls' Athletic Association, writing in 1911, blended the Victorian emphasis on morality and character with Christian ethics in an essay entitled "The Ladder of Character," a portion of which reads: "We bring into the world different gifts ... gold ... marble ... or clay. It is for us to fashion these substances. We can make them what we will. Environment sometimes plays an important part in the moulding of our character.... Many of our greatest men have come from the hovel and the plow. Then it is not money, but Christian influence, which gives us noble men and virtuous women ... steadily, patiently do we soar from the cradle to the grave.[9]

Much of the prose and poetry written by ACC students between 1908 and 1912 reflected concern with the human spirit and with man's quest to bring justice and morality to a world threatened by evil. Threads throughout these writings connect historical events and heroes from Socrates, Luther, Shakespeare, Pope, Tennyson, and Dickens to God's plan for man as revealed in scripture. A November 1908 editorial praised the increasing number of colleges and universities offering Bible classes and expressed hope that the trend would lead all colleges to require Bible studies as a condition for graduation.[10]

College students of the era found themselves on the threshold of a dynamic new century where the values of their elders frequently conflicted with doctrines brought by social and technological change. As eastern North Carolina's young adults questioned the religious conservatism and Victorian ideals of their parents, they also encountered the Progressive Movement, a middle-class reform spirit that swept through early twentieth-century America. The Progressives emphasized a need to clean up corrupt government, dissolve business monopolies, prohibit the sale of alcoholic beverages, create a square deal for factory workers, and enact legislation aimed at conservation of the nation's natural resources. Reformers hoped to cause the nation once again to reflect high democratic and moral standards, which they believed to have permeated early America.

Historians have noted that middle-class women provided significant leadership to the turn-of-the century revolt against Victorian restraints. Central to the struggle was the new feminist crusade, which swept the country in the early decades of the twentieth century. Reformers were not happy that little change had occurred during the half-century since the 1848 Women's Rights Convention at Seneca Falls, New York, had declared equal rights for females. When Atlantic Christian College first opened its doors in 1902, women remained nearly two decades away from possessing the right to vote. Not surprisingly, the subject of gender equity remained a lively issue on the American college campus.[11]

Bess Hackney, a Wilson co-ed who served as wit editor on *The Radiant* staff and president of the Girls' Athletic Association, argued in May 1909 that "The Educated Woman" was the greatest achievement of the civilized world. Tracing women's progress from classical Greece and Rome to the present, Hackney praised such notable women as Queen Elizabeth, Jane Austen, George Eliot, and Helen Keller. She noted that women already voted in elections in England, Scotland, and Ireland and had begun to participate at political conventions of both national parties in the United States. She found it particularly significant that a woman had formally seconded the nomination of presidential candidate William Jennings Bryan at the Democratic Convention of 1900.[12]

A 1910 article, entitled "Woman's Influence and Position," by senior class president Verdie Noble, a Kinston native and assistant editor of *The Pine Knot*, contended that a woman's position in society determined the level of sophistication attained by a nation or race. Noting that women had made important contributions to the national prohibition movement and occupied most positions open to men in general, Noble suggested that women continue to receive equal opportunities for intellectual, cultural, and spiritual growth because "their elevation results in the elevation of humanity."[13]

Male students sometimes joined female colleagues in supporting equality between the sexes. Hayes Farish, business manager of *The Radiant* and Washington, D.C., native, contributed two articles during the school year 1910–11 which forcefully argued the case of women's rights. Noting that American women had already held practically every office open to men with the exception of chief executive, he suggested that the election of a woman president would be a positive step for the national prohibition movement, with the result that "the beautiful white flag of temperance would wave over every state and territory of our grand Republic." Farish called for equal education of women and deplored the double standard that held females to a stricter moral code regarding dating, smoking, and drinking. He argued that real social and moral reform could not occur until men and women were held equally accountable.[14]

Senior class president Mattie Phillips, a Kinston native, also lamented the existence of the double standard. Writing in the June 1911 issue of *The Radiant*, she stated that the woman who made the best wife and mother was the woman with a "trained mind." Voicing a concern shared by modern Americans, she wrote, "It is a common idea that the children of today have no conscience, and have no knowledge of God because their mothers are club women, who see too little of the children." In addition, Phillips argued that the "foolish cry that 'the place for a woman is in the home' has given way to 'the place for a woman is where she fits.'" In the future, she predicted that women would become adept at flying "aeroplanes," which she phrased as "driving 'the automobiles of the sky.'" Phillips's remarks were aimed at the great expansion of women's clubs during the last three decades of the nineteenth century, which tended to thrust the American club woman into greater public view.[15]

With the exception of C. Manly Morton, no student's writing appeared more in early student publications than that of Lossie Davis. A freshman literary major from Lucama, Davis served as literary editor of *The Radiant* in 1908.

Her fellow students may have been amused by the essay "My Ideal Man," appearing in the second volume of the college magazine. The perfect man of Lossie Davis' dreams was handsome, graceful, intelligent, and loyal, in addition to being a devout Christian and music lover, whose only weakness was an inability to refrain from purchasing more neckties than he either needed or could afford. The casual reader might have taken the article's author for a typical love-struck co-ed, obsessed by the thought of finding her ideal male on the AC campus. Those acquainted with Davis knew that such an impression was a mistake. Lossie Davis was intelligent, pragmatic, and reform-minded. Her critique, "Elizabeth Barrett Browning—The Woman," reveals a broad knowledge of Western literature. Acknowledging that Browning was helped by other writers, Davis argues that she was largely self-taught and had been forced to conquer both physical difficulties and the prevailing prejudice against female writers. Elizabeth Barrett Browning survived these challenges to become a respected poet. One measure of a poet's greatness, Davis argues, is the ability to infuse her writings with "a refining, chastening and elevating influence, breathing forth an unwavering trust in God and in immortality."[16]

Another of Davis' essays, "Beyond the Altar Lies the Washtub," blends idealism, humor, and practical advice in warning women against the perils of rushing into marriage only to be awakened to life's "harsh realities." Her advice to young women is to develop their God-given powers of womanhood while demanding purity and manhood in the man who will be her husband. In perhaps her best essay, "The American Woman of To-Day and Yesterday," written in 1911, Davis demonstrates a keen understanding of the woman of her own age as well as those of her mother's and grandmother's generations. She sees nothing wrong with females of her generation inviting men to escort them to a dance or the theater and no harm in offering carriage and automobile rides to male friends. Davis boasts that in comparison to European women, the modern American female is like "bottled lightning." She argues that:

> The Woman that the new South needs is not less womanly than her sister of 'old days,' but she is better educated, and therefore, more fit for the problems of the future. Her horizon is broadened, her outlook on life is far wider.... The South needs the college bred woman because she will best conduct the home, and thus indirectly uplift the nation.... The daughters and future wives of American men must be resourceful, clever, intelligent. They can never become so through quietly sitting by and listening to the

tales of mid-Victorian courtesy. . . . our entire attitude must differ in many respects from that of the girl of yesterday.[17]

Davis did not differ from many college women in appreciating the heroic efforts made by suffragettes while arguing that most women remained uninterested in attaining the right to vote. She also applauded recent statistics indicating that the number of American women actively involved in businesses had increased dramatically between 1880 and 1911. Davis demonstrated the dilemma faced by her generation in welcoming newly won freedom and increased opportunities but cautioned that modern women must retain qualities of "gentleness and generosity" as well as high standards of morality.[18]

Wilson would seem to some an unlikely meeting place for a different reform movement announced in the November 1908 issue of *The Radiant*. Male students had organized the "Anti-tobacco Club of Atlantic Christian College." The group had begun an investigation into "the many deleterious effects of this noxious weed upon all those who have formed the habit of using it." Displaying great enthusiasm for the project, the club vowed to hold an open meeting on their findings in December. An announcement that the meeting would be restricted "to the student body only" indicated a decision to temper crusading reform with caution. The opening of the Wilson tobacco market in 1890 had been followed by steady sales growth. By 1908 the city had become a leading state and national tobacco marketing center. In addition, tobacco sales furnished financial support for the college, including aid to student publications, which listed tobacco warehouses among their patrons.[19]

AC College students who supported reform organizations represented the nation's typical citizens of this era. Historians studying late nineteenth and early twentieth-century America have argued that the Gilded Age trend of organizing was an essential step toward building the modern nation of the twentieth century. Significant new organizations of that time included the National Education Association, the American Bankers Association, the American Bar Association, the National Collegiate Athletic Association, and the American Federation of Teachers. None of the new groups became as controversial as those started by the working man, including the American Federation of Labor, which began in 1886. From the days of its first appearance, conservative Americans harbored strong distrust of big labor. Labor unions struggled to gain acceptance in North Carolina, especially in conservative areas of the state, but frequently found more receptive audiences on college and university campuses. The topic of the only speech delivered by a graduating senior at ACC com-

ACC student writers (top to bottom, left to right) C. Manly Morton and Lossie Davis, Julia E. Farmer and Verdie Noble. 1910 Pine Knot.

mencement exercises in May 1910 likely surprised the audience; they may have been even more startled that the prolabor union speech was delivered by a demure co-ed from Wilson.[20]

The commencement speaker was Julia Estelle Farmer, senior class vice-president and the lone literary department graduate of 1910. Ministers, lawyers, and doctors had formed organizations to benefit their professions, Farmer noted, suggesting that the "'spirit of organization' and the 'spirit of progress'" were actually the same thing. Admitting that radicals had sometimes caused unions to act rashly, she maintained that positive aspects of organized labor outweighed negative factors. Labor unions benefited workers by bringing salary increases, improving working conditions, and supporting better city playgrounds and schools. Furthermore, Farmer stated that the record showed that unions "aid their members in times of need, protect widows and orphans, pension the aged members and benefit them in many other ways." After using a prolabor quote from philosopher Thomas Carlyle, she ended her speech with a bold assertion: "It is now generally admitted by nearly all really educated and honest men that a thorough organization of the entire working class . . . is one of the most vital necessities of the present day."[21]

The editorial staff of *The Radiant* labeled Farmer's speech "profound" and considered the style "clear and forceful." Farmer's remarks demonstrated insight into forces which had brought extraordinary growth to both labor and business and revealed an understanding of current reform issues, including the Progressives' drive to secure child labor legislation and safer working conditions in American factories. Yet, the most significant aspect of Julia Farmer's address was likely the fact that a small liberal arts college in conservative eastern North Carolina readily provided her with a podium from which to challenge such controversial issues. At this time, the rest of the nation did not differ significantly from North Carolina in its hesitancy to confront divisive issues. With American women of 1910 still a decade away from obtaining the right to vote, both Farmer and the college took a bold stand in support of academic freedom.[22]

The main graduation address, which followed Farmer's speech, came from one of the state's most illustrious native sons, Josephus Daniels, editor and publisher of the Raleigh *News and Observer*. Daniels had grown up in Wilson, where he gained experience as editor of the local newspaper while still a teenager and earned a statewide reputation as a promising young journalist. A lifelong active member of the Democratic Party, Daniels later served as Secretary of the Navy and Ambassador to Mexico under Presidents Woodrow Wilson and Franklin Roosevelt. In *Tar Heel Editor*, his autobiography, Daniels recalled his happy boyhood in Wilson. He had also found the capital city of Raleigh, where he spent most of his adult life, to be a good place to live and a solidly Democratic city. Wilson, however, was special to Daniels, because as he explained, it was both Democratic and a democratic city. Daniels thanked President Caldwell for the invitation to return to his hometown and deliver the college commencement address. Surveying his audience, the veteran editor announced to the amused group that he had taken his topic from "the seventh verse of the fourteenth chapter of Uncle Remus." In that passage the terrapin proclaims, "I carries my own house upon my own back. I messes with nobody and lets nobody mess with me." Daniels warned graduating seniors and guests that demands made by a rapidly changing world had rendered the terrapin's philosophy obsolete. He advised the graduates to go out into the world and become involved, to "'mess' with people and let people 'mess'" with them. Arguing that mankind must be willing to sacrifice individuality in order to serve others, Daniels ended his remarks with a reminder that nothing important in life is accomplished apart from the power of Almighty God.[23]

ACC students hailed Daniels' speech as a "masterpiece of thought and diction . . . filled with 'good sound doctrine.'" *The Radiant* proclaimed that the college community and Wilson were honored by the opportunity to hear remarks from the respected journalist and looked forward to his return to the area. However, long before hearing Daniels' wise words of advice, students at the college had taken the initiative to "mess" with others. The editorial staff of *The Radiant* had begun in 1908 to participate in an exchange of magazines with other academic institutions. The first exchange publications to reach the ACC campus included *St. Mary's Muse* and a publication from the Baptist University in Raleigh entitled *The Acorn*. By the summer of 1910, *The Radiant* staff members were benefiting from a spirit of "fellowship" created by the exchange program. They had divided incoming journals into three categories. Ranked in the first class were those considered "breezy and alive with school spirit." These magazines featured short, invigorating articles, and their editors appeared to be alert and effective. The second class, described as "classical," dealt with deeper articles, especially valued by intellectual readers. Magazines rated in the third class were deemed below standard. The efforts put forth by the staffs of these journals were described as "feeble," and, critically speaking, their poor condition indicated the possibility that they originated from "a dead student body." Obviously, student editors took seriously their responsibility to provide frank literary criticism. Fortunately, few exchange issues arrived on campus that deserved placement in category three.[24]

The staff of ACC's student magazine received exchange journals from across the nation during the 1910–11 academic year, including Lexington, Kentucky; Meriden, Connecticut; Kearney, Nebraska; Detroit, Michigan; and Fort Worth, Texas. The editors singled out several North Carolina journals for special praise. *The Guilford Collegian* of Greensboro and *The Blackboard* from Rocky Mount were cited for attractiveness and high literary quality. The exchange program brought new ideas to the campus, provided the college with national exposure for the first time, and created an exhilarating sense of sharing student-created literature with kindred spirits from faraway campuses.[25]

The Radiant staff attempted to provide humor for the magazine's readers. The following examples, listed under such headings as "Why We Laugh," "On the Funny Side of Life," and "On the Funny Bone," appeared in issues of *The Radiant* between April 1908 and June 1911:

Lady Turnage—The automobile is being used more than horses now.
Reide Lang—Yes, I found a piece of rubber tire in our sausage yesterday at breakfast.

"Old Maids' Club." *1910* Pine Knot.

>Miss Myrtle—Albert, tell me what you know of the Mongolian race.
>Albert—I wasn't there. I went to the football game.
>
>Of all sad words of tongue or pen,
>The saddest are these: I've flunked again.
>
>On the 10th of May the college girls saw an object moving through the air above the campus, and being unable to ascertain what it was, they ran from it. But when it neared the ground and proved to be a balloon with a man in it they ran toward it. Why?
>
>Wanted—To know where is the wit of the wit editors? Readers.[26]

While attempting to produce laughter, which lifted the spirit, *The Radiant* also occasionally found it necessary to report news that saddened the college community. A brief article in the April 1908 issue noted that "Bro. Outlaw," a ministerial student from Wilson, had recently returned to the college community with his wife after being away from school for nearly two months. His lengthy absence at a critical time in the spring semester had been caused by "the death of his little son, and the subsequent illness of his wife." The toddler's death, rapidly following the unexpected loss of President Harper, had been a second severe blow to the religion department and spread grief throughout the college community.[27]

Cecil F. Outlaw, member of the class of 1911, later served as vice-president of the junior class, treasurer of the Alethian Society, and corresponding secretary of the ministerial association. Although stylistically not among the best-written poems published in the college magazine, Outlaw's tribute to his son contains hauntingly beautiful words that attest to the depth of the young couple's loss. "Our First Born," appearing in the May 1909 issue of *The Radiant*, ends with these words:

In the midst a tiny grave lot, / Is a sacred little mound,
There our precious darling sleepth, / 'Neath the damp and chilly ground.

At the head a shaft of marble, / Marks the little mound of clay,
Where we go to scent the flowers, / And the tears to wipe away.

On that little shaft of marble, / Is our darling's name so sweet,
It is little "Cecil Junior." / Oh! in heaven may we meet.

'Tis a little grave I grant you, / But my friend you'll please use care,
When that way you tread to view it, / World-wide hopes are buried there.[28]

Outlaw's solemn words reflect a simple, yet profound, spiritual faith which lay at the core of Atlantic Christian College and helped to sustain those who served and attended the school. The young ministerial student, himself then in the process of learning how to help others deal with tragedy and grief, would have found a nurturing environment at the small Christian college, which was well equipped to aid a young couple struggling to deal with great loss.

In addition to articles on nature, beauty, joy, and grief, student poems and essays during the first decade of the college's existence voiced pride in North Carolina and the South, discussed political issues, and explored Social Darwinist themes of imperialism, nationalism, and racial pride. Others addressed ethical and/or religious concerns. C. Manly Morton continued to serve as associate editor of *The Radiant* as a post-graduate student after leaving the college. *The Pine Knot* of 1913, which lists him as an alumni editor, also praises his work as pastor of the First Christian Church of Winston-Salem.[29]

Atlantic Christian College's earliest student writers created a legacy that has stood for nearly a century. Through hard work and tenacity, and with help and encouragement from faculty and administrators, they honed their writing and editing skills, shared ideas with distant institutions, and exerted an impact throughout the Wilson community and beyond. Their efforts and those of student writers who followed built a solid literary foundation for such later publications as *The Collegiate* and *Crucible*. As the college celebrates its one hundredth year, The Sam and Marjorie Ragan Writing Center stands as both a tribute to Barton's literary heritage and a resource for present and future generations of young writers who will build upon that tradition.[30]

FOUR

He Won't Let Us Dance but He Wants Us to Walk

AS THE COLLEGE prepared to celebrate its tenth anniversary in 1912, the price of a postage stamp was two cents, gasoline sold for seven cents a gallon, and the average American house listed for $4,800. The huge British liner *Titanic*, considered the safest ship afloat, left on its maiden voyage from England to New York. Roy Rogers, Dale Evans, Perry Como, and Art Linkletter were born, and, in November, Woodrow Wilson became only the second Democratic president elected in more than half a century. On the Barton campus, Jesse Cobb Caldwell completed his fourth full year as president, and Mamie Doss Jennings, director of expression, began her second year on the faculty.[1]

Mamie Jennings described President Jesse Caldwell as "one of the most delightful men I have ever known," and stated that she had enjoyed working on the faculty under his leadership. Nevertheless, she never forgave Caldwell for a perceived slight rendered on a winter night in 1910, which caused her to reevaluate her decision to come to the college. Recalling the event during a 1992 interview at her home on Wilson's West Nash Street, Mamie Jennings Lucas, lucid and remarkably spry at the age of 106 years, shared her thoughts about events spanning more than eight decades.[2]

Jennings, a Nashville, Tennessee, resident and recent college graduate in the autumn of 1910, learned of a teaching position which would be available the following January at a college in eastern North Carolina. Overriding the objections of parents and friends who disliked her moving so far away, she accepted President Caldwell's offer to join the faculty at Atlantic Christian College and began preparations to move to Wilson. In late December 1910, Jennings said goodbye to friends who had gathered to see her off despite the lateness of the hour and boarded a midnight train for North Carolina. Hours later, as her train rumbled east through the Great Smoky Mountains, she wistfully recalled a warning from the boy who had lingered longest to say goodbye. "Mamie," he had predicted, "you're going to get tar on your heels and you'll never come back." Her flippant reply did not reveal the uncertainty that she felt: "You don't know what you're talking about." Recalling the event nostalgically after more than eighty-one years, she stated, "But I never did [return to Tennessee]."[3]

Her journey through North Carolina ended about twenty-four hours later at the Wilson depot where she expected a warm reception following her long, lonely trip. The freight agent, to her dismay, reported that Dr. Caldwell had requested that he look out for her arrival and directed her to a solitary figure waiting beside a horse and carriage near the train station. The traveler and luggage were placed on board a "little surrey with a fringe on top" and driven west by a small black man along a very dark Nash Street toward the college campus. Jennings' reception upon arrival at the women's dormitory of Kinsey Hall was no warmer than her experience at the depot. Her knock on the door was answered immediately by a grim-faced woman in nightclothes who escorted the weary traveler upstairs to a stark little room near the tower. Recalling that the room contained a fireplace, bed, and little else, Jennings stated curtly, "She left me, a young woman, in that awful position. I was treated rather shabbily that first night or two." She soon learned that her hostess was "Miss Myrtie" Harper, who served officially as librarian and unofficially as "the general manager of the school—whatever was going on, she knew about and had a hand in it." Fortunately, Miss Myrtie decided that the newcomer was acceptable and assigned Jennings a more suitable room on the second floor which she enjoyed during the remainder of her stay at the college.[4]

Jennings found her teaching responsibilities both challenging and rewarding as she became active on the campus and in the Wilson community. College publications show that she quickly became a respected and productive member of the faculty. Her remarks regarding memories of President Caldwell, shared in 1992, were overwhelmingly positive. Typically, however, positive comments were followed with the admonition: "But I never did forgive him for not meeting me that night."[5]

President Jesse Cobb Caldwell observed his thirty-ninth birthday with his wife and two daughters on 15 January 1912 in the spacious, two-story frame structure known as the President's House, located opposite the eastern corner of the campus. A short, dapper man of slender frame, he parted his dark hair in the middle and sported a well-trimmed mustache and short goatee. Dr. Caldwell was a gentle, kindly man best known for his abilities as a speaker and for his scholarly classes in sacred history. Mary Settle Caldwell, described as a quiet, gra-

Mamie Jennings, director of expression. 1913 Pine Knot.

cious lady whose time was devoted largely to rearing the couple's two young daughters, Elizabeth and Mildred, occasionally served as a substitute teacher on the campus. Although the Caldwell family was fashionably and neatly dressed and seemed to get along well, their life-style was rendered somewhat Spartan by the lack of outside income to supplement Dr. Caldwell's modest salary of $125 per month.[6]

Caldwell had accepted the presidency of the college at a critical time for both the institution and the Disciples of Christ Church in North Carolina. While both previous presidents had realized notable achievements, the school that Caldwell headed remained caught in a long-standing struggle to free itself from a condition of debilitating indebtedness in an era when colleges throughout the nation faced adverse economic conditions. The most significant problem was the lack of an endowment large enough to afford retaining a faculty capable of offering quality academic programs. Historian Charles C. Ware quoted remarks made on that issue by President Ely Von Zollars of Hiram College, a sister Disciples school in Ohio. Referring to the poor financial status plaguing American church-related institutions, Dr. Von Zollars charged that religious groups across the nation challenged their colleges "to make bricks without straw."[7]

At commencement ceremonies in May 1911, Atlantic Christian College finally celebrated its freedom from the school's original indebtedness by publicly burning the bonds in a festive ceremony on campus. Numerous friends from the Wilson community attended the celebration. "Colonel" J. F. Bruton, president of Wilson's First National Bank, who had been invited to address the crowd, praised the commitment and leadership of both Harper and Caldwell and noted that their good works had won the love and respect of the entire Wilson community. The celebration also called attention to the new dormitory for men, which was nearing completion, and to additional construction underway on Kinsey Hall which promised to provide additional living space for young women. A campaign to name the new dormitory in honor of Dr. Caldwell was stopped at the request of the modest president, and the handsome, three-story brick building, located north of Kinsey Hall, was called the Boys' Dormitory initially. Months later, trustees ignored the president's protests and officially named the building Caldwell Hall as a tribute to the school's popular leader.[8]

After a decade of being shuffled between neighboring boarding houses, male students finally began living on the campus. Trustees and school officials hoped that the modern new dormitory would attract additional young men to ACC. The building also provided space for administrative offices and a laboratory for natural sciences, freeing areas of Kinsey Hall for additional dormitory and classroom use. Total construction costs were approximately $20,000. The need to upgrade campus facilities forced the college to assume new indebtedness at the very time that the institution had finally paid off the old debt. Charles C. Ware noted the irony in the fact that the new construction expenses diminished chances of attracting crucial endowment funds during the first twenty years of the school's existence. Ware referred to the existence of an unwilling, albeit "ungenerous and illogical" trend among potential contributors to withhold endowment giving while outstanding debt existed. Praising early leaders for creating successful academic programs despite a lack of adequate financial support, Ware called their accomplishments "a superlative memorial" to the college.[9]

Caldwell's efforts to make ACC into a first-rate college, while simultaneously working to increase membership within Disciples congregations, were impressive. The Caldwell family had arrived in North Carolina at an opportune time for church growth. While the denomination continued to prosper in rural areas, the traditional stronghold of the church, metropolitan areas also became increasingly receptive to the Christian Church. Caldwell worked diligently and traveled extensively in support of church projects. While continuing to make visits to traditional sites, including Ayden, Belhaven, Farmville, Goldsboro, Greenville, Kinston, and Williamston, he also broadened his travels. Responding to invitations from such geographically diverse areas of the state as Wilmington and Asheville and from Piedmont churches in Raleigh, Winston-Salem, and Charlotte, Caldwell quickly became an extremely popular champion of Disciples causes. He agreed to help South Carolina churches requesting assistance and visited Charleston, home of the largest Disciples church in that state. Caldwell's value to the Disciples within the two states increased to the point that national church officials considered him one of the most effective leaders in the South and referred to him as the "Bishop of the Carolinas."[10]

Caldwell's extensive efforts on behalf of the college and the church became so demanding that friends were concerned about his health. In an effort to demonstrate their appreciation for his contributions and also to convince him to reduce his work load, trustees and friends decided to reward the president with a paid trip abroad. Typically, the self-effacing Caldwell proposed an alternative idea, suggesting a monetary gift to upgrade the college library. Students and friends finally changed his mind by stressing the value that a trip to the Holy Land would have to a dedicated teacher of religion. Caldwell finally relented, and the voyage was scheduled to begin in early February 1912.[11]

Disciples newsletters praised the idea of a pilgrimage to Palestine as a reward for the popular college president and attempted to attract financial support from church congregations throughout the state. In January 1912, *The Evangel*, published in Wilmington, cautioned that the scheduled departure date was drawing near and urged that pledges to raise the estimated $1,000 gift be paid at once. With the requisite pledges finally collected, a February issue of *The Evangel* outlined the traveler's itinerary. He would travel by train to New York and depart 8 February aboard the *Arabic*, a steamer belonging to the White Star Line. The first stop would be the island of Madeira, off the African coast, followed by visits to Cadiz, Seville, Gibraltar, Algiers, and Malta.

Tours of Athens and Constantinople would precede the main visit to the Holy Land, with side trips to Ephesus, Smyrna, and Damascus.[12]

Caldwell would spend four to six weeks in Palestine, during which time he would also visit Egypt and travel the Nile River as far inland as the city of Luxor. He would be gone an estimated three months. The editor of the college magazine, a ministerial student under Caldwell's tutelage, referred to the trip as outstanding in its own right and predicted that it would prove to be "of inestimable worth to a student and teacher of Sacred History." Providing additional news about the extended scope of the trip, *The Radiant* added that the traveler had also decided to tour Europe for a few weeks. In its April edition, the student magazine reported that Mrs. Caldwell had received cards and letters from the president at every port. He also corresponded with his children, having sent Elizabeth a beautiful picture postcard of the famous Rock of Gibraltar. The traveler remained in splendid health and was thoroughly enjoying his tour. Caldwell's trip was enhanced by the companionship of E. M. Waits, a friend from Transylvania College days. Waits was a preacher at First Christian Church in Fort Worth, Texas, and later served as president of Texas Christian University.[13]

Caldwell's trip undoubtedly produced considerable anxiety in Wilson and other Disciples strongholds of North Carolina when people learned the shocking news of the tragic sinking of the *Titanic*, which, like the *Arabic*, was a British steamer owned by The White Star Line. On the night of 14 April 1912, the "unsinkable" *Titanic*, the world's largest vessel, sank after striking an iceberg in the north Atlantic, about 1,600 miles northeast of New York City. Many of the approximately 1,500 passengers who died were Americans. The coincidence that both the *Titanic* and *Arabic* not only belonged to the same shipping line but shared identical port destinations could hardly have been lost upon the college community.

Caldwell returned to a warm welcome at the college in May and discovered his schedule filled with tasks and invitations that had accumulated since early February. Among the returning president's first priorities was acceptance of a unanimous request from the graduating seniors to preach the baccalaureate sermon during commencement exercises scheduled to begin the week of 26 May. Other tasks requiring immediate attention included final preparations of the *College Catalog*, hiring new faculty, and recruiting students for the fall semester. As the trustees had hoped, the overseas trip not only had broadened Caldwell's global perspective and provided extensive insight into the geogra-

President James C. Caldwell, 1908–16. 1910 Pine Knot.

phy of important biblical sites but had also afforded quality time to reflect and plan for Atlantic Christian College's future.[14]

The opening of fall semester on 10 September 1912 proved very successful. All dormitory rooms were filled to capacity, and students planning to arrive later had to be notified that their enrollment would be delayed until arrangements could be made. Other positive news included rumors that friends of the school planned to raise $150,000 to provide an endowment for the college. Addressing the Disciples State Convention, held in Farmville during November, Caldwell thanked supporters for financing his trip to the Holy Land and emphasized that an endowment was critical to the school's ability to reach its potential. Student leaders echoed their president's call for an endowment in the February 1913 issue of *The Radiant*. Appealing to friends of the college to raise at least $100,000, the editors promised that once the endowment funds were raised, "we will show you what Atlantic Christian College can do." The magazine further noted that although pledges had been made to create an endowment, no leader had been named to head the campaign.[15]

Attempts to raise an endowment apparently made little progress, and the popular president's travels and speeches were seldom rewarded with money for the school. The Education Committee of the North Carolina Christian Missionary Convention, meeting in Greenville in November 1914, requested that $3,000 be raised to support the college by 1 January 1915. The committee argued that the money was needed because the church had conducted no statewide attempt on behalf of the institution "during the last two or three years."[16]

Disciples leaders and editors argued repeatedly that most church members did not appreciate the college's true value to the denomination in North Carolina. Responding to this problem, in September 1913 the college formed the Ministerial Association of Atlantic Christian College for the purpose of determining how the institution might better serve the church. The group consisted of all ministerial students, four faculty members, and Wilson Christian Church pastor Richard Bagby, who served as chairman. In August 1914, the editor of *The Watch Tower* urged readers to support ACC and cautioned them not to forget that the college remained the "greatest asset of the Disciples of Christ in North Carolina." The December 1914 issue of *The Radiant* also addressed the problem, pointing out that ministerial students at the time preached in thirty-one churches within the state and during the previous year had preached more than 900 sermons and baptized more than 300 believers.[17]

Students and faculty members often accompanied President Caldwell on trips to conferences and to individual churches, where they assisted with programs, helped to draw attention to the college, and enhanced the image of their school. Ministerial students added a youthful perspective, impressed their elders by their commitment to the ministry, and shared information concerning current activities on campus. Musical groups, such as the glee club, chorus, or quartet, were especially well received because they contributed special music, which entertained and energized the sessions.[18]

Many members of the college community perceived that a problem between the campus and the town persisted during the early years of Caldwell's administration. The prevailing view on campus throughout the school's first decade was that, other than the members of the local Christian Church, Wilson residents tended to exhibit an attitude of indifference toward ACC. Thus, when a group of Wilsonians sponsored an informal reception to welcome incoming college students in September 1912, the college eagerly embraced the social occasion. Editors of the student magazine remarked that the reception, which was held in the "circular room" of Kinsey Hall, caused students to "feel that Wilson is no longer a strange city." A second reception, designed to honor both students and faculty, packed the college auditorium and became a delightful occasion. In addition to refreshments and introductions to the faculty, the event featured musical performances by Harriet Settle, soloist, and Ed Stallings Jr., violinist, both from the college music department.[19]

Barton College's Wilson students led the way in making the welcome-back-to-school reception into an annual affair. Students Bess and Lula Hackney, whose family had strongly supported the school from the beginning, helped organize the September 1914 reception. The editor of *The Carolina Evangel* considered the social such a success that he remarked that the town-gown affair represented "a fortunate omen for the future growth of this school." The February issue of the college magazine reported that faculty and students honored Bess Hackney at a campus social prior to her marriage to William Dennis Adams, which occurred in Wilson's First Christian Church on 30 January 1915. Editors of *The Radiant* praised the bride, who was a daughter of trustee chairman, George H. Hackney, as a loyal friend of the college and a key factor in improving social life on the campus.[20]

By 1916, a decade and a half of religious, cultural, and economic interaction between the institution and the Wilson community had provided ample opportunity for town-gown relationships to develop, and both parties benefited in a variety of ways. Students, faculty, and staff contributed to the local economy as consumers. Financial contributions from city businesses provided support for special campus events, and local merchants bought advertising space in the college magazine and yearbook. Some businesses, including P. D. Gold Publishing Company, owner of both *The Daily Times* and *Semi-Weekly Times*, provided scholarships to the college. Wilson residents who were not regular students enrolled in art or music classes, and some took individual instruction from professors in the visual or performing arts. Musical performances and drama productions were open to the public as were other campus events. A January 1916 recital, featuring violinist Ed Stallings, and vocalists Harriet Settle, Maude Bowen, Ruth Hardy, and Professor Albert Muilberger, played to a large and enthusiastic crowd. The Raleigh *News and Observer* praised the event as an outstanding program of classical music.[21]

Students and faculty members frequently presented cultural, religious, and intellectual programs both on and off the campus, including those at localities beyond the Wilson community. Famous speakers and artists from various parts of the country came to the campus and presented a broad array of informative and entertaining programs. In March 1916, faculty members Settle and

Stallings held a music recital in Dunn. In early May of that year, an enthusiastic audience filled the college auditorium to see and hear Helen Keller, "one of the world's leading celebrities." The famous author and lecturer, whose life inspired millions and whose books were translated into more than fifty languages, captivated her audience with an inspirational program on the topic of "Happiness." Keller, who was thirty-six years old in 1916, visited the college at the invitation of Frances F. Harper, professor of mathematics. Editors of *The Watch Tower* described her presentation as "a mechanical marvel."[22]

Students willingly attended such cultural events as recitals and lectures but typically demonstrated greater enthusiasm for less formal, popular forms of entertainment, especially events providing opportunities to mix socially with members of the opposite sex. Approaching holidays were eagerly anticipated at the college and frequently resulted in elaborate preparations, which preoccupied the campus community for days. With the exception of commencement week, Halloween and Valentine's Day apparently generated the greatest excitement and resulted in the most memorable social occasions. Thanksgiving and Christmas also stimulated excitement and special events but usually did not match Halloween or Valentine's Day, probably because the former holidays occurred when the college was not operating and students had gone home.[23]

The young women usually prepared elaborate Halloween celebrations with assistance from faculty members. Excitement for a "Night of Ghosts and Goblins" began to build several days before 31 October 1912, triggered by a document circulated during chapel exercises. The paper summoned all males, student and faculty, to appear at the Kinsey reception hall promptly at 7:30 PM on Halloween. Failure to obey the injunction placed the individual at risk to a "dreadful calamity." When the festivities began, the girls appeared in Halloween costumes, received each guest individually, and led the victim into a "haunted woodland forest." During some years, the poor victim was blindfolded and led helplessly stumbling and groping through a carefully designed horror chamber, seemingly filled with every imaginable eerie sensation. Editors of *The Radiant* referred to the Halloween party as a premier social event of each year and praised 1914's festival as the most entertaining in school history. Among the most enjoyable features was the fortune-telling booth, operated by the clairvoyant Louise Davis.[24]

The opening of the boys' dormitory finally enabled young men to hold their own social events on campus. They quickly made the new dormitory into a suitable site for galas especially designed to impress young ladies. While Caldwell Hall became the scene for numerous social gatherings, Valentine's

Caldwell Hall, boys' dormitory. 1913 Pine Knot.

Day celebrations were the featured attractions. Beginning in 1913, the faculty formally designated 14 February as the annual date for male students to host a reception in honor of the young ladies and the faculty. The event became "a night of hearts and flowers, mirth and song, laughter and good cheer," which rated among the most memorable social triumphs each year. Festivities on the evening of 14 February 1913, began with a banquet featuring President Caldwell as toastmaster, followed by remarks from several faculty members. In addition to decorating the dormitory in red and white, the young men formed a receiving line that welcomed their guests and led them to appropriate refreshments. Valentine's Day 1916 included several enjoyable contests followed by violin solos and a performance by the college orchestra. The young men reportedly performed as very charming hosts.[25]

Literary societies also continued to function as key instigators of cultural and academic events. Alethians, Demosthenians, and Hesperians hosted receptions, invited guest speakers, and sponsored dramatic presentations. A mock trial held in the auditorium by the Demosthenians, in January 1914, provided a delightful evening of comedy. The defendant, James Edmund Lingan, was charged with "intent to murder a chicken, carrying a concealed weapon, vagrancy, larceny, burglary, egotism, and flirtation." Following a guilty verdict by the jury, the judge sentenced the criminal to talk to three co-eds, Hattie Newborne, Willa Chestnutt, and "Tiny" Brook, for two hours each. If that ordeal did not kill the unfortunate man, the sheriff would "complete the job." The trial's climax came during the judge's charge to the jury. His honor declared that if the defendant was found guilty, "the teachings and training of the 'State of Caldwell' were as 'sweets wasted on the desert air.'" The judge also caricatured members of the faculty and explained how each teacher had failed to meet his responsibilities to the defendant.[26]

Literary societies also helped students develop skills in critical thinking, debating, and public speaking. The importance of these efforts became evident in 1913 and 1915, when the college's representatives to the Inter-Collegiate Peace Contest gained distinction for themselves and their school. First held in 1912, the contest attracted participants from nine North Carolina colleges to a public speaking competition on topics related to world peace. Other schools represented were A & M (later NC State University), Davidson, Elon, Guilford, Trinity (later Duke University), the University of North Carolina, and Wake Forest. On 28 February 1913, Horace Settle of ACC's Hesperian Society won second place in the contest. A full-page feature on Settle appeared in the 1913 yearbook, listing him as a member of the ministerial association, former editor of *The Radiant*, president of the choral club, and member of the glee club. *The Pine Knot* praised him as a sincere, honorable, and deeply committed young man of uncommon grace and skill, whose pleasant nature made him one of the college's most popular students.[27]

Horace and Harriet Settle, younger siblings of Mary Settle Caldwell, had followed their sister and brother-in-law to Wilson. The talented and active students from Owenton, Kentucky, frequently performed in musical recitals, and Horace preached in area churches. He received his degree in religion in 1912 but remained at the college to take postgraduate courses and, apparently, to continue courting Agnes Spain, a classmate also enrolled in post-graduate classes. Following their marriage, the couple moved to Greenville, North Carolina, and then to Aniston, Alabama, where Settle served as pastor of Disciples churches. His younger sister Harriet completed studies in pianoforte and voice and earned a B.M. degree. She taught music as a member of the college faculty for several years before resigning to marry Wilson businessman B. B. Plyler. Harriet Settle Plyler continued to teach music and served as choir director and/or organist in most of Wilson's mainstream churches prior to her death in 1984. Today, the Harriet Settle Plyler Memorial Scholarship is awarded to an upperclass music major at Barton College.[28]

Harriet Clay Settle, class of 1911 and instructor of piano. 1916 Pine Knot.

Two years after Horace Settle's prize-winning speech, S. Lee Sadler, another member of the ministerial association, won first place in the Inter-Collegiate Peace Contest, held on the Meredith College campus. Sadler's speech, entitled "The New Empire," argued that an empire based upon the brotherhood of man could rise from "the blood drenched battlefields of Europe." Sadler served as president of the Demosthenian Society and exchange editor of *The Radiant* and an officer of the Athletic Association. The April 1915 issue of the student magazine printed Sadler's speech and boasted that during the four years in which the contest had been held, ACC students had performed successfully against contestants from the best schools in the state. Specifically, *The Radiant* editors noted, the college had furnished 11 percent of the contestants (8 of 72) and won 25 percent of the prizes (2 of 8.) Editors of Disciples publications also lauded Sadler's performance and pointed out that first prize had been $75. The entire student body met the train returning the victorious speaker to Wilson. Excited students hauled the state oratorical champion from the train, hoisted him upon the boys' shoulders, and carried him to "an elaborately decorated vehicle." Cheered along by shouts from the crowd, the hero rode back to the campus in triumph. After graduation, Sadler earned a master's degree from Vanderbilt University and joined the faculty of his alma mater as a history and social sciences teacher in 1920.[29]

In addition to impressive accomplishments in public speaking, other achievements indicated that the college was improving academically. Caldwell's earlier trip abroad had afforded quality time for brainstorming and discussions with a learned colleague upon a variety of college-related issues. During the months following his return, the president implemented a number of changes aimed at strengthening academics at the school. A visitor to the campus in the summer of 1913 noted the addition of new bookcases for the library, which he estimated contained 3,000 volumes, and was impressed by the large number of magazines on display. He also approved efforts by Miss Myrtie Harper to make the place attractive and orderly. A later edition of *The Radiant* reported that the college had changed the preparatory program significantly by dropping the lower grades and retaining only grades ten and eleven. Apparently, Caldwell, who had voiced concern that entering students encountered difficulty in qualifying as bona fide members of the freshman class, decided that strengthening the preparatory program could improve that situation. Student editors applauded the change, arguing that the revisions helped put the academic quality of the college on a plane equal to any institution in the state.[30]

Writing from Belhaven in 1913, a recent graduate identifying himself only as "An Alumnus" argued that Caldwell's leadership had substantially improved the academic reputation of the college. As evidence, he noted that graduate schools at both Transylvania and Yale had quickly approved his application for enrollment while delaying decisions about graduates of much older institutions. He expressed pride that his alma mater had attained such a positive reputation and urged Disciples throughout the state to provide greater support for the college. Charles C. Ware argued that Caldwell's declining to award honorary or postgraduate degrees provided another indication of the president's serious attitude about maintaining high academic standards.[31]

The ability of the school to retain more key faculty members during his tenure may have helped convince Caldwell that the time was opportune to raise academic standards at the college. Counting Caldwell, who served as professor of biblical literature and church history, seven members of the faculty of 1913 had served two years or more, and five had been there at least five years. Among the faculty of 1916, seven members had served at least five years.

Faculty who boasted the greatest longevity during this time included Frances Harper, professor of mathematics, since 1904; Kathleen Salmon, professor of English, 1906; Myrtle Harper, instructor of history, later librarian, 1907; J. C. Caldwell, 1907; Albert Muilberger, director of music, 1909; E. L. Barham, professor of Latin and Greek, 1911; and Johnnie Speer Barham, instructor in piano, harmony, and history of music, 1911.[32]

Others who served shorter periods joined their colleagues in working diligently and skillfully to improve the college. Mamie Doss Jennings, director of expression from 1911 to 1913, when she took leave to get married, returned to the college in the 1920s. In addition to expression classes, she taught literature, English grammar, and physical education. In physical education classes, which met daily, she taught the young women of the college different methods of exercising, how to stand correctly in order to avoid tiring, how to sit and walk gracefully, and how to relax. Her grammar and literature classes emphasized extensive memorization, which Jennings considered essential to academic success. She also recalled that faculty duties extended to the cafeteria where students learned proper dining etiquette. During her relatively brief tenure on the faculty, Mamie Jennings Lucas developed a love for the college that remained until her death in 1995 at the age of 109.[33]

Jesse C. Caldwell spread his talents across a broad array of responsibilities: teacher, mentor, preacher, organizer, and college president. In the latter role, he stood among those rare individuals capable of effectively leading an institution while forming close associations with those being led. Campus publications indicate that students held great respect for their president and mentor but also felt comfortable engaging him in good-natured banter. A verse from the poem "The Faculty Song," which appeared in the college yearbook, details this fact:

> To Dr. Caldwell we'll drink with loud cheers;
>   Viva our J. C. C.!
> Grape Juice is our toast—no intoxicants here—
>   Viva sobriety!
> He won't let us dance but he wants us to walk;
> He won't let us drive, for Prince might kick or balk;
> Of college ideals, he will evermore talk.
>   Viva la propriety!

"Prince," the college pony whom the students were not permitted to drive, likely pulled the carriage on the night of Mamie Jennings' unforgettable in-

"Prince" pulling the college cart. 1916 Pine Knot.

troduction to Wilson and the college. The 1916 *Pine Knot* mentions "Prince" as the only pony owned by ACC at that time.[34]

Soon after the spring term opened in 1916, Caldwell decided to leave the college and return to the Midwest. In early February, he announced that he would accept an appointment as dean at Drake University in Des Moines, Iowa. Students, faculty, friends of the college, and Disciples from various parts of the nation praised the quality of Caldwell's impact upon the college and the church. Charles C. Ware, who had moved to North Carolina in 1915 as registrar at the college and state secretary of the Disciples of Christ Church, had worked closely with Caldwell upon a variety of endeavors. In his history of the college published in 1956, Ware praised the president's leadership and accomplishments. Caldwell's greatest impact upon the institution, in Ware's opinion, resulted from his close association with the students and his positive influence upon their lives. The popular president had "entered into all phases of their life [sic] religious, academic, aesthetic, forensic, and athletic."[35]

Several factors may have contributed to the president's decision to leave Atlantic Christian College after serving nine years. Enrollment, which averaged 173 students between 1911 and 1914, dropped to 105 in the autumn of 1915. Unfortunately, the enrollment decline coincided with an increase in the size of the faculty to eighteen members, the largest in the school's history. As a result, the college incurred a shortfall of $3,000 for the 1915–16 year, bringing total indebtedness to $24,000. Mamie Jennings Lucas recalled that Mary Settle Caldwell's health had deteriorated as her migraine headaches increased, and a move to a different climate might have been considered helpful. Also, Caldwell's new position as academic dean would mean more involvement in scholarly activities and fewer administrative duties. The key reason for the move, however, was likely Caldwell's growing disappointment with the inability of the Disciples of Christ in North Carolina to produce adequate financial support for the college. The best efforts of the president and of a few committed Disciples leaders had produced neither an endowment nor other significant monetary contributions to the institution, compelling reason in itself to look elsewhere.[36]

In dedicating the 1916 yearbook to Dr. Caldwell, the editors lauded his high ideals, devotion to duty, and interest in every student. The *Pine Knot* also praised the president's hard work and identified a number of areas where he had succeeded in advancing the interests of both the college and the Christian Church. Praising Caldwell as a man of "innate grace" who had encouraged growth in every aspect of the college, the editors predicted that his spirit would continue to inspire the school and the students whom he had taught. To Caldwell and his family, students expressed best wishes for a successful move to their new home and for continued good fortune as their former president assumed the position of dean of the Bible College at Drake University.[37]

FIVE

Greet Us with Beauty and Fragrance When We Return in September

IN LATE FEBRUARY 1916, the board of trustees invited Raymond A. Smith, an Indiana native, to become the fourth president of Atlantic Christian College. Smith had taught at the college in 1905–06, and, reportedly, John J. Harper had been so impressed with the professor's potential that he requested that Smith remain on the faculty and consider succeeding him as president. A veteran of the Spanish-American War, the forty-one-year-old Smith had spent seven years as an Indianapolis businessman and had compiled impressive records as an educator and preacher in Indiana, Pennsylvania, and West Virginia. He had earned degrees from Vincennes University, Butler College, and the University of Indianapolis prior to completing a B.D. at Yale in 1905. Smith had served as school superintendent in Beckley, West Virginia, from 1913 to 1916. After agreeing to become president of ACC, Smith and his wife Grace prepared to move to Wilson with their three children. *The Radiant*, quoting *The Daily Times* of Wilson, reported that the incoming president would assume his new duties in June.[1]

As the Smith and Caldwell families adjusted to new surroundings during the summer of 1916, President Woodrow Wilson prepared for fall elections. Democrats reminded Americans that the incumbent President had kept the country out of the Great War then raging in Europe and reassured people that the nation's neutrality policy would continue. Even though the United States retained claim to an empire since the Spanish-American War in 1898, Americans typically considered European conflicts, especially those involving such remote areas as Serbia and the Balkans, as none of their business and better left alone. In fact, in 1916, national and state newspapers paid more attention to the revolution occurring in Mexico than to the war in Europe. As the Great War continued to expand, however, involving more horrible and increasingly lethal weapons, including tanks, machine guns, airplanes, and poison gas, the event became virtually impossible to ignore. American concern increased in the summer of 1916 as the conflict between the Allied and Central Powers moved into its third year. In July, the great Battle of the Somme alone brought more than a million casualties with no end to the devastation in sight. Newspaper descriptions of clashes involving unbelievably high death rates on French battlefields helped convince Americans that the carnage must stop.[2]

On American college campuses, including Barton's, the Great War provoked students to write essays and poems devoted to world peace. A few daring young Americans, several North Carolinians among them, ignored their President's call for neutrality and joined the Allied war effort, including a few pilots who served in the famed Lafayette Escadrille. Many American women, answering a plea from the International Red Cross, volunteered to prepare bandages to aid the recovery of wounded soldiers in overseas hospitals. At Atlantic Christian College in the spring of 1916, student writers began to address issues relating to "the terrible European conflict" in prose and verse. Yet, as summer passed and autumn approached, most students, like Americans generally, continued to consider the war as too distant to pose a serious threat to the United States. Few, if any, could have known by election day that November that within six months America would enter the Great War and that the conflict would continue for another two years.[3]

Thus, it seemed quite normal for students and faculty returning to school in the fall of 1916 to be far more concerned with academic matters and with establishing a good beginning under a new president than with a war in faraway Europe. Besides, Dr. Smith remained unknown to almost everyone on campus until some students suddenly found themselves enrolled in his classes. Like the college's three earlier presidents, Smith's responsibilities included classroom teaching. His title read President and Professor of Education and Biblical Literature.[4]

J. C. Caldwell's departure left his successor with major challenges, among them improving the college's financial situation and continuing to graduate Disciples ministers of high caliber. Perhaps Caldwell's most important contribution to the school and to the Christian Church was the success with which he nurtured and motivated young preachers while building a strong ministerial studies program at the college. By the time he left to assume leadership of the Bible College at Drake, fully one third of all active Disciples preachers in North Carolina had been educated at Atlantic Christian College. Caldwell's impressive work in that area, in addition to attracting the interest of Drake, had provided ACC with a rich legacy, which friends and alumni desired to

President Raymond A. Smith, 1916–20. 1920 Pine Knot.

maintain. Raymond Smith likely was aware of those challenges when he made a commitment to move to Wilson. What he could scarcely have foreseen was that in March, months before he departed West Virginia, one of his own former ministerial students would question publicly Smith's fitness either to lead or teach at the college. The resulting controversy, which Charles C. Ware labels a "flash heresy trial," soon became the most immediate challenge confronting the president-elect.[5]

During his year on the ACC faculty in 1905–06, Smith had used textbooks and recommended other books written by "modern scholars" that some conservative students had found difficult to accept. *The Watch Tower* of 19 April 1916 quoted from a letter written to the board of trustees by one of Smith's former students. It charged that Smith held religious views that deviated from the beliefs of the Disciples church regarding the critical issues of the "birth, life, miracles and teachings of our Lord." The letter, written by Cecil Outlaw, further charged that Smith's radical views had so upset some Disciples ministers that President Harper had felt obligated to make a public apology regarding the matter to the annual Disciples convention in 1907. The following month, *The Watch Tower* carried articles refuting Outlaw's charges, including a letter by outgoing President Jesse C. Caldwell supporting Smith. Caldwell also produced a 1907 letter that proved that J. J. Harper had asked Smith to consider the idea of succeeding him as president of the school. *The Watch Tower* contained messages from several other prominent Disciples ministers praising the newly appointed president and noting that he had received the unanimous endorsement of the North Carolina Christian Ministers' Association as "President and Bible teacher elect."[6]

The 7 June 1916 issue of the Disciples newspaper contained a letter signed by Outlaw in which he stated that he did not question Smith's honesty, ability, or scholarship, but he repeated the charge that the latter's reliance upon "modern thought," as written by "modern scholars," was not in harmony with the views of "the ministry and masses of the brotherhood in the two Carolinas." Outlaw also argued that Disciples in the Carolinas would be reluctant to send students or financial support to ACC as long as its leader was known to hold Smith's views on the holy scriptures. Smith's defense, printed under the heading "Reply to Bro. Cecil F. Outlaw's Objections," immediately followed "Outlaw's Protest." The newly appointed president listed the complete bibliography that he had used in teaching the ministerial course in question. He then refuted the charges against him and noted that he possessed letters from elders of every church which he had served, beginning in 1898, each of which confirmed "my soundness in the faith."[7]

Ware, who knew all of the parties involved, argued that, ultimately, the controversy likely proved to be positive for the Disciples because it "spiced their consolidated fellowship." Ware attributed the controversy to immaturity and confusion on the part of Smith's students and to the fact that the new professor used a more modern historical approach to studying scripture than the traditional style to which they had been accustomed. Ware doubted that anyone as radical as Smith's critics portrayed him as being could have survived in conservative Wilson. He pointed out that, on the faculty at ACC alone in the academic year 1916–17, there were seven other preachers, several of whom were "unequivocal conservatives." In evaluating the controversy years later, Ware labeled the event "a case of mythical heresy" which time had turned into a "treasured legend of forgotten lore." C. F. Outlaw later returned to the college, completed his degree, and loyally supported the institution as an alumnus. His views of Smith also changed over time; a 1939 publication by Outlaw mentioned Smith's writings in the bibliography.[8]

As theological squabbles waned among Carolina Disciples in the early spring of 1917, a much more ominous conflict threatened the entire nation. Assenting to President Wilson's request, Congress formally declared war on Germany on 6 April. The President called upon the United States to join the Allied Nations in a humanitarian crusade to defeat the Central Powers and thus "make the world safe for democracy." Both public opinion and the national press had increasingly hardened toward Germany as her submarines sank unarmed vessels and threatened beaches along the Atlantic coastline, including those of North Carolina. The wave of patriotism that greeted the nation's entry into the war was particularly evident upon college campuses. President Smith and the trustees were concerned about the prospects for enrollment in the fall of 1917 because of a national trend among college-age males to indicate a readiness to enlist in military service. President Wilson somewhat alleviated the apprehension by suggesting that colleges and technical schools maintain normal activities and by urging young men already enrolled in college to continue their studies in preparation for future leadership roles within the country. Writing in "The Patriotic Number" of *The Radiant* in March 1918, news editor William Thomas Mattox, a senior from Stantonsburg, echoed the President's advice. Noting that some young men claimed that they volunteered to avoid being classified as unpatriotic, Mattox argued that there was no disgrace in waiting to be drafted.[9]

The American Red Cross, which began supplying humanitarian aid to war victims very early, realized a significant increase in support from the surge of patriotism then sweeping the country. Prior to America's entry into the war, the Red Cross collected clothing, taught first aid classes, made surgical dressings for use overseas, and later served refreshments to soldiers leaving for Europe. North Carolina historian Sarah M. Lemmon, tracing the state's role in World War I, wrote that, by the autumn of 1917, Wilson businesses were actively supporting Red Cross activities, citing the case of a local tobacco warehouse which pledged one half of its October commissions to the state chapter. Atlantic Christian College also cooperated with the Red Cross, offering a special class devoted to making bandages and surgical dressings and another class in first aid. The former class was taught by Cora A. Lappin, a member of the music faculty, who served as Instructor in Red Cross Work at the college for the 1917–18 academic year. Anna F. Moore, dean of women and director of the school of expression, taught the class in first aid. Lappin earned a certificate and instructor's card after receiving special training in Red Cross Work held in Chicago during the summer of 1917. Her class at ACC the following fall numbered twenty-one students, who were engaged in helping to meet an urgent plea that North Carolina Red Cross units send 330,000 surgical dressings to France by 1 February 1918. During World War I, the state of North Carolina contributed nearly 2 million surgical dressings and over 200,000 articles of clothing through the Red Cross. By March 1918, the state claimed 119 chapters with 114,348 members.[10]

ACC's student magazine in November 1917 urged more students to take the special course in Red Cross Work, noting that the college furnished all required materials and that a tuition fee of five dollars covered the entire year. *The Radiant* editors also emphasized the importance of volunteer efforts by printing Gerald Lively's poem, *The Song of a Surgical Dressing*, a portion of which reads:

> I'll be used on the fields of France,
> Where Life or Death is the gift of Chance;
> And ever and always the order runs—
> Men and more men for the greedy guns:
>
> * * * * * * *
>
> But why was I made, and why do I go
> From a place of peace to a place of woe?
> I serve no King and I serve no State—
> I'm the answer of Love to the song of Hate;
> Or comrade or foeman is one to me—
> From tunnel or trench, or sky or sea;
> When the last gun's fired and the war-flag's furled
> May I heal the hurts of a wounded world.

The patriotic fervor that dominated the campus during the autumn of 1917 prompted the senior class to cancel plans to publish an annual. After reassessing the matter, the class voted to discontinue all work upon a "record of its happiest days" and channel its energies toward "War Relief Work." The student magazine also reported that the seniors had offered to work through the local chamber of commerce to support their country in its "hour of supreme need."[11]

Joel E. Vause, class of 1919 and a native of Kinston, wrote in *The Watch Tower* in August 1918 that he had found President Smith confident regarding prospects of a large enrollment for the 1918–19 school year. Vause had learned, however, that many of "the old boys" would not return to their classes because they had "answered the call to the colors." Professor W. O. Lappin, for example, had left the school to volunteer his services as a chaplain. The administration expected that the girls' dormitory would be filled and asked that churches send the college more male students to prepare for ministerial careers. Vause also wrote that the Young Men's Christian Association (YMCA) still needed volunteers and noted that several of the college's ministerial students had withdrawn from school to take positions with that organization.[12]

Perhaps the most visible change that the war brought to the campus was the addition of close order drill and military discipline. Atlantic Christian College joined other American colleges and universities in forming a unit of the Students' Army Training Corps during the fall semester of 1918. At some schools "military French" was also added to the curriculum. Male students who joined S.A.T.C. carried eleven hours of military training and three hours of recitation each week, in addition to their regular classes. Professors Perry Case and Warren Lappin, along with student Magruder E. Sadler, took special training at Plattsburg, New York, during the summer of 1918 in order to lead S.A.T.C. exercises at the college. Class history features contained in *The Pine Knot* for both 1920 and 1921 reveal that S.A.T.C. became a dominant feature of campus life for most male students during the autumn of 1918. A total of fifty-four men, 55 percent of all male students, participated in the military training class.[13]

Joshua Ernest Paschall, editor-in-chief of *The Radiant* in 1917–18, likely reflected sentiments held throughout the college community regarding the Great War in his poem *Prayer* printed in December 1917, a portion of which reads:

> Our nation's God, to Thee we raise,
> In hopeful hearts our grateful praise;
> From North to South the anthems rise;
> Accept our nation's sacrifice.
>
> * * * * * *
>
> Grant us Thy strength, Thy love, we pray
> And bless the bleeding world today;
> Inspire the world to speed Thy plan:
> The Kingdom of the Son of Man.[14]

In an editorial entitled "Perseverance" in *The Radiant* of March 1918, Paschall, a senior from Black Creek, commented upon the special challenge that the war presented for college students because so many throughout the country had left school to join the army or navy. He also noted volunteers who worked as active Red Cross workers and as leaders in the YMCA. Paschall challenged all readers of the student magazine, whether leaving to enlist or remaining to continue their studies, to persevere and make the best use of their time. *The Radiant* of March 1918 was labeled "Patriotic Number 1918" and was devoted almost entirely to war-related issues. Student editors were complying with a national government request that magazines and papers throughout the country "carry on a Patriotic Campaign during March." In addition to pointing out the duty of all citizens to support their country, the issue praised black Americans for loyal and vigorous support of the war effort and suggested various ways that women could contribute other than through Red Cross activities. The issue quoted advice to American college students provided by a French army officer then teaching at Harvard. The lieutenant cautioned young men not to be too impetuous about leaving school to enlist in the armed forces. In most cases, he said, the student should put completion of college ahead of military service because the period of reconstruction following the war would require "trained minds."[15]

World War I prompted a total of sixty-two enlistments, counting alumni, from Barton College, nine of whom were ministers serving either campuses or churches in the Carolinas. Ernest Paschall enlisted in the navy soon after graduation in 1918. Many volunteers from ACC became chaplains or participated in YMCA work. Hayes Farish, class of 1914 and pastor of the Belhaven Christian Church, served as a lieutenant and chaplain overseas. He was assigned to a YMCA unit with the American Expeditionary Force. The YMCA and Young Women's Christian Association (YWCA) sought to provide a relaxed and interesting environment for men who were away from the front lines by holding vesper services, organizing baseball and football games, staffing canteens, and providing social workers in France and England.[16]

At a special patriotic program held on campus 22 February 1918, the college unfurled a service flag in honor of the young students engaged in military service. Students donated material for the flag, which was made by Cora Lappin and the Red Cross class. The flag featured thirty-five stars, representing the number of ACC boys in military service, some of whom were killed in action. *The Watch Tower* of 21 August 1918 reported that the college service flag contained two gold stars honoring Robert B. Anderson and J. B. Farmer, both killed in France. Anderson, who played shortstop on the 1910 baseball team, became the first Wilson County casualty of World War I. His sacrifice is memorialized by the local American Legion Post, which bears his name.[17]

The guns of Europe finally fell silent as an armistice went into effect 11 November 1918. While the armistice ended the shooting, the dying continued that autumn for many returning soldiers and for some who had not served in the military. One of the most deadly influenza epidemics in the nation's history swept the country, almost exactly coinciding with the opening of ACC's fall term in 1918. Initially believed to have been brought from Europe by returning soldiers, the "Spanish Flu" spread through cities and communities between September and November, killing an estimated 450,000 Americans. In North Carolina, alone, although churches and schools closed because of the danger, approximately 13,000 died. Atlantic Christian College suffered the effects of the deadly disease as those most vulnerable to the epidemic proved to be adults between the ages of twenty and forty. The sophomore class in 1918–19 had a particularly difficult time in struggling to deal with the influenza epidemic while adjusting to the newly implemented S.A.T.C. program. Kathlyn Jackson, historian for the class of 1921, noted the impact of influenza and wrote that tough examinations had caused other students to leave during the year. Her class of twenty-five entering freshmen in 1917 had dwindled to only seven members by their junior year. Students transferring to the school only managed to increase the senior class of 1921 to eight graduates.[18]

President Smith managed, with some difficulty, to keep the college operating during those particularly challenging years. Successful fund-raising was a vital accomplishment of his brief tenure. The total debt of the college when Smith assumed leadership of the school in the summer of 1916 stood at $24,000, and the institution continued to operate without an endowment. Earlier ACC had received a pledge of $50,000 from The Men and Millions Movement, a national fund-raising campaign launched by the Disciples church in 1913, but had gained no money from that program by the time that Smith arrived as president. Taking advantage of a network of contacts established by his predecessors and utilizing the talents of his faculty and staff, Smith moved immediately to improve the financial position of the college by seeking pledges from Christian Church leaders and congregations throughout eastern North Carolina. The results of a campaign launched by "men from the college," faculty, staff, and students, were gratifying. Gifts from the Carolinas churches improved by over 700 percent between 1916 and 1920. In addition, by April 1919, the college had received a total of nearly $17,600 from The Men and Millions Movement. A generous gift of $30,000 from the estate of Wilson native Charles N. Nurney, which Charles C. Ware called the beginning of a permanent fund for the school, was particularly significant. The largest coup came with the "Carolina Enlargement Campaign" adopted by the Disciples Convention meeting in Robersonville in 1919. Scheduled to begin in June 1920, the campaign set a total goal of $250,000, of which 80 percent would go to Atlantic Christian College. That $200,000 pledge, to be raised over a five-year period, represented the Disciples' largest financial commitment to the college.[19]

Smith also demonstrated a willingness to take risks in efforts to improve the financial condition of the college. Apparently impressed by the idea that the school might attract and educate needy and worthy students by providing tuition grants for manual labor, he suggested that the college purchase a large local farm. Despite the existence of a rather large indebtedness already facing the institution, the trustees agreed. In January 1918, Atlantic Christian College accepted an additional debt of $72,500 for the purchase of a tract of 252 acres from Robert Hart Rountree known as the Malvina Rountree Tract. The property lay just outside the Wilson city limits, bordering West Nash Street and extending southwest all the way to Hominy Swamp. The trustees planned to use this prime piece of property, which was close enough to the existing campus to be within convenient walking distance, for future expansion of the college. The *College Catalog* for 1918–19 stated that the land, which included a modern dairy, would be cultivated temporarily as a working farm by the college, thus enabling the school to "furnish the best possible food at reasonable rates." The college actually farmed the land for two years, mainly utilizing students not called to military service for planting, tending, and harvesting crops and vegetables. A cartoon in the 1920 yearbook depicted "Gardener Smith" returning from the fields with a wheelbarrow filled with corn, squash, carrots, and cabbage. The caption read, "From Gardenville. Bringing them in fresh and green."[20]

No information has appeared to indicate what financial returns the college gained from operation of the farm. Continuing concerns about retiring outstanding debts prompted trustees to sell the entire farm in 1920 for $100,000, a sum that permitted paying off the college's total debt. The sale also meant that the school could retain the sum of $30,000, realized from the sale of the estate of C. N. Nurney, as a contingency fund for the school. However, the size and location of the property made it a prime real estate investment and rendered its hasty sale one of the most unfortunate monetary decisions in the college's history. Instead of the often repeated adage, "too little and too late," this business deal was a case of "too much and too soon."[21]

"Gardener Smith" cartoon. 1920 Pine Knot.

Bringing them in fresh and green.

From Gardenville.

President Smith had pleased students and other members of the college community by supporting the establishment of a Sunday school on campus in the autumn of 1916. Students in the ministerial program and some co-eds enrolled in religion classes assumed leadership of the Sunday school. The initial officers were Maude Russell, class of 1917, superintendent; Claire Hodges, class of 1917, secretary; and Elsie Respass, class of 1918, treasurer. Marion Brinson, class of 1921, served as superintendent from 1917 to 1919.[22]

Another precedent established by Smith in February 1917 was a formal presidential inauguration ceremony, which *The Watch Tower* described as a "new era in the history of education in eastern N.C." The inauguration was held in conjunction with a meeting in Wilson of the North Carolina Christian Missionary Committee. The March issue of the student magazine provided a more complete description of the scheduled proceedings, planned for Tuesday, 22 March, at 11 AM. Although the entire details of the ceremony had not been completed, *The Radiant* announced that the approximate order of the program would include the following events:

A piano processional.
Singing by the audience.
Invocation.
Presentation of the charter and seal of the college to Dr. Smith.
Congratulatory addresses.
Inaugural address by Dr. Smith.
A sacred song.
Benediction.[23]

Following the formal proceedings, President Smith would greet guests in the college library. The trustees planned to host a luncheon for invited guests at 3 PM in the Briggs Hotel. The faculty and representatives of other colleges would march in academic costume. The editors of *The Radiant* urged every student to:

help to make this function the biggest thing ever held at A.C.C.
Keep the ball of enthusiasm rolling. Let our prexy feel our loyalty, see our loyalty, hear our loyalty.
Let A.C.C. be placed in bright colors on the map of eastern N.C.
A.C.C. is our college, and Dr. Smith is our president, and they are both 'all right.'[24]

The records indicate that students highly respected the presidents and faculty of the college during the school's early years; there is little evidence of serious cases of misbehavior. One prank involving residents of the girls' dormitory prior to Christmas vacation in 1919, however, struck the students as both humorous and unusual enough to record for posterity. Descriptions of the prank appear in both the yearbook and student magazine, and the event is captured in verse. The great "faculty kidnapping or hostage taking" reportedly occurred two days before the Christmas break. Student pride and pleasure in accomplishing the devilish deed were so greatly relished that the poem, "A Christmas Revel," written by sophomore class president Mary Moore, is printed here in its entirety (with apologies to Clement Moore and "Twas the Night Before Christmas").

'Twas the night before leaving and all through the dorm
The students were taking the teachers by storm.
Some teachers were tied and the rest were all locked;
Twas all done in fun, so please don't be shocked.

Through the halls 'Sh! Sh!' whispered the girls, every one.
'Now won't we be having just great heaps of fun!'
As they tip-toed along by the stern teachers' doors
Such loud creaks and wild squeaks came from under the floors!

They had yards of strong rope and big keys by the score,
'We will tie every room up or lock every door!'
To the third floor they crept without making a sound.
'Twas for Ivy Mae Smith and Nelle Krise they were bound.

'Get away from here, burglar; you burglar, so bold!'
Cried the frightened Miss Nelle, all a-shivering with cold.
'There is one at the door!' shrieked the pale Mrs. Grim.
'Oh dear Ferrell, wake up and s-speak out t-t-to him!'

When the Harpers were locked and the Dean was safe-tied,
Feeling safe from the foe the new captors all sighed.
Every girl in the dorm was awaken'd for the feast.
Not a girl was left sleeping, not even the least.

To the Art Room they ran when the work was all done.
There the table was spread and the fun was begun.
'Please ma'am' and 'Thank you' were words not to be found;
Nor none thought of their manners when the 'eats' went around.

When the table was spread by them right on the floor
There were pickles and crackers and sausage galore.
'Kat,' 'Sammy,' 'Margaret' and others were there,
And none was too sleepy to grab her full share.

Very soon they were giddy and ready to shout,
So they laughed and they joked, and they danced all about.
Through the halls they then marched in a 'coat-tail' parade,
While resounding abroad a barnyard serenade.

At last a loud crow from the gay chanticleer
Announced that the dawn was a-drawing quite near.
So their yells being all over and their fun, too, being sped,
All the revelers quietly stole off to bed.

All over! Nay, think not the fun ended here.
Why, at breakfast next morn did a teacher appear?

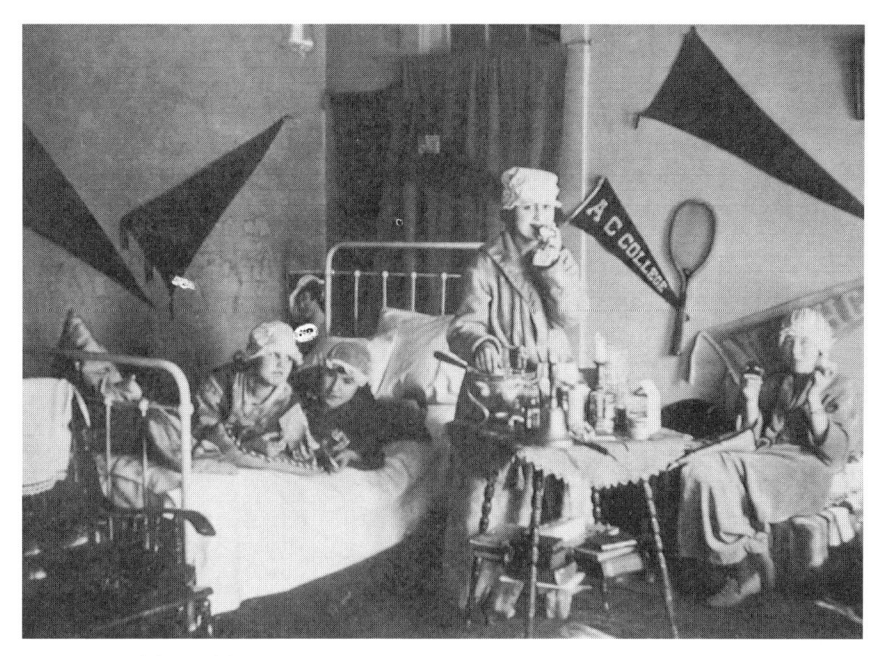

Dormitory life in old Kinsey. 1920 Pine Knot.

No, indeed! let me tell you, they enjoyed a nice nap
Or they tried to release themselves out of their trap.

There's one little thing we would just like to know—
How Miss Ivy Mae Smith through her transom could go.
Oh, they all wiggled out in a magic-like way ;
How they managed to do it, no one can yet say.

Such fun as we had and what a good joke,
Though we've all gotten back now under our yoke;
We will try something better for our new stunt next year,
So the teachers have something to look for and fear.[25]

The Pine Knot of 1920, recording the academic year of 1919–20 as a month-by-month calendar of events, carried these last two lines for December: "17. Midnight revelry in girls' 'Dorm'; barnyard serenade; teachers overcome and roped in by students. 19. One teacher at breakfast. Homeward bound." Interestingly, nothing is mentioned for December 18. Ivy Mae Smith was director of the school of music, and Nell Krise was instructor in history and domestic science. Ethel M. Grim served as professor of English, and Frederick Grim was professor of education. Frances F. Harper was professor of mathematics, and Myrtle L. Harper served as librarian. Charles C. Ware did not mention the occasion, and it is quite possible that the event occurred only in the minds of the young women and that both the prank and printed accounts were a hoax. If such was the case, perhaps one or more of the ladies involved later confessed to her role in the deceit.[26]

A few months earlier, headlines in the Disciples newspaper carried an article filled with accusations against Dr. Smith which friends of the man and the school likely wished could be dismissed as a prank. *The Watch Tower* in April 1919 contained a front page feature declaring "Dr. Smith, Head of A.C. College Publicly Announces Himself as An Advocate of Higher Criticism." Attributed to remarks by former ACC president James C. Coggins, the article resurrected the earlier heresy charges against Smith and identified an accuser in addition to Cecil Outlaw. Coggins claimed that during the 1905–06 academic year, Glenn Cole, a member of the faculty, had spoken to him in confidence about some of the same criticisms contained in Cecil Outlaw's indictment. Moreover, the article charged that Smith, during a public address made at a recent meeting at Plymouth, had again voiced support of Higher Criticism while demonstrating his view that "the whole New Testament record is a baseless fabrication of falsehoods." The newspaper leveled numerous other serious accusations against Smith. A related article written by J. H. Adams of Pungo appeared in *The Watch Tower* two weeks later. Adams also raised doubts about the soundness of Smith's interpretation of scripture while lauding Coggins for an address delivered in his church 20 April. Adams praised Coggins for preaching "some more of his old Jerusalem Gospel sermons just like we need." Finally, Adams indicated his opinion that there was too much "modern thought, German culture, and higher criticism floating around" and too much denying the miracles of Christ.[27]

Not until midsummer did the pastor who had invited the college president to preach at Plymouth in April break his silence to defend Smith. In the 6 August issue of *The Watch Tower*, W. H. Marler wrote that he would soon invite Smith to revisit his congregation and speak on the college's relationship to the church. Marler denied that he had ever criticized Smith although some people had misrepresented him as doing so. Referring to Smith's message, which had disturbed both J. C. Coggins and W. H. Adams, he wrote: "His sermon on the pre-eminence of Christ . . . was one of the most masterly sermons on the subject I ever heard, and I have no criticism whatever." Marler wrote that he joined members of his church in encouraging young people in

Plymouth to attend Atlantic Christian College and receive a Christian education or prepare for the ministry.[28]

In February 1920, after festering for another six months, the heresy controversy took a new turn, placing Atlantic Christian College and Charles C. Ware at the center of the dispute and threatening to create a major split among Disciples churches of the state. The event concerned the launching of a new monthly newspaper, the *North Carolina Christian*, intended to represent the Christian Church in North Carolina. Volume I, Number 1 announced that the Carolina Publishing Company grew out of an agreement between the college trustees and the board of managers of the North Carolina Christian Missionary Committee at a meeting at the Christian Church of Greenville, North Carolina, 24 November 1919. Under the heading "What Is This Paper?" managing editor C. C. Ware wrote:

> It has been recognized as a virtual necessity that our College and our State Missionary Service have a direct, distinct, and responsible medium of communication edited at and distributed from Wilson, where both the College and the State Headquarters of the disciples are located. . . . it cannot be rightly construed that we are in opposition or competition with any other paper that may now circulate within the State. . . . We will seek deliberately to serve not merely a part of our brotherhood, but, all of it. . . . we appeal to our brethren of the State for their enduring substantial support of this paper.[29]

The Watch Tower's immediate response to the creation of the Carolina Publishing Company went straight to the point. An article by J. R. Tingle of Ayden entitled "Where Are We Drifting?" stated that reports in the Inter-church Bulletin indicated that officers of the national Disciples church planned to unite with the Inter-church Movement at the Charlotte meeting scheduled for 8–10 March 1920. It also noted that State Secretary Charles C. Ware had urged preachers to attend the meeting. The article also charged that a $250,000 pledge made to Atlantic Christian College and the Raleigh church at the last North Carolina Disciples Convention was to be routed through the Inter-church Movement. Tingle argued that the Disciples of the state were being pushed into joining a world church association referred to as the "Federation and Inter-church Movement," which would strip the Christian Church of its identity. An editorial in the same issue invited anyone doubting the veracity of Tingle's charges to contact any minister who had received an invitation to the Charlotte meeting. J. H. Adams wrote in a separate article that the "good old

Charles C. Ware, general secretary of the North Carolina Christian Church and college registrar, archivist, and historian. 1920 Pine Knot.

Tower" had served the brotherhood well since being founded by John T. Walsh in 1872 and questioned the need for a new newspaper. He urged Disciples to continue supporting *The Watch Tower* and to work together toward the same goals.[30]

After additional charges and counter charges appeared in April and May, the 23 June issue of *The Watch Tower* printed several articles suggesting an end to the quarrel. The lead article, written by J. R. Tingle, described a meeting held in Washington on 15 June to discuss the Inter-church Movement. Ware had assured those present that Atlantic Christian College was not connected with the Inter-church Movement in any way and promised that all funds designated to the college would go straight to the school and not to the Inter-church Movement. Ware also told the gathering that instruction and textbooks would always be open for examination and complaints would be welcomed at any time. In addition, J. H. Mohorter assured the group that there was absolutely no connection between the Disciples Benevolent Association and the Inter-church Movement.[31]

The Washington meeting apparently had the effect of clearing the air and helped to restore a sense of unity among church members. The group voted unanimously to support the $250,000 fund-raising campaign on behalf of the college and the Benevolent Association. In addition, the 23 June issue of *The Watch Tower* quoted A. F. Leighton of Scotland Neck as protesting that his earlier comments had been misunderstood and denying that he suspected anyone at the college of being "false to the Apostolic plea." He voiced great respect for Harper, Caldwell, and Smith and reported that he had heard rumors indicating that the former presidents had paid large debts owed by the school out of their own pockets. If such rumors were true, Leighton suggested, the situation was a disgrace to the Disciples church.[32]

College trustee A. J. Moye of Farmville, whose family had furnished students and teachers to the college for nearly twenty years, praised *The Watch Tower* but added that "one communication in your last issue cut me to the core." The article in question implied that ACC had strayed from its proper course and was turning out heretics. It further suggested that Disciples send their sons and daughters to another college. Noting his ten years of service on the board of trustees, Moye argued that if any Atlantic Christian College president, professor, or student had ever "gone astray . . . [or] if there had been any destructive criticism taught I should have heard of it." Considering the fact that the school had usually lacked sufficient financial support, he labeled the college's performance superb and argued that adequate funding would result in an even better achievement by the college. Moye ended his letter with a plea for unity: "Let's be brethren—Let's be reasonable—Let's be charitable—."[33]

What had begun as a classroom disagreement over church doctrine and scriptural interpretation during the school's formative years had lain benign for more than a decade before Smith's appointment as president in 1916 resurrected the matter and brought the dispute to the attention of the Disciples newspaper. Following an exchange of views, the controversy again subsided until the spring of 1919, when changing world events suddenly made the issue appear sinister and more serious in nature. The Red Scare, which swept the Western world after World War I ended, frightened Americans and threatened to split many organizations, including churches. Stirred by a large influx of immigrants from southern and eastern Europe, prejudices were heightened by irresponsible newspaper reports of radicalism and violence associated with labor unions and striking workers. The Inter-church World Movement was but one of many groups investigated by the American government for its perceived danger to the nation during 1919 and 1920.[34]

Higher education's standing commitment to free thought rendered colleges and universities especially vulnerable to criticism during the surge of antiforeign sentiment in postwar America. On the campuses of numerous church-related colleges, where a discomfiting fear of modern scholarship had troubled orthodox Christians for decades, serious splits developed among faculty members. For some religious conservatives, conformity regarding the sanctity of the Holy Bible became the last refuge in a turbulent world bombarded by radical philosophies. At Transylvania College in Lexington, Kentucky, a sister institution of Atlantic Christian College, a "heresy trial" in the spring of 1917 produced deep divisions within the entire college community which continued to divide Disciples churches for years.[35]

The March and April 1920 issues of the *North Carolina Christian* reported that Dr. Smith would leave the college at the end of June to become chairman of the education department at Texas Christian University. The paper praised Smith's success in leading the college's rise to the "front rank among the religious educational institutions of the South." The departing president had enjoyed continuous support from Christian churches throughout the state and additional praise for his leadership came from students, faculty, and colleagues. Editors of *The Radiant* lauded Smith's value to the institution, mentioning his early action to separate the preparatory department from the college, designating a different faculty for each school. Two faculty members admired the president so much that they dedicated the college's first song in his honor. *Hurrah For Our A.C.C.*, composed by Professors Frederick F. Grim and Ethel M. Grim, was "Inscribed to our friend, President Raymond Abner Smith."[36]

Smith's legacy included the establishment of a popular Sunday school on the campus. He also established a tradition of recognizing outstanding student achievement, including an award to "the best all-round college student of the year," as selected by vote of the faculty. Presented in 2001 to a graduating senior, this award survives as the Coggins Cup (formerly the Faculty Cup). Smith also began the practice of presenting a medal to the most outstanding debater on campus, initially sponsored by Denny Brothers Jewelers. Now known as the Hilley Cup, the award goes to the graduating senior who has earned the highest grade point average throughout his or her college career. The first recipients, juniors Mabel Lynch of Dunn and Marion Brinson of

Arapahoe, respectively, were awarded these honors at commencement in June 1920.[37]

Raymond Smith's experience as businessman, educator, military veteran, and preacher made him well suited to guiding a college through fund-raising challenges, improving competence in managing business affairs, and adjusting to turbulent conditions created by the Great War. He also demonstrated restraint in responding to personal criticism and helped to stimulate innovative communication between campus, church, and community through the publication of the *North Carolina Christian*. The commencement issue of the student magazine, which featured a full-page photograph of Dr. Smith, voiced regret at his decision to depart and offered best wishes as he began a new position at Texas Christian University. Editors of *The Radiant* also expressed approval of the trustees' swift action in appointing Howard S. Hilley as dean and acting president of the college. The June 1920 issue featured a brief article written by the newly appointed president, commenting on the condition of the institution and announcing an enrollment goal of 250 students for the following year. Hilley and his wife, Maggie, had accepted President Smith's offer to join the faculty in 1919, as professor of ancient and modern languages and instructor in voice, respectively.[38]

As the college celebrated the completion of eighteen years of service with commencement exercises in 1920, members of the faculty and the student body acknowledged that the young school stood at a crossroads. In an article entitled "Today's Task," Professor Frederick F. Grim wrote that the futures of the church and the college were intertwined. Suggesting that success for both depended upon increased support from Disciples in the Carolinas, he estimated that pressing needs of the college would require raising $1 million over the next five years. Student writers, showing the exuberance and optimism of youth, evaluated the previous year as "above normal" and predicted a bright future for the school. Editors of *The Radiant* and *The Pine Knot* noted that renewed interest in ACC athletics and brighter prospects for a successful intercollegiate sports program had stimulated great anticipation for the next school year. Returning students wrote wistfully of looking forward to the fall term, when they hoped to find the campus overflowing with newly planted flowers to "greet us with beauty and fragrance when we come again in September."[39]

SIX

Here's to Next Year's Team

AT THE TIME that Barton College was founded, America was experiencing a revolutionary growth in athletics, and the increasing popularity of baseball, basketball, football, and tennis exerted a strong impact upon the young school. Baseball, the oldest of the four sports, had spread to southern college campuses including the University of Georgia, Wake Forest College, and the University of North Carolina in the 1880s. By the late nineteenth century, baseball had become the favorite team sport of Americans and was well on its way to becoming the national game. Male students at Atlantic Christian College shared the country's growing fascination with baseball, which became the early favorite sport played at the school. Efforts to organize baseball and other athletic teams during the college's formative years were hampered by a lack of adequate playing fields, difficulty attracting and retaining coaches and team managers, and lack of funds for travel and other basic expenses.[1]

Early Atlantic Christian College publications emphasized opportunities for participation in physical activities, specifically mentioning that "Croquet, tennis, basketball and other open-air amusements are encouraged." By the spring of 1908, the college girls had organized a basketball team and enjoyed spirited competition on the outdoor campus court. Tennis also was popular among students, and members of the first tennis club honed their skills upon the newly remodeled court adjacent to the girls' dormitory. Although organization of the baseball team remained unfinished, the boys practiced hard and appeared to be "rounding into first class shape." Some positions had been determined for the 1908 team; Horace Settle would be at first base, G. Hinton "Crump" Crumpler appeared set at third, and James J. Walker would pitch and likely serve as team captain.[2]

Soon after Will Upton Guerrant, a Kentucky native and recent graduate of Davidson College, arrived on campus in September 1908 as professor of philosophy and Greek, *The Radiant* reported that he was already well known throughout North Carolina and had organized an athletic association at ACC. The status of ACC athletics became a favorite topic of conversation during the autumn months. Rumors persisted that the college would build three excellent tennis courts on campus and planned to organize two clubs, which would permit "thirty boys and girls to enjoy the scientific sport every afternoon." Goals for the spring semester included a tennis tournament in which a prize would be awarded to the winning team. Student dreams of mid-November also included reorganizing girls' basketball and starting a "'cross country run' team for the boys." Student publications reported that the campus was caught up in a virtual "whirl of foot ball talk." Will Guerrant also served as athletic editor of *The Radiant* and was the likely instigator of much of the rising anticipation regarding the future of ACC athletics. When Guerrant turned his attention to "the attractive game," baseball, he boldly predicted a successful spring season with a glibness that might be envied at a much later annual gathering of the Wilson chapter of the Hot Stove League:

> Beginning in February we hope soon to be able to meet any and all comers this spring and at the same time furnish a guaranty of our presence in the thick of battle. We are arranging a schedule and we promise some very interesting games to the people of Wilson with most of the first institutions of learning in the State. We have some very promising material to select from, for example, Stallings, Winstead, Leach, Walker, Rawlings, Lane, and others. As we agree with the one who said, 'Actions speak louder than words,' we will leave the rest for you to see with your own eyes, and we hope to put up an article of ball worth your time and money to see.[3]

Will Guerrant had indeed been busy since arriving in Wilson. *The Radiant* of November 1908 listed him as the only member of the college "Executive Committee" besides President Caldwell. In addition to serving as athletic editor of the student magazine, he was manager of both the "Base Ball Team" and boys' tennis club. Guerrant's 1909 baseball team, pictured in the May issue of *The Radiant*, was reportedly the college's first team to play against outside competition "to any great extent." The opposition came from military academies, high schools, and league (city) teams, including Rocky Mount, Goldsboro, Raeford, Oak Ridge Military, Groves Academy (Oxford), and Bingham School (Mebane). ACC finished the season with a record of nine wins, eight losses, and one tie. The team earned two key victories against the league team at Fayetteville and gained a split at Wilmington where each team

The first ACC baseball team of record. The Radiant, *May 1909.*

won by a 1–0 score. A low point came in Wilson where the league team defeated ACC by scores of 8–2 and 13–0.[4]

Early baseball games between colleges, league teams, and high schools were usually played on the high school level, with rules not rigidly enforced. League teams existed in many Tarheel towns during the late nineteenth and early twentieth centuries when scheduling competitive opponents could mean an overnight stay. Josephus Daniels, revealing a youthful passion to play baseball from dawn to dusk, described being chosen captain of the Wilson Swift Foot baseball team as his "greatest honor." Daniels' biography, *Tar Heel Editor*, recounts a trip by the Swift Foot nine to play at Snow Hill, a round trip of some fifty miles. Traveling in a large wagon containing no seats and drawn by mules along sandy roads, the Swift Foot team emerged from the challenging trip victorious. Daniels considered the win especially gratifying because the Wilson squad overcame the additional adversity of the two star players having become intoxicated at a dance held the evening before the game.[5]

Baseball as played by collegiate teams around the turn of the century differed markedly from today's game in ways other than the makeup of the opposing teams. Many baseball diamonds were recently cleared fields with the typical infield so rough and unpredictable that routine ground balls sometimes became airborne missiles. Also, in a time before strict regulations, college teams frequently included players who were not officially enrolled as students. For example, Will Guerrant played third base and managed the team while serving on the faculty. Also, Mamie Jennings Lucas remained impressed in the late twentieth century that the 1912 ACC team included Bunn Hearn, a professional athlete, who played organized baseball in Wilson and coached at Elon College. *The Radiant* of February 1912 proclaimed that Hearn "will matriculate and be a *bona fide* student, hence he can participate in the games." Hearn served as coach and was considered the school's ace pitcher, despite the fact that his name did not appear on the official list of students. Unfortunately for the college team, Hearn was ordered to report to his professional team at Omaha earlier than expected, causing the 1912 season to be "cut short." Although ACC was able to play only seven of twelve scheduled games, the team compiled a record of four wins, two losses, and one tie and gained a key 4–0 victory over Elon College. Hearn rejoined the college team for the 1913 season.[6]

Americans who had been raised according to strict Victorian standards were not particularly thrilled by the sudden growth of athletic participation. The frivolity and apparent wasted time associated with organized play engendered much criticism. At Wake Forest College, which was then located in eastern Wake County and was an early opponent for ACC athletic teams, sponsorship of the baseball team became controversial because of reported rowdiness, drunkenness, and general misbehavior associated with baseball players. This factor, when added to a growing concern over the alleged brutality of football near the turn of the century, prompted the Wake Forest College administration to advocate drastic measures. President Charles E. Taylor summed up the prevailing opinion in a speech to trustees: "The faculty has sought to reduce to a minimum the interruption to study by intercollegiate games. Intercollegiate football is entirely prohibited, and the number of games of baseball is strictly limited. I should be glad if the Christian Colleges of the country . . . could unite in [abolishing] all collegiate games; but it is my opinion that, as things now are, it would not be wise for individual colleges to attempt such a total abolition."[7]

At the time Atlantic Christian College was founded, some Americans were made uneasy by persistent stories regarding the dangers of college sports. By 1905 this growing national concern over collegiate athletic problems, particularly a pattern of violence in college football, prompted President Theodore

Roosevelt to address the issue. Speaking to representatives from Harvard, Yale, and Princeton, Roosevelt suggested that the schools "come to a gentlemen's agreement not to have mucker play." The mild resolution adopted at the conference, which promised to eliminate violence and foul play, satisfied few critics, although numerous colleges did discontinue football, including Wake Forest, which dropped the sport between 1895 and 1907. The excitement generated by football had created such widespread fan support, however, that reinstatement of the game was practically inevitable. Even at schools that had never fielded a football team, such as Atlantic Christian College, students lobbied to add the sport. The athletics editor of *The Radiant*, in November 1911, argued that football on many college campuses had been influential in "instilling discipline and developing manly virtues."[8]

Although baseball and tennis were active sports on the Wilson campus in 1911, students complained that basketball and football received inadequate support. The students were in tune with sports enthusiasts who clamored nationally for inclusion and expansion of those very popular sports. The college magazine commented sarcastically that "as the college does not support a football team, there is little to report concerning athletics." At the time, baseball was the only sport that ACC played competitively.[9]

Still a young sport by the beginning of the twentieth century, basketball was first played in a gymnasium belonging to the Springfield Massachusetts YMCA in 1891. The game quickly became popular among both men and women because it was inexpensive, required little space, had simple rules, and stressed teamwork. The sport soon spread to other YMCA gymnasiums and to college campuses including Yale's, where a team was organized in 1895. The lack of a gymnasium at Atlantic Christian College and at many other small colleges was a factor that delayed intercollegiate competition.[10]

Meredith, a later opponent of ACC teams, was among the earliest North Carolina colleges to play women's basketball, organizing a team in 1903. The basketball and tennis courts at Meredith, located northeast of Main Building, were almost on the street. Victorian social standards prompted trustees to order building a tall wooden fence to "protect the young ladies from the gaze of passers-by." During basketball games with St. Mary's in 1904, the young women temporarily abandoned Victorian decorum in the heat of competition. Following a tie and a victory earned by Meredith in the two games, plans for future contests between the schools were canceled. The decision resulted from rising tempers and harsh words between players and fans when "unladylike language was used on both sides." St. Mary's supporters contemptuously referred to their opponents as "bourgeois," and the Meredith contingent responded by questioning the "educational limitations" of their rivals. American playgrounds continued to provide tests of Victorian mores as feminist goals and values clashed with the athletics revolution of the early twentieth century.[11]

The 1912 *College Catalog* stated that Atlantic Christian College officially encouraged the sports of basketball, baseball, and tennis and boasted that the school had excellent tennis courts and a baseball park that ranked among the finest in the state. Early ACC women appear to have been as interested in basketball as the men. *The Radiant* of November 1912 reported that a "craze for basketball has spread over the girls, and a nice team has been organized." The women's team of 1912–13 acquired Annie Starr, former captain of the Wilson High School team as coach and Eunice Andrews of Wilmington as manager. Both Starr and Andrews brought several years of experience to the college team. New basketball goals had been erected on outside courts on campus, and the girls hoped to compete against teams from other schools in the spring of 1913. Although their goals did not materialize immediately, the young ladies remained optimistic. The student magazine noted that basketball had become the leading sport on campus by the autumn of 1913. Under the direction of coach Pearl Fay Monk, faculty member and vice-president of the athletic association, the girls quickly learned the game. The basketball goals were located close enough to the city street bordering the campus to attract the interest of spectators, and local residents enjoyed the opportunity to "stand on the street and watch them play." In Wilson, social attitudes regarding athletic participation by young women apparently had become more enlightened during the decade following construction of Meredith's protective fence.[12]

Basketball remained the rage on campus in the fall of 1914. Under Coach Monk's guidance, the girls formed both a senior team, led by captain Mary Belle Smith, and a junior team, captained by Claire Hodges. Wilson resident Mary Hunter Deans had joined the college team, and the girls invited players from the local high school to practice with them. *The Watch Tower* of 22 March 1916 noted that the ACC girls finally succeeded in scheduling games with outside teams and had split games with Smithfield High School by scores of 14–7 and 2–13.[13]

The 1916 girls' team had only eight players and was coached by Ruth Lackey, a 1915 graduate of Transylvania College who also served as professor of modern languages. Ruth Hardy, a senior from Waycross, Georgia, was team manager and played forward. The other starting forward was sophomore

Girls' basketball club team. 1916 Pine Knot.

Mary Proctor, team captain. The 1916 annual shows team members standing on a tall ladder against one of the crude wooden backboards featuring iron goals without nets. They played on an outdoor, sandy court which ran vertical to Lee Street, approximately where Hardy Center and Belk Building now stand. Interest in girls' basketball at the college declined during the next two years. *The Radiant* listed no women's team for the spring of 1917, and no opponents had been scheduled as late as the following November. College publications of 1920 and 1921 contain pictures of a girl's team but focus upon expectations rather than actual accomplishments. The 1921 team was apparently the largest up to that time, with twelve players pictured in *The Pine Knot*.[14]

As athletics became increasingly significant on American college campuses, faculty and administrators became alarmed that sports were becoming a threat to academics. They also began to address issues of funding, maintaining control over composition of teams, procedures for selecting and dismissing coaches, creation of adequate facilities, etc. Harvard had led the way in addressing these issues in 1888, creating an athletic committee which, equally representing students, faculty, and alumni, became a model for many colleges. At Atlantic Christian College, the 1908 student-led athletic association created by Professor Guerrant was intended mainly to provide organization and increased support for sports programs. Beginning with the 1912–13 academic year, nonstudents playing on college teams became a major concern and brought a move to strengthen the athletic association by appointing a faculty member as president. C. M. Farmer, instructor in mathematics and English and principal of the boys' dormitory, became the group's leader. *The Radiant* in 1913 reported that the athletic association, now under the lead of a new president, professor Gilbert Fern, exerted greater control over sports and had convinced the college to upgrade facilities. The *College Catalog* for 1913 reported that a newly reorganized athletics committee of four members had drawn up specific rules for student-athletes: "While athletics is generally cultivated by the student body and encouraged by the faculty, it has not become the chief factor of our student life. Those who make the ball teams are required to be bona-fide students. We do not desire a man who comes preeminently for athletics. Students who play match games with other colleges must have a class standing of passing grade at the time of the contest. Not more than five days absence during any term is permitted of any student for the purpose of sport."[15]

Another innovation was the creation of an athletic fee required of every student beginning with the 1913–14 academic year. The fee entitled each student to play on the grounds and gain admission to all games played on college fields. Revenue provided by the fee aided athletic teams in a variety of ways, including improving communication with potential opponents and enhancing public relations. Manager M. A. Bishop used special basketball department letterhead stationery purchased for the 1913–14 season when scheduling away games. The Raleigh YMCA team agreed to host a game with ACC on 1 December 1913, providing the game be played under YMCA rules. The YMCA offered to pay the college athletic association twenty dollars to cover travel expenses. That arrangement is a reminder that the college operated under a handicap by not owning a gymnasium that could help attract visiting teams to Wilson. Not until the mid-1920s, when the college succeeded in gaining use of the newly built Charles L. Coon High School gymnasium, did ACC have the benefit of consistent use of a home court.[16]

The 1914 men's basketball team, under the leadership of coach Al Branch and captain T. V. Polter, began scheduling more outside opponents. *The Radiant* noted that the team had defeated two or three opponents by "a big score" and anticipated playing the top college teams in the state. The following year, with the season almost completed, the student magazine reported that the men's team had defeated some of the best high school teams in the state. Even in contests that ACC lost, the editors boasted that ". . . our boys have always made their opponents admire them for their manly and scientific playing." Professor and coach C. F. Farmer was praised for "scientific coaching and patience" in developing the 1915–16 team. Prior to the development of modern cheerleading when the activity would gain acceptance as a sport, the college co-eds urged the boys on to victory with repetitive chants of "Our boys are sure to win." Continuous use of that particular yell during the next three years may have been the factor motivating Wilson businessman Jonas Oettinger to offer a prize to the boy and girl who composed "the best original college yells." The athletic association attempted to improve the cheering section by appointing Marion Brinson "college yell leader" and called for new cheers "full of life and enthusiasm."[17]

The 1916–17 men's basketball team, not yet playing rival colleges, defeated the high school team from Rock Ridge in a home game by a score of 43–9. Guard Guy Carawan and forward Leamon Whorton led the college in scoring. The two players "tied in the number of goals thrown from the field, each cageing [sic] the ball six times." Warren Lappin, a forward from Illinois, contributed seven "Foul goals." In away games the college beat Fremont High School, 36–24, and the Wakelon team of Zebulon, 18–11. In the Fremont game, Lappin and Whorton led the way with eighteen and twelve points, respectively. The "big game" with Wakelon brought most of the student body to Zebulon to support the college team. Guard Roy Carawan with six points and Lappin with four were scoring leaders. Other players on the team were James B. Anderson and Joel E. Vause. Editors of *The Radiant* credited the unusually large student cheering section with inspiring the ACC boys to victory.[18]

While tennis club members continued to compete against each other, Barton's 1918 baseball team resumed intercollegiate play, finishing their brief season with a split of the six games played. After opening with three losses on the road against State College, Trinity Park, and Elon, the team returned to Wilson and finished the season on a victorious note against Fremont, Wakelon, and Donaldson Military Academy.[19]

The negative impact of the Great War severely limited the activities of the college's athletic programs. The May 1918 issue of *The Radiant* contained only a brief mention of baseball and reported that the athletic association and faculty had scheduled an interclass field day for commencement week. Issues of the magazine between September 1919 and June 1920 fail to mention athletics and list no athletics editor for that period. While lamenting the poor state of athletics at the college, *The Pine Knot* for 1919–20 named Marion B. Brinson as athletics editor and featured a brief section on baseball, basketball, and tennis. The tennis club pictured only eleven male members, the girls' basketball team had seven players, and there were eight members on the boys' team. A picture of the baseball team, coached by Sollie Meadows, showed only eleven men in uniform. Another telling factor regarding the limited resources of athletics was the listing of H. S. Hilley as baseball team manager. The college dean had assumed a new responsibility.[20]

While early Barton basketball teams practiced to prepare for competition against outside teams, tennis quietly became the most popular sport on campus, attracting the largest number of participants and furnishing more opportunities for significant exercise. Invented by a British army major in the 1870s and originally played mainly by wealthy Englishmen, tennis spread to the United States by 1874. Both Yale and the University of North Carolina formed organized tennis clubs during the 1880s. Tennis clubs for both sexes were formed at Atlantic Christian College soon after the school was founded, and by the spring of 1908 tennis was widely played on campus, with club members busily improving skills and enjoying the game. By the summer of 1908, the campus tennis court, located south of Kinsey Hall and parallel to Lee Street, had received enough wear to merit remodeling. A photo of the girls' tennis club in the 1910 *Pine Knot* shows twenty-two members dressed in white physical culture class uniforms, featuring full ankle-length skirts, cotton blouses, and dark scarves. Leaders of the young men's tennis club in the autumn of 1911 were Leon Garner, Arthur Riley, and G. D. Woodley, while Agnes Spain, Vernice Lang, Susie Gray Woodard, and Marie Bailey served as officers of the young ladies' club. Students consistently voiced the need for additional courts, and by the autumn of 1912 campus courts were in such demand that club members were forced to reserve playing time in advance. *The Radiant*

Girls' tennis club. 1910 Pine Knot.

noted that lumber had been donated to construct back nets and stated that students would appreciate it if "some kind citizen" would contribute several loads of sand and clay to further improve the courts.[21]

Tennis clubs at ACC remained popular into the early 1920s without significant play against outside competition. Although various issues of the student magazine mention an intent to schedule tournaments, evidence suggests that no such events were actually held. The athletics section of the 1920 school annual pictures the largest men's tennis club to that time with eleven members. *The Pine Knot* of 1921 reported that tennis remained a favorite sport of both sexes and that the courts were in use during the fall and spring seasons "from early morn until dusk." The 1921 tennis club may have established a first in athletics at the college by reorganizing as a coeducational group composed of twelve men and six women.[22]

While Barton's early baseball and basketball teams continued to schedule and compete against outside foes, hopes of fielding a football team did not totally disappear. The first serious attempt to bring that sport to the campus apparently came during the 1908–09 academic year. *The Radiant* reported that the "whirl of foot ball talk has been so intense and so far-reaching in its results this fall, that A.C.C. has decided to combat some of her worthy foes on the gridiron during the fall of '09." A plan to field a team for the autumn of 1908 had been deferred because of the "small number of large boys" and the difficulty of scheduling opponents. Athletics editor Will Guerrant, attempting to shame male students into coming out for the team, argued that football would make "some of these little puny mama baby boys" into real men. Responding to critics' warnings that football was too dangerous because players were injured and several had died on the field, he noted that automobiles and trains also were dangerous but had not been banned and argued that far more men were strengthened than hurt by the sport. Football, Guerrant wrote, challenged young men to develop discipline, helped to build confidence and character, and prepared them for "the battle of life."[23]

Guerrant's challenge went unanswered. Two years later, athletics editor Paul Howard complained that the lack of a college football team meant there was little athletics news worth reporting. Guerrant and Howard were ahead of their time in calling for the addition of football at AC College, and both would be gone from the campus long before the school adopted the sport. The combination of wishful thinking and a rush to meet publication deadlines may have prompted editors of *The Radiant* in the autumn of 1912 to announce erroneously that football was among the sports which had been organized on campus.[24]

Athletically, the 1919–20 academic year appears to have been a disaster for the college. Writing in February 1920, the yearbook editors had little to say about the sports programs beyond voicing hope that the future would be kinder to college athletics than the rather disastrous past. They appealed for the college community to remember the lessons of history, especially regarding the benefits provided mankind by the Olympic games of the ancient Greeks. As for athletics at ACC, the negative slant of the one paragraph devoted to sports told the story: "Athletics will go at A.C.C. Our college is young and has not yet been able to develop teams to cope equally with older and bigger colleges of the State. Then, too, our athletics has [sic] been stunned by the reluctance on the part of some to see the value in it." When school had ended the previous June, students departed expecting to "play real games this year." Disappointed that those expectations had not been realized, the student editors called for greater emphasis upon athletics in the future. The impact of World War I and the influenza epidemic were other factors adversely affecting the school's athletic teams.[25]

Administrators and trustees, also dissatisfied with the condition of athletics,

The 1920–21 ACC basketball team. 1921 Pine Knot.

decided to make changes, including hiring three new coaches for the 1920–21 academic year. M. H. Grant would coach basketball and baseball, Mrs. Grant would coach the ladies' teams, and Casey L. Blackburn would coach football. In retrospect, it seems entirely appropriate that the exciting, albeit controversial, game that many in the college/Wilson community had wanted for many years would arrive at the start of "the Roaring Twenties." During a decade characterized by prosperity, excitement, and revolutionary social change, Americans became determined to have a good time. The introduction of football at the college significantly energized social life on the campus and within the surrounding community.[26]

Information is sparce regarding C. L. Blackburn's experience, and other qualifications to lead a football team at ACC is sparse. What may be assumed is that Coach Blackburn was a very brave individual. When he accepted the task of fielding the first football team in the school's history, there was a grand total of nine males enrolled in the sophomore, junior, and senior classes combined. Moreover, only three of those students reported for football practice. Fortunately for the coach and the college, the entering freshman class was either not easily intimidated or, perhaps, blissfully unaware of the challenges which lay ahead. Eight freshmen bravely showed up for fall practice. The prep classes also contributed, furnishing three additional candidates—two high school juniors, and one senior. The team total of fourteen players was not enough for a scrimmage, but barring multiple injuries the team could put eleven starters on the field on game day.[27]

In addition to the small number of players, the "Little Christians" team that trotted onto the field that autumn to begin the football season lacked size and experience. The squad's average weight was approximately 145 pounds, and only four players had ever played football. Between late September and Thanksgiving of 1920, the college team won two of nine games against competition furnished mostly by high school and military teams. Despite a dismal record, the young team became an instant success with the students. *The Radiant* that fall devoted two full pages to the coverage of football without so much as mentioning other sports. The football team, the magazine boasted, "was never disgracefully beaten and the spirit in which it fought was wonderful. . . . It was a real credit to the College and it won the admiration of the entire school." The article listed each of the starting eleven players by name and nickname. Led by sophomore captain Milton Jefferson and manager Marion Brinson, the lone senior, the team had boldly accepted the challenge of competing in "the real man's game." The realization that the little team had fought hard against every opponent instilled pride throughout the college community. Coach C. L. Blackburn, dedicated, witty, and committed to fostering "good clean sportsmanship," quickly won the affection of his team and the entire student body. *The Radiant* editors reflected the college's pleasure with its new team in the closing sentence: "May football continue [at] Atlantic Christian College, so here's to Next Year's Team."[28]

Reliable sources regarding the performance of the first football teams are quite limited. An unpublished history compiled by Milton H. Lewis and located in the college archives contains information about the teams of the 1920s. Coach Blackburn, one of the coaches interviewed by Lewis, recalled that the 1920 team had beaten the Wilson High School team by a score of 13–0. Notations later added to Lewis' manuscript, which was written in 1949, indicate that their other victory was against the high school from Washington, North Carolina. Additional opponents played during that first season included Rocky Mount, Wilmington, and Red Oak. Elon, apparently the only college team played, proved to be the toughest foe. Playing at Elon on Thanksgiving Day, the thoroughly overmatched ACC team was beaten 88–0. A dismal initial season, which ended with a one-sided defeat, failed to diminish the students' enthusiasm for their football team. *The Pine Knot* editors praised the effort and determination displayed by the AC squad and credited Coach

The 1920 "Little Christians," ACC's first football team. 1921 Pine Knot.

Blackburn with developing a team which was described as "a splendid working machine . . . full of fight from the beginning until the final whistle."[29]

The players who struggled to master the intricacies of football on Barton's first grid team were student-athletes of high caliber. Marion Brinson, the only senior on the team, was perhaps the busiest student on campus. A native of the Pamlico County town of Arapahoe, Brinson served two terms as president of the Hesperian Literary Society, was editor-in-chief of *The Radiant*, 1919–20, and *The Pine Knot*, 1920–21, won Annual Inter-Society Debate honors, and served three years as superintendent of the college Sunday school. Brinson also was vice-president of his junior class, a member of the tennis club, and the senior member of what might be termed "the Arapahoe connection," a definite force in the early years of ACC athletics. Arapahoe natives joining him on the 1920 football team were Zeb Brinson, class of 1923, and Archie Reel, class of 1924, both of whom were active in campus activities and good academic students. Zeb played tackle on the football team, was manager of the basketball squad, and served as captain of the baseball team. Reel displayed skill in all sports, as halfback and quarterback in football, guard in basketball, and a starter on the baseball team. He was a member of the tennis club and was described in campus publications as a "campus character." Upon arriving as a freshman, Reel sported a large button which read "Watch Arapahoe Grow," and grow it would. During the 1920s and beyond, a continuous flow of skilled student-athletes from the small town enriched the classrooms and athletic fields of AC College.[30]

Football teams during the four years following 1920 continued the pattern established by the initial squad, playing hard but losing far more games than they won. The 1921 team managed to win three games and closed the season on Thanksgiving Day with a hard fought 14–13 victory over the Wake Forest reserves. President Hilley honored the team at a chapel service 2 January 1922 by presenting players white sweaters monogrammed with a handsome letter "A." The 1922 team was less successful, opening the season with a 34–0 loss to the varsity team at Wake Forest College and ending with a 85–0 loss at Raleigh to a strong NC State freshmen team.[31]

Football and organized cheerleading apparently arrived on the Wilson campus about the same time. While describing the football season of 1920 and praising the college girls for promoting school spirit, *The Radiant* singled out "'Kat' Jackson, cheer-leader" for special mention. A resident of Washington, North Carolina, Kathlyn Jackson was credited with putting "'pep' into the College life" and was the only graduate of the class of 1921 listed as a cheerleader. "Kat" Jackson also appears to have been the key organizer of the "A-1 Club" on campus. While no records indicate that this group was officially a cheerleading squad, the fact that it was led by the cheerleader and developed the following yell provides compelling evidence:

> Rack-a-Chick-a-Boom!
> Rack-a-Chick-a-Boom!
> Rack-a-Chick-a-Rack-a-Chick-a!
> Boom! Boom! Boom!
> Rip! Rah! Ree!
> Rip! Rah! Ree!
> A No. 1's, A No. 1's,
> 'A.C.C.'

Later yearbooks picture the A-1 Club with five to seven members and identify officers of the organization. At least four other clubs adopted yells in the early 1920s, which indicates competition in displaying school spirit at athletic events. Sororities and fraternities, which were also beginning to appear on the ACC campus in the 1920s, adopted similar activities. The A-1 Club, the D. D. Club, and Sigma Tau Chi Sorority were organizations listing yells in the 1926 yearbook.[32]

By 1922, the Athletic Association and Faculty Athletic Committee controlled all athletic matters. The Athletic Association, which included all students and faculty members who paid the annual athletic fee, was responsible for electing managers for each of the teams and raising funds to pay expenses. Led by President Archie Reel, the group convinced the trustees to provide a larger budget by raising student fees by five dollars, the increase to go directly to the association to support athletics. The formula for granting funds gave one-fourth of the total to girl's basketball while football, baseball, and boy's basketball divided the remaining three-fourths, using the ratio of 3:2:1, respectively. The 1924 annual reported that the new funding arrangement had improved the budgeting system.[33]

Efforts to upgrade athletics included the appointment of F. M. Pearce, a native of Zebulon, as the school's first athletic director in 1923. Pearce was a recent graduate of Wake Forest College, where he played baseball, basketball, and football. Despite reorganization and increased funding, the sports teams of the early 1920s continued to struggle. With only five veteran players returning from the previous year and a schedule featuring college and military schools, the 1923 football team's season ended with a record of one victory, one tie, and four defeats. Among the few positive developments was a more attractive schedule for the 1924 baseball team, featuring games at Wake Forest, NC State College, Oak Ridge, Elon, Guilford, and Lenoir. Home games, eagerly anticipated by the Wilson community, would be played at League Park, "one of the best diamonds of the Virginia League."[34]

Even the dismal record of the 1923 football team must have been envied the following autumn by a squad that apparently lost all of its games except one, which ended in a tie. In addition to building character, however, the 1924 team also built for the future, and teams of the following years reaped the benefits. Coached by John Barclay and noted for playing tough defense, the 1925 team produced ACC's first winning football season, claiming four victories and three defeats. Key games of the season were a 2–0 win over Catawba and a 19–0 shutout of Elon, the latter game considered one of the biggest upsets in the state that year. At the end of the season, the sports staff of the Raleigh *News and Observer* rated the 1925 team the equal of any small college squad in the state. In addition, the football team's newly discovered success seemed to spread from the gridiron to other sports. Against competition provided by college and YMCA teams, the boy's basketball team compiled one of the school's best records with thirteen victories and six defeats. Editors of the 1926 yearbook, expecting a veteran baseball squad to take the field later that spring, boldly predicted the best year for athletics in the college's history.[35]

Fans of Atlantic Christian College, pleased as they were with the success of their 1925–26 athletic teams, could hardly have hoped for what was in store. The next autumn the football staff produced the best grid team in the college's history. In fact, the 1926 "Little Christians" came within a single touchdown of an undefeated—and unscored against—season. High Point College, with a 7–0 victory, became the only opponent to score on the 1926 grid team, and ACC gained a measure of revenge by holding the Panthers to a scoreless tie in a rematch later that season. When the 1926 season ended, Atlantic Christian College had outscored the opposition by the remarkable total of 139 to 7.

RECORD OF THE 1926 ACC FOOTBALL TEAM

ACC	6	Elon	0
ACC	50	Blackstone, Va.	0
ACC	6	Guilford	0
ACC	0	High Point	7
ACC	6	Wilmington Light Infantry	0
ACC	37	Fort Bragg	0
ACC	34	Catawba	0
ACC	0	High Point	0[36]

Legendary coach D. C. "Pea Head" Walker led the 1926 team, which received statewide attention and garnered praise from alumni and local citizens as no previous ACC team had done. The announcement of Coach Walker's hiring in August reportedly caused a large number of promising athletes to register at ACC in September. Like many other coaches affiliated with the college during its first quarter century, Walker left the school after only one season. Nonetheless, "Pea Head" Walker and the members of the 1926 football team had provided fans of the college with memories that would linger for years. In 1937 Walker began a highly successful coaching career at Wake Forest College which would make him a legend in the Southern Conference and the state of North Carolina.[37]

With the addition of football, Atlantic Christian College became competitive with other small colleges of the state in adopting expanded athletic programs. Athletics benefited the college and the local community by providing opportunities for participants and fans and expanding name recognition for the college. It is evident, however, that the growing popularity of sports ultimately had a negative impact upon student publications. With a limited number of upperclassmen, the demands of writing and editing, fund-raising, etc., sometimes became overwhelming. Writing in the April 1911 issue of *The Radiant*, a staff member described the difficulty of resisting the temptation of "'hanging around'" with friends or of leaving the office early to join a game of tennis or basketball. Football's arrival in 1920 may have rendered the decision less difficult. The last issue of the popular student magazine appeared the month after the initial football season ended. Editor Marion Brinson was team manager and a starting end on the football team. Several other football players, including Zeb Brinson, Archie Reel, and James Manning, were also members of the publications staff.[38]

Football became the main game on campus during the 1920s. The sport dominated the headlines and gained the envy of players on other athletic teams at the college. *The Pine Knot* clearly indicated football's exalted status. Unfortunately, the four teams following the great 1926 team failed to attain winning seasons. Coach Edward R. Tweddale's arrival from Eureka College in 1927 proved that dedication and hard work could not replace experience and talent in assuring success on the gridiron. The 1927 team defeated only Wilmington Light Infantry and Guilford, while losing to Campbell, High Point, Catawba, Roanoke College, and Paris Island. The key win came in the homecoming game against the Guilford "Quakers" when "swift footed" defensive back C. L. Riggan returned an intercepted pass for a touchdown.[39]

Even the inspired leadership of new coach Mark Anthony, who had won All Southern Conference honors while playing at the University of Georgia, was not enough to end the string of losing seasons. The popular coach stayed at ACC for three years, even though his initial season of 1928 failed because "a jinx 'grabbed' the team" and produced a rash of injuries and fumbles resulting in a record of one win and seven defeats. Despite the team's poor record, the young coach retained the players' respect. Determined to honor their leader, the players formed a campaign, which adopted a new nickname for the college—"Bulldogs." Mark Anthony had starred for the Georgia "Bulldogs," the source of the new nickname. The yearbook of 1929, then named *The Collegiate*, pictures the team with "Mutt," the college's first mascot. Unfortunately, the 1929 "Bulldogs" played only slightly better than the "Little Christians" of the previous two years, finishing the season with two wins and four losses. The two victories were over Campbell and Lynchburg.[40]

Coach Anthony returned for his third and final season in the fall of 1930, the last year that the college sponsored a football team until after World War II. The team suffered one of the worst seasons in the school's eleven years of football competition, matching the 1928 record of one win and seven defeats. Unable to find a suitable quarterback and suffering a shortage of talent at other positions, ACC fell victim to opponents by lopsided margins. The only highlight besides the single victory that autumn was the selection of "Big Center" Bob Hawkins to the All State Football Team by the coaches of the Little Seven League. The trustees, likely anticipating funding problems resulting from the declining economy in 1930, voted to discontinue football for two years.[41]

The 1928 basketball team, upon which star football player Bob Hawkins also played, struggled unsuccessfully to equal the record of the 1927 team, which won the Little Five State Championship. Guard Roy Dunn had led that championship team, assisted by teammates Monroe Fulghum, Clifford Hill, Randolph Munn, Cecil Reel, and C. D. Riggan. As the school reached its twenty-fifth birthday in 1927, alumni and fans undoubtedly reflected upon past accomplishments while pondering future challenges. Atlantic Christian College's first quarter century of athletics had been a difficult, frustrating period; its attempts to build competitive teams were hampered by modest budgets and a limited number of male athletes. Organizational and administrative problems had also proven difficult to resolve. The heterogeneous assortment of opponents faced during the school's formative years, featuring high school, YMCA, military school, military based, and community league teams, with a few games against college freshmen and reserve squads, frequently rendered assessment of team progress quite difficult.[42]

The *Pine Knot* of 1928 featured an analysis of the importance of athletics to the college with a special emphasis upon football. Baseball and boys' basketball received minor coverage while tennis and girls' basketball were ignored altogether. A perceptive editorial in an earlier issue of the student magazine analyzed the value of athletics to students, school, and community. The writer pointed out that by the 1920s Atlantic Christian College had become an important source of culture and entertainment in eastern North Carolina and mentioned the contributing role of athletics. *The Radiant* argued that the American people demanded entertainment and noted that athletics (during a time preceding the appearance of radio) increasingly provided that entertainment. In outlying areas such as Wilson, "a place where a good theater or opera is not within reach," sports events filled a cultural and social void. In addition, the article suggested, "more and better athletics for A.C.C." would continue to provide the exercise necessary for building healthy brains in healthy bodies. The articles were apparently written by seniors James T. Lawson of Rural Hall and Marion Brinson of Arapahoe, editors-in-chief of *The Pine Knot* and *The Radiant*, respectively. By the time that the school celebrated a quarter century of service, collegiate athletics had become firmly entrenched on the campus and attracted loyal fans from communities surrounding Wilson. The adversity experienced by athletic teams during the school's early years helped to lay the foundations upon which more competitive and successful Bulldog teams would be built.[43]

SEVEN

The Professor Who Cannot Walk Slow

DURING PRESIDENTIAL ELECTION YEARS, politics temporarily outranks baseball as America's national pastime. Such was the case with presidential campaigns of the 1920s, a decade of economic success which historians have labeled an era of "Republican prosperity." Three successive GOP Presidents, Warren G. Harding, Calvin Coolidge, and Herbert Hoover, occupied the White House and helped their party dominate the period politically. During the 1920 presidential campaign, the first following World War I, Harding's call for a "return to normalcy" encouraged Americans to turn their attention away from foreign concerns and focus on domestic issues, especially education and the economy. On the Barton College campus, Howard Stevens Hilley, Raymond Smith's successor, prepared to do just that, assuming new duties as both dean and acting president. *The Wilson Daily Times* reported that Hilley, a native of Acworth, Georgia, had earned an A.B. degree from Transylvania College prior to receiving a Rhodes Scholarship to attend Oxford University in 1914. He earned both a B.A. and M.A. at Oxford before returning to America and his native state.[1]

Indeed, the age of normalcy seemed an appropriate time for the Wilson college to be led by a gifted young scholar who studied abroad during the war and served as an orderly in a French military hospital prior to returning home to begin a teaching career. Hilley taught at Southeastern Christian College in Auburn, Georgia, in 1917–18 and acted as director of vocational guidance for the Atlanta city school system during the following year. In September 1919, both he and Maggie Tucker Hilley, his bride of fourteen months, joined the Atlantic Christian College faculty, Hilley as professor of ancient and modern languages and Maggie as instructor of voice.[2]

Howard Hilley's status as a Rhodes Scholar and Oxford graduate would have impressed educators and administrators at any American college of the 1920s. Certainly, few small Southern colleges boasted faculty members with such impeccable credentials. Still several days short of his twenty-seventh birthday upon arrival on the Wilson campus, the new professor quickly demonstrated that he also possessed such positive qualities as commitment, maturity, and a seemingly endless supply of energy. Student editors of the June 1920 issue of *The Radiant* expressed their approval of Professor Hilley's obvious skills:

> He is known around the campus as 'the Professor who cannot walk slow.' The one thing that stands out in his classwork is thoroughness. He has broad and accurate information, founded on common sense, and shows . . . a desire to make the student familiar with the subject. . . . He is always optimistic and cheerful, and the students love to come in contact with him. Being a man of vast information, of unbounded energy, and of high ideals, we feel that his coming means the greatest of success for A. C. C.[3]

That students found Hilley to be "cheerful" was an interesting observation. Former students and faculty members who worked closely with Hilley normally described him as strict, intense, high-minded, and deeply committed, but cheerfulness was not typically a characteristic mentioned. Mamie Jennings Lucas, who returned to the college as director of drama from 1925 to 1934, remembered Hilley as intense and domineering, a man whom faculty and staff respected but often found intimidating. Photographs of Hilley appearing in student publications of the 1920s and 1930s reveal an alert, stern-faced college official, apparently intent upon fulfilling the duties of his office. In dedicating the 1928 *Pine Knot* to the president, the editors praised his leadership and assessed the intensity that photographs reveal: "Hilley . . . brought to this young institution all the boundless energy of youth, together with the genuine enthusiasm of a man who works for a cause which he believes is worthy of his very life." Hilley would need all of those qualities in leading the institution for nearly three decades, the longest tenure of any president. During the 1920s alone the school struggled to maintain enrollment, launched large fund-raising campaigns, experienced increasing global awareness, welcomed new campus social organizations, and made the decision to relocate the college.[4]

Charles C. Ware, who worked closely with Hilley for three decades, points out that as chairman of the publicity committee during his initial year on campus, Hilley prepared a meticulous chart listing annual enrollment and graduation records for the school's early years. Ware regarded Hilley's chart as "a graphic and concise exhibit, [which was] a characteristic item in his thirty years' service at Wilson." The intensity with which Hilley approached his responsibilities is revealed further in an article written soon after his appointment as acting president. Entitled "Toward 1920–21" and appearing in the June 1920 issue of *The Radiant*, Hilley's words challenged the entire academic community to demonstrate "loyalty and passion for the College" and expressed conviction that the students, faculty, and administration possessed the qualities to make ACC one of the best schools in the state.[5]

In a surprisingly bold move for a new acting president, Hilley revealed a goal to enroll 250 students for the fall term. His chart, which appeared in the first issue of *North Carolina Christian*, showed that the college enrollment for 1919–20 was 125 students. Considering enrollment trends of the institution's early years, an achievement of doubling the student body by the fall term would be almost miraculous. Hilley acknowledged that producing a much larger enrollment depended on hard work from everyone. However, as a biblical scholar, he believed in the possibility of miracles, making reference to the prophet Isaiah's experience of witnessing a desert mirage turn into a pool of water. Hilley's brash forecast may also have been a rare display of youthful exuberance. The youngest college president in the state in 1920, he would not reach his twenty-eighth birthday until September. Although the 1920–21 enrollment did not reach the predicted number, the student body grew to 187 members, an increase of 67 percent.[6]

Hilley's positive outlook was also consistent with the optimism of the new decade. The spirit of the Roaring Twenties seemed to promise an era of excitement, progress, and economic success well beyond the conditions of previous decades. Especially encouraging in the case of Barton College was an overwhelming demonstration of support from Disciples leaders for the new "Carolina Enlargement Campaign." Scheduled to begin in the summer of 1920, the economic plan included a commitment to raise $200,000 for the school. The May issue of *North Carolina Christian* outlined specific campaign goals. Designating the college as the major recipient of fund-raising efforts, the newspaper listed four goals: an enrollment of 250 students for ACC in 1920–21, 50 of whom would be majors in religious service; the addition of 2,200 new members for Churches of Christ in the Carolinas; raising $200,000 for AC College from North Carolina, $25,000 for the Raleigh Church, and $25,000 for Benevolent Homes of Disciples at Atlanta and Jacksonville, Florida; raising $3,000 for ACC from South Carolina, $4,000 for Constructive State Work in South Carolina, and $3,000 for Benevolent Homes in Atlanta and Jacksonville.[7]

Stressing the value of the college to the Christian Church in North Carolina, the *North Carolina Christian* also named twenty-two counties, containing fifty-nine churches, being led by "A. C. College men." Under the heading "Atlantic Christian College Needs," the paper listed an endowment of at least $100,000, a new site and adequate equipment for college enlargement, a library building, a gymnasium, a central heating plant, a music hall, a science hall, additional residences for faculty, adequate compensation of faculty, temporary improvements of present buildings at a cost of approximately $6,000, and funds to provide for special needs of the music and science departments. The May 1920 feature on the Carolina Enlargement Campaign ended with statements of support from twenty-two Disciples from the Carolinas. The 1920 fund-raising campaign was the most ambitious of the school's early history. Significantly, the campaign produced the first public mention that the college might move to a different site. The large monetary drive had actually been planned and approved in 1919–20, the final year of President Smith's tenure. Ware, appointed director of the campaign, supervised three teams composed of seven "regular workers" and fourteen active church ministers assisting on a part-time basis.[8]

Members of the college faculty quickly joined Hilley, trustees, and church leaders in supporting the fund-raising effort. Frederick F. Grim described the start of the campaign as "the dawning of a new day." In the June 1920 issue of *The Radiant*, the education professor suggested that college needs over the next five years would require a million dollars, a "new location, new buildings, adequate endowment and an increased teaching force." He argued that the church in the Carolinas had never experienced a more opportune time for growth and challenged Disciples to "unite in one great response."[9]

The trustees appointed Hilley president of Atlantic Christian College at the board's 18 May meeting. While student, faculty, and trustee approval of his performance may have been gratifying, Hilley remained dissatisfied with enrollment and fund-raising results. An additional but closely related problem had also proved vexing to his predecessors—convincing Disciples to send their sons and daughters to AC College. Even lifelong church members and leaders who had contributed money and rendered loyal support to the school often opted to send their children to larger, better established colleges and universities rather than to Atlantic Christian College. That particular problem continued to provide the college with one of its most troublesome dilemmas. Writing in the April 1925 *North Carolina Christian*, Hilley revealed dismay that only 78 of 248 college students from North Carolina Disciples churches were

President Howard S. Hilley, 1920–49. 1923 Pine Knot.

enrolled at ACC. Pointing out that size, buildings, and furnishings alone did not determine quality, he stated that "the great majority of leaders in . . . our Nation have come from small colleges. A.C.C. is worthy of your loyalty. It merits your support in every way."[10]

The young school at Wilson had long suffered an image problem in comparison with older and larger universities, especially those offering graduate programs. It was also troublesome that some graduate schools did not award ACC graduates full credit for work completed, granting only two years credit for four years of undergraduate study. In addition, ACC graduates hired as teachers by public schools were not always compensated fully for their degrees. Therefore, when in 1922, leading North Carolina colleges launched a cooperative plan to adopt definitive standards for judging "A Class" colleges, Atlantic Christian College promptly joined the group. The State Department of Education would administer the higher standards. On 26 May 1922, the Raleigh *News and Observer* reported that ACC was making progress toward strengthening its library, faculty, and academic departments. Assurances from trustees that the college would continue making improvements convinced the State Department of Education to announce in 1922 that the institution was on track to become an "A Grade College." The announcement meant that ACC was among twelve colleges recognized by the state as either already meeting standards or very close to official recognition. The first ACC class to graduate from an institution officially rated as "A" was the class of 1923.[11]

Hilley and the trustees realized that maintaining compliance with the state's higher new standards required that maximum priority be given the needs of bona fide college students. That decision prompted the school to discontinue the high school department that it had supported for twenty-two years. Ten students received certificates as the last "prep" class to graduate from ACC during the 1924 commencement. The decision appeared prudent when the college's enrollment began to increase markedly. The 1928 commencement marked two milestones in the history of the institution: the largest graduating class and the largest total student enrollment. Twenty-eight graduates received A.B. degrees, and 187 students enrolled for the 1927–28 academic year. Included in the latter number were twenty-three pupils listed as "students preparing for religious work."[12]

Raising the quality of the faculty was an obvious priority toward the goal of improving the quality of academic programs. Hilley had inherited a small but experienced group of teachers, headed by Perry Case, professor of philosophy and religious education; Ethel M. Grim, professor of English; Frederick Grim, professor of education; and Frances F. Harper, professor of mathematics. President Hilley also remained an official part of the faculty, continuing to teach Latin, Greek, and religion courses. Frances and Myrtle Harper held the longest tenure with the college, having served on the faculty and staff since 1904. Hilley encouraged faculty members to continue graduate studies and to travel and study abroad. During his early tenure, members of the faculty studied at Columbia University, the University of North Carolina, the University of Indiana, the University of Rome, Emerson School of Oratory, and Chautauqua College of New York. Faculty travel destinations during the same period included England, France, Germany, Holland, and Spain.[13]

Other individuals who served Atlantic Christian College with distinction over an extended period as faculty members and in various other capacities were Charles C. Ware, John Barclay, and Charles H. Hamlin. Ware had been a

"Captain John" Barclay, Disciples of Christ pastor, civic leader, civil rights activist, and unofficial ACC chaplain. The Collegiate, September 1941.

member of the faculty and staff since his arrival in Wilson as Disciples state secretary in 1915. He served successfully as registrar and fund-raiser and was managing editor of the *North Carolina Christian*. Ware's articles and editorials on behalf of the church and the college circulated throughout North Carolina and beyond. He also became archivist and historian to both the church and the college and established the North Carolina Discipliana Collection, currently housed on the Barton campus. Although Ware's history of the college lists his tenure as 1915–26, his contributions as liaison between the church and college continued into the 1950s.[14]

A thirty-one-year-old Kentucky native, John Barclay arrived in Wilson as pastor of First Christian Church in the late summer of 1924. In addition to holding a bachelor's degree from Transylvania and a master's from Columbia, Barclay had served as an infantry commander in France during World War I and had gained a reputation for his knowledge of athletics, largely by coaching a national champion high school basketball team in Chicago. Adapting quickly to the Wilson area, Barclay helped build a closer association between the church and the school. Commenting on his value to the community, the

October 1925 issue of *North Carolina Christian* reported that "Mr. Barclay as college pastor, assistant athletic coach, and friend to everybody is highly esteemed at Atlantic Christian College." In addition to forming a special association with ACC students, he also received praise for helping to improve race relations within the Wilson community. Leading educators in Wilson's black community recalled Barclay's visits to Darden High School, where his addresses to the student body on social justice, ethical behavior, and character building were eagerly anticipated and highly regarded.[15]

Perry Case came to ACC in 1916 as professor of natural science but soon was reappointed registrar and professor of religious education. The Indiana native held A.B. and B.D. degrees from Butler College. His outgoing personality, cheerful disposition, and interest in every aspect of college life made him a popular faculty member. Case's wife, Mable Catherine, also joined the faculty as an English instructor in 1918 and later became associate professor of education. Both husband and wife shared a deep commitment to the school, as they proved by funding a full student scholarship valued at $305 in 1923. Offered to the returning ACC student who recruited the largest number of entering students, the grant covered tuition, room and board, and matriculation fees. Sadie Greene, a rising senior from Pantego, won the scholarship for 1923–24 by attracting thirteen new students. Greene may have been a natural-born recruiter, as she also won an oratorical award and captured the Oettinger prize, which went to the winner of a Yell Contest. Following a leave of absence to complete graduate studies, Perry Case returned to serve as teacher and administrator until 1960. Case Art Building, built in 1966, bears the name of this dedicated professor.[16]

Charles H. Hamlin, a native Virginian, came to ACC as professor of social science in 1925 and became one of the best-loved and most controversial individuals in the college's history. A productive author, scholar, teacher, and mentor, Hamlin was also a confirmed pacifist and advocate of social justice. Many of his liberal views, especially those regarding racial equality and civil rights, made him appear radical in conservative eastern North Carolina. The C. H. Hamlin Student Center, built in 1967, was named for this distinguished professor, whose tenure on the faculty was the longest and among the most productive in the school's history. The Hamlin Society is a student organization sponsored by Barton's school of social work.[17]

Professors Charles Hamlin and Frederick Grim were among the faculty members who first began to teach summer school classes at ACC during the 1920s, largely to benefit teachers desiring to upgrade their certification. In

1920, Grim directed the first state-approved summer school taught at the college. Grim and his wife, Ethel McDiarmid Grim, professor of English, were both talented and highly respected teachers who joined the faculty in 1918. In 1925, Frederick Grim became dean of the college. Hamlin taught in the Oriental Seashore Summer School operated by Duke University in 1926 and 1927. ACC sponsored a twelve-week summer school at Neuse Forest near New Bern in 1928. Also teaching summer school were professor of English Cortell K. Holsapple and B. G. Carson, professor of science. Carson, who arrived in 1927 with a Ph.D. from the University of North Carolina, was the first member of the science faculty with a doctorate.[18]

The faculty club of Atlantic Christian College, organized during the autumn of 1927, consisted of faculty members and spouses. The group met monthly at various campus locations or in the homes of members. During the Christmas holidays of 1927, W. A. and Mamie Jennings Lucas hosted the event at their home on Nash Street. After singing several carols, the members heard Professor Holsapple read a paper on the origin of Christmas. President and Mrs. Hilley joined approximately a dozen members for the program and refreshments. Club president Frances Harper usually opened the meetings, and programs typically consisted of book discussions, stimulating mental games, and/or current events discussions. Most sessions also featured music and refreshments.[19]

By the spring of 1930, the college faculty met three times per month with the first two sessions devoted to curriculum revision, catalog changes, committee reports, and student advising. In ACC's regular column printed in *North Carolina Christian*, Frances Harper wrote in April 1930 that "Running through the routine of business is the earnest desire to build into all teaching the principles of Christian character." The third meeting each month resembled the original faculty club socials and included popular programs. At the third meeting in March 1930, Ruth French, chair of the music department, read a paper on "Beethoven and the Fifth Symphony," then treated those present by playing Victrola records of the symphony.[20]

With the exception of a certain aura typically accorded newly arrived faculty members with exotic sounding credentials from foreign universities, serious interest in international matters developed rather slowly at the college. President Caldwell's well-publicized 1912 trip to Palestine and Europe had stimulated academic interest in global issues, and the outbreak of World War I awakened the college abruptly to the importance of the world beyond America. The news of horrible casualty rates stirred emotions and quickly caused the campus to become far more world conscious. Direct involvement by sons and daughters of the college in events of the war graphically demonstrated the extent to which ACC and the world were interrelated.

During the 1920s, the college community's awareness of global issues increased significantly because of a continuous stream of world travelers to the Wilson campus, including renowned missionaries and biblical scholars. A commitment by the Disciples of Christ Church to a broad range of missionary programs also increased global interest at a time when more alumni chose careers in foreign service. The revolutionary modernization of communication and transportation also contributed by spreading news of world events faster and in greater detail than ever before. Newspaper circulation increased significantly, and, following an important first broadcast of a presidential election—that of President Harding in 1920—the infant medium of radio grew rapidly. Improvements in both air and rail travel seemed to shrink the world still further, and automobiles became increasingly available in small towns such as Wilson as Henry Ford's assembly lines turned out greater numbers of the "Model T." By 1926 there were nearly ten thousand Ford dealerships in the country.[21]

Missionaries speaking on campus and at local churches frequently stayed several days. To students who seldom ventured outside eastern North Carolina, stories of strange-sounding peoples in Latin America or Africa could be fascinating. Lecture sessions could now be enhanced by the use of slides, as Mr. and Mrs. C. Manly Morton demonstrated during a missionary rally at ACC held 19–21 January 1922. Active as missionaries in Paraguay and Puerto Rico for years, the Mortons frequently visited the college to share their experiences and recruit talented young adults to the foreign mission field. As the *North Carolina Christian* noted, the rally gave valuable information on Latin America's natural resources, architectural features, and the dress and customs of the people. Their "stereopticon slides," demonstrating the natural beauty of the countryside, were described as "beautifully tinted" and enthusiastically received. When the rally ended, five ACC students volunteered for work "on the foreign field," and twenty-eight students agreed to give the matter additional thought.[22]

Morton's importance to the college prompted the editors of the 1925 annual to write: "To C. Manly Morton, an outstanding alumnus of our college, the editor of our first *Pine Knot*, the living link of our Wilson Church, whose work in the field of education and religion has endeared him to the heart of his alma mater, we dedicate this 1925 volume of our *Pine Knot*." The tribute to the 1909 graduate followed an earlier honor paid by the school. As a part of commencement week in 1923, Reverend Morton preached the baccalaureate sermon to graduates and their guests at Wilson's First Christian Church.[23]

Other missionaries visiting Wilson during the decade worked in Mexico, Argentina, China, India, Japan, and Java. Topics addressed by the distinguished guests ranged well beyond standard religious themes. In December of 1925, Dr. Alva W. Taylor, head of the social welfare service of the national Disciples Church, stressed the importance of settling national disputes through the World Court. Not all of the important visitors represented the church. Lucia Ames Meade, renowned representative of the National Council for Prevention of War, spoke to an attentive audience on the campus in November 1926. Meade, who had attended the 1919 Woman's Peace Conference at Zurich with Jane Addams, the world-famous pacifist and social worker, had also served as a delegate to peace conferences at Glasgow, Lucerne, London, and Munich. Invitations to scholars of international affairs by other campus groups, including literary societies and the faculty club, provided students and faculty with opportunities to become well versed on global issues. Sketches and cartoons appearing in the 1925 and 1926 issues of *The Pine Knot* depict male and female graduating seniors, dressed in academic garb and with diplomas in hand, appearing eager and ready to meet the challenges of a global community.[24]

Both global and domestic issues formed the basis of the curriculum of the Wilson County Public Schools, which Charles L. Coon led as superintendent. The close proximity of the renowned educator's home to the campus and his interest in the college made Dr. Coon a frequent visitor to the school. The superintendent's commitment to establishing closer relations between the public schools and the college caused Coon to play a significant role in helping ACC upgrade its teacher education program. He also supported the idea of summer school programs at the college as a means of facilitating teacher certification in eastern North Carolina. The Wilson public school classrooms, which Coon opened to student teachers, helped the college to meet state requirements for accreditation. In April 1928, the *North Carolina Christian* reported that all of the students in ACC's "Education 66 class" were fulfilling requirements for careers as teachers by practice teaching in the Wilson grammar school. Coon also participated in the college's twenty-fifth anniversary celebration, speaking on the topic, "Wilson and Atlantic Christian College." Emphasizing the importance of a Christian college to the community, Coon called the institution one of Wilson's most valuable assets. He also noted that twenty-five graduates of ACC were then teaching in Wilson's public schools.[25]

Recognition of the college's twenty-fifth year of service during commencement week of May 1927 began on Saturday evening with a Joint Society program, followed by the baccalaureate sermon on Sunday morning. Monday's events featured College Class Day, a baseball game, and a play presented by the dramatic club. Tuesday's calendar included the commencement address, an alumni banquet, and a Founders' Day program. All events were open to alumni and friends of the college. "The Meaning of a Christian College" was the theme of Hilley's baccalaureate sermon at the First Christian Church. Reverend John Barclay, delivering his annual farewell sermon to the senior class on Sunday evening, urged graduates to continue to appreciate the fullness of life by focusing on "the beautiful and the essential in literature, history and science." The commencement play, "Dulcie," a three-act comedy directed by Mamie Jennings Lucas, played to an appreciative full house on Monday evening.[26]

The alumni association held its banquet in the Christian Church on Tuesday afternoon with Sadie Greene presiding. Following an address by Frances Harper on "The Twenty-fifth Anniversary," John Barclay and Marion Brinson reported on athletics, and Sidney Bradley and John Waters provided an update on the capital campaign. Speaking on "The College and the Future," President Hilley urged all alumni to continue to support their alma mater. In addition to President Greene, officers of the alumni association were Mable C. Case, vice-president; Annie Kate Oakley, secretary; and J. Ernest Paschall, treasurer. Students receiving awards at the twenty-fifth commencement included Ethel Morgan of Stokesdale, who won both the Denny cup for the best essay on the college motto and the Kiwanis scholarship cup; Monroe Fulghum of Wilson, who won the Rotary Club cup, presented to the best all-around athlete; and Clem Banks of Arapahoe, who gained the Faculty Cup, which went to the best all-around student. Ironically, of only two years in the 1920s when students failed to publish an annual, one was the anniversary year of 1927, and the other was 1922.[27]

Much of Howard Hilley's success as president and teacher at the college was based upon a positive relationship with students. A feature article appearing in the 1924 *Pine Knot* lauded Hilley's faith in people, consecration, and executive skills, and explained the youthful president's special appeal:

> With the natural energy and enthusiasm of youth, he brought also to his work foresight and judgment beyond his years. He has made the college work his work, the college interest his interest, and with the spirit of 'This one thing I do' he has applied himself to the task to which he was called.

ACC "flappers"—seniors Eunice Aycock of Lucama and Nona Godwin of Kenly. *1928* Pine Knot.

The students find in him a wise counselor, just in his judgments, and withal kind. With true devotion to a cause which lies on his heart, he plans and works with untiring zeal, looking steadfastly toward the fruition of his hopes for A.C.C. And yet, there is no thought or complaint of self sacrifice. President Hilley works for Atlantic Christian College because he loves it, and believes in it.[28]

Photographs in college publications indicate that the students taught by Hilley and other faculty as Atlantic Christian College approached its second quarter century of service were enjoying the Roaring Twenties. By the middle of the decade, radical changes in clothing and hair styles, which had arrived earlier in American cities, began to alter the appearance of the campus in Wilson. Photographs in *Pine Knot* issues of the 1920s reveal that, with the single exception of high hemlines, ACC co-eds preferred the flapper look over more conservative styles. The greatest changes seem to have occurred about mid-decade. The class of 1926, including senior class president Macon Moore of Wilson and fellow class officers Nannie Pearl Quinerly of Grifton, Esther

Bryant of Lucama, and Moses Moye of Farmville, clearly merited recognition as fashion-conscious graduates. Seniors Mittie Wiggins of Elm City, Annie Harper and Anderson Boswell of Wilson, Jannie Manning of Middlesex, and Mae Reel of Arapahoe all reflected the popular styles of the 1920s.[29]

These style-conscious students participated in religious associations, athletics, literary societies, fraternities and sororities. Other popular extracurricular activities in the 1920s were affiliated with the schools of music and drama. Two-thirds of the graduates of the class of 1923 listed memberships and activities involving music and/or drama. Extensive coverage of these groups in college publications reveals their significant impact upon the college community. Ivy May Smith, director of music, 1916–27, served as adviser to piano and voice majors, arranged recitals, and provided leadership to large numbers of participants in glee club, ensemble club, and other music groups. Mamie Jennings Lucas served as adviser to the dramatic club and directed the group's numerous theatrical performances. In addition to providing a broad range of experiences for ACC students, these activities furnished a continuous source of entertainment for the college community and surrounding area. Faculty and students eagerly anticipated the productions, which typically featured elaborate musical and dramatic presentations prior to Christmas vacation and commencement week. Literary societies maintained lively rivalries and continued to provide quality programs, and fraternities and sororities gained popularity during the decade. By 1928 there were four Greek organizations (Phi Sigma Tau and Sigma Tau Chi sororities and Phi Kappa Alpha and Sigma Alpha fraternities) adding to social life on campus.[30]

Yearbook photographs also reveal the growing numbers of vehicles on the campus as the 1920s advanced, particularly parked in front of the girls' dormitory. As social historians have noted in evaluating the twentieth century, the automobile exerted radical cultural and psychological changes that extended beyond transporting travelers from point A to point B. Although hardly foreseen by Henry Ford and other early car builders, innovative social uses of the automobile dramatically altered courtship patterns and contributed to the sexual revolution of the 1920s.[31]

Although most students who lived off campus either walked or rode bicycles, increasing numbers commuted to the college by automobile. Coinciding with the growth of intercollegiate athletics, increased availability of automobile travel permitted teams to play away games more frequently and allowed numerous fans to follow their team to the courts and athletic fields of opposing teams. The streets surrounding the college were paved in 1925, providing more convenient access to the school and improving the aesthetic beauty of the campus. Circulating rumors that sidewalks surrounding the school would also be paved in the near future produced additional excitement within the student body.[32]

Advertisements appearing in student publications provide further evidence of the local availability and impact of the automobile. Hackney Brothers, consistent financial supporters of the college, advertised their business in the 1916 *Pine Knot* through an ad featuring a drawing of a single-seated, horse-drawn carriage. An ad for T. G. Pettus Company on South Goldsboro Street listed buggies, wagons, harnesses, horse blankets, lap robes, and bicycles for sale. However, by 1920 *The Pine Knot* listed Hackney Brothers as a distributor in the Carolinas for "Standard Eight: A Powerful Car." The firm's ads for subsequent years in the college annual and Disciples newspapers pictured a "Closed School Bus Body" and "Special Truck Bodies." Other ads featuring automobile services and sales listed Grant Six Motor Cars and Trucks, Red Seal Continental Motor Trucks, and Hudson-Essex Motor Cars. The changes also influenced the provision of medical services for ACC. Ads of the 1916–23 period show the Wilson Sanitorium located on Nash Street with two or three automobiles parked out front, evidently owned by doctors E. T. Dickinson and A. F. Williams, "the College Physicians and strong friends of the Atlantic Christian College." Interestingly, the other vehicle in each of the sanitorium ads is "The Wilson Sanitorium Ambulance," pictured in the earlier photograph as drawn by a single horse and in the latter as hitched to two mules.[33]

With the lone exception of the arrival of football, the most exciting change anticipated by Atlantic Christian College during the 1920s was the prospect of relocating the school. ACC's purchase of the large farm during Abner Smith's presidency, followed by state recognition of the institution's A Grade status, increased anticipation that significant growth of the college would follow. Student disappointment with the slow rate of change prompted three successive yearbook editors to address the problem, beginning in 1924. C. Bonner Jefferson of Washington, North Carolina, under the title "A Look Forward," noted that the college was approaching its twenty-fifth year of service. He challenged friends and trustees to provide a "new location containing at least fifty or sixty acres" in order to accommodate adequate buildings, athletic fields, and research facilities. He added that immediate needs included dormitory rooms and office space to serve 200 students, a new library, laboratory facilities, a central heating plant, and a gymnasium. The new campus should be planned and developed "with some view to artistic design and architectural beauty." Jefferson advocated increasing the enrollment to 250 students, the creation of an endowment of $500,000, and the provision of a maintenance budget of $25,000.[34]

Charlie Grey Raulen of Wilson also called for a larger campus and an auditorium in her editorial in the 1925 *Pine Knot*. Additional needs were reception rooms, comfortable dorm rooms, and visually enhanced grounds featuring beautiful plants, attractive walks, charming benches, and paved driveways. Academic needs included modern research equipment and a larger library containing a broader selection of books. The 1926 editor, Nannie Pearl Quinerly, a graduating senior, chose to compare her school's economic woes and limited facilities to problems encountered by a plain, single young woman facing a choice between unwanted marriage proposals and spinsterhood. In a feature entitled "Miss Atlantic Christian," Quinerly wrote: "She has had a hard time these twenty-three years . . . she does not dress quite as expensively as some of her friends. . . . Her parents are not by any means wealthy . . . she has hoped that some rich friend would help her . . . [but] No one has thought enough of her to buy her pretty clothes and luxuries that a girl of her A grade standing needs." "Miss Atlantic Christian" had received offers from suitors enticing her to marry and move to Raleigh, Winston-Salem, or Rocky Mount but preferred to remain where she was, provided her "Wilson friends show a little affection for her." She hoped to settle where she was most wanted, to become better dressed, and to be housed in a beautiful home with a large yard of twenty-five to fifty acres. Also, she had become very much "inclined to be an old maid, and her own boss." [35]

College leaders were well aware of the critical status of the institution. Rumors circulating at the Disciples state convention at Wilson's First Christian Church in November 1925 predicted that the college would be relocated. George F. Cuthrell of Raleigh, reporting for a steering committee of college trustees and representatives of the church, verified the rumors. In order to maintain its A Grade rating, Cuthrell argued that the college must have a campus of at least twenty-five acres, equipment valued at $300,000, and an endowment of $250,000. The convention also directed that the question of relocating the school be resolved by the state convention.[36]

The January 1926 *North Carolina Christian* reported that consultant F. W. Reeves of Chicago had visited Wilson the previous month, "making a survey of the College and its field. Proposed locations were visited and points of desirability noted." Based on Reeves' report and recommendations by the steering committee, the state convention in March 1926 voted to build and operate "in Eastern North Carolina a Standard Senior College" which would open by 1 September 1929. The church would raise a minimum of $220,000 for buildings and $250,000 for endowment, enabling the college to gain accreditation by the Southern Association of Colleges and Secondary Schools. The site of the college would be the city, which, in the judgment of the steering committee, submitted the most attractive offer. The school would include an administration and classroom building, separate dormitories for girls and boys, and a gymnasium. The church would provide a maintenance fund of $10,000 per year. A more immediate problem was finding the money to allow the school to pay its immediate debts. Urgent requests for gifts of nearly $20,000 appeared in the January–April issues of the Disciples newspaper. By May 1926, the college maintenance fund had received slightly over half the money needed, and, with less than a month remaining in the fiscal year, a shortfall of nearly $3,000 remained. May 1926 also brought an agreement between trustees, the church, and the citizens of Wilson to keep the school at its original site. Wilson leaders pledged to contribute $100,000 to the college by 15 November 1927. If the community raised an additional $50,000 by the spring of 1927, the school would move to a different site in Wilson, which had been offered by residents of the city.[37]

Declining agricultural prices throughout the 1920s made fund-raising efforts by the college and the city particularly difficult. The stagnant agrarian economy persisted throughout the state and was especially felt in eastern North Carolina. Thus, although fund-raising efforts by the college during the decade aimed higher than previous drives, results were disappointing. Three years after the campaign started, the *North Carolina Christian* announced that, of the $250,000 original goal, North Carolina and South Carolina Disciples had raised $100,190.86, slightly over 40 percent of the objective. Only $63,698.37 of that amount was in cash and government securities; the remaining $36,492.49 was in the form of personal notes.[38]

In his history of the college, Charles Ware reported that eventually two-thirds of the campaign pledges were "paid in full or in part" and blamed the shortfall on the depressed condition of agriculture which lingered throughout the decade. Disciples leaders tried again at the state convention of 1923, establishing a new drive to raise $300,000 for endowment and $19,000 per year for maintenance at the college. Although some 3,000 pledges, amounting to approximately $320,000, had been received by midsummer 1927, documents fail to reveal the actual income collected. The urgent tone of appeals for support of the school published in the *North Carolina Christian* issues of the late 1920s demonstrated serious concern that the second drive would also fail to attain its goal.[39]

The two campaigns did have positive results. First, the critical money shortage during the 1920s increased efforts by college officials and Disciples leaders to spread the influence of the church and the college beyond traditional areas of impact in rural eastern North Carolina and into such urban areas as Raleigh, Greensboro, Winston-Salem, Charlotte, and Asheville. Second, the campaigns identified several new donors and potential donors, who provided generous support, including James W. Hines, a Disciple and successful businessman in Wilson and Rocky Mount, and Mrs. Heber L. Coward of Greenville. In 1927, Hines offered to contribute $100,000 toward the campaign's $300,000 goal, provided the remaining $200,000 was secured by 1 January 1930. An editorial, appearing in the *News and Observer* on 2 February 1927, by Josephus Daniels, a former classmate of Hines at the Wilson Collegiate Institute, praised the generosity of the benefactor. Daniels also touted Wilson's progressive record in education, superintendent Charles L. Coon, and Atlantic Christian College. Gertrude Hooker Coward, a native of Greene County and a member of the Eighth Street Christian Church in Greenville, died in July 1929. Her will provided gifts to several worthy causes; the largest, a sum of between $40,000 and $50,000, went to Atlantic Christian College. *Pine Knot* editors recognized the generosity of Hines and Coward in yearbook dedications of 1923 and 1928, respectively.[40]

Despite the stagnant agricultural economy, pledges of monetary support from Wilson citizens encouraged college officials to purchase a larger site for the school on the western outskirts of the city limits. By March 1928, conversation at the college was filled with speculation about moving to the new site. Trustees had agreed to buy a forty-two-acre tract approximately one-half mile from the western city limits and two miles from the original campus. Located near the present intersection of Raleigh Road and Ward Boulevard and fronting the Norfolk Southern Railroad, the tract was covered by an impressive stand of trees and promised to be an attractive site for future buildings, athletic fields, and other facilities required to build "a greater Atlantic Christian College." The Disciples newspapers of April and May 1928, announcing that an architect had been hired, also called upon friends of the college to support this worthy venture. Groundbreaking for two dormitories, an administration building, a gymnasium, and a central heating plant would start soon.[41]

When the college opened for fall semester, the news spread that workers were preparing the sites of the girls' dormitory and a heating plant. The Wilson

Garden Club announced that it would help beautify the site by planting crepe myrtle trees along the entrance to the new campus. On Sunday, 18 November 1928, the college celebrated laying the cornerstone for the girls' dormitory and honored both George Hackney and J. W. Hines. Hackney had served on the board of trustees since the founding of the college, most of the time as chairman. His leadership established an important precedent by encouraging his family, whose selfless leadership and philanthropy now spans a century, to become Barton College's "first family." Hines' faithful support also coincided with the creation of the institution, and he ranks as the greatest individual benefactor of the school's early history. Acting on behalf of the trustees, Dr. George F. Cuthrell, pastor of Raleigh's Christian Church, presented oil portraits of the honorees in a ceremony held in the chapel. In accepting the gifts, President Hilley told the large audience that it was appropriate for the portraits to hang on the walls of an institution that the honorees had helped to create and sustain. Hackney Hall, built in 1960, Roma Hackney Music Building (1963), and Willis N. Hackney Library (1977) are named for the Hackney family. J. W. Hines Hall (1956) serves as Barton's largest classroom building.[42]

Following the presentation, the group traveled to the new site to witness the laying of the cornerstone of the first building. Program participants were Galt Braxton of Kinston, chairman of the building committee; Dr. Doane Herring of Wilson, chairman of the finance committee; Bryce Little, president of the Wilson Chamber of Commerce; A. E. Cory of Kinston; Howard S. Hilley; John Barclay; and the contractor, a Mr. Jones. Coming so soon after the observance of ACC's twenty-fifth birthday and so near Thanksgiving, the ceremonies stirred emotions and memories among a crowd that included representatives from twelve churches. Frances Harper's description captured the moment: "It was a day fraught with memories of incidents and persons in the quarter of a century of the institution's history, and yet it was a day charged with promise, and replete with plans for a greater Atlantic Christian College."[43]

Two weeks and two days before the nostalgic but cheerful crowd met to celebrate and socialize on the attractive new campus, America had elected a new President. A man of the American Midwest, who had triumphed over adversity by hard work, sterling character, and a strong will, Herbert Hoover appeared to be the ideal leader to insure a continuance of "Republican prosperity." Some within the group may have noticed similarities between the lives of a popular new President and a promising young college. Both had faced great challenges, struggled, and prevailed. Both had reason for optimism regarding a future that appeared to promise great success. As the crowd watched Rev-

The Pine Forest Apartments building (intended to be a women's dormitory) and heating plant smokestack, remnants of the "new campus" of 1928–29 located near the intersection of Raleigh Road and Ward Boulevard. Photos by Keith Tew, 2001.

erend Barclay lay the first cornerstone, there was little reason to doubt that the new campus would soon contain many buildings. Perhaps some remembered positive feelings brought about by the confident ring of the newly elected President's campaign speeches. Hoover had predicted that "we in America today are nearer to the final triumph over poverty than ever before in the history of any land. The poor house is vanishing from among us." The words seemed to convey accurately the mood of warmth and optimism in an exciting age of prosperity that many Americans believed would last indefinitely.[44]

EIGHT

The Very Sweetest Way I Ever Heard of Getting Through College

FOR MANY AMERICANS, the economic crisis of the 1930s was as unexpected as it was difficult to comprehend. As hard times spread across the nation, it was far easier to understand plunging agricultural prices, a severe shortage of money, and a growing number of jobless people. The Great Depression, which followed the disastrous plunge of the national stock market known as Black Thursday on 24 October 1929, posed the most serious threat to America since the Civil War. No one on the Atlantic Christian College campus that autumn could have predicted the severity of the future struggle nor the changes that the school would be challenged to devise and implement during the turbulent decade that lay ahead.

On Thanksgiving Day, exactly five weeks after the stock market plunge, the ACC community suffered a much smaller, albeit more easily understood, disappointment when the football season ended at Catawba in a hard-fought 13–6 Bulldog defeat. During the return home, some AC players and fans were already anticipating the opening of basketball season less than three weeks away. Coach Marc Anthony's squad had begun practicing in the Wilson high school gymnasium for the 17 December game at Wake Forest. In the college chapel that day, Reverend John Barclay delivered a stirring Thanksgiving address by expressing gratitude to God that Americans lived in a "creative generation." He warned the congregation that democracy faced its greatest challenge since the American Revolution. Troublesome uncertainties which he specifically noted were a weak, fledgling League of Nations and changes occurring within the Soviet Union, "a great new nation feeling her way toward a new outlook on life." Despite growing concerns about the declining economy in the autumn of 1929, it was still too early to suspect that America's greatest tests in the coming decade would come from chaotic conditions within rather than from problems which seemed to loom abroad.[1]

As Christmas 1929 approached, the mood within the college community was festive but deeply attuned to the spiritual meaning of the season. Strong Christian faith had continually been the central guiding force for Atlantic Christian College, and the celebration of Christ's birth always held special significance. The Young Women's Christian Association opened seasonal activities with a service enhanced by a chapel decorated with beautiful holly and native pine, the singing of carols, and a biblical reading of the journey to ancient Bethlehem. Professor Frances Harper wrote that by the end of the program "... the true spirit of the Christmas seemed to linger with each one." On Thursday evening prior to Christmas break, the dramatics club, directed by Mamie Jennings Lucas and joined by several faculty members, treated the college to *Southumberland*, an elaborate and artistic pageant featuring such Old English customs as entertainment by a jester and bringing in the Yule log. In addition to charming the large audience that packed the auditorium, the program seemed to set a perfect tone for beginning the holidays.[2]

Ten days into the spring semester of 1930, Frances Harper, rising shortly after daybreak, marveled at the beauty of a quiet snow-covered campus. She described a majestic scene of towering pine trees that appeared to be "sentinels, keeping watch over a sleeping campus." For Howard Hilley, then nearing the completion of his tenth year as president, the longest tenure of any ACC chief executive, the unexpected snowfall provided an opportunity to reflect upon institutional problems. The new semester had brought evidence of approaching economic troubles, but neither Hilley nor anyone else could have predicted the extent of the changes that the depression soon would bring, including shifts in plans for the new campus and forces which threatened to cause the school to close its doors. In rising to meet those challenges, the college suffered numerous adversities but also increased admissions, improved retention, constructed new buildings, created new traditions, and graduated talented, young leaders prepared to contribute positively in a broad range of professional fields. Those achievements, realized during a period of great sacrifice, made up one of the most compelling episodes of Barton College's history.[3]

April 1930 brought both negative and positive financial news for the college. Disciples church funding for the school, which had averaged $5,000 per year for the past decade, fell drastically for a second straight year. Far more positive was President Hilley's announcement during chapel service that the college had been awarded the J. W. Hines gift of $100,000. That gift, plus the $200,000 raised by the college in matching funds, brought the size of the endowment above $400,000. The Disciples newspaper reported that work would soon be resumed on the new forty-two-acre campus.[4]

Commencement exercises in 1930 produced the college's first honors graduates. F. W. Wiegmann and Ray Moses graduated magna cum laude, while Fred Hardison, Margaret Sasser, John Hyatt, Needham Bryan, and Mrs. Jack Barnes graduated cum laude. President Hilley preached the baccalaureate sermon on the college motto, formally adopted in 1923, "They Shall Have the Light of Life." Taken from John 8:12, the scriptural passage became a traditional theme of Hilley's baccalaureate addresses.[5]

An additional notable event that spring was the college's first radio broadcast. The ACC column in the May issue of *North Carolina Christian* announced that the college male quartet, accompanied by Lottie Carawan, had broadcast a program of religious music from Raleigh radio station WPTF. The performance featured such traditional favorites as *Steal Away* and *Standing in the Need of Prayer*, included a piano solo by Carawan, and ended with the college song. The event stirred excitement on the campus and created anticipation for the quartet's next scheduled broadcast on 15 May. Following a performance by the quartet in February 1931, the Raleigh *News and Observer* commented that the quartet's numerous WPTF broadcasts had "won many friends throughout the radio audience, particularly for their interpretation of religious music." The college glee club of thirty-six members, featuring Martha Edmonston and D. E. Poole as soloists, also broadcast programs on 20 November 1930 and 23 April 1931. Carawan was a senior education major from Bath and pianist for the Alethian Society, Edmonston was professor of modern languages, and D. E. Poole was president of The Fellowship group.[6]

The Wilson campus of the 1930s found students and faculty members tuned in to radio broadcasts. Frances Harper wrote that Martha Edmonston and Elizabeth E. Yavorski, dean of women and director of music, had an "Echophone" radio installed in their room and that ". . . very good music comes over." Interested individuals came by to listen to President Hoover, King George, and other famous people. A few months later, an innovative "Birthday Party" fund-raiser for students and faculty raised money to purchase radios for the parlors of the girls' and boys' dormitories.[7]

Much of the news in broadcasts of the 1930s, whether national or local, was far from positive. Bank failures, unemployment, struggling businesses, and stories of human poverty, as well as reports of financially stressed churches and colleges filled news broadcasts of the decade. In September 1930, as ACC opened for its twenty-ninth year, *The Wilson Daily Times* ran a full page of ads purchased by local businessmen voicing support for the institution and included an editorial praising the school. President Hilley addressed the Wilson Kiwanis Club on the state of the college. Admitting that times were hard and money scarce, he stated that the institution was going forward and would eventually "work out its building program."[8]

Plunging economic conditions also threatened tens of thousands of churches across the country, including those of the Disciples of Christ. The *North Carolina Christian* reported that, as of 1 January 1931, ten Disciples churches in the state owed outstanding building loans of over $70,000. Churches at New Bern, Raleigh, and Charlotte owed the largest debts, amounting to between $15,000 and $20,000. Although First Christian Church of Wilson did not share that problem, church membership had fallen 7 percent, the number of pledges were down 26 percent, and the total amount pledged had declined 16 percent. Disciples state secretary Charles C. Ware, who continued to edit the state newspaper from Wilson, wrote in May 1931 that bank failures had cut state missions receipts by 50 percent and forced the fund to borrow heavily in order to meet the church's needs throughout North Carolina. Listed among disbursements by the state's Woman's Christian Missionary Society was the figure $37.98 labeled "Lost in bank closing."[9]

Some Disciples among North Carolina's cotton farmers devised an innovative way to pay commitments to the national pension fund, an idea that reportedly swept the eleven cotton states. The idea was "Pay it With Cotton." The pension fund agreed to accept cotton at the rate of ten cents per pound as payments on the $8 million pension fund drive. The church headquarters in Indianapolis would store the cotton for up to a year, selling only if the price rose to ten cents per pound. Several Sunday school classes had volunteered to pick the cotton donated to the pension fund. A New Bern Disciple and farmer suggested another innovative approach. In a letter to Charles C. Ware, 17 February 1932, R. C. Holton offered to contribute livestock: "In your travels for the Master if you find a brother who wants a registered Duroc-Jersey pig (now thirteen weeks old,) I will deliver it in New Bern for him if he will give you $10 for State Missions. These are blue-ribbon stock and really worth more by several dollars, but I have them for sale in the depression."[10]

These attempts to deal with adversity came from areas where many ACC students lived and further warned supporters of the college that hard times lay ahead. By the spring of 1931, the declining economy prompted trustees to halt construction on the new college campus on Raleigh Road. After several meetings with Wilson community leaders on the matter, they decided to con-

Marsh Knott '38 and Sue Todd '34, resourceful students who helped President Hilley and ACC to weather the Great Depression. 1934 Collegiate *(yearbook) and 1938* Pine Knot.

centrate on improving the original campus. Plans called for renovations with special attention to heating and plumbing systems and repairing and repainting woodwork, walls, and floors. Representatives of the college and the Wilson community also agreed to build a gymnasium on the campus.[11]

The small Disciples college was also challenged to develop innovative methods to help reach President Hilley's goal that no student should be denied an education because of inability to pay. Several boys received permission from their families and the college to keep cows on the outskirts of the campus. Each boy would tend to his cow and provide fresh milk to the college dining hall as payment-in-kind for tuition and room and board. *The Collegiate* column "Around the Campus" poked fun at senior Marsh Knott's preference for raising dogs and hunting over academics and reminded readers of his other agrarian interests: "In the fall of 1934, Atlantic Christian College received two new members, Marsh and his cow. For three years this cow has carried him through school, not literally speaking, of course. In addition to this, Marsh has been known as the campus barber and is noted for making boys' heads look like Fuller brushes. . . . In spite of the fact that he must get up at daybreak to milk a cow and is always in demand as a barber, he has managed to make good grades and maintain his popularity on campus."[12]

Onnie Cockrell, Wilson resident and class of 1938, remembered fellow classmates Marsh Knott of Wendell and Hugh Cherry of Rocky Mount tending and milking their cows. Students good-naturedly accused the boys of adding water to the milk in an effort to meet their quota to the college dining hall. Another in-kind product eagerly anticipated by students was seafood brought to the dining hall by the daughter of a New Bern commercial fisherman. Fresh seafood greatly improved the typical dining room fare remembered by former students as being plain but filling. Sue Todd of Wendell recalled a father with three children at ACC furnishing a carload of beef, and added: "Potatoes, chickens, corn, all kinds of canned vegetables, fruits, and the like are sold to the kitchen, which helps out immensely in meeting one's obligations. The very sweetest way I ever heard of getting through college was two girls who gave molasses in exchange for their education." Bread and molasses became mainstays of the college food service during this period. Todd also recalled a student canning over 200 half-gallon jars of tomatoes to help pay her educational expenses.[13]

Ashley Futrell Sr., who worked for a local tobacco company and served on the staff of *The Wilson Daily Times*, remembered a legendary campus tale of the 1930s. Perhaps no story better illustrates President Hilley's tireless efforts to keep the college's kitchen well stocked with food during the Great Depression. While returning one afternoon from a recruiting trip to a high school near Pinetops, Hilley accidentally struck and killed a stray cow that had wandered onto the road. Seeing no farmhouse in the area where the likely owner of the unfortunate animal might be found, Hilley decided to make the best of a vexing situation. Driving back to the college for a truck and additional manpower, he returned to the scene of the accident. For the next week, well-fed students pondered the identity of the generous benefactor who had contributed fresh beef to the AC dining hall. A frequent visitor to the campus during the 1930s, Futrell developed a friendship with Hilley while working with the baseball team as an assistant coach. He later moved to Beaufort County and developed the *Washington Daily News* into a Pulitzer-Prize-winning newspaper.[14]

Hilley's efforts to make the college affordable became a strong selling point in recruiting students during the Great Depression. Following a WPTF broadcast of a glee club program in the spring of 1932, the president himself went on the air to promote the school. He told the radio audience that four distinctive features characterized Atlantic Christian College:

> First: It is unique in its field of service . . . situated in a section of North Carolina not adequately served by any other four-year college of liberal arts . . .
>
> Secondly: The college is a friendly college—a homelike place . . . [a] 'big happy family . . . [with] a friendly spirit and a helpfulness that is a joy to all who share in it.

Thirdly: the college endeavors to be distinctive in its low cost. Our rate for board, room rent, tuition and fees . . . [is] lower than any other four-year privately-operated college in North Carolina.

. . . . In these days of hard times . . . it is our ambition to put a college education in the reach of worthy students of limited means. In fourth place, it is our hope to be distinctive in our religious emphasis. . . . We are working upon the theory that an educated man needs religious faith to unify, integrate, and motivate his personality and service—that education without religion is a menace. . . . Without sectarian prejudice or denominational bias we want the lives and service of our students to count for Christ.

Hilley revealed that he and the trustees planned to reduce the total cost of attending ACC from $335 (the 1931–32 total) to $300 for the 1932–33 year.[15]

ACC's recruiting efforts resulted in a larger enrollment in 1932 than that of the previous fall. Frances Harper wrote in the Disciples newspaper that families willingly sacrificed to send sons and daughters to college and noted that "An excellent school spirit prevails." Campus activities that Harper mentioned included education club meetings, led by president Sue Todd and entertained by songs from the trio of Jack Brinson, Sam Freeman, and Ira Langston. The young ladies enjoyed beautiful October weather while competing in volleyball, soccer, tennis, and archery. The faculty perceived the student body of the early depression years as focused, hardworking, and intent upon mastering their studies. Christian principles prevailed and "integrity of character [was] emphasized."[16]

Langston, Freeman, and Brinson served as officers of the class of 1933, and remained loyal supporters of the college. A native of Dunn, Langston was president of the Hesperian Society, a member of the football and basketball teams, and was elected King of the May Day Festival of 1933. He received an honorary Doctor of Divinity degree from his alma mater in 1954. Sam Freeman of Washington, an Inter-Society Debater and a member of the May Day Court of 1933, received an Alumni Achievement Award in 1993 and was the recipient of a Doctorate of Laws in 1956. Jack Brinson of Arapahoe served as president of the Hesperian Society and participated in the May Day Festival of 1933. The college awarded him the Alumnus of the Year Award for outstanding service in 1983. Brinson and his wife Elizabeth later established the Elizabeth Faye Brinson Memorial Scholarship in honor of their daughter. The scholarship is awarded to a student preparing for a career in church vocation. The board of trustees recognized Brinson's distinguished service to the college with the designation of Trustee Emeriti following his retirement from the board in 1983.[17]

Sue Todd, class of 1934, was president of the Women's Dormitory Council and vice-president of both the YWCA and Alethian Society. She won the Faculty Cup as the student with the best general record at the college in 1933 and the Rotary Cup for having the best academic record in both 1933 and 1934. Years later Sue Todd Holmes endowed a scholarship in honor of her parents, Mallie C. and Martha M. Todd.[18]

Members of the faculty took pride in students who won leadership and academic achievement awards and were also pleased with the overall high quality of graduating seniors of the 1930s, closely monitoring their success in graduate schools and vocations. In 1932 ACC graduates pursued advanced degrees at nine universities including Columbia, Cornell, and Yale. As professor Frances Harper noted two years later, eight ACC graduates served as principals of schools in Wilson and surrounding counties. By October 1934, all thirty-one members of May's graduating class were employed, twenty-two as teachers. Miss Harper's interesting description of the 1933 graduates also demonstrates how the meaning of language has changed with the passage of two-thirds of a century. Ten members of the class were teaching, she wrote, six were in graduate school, "one is in farming, one is in the drug business, and two are in a State hospital." The respect between faculty and students was mutual. In May 1934, Sue Todd wrote, "I came here to school largely because of the faculty. My personal contact with members of the faculty here has meant more to me than any other phase of the college life."[19]

Atlantic Christian College's graduates of the 1930s strengthened the alumni association and worked hard in support of the college. A 1930 business meeting of the association, led by President C. Bonner Jefferson, class of 1924, passed several important resolutions. The association agreed to require the secretary to compile a list of all individuals ever enrolled at ACC and invite them to join the Alumni Association, appoint a committee to raise money to build "a gymnasium, alumni building, or whatever the organization wished to donate to the college," sponsor *The Collegiate*, and declare homecoming an annual event, with the executive committee designating the day. Twenty-two alumni attended, traveling from such places as Deep Run, Arapahoe, Pink Hill, and Richmond, Virginia, and representing classes ranging from 1916–30. At the association's business meeting of May 1931, John Waters, reporting for the committee making plans for an alumni building, stated that depressed financial conditions had caused temporary postponement of that goal.[20]

Annual debates between the Alethians and Hesperians frequently brought numerous graduates back to their alma mater, sometimes from as far away as Georgia, Virginia, and New York. The subject debated by the societies in 1933 was a key issue then facing Congress and the country as a part of President Roosevelt's New Deal: "Resolved, That State and Federal governments should own, develop, and control the sources of hydro-electric power in the United States." Speaking for the affirmative and representing the Alethians, Hazel Windley of Pantego and Lalah Driver of Wilson defeated Hesperians Ira Langston and Sam Freeman, who took the negative side.[21]

During commencement week of 1933, the alumni association continued a recently established tradition by hosting a banquet for the seniors at the Wilson Country Club. New officers elected prior to the dinner included president Zeb Brinson of Stokes, vice-president Christine Whitley Davis of Clayton, secretary Neva Banks of Arapahoe, and treasurer Agnes Peele of Wilson. In an effort to build greater loyalty and unity between alumni and the school, the association voted to request that the college secure a full-time alumni secretary who would also serve on the faculty as an instructor. At homecoming day on 4 November, the college appointed faculty member Dallas Mallison of Oriental, an ACC alumnus, as the first permanent alumni secretary. His duties would be evenly divided between alumni affairs and teaching in the social sciences department.[22]

With the help of alumni and churches, recruitment efforts of the 1930s resulted in the largest sustained enrollment growth in ACC history. The size of the student body was a record high in 1932–33, and the growth trend continued during subsequent years. When enrollment figures passed the 250 mark for the first time in the fall of 1933, President Hilley placed notices in *The Wilson Daily Times* that no more students would be accepted. The rapid increase of commuting students contributed to the impressive growth, and September 1934 found Hilley again terminating enrollments after the student body size passed 300. Dixie Barnes and John Edmundson of Fremont were among commuting students of the early 1930s who helped to swell enrollment. They drove from Wayne County to Wilson in a Model A Ford and less frequently in a large green Cadillac with several other commuters. Barnes recalled that students who lived on campus made the day students feel welcome. Praising the faculty and the high standards of the school, she added, "The opportunity was here. They taught you here. There was a strength here." After receiving her degree in elementary education, Barnes taught for thirty-one years in Wayne County, mostly at Fremont. She later married John Edmund-

Co-eds beside ACC school bus. 1940 Pine Knot.

son, and they became the first of three generations of the family to attend Barton College.[23]

The sudden enrollment surge prompted the administration to purchase a bus to pick up commuters and brought alumni and others to call for a new dormitory to enable more students to live on campus. The college bought a new Ford V-6 bus from Hackney Brothers Body Company in the autumn of 1934 and began transporting students from the Rocky Mount area. George Stein of Rocky Mount drove the bus, which also made stops in Sharpsburg and Elm City. Bus service was soon provided to Smithfield, Selma, Rock Ridge, and other areas.[24]

Several students arriving in the large freshman classes of 1932 and 1933 formed lifelong associations with the college. After discovering that the money that she had made working in tobacco and saved for college expenses had been lost in a bank failure, Sarah Loftin tried to enroll in an extension class offered by ACC in her native Kinston. When the class failed to make, President Hilley persuaded Loftin to enroll at the Wilson campus by promising a scholarship and part-time work. Georgia and Mary Brewer from New Bern had, like Loftin, been raised in a Disciples family. The Brewer twins had participated in church youth programs in the summer held at Bonclarken, a retreat in the North Carolina mountains. While there, they had met members of the AC College faculty, including Hilley, Ware, Barclay, and Charlotte Hill. Loftin later joined the Brewers in attending Bonclarken, and the three co-eds became active church workers on campus and within the Wilson community. Each served as a leader in the YWCA, Fellowship Club, student government, Phi Sigma Tau Sorority, and the dramatic club, as well as on the girls' athletic club cabinet. Like many other students, Loftin and the Brewer twins helped to pay expenses by holding part-time jobs while keeping up with studies and participating in extracurricular events. Georgia Brewer won election to the May Day Court of 1933, which honored Queen Maude Boswell of Wilson and King Ira Langston. Mary Brewer and Loftin served in the 1934 court ceremonies held at "Rustic Gold Park," which honored Queen Maria Brinson of New Bern and King Jack Aycock of Black Creek.[25]

A lanky Johnston County farm boy, who later became acting president of Atlantic Christian College, arrived at the campus riding on the back of a farm truck and carrying a small trunk in September 1933. Loaded with tobacco, the truck traveled to the Wilson market from Newton Grove. That rustic arrival seems natural for Milton Adams, who paid his way through college by working a variety of jobs on the campus and at Bissette's Drugstore downtown. While earning his degree in mathematics, Adams found time for studying and participating in student government, the YMCA, and the Hesperian Society. During 1936–37, his senior year, Adams served as student body president and reigned as King of the May Day Festival. Following a stint in the army after graduation, Adams worked at Branch Bank prior to joining the college as business manager, a position that he filled for thirty-two years. Like many ACC students, Adams fell in love on the college campus, where he met and courted his future spouse, Sarah Loftin. Adams's distinguished service to the school brought him an honorary Doctor of Laws degree from his alma mater in 1978. In 1985 the school recognized Adams' contributions as director of athletics by inducting him into the college's Athletic Hall of Fame.[26]

Amos C. Dawson Jr., a graduate of Wakelon High School in Zebulon, joined Adams in the 1933 freshman class. Dawson joined the Hesperian Society, was voted most popular male student, and served as president of the junior class. A three-sport athlete, he became captain of the baseball, basketball, and tennis teams. Dawson's performance in baseball brought him the label "Iron Man" for pitching both games of a double-header against conference foe Guilford College. His value to ACC's athletic program was proven in the spring of 1935 when, playing the number one position on the tennis team, he led the Bulldogs to a 7–1 victory over High Point. *The Collegiate* noted that the win was the first of the year over a conference team in any sport. Dawson's 2–1 pitching victory over Guilford may have been the Bulldogs' second conference victory. Honored by his alma mater for his contributions, Dawson was inducted into the Atlantic Christian College Athletic Hall of Fame in 1983. Following two decades as teacher, principal, and superintendent with the Southern Pines City School System, Dawson served nineteen years as Executive Secretary of the North Carolina Association of Educators before retiring in 1978.[27]

Onnie Cockrell, another graduate of Zebulon's Wakelon High School, enrolled in the autumn of 1934, joined Dawson on the baseball and basketball teams, and became a three-sport star in his own right by capturing the school's trophy in track for 1936. Cockrell served as president of the Alethian Society and Sigma Alpha Fraternity, edited *The Collegiate* and *Pine Knot*, was president of the class of 1938, and found time to play saxophone in the college band. The hard-hitting center fielder earned All North State Conference honors in 1937 and was inducted into the Barton College Athletic Hall of Fame in 1990. Cockrell taught and coached in Bertie County and served in the military prior to joining Wilson County's Rock Ridge High School as teacher, guidance counselor, and coach in 1948. His football, basketball, and baseball teams won over forty conference and district titles. Cockrell served as director of federal programs for the Wilson County Schools prior to retiring in 1980 and held numerous civic positions, including eight years as Wilson County commissioner.[28]

A. C. Dawson and Onnie Cockrell were fortunate that the college chose to upgrade athletic facilities during their playing days. In November 1933, the college newspaper announced that the school had secured a convenient location near Maplewood School for athletic events and that students had already laid out a soccer field. During homecoming exercises on 4 November, the Alethian boys' soccer team defeated the Hesperians, and the freshman class won a major victory in an "Inter-Class-Tug-of-War" held on the spacious field. Facing the opponent across a huge puddle of water furnished by a Wilson fire truck, the exuberant freshmen struggled mightily before pulling the upperclassmen through the muddy water. Students anticipated using the new athletic field for a variety of other events, including baseball practice, archery, and track and field. Years later, Milton Adams remembered the excitement of competition on that field when he lost a 100-yard dash, "by an eyelash," to Charlie Ware.[29]

At homecoming 1933 the alumni association formally committed to raise $500 to help build the athletic facility which the college had needed longest and desired most—a gymnasium. *The Collegiate* of 15 December 1933 listed an Alumni Honor Roll naming thirty-four members who had already contributed to the fund. Meanwhile, the boys' basketball team still trudged the mile and a quarter distance across town each night to practice in the Charles L. Coon high school gymnasium. The Alethian and Hesperian girls' basketball teams also practiced in the high school gym on Tuesday and Thursday nights.[30]

When the college opened for fall semester in September 1933, students dreamed of having the new gymnasium available for the beginning of basketball practice in November. When mid-November arrived, however, with no progress toward construction discernible except for a large stack of lumber dominating the west side of campus, students angrily questioned the delay. Hilley promised that work would start soon and explained that he awaited word from New Deal agencies, including the Public Works Administration (PWA), regarding a college request for government funds to help finance the gym. With work still not underway by early January, the lumber now "darkening with age" and a recent "home court" loss to the High Point Panthers by a single point, the students' patience neared the breaking point. Finally, in mid-March, the college newspaper announced that workers had begun excavating the foundation for the gym. A foreman had been hired and was directing work by several college boys at the site. ACC had secured a Federal Emergency Relief Administration grant that permitted a college or university to use up to 10 percent of its student body for work around the school. For ACC the grant meant that twenty-four students could be hired at thirty cents an hour for approximately thirty hours per week. Construction of the long-awaited structure would now move along, although not as rapidly as the college would have preferred.[31]

NEW GYMNASIUM AT A.C. COLLEGE WILL BE OPENED TONIGHT
ALUMNI PLAYS VARSITY IN TONIGHT'S OPENER

That headline, which appeared in the 15 December 1934 issue of *The Collegiate*, related news that had been anticipated for months. The editors added that the chances of the Bulldogs' athletic teams had been handicapped for years without a gymnasium. Basketball teams were forced to either "work in the open, or use the high school gymnasium at night . . . [which] besides being inconvenient, has greatly cut down on the efficiency of the teams." That disadvantage became especially noticeable when the team began intercollegiate competition. Another headline proclaimed HIS CANINE MAJESTY TO APPEAR TONIGHT. The college had procured another live bulldog mascot,

The college's first basketball arena, Wilson Gymnasium. 1937 Pine Knot.

and the canine, yet to be named, would make his initial public appearance at the 15 December game. The official opening of the gym would not occur until 5 January 1935 when ACC would host the High Point Panthers in the first conference game of the season.[32]

Erected at a cost of nearly $15,000, the gymnasium was a red brick building that measured seventy feet by ninety feet and featured a maple playing floor and bleachers with a seating capacity of approximately 400. The basement, when completed, would contain dressing rooms, showers, and lockers. In addition to providing a modern playing court for Bulldog basketball, the facility enabled the school to offer programs leading to teacher certification in physical education and coaching. The ACC boxing team, which began intercollegiate competition in 1935–36, shared the facility and became a success in its initial season, winning three of four scheduled matches under Coach W. P. "Bill" Wright. Most important of all, the student body now had a suitable place for a variety of uses, including a temporary auditorium and the expansion of the intramural program.[33]

The gymnasium was the first of several expansion projects which the college accomplished in the mid-1930s. In 1935 trustees purchased an "entire block adjoining the old campus on the north" for approximately $23,000. A gift of $10,000 by Greene County native Clarence Leonard Hardy in memory of his nephew, Bert Clarence Hardy, enabled the college to build a dining hall on the site between August 1935 and October 1936. R. B. Whitley of Wendell contributed 50,000 bricks toward construction of the dining hall. With seating space for 300 people, the new facility enabled all of the college community to dine together, eliminating the need for divided shifts at meal times. Serving in 2001 as a formal meeting and dining facility, Hardy Alumni Hall housed the Trustees' Room and provided basement office space for the physical plant staff.[34]

Hardy Dining Hall was one of several places affected by the Eureka Plan, which President Hilley implemented in 1934. Based upon an innovative system begun at Eureka College in Illinois, the plan employed student workers throughout the college. In return for student labor, the school reduced the cost of tuition and room and board. Students performed practically all work done on campus with the exception of cooking the meals served in the dining hall. The school hired adult cooks to work under the supervision of the school dietitian, Gladys Charles. The faculty approved the student board of managers under the Eureka Plan, which included a supervisor for office work, grounds, buildings, and two supervisors for the dining hall. A faculty committee met weekly to advise student managers, and each supervisor had a faculty advisor.[35]

Sam Ragan, a junior from Varina, was among the students taking advantage of the new facilities. Transferring to ACC in the autumn of 1934 from Textile Institute, where he had gained experience in debating, Ragan promptly demonstrated impressive literary and leadership skills. He became associate editor of *Pine Knot* and chaplain of Sigma Alpha Fraternity and served on the Inter-Collegiate Debating Team. In 1935, as editor-in-chief of both *Pine Knot* and *The Collegiate*, Ragan honed skills that continued to win acclaim when he served as an editor with *The News and Observer*. Ragan also edited *The Pilot* in Southern Pines and won distinction as poet laureate of North Carolina. ACC awarded Ragan an honorary Doctorate in Literature in 1972 and the Alumnus of the Year Award for 1990. Barton College further recognized the contributions of Ragan and his wife with the dedication of The Sam and Marjorie Ragan Writing Center on the campus in the autumn of 1999.[36]

One of Ragan's classmates, Sarah Bain Ward, was astonished upon arrival from Kinston as a freshman in September 1934 to find the college grounds literally covered with pea vines. The lovely campus that she had envisioned appeared, instead, to be a farm. Ward learned that the unsightly pea patch was part of President Hilley's scientific farming scheme to create a healthier lawn by planting soybeans and enriching the soil. Ward's initial thought upon encountering the rustic scene was that she should have followed her first impulse and enrolled at Meredith College. Realistically, she knew that her father would never have agreed to such a move. George Roberson Ward had roomed with C. Manly Morton during the one year that he attended Atlantic Christian College. That brief experience and his commitment to the Disciples church were enough to convince him that his daughters also belonged at ACC. Sarah Bain Ward adjusted quickly to AC College, displaying strong leadership skills, which, along with a good mind and an aptitude for hard work, enabled her to flourish on the Wilson campus. Active in YWCA, glee club, and dramatic club early in her college life, Ward served as supervisor of the girls' building and offices during her junior year. In her senior year, 1937–38, she became president of the Co-operative Association. As her colleagues discovered, Ward was precisely the type of student that Hilley envisioned when he decided to involve students more fully in running the college. As Ward remembered forty-five years later, "Dr. Hilley and I were on really good terms because we were both sort of authoritarian and bullheaded and stubborn, but we kinda got along well together." Although she could hardly have realized it by the time she graduated with a degree in mathematics in 1938, Ward was not finished helping Hilley run the college. After teaching six years at Selma in Johnston County, she received a call from Hilley asking her to consider returning to ACC and joining the staff in the summer of 1944. During the thirty-six years that Ward served as dean of women, under nine college presidents and acting presidents, AC College became her life. Long before retirement in 1980, she had become the epitome of "The Harper Hall Woman," a title that she herself suggested as she helped to shape hundreds of young women into cultured, self-assured college graduates who became role models for others. Ward's contributions earned her an honorary Doctorate of Laws degree from her alma mater in 1969 and the alumni of the year award in 1980.[37]

Ward had succeeded Milton Adams as leader of student government for the 1937–38 academic year. The Co-operative Association was organized in 1936 in an effort to create a governance structure satisfactory to both students and faculty. Labeled by ACC as unique among colleges in the South, the system placed all campus governance except that retained directly under auspices of the president in the hands of students. After a year's trial, the *Pine Knot* praised the success of the new government and noted that the system had won the respect of the student body. The Executive Council of the Co-operative Association included seven students—the president, vice-president, secretary, treasurer, presidents of the men's and women's dormitory councils, a representative at large—and four faculty representatives.[38]

While a variety of issues apparently caused the college community to create the Co-operative Association, growing concern over reports of student cheating seem to have been a significant factor. President Hilley addressed the student body on the issue in December 1933, prompting editors of the student newspaper to lament the fact that cheating had "become so prevalent on this campus that the majority of the students have grown accustomed to it." The situation apparently grew worse the following year, bringing headlines in *The Collegiate* announcing "Groups Plan to Abolish Class Room Cheating." Fraternities, sororities, and the "A Club" had accepted a faculty suggestion that enforcement of the existing honor code would improve the moral tone on campus. The Greeks and the "A Club" presented the plan at a weekly chapel meeting, urged other groups to sign the pledge, and announced that the new plan would go into effect one week after the end of the Christmas holidays.[39]

Editorials and letters in the college newspaper indicate that cheating rumors continued to haunt the campus. A letter signed by "A Senior," appearing in the column Open Forum, stated that cheating had declined on campus. He credited the improvement to increased strictness by professors and, more significantly, to a positive change in attitude among students. Editors of *The Collegiate*, however, convinced that cheating on the campus remained excessive, continued to campaign against dishonesty. Campus leaders created the Golden Knot Honor Society in 1938 as a new organization designed "to give recognition to those who have measured up to the ideals of the college, and to develop and foster attitudes among the students that would make for the attainment of these ideals." Sarah Bain Ward and Griffith Hamlin were among the organization's ten charter members. At a chapel program in February 1939, the Golden Knot polled the student body through a questionnaire to be completed anonymously. The four questions asked were: 1) "Did you cheat on exams? 2) Did you see any cheating? 3) Was there much cheating on exams? 4) Are you willing to help eliminate the problem? The student responses to the questions were: 1) Yes—4, No—158; 2) Yes—77, No—85; 3) Yes—11, No—141, Uncertain—10; 4) Yes—160, No—2. *The Collegiate*'s editorial response, headlined "Cheating on a Cheating Poll," called the results of the poll "amazing" but argued that they could not be considered valid since anyone who would cheat on an exam would not hesitate to lie about the matter.[40]

In the 1930s, conservative eastern North Carolinians considered dancing at least as great a danger to society as cheating on school work, and dancing was the fad seen by some as a threat to undermine morality on the ACC campus. Long opposed by certain religious sects, dancing between members of the opposite sex remained sinful to those who interpreted the Bible literally. Therefore, a column appearing in *The Collegiate* of 15 December 1933 disturbed some people within the college and the surrounding community. "Evidently students of Atlantic Christian College do not adhere to the old belief that dancing is detrimental to the normal standards of a Christian institution." The student newspaper referred to the results of a straw vote on dancing taken of the student body in the college auditorium Saturday morning, 25 November 1933. The results of the poll showed that 178 students voted; 148 voted to permit dancing; 26 voted not to permit; 4 had no opinion. The poll further revealed that 135 knew how to dance while 43 did not. In addition, the parents of 138 students approved of dancing, while those of 36 did not. The newspaper suggested that the Student Council had no intention of presenting a petition to the trustees regarding the matter at that time.[41]

Apparently, reports of a shenanigan involving Guilford College students prompted the ACC poll on dancing. According to the High Point College newspaper, *The Hi-Po*, Guilford students revolted against a ninety-seven-year ban on dancing on the Quaker school campus. The controversial incident followed a pep rally on the eve of a football game scheduled with Elon. Taking advantage of the college orchestra's presence, students had shoved back tables in the dining hall and "danced for some time." The student editor remarked, "This is another indication of the revolt of youth against age-worn and senseless rules, another proof that Guilford students have begun to think."[42]

As *The Collegiate* observed, ACC students wasted little time in emulating the Quakers, but on a neighboring campus: "On Friday night, January 17, 1934 Atlantic Christian College played the co-eds of ECTC, in a spirited game of basketball." Actually the game was played between the boys' teams of the two schools, but, prior to the game, the ACC players had become smitten by a swarming group of vivacious Eastern Carolina Teachers College co-eds. Writing under the headline "Coach Has Hard Time Keeping Boys Under Wing," the sportswriter argued that basketball had not been foremost on the minds of the Bulldog players that evening, and, as a result, the ACC boys were unable to concentrate on their play. In the opinion of the sports scribe, the Bulldog players had managed to lose the game before it had even begun.[43]

After arriving early at the gymnasium in Greenville, the visitors were startled to find themselves surrounded by a lively group of ECTC co-eds, including "four beautiful blondes." Momentarily forgetting the purpose of their mission, several of the young men "participated in a little lively dancing. Of course the AC Boys were rushed off their feet by the girls—and seemed to stay in a whirl until after the game. Gladys Charles and Russell Roebuck graciously furnished music for the occasion." The exasperated coach, F. A. Hodges, who was also professor of science, had a difficult time settling his players down. Several missing Bulldog players had to be summoned to dress for the game by the loud use of "two or three war whoops," from the coach. Cocaptain George "Red" Amerson, a junior from Wilson, still remained absent. To the great delight of his teammates, Amerson finally appeared "his face as red as his hair—but with lipstick—and insisted that he had only been out for a stroll in the moonlight." The contest was thirty minutes late beginning, and, of course, was won handily by ECTC. Convinced that his beloved Bulldogs had fallen victim to a bit of underhanded Pirate chicanery, the chagrined sportswriter wrote, "Did AC boys get the horse laugh? We might say that A.C.C. has never won a basketball game from E.T.C.C. at Greenville. Do you wonder why?!!"[44]

Editors of *The Collegiate* joined other students and faculty members in speaking out against dancing on the Wilson campus. In the 20 January 1934 issue, editor-in-chief Collins Yelverton wrote, "It is our wish to sponsor those things which elevate and make a better 'Atlantic Christian College.' If one wishes to dance he can find plenty of places to do so without making A.C.C. a social club." A brief article in the same issue added, "One of our professors when asked his views on allowing dancing at AC said, 'I want to see Atlantic Christian College the intellectual center of Eastern North Carolina and not the social center.' That's putting it in a nutshell for you, and he's right." The Open Forum column carried a letter by "A Ministerial Student" stating:

> It is very strange why thinking students think they can get dancing in our school. The good Christian men and women who own the institution would not allow it. It would be pathetic to see a student or group of students present a petition to the State Disciples' Convention. I would like to know if dancing improves thinking ability or social standing. Will the leadership of tomorrow come from night clubs and dance halls, or from those who have humanity at heart. To me dancing is not a religious matter. It is nonmoral. . . . Atlantic Christian College is just not the place for dancing.

The writer claimed to represent the twenty-six students who, he argued, by voting against dancing on campus, had chosen not to "lower the dignity of the school."[45]

Although many students and many parents did not agree with the position

The college celebrates May Day on Kinsey Hall's front lawn bordering Whitehead Avenue. 1938 Pine Knot.

stated in the letter, the ministerial student and those who regarded dancing as immoral represented the majority opinion. The issue apparently soon lost momentum at the college, however. The only dancing between members of the opposite sex permitted on campus for decades occurred in dramatic presentations, including the elaborate May Day festivals, which became traditional during the 1930s. Dances upon these occasions were structured and controlled in such a way as to ensure that performances maintained strict rules of etiquette that many college students deemed more appropriate to the age of their parents or grandparents.

In many ways the May Day pageants which appeared on American college campuses and elsewhere in the 1930s represented a formal and final farewell to Victorian social rules which had dominated Western culture for a century. Begun in May 1932 by the physical education department under the direction of Charlotte Hill, the May Day Festivals featured brilliant pageants which became major social events in the community. Males and females danced individually and as couples in a variety of formal, ethnic, and folk dances. Among the largest was the celebration of 1935, led by Queen Ina Rivers Tuten of Aurora and King Donahue Bryant of Saratoga, which attracted an audience of over 1,500 people. The performances included eight folk dances and a minuet. May Day exercises of 1938 with Queen Edna Barnhill of Stokes and King Robert Carr of Clinton were also elaborate, featuring numerous dances and the ACC Band directed by Millard Burt. Ruby Barnes of Fremont, Helen Godwin of Kenly, A. J. Moye of Farmville, and Hugh Cherry of Rocky Mount served as attendants to the royal couple. Ruby Barnes Brown, class of 1939, recalled the experience as a highlight of four enjoyable years at the college. She described the excitement among members of the court and stated that the May Day Festival was eagerly anticipated on campus as the social event of the year. Sarah Bain Ward commented on both the beautiful appearance and expense of the gowns and recalled that many young women later wore them as wedding dresses. An example was Ina Rivers Tuten, who married Cecil Jarman, dean of men and instructor in religious education, in the dress that she had worn as May Day Queen.[46]

Memories of the school's fifth May Day Festival faded as students worked to meet the challenge of fall classes. The passing of Atlantic Christian College's thirty-fifth birthday in 1937 prompted editors of *The Collegiate* to reflect upon changes which had occurred on the campus within the past five years. In 1932 ACC had consisted of only two main buildings, the girls' dormitory and the boys' dormitory. When classes convened in 1937, the school could boast of three additional buildings: a dining hall, a gymnasium, and a new heating plant, which had been built behind the dining hall. Furnished with such attractive features as indirect lighting and other modern equipment, the Bert Clarence Hardy Dining Hall immediately became popular with students and faculty. This handsome building provided badly needed space for a variety of uses. The commercial department moved into the large basement, offering classes in typing, shorthand, bookkeeping, commercial law, and other subjects. The college band anticipated holding rehearsals in yet another large room in the basement. The school had also procured additional dormitory space for a growing student body by renting several houses near the campus. Finally, the newspaper noted, President Hilley remained diligent in his efforts to build another girls' dormitory and a new chapel.[47]

The additional space provided by the new dining hall permitted other changes on the campus that benefited students and faculty in significant ways. The library was improved by the purchase of new equipment and moved into the room in Kinsey Hall that had formerly housed the dining hall. The old library area became the girls' parlor, and a nicely furnished town girls' room was fashioned from a classroom in Kinsey Hall. The biology laboratory was upgraded and relocated to a larger room with better lighting, and the chemistry laboratory, located in Caldwell Hall, received modern equipment.[48]

During the brief periods when Howard Hilley had time to reflect upon the fortunes of the college during the 1930s, he must have marveled at the school's achievements in such areas as increasing enrollment, improving landscaping, constructing buildings, and creating innovative programs. Considering that the accomplishments came in the midst of dire circumstances, the progress was rather remarkable. After convincing trustees to cut tuition rates, Hilley resolved that no student would be denied a college education because he or she lacked money. Students could work, apply for scholarships, and/or meet the costs of tuition and fees through payments in-kind.[49]

Hilley also kept costs low by delaying payment of faculty salaries. Faculty living on campus received room and board and were paid when money became available, while those who lived off campus received IOUs. Mamie Jennings Lucas labeled the period one of both sacrifice and benefit for faculty members, who realized that the times were so bad they could hardly expect anything better. Since Lucas lived at home and shared the benefit of her husband's income, payment of her salary was delayed. "I was years getting my money; [but] I got it all," she remembered. Her assessment that Hilley's authoritarian means were necessitated by the demands of the times was shared by students as well as faculty. Lucas characterized Hilley as a "ruthless" leader who knew how to economize, adding "I am quite sure that if it had not been for him the college would have gone under." Alumni who attended ACC during the Great Depression tend to agree with Lucas and, virtually without exception, share the view that they were part of a remarkable experience at a defining time in history. In addition to preparing themselves for careers and for life in general, they developed strong character, savored glorious moments, and made firm and lasting friendships on the AC College campus during the years of the Great Depression.[50]

NINE

Some of Our Friends, Relatives, and Brothers May Be Leaving

NORTH CAROLINIANS STRUGGLED to cope with severe economic conditions as the decade of the Great Depression moved toward an end. Despite hard times, Wilson businesses remained open, and Barton College's enrollment, buoyed by large freshman classes, steadily increased. Between 1932 and 1937, total enrollment rose by 97 percent (405 to 786), and the size of the freshman class increased by 76 percent (100 to 176). With surging enrollment straining college facilities, President Hilley asked local businessmen and alumni to help raise money to build a new chapel and a women's dormitory. Earlier expansion of the campus had added two houses, which the college rented to fraternities. As early as 1932, ACC provided interim student housing by renting private homes near the campus. A new chapel was an even more urgent need because the existing, badly deteriorated structure also served as an auditorium. Physically attached to the east wing of Kinsey Hall, the chapel had been condemned by the city in 1936 for safety reasons. In February 1937, *The Wilson Daily Times* reported that Hilley had challenged the city chamber of commerce to help raise funds to build a new chapel-auditorium. Sarah Bain Ward recalled that Hilley, John Waters, and Perry Case organized teams of students to speak in area churches about the urgency of the problem.[1]

By 1937 the town of Wilson was a bustling commercial center of 15,000 residents in the state's leading farming region. Local businesses, which patronized college publications and competed for customers among the growing student body and faculty, sometimes ran ads specifically targeting the college community. Oettinger's ladies' clothing department advertised "Campus frocks . . . as . . . Smart as her Professor" at $4.98 each. Lucielle's Dress Shop, The Vanity Shop, and London Shop also catered to female shoppers. Ellis "Beau" Rabil, Bruce Lamm Men's Shop, and Thomas-Adkins, Inc., featured stylish clothes for the campus male, while Leder Brothers and Oettinger's carried clothing for both sexes. Sandwiches and meals were available at Central Lunch on South Tarboro Street, Bill's Quick Lunch offered "any style" of oysters, and The Karl's Lunch claimed to be the "Collegians After Hours Meeting Spot." Dick's Hot Dog Place on West Nash Street featured five-cent hot dogs served at " The Best Place to Eat . . . [and] Cleanest Place in the State."[2]

Businesses offering services to the community included Sanitary Cleaners, Rex Shoe Shop, Red's Barber Shop, and Denny's Credit Jewelers. The Arcade Beauty Shop and LaBelle Beauty Shop both advertised a "shampoo and finger wave" for fifty cents. Wilson Drug Company and Bissette's Drug Store advertised in *The Collegiate*, the latter listing desk lamps for ninety-eight cents, toothbrushes for nineteen cents, and pocket combs for nine cents. Em-Jay Sporting Goods Company and Wilson Hardware carried athletic and recreational equipment. For those seeking entertainment, Wilson Smoke Shoppe offered "Last Minute Football Scores" along with ice cream, candies, drinks, and "One Minute Delivery Service." S & M Pocket Billiards and Wimpy's, both on South Tarboro Street, offered recreation, and Wilson station WGTM carried a variety of radio programs. Movies playing at the Carolina or the New Wilson Theatre included *The Bride Wore Red* starring Joan Crawford, *Life Begins at 40* starring Will Rogers, and *Her Jungle Love* starring Dorothy Lamour. For those finding shopping unsatisfactory in Wilson, Norfolk Southern Railroad offered speedy, safe, and comfortable transportation out of town at the rate of two cents per mile.[3]

In addition to purchasing goods and services, ACC helped the Wilson economy by attracting visitors to various events including intercollegiate athletic games. A popular basketball tournament begun in 1935 brought between twenty and thirty eastern North Carolina high school teams into town for three days each February. Playing in the college gymnasium, teams in the tournament competed in one of two divisions determined by size of enrollment. Organized by the ACC athletic director, the annual event was a public relations coup for the college and a significant boon to the local economy. Wilson merchants provided trophies for champions and runners-up in each division.[4]

Fans in the Wilson community who attended athletic matches and supported college teams through monetary contributions were as disappointed as students by the inability of the Bulldogs to win consistently within the North State Conference. Among the major sports of baseball, basketball, and tennis, only the latter could be labeled a consistent winner. Sports editor John Yavorski's perceptive editorial in *The Collegiate* of 21 February 1938 examined the

Mascot "Bo" and the famous "Bo-Hun-kus." The Collegiate, March 1955.

situation. The sophomore from Elmira, New York, argued that ACC remained near the conference cellar because the college neither recruited athletes nor provided athletic scholarships. Elon, Catawba, High Point, and Lenoir Rhyne awarded scholarships and led the conference. ACC, Guilford, and Western Carolina Teachers College did not offer scholarships and typically finished last in conference rankings. Providing athletic scholarships would not necessarily lower academic standards, Yavorski contended, and would enable Bulldog teams to compete successfully within the conference. The fact that ACC's first conference win of the 1937–38 basketball season came against a weak Quakers team in mid-February supported Yavorski's argument. That "colorless game" avenged an earlier loss at Guilford but drew the season's smallest crowd to the local gym.[5]

Anticipating little help from an economically strapped administration in his efforts to infuse new life into the college's slumping athletic fortunes, the sports writer devised an ingenious plan. Perhaps influenced by the intensity of the Duke-Carolina football rivalry over possession of the "victory bell," Yavorski suggested creating a trophy symbolic of the rivalry in athletics between Atlantic Christian and East Carolina. Meeting in the Wilson gymnasium with Jack Daniels, sports editor of *The Teco Echo* of ECTC, at the February 1938 basketball game between their schools, the two scribes created the "Bo-Hun-Kus." The trophy was a "common wooden bucket" owned by the sports divisions of *The Collegiate* and *The Teco Echo*. One side of the bucket was painted Bulldog blue and white; the other, Pirate purple and gold. Pictures of a pirate and a bulldog adorned the appropriate side, and there was space to mark scores in four sports—basketball, baseball, boxing, and tennis. Possession of the trophy would be determined by and immediately follow the completion of each contest.[6]

Since the Bo-Hun-Kus trophy was prominently displayed at each athletic event played between the teams, the symbol served as a strong incentive to players and fans of the schools, resulting in hotly contested games and close scores. *The Wilson Daily Times* noted that on 9 January 1939 the ACC basketball team won its first game ever in Greenville. The May issue of *The Collegiate* listed the results of the first year (1938–39) as three wins and a tie for the Pirates and four wins and a tie by the Bulldogs. Most importantly, the newspaper bragged that since the AC baseball team had won the year's final game, the coveted bucket would remain on display in the college library until fall semester. The same issue carried a front-page photograph of the popular Yavorski and announced his election as editor of the *Pine Knot* for 1939–40.[7]

Boxing, listed as a minor sport, became ACC's most successful athletic pursuit of the 1930s. Interest in the sport on the college level increased after World War I when Southern universities, including North Carolina and Virginia, joined Harvard, Yale, Army, and Navy in building strong teams. College boxing matches consisted of three two-minute rounds separated by one-minute rest periods. Boxers used six-ounce gloves and fought in a ring that was eighteen feet square and covered by a canvas floor. A national college tournament determined the annual champion. Upon forming its first boxing team in 1935, the college became an immediate winner and was competitive against such larger schools as Wake Forest and North Carolina State. Early ACC boxing teams easily defeated Campbell, ECTC, Louisburg, and most North State Conference teams. Although supporters of boxing downplayed the brutality of the sport, preferring to emphasize its appeal as "a fast-moving, scientific sport," some students protested. While letters to the campus newspaper objected to bloody aspects of the fights, labeling the matches "beastly" and calling boxing incompatible with a Christian school, the team's success helped to blunt the criticism. *The Wilson Daily Times* reported in December 1938 that the undefeated team had been invited to participate in a tournament at the University of Wisconsin. Following their second loss by a single point to Wake Forest in February 1937, the local pugilists recorded two undefeated seasons and reportedly compiled the longest winning record of any boxing team in the state. An exceptionally strong North Carolina State "B" team ended the Bulldog's winning streak in January 1940.[8]

Unfortunately, ACC's other athletic teams proved unable to win consis-

The 1937–38 ACC boxing team. 1938 Pine Knot.

tently. The weakness of the ACC basketball program may have been a factor in motivating UNC to add Atlantic Christian College to its 1938–39 schedule for the purpose of formally dedicating Woolen Gymnasium. Traveling to Chapel Hill in January 1939, the Bulldog team fulfilled its sacrificial role admirably by bowing to the UNC team, then known as the "White Phantoms," by a score of 57–18.[9]

Although seldom attracting numerous fans or boosting the local economy, the school's intercollegiate debating team gained a reputation for successful competition and furnished talented students with opportunities to enhance their critical thinking and public speaking skills. Campus debates between the Alethians and Hesperians during the school's first thirty-five years proved both popular and intellectually stimulating while showcasing their debating skills. The demise of the literary societies after 1937, however, created a certain void regarding intellectual competition which the new sororities and fraternities did not fill. Strong debating teams of the 1930s helped to fill the void and created positive publicity for the college. Teams debated by the ACC squad included Campbell, North Carolina State, Wake Forest, and William and Mary. Leaders of the particularly strong team of the 1937–39 era were Cyrus Lee of New Bern, Hugh Kelly of Pfafftown, James E. Miles of Wilson, Ray Silverthorne of Washington, Julian Roebuck of Robersonville, and Eugene Ogrodowski of Sayreville, New Jersey. The team visited Rock Hill, South Carolina, in December 1938 to participate in the Dixie Tournament, the nation's second largest collegiate tournament, hosted by Winthrop College. The 1938–39 team made an impressive showing, competing with 250 students representing thirty-six colleges from states including New Hampshire, Alabama, and Florida. Cyrus Lee, team captain, finished the contest in fourth place. The December issue of *The Collegiate* expressed the student body's pleasure with the team's success and described the results under a large headline: "Lee Chosen South's Fourth Debater." Lee served as student government president, became associate editor of *The Collegiate*, and was inducted into the Golden Knot Honor Society. Following graduation from law school, he established a successful legal practice in Wilson. Ray Silverthorne was active in YMCA, a member of Campus Religious Council and the Ministerial Club, and *Pine Knot* business manager in 1940 and editor in 1941. Silverthorne later practiced medicine in Washington and served the college as a member of the board of trustees from 1970 to 1991.[10]

Leading issues debated and discussed on American college campuses during the second quarter of the twentieth century included racial justice and world peace. Jim Crow racial segregation laws prevailed in eastern North Carolina and throughout much of the nation. At Atlantic Christian College, Charles H. Hamlin, professor of social sciences and the grandson of a Virginia slaveowner who had opposed secession, became a spokesman for racial equality and a member of the National Association for the Advancement of Colored People at a time when few white southerners were involved. Hamlin endeared himself to students through his popular classes and a reputation for helping impoverished students remain in school. More than half a century later, former students and colleagues still credit the genial but forthright teacher with encouraging them to reexamine controversial issues and accept a broader, more inclusive view regarding racial issues.[11]

By the invitation of N. C. Newbold, a state board of education official assigned to work with the black schools, Hamlin joined the North Carolina Commission on Interracial Cooperation in 1926. Students sometimes accompanied the slender, bespectacled professor to black churches in Wilson, especially Calvary, "the colored Presbyterian church," where H. H. George was pastor. The white social scientist and the black preacher cooperated to organize the first troop of black scouts in the city and gained official recognition from the Boy Scouts of America. Having won the trust and respect of black leaders, Hamlin accepted invitations to aid voter-registration drives in Goldsboro, Rocky Mount, Kinston, and other eastern North Carolina towns. While his activism made him a controversial figure, Hamlin recalled facing physical danger only once. During a visit to a black church in Enfield in 1935, white policemen with pistols drawn appeared at the door and demanded that Hamlin step outside. The professor was escorted to the police station and questioned for approximately an hour before being allowed to leave.[12]

Christian Church minister John Barclay, widely trusted and respected within Wilson's black community, likely promoted Hamlin's early association with black church leaders. Barclay and Hamlin also attempted to broaden the perspectives of eastern North Carolina white citizens by bringing interracial groups and noted liberal speakers to Wilson. In the spring term of 1937, Hamlin began teaching a new class called Forum Techniques sponsored by the National Forum. Barclay served as director of the National Forum project over an area of seven counties including Wilson. The national education experiment enabled directors to invite "educators of recognized ability" to address the forum.[13]

Efforts by Barclay and Hamlin on behalf of racial justice undoubtedly helped convince individual students and college organizations to join the quest. Hamlin served as faculty advisor to the YMCA, which his son, Griffith, led as president in 1937–38. The YMCA, joined by the YWCA, invited black glee clubs from Wilson's Darden High School and the State Normal School in Elizabeth City to perform on the ACC campus in 1938 and 1939.[14]

A 1938 winter issue of *The Collegiate* included a front-page feature praising the Darden High School glee club performance on campus, noting that an enthusiastic student body applauded a program of "classical music . . . followed by some beautiful negro folk songs and spirituals." Another front-page article reported a January 1939 address at ACC by N. T. Harvey, a black graduate of New York University and the president of Youth Conferences in America. Harvey addressed key problems facing the youth of America—war and peace, relations between business and labor, and racial prejudice. He concluded that solutions to each of the challenges depended upon awareness, communication, and education. Harvey advised America's youth to oppose unfair economic conditions and to participate in "student strikes and demonstrations against war."[15]

Efforts by Barclay and Hamlin to provide a Wilson forum to address racial issues may have influenced the North Carolina Commission on Interracial Cooperation to select the city for a public conference in May 1938. Governor Clyde R. Hoey, University of North Carolina president Frank P. Graham, and Dr. Walter J. Hughes, a black member of the state health department board, addressed the session. Hughes was reportedly the first of his race to hold such a post in the United States. Discussions focused on improving health care and education in rural areas, cooperation between blacks and whites to create a stronger North Carolina, and the need for greater federal aid for education. The commission adopted a resolution supporting a graduate school for blacks in North Carolina. John Barclay and Dr. C. C. Weaver of Charlotte were named cochairmen of the organization.[16]

The next three years brought several prominent black speakers to the college including L. A. Oxley, Assistant Secretary of Labor. A graduate of Harvard University and the highest-ranking black official in America, Oxley lectured to four ACC social science classes. He concluded that unemployment, the South's number one problem, would be solved only through racial cooperation. The college hosted a meeting of the North Carolina Commission on Education and Race Relations in January 1941. Raymond Morgan, associate professor of social science at Atlantic Christian College and editor of a pamphlet on racial issues, served as chairman of the conference. Featuring N. C. Newbold as the principal speaker, the meeting was attended by representatives of nine colleges.[17]

A few black Wilsonians worked at the college as janitors and maids from the time that the school was founded. President Caldwell had employed a black man to serve as a general handyman, which included driving a horse-drawn wagon and cart to transport students and faculty between the college and the Wilson train station. Early yearbook pictures reveal black male and female workers on the campus. During Hilley's tenure as president, students did almost all work on campus, including caring for buildings and grounds. Four exceptions were Hilda Thompson, Charles Kendall, and two black workers known to the students only as "Red" and "Shortie." Thompson was a young black maid who had gone to school in Stantonsburg and loved going to the movies and reading *The Collegiate*. Kendall, a janitor and handyman, was a favorite of the students and remembered warmly by alumni half a century later as a popular employee and campus character. Historian Charles C. Ware wrote that "Charley Kendall" enjoyed the trust of the entire college community, including that of President Hilley, who relied upon Kendall's skills as a campus worker and included him as a companion during occasional trips in the "college car." Former students remembered "good old Charley" for his friendly manner and strong devotion to students and the school. Sarah Bain Ward recalled Kendall's adhering to the policy requiring all males entering the girls' dormitory to announce their presence. Charley Kendall would immediately call out loudly,

"MAN ON THE HALL! MAN ON THIS HERE HALL!" His faithful labor in cranking the large freezer to produce gallons of delicious ice cream became a Sunday ritual eagerly anticipated by all. According to college lore, Kendall nicknamed the president "Cannon Ball" because of Hilley's energy and active nature. The nickname was quickly picked up by the students, who named the school mascot—a large, rotund bulldog—"Cannon Ball, Jr." Both nicknames stuck and enjoyed widespread popularity across the campus.[18]

Hilley's daughter, Elizabeth, who grew up in the president's house on the corner of Gold Street and Whitehead Avenue, remembered Charles Kendall after six decades as a quiet, strong, and personable man and recalled her friendship with Kendall's daughter, Myrtle, a childhood playmate. She also furnished the story behind Kendall's selection of the nickname "Cannon Ball." Charley Kendall described Howard Hilley: "When he goes, he goes in a hurry and when he gets there he busts things wide open." It is unlikely that anyone will provide a better description of the college's fifth president than that of the affable man whom Hilley valued as both employee and friend.[19]

Naomi S. Hunter and a janitor named Faison joined Kendall as black employees during the 1940s. Hunter was the only member of the custodial staff featured in a special article and photograph in *The Torchlight*. Mary McDaniel, a junior from Trenton and literary editor of the new student magazine, praised Hunter's commitment, efficiency, and personal warmth in the February 1945 issue. Hunter worked as a maid in the girls' dormitory, where her smiles and cheerful greetings lifted the students' spirits. A proud young woman who carried herself in a "queenly way," Hunter had a no-nonsense approach to her duties that was appreciated even when she had to scold the girls to keep Kinsey Hall clean. McDaniel recalled her embarrassment when her explanation to Naomi as to why she was parading down the hall in her "best gown" had prompted Hunter's stern reply, "Well, no matter . . . git offen this floor 'til it dries." Even then, the effect of the commanding tone was softened by a "contagious giggle."[20]

Early efforts to improve race relations were important to individuals at the college and within the church and community, but racial equality remained an elusive goal for many years. Historians contend that the revolutionary impact of World War II not only ended the Great Depression but also ignited the spark of the civil rights movement of the 1950s and 1960s, which ultimately ended racial segregation. C. H. Hamlin, far ahead of his time in advocating integration, predicted that at least twenty-five years would pass before the federal courts would finally strike down Jim Crow laws as unconstitutional. Re-

Professor Charles H. Hamlin. 1939 Pine Knot.

calling that prediction years later, Hamlin said that he had made the forecast in 1930 and missed by one year—the decision of *Brown v. Board of Education* occurred in 1954. For Barton College, as was the case for many other schools in the South and elsewhere, integration of classrooms did not come until the 1960s.[21]

As the prospects of war in Europe and Asia increased during the 1930s, racial justice competed with the issues of pacifism, socialism, and fascism as topics of discussion on college campuses. At Atlantic Christian College, Howard Hilley and John Barclay urged students to become more knowledgeable about international affairs. The college president spoke frequently to civic groups on world events, including giving a March 1932 address to the Rotary Club on the Sino-Japanese conflict, an event which historians now consider the beginning of World War II. Barclay's Tuesday morning chapel services typically focused upon world issues. Among the students benefiting from Barclay's knowledge and passion for international issues was Elizabeth Hilley, class of 1940, who recalled learning much about world affairs, although not being particularly fond of history or the social sciences. Growing student and faculty interest in national and world issues, including conflicting political and economic systems, caused ACC to bring numerous visiting speakers to the campus during the last half of the 1930s.[22]

The Collegiate of 20 April 1935 noted the ACC students' role in bringing socialist leader Norman Thomas to Wilson and stated that the crowd that gathered in the local courthouse to hear the presidential candidate speak included members of the college community. C. H. Hamlin was an avid supporter of Norman Thomas and had served as an elector during his political campaign. Another campus visitor was Minnesota native Howard Y. Williams, national leader of the Farm Labor Party and editor of the *Farm Labor Leader*. Williams advocated socialism as a solution to economic problems facing agrarian workers in a speech to ACC's Forum Technique class.[23]

Many distinguished visitors to the campus focused on the growing threat of another major war. Pacifist speakers at the school in 1935 and 1936 included Mary Ida Winder, secretary of the National Council for Prevention of War; Irma Liegey, a native of France; and Dr. Donald Grant, world traveler and author from Scotland. At an April 1936 chapel assembly, John Barclay led a discussion of the Emergency Peace Campaign then spreading among the nation's colleges and universities. Approximately 150 students and faculty responded by standing up to vote yes on specific questions. On the question of supporting American disarmament to the extent that other nations complied, 145 voted yes. An equal number supported the United States "waging peace." American participation in the League of Nations and the World Court drew 142 yes votes, while 102 indicated that they would fight only in a defensive war.[24]

During the following February, First Lady Eleanor Roosevelt and Admiral Richard E. Byrd, then retired from the United States Navy, publicly endorsed the Emergency Peace Campaign goal of "No Foreign War." *The Collegiate* printed their appeal for the nation's youth to join the drive and help establish a permanent world peace. Two months later, Atlantic Christian College students took a stand against war by participating in a national college peace march. A three-day antiwar rally began on the campus 20 April 1937. Following pacifist speeches, the students adopted a position statement: "We won't fight. We will not go to war if there is another one." Activities the following day culminated with an evening bonfire in front of Kinsey Hall. On Thursday morning approximately 250 students gathered in front of the gymnasium to hear remarks by John Barclay before marching down Nash Street with banners proclaiming: "We won't fight ... Schools not arms ... No Flanders Fields ... To Hell with war." Costumed characters in the march included the God of War, Youth, and a Future Gold-Star Mother. The march ended in front of the courthouse with more speeches, including an emotional proclamation from Reverend Barclay, "I have decided against war, and I am going to yell about it, even if I have to do it through the bars."[25]

Among those taking strong positions against war were Hamlin and Kirby Page, a gifted lecturer and famous pacifist. Hamlin, whose pacifist beliefs had been strengthened by the failures of World War I, wrote a short book, *Educators Present Arms*, in which he accused the national government of spreading false information in American schools and charged that academic freedom is denied during times of war. In late February 1939, Page spent a full day on the campus addressing the student body and the college International Club. Remaining in town to speak at the black high school and to a public forum at the Christian Church, Page provided graphic and unsettling details of the world situation in 1938, warning that "civilized forces" throughout the world seemed to be retreating. Employing scriptural references to make his point, Page reminded the audience that "There is a God and moral judgment.... [and] whatsoever a man soweth, that shall he also reap." Less than a month after Page spoke in Wilson, German occupation troops invaded the remainder of Czechoslovakia, breaking Hitler's promises to Britain and France made at the Munich Conference of September 1938.[26]

When international traveler and missionary Sherwood Eddy spoke in the college gymnasium in March, the world knew the grim fate of Eastern Europe. Eddy criticized Hitler for crushing the democratic nation of Czechoslovakia and charged that in a period of nine months the German Fuhrer had murdered 3,000 people and imprisoned over half a million others, mostly in concentration camps. Charging Germany with creating the world's greatest crisis, he warned that Americans would soon have to choose between pacifism and realism, challenging the audience to "make your choice now ... for it will be too late when the band starts playing."[27]

Even experts like Sherwood Eddy could be mistaken, of course, and the presence of warfare on a distant continent during the spring of 1939 did not prevent students from pursuing the joys of college life, including the time-honored drive to improve relations with members of the opposite sex. *Enchanted April*, "an especially clever and humorous comedy," was the title of the commencement week play. Apparently, the title perfectly reflected the mood on campus as ACC prepared for graduation. The May Day festival was both regal and beautiful, the Bo-hunk-us was in Wilson for the summer, and *The Collegiate*, led by editor-in-chief Elmer Mottern, became the first ACC newspaper to win national recognition when the Associated Collegiate Press awarded it a second-class honor designation. Mottern's staff of twenty-one members included Eugene Ogrodowski, managing editor; Cyrus Lee, associate editor; Mary Matthews of Englehard, society editor; John Yavorski, sports editor; Robert Windham of Farmville, business manager; Basil Bowden of Dudley, assistant business manager; and John K. Wooten of Grifton, circulation manager. A junior from Asheville, Mottern served as student body president, was a member of the glee club, the debating team, and Golden Knot Honor Society, and served as a captain and a four-year member of the boxing team.[28]

Local theater marquees carried the titles of movies scheduled for autumn which seemed to blend perfectly with developing world news, including *Whispering Enemies* and *Each Dawn I Die*, which played at the Wilson Theatre and featured James Cagney and George Raft. On 1 September 1939, Germany's dramatic invasion of Poland drove European nations into the largest and most expensive war in history. As concerned Americans followed war news with interest, Congress officially declared the neutrality of the United States.[29]

The college newspaper of September 1939 welcomed the freshman class and proclaimed: "Class Of 1943 Largest In History." Borrowing a phrase from world headlines, the editors wrote that 184 freshmen had "invaded" Atlantic Christian College on 7 September to begin orientation week. Freshmen met with student leaders, toured campus facilities, and took placement tests to determine class schedules. In addition to providing typical information for the start of a school year, the newspaper carried a seven-question poll to ascertain students' attitudes toward the existing war. The results of the poll appeared in *The Collegiate* of 20 October and showed that, of 159 students responding, 94 percent said that the United States should not enter the European war under current conditions. A majority favored both selling munitions to belligerent nations on a cash-and-carry basis (60 percent) and increasing the size of the American armed forces (68 percent). Although 86 percent said that they would fight if the United States were attacked, 72 percent of the respondents said that they would decline to fight if another country in the western hemisphere were attacked, and only 53 percent indicated that they would fight if American ships carrying American passengers were sunk.[30]

National poll tabulations indicated that the ACC students' antipathy against war was shared by students across the country. A Hollywood film then attracting crowds to theaters in Wilson and elsewhere added a touch of irony to the autumn of 1939. The film version of Erich Maria Remarque's classic book, *All Quiet On the Western Front*, regarding the senseless slaughter of World War I, appeared at Wilson's Rialto Theatre in November.[31]

ACC students attempted to put the war into perspective and to continue their focus on academics while also enjoying activities and friends. Editorials and letters to the editor expressed concerns about whether upperclassmen were setting good examples for freshmen, appropriate student conduct at formal dinners, and student absences during chapel services. On 3 and 4 November, alumni and friends joined the college community for the official dedication of the school's handsome new chapel named for Curtis William Howard. At the first service in the new building held Friday evening, 4 November, the glee club led the congregation in singing a hymn, followed by a devotional and a brief address by professor Perry Case. At the dedication on Saturday morning, Charles C. Ware summarized the life of Dr. Howard, a distinguished Disciples preacher and a trustee and benefactor of the college prior to his death in 1932. Dr. Stephen A. Corey, president of the College of the Bible in Lexington, Kentucky, was the featured speaker.[32]

Howard Chapel became a site of mourning in January 1940 when Frances F. Harper, popular math teacher and the oldest member of the faculty, died following a two-month illness. Arriving on campus in 1904 when their father became the college's second president, Frances and Myrtle Harper literally grew up with the college and became legendary figures. More than half a century later, alumni recalled elaborate May Day festivals on Old Kinsey's front lawn under the shade of two large oak trees, which the students had named "Miss Fannie" and "Miss Myrtie." The revered math teacher died in the Wilson hospital at age sixty-five. Her body lay in state in Howard Chapel prior to funeral services conducted by John Barclay and Howard Hilley at Wilson Christian Church.[33]

The class of 1940, largest in school history, became the first to hold commencement exercises in the new chapel. The featured speaker was Dr. Charles Clayton Morrison of Chicago, internationally known editor of the *Christian Century*. Morrison had won acclaim for his efforts to outlaw war, which resulted in the Kellogg-Briand Pact of 1928. President Hilley delivered the baccalaureate sermon, and John Barclay presented his annual farewell sermon to sixty-four seniors. Special exercises included an announcement of a loan fund established in honor of Frances Harper by former students and the presentation of a portrait of "Miss Fannie" to the college by the YMCA and YWCA.[34]

Despite Germany's invasion of northern and western Europe in the spring of 1940, campus publications made little mention of the war. On 28 May, the day after the class of 1940 graduated, Belgium surrendered to Nazi Germany. With Hitler's military forces controlling Europe, Britain faced German and

Howard Chapel. Photo by Keith Tew, 2001.

Italian armies alone. The determination of President Roosevelt and Congress to save democracy in Europe resulted in huge shipments of war goods to Britain. In September, Germany and Italy signed the Tripartite Pact with Japan, creating the Axis Powers, an alliance that threatened democratic nations everywhere.[35]

At Atlantic Christian College the summer of 1940 passed quietly as school leaders considered how best to resolve the needs of a student body that had outgrown existing facilities. Fortunately, the school's financial situation appeared to be in its best condition in two decades. The top priority was building a modern women's dormitory to provide adequate housing for students rather than having them room in four separate houses. The second priority was a modern library building, and the third was a larger athletic field owned by the college. ACC continued to use the athletic field at nearby Margaret Hearne School.[36]

A new entering class of 159 members reported 5 September to begin Freshman Week, attend a reception at the home of President and Mrs. Hilley, and enjoy a Jamboree at nearby Gold Park. Returning students noted few changes other than new faculty members and the news that the college had dropped boxing as a sport. The news that the recreation committee had declared 9 November Sadie Hawkins' Day on campus may have alarmed a few shy males. Based on the popular cartoon *Li'l Abner* drawn by Al Capp, the fad was sweeping American colleges. The motive behind the event was to suspend temporarily the standard social rules between the sexes by setting aside one day in the year for females to pursue males openly and shamelessly. *The Collegiate* explained that the intent was to allow students to "woo Dog Patch style . . . the victims are the Single Eligible Males, the victors the hungry, lonesome hags of Dog Patch." The college newspaper provided publicity for the big race, featuring cartoons of Dog Patch characters a week prior to the scheduled event. On Saturday evening, 9 November, "A. C. Dog-patchers" gathered in front of the gym for the 8:00 PM race. The noisy chase continued back and forth across campus until every male was caught, except for one shaken individual, who, in desperation, had climbed a tree. After the race, "catchers and catchees" returned to the gym for games and refreshments. *The Collegiate* of 18 November provided a hilarious account of events and labeled Sadie Hawkins' Day a success.[37]

An eighteen-year-old freshman commercial studies major from Wilson County received brief mention in the college newspaper for catching her beau in the Sadie Hawkin's Day Race. Tall, strikingly beautiful, and a vivacious tomboy, Ava Gardner grew up during the Great Depression on a Johnston County farm where her father was a sharecropper. After relocating to Newport News, Virginia, the Gardner family returned to North Carolina in the late 1930s, settling in Wilson County. Ava enrolled at Rock Ridge High School while her mother ran the local teacherage, providing room and board for female schoolteachers. Following graduation, Ava entered Atlantic Christian College in September 1940, enrolling in the one-year business certification program. By the time of the November race, Ava apparently had become noticed by most of the school's male population, including the newspaper reporters. Her name was the first one mentioned in *The Collegiate*'s coverage of the event, with a remark that "David Snipes didn't have a chance. That Gardner girl was bigger'n he was in the first place."[38]

An article near the bottom of page one of that same day's newspaper carried a more somber headline—"The Boys Are Marching." The first group of young Americans between ages twenty-one and thirty-five had been ordered to appear for one year of military training. Noting that voters had approved the new conscription law, *The Collegiate* concluded, "there is the grim reality

Some May Be Leaving

ACC's Ava Gardner shown in beauty queen contest and freshman class photographs. 1941 Pine Knot.

that before long some of our friends, relatives, and brothers may be leaving." The newspaper forecast that a year could seem a long time and would change people's lives. Three ACC students had already been drafted: Jackie Bullock of Zebulon, Charles M. Byrd of St. Pauls, and Frank Wiley of Grantsboro.[39]

The typical college student in the late autumn of 1940 likely considered threats of war and military service too remote for concern. The approaching Thanksgiving holidays promised a visit home, followed shortly by an eagerly anticipated Christmas break. For serious basketball fans, which seemed to include most of the college community, early December also promised a rare treat. North Carolina State College, a big school and member of the Southern Conference, was coming to play the Bulldogs on ACC's home court. In the 18 November issue of *The Collegiate*, a sports writer using the name "Bull" predicted that a good effort by the home team, aided by a boisterous crowd and an overconfident State team, could produce a major upset. To the delight of local fans, "Bull's" prediction came true. The hustling Bulldogs, led by center

Marion Lassiter's game high of thirteen points, won an impressive, hard-fought 26–25 victory in a game the local newspaper called "a blood tingling thriller such as never before staged on the college court." After Johnny Hicks' foul shots clinched the game, delirious students rushed out of the gym and snake-danced around the campus shouting victory yells.[40]

Following an unusually enthusiastic and well-attended Homecoming festival, the Bulldogs' dramatic, home-court triumph over the "Red Terrors" of North Carolina State electrified the campus and added luster to the successful autumn of 1940. The fall term also witnessed impressive student and faculty presentations at the annual Disciples state convention and a generous $100 donation to the women's dormitory building fund by the men of Phi Delta Alpha fraternity.[41]

Writing in the December issue of *North Carolina Christian*, President Hilley commented that students and faculty who had remained on campus for the traditional Thanksgiving feast had been treated to an outdoor religious service and an entertaining "Turkey Bowl, [a] six-man football game" played by the boys. Hilley stated that the college community looked forward to the Christmas season, especially the annual Christmas pageant for underprivileged children. On Sunday, 15 December, for a tenth straight year, the college students provided gifts for Wilson's indigent children. After drawing names from lists furnished by the local welfare department, students bought and wrapped a small gift for each child. On Sunday, a local minister read the story of the birth of Christ, followed by the presentation of gifts. Mrs. Grainger, director of the Wilson Welfare Association, claimed that ACC was the only college "in this part of the country" which gave gifts to children at Christmas. Other seasonal events eagerly anticipated by the college community included religious services and the singing of carols. Although the college tried hard to maintain a sense of normalcy during the days prior to celebrating the birthday of the "Prince of Peace," faculty and students sensed that war had become a serious threat to America. The troubling atmosphere of uncertainty lingered as the school closed for the holidays and students headed home to celebrate Christmas 1940 with family and friends.[42]

TEN

The Dawn of a New Day

WHEN STUDENTS RETURNED from their Christmas break in January 1941, American neutrality regarding the war in Europe was no longer a viable option. Three months earlier, newspapers had carried Germany's demand that both the United States and the Soviet Union announce their intent to enter the war on either the side of Britain or the Axis Powers. If Hollywood films accurately reflected national sentiment as spring approached in 1941, the marquee crowning the front of a Wilson theater revealed both America's choice of allies and her primary means of travel to the battlefront. Movies playing at the Carolina Theatre, as advertised in *The Collegiate* of 15 March 1941, were *Hitler, Beast of Berlin* and *Here Comes the Navy*. A large front-page photograph in the student newspaper also indicated that the American Air Corps intended to play a major role in the nation's military future. The article accompanying the photograph, showing pilots revving military aircraft engines at Randolph Field, Texas, stated that Atlantic Christian College graduate Leland B. Farnell Jr. was a student at the "West Point of the Air." A native of Jacksonville, North Carolina, Farnell was one of the first "flying Cadets" to complete basic training and to receive the prestigious wings emblem worn by military pilots. The class of 1939 graduate had been a member of the YMCA, president of Phi Delta Gamma fraternity, assistant business manager of *Pine Knot*, and a member of the boxing team. *The Collegiate* in early 1941 also announced that the YMCA and YWCA had raised $108 in their joint effort to adopt a war orphan. Campaign workers placed milk bottles around the campus to collect donations, and dining hall students voted to give up dessert for a week and contribute the money to support a refugee child who would live in England with a foster family.[1]

The college attempted to operate as normally as possible as the nation increased its military preparedness policy. Trustees met with area ministers and other friends of the college on 4 March to discuss the campaign to construct a women's dormitory and agreed to build a two or three-story building at the corner of Lee and Rountree Streets. The L-shaped structure would adjoin Hardy Dining Hall, house 115–120 women, and cost between $75,000 and $80,000. Plans also called for Kinsey Hall to be modernized and converted into classrooms and administrative offices, thus freeing additional space in Caldwell Hall for male student housing. Student and faculty news included a report that C. H. Hamlin, who had rejoined the social sciences department after spending a year at Peabody College, would receive a Ph.D. in history in June, and that M. E. Sadler, a 1919 ACC graduate, had been named president of Texas Christian University. Also, editor-in-chief James V. Creasy Jr. and staff had led *The Collegiate* of 1940–41 to a high national ranking by the Associated Press for a second straight year.[2]

The large freshman class of 1941–42, arriving 4 September to begin orientation week, soon found the gaiety surrounding the opening of school tempered by news from returning students that Reverend Barclay was leaving Wilson. "Captain John" Barclay, who would become pastor of a Christian church in Austin, Texas, had proven to be a uniquely valuable friend to the college and an effective leader in local and state affairs for twenty years. The college newspaper noted that Barclay's commitment to civil rights, economic justice, and other humanitarian causes had endeared him to those who remained outside the mainstream. His energy and devotion to the church, the college, and the broader community had gained distinction for the popular minister as one of Wilson's foremost progressive leaders.[3]

Both the September and October editions of *The Collegiate* noted the absence from campus of another member of the AC College community in the autumn of 1941. While visiting relatives in New York during the summer, Ava Gardner had attracted the attention of a Hollywood talent scout. Soon after her discovery, Gardner began realizing a dream held by many an American girl—the opportunity to move to Hollywood and become a movie star. *The Collegiate* recalled that during the previous year the young "glamour girl" had been chosen one of the most beautiful girls on campus and added: "Those who remember Ava will have no trouble remembering her unique and pleasant personality. No matter when she was seen or in whose company she was in, there was always an air of pleasantness about her. Soon she will be seen on the silver screen. Her natural wavy medium brown hair, her green eyes that seem to haunt you together with her graceful, slender figure will make such a striking picture that you will be proud to say, 'We were school mates together.'" The young reporter might also have listed another attractive physical feature that Gardner mentioned years later in her autobiography, the "magnificent creamy porcelain skin, which all we Gardner girls inherited."[4]

Photographs of the young starlet then under contract with Metro-Goldwyn-Mayer Studios appeared on page one of *The Collegiate* on 15 October 1941 and on 15 January 1942. Over half a century later, Milton Adams remembered explaining banking activities during a tour of Branch Bank facilities to a college business class that included Ava Gardner. He recalled that she had asked more questions than her colleagues and that her questions were well chosen. A standing joke at Barton College is that every boy on the campus during the 1940–41 academic year "remembered" that he had once dated Ava Gardner. The campus newspaper of January 1942 included her photograph from the 1941 *Pine Knot* under the caption "She's Mrs. Rooney, Now" and explained that the young starlet had become the wife of "Hollywood's No. 1 box office attraction, Mickey Rooney."[5]

Ava Gardner's importance to the college is that of a true Cinderella figure—a beautiful girl from a tenant farm background who became one of few North Carolinians to gain international fame. A life of glamour, adventure, and renown saw her become leading lady to the silver screen's greatest male stars: Clark Gable, Richard Burton, Burt Lancaster, Tyrone Power, Gregory Peck, Humphrey Bogart, Stewart Granger, Howard Duff, and Robert Taylor. She also was married to Artie Shaw and Frank Sinatra. After winning world acclaim as a movie star, Gardner included memories of ACC in her autobiography. Answering questions regarding her educational experience at her screen test in New York City, she replied, "Yes, I'm at the Atlantic Christian College in Wilson, North Carolina. . . . I'm taking a secretarial course in shorthand and typing." Memories of her days as a college student included these remarks about ACC: "Atlantic Christian may not have been Harvard, but it was a fine college, and it included all the odds and ends that go with a college education: sororities, football and baseball teams, drama and debating societies. Once again, I concentrated on shorthand and typing. We still had no money, and I had to be driven in every day by a girlfriend who lived nearby, and driven back every evening." Although Ava Gardner left school before earning a degree, she remains an intriguing part of Barton College history and legend. Numerous relatives followed her to the Wilson campus and are alumni of the school. An autographed photograph of the screen goddess has graced the office of a Barton professor for twenty years, courtesy of Gardner's cousin, Rachael Thorne of Elm City. Bill Smith, director of alumni affairs, became so excited upon receiving a contribution to the general fund from the star that he had to be persuaded to cash her check rather than display the famous signature throughout the campus. A Barton sorority claimed Ava Gardner as a former member and included her name in their song in the late twentieth century. Research by college archivist Edward B. Holloway in the 1990s proved that the claim was probably not valid.[6]

Hollywood stars joined millions of other Americans in hearing startling news from the Hawaiian Islands on Sunday, 7 December 1941. The Japanese surprise attack upon the American naval base at Pearl Harbor threatened to change millions of lives. The news of the assault spread rapidly across the AC campus, dominating almost every conversation. *The Collegiate* estimated that every radio at the school was tuned in the following day to hear news of President Roosevelt's request to Congress for a declaration of war against the Empire of Japan. President Hilley, learning that several boys had already announced intentions to volunteer for military service, urged prudence. Speaking at the chapel service on Tuesday, 9 December, he advised students to think clearly and weigh their responsibilities carefully. Later that week, after conferring with other educational leaders, Hilley offered the opinion that students ought to remain in college and should definitely complete the current school year.[7]

The college formed a "War Plan Group" to encourage patriotism and help the college adjust to war. Patriotic activities included participating in the city of Wilson's blackout drills, promoting the sale of war bonds, and sending delegates to Chapel Hill to hear Eleanor Roosevelt speak on "Youth's Stake in War Aims and Peace Plans." *The Collegiate* of 18 February 1942 announced that four boys had left school for military service following January's examinations and noted that twenty-six additional students were eligible for the draft under the latest registration drive. Several ACC students and former students opposed war for religious and humanitarian reasons and requested to be listed as conscientious objectors. They were allowed to fulfill their national obligation at conscientious objector camps, where they worked on nonmilitary projects such as construction and reforestation. Ironically, Marvin Jackson, class of 1937, who initially requested conscientious objector status, changed his mind, enlisted, and became ACC's first student or former student killed in the war.[8]

The 18 March 1942 school newspaper featured front-page pictures of three former students in aviation cadet flight gear: James Banks of Arapahoe, Claude Garner Jr. of Wilson, and James D. Walters of Jamesville. An editorial

Former ACC students and aviation cadets prepare for World War II duty. Completing basic flight training at Randolph Field, Texas, are, from left, Claude Garner Jr. of Wilson, James D. Walters of Jamesville, and James B. Banks of Arapahoe. The Collegiate, *February and March 1942.*

announced that Wilson County would distribute allotment cards limiting each student to one-half pound of sugar per week and suggested putting "that sweet tooth on a diet for the duration." The junior class of 1942 substituted a "wiener roast and theatre party" for the traditional junior-senior banquet and purchased saving bonds with the money saved. They wisely made the bonds payable to the senior class of 1943 with plans to redeem the bonds and use the money for their senior gift to the college.[9]

In the spring and fall of 1942, increasing numbers of students and graduates of the college either volunteered or were drafted into military service. The student newspaper of September printed the names of forty-two students, representing every class at the college, who were either on active duty or awaiting a call to duty. Included were senior Marion Lassiter of Conway, junior Kirby Watson of Wilson, sophomore Howard S. "Steve" Hilley Jr. of Wilson, and freshmen Howard Chapin of Kinston and Vincent Colombo of Brockton, Massachusetts. The newspaper also reported two former students, George

Marvin Jackson of Elm City and C. H. Rowland Jr. of Varina, as missing in action. Jackson died in July 1942 as member of a gun crew on a merchant vessel that was sunk off the Denmark coast. "Windy" Rowland, a promising freshman on the 1940–41 Bulldog basketball team, survived the ordeal as a Japanese prisoner of war.[10]

Men from ACC fought in every theater of World War II including campaigns in North Africa, France, Germany, Italy, Okinawa, Saipan, and the Philippines. Their departure for military service exerted tremendous pressure upon the school. *The Collegiate* consistently reported their activities under the column "In The Service," and many former students visited the campus while on leave from duty. The college post office did a thriving business as the boys in service wrote to favorite co-eds and received letters in return. The student newspaper reported in May 1943 that the campus post office had sold over $607 worth of stamps since January. Of the 231 letters mailed each day, two-thirds bore the addresses of soldiers, sailors, and marines. The co-eds also sent their favorite service men birthday cards and news of the college, including copies of *The Collegiate*, along with packages containing books and cigarettes.[11]

In January 1943 the college graduated eleven seniors in its first midyear graduation ever. Of the eleven, three males were entering military service and four females were departing for defense work in Arlington, Virginia. The drafting of twenty-six additional students in April left fewer than thirty male students enrolled. For the first time in its history, the college allowed seniors to graduate early and awarded degrees to seniors who were drafted in April. Undergraduates ordered to report before the end of the term received credit for one-half of a semester's work. Military inductees from the college compiled distinguished records during the war. "In the Service" reported in March 1943 that Army Air Corps pilot James D. Walters had shot down a Japanese airplane and that Russell Roebuck had recovered from wounds received in the North African campaign. Vincent Colombo, a star athlete at ACC, recorded the second-highest score on an intelligence test taken at Fort Devens, Massachusetts, as an army private in the spring of 1943. Howard E. Blake of Fairfield, North Carolina, former president of the ACC student body, made the highest score of 1,200 midshipmen tested at the University of Notre Dame during the same period. Talmadge Narron of Kenly, vice-president of the 1942–43 freshman class, received an appointment to West Point, effective 1 July 1943. Narron's older brothers, Homer, Jarley, and Donnell, all former ACC students, were already enrolled in military service.[12]

Troubling thoughts about the future, including possible upheavals and dangers posed by a foreign war, prompted some young men to write whimsically about the pleasures of college life and about what fighting for their country meant to them. Bill Osborne of Charleston, South Carolina, a sophomore and a member of *The Collegiate* staff, wrote in "Bill's Column" in February 1943 that after being on campus for two years or more, "one acquires that spirit of lightheartedness yet seriousness, that spirit of flippancy and gaiety so typical of, and peculiar to . . . college life. . . . You become so attached to college you're really disappointed to see the four years slip by so quickly. . . . College gets in your blood!!" In *The Collegiate* of the previous December, Osborne had commended American women who entered military service in the nation's defense. He wrote that, in addition to reasons of honor and patriotism, he believed that American men and women were "fighting to preserve this season of the year. . . . They are fighting to keep Christmas what it has been—a season of merriment, gaiety, happiness, yet one of humbleness, reverence and piety."[13]

A number of female ACC students and former students joined the military service, entered Red Cross work, or took defense-related jobs. Clyde Deans of Wilson, class of 1937, left her job as a Stantonsburg schoolteacher upon receiving appointment to officers' candidate school. She became the first Wilsonian and the first ACC graduate to pass the Navy's rigorous entrance examination for acceptance into the WAVES. Captain Kathleen Eagles of Wilson, class of 1935, served as an army nurse, and Ruth M. Strickland of Elm City, class of 1937, became a medical technician with the Women's Army Corps (WAC). Madeline Brooks of Wilson, class of 1938, served with the American Red Cross.[14]

Those remaining on the campus dealt with new policies from the school's War Defense Committee, including the suggestion that students take a minimum of three semester hours of physical education and a course in first aid. The library became "The War Information Center," providing newspapers and maps to help trace areas of combat and identifying radio programs and articles regarding the war. Responding to calls for help from local farmers whose labor force had dwindled because of defense demands, students became temporary field hands, picking cotton in the autumn of 1942. The junior class won the competition between classes by picking the largest amount. The school added patriotic touches to traditional campus events by buying defense savings stamps with profits realized from Sadie Hawkins' Day events and conducting May Day 1943 festivities according to a "Victory Garden" theme, complete with costumed vegetables and bugs. The college science club, called the "Dodo-Bio Club," planted a real victory garden beside Hardy Dining Hall. The gardeners' plan was to support the war effort by "eating vitamins from our own garden."[15]

The World War II demand for servicemen brought drastic changes to intercollegiate athletics by reducing the number of males on campuses and creating new service teams that looked to colleges for athletic competition. Fan excitement grew in Wilson during late autumn of 1942 following rumors that Fort Bragg, a new opponent on the Bulldogs' basketball schedule, had a tall, talented team which included Horace McKinney, a former star player at North Carolina State. In a contest played in Wilson, "Bones" McKinney and the Fort Bragg team dominated by a score of 42–19. Fewer available players and restrictions on travel because of gas rationing forced cancellation of many North State Conference games of the 1942–43 season. *The Collegiate* of 15 April reported that, following the recent draft of twenty-six students, intercollegiate sports had been "curtailed here for the duration." One consolation was the success of recent Bulldog teams against their arch rival, East Carolina. A 10 December 1942 basketball victory in Greenville by a 42–22 score marked the ninth straight athletic victory over ECTC and insured retention of the Bohunkus for "the duration." The jubilation among Wilson fans over Bulldog domination of Pirate athletic teams soon vanished with the cancellation of baseball in 1943. Lamenting the loss of intercollegiate sports in the student newspaper of 15 May 1943, "Spectator Sid" wrote, "By turns the air around the gym has been filled with tennis balls, shuttle cocks and horseshoes. . . . intercollegiate sports are dead, intramurals are the thing now. . . . Horseshoe pitching is the most popular [sport.]"[16]

When America declared war, President Hilley immediately realized that future changes would reach far beyond athletics. He spent much of the 1941 Christmas break meeting with state and national college leaders and Disciples officials to discuss the war's impact upon small colleges. The school also increased efforts to attract female students by inviting high school senior girls from the surrounding area to spend the first weekend of May 1942 on the ACC campus as guests of the college. The following year the program was broadened to cover most of the state when 75–100 high school seniors received invitations to visit co-eds on the campus and be introduced to college life. By the start of spring semester 1943, with most remaining male students expecting a call into military service, Hilley shared his sense of urgency in the *North Carolina Christian*, writing that the college faced far greater concerns than the cancellation of intercollegiate athletics. Next year's enrollment and the college's future were at risk. Meeting these challenges would force the school to recruit students from four pools: women, ministerial students, men who were physically unfit for either the armed forces or defense work, and young men under eighteen years old.[17]

Young men who remained on campus after their colleagues departed in 1943 faced problems other than waiting for orders from their draft boards. The school Defense Committee's decision to hold "open house" for servicemen on alternate Sundays in Caldwell Hall and Kinsey Hall attracted numerous young men in uniform to the campus. Writing in *The Collegiate* of mid-April 1943, Bill Osborne expressed the feelings of jealousy experienced by the male students. Osborne complained that "As each Sunday afternoon rolls around, the male specie of A.C. College cannot get within a five-mile radius of Caldwell and Kinsey Halls. . . . [because of] men in khaki, green or navy blue." Moreover, co-eds spoiled the servicemen by serving tasty sandwiches, teacakes, and punch, treating the invaders far "more royally" than they did their envious male colleagues. Osborne's good-natured complaints ended with a simple plea, "How about giving us a tea some Sunday in the future—a tea which servicemen cannot attend?" Osborne's problem was solved within less than a month when he, too, donned a military uniform. From his new home at Fort Jackson, "Pvt. Bill Osborne" wrote his last column about the fun-filled hours of basic training. He had learned to make his bed so professionally in the "Army Style" that he had been requested to make up his sergeant's bed each morning. Military uniforms, however, continued to bother Osborne, who wrote, "My shoes are so large that Uncle Sam could rent them as gunboats."[18]

Throughout the World War II era, strong Christian and humanitarian values within the college community encouraged students to resist all inclinations to hate the enemy and to demonstrate a spirit of brotherhood in the postwar world. The editors of *The Collegiate* advocated respect and equal treatment for everyone, including the Germans and Japanese. *The Collegiate* of 15 February 1943 published a poem by an American citizen of Japanese ancestry imprisoned in a relocation center camp. The author stressed his patriotism and loyalty and asked that his value as a human being not be dismissed because of his Japanese ancestry. He wrote, "I'd fight for 'freedom and liberty,' / I'd die with the best of you. / But here behind this barbed wire fence / What can a patriot do?" The Golden Knot Honor Society also advocated brotherhood and peace in a postwar world. In the spring of 1943, the organization raised money to bring a refugee from a war-torn country to study at the college. The honor society set a goal of $350 for the project, suggesting that $200 be raised on campus and asking Wilson civic clubs to contribute the remaining sum. A supportive article in the student newspaper suggested that the foreign student's presence could help reduce prejudice and hatred while broadening the experiences of ACC students.[19]

As war placed increasing demands upon the American people, Atlantic Christian College struggled to adjust and survive. Between 1940 and 1945, the college lost 334 students, almost half of its total enrollment. During the two worst years, 1942 to 1944, the school lost 281 students, leaving a total of 373 students enrolled in 1944. Enrollment had peaked at 786 in 1938, counting 367 regular semester students and 419 enrollees in summer school and extension classes. Enrollment bottomed out in 1944–45 at a total of 367, including only 261 regular semester students. In January 1945, the service roll posted in Kinsey Hall listed nearly 400 names of former students in the armed forces. In addition to draining the school of male students and causing cancellation of intercollegiate athletics, the war delayed plans for new buildings and prompted the administration to restructure recruiting efforts in order to survive. The loss of student leaders also brought the demise of both *The Collegiate* and *Pine Knot* following the spring semester of 1943 when the college merged the two publications into *The Torchlight*, a new magazine of 16–24 pages published eight times a year.[20]

Crises regarding declining enrollment and insufficient operating funds convinced the trustees to form a strategic plan in the summer of 1945. The board voted to maintain college enrollment at its current level of approximately 275 students, increase the numbers of both Disciples and ministerial students, request that the churches furnish $10,000 for a maintenance fund, increase the endowment, provide a blueprint of future building needs, and continue promoting cooperation between the school and the Wilson community. President Hilley was nearly as concerned over declining numbers of Disciples and ministerial students as with the overall enrollment drop. Using the college's monthly column in *North Carolina Christian*, the president consistently called upon the churches to support the school with students and money, noting that ACC expected only four or five new ministerial students for the fall semester of 1944 when the number should be ten to fifteen. Clarence L. Hardy, a Christian Church stalwart and trustee from Greene County, came to the aid of the college by pledging $50,000 to the school's building campaign on condition that supporters raise an additional sum of $150,000.[21]

Other plans for the college, including a new dorm, library, and student union, were delayed by military priorities while the college community awaited news of colleagues, friends, and family involved in the war. Military reports included news of several ACC servicemen who gained distinction while fighting in European and Pacific campaigns. Elton D. Winstead III of Elm City became Wilson County's first prisoner of war when General Douglas MacArthur's former Philippine headquarters at Corregidor fell to the Japanese in May 1942. Winstead survived the war and returned to Wilson County and a hero's welcome. After retiring from the Army, Colonel Winstead graduated from ACC, class of 1960, earned a doctorate at Duke University, and taught in the education and mathematics departments of his alma mater between 1962–77. Raleigh native Ellis W. Williamson, class of 1940, was decorated for exemplary leadership and courage following European military engagements that included the Battle of the Bulge in December 1944. At ACC, Williamson had served as director of the college band, as chaplain of Sigma Alpha fraternity, and as treasurer of his junior and senior classes. He earned graduate degrees at Harvard and George Washington Universities and retired from the United States Army with the rank of major general. Lt. Robert Webb Winstead of Wilson, a member of the sophomore class of 1942, completed approximately fifty bombing missions over Nazi-held Europe as a member of the Army Air Corps. He graduated from Georgia Tech after the war and settled in Richmond, Virginia. Charles C. Ware lists the names of twenty former ACC students "reported as killed in action" while serving in World War II.[22]

On V-J Day, 15 August 1945, the day that Japan formally surrendered, ACC mailed letters to all former students in military service, reminding them of the college's continued interest in them and asking for their support. The response began almost immediately and was overwhelmingly positive as a few GIs enrolled for the 1945 fall term. In January 1946, when the school welcomed nearly fifty additional students, most of them veterans, President Hilley remarked at a chapel assembly that "the college looked more like itself" than at any time since 1941. Hilley's assessment may have been accurate for the moment, but the veterans appeared in great numbers, tended to be older and more mature than typical underclassmen, and, in the president's words, "added tone and variety to the life of the college." The administration quickly learned that adjusting the school to the postwar era would prove as vexing as adapting to the war itself. The surging enrollment quickly caused overcrowding and brought creation of a waiting list for additional male students. Within five years, 1945–49, regular semester enrollment increased from 261 to 576 (120 percent), and total college enrollment, including summer school and extension students, increased from 367 to 940 (156 percent.) President Hilley consistently appealed to friends of the college and to Wilson's city government for assistance in dealing with an emergency shortage of student housing.[23]

President Hilley also requested federal assistance to provide temporary housing and additional classroom space for the large number of veterans attempting to enroll. In April 1946, the Atlanta office of the Federal Public Housing Authority approved funding for adding twenty-five dormitory rooms and three family housing units on the campus. Eleven months later, Hilley announced that the Federal Works Agency had agreed to furnish building materials for a one-story, four-classroom structure to be located on the corner of West Lee and Rountree Streets adjoining the dining hall. In December 1946, the *North Carolina Christian* reported that the veteran's housing project had been completed and that the GIs had named the units "Kilroy's Kennels." The classroom building, a white wooden structure, was completed in August 1947 and called "The White House." *The Collegiate* of 15 February 1949 reported that the "G. I. Barracks" had been remodeled and renamed "Murray Hall" in honor of Leslie L. Murray, dean of men.[24]

The resurgence of male students prompted trustees to approve resumption of intercollegiate athletic competition within the North State Conference, and the 1946 baseball team enjoyed its greatest season ever, winning thirteen games and losing only two to rank at the top of the conference. The Bulldogs defeated Wake Forest, lost only one conference game by splitting two contests with Lenoir Rhyne, and swept rivals High Point, ECTC, and Elon, defeating the latter team four times. Unfortunately, the team was denied the conference championship because coach and director of athletics M. J. "Red" Bird learned that star player Vincent Colombo had played for the Wilson Tobs team in the Hi-State League in 1942. Bird reported his findings to conference officials, who declared Colombo ineligible and designated the second-place team, Lenoir Rhyne, the official conference champion.[25]

Bulldog fans welcomed the news that President Hilley and the trustees had agreed for ACC to resume competition in football on the condition that adequate private funding be raised to equip a team. After meeting with Athletics Director Bird, Wilson Disciples leader and businessman Willis N. Hackney headed a successful drive to raise $3,000 within the local community, and on 21 September 1946, the Bulldogs returned to gridiron play for the first time in fifteen years. While the team struggled to compile a record of two wins, four losses, and one tie, most games were close, and fans demonstrated impressive support. The Bulldogs defeated Campbell and Norfolk Naval Base

Willis N. Hackney, loyal Bulldogs' fan and college benefactor. Undated photograph in college archives.

team and tied ECTC, 6–6, at Greenville. The season's big disappointment came 9 November during the season's final game held in Wilson. Playing in Municipal Stadium before the largest homecoming turnout in school history, the Bulldogs lost the rematch to East Carolina by a score of 26–6.[26]

During the next few years, virtually none of the four ACC athletic teams matched the success of the 1946 football squad. The first college tennis team formed since the war lost its only scheduled game of the 1947 season. Although the Bulldogs slumped badly, losing all eight football games in the "disastrous" season of 1947 and winning only two of seven contests the following year, the team retained a cadre of hard-core supporters even in defeat. The community honored the winless squad, which had been outscored by a total of 168–19, with an appreciation ceremony at the Wilson Theatre. Radio station WGTM and the Wilson Junior Chamber of Commerce, sponsors of the event, presented the most valuable player (MVP) trophy to freshman Harry "Lefty" Helmer of Goldsboro, a triple-threat tailback and one of the best punters in the North State Conference. The MVP award was the first ever received by an ACC athlete. The 1948 grid squad won only two games but excited its fans, including the normally somber college president, by rallying late to end the season "in a muddy blaze of glory" with a stunning upset win over East Carolina in Greenville by a score of 6–0.[27]

Helmer, James Fox, and Charles "Ned" Liggon were considered the stars of the team. Fox, an outstanding blocking back from Hilton Village, Virginia, won the second MVP award in 1948. Liggon, a sophomore guard from Wilson on the 1948 team, became the first ACC athlete to receive any type of All-American designation. The Associated Press named him an honorable mention member of the 1948 "Little All-American" team. The problem with ACC football was that, except for Fox, Helmer, Liggon, and perhaps a few others, the players lacked the ability and experience to form a squad which could compete with the top teams in the conference. *The Collegiate* sports staff echoed an earlier assessment made by John Yavorski that consistent success in intercollegiate sports required enrolling better athletes, which meant offering athletic scholarships. College leaders finally decided to discontinue intercollegiate football. The 1950 squad, which won only two games, became the last football team sponsored by Barton College.[28]

Even though many Bulldog teams of the 1940s struggled to win in the North State Conference, several great individual athletes represented ACC during those years and are members of Barton's Athletic Hall of Fame. They included Harmon W. "Red" Broughton of Garner, Joe Holliday of Jamesville, Howard Chapin of Kinston, Ed Smith of Micro, Vince Colombo of Brockton, Massachusetts, William Troy Godwin of Dunn, James Daniel "J. D." Thorne of Elm City, and Henry "Hank" Davis of Wilson. Most of these outstanding athletes were also good academically. Some of them played professionally following graduation, and many became successful teachers and coaches.[29]

Players and fans associated with Bulldog sports of the 1940s appeared to agree that competition for the "Bohunkus" added a tremendous incentive in games against arch rival ECTC. ACC held the coveted bucket during most of the World War II period, 1942–1946, and were crestfallen when East Carolina regained the trophy in November 1946. *The Collegiate, The Wilson Daily Times,* and *North Carolina Christian* mentioned the Bohunkus in articles about games between the schools. Headlines in the student paper four days before the 19 November 1948 football contest stated "Famed Bucket At Stake in Classic Duel." An accompanying article argued that "the old wooden bucket makes each athlete put out the best that is within him." The rivalry's intensity brought a few fans to violate the standards of good sportsmanship. At a November 1948 chapel meeting, Dean Leslie Murray and Coach "Red" Bird asked students to keep athletics in proper perspective after an unspecified case involving "wanton destruction of personal property" regarding East Carolina. They cautioned that further destructive acts could end an important rivalry and possibly endanger the college's membership in the North State Conference.[30]

The pep talk may have inspired the players; by the following February the Bulldogs not only possessed the bucket but had a four-game winning streak over ECTC. The college's honor society proved that the "Bohunkus" had attained a status that actually transcended athletics. In an innovative campaign for The March of Dimes in February 1949, students circulated the famed bucket at a home basketball game, collecting over $32 to benefit polio research, and repeated the appeal at a chapel assembly, collecting another $29. During the process, the scholars also revealed that the revered "Bohunkus" had assumed human dimensions. When asked to aid this worthy cause, *The Collegiate* reported, "Bohunkus . . . went all out for the March of Dimes. . . . He used the slogan, 'Give that they may play.'. . . Bohunkus is one who can appreciate fair play and sportsmanship.'"[31]

The realm of athletics was not the only area of student life significantly affected by the presence of returning GIs, WACs, WAVES, and Red Cross nurses after World War II. The veterans brought a liberating spirit that led to a broad range of social and recreational activities at ACC. Members of the *Pine Knot* staff, led by editor Eugene Barnes and business manager Mary Lee Tanner, chose a prophetic slogan and appropriate symbol for the opening page of the 1948 yearbook: "The Dawn of a New Day." The phrase seemed to capture the spirit of AC College in 1947–48, just as the slogan of the junior class, "Nothing Can Stop Us Now," appeared to describe the air of confidence, even cockiness, which prevailed on the campus. For the first time in the institution's history, a photograph of youthful couples dancing to their own music appeared in a college publication. A new social committee, appointed by the executive board, assumed responsibility for planning and promoting social activities involving "full student participation." Specific activities that the students planned to support included athletic contests, bull sessions, concerts, dating, and dances.[32]

One event in the autumn of 1947 which stimulated additional social opportunities was the school's decision to name a "Queen of the *Pine Knot*." In October, Elizabeth Ann "Lib" Leach, a junior from Wilson, had a memorable experience that remains unique in the history of the college. She not only became the first "Queen of the *Pine Knot*," but she was also chosen by a future President of the United States. Movie stars Ronald Reagan and Jane Wyman

Our Judges

RONALD REAGAN and
JANE WYMAN
of Hollywood, California

10-29th-47

Dear Friends,

This is just a brief note to thank you for choosing us as judges in the selection of your Queen.

Incidentally this is the first time either of us have ever said "Thanks" for a tough job.

We finally chose Lib Leach as Queen. Our second & third choices were Lois Harper and Mary Alice Beasley.

I'm sure these three girls will understand — when we say that our real first choice would have been to return all the pictures and say — "They were all Queens."

Again our thanks to you and our Congratulations to Atlantic Christian — for what must be a fine student body.

Sincerely,
Jane Wyman
Ronald Reagan

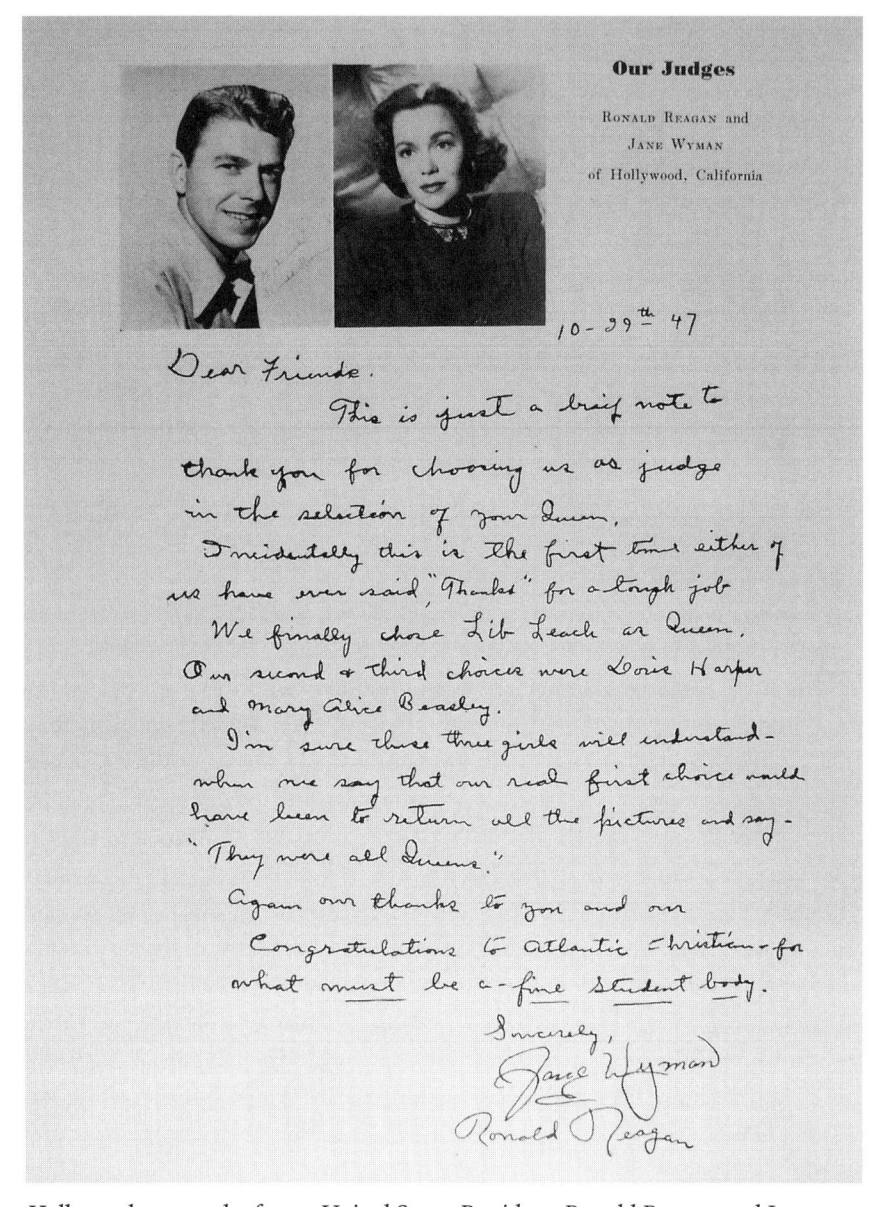

Hollywood stars and a future United States President, Ronald Reagan and Jane Wyman, selected an ACC beauty queen in 1947–48. A letter to AC College students from the contest judges. 1948 Pine Knot.

selected the queen along with first and second runners-up from photographs of fourteen ACC co-eds. In a gracious and complimentary letter to the ACC students, the two stars named Leach as queen, Doris Harper, a sophomore from Spring Hope, as first runner-up, and Mary Alice Beasley, a junior from Four Oaks, as second runner-up. Reagan and Wyman thanked the students for inviting them to serve as judges and added ". . . our real first choice would have been to return all the pictures and say—'They are all Queens.' Again our thanks to you and our Congratulations to Atlantic Christian for what must be a fine student body. Sincerely, [signed] Jane Wyman & Ronald Reagan." Barnes, the *Pine Knot* editor, crowned the queen at an informal dance for the student body at the Wilson Country Club on Saturday, 22 November 1947. *The Collegiate* announced that the yearbook staff planned to make the contest and dance an annual event on the campus. Students planning to hold dances on the campus in the 1940s were disappointed. College lore has maintained that Hilley had informed trustees upon several occasions that he would resign as president if they permitted either drinking or dancing on the campus. ACC students of the 1940s mockingly referred to their campus as "God's little acre."[33]

The students decided to find appropriate chaperones and hold their dances off campus. An editorial in the student newspaper of May 1947 reported that a few students had already been dancing since the previous spring at "Harper's . . . little store, just off campus." Recently, however, students had become upset because the administration was, reportedly, trying to prevent future dancing at the store. The annual junior-senior banquet on 9 May 1947 was made especially enjoyable because many students rushed from the dinner, held in the Carolina Room of the Christian Church, to a dance at the Country Club. The memorable event ended promptly at 11:30 PM because the dormitory girls faced a midnight curfew. Sarah Bain Ward, who returned to the college in 1944 as dean of women, recognized that dancing had become vital to the social life of the college. As a member of the executive board of the Cooperative Association and as faculty chairman of the social committee, Ward used her position to render significant support for student dances and to attend the events as an appropriate chaperone. The college social committee and Sigma Tau Chi Sorority both sponsored off-campus dances during March 1948. Sigma Tau Chi held a "Leap Year Dance" at the Wilson Country Club on Friday, 5 March, at which the girls asked the boys to go dancing and paid for the tickets. The social committee dance, which had Easter and the beginning of spring as a theme, occurred Friday, 19 March, at the Wilson armory. As the popularity of dancing increased, students added the Briggs and Cherry Hotels as other sites for their socials. *The Collegiate* of March 1948 saluted the social committee for its active and successful role in organizing and planning the dances.[34]

Interestingly, the college's first dance held on campus was a square dance and, apparently, a compromise between the administration and students. Sponsored by the Golden Knot Honor Society, the dance occurred in April 1948 in Hardy Dining Hall. Dr. Harold J. Dudley of Wilson's First Presbyterian Church served as caller for the dance and provided instruction to those unfamiliar with square dancing, which included most of the crowd of about seventy students. Editors of *The Collegiate* wrote that students welcomed the opportunity to dance on campus, even at a square dance, and predicted that the dining hall would become a site for future dances.[35]

While students readily welcomed dancing on the campus, they were less pleased with other functions of the dining hall. The student newspaper argued that, despite an increase in the boarding fee to $97.50 per year, the quality of the food served in the autumn of 1947 remained "fair" at best and the staff provided little variety. The typical menu for lunch was "slaw, potatoes, beans, while the supper menu was slaw, potatoes, fish." Food had always been served family style, and dormitory students paid for all meals without the option of different meal plans. An unusually critical student editorial in November 1947 complained of unsanitary conditions in the dining hall and suggested that the school switch to a cafeteria plan and offer meal tickets. Ultimately, the continued griping proved too much for those who saw themselves at the center of the controversy, the food service staff. That small group initiated an action which, apparently, had never before occurred at Atlantic Christian College; they staged a protest and walked off the job. At precisely 10:30 AM on 17 November, just prior to the lunch hour, the four cooks left their posts and headed for the president's office. Apparently, Hilley was unavailable at the time, and the four disgruntled staff members, identified as "Tilly, Lanie, Tina and Sue," sat down to discuss the matter with the individual who, according to Sarah Bain Ward, Milton Adams, Sarah Loftin Adams and others, "really ran the college," Mildred Ross. Although officially listed as the college "bookkeeper," Ross was far more than that. *The Collegiate* suggested that Ross applied "successful persuasive efforts" in successfully arbitrating the issue with the cooks, and the women returned to work. In early October 1948, the college began offering a cafeteria style of service, providing students with more choices of food. While the new style was introduced on an experimental basis,

Mildred Ross, "Miss Mildred," revered staff member and campus character. 1943 Torch Light.

The Collegiate noted that students seemed happy with the change and predicted that the cafeteria style would continue.[36]

Mildred D. Ross joined the college staff in 1927 and gradually assumed sufficient administrative duties to rank her unofficially as an assistant to the president. Occupying an office next to Hilley's in Caldwell Hall, she was known for her work as office secretary, business manager, and postmaster and for her deep commitment to virtually every aspect of the college. The school annual of 1943 pictured Ross on a bicycle above the caption "Rural Free Delivery" and suggested that her skill in managing money greatly exceeded her limited ability to ride a bike. Bob Clark, feature editor of *The Collegiate* of 1948, thanked Ross for successfully "handling public relations" in the property destruction case which threatened to end ACC's heated but valued rivalry with East Carolina. One of the most jovial and helpful people on the campus and a huge fan of Bulldog athletics, Mildred Ross remained best known for her interest in students and for her inability to drive an automobile safely. Clark mentioned Ross's driving problems, suggesting that she hold her speed below sixty, and adding "the only way Mildred knows when she is getting near town is that she is hitting more people." One of the more humorous college legends involves Ross and Willis Hackney, who shared Ross's love of Bulldog athletics. Ross was driving in Wilson's downtown area near midmorning one day when, straying well across her side of the public street, she rammed Hackney's automobile, smashing a fender. Getting out of their cars, the drivers approached each other as a small crowd began to gather on the sidewalk. Hackney immediately assumed a defensive position, extending his arms with hands in front, palms open and fingers spread. In a loud, serious voice, he blurted, "Mildred it's my fault, all my fault. I knew you were coming to town this morning. I should have known better than to be down here."[37]

Alumni continue to remember Ross's generosity in lending money to financially strapped students and recall that her desk drawer was often filled with IOUs bearing student signatures. Howard Hilley, apparently alarmed upon learning about the size of Ross's loan service, suggested that the practice stop. Ross answered that it was her money and the college president should mind his own business. She later told friends that during the four-plus decades that she had loaned money, only two students failed to repay her. The college's veterans' club also appreciated Ross's kindness and assistance on behalf of the GIs. At an assembly meeting in Howard Chapel, 20 January 1949, the group presented her with a puppy as a token of their appreciation and affection. *The Collegiate* carried a photograph of the event and an article that stated, "Mildred . . . has done many things quietly for students which are not generally known. She is A.C.C. at its best, one of the finest of them all."[38]

AC College needed the skills of Ross and of all the faculty and staff when tragedy struck during the summer of 1947. While returning from a meeting in Edgecombe County on Wednesday, 2 July, President Hilley and students Ivan Adams and John Goff Jr. were involved in a serious automobile accident when Hilley's car collided with another vehicle at Cobb's Crossroads near Pinetops. Both cars overturned and were practically demolished. Adams was treated and released at the Tarboro hospital. Goff and Hilley both suffered concussions and remained hospitalized. While Goff's situation began to improve the following day, Hilley remained unconscious in critical condition and was transferred to Duke Hospital four days later. The college president's health

The Dawn of a New Day

improved gradually, allowing him to resume his duties when school opened in September.[39]

While Hilley continued to regain strength, ACC suffered the loss of one of its greatest friends when George Hackney, one of the founders of the college and a venerable Disciples leader, died at the age of ninety-three. An honorary member of the board at the time of his death, Hackney had been chairman of the board of directors of Kinsey Seminary and served as a trustee of the college, usually as chairman, from 1902–48. As civic leader, member of the local board of education, active church layman, and faithful supporter of the college, George Hackney left an impressive legacy. It was also significant to the future of the college that when the elder Hackney stepped down as trustee chairman in 1931, his son, Thomas J. Hackney Sr. was a board member. Following a two-year stint as chair by another faithful trustee, N. J. Rouse of Kinston, the younger Hackney became chairman in 1935.[40]

An important announcement in the spring of 1949 shocked and saddened friends of the college. On 16 April, Howard S. Hilley informed trustees of his decision to resign as college president effective 1 July. *The Wilson Daily Times* and *North Carolina Christian* announced that trustees had granted Hilley a year's leave of absence with pay and, as of 1 July 1950, would designate him as "President Emeritus For Life." Hilley's resignation came after thirty years of service at ACC; his twenty-nine-year presidency was the longest in Barton College's history. He was the only ACC president that many of the younger adults among the school's alumni had ever known. For the first time in nearly three decades the institution began the search for a new leader.[41]

ELEVEN

Come, and Trip It as Ye Go, On the Light Fantastic Toe

AS HOWARD HILLEY PREPARED resignation remarks for the board of trustees in the spring of 1949, the cold war enveloped much of the world, and Americans soon would endure the politically divisive phenomenon known as McCarthyism. In the nation's capital, President Harry Truman signed the North Atlantic Treaty committing the United States to help protect Europe and the western hemisphere from communist aggression. In Asia, North Korean communists devised plans for an invasion to the south that would explode into a major military conflict and involve American college students. In Wilson, trustees met to begin the search for a new president who would lead Barton College into the second half of the twentieth century.

Trustees and Disciples leaders praised the accomplishments of President Hilley and acknowledged that he would be a difficult leader to replace. The growth of the institution between Hilley's appointment in 1920 and his resignation in 1949 was impressive. With an enrollment of only 127 students, the college of 1920 consisted of two buildings on a single block of land. The school had a total value of approximately $75,000, no endowment, and a debt of $10,000. In 1949, the college had an enrollment of more than 900 students and a campus of three city blocks with six buildings and a seventh under construction. The total property value was approximately $1,400,000; the school claimed an endowment of over $400,000 and was almost debt free.[1]

The board praised Hilley's integrity, commitment, exemplary leadership, and influence upon the life of the college and upon the lives of countless students. Charles C. Ware, who had worked closely with the departing president for three decades, lauded Hilley's devotion to duty, close attention to details, and leadership of both the Disciples church and the college. Ware also noted that one of the president's qualities that had not been fully appreciated was "his grim frugality of institutional resources." Former students and faculty continued to add to the accolades in the late twentieth century, remembering Hilley as a serious disciplinarian who cared deeply about people, theology, and Atlantic Christian College. Recalling the former president more than four decades later, Mamie Jennings Lucas, Sarah Bain Ward, and James B. Hemby Jr. remained convinced that Hilley had saved the college from closing. Hilley's commitment, hard work, and impeccable character won respect within the Wilson community, which enabled the president to guide the school through the perils of the Great Depression and World War II. More than half a century later, Hilley's daughter remembered her father's comment that ACC's credit rating had been so bad when he became president that the school "could not charge a loaf of bread in Wilson."[2]

Hilley's leadership had laid the foundation on which Barton College continued to thrive following his resignation. The class of 1950, the first in nearly three decades to miss Hilley's baccalaureate sermon on the topic *Habebunt Lumen Vitae,* graduated during the administration of acting president Cecil Jarman, who was also pastor of the Wilson Christian Church. Jarman reached an agreement with the church enabling him to remain pastor while also serving as acting president of the college, effective 1 July 1949. A native of Richlands and graduate of ACC, Jarman held a masters's degree from Emory University, a divinity degree from Yale, and a Ph.D. from the University of North Carolina. He had served his alma mater for nine years as associate professor of religious education and dean of men, and, from 1944–45, as professor of education and dean of the college.[3]

Listing changes that had occurred since their arrival in 1946, the class of 1950 mentioned women's fashions going "from short skirts and long hair to long skirts and short hair." They also recalled dancing to such favorite songs as "I Love You for Sentimental Reasons," "It's Magic," and "Some Enchanted Evening." Along with introductions to homecoming, Bohunkus, and Tweetie, the seniors of 1950 remembered the construction of the new girls' dormitory, the ground breaking for the new library, and the resignation of John M. Waters, respected business manager and professor of religion. The class of 1950 also recalled the closeness they had felt to colleagues and to members of the faculty and staff. Dr. Mildred Hartsock impressed them with her knowledge and teaching skills and with her practice of serving coffee to the English majors. They also remembered that during their sophomore year, the biggest snowfall that anyone had ever seen caused the kitchen staff to become snowbound and Chef Dean Ward came to their rescue by producing breakfast on a snow-covered Sunday morning.[4]

Professor Hartsock teaching an English class. 1955 Pine Knot.

Mildred Hartsock and Sarah Bain Ward assumed critical roles in assisting Cecil Jarman during his tenure as acting president and in enabling the college to prosper during a critical time of changing leadership. Few people knew the institution as well as Ward, who had worked closely with Hilley prior to graduating in 1938 and for five years as dean of women. At the time of her retirement in 1980, Ward had served the longest tenure as dean of women in Barton College history, thirty-six years. Hartsock, an Ohio native, had joined the faculty as a young, but experienced professor of English in 1940 after brief teaching stints at Kentucky Wesleyan and Lynchburg College. She quickly became one of the busiest and most respected faculty leaders, a status retained until her retirement in 1973. Both women remained single, devoting their lives to the college and bringing distinction to the school and to themselves. The college honored Hartsock with an honorary Doctor of Literature degree in 1962 and Ward with an honorary Doctor of Laws in 1969.[5]

Other veteran members of the faculty and staff in 1949 were Perry Case, registrar, director of personnel, and professor of philosophy; Dorothy Eagles, instructor in English; Ola Fleming, librarian; C. H. Hamlin, professor of social science; Doris Holsworth, assistant professor of English and dramatics; Bethany Joyner, secretary to the registrar; Esther Long, professor of modern languages; Mary Wilson, college nurse; and Mildred Ross, bookkeeper. Several new members joined the veterans between 1949 and 1956 and remained with the school to provide continuity and stability. They included Milton Adams, 1949, business manager; Jesse P. Tyndall, 1949, science; Russell Arnold, 1951, art; Edna Long Boykin, 1951, languages; John Dunn, 1951, mathematics; Kathryn Lamm, 1952, secretary; Edward L. Cloyd Jr., 1953, physical education; Hugh B. Johnston Jr., 1953, history; Allan Sharp, 1953, religion; George Harry Swain, 1953, business; Robert Capps, 1954, sociology; Robert P. Hollar, 1954, science; Myrtle T. Swain, 1954, mathematics; James D. Daniell, 1955, public relations; and Doris Capps, 1956, psychology.[6]

The trustees' appointment of Denton Ray Lindley as president of the college in February 1950, effective 1 July, likely came as no surprise to friends of the school. In the autumn of 1948, leaders and friends of ACC had met Lindley at the Disciples' annual state convention in New Bern. Lindley, then dean of Brite College of the Bible, which was affiliated with Texas Christian University, was the featured speaker at the convention. The *North Carolina Christian* praised Lindley's impact upon the convention, which drew an estimated 1,200 delegates. Some who heard Lindley speak at New Bern probably already knew him because of the close association between North Carolina Disciples and Texas Christian University. Relationships existed with current students and graduates, as well as with members of the faculty and staff. Texas Christian president M. E. Sadler was an Atlantic Christian College graduate, and TCU professors Raymond A. Smith and Cortell K. Holsapple had served, respectively, as former president and faculty member at the Wilson school.[7]

D. Ray Lindley was born in Brown County, Texas, in 1905. He held an A.B. degree from Phillips College, a B.D. from Brite, and a B.D., M.A., and Ph.D. from Yale. He and Mrs. Lindley, the former Maybon Marie Torrey, had two sons, Gene and Neil. Gene was a senior pre-med student and Neil a freshman at TCU. The February 1950 issue of *North Carolina Christian* described Maybon Lindley as a writer who had recently published a volume of poems. The president-elect spent a week in Wilson during early April 1950, meeting many local residents and interacting with the college community at two chapel services. He held nightly services at the Christian Church and preached the sermon on Easter morning.[8]

In addition to welcoming a new president, students returning to campus in September 1950 were anxious to use the facilities of the recently completed

President D. Ray Lindley, 1950–53. 1952 Pine Knot.

residence hall for women. The first permanent residence hall to be built on the campus since 1911, the imposing structure was only the second dormitory constructed by Atlantic Christian College. As the building neared completion in the spring of 1950, *The Collegiate* praised the attractive dormitory rooms and described the laundry room, parlors, and beautiful reception room. The building also provided living quarters for the dean of women, and, most significantly, a huge recreation room with an impressive fireplace. The newspaper reported that the game room already included sofas and ping-pong tables and noted that sororities and fraternities had promised to purchase additional furniture and had challenged other student organizations to provide card tables and folding chairs. The presence of storage space for recreation room furniture meant that students finally had a suitable place for social dances on campus. On 27 May 1951, trustees officially named the new women's dormitory Harper Hall in honor of the college's second president.[9]

While young women appreciated the new living quarters and other modern facilities, as well as the social opportunities afforded by the recreation room, the new residence hall did little to bring relief from the oppressive restrictions that continued to hamper the lives of ACC women. Female students could not ride in automobiles except in the company of parents or a member of the college staff, even if caught downtown in the rain. They had to sign in and out of the dormitory when leaving and returning to campus. Strict curfews regulated their activities every evening of the week. Quiet hours or study hours applied to the women' residence hall but were either nonexistent or unenforced in the men's dorm. Interestingly, students delighted in telling the story of how Sarah Bain Ward, who, as a senior and president of both student government and the YMCA, had ridden in a car to Kinston with classmate Griffith Hamlin in 1938. When they returned, Ward was "strictly" campused while Hamlin "stood by regretful." Bob Clark of Atlanta, a feature editor of *The Collegiate*, first printed the story in 1949. His account was reprinted in the student newspaper in 1951 and 1952. When confronted with the story by Clark, the dean of women replied impishly, "Don't put Miss on my gravestone because I haven't missed half as much as you think I have."[10]

Although frequently forced into the role of martinet by her sense of responsibility to the college, the good-natured dean of women was deeply committed to fair treatment for everyone. In a 1984 interview, four years after her retirement, Ward stated that she, Hartsock, and other members of the faculty-staff had begun to press the administration gradually to ease its strict policies regarding females. She also chaperoned dances, both on and off campus, and joined other faculty and staff members in taking dancing lessons from Gene Barnes. The dean remembered Bob Hollar and Herb Jeffries learning to dance in the game room of Harper Hall. She also recalled dancing with fellow chaperone J. P. Tyndall, an excellent dancer, in the ballroom of the Cherry Hotel. During one of the dances Tyndall "flipped" her too far, and Ward landed on her back side. The dignified dean referred to the event as "a most embarrassing moment."[11]

In the autumn of 1950, Ward and the rest of the college community anxiously awaited induction ceremonies for the school's sixth president. On 1 November 1950, a long and colorful procession of trustees and faculty, joined by officials of the Christian Church, Disciples of Christ, and representatives of numerous colleges and agencies marched in academic regalia from the front of Harper Hall to Howard Chapel for Dr. Lindley's inauguration. The college band played the inaugural march, and students of the class of 1951 lined the path of the procession. Dr. Liston Pope, a native North Carolinian and dean of the Yale University Divinity School, presented the charge to the new president and, following Lindley's inaugural address, spoke at a formal luncheon in Bert Hardy Dining Hall. Since the occasion had been planned to coincide with the annual Disciples of Christ state meeting held in Rocky Mount, many national and state church leaders attended the inaugural events.[12]

Editors of the 1951 *Pine Knot*, analyzing the significance of Lindley's inauguration, remarked that the new president's assumption of leadership symbolized the "opening of a new era," which also promised to continue important goals of Hilley's administration. In addition to expanding the college by erecting a new residence hall and starting construction of a library building, Hilley had convinced the city to close Rountree Street between Lee and Woodard Streets, thus physically connecting the campus while eliminating public traffic between the gymnasium and the dining hall. President Lindley started an evening program in an attempt to share the "cultural life of the college" with the broader community. He also began to strengthen the religion department and to place greater emphasis upon athletics. As a step toward increasing the influence of religious offerings, Lindley added faculty. Counting the president as an instructor in religion, the department numbered six faculty, with four holding doctorates. Lindley also added the position of assistant to the president, bringing in a promising young man by the name of Arthur D. Wenger, who also served as instructor in religion.[13]

While smaller in size than the religion department, the English department continued to gain in popularity and prestige during the 1950s. Mildred Hartsock, professor of English and head of the department, and Doris C. Holsworth, instructor in English and dramatics, exerted a profound impact on numerous students. The yearbook staff paid tribute to Hartsock by dedicating the 1951 *Pine Knot* in her honor. The dedication page praised the master teacher, faculty leader, and prodigious scholar as the epitome of the teacher whom students aspired to emulate. Holsworth, a native of Windsor, Connecticut, joined the faculty in 1947. Known on campus as the "Duchess," Holsworth attracted some of ACC's best students to Stage and Script, a dramatics group open to all students. Stage and Script members aggressively publicized productions, which included modern comedies, folk plays, Shakespearean dramas, European and American classics, and religious pageants. Hartsock taught Shakespeare in the classroom, while the "Duchess" taught the great playwright on the stage. The dramatic productions frequently played to a packed house.[14]

Among the most talented members of Stage and Script were English majors Cecil Willis from Rocky Mount, class of 1954, and Paul Crouch from Ellenton, South Carolina, class of 1955. Willis was the most experienced member of the dramatics club, having appeared in several Stage and Script productions while directing the Shoestring Players, Wilson's professional community

The "Duchess" directing Stage and Script. 1955 Pine Knot.

theater. Willis had also appeared in Broadway productions, won first place in the National Collegiate Playwriting Contest in the spring of 1953, and received a prestigious Morehead Scholarship for graduate study at the University of North Carolina in April 1954. Crouch was a regular cast member of Stage and Script productions between 1951 and 1955 and participated in such behind-the-scenes tasks as scenery, make-up, and publicity. He was the president of Stage and Script his senior year, a soloist in mixed chorus, and a member of Golden Knot Honor Society. Crouch also served as student director of *Heat Lightning*, a one-act murder mystery, in the spring of 1954.[15]

Stage and Script plays drew criticism occasionally when productions contained "the language of the vernacular in our society." One such presentation was Robert E. Sherwood's Pulitzer Prize winning play *Idiot's Delight*, which appeared on the Howard Chapel stage on 12–13 November 1953. The fact that a few critics called the play "trash" and "immoral" did not faze Holsworth, who did not favor censoring good writing when the content contained realism or minimal cursing. Recalling experiences with both Stage and Script and the Duchess nearly forty years later, Crouch remembered a male member of the cast panicking during rehearsal in 1954. Recognizing a word in his part of the script as a mild vulgarity, the student continued reading his lines but substituted the word "pox" for the offending four-letter word. From the back of the chapel, came the stern, admonishing tone of the Duchess's voice. "The word," she said, "is F - - T!" Today, the Duchess Trophy, awarded to the outstanding participant in dramatics, honors Holsworth who retired in 1962. Crouch also remembered that Stage and Script included mischievous individuals and free spirits, and he admitted that he had spiked drinks served on stage during the final night's performance of *Idiot's Delight*. Crouch recalled several raucous postproduction parties and remarked that the college dances held off campus during the 1950s typically featured two punch bowls, one of which was spiked.[16]

Crouch and James B. Hemby Jr. were graduates of the class of 1955 who used their English majors and experience in Stage and Script as stepping stones to teaching careers. After earning a master's degree at the University of North Carolina at Chapel Hill, Crouch returned to ACC as assistant professor of English and director of drama in 1967. He also spent summers as a member of the cast of *The Lost Colony* and earned his Ph.D. at Florida State University in 1979. Crouch retired from the faculty in 1995. Hemby, an Ayden native, double majored in English and religion and was an active member of both Stage and Script and Golden Knot Honor Society. He spent a busy senior year as editor-in-chief of *The Collegiate* and as president of the student body. After receiving a B.D. degree from Vanderbilt, Hemby joined his alma mater as director of admissions and religious life in 1959. He left to pursue graduate work at TCU in 1962, returning to ACC as assistant professor of English in 1965. Hemby succeeded Mildred Hartsock as department chairman upon her retirement in 1973, and in 1983 he became president of the college. Other 1955 graduates who served lengthy careers at ACC were Zeb Whitehurst of Farmville, who became dean of students, and Ashton Wiggs of Pine Level, who returned to ACC as assistant professor of business.[17]

While theatergoers flocked to Howard Chapel to enjoy Stage and Script productions, a drama with more serious consequences was unfolding in Asia. On 25 June 1950, six days before D. Ray Lindley became president of the college, military conflict broke out in Korea. During the following April, Arthur D. Wenger explained draft and military options to approximately seventy male students. The college had been designated as a testing center where students applying for deferments were tested in May, June, and July of 1951. The first recorded mention of a serviceman in Korea with AC College ties came in the October 1951 issue of *The Collegiate*. First Lt. Carl N. Church of Wilson, a business major in the 1930s and a veteran of World War II, was attached to the United Nations Civil Assistance Command in Korea. In November 1952, the student newspaper reported that Sergeant Joseph T. Gurganus, an alumnus and a former guard on the Bulldog football team, had been decorated for bravery in Korea. While on patrol in "no man's land, near Kumsong," on 14 June 1952, Gurganus had ignored heavy enemy fire to rescue a wounded comrade.[18]

An early and unexpected Christmas gift from Korea, which arrived at ACC in late autumn 1952, was a reminder of the sacrifices borne by American servicemen away from home. *The Collegiate* labeled the $100 check a gift from the college's "G.I. Santa Claus." A letter accompanying the check was addressed to President Lindley and the college and signed by James B. Blunk, chaplain of the 40th Infantry Division located on "Heartbreak Ridge" in Korea. Blunk wrote that each month voluntary offerings collected at religious services went to worthy causes in Korea and in the United States. He added, "We are delighted to make this small contribution to Atlantic Christian College." Reporting that the division was occupying a site on the ridge called the "Punch Bowl," the chaplain ended the letter by writing, "Our casualties are quite heavy."[19]

In an editorial examining the serious business of sending young Americans to war, the student newspaper of February 1953 noted that draft boards usually exempted students making satisfactory progress toward a college degree. The writer supported bona fide student exemptions but suggested that anyone misusing the privilege as "a hiding nest from the draft board . . . [was] an enemy of student society" and deserved punishment. Although no record was found to indicate that any student was drafted out of school and sent to Korea, Charles C. Ware estimated that approximately seventy-five students and graduates of ACC served in the Korean War. Among them, the only combat casualty was Lee E. Brinson from New Bern, who apparently volunteered for service after dropping out of school. An ACC freshman, Brinson had barely begun his studies at the college before enlisting in the armed forces in November 1952.[20]

The Korean Conflict did not dampen commencement festivities of May 1952, which also began a year-long celebration of Atlantic Christian College's fiftieth birthday. President Lindley's baccalaureate sermon at the Christian Church on Sunday morning, 25 May 1952, preceded graduation that evening. Seventy-eight seniors received diplomas during "open-air commencement exercises" on the front lawn of the college. Dr. Magruder Ellis Sadler, native of Hobucken, North Carolina, ACC alumnus, and president of Texas Christian University, served as commencement speaker. During the commencement, Lindley became only the second president of the college and the first since 1904 to award honorary degrees. The four alumni recipients and the degrees awarded were: Sadler, Doctor of Literature; Cecil Jarman, Doctor of Divinity; John Mayo Waters, Doctor of Divinity; and C. Manly Morton, Doctor of Divinity. H. Galt Braxton of Kinston, distinguished trustee of fifty-one years, and Perry Case, whose association with the college spanned thirty-six years, both received the Doctor of Laws degree. The alumni association, led by J. P. Tyndall, sold special fiftieth anniversary commemorative plates featuring a handsome drawing of the Harper doorway of Kinsey Hall, bordered by smaller drawings of campus scenes interspersed with dogwood blossoms.[21]

The college officially celebrated in the autumn with a Fiftieth Anniversary Convocation in Howard Chapel on Thursday evening, 18 September. The featured speaker, newly appointed academic dean James Moudy, would officially replace Perry Case at the end of fall semester. *The Collegiate* described the new dean as a native Texan and an ordained Christian Church minister with a wife and two young daughters. Moudy held A.B. and B.D. degrees from Texas Christian University and Duke, having won honors from the Duke school of religion and election to Phi Beta Kappa. Moudy completed his dissertation at Duke during the spring semester and received the Ph.D. degree in June 1953. The fiftieth birthday celebration would continue during homecoming weekend, which was scheduled for 17–19 October 1952 and was expected to be the largest in school history. In addition to an alumni association meeting and homecoming dance, the classes of 1912, 1922, 1932, 1942, and 1952 would hold their first anniversary reunions.[22]

The student newspaper of March 1953 also carried a letter from President Lindley explaining his decision to resign. The popular leader reported that personal interests in his native state had caused him to accept the position of administrative vice-president of Texas Christian University, effective 1 June. An editorial in the same issue expressed appreciation for Lindley's leadership and voiced surprise and regret at his resignation. Trustees appointed newly installed academic dean James Moudy as acting president and, once again, began the search for a new leader.[23]

The search ended 13 May 1953, when Travis Alden White agreed to become the college's seventh president, effective 1 August. The student newspaper reported that both Lindley and White would participate in graduation exercises, the former preaching the baccalaureate sermon on Sunday morning, 31 May, and the latter speaking at graduation in the evening. Included in the class of 1953 were Robert Frazier of Henderson, a mathematics major, member of the Golden Knot Honor Society, and president of the science club, and William E. Tucker of Greenville, an English, religion, and social studies major, member of the Golden Knot Honor Society, and president of the student body. Both young men later returned to Wilson and served their alma mater as professors and as department chairmen.[24]

D. Ray Lindley's administration, although brief, held great significance for Atlantic Christian College. Lindley's accomplishments included completing and furnishing Harper Hall in 1950 and Hardy Library in 1951. The library building honored Clarence L. Hardy, a successful Greene County farm owner and one of the school's most generous benefactors, who served on the board from 1926 to 1949. In addition to paying off the building debt and renovating Caldwell Hall, Lindley brought both vigor and an innovative style to ACC, which helped to launch the school into a new era of growth. The number of faculty holding doctoral degrees increased, and, for the first time, the college granted permanent tenure to faculty members. *The Collegiate* of May 1952 reported that the board of trustees had granted tenure to Dr. Hartsock and Dr. Hamlin, as well as to Dr. Esther Long, head of the modern languages department, and Dr. Lawrence Smith, acting head of the science department. Lindley's administration opened an evening college on campus in the autumn of 1951, providing opportunities for residents of the community who were unable to attend day classes. In 1953 the college awarded honorary degrees to the following men: Thomas J. Hackney Sr. of Wilson, chairman of the board of trustees, Doctor of Laws; F. W. Wiegmann, class of 1930, pastor of the Downey Avenue Christian Church of Indianapolis, Indiana, and trustee from 1940–43, Doctor of Divinity; and George Walter Buckner of Indianapolis, Indiana, editor of *World Call Magazine*, Doctor of Literature.[25]

During an interview in 1996, James B. Hemby Jr., a member of the sophomore class in 1953 and the tenth president of the college, recalled the administrations of D. Ray Lindley and Travis White. Hemby considered Lindley one of the college's most talented chief executives and rated White among the most eloquent speakers he had heard. Travis Alden White, a native of Shreveport, Louisiana, came to Wilson from the First Christian Church of Lubbock, Texas. An ordained Disciples minister, he held A.B. and B.D. degrees from Texas Christian University, which awarded him an honorary Doctor of Divinity degree in 1949. White and his wife, the former Evalyn May VanKeuren, a native of Dighton, Kansas, and an accomplished musician, were the parents of three children. Travis Jr. was enrolled as a science major at TCU, Ned was a fifteen-year-old student at Charles L. Coon High School, and daughter Diana was four years old. A warm and energetic man, the new president wrote a letter that was printed in the school newspaper of October 1953 challenging each

President Travis White, 1953–56. 1955 Pine Knot.

student to help him make ACC an even better school. Dr. White was formally inaugurated as the college's seventh president on 30 April 1954 in an elaborate outdoor ceremony on the front campus. Veteran Congressman Brooks Hays of Arkansas delivered a special address at a luncheon at Hardy Dining Hall, and alumnus Ira W. Langston, class of 1934, minister of the Park Avenue Christian Church in New York City, presided over the inaugural ceremonies.[26]

Among President White's main priorities at the school was the launching of a ten-year campaign to raise $2 million for construction and renovation of buildings. In March 1954, he announced that the first $100,000 had been pledged toward a new science building and an infirmary. Trustees had also approved restoration plans for the chapel and dining hall to begin immediately. When students returned from spring break, renovations were in progress on the chapel, and the college had moved two houses from Gold Street in preparation for ground breaking for the science building. The school had sold two additional houses on Gold Street that would be moved to allow construction of an infirmary. At a meeting called to consider new construction on the campus, the faculty and staff had voted in favor "of having a functional type-building instead of the traditional Georgian type now prevailing on campus." While the vote allowed planning and building to proceed, the decision to open the way for functional structures of varied styles and designs remained controversial nearly half a century later. Perhaps anticipating such controversy, a word of caution arose from Cove City freshman Elaine Mitchell, who wrote to *The Collegiate* in April 1954. Mitchell stated, "Lest we go overboard for the 'Functional,' something else has been added to our campus for sheer beauty. There are two new sugar maple trees and a new fir tree. On the west side of the White House is a new rose garden."[27]

In the opinion of many students and ACC supporters, the building most in need of renovation or replacement was the gymnasium. Since dropping football in 1951, Bulldog athletic fans were left with intercollegiate competition in only basketball and baseball. Touch football became extremely popular on the campus, especially among fraternity men and residents of Caldwell Hall, and *The Collegiate* diligently published game results and team standings. For rabid fans, however, the most attractive sport at AC College was basketball, and, despite several consecutive losing seasons, spectators continued to pack the gymnasium. At the opening home game of the 1953–54 season, many fans had to be turned away because of insufficient seating. Jim Peebles, a junior from Raleigh and sports editor of *The Collegiate*, called for a new gym. Despite two earlier renovations that had enlarged the capacity of the Wilson Gym, the need for additional seats was so great that the home game with East Carolina, scheduled for 20 February 1954, was moved to the Elm City High School gym. That gymnasium was located only seven miles from the campus and offered a significantly larger seating capacity. Later, perhaps during a slow news time, Peebles also suggested that since so many schools were called Bulldogs, a new nickname might be in order. Two names that sprang to his mind were "Crusaders" and "Hurricanes." Had he waited a few months, until the autumn of 1954, an unwelcome visitor named "Hazel" would have rendered the latter suggestion particularly appropriate.[28]

Jack McComas, a native of Indiana and star on three strong North Carolina State teams coached by Everett Case in the 1940s, was hired in 1951 to build a Bulldog team that would be competitive within the North State Conference. McComas's first ACC team had promising athletes but little experience. Senior Jay Clark and sophomore Gilbert Ferrell, local favorites who had starred at Charles L. Coon High School, were practically the only experienced players. The new coach and his young team suffered through a "character building" season, losing nineteen of twenty-one games, many by lopsided scores. An interesting road trip at the start of the season against Presbyterian College was a match between former NC State Wolfpack stars and teammates, coaches McComas and Norman Sloan. Sloan's veteran cagers proved too strong for the Bulldogs and won two games handily. North State Conference competition also proved difficult for the Bulldogs, who continued a string of fifteen consecutive conference losses with an 84–62 defeat at East Carolina.[29]

McComas, serving double duty as baseball coach, had little time to regroup before discovering that North State Conference diamond teams were also strong. The Bulldogs struggled through an early schedule which brought two losses to arch rival East Carolina and left the Bohunk in Greenville. McComas' team refused to quit, however, rallying behind the pitching of Gilbert Ferrell to win the last two games against the Pirates. A proud sports writer boasted that ACC had brought the revered bucket "home, 'where it belongs.'" Bold headlines carried on the sports pages of *The Collegiate* in May 1952 voiced satisfaction likely felt across the campus: BOHUNK STAYS HERE FOR SUMMER.[30]

The large crowds that continued to fill Wilson Gymnasium early in the 1952–53 basketball season witnessed a quicker and more competitive Bulldog team, but one which won only six victories against sixteen defeats. In the autumn of 1953, McComas welcomed the arrival of ten freshmen, including John Marley from Franklinville, Bill Tomlinson from Wilson, and Billy Widgeon from Newport. In addition, junior Ronald Percise of Goldsboro transferred to ACC from Campbell Junior College. They joined veterans Jim Peebles, Bill Beacham from Rocky Mount, and Jerry Williams of Fuquay Springs to give the Bulldogs a taller and more talented squad. Big John Marley was six feet, eleven inches tall and Bill Beacham was six feet, seven inches.[31]

The 1953–54 team compiled an overall record of eighteen victories against nine defeats and a conference mark of eleven wins and eight losses. For the first time, ACC won two games in the conference tournament while also setting a new scoring record in a 100–74 win over Catawba. The Bulldogs whipped powerful Lenoir Rhyne, 77–73, before losing the final game at Lexington to East Carolina by 86–75. Local fans followed the team to Lexington and provided enthusiastic support throughout the tournament. Wilson's pride in the Bulldogs reaching the championship game brought Mayor John D. Wilson, an alumnus of the class of 1934, to present the team with a key to the city.[32]

Faculty and staff enthusiastically joined the basketball spirit sweeping the campus in the 1950s, supporting the team and participating in faculty-student games. On 24 March 1953, a team led by "Pro" Tomlinson and including such stars as "Butch" Hartsock, "Hotshot" Holsworth, and Mildred Ross won a thrilling contest against the Women's Athletic Association. In the men's game that followed, the faculty team of "sharp shooting" McComas, Milton Adams, Russell Arnold, John Dunn, Jim Fulghum, and "Speedy" Smith almost emerged victorious before the students rallied to win. During the following spring, a packed gymnasium was the scene for a junior-faculty game that ended in another narrow victory for the students.[33]

The Women's Athletic Association (WAA), led by a student athletic cabinet and the director of physical education, provided opportunities for co-eds to engage in healthful living and develop leadership skills while participating in intramural sports and recreational activities. The WAA also presented opportunities for competition at "Play Day" events in basketball, volleyball, and tennis on campuses at Greensboro College and East Carolina. "Play Day" competition served as a prelude to the arrival of full-fledged women's intercollegiate athletic programs during the next decade. Rebecca Tomlinson, a native of Black Creek, joined the faculty in 1951 as an instructor in physical education and helped develop the WAA, which changed its name to the Women's Recreational Association (WRA) in the autumn of 1955. Ed Cloyd's arrival in September 1953 also brought changes in the college's physical education department and contributed to the growth of women's athletics on campus. A Raleigh native with degrees from Davidson and UNC-Chapel Hill, Cloyd served as professor in the physical education department until retiring in 1984. Tomlinson, Sarah Bain Ward, and Ed and Ann Cloyd accompanied the women athletes to "Play Day" events, serving as coaches and chaperones.[34]

Coach Cloyd made plans to revive the ACC tennis team in the autumn of 1954, as growing excitement over the approaching basketball season enveloped the campus. The Bulldogs' success in reaching the conference tournament the previous March and the knowledge that most of the team would return created great anticipation for the approaching season. During the summer, workers had renovated the gymnasium, increasing seating capacity to approximately 1,200 and adding a new lighting system that prompted students to brag that their facility was one of the better gyms in the conference. Among the most popular new features was a "colorful bulldog" image painted in the center circle at midcourt by art professor Russell Arnold. The college's purchase of a new activity bus, painted ACC blue and white, brought a headline in *The Collegiate* boasting "Dogs Ride in Style."[35]

In early November, the college showcased the team to the fans at a special pregame event for the Century Club, a group of local businessmen who supported ACC athletics. Coaching legend Everett Case of North Carolina State was the featured speaker at the initial banquet of the club and remained for the blue-white game. Wilson's basketball fans eagerly awaited the season-opening game with Lynchburg College scheduled for homecoming weekend.[36]

Homecoming 1954 was one of the most successful in AC College history, starting with a huge pep rally led by the cheerleaders on Thursday evening. Friday's events included an elaborate parade along Nash Street featuring the college marching band, cheerleaders, several visiting bands, homecoming queen contestants, and eleven floats representing the classes and various clubs. Homecoming queen Judy Lane, a freshman from Wendell, was crowned at half time of the basketball game, which featured a rousing Bulldog victory over Lynchburg by a score of 104–71. Saturday's activities included an alumni association luncheon, tours of campus buildings, and a homecoming ball in Hardy Dining Hall featuring music by *The Dreamers*, a dance band group of the college band.[37]

After losing away games to Presbyterian and Erskine, the Bulldogs won twelve of their next thirteen games and ended the regular season with an overall record of seventeen victories and six defeats and a conference mark of sixteen and three. Entering the conference tournament as the second-seeded team, they defeated High Point and top-seeded Lenoir Rhyne to claim the school's first North State Conference championship. Guard Billy Widgeon was named most valuable player and joined center John Marley on the all-tournament first team. Forward Jerry Williams won second team honors, and forward Kim Buchanan and guard Ronald Percise gained honorable mention designation. One of the team's most loyal fans also received a special honor at Lexington. The college had surprised Mildred Ross on Saturday morning with a sixtieth birthday party in the president's office featuring cake and coffee and a corsage for the honoree. On Saturday evening, in Lexington's YMCA gymnasium as fans waited for the championship game to begin, "Miss Mildred" received a second surprise. President White summoned her from the crowd to join him at courtside where, in front of bleachers filled with hyper Wilson fans, he presented her with a gold wristwatch. *The Collegiate* noted that the gift came from students, faculty, and staff in appreciation for Ross's thirty-four years of dedicated service to the college. Around ten o'clock that evening, excited fans stormed the court to join happy players, coaches, and cheerleaders in a victory celebration. The newspaper wrote, "Miss Mildred felt sure they'd won the tournament as a birthday gift to her."[38]

The 1954–55 championship basketball team. 1955 Pine Knot.

The Bulldogs added to their championship victories two more wins over conference foes East Carolina and Lenoir Rhyne for the District 26 championship and a trip to Kansas City and the National Association of Intercollegiate Athletics (NAIA) tournament. In winning a trip to the national tournament, the ACC Bulldogs defeated every opponent on their schedule at least once, a school record which still stands. Their first contest in Kansas City was with Evansville College of Indiana. After receiving a pep talk from legendary professional star George Mikan the night before the game, the Bulldogs defeated Evansville 95–88. Powerful Arkansas Polytechnic Institute brought an end to ACC's sensational season and to their stay in Kansas City by defeating the Bulldogs 93–74. The Kansas City trip was a memorable experience for players, coaches, and fans, and the excitement was shared by fans back home through radio broadcasts over Wilson station WVOT. Wilson welcomed its team home with praise, banners, and banquets. While congratulating the team for an outstanding season and for positive publicity for ACC and Wilson, *The Collegiate* also praised the support of the fans. The newspaper stated that "Wilsonians have shown their appreciation by showering honor upon honor and meal upon meal upon meal on the 'Champs.'"[39]

As memories of the banner basketball season began to fade, members of the class of 1955 thought of graduation and the future as well as of their past four years as college students. The school had changed while they adjusted to two presidents and one acting president between the fall of 1951 and midspring 1955. A successful evening program now offered classes on each weeknight, plus sessions on Saturday mornings and afternoons. The student body had increased between their freshman and senior years by over 20 percent with regular enrollment up from 410 to 495 students. The faculty-staff had grown and changed as senior members retired and younger scholars brought new ideas, which included creation of a dean's list.[40]

Among the more popular changes on campus were the new dancing classes added to the physical education curriculum. The college hired Gene Barnes to teach dancing classes in the recreation room of Harper Hall during spring semester 1955. Beginning in early February, Barnes taught a variety of dance styles on Tuesday and Thursday nights, including the foxtrot, jitterbug, mambo, rumba, tango, and waltz. A feature article in *The Collegiate* of April 1955 carried the heading, "Come, And Trip It As Ye Go, On The Light Fantastic Toe." The newspaper saluted Barnes for enhancing social life on campus and added that "With this enjoyment comes poise, self-confidence, and improvement in posture which carry over into other phases of life." The classes were considered so successful that Barnes was retained as adjunct instructor in dancing through the remainder of the decade.[41]

Additional changes included new uniforms and instruments for a revitalized marching band. Reorganized in 1953 by Millard Burt, professor of education and band director, the improved band rapidly became an asset to the college and the community. Drum major Richard Ziglar and majorettes Annie Morris Barnes, Jo Ann Crumpler, Joan Edwards, and Nettie Sue Phillips made an impressive sight as they led the Atlantic Christian College marching band along Nash Street in homecoming parades and through downtown Wilmington during the Azalea Festival. The forty-five-member band also added to the pomp and pageantry of President Travis White's inauguration. Dr. Burt, class of 1938, had first organized an ACC band as a student. He later directed army bands in Europe and the United States during World War II and, subsequently, the Raleigh municipal band. The Wilson Kiwanis Club recognized the band's value to the community and generously provided new uniforms for the group.[42]

The Chamber of Commerce Day held on Tuesday, 12 April 1955, demonstrated that a new appreciation existed between the college and Wilson business leaders. Members of the faculty and the championship basketball team officially welcomed approximately 100 members of the chamber to the campus. Photographs in *The Collegiate* show President White and trustee chairman T. J.

Hackney Sr. greeting Moseley Hussey, chamber of commerce president, and Harold Seburn, chairman of the chamber's college cooperative committee. Following lunch and a band concert, the guests toured campus buildings, including the $250,000 science building then under construction, and met in Howard Chapel to discuss mutual interests shared by the college and the community.[43]

The college also welcomed the new technology of television to campus during the 1950s. Caldwell Hall residents purchased a Westinghouse television for their parlor and installed the set themselves. The young men enjoyed relaxing in pajamas and robes while watching their own TV instead of having to dress and go elsewhere to see entertaining and educational programs. Students could also watch their colleagues and teachers perform on the new medium. The ACC mixed chorus appeared in a half-hour program on station WNCT, Greenville, in May 1954, and students joined faculty and alumni in presenting an hour-long program over WUNC-TV, Chapel Hill, in March 1955. Mrs. Edward Rider, the former star of stage and screen Mary Ann Matthews and the wife of an assistant professor of social science, organized the latter program, assisted by Paul Crouch who also served as master of ceremonies. Mrs. Rider had taught dramatics at Sam Houston State Teachers College in Huntsville, Texas, before coming to Wilson. By May 1955, the college was presenting a half-hour program each Wednesday morning over WNCT.[44]

The most important day of the 1954–55 academic year, graduation day, arrived Sunday, 29 May 1955. Sixty-two seniors were featured guests at one of the college's most elaborate commencement ceremonies. Former graduates joined the alumni reception Saturday evening and were invited to remain for the graduation ball on the Harper Hall terrace. In addition to the graduating seniors, the college recognized three distinguished men with honorary degrees: George F. Cuthrell, Doctor of Divinity; Amos C. Dawson, Doctor of Laws; and Howard S. Hilley, Doctor of Laws. A native of Pamlico County and minister of the First Christian Church of Brunswick, Georgia, Cuthrell had served as a Disciples preacher for over half a century. Dawson, class of 1937, was former president of the North Carolina Education Association and principal of Southern Pines High School. Hilley had previously received an honorary doctorate from Transylvania University. The presentations brought the number of honorary degrees awarded by Travis White to a total of five. In 1954, he had bestowed the Doctor of Divinity degree upon Ira Wright Langston, trustee and alumnus, class of 1933, and the degree of Doctor of Literature upon Charles Crossfield Ware.[45]

Preparing the college to serve the future while honoring the past, the board of trustees had approved groundbreaking ceremonies for a new classroom building. Current and former faculty participated in the symbolic shoveling of earth, which occurred Sunday afternoon prior to graduation. Perry Case, dean emeritus, directed the ceremony. A concert by the college band and chorus, led by Dr. Burt, was followed by graduation at 5:00 PM. Chief marshal Mary Hadge of Wilson and marshals representing each class led the commencement procession. The graduation speaker was Lloyd Griffin of Raleigh, head of the North Carolina Citizens' Association. The pomp and pageantry, which complemented the formal presentation ceremony, brought an end to graduation day 1955 and culminated one of the most significant years in the college's history.[46]

TWELVE

The Cotton Still Grows

PRESIDENTIAL POLITICS, featuring campaign posters and buttons with slogans including "I Like Ike," dominated the national news media as the college welcomed a new freshman class in September 1956. The 204 members of Atlantic Christian College's class of 1960 would reach adulthood in an age of economic prosperity and domestic tranquility often associated with the presidency of Dwight D. Eisenhower. Affectionately known as "Ike," the popular World War II hero and grandfather figure became the symbol of America during the post–Korean War era. Most of ACC's new and returning students, who boosted the school's enrollment total above four figures for the first time, were yet to reach voting age and may have held little interest in elections or party politics. They were more anxious to gather with classmates at Tweetie's for snacks and conversation, to enjoy the raucous atmosphere of Wilson Gymnasium basketball games, and to join in the intriguing and cliquish social life offered by fraternities and sororities. College students of the mid-1950s were also highly motivated, anxious to improve their leadership skills and compile strong resumes that would help them attain career goals. Many students arrived on campus with strong religious backgrounds and sought new opportunities for spiritual growth. For the 1,045 members of the college's 1956–57 student body and for the faculty and staff greeting their arrival, the next few years would prove both challenging and memorable.[1]

The freshman class of 1956 also became the first entering class in Barton College history to graduate from a regionally accredited college. The school had begun the lengthy process of fulfilling the academically rigorous accreditation standards required by the Southern Association of Colleges and Secondary Schools (SACS) during D. Ray Lindley's tenure as president. President Travis White and Dean James Moudy led continuing efforts to gain accreditation. In early October 1955, an inspection committee visited ACC to determine the school's progress toward meeting SACS standards. In late November, White and Moudy flew to Miami to meet with officials and complete the five-year accreditation process. *The Wilson Daily Times* of 2 December 1955 carried a large photograph of the smiling ACC leaders, accompanied by headlines announcing that Atlantic Christian College's recently acquired accreditation status ranked the institution with the leading colleges in the South. President White labeled the feat "the greatest single step taken by the college since it was established 54 years ago."[2]

According to the *North Carolina Christian* and *The Wilson Daily Times*, the college's new status would also make ACC eligible for Ford Foundation grants to increase faculty salaries. Low faculty pay, one of several weaknesses identified in the SACS report, required immediate attention. Other cited problems included inadequate endowment, insufficient faculty size, the deteriorated condition of the physical plant, and inadequate space for expansion. The newspapers commented that the current building program on the campus, with both an infirmary and a science building nearing completion and new classroom and administration buildings under construction, had helped influence SACS officials to grant accreditation.[3]

Buoyant spirits produced by the positive SACS report were diminished in May 1956 upon President White's resignation. He informed trustees and the college community of his acceptance of an offer to become president of Midwestern University in Wichita Falls, Texas, effective 15 July. Supporters of both the college and the Disciples Church expressed regret at the popular leader's decision and praised his accomplishments. During White's three-year tenure, enrollment had nearly doubled, and the $2 million building campaign had made steady progress. The board of trustees named James M. Moudy acting president for a second time and launched a search for a new college leader.[4]

While presiding over graduation ceremonies on 3 June, White presented four honorary degrees, including a Doctor of Laws to Samuel F. Freeman Jr., who preached the baccalaureate sermon. An alumnus of the class of 1933 and a loyal supporter of his alma mater, Freeman was pastor of the First Christian Church of Winchester, Kentucky. Another special feature of graduation exercises was the dedication of the $275,000 science and mathematics building in honor of Lawrence A. Moye of Maury, a trustee of the college from 1950–84. Some of the crowd of approximately 2,000 people toured the new infirmary building, later named in honor of Mr. and Mrs. Don E. Lee of Arapahoe, friends and benefactors of the college. Visitors likely also noted the new classroom and administration buildings nearing completion in preparation for the beginning of fall term.[5]

The structure eliciting the greatest reaction from campus visitors during late spring and early summer 1956 was Kinsey Hall, the only building older than the college itself. Built as Kinsey Seminary and the center of Atlantic Christian College life for over half a century, Old Kinsey was demolished between April and July. Everyone enrolled at the college between 1902 and 1955—more than 10,000 students—had attended classes in the venerable structure. In dire need of repairs for some time, the upper floors of the building had been closed off for nearly three years, leaving only first-floor classrooms and a few faculty offices in continued use. A photograph in the July 1956 issue of *North Carolina Christian* shows the skeletal frame of the building and the tower awaiting demolition. The white marble crescent which once crowned the front entrance, containing the college name and founding date, was preserved along with bricks to be used in building a new house for the college president. Members of the Kinsey family joined President James B. Hemby Jr. in unveiling a plaque marking the former site of Kinsey Hall during Founders' Day ceremonies on 1 May 2000.[6]

A concrete terrace was the lone remaining remnant of Kinsey Hall when upperclassmen joined the class of 1960 on the campus in September 1956. Expeditious work by the search committee also enabled newly appointed president Arthur D. Wenger to join students, faculty, and staff at the opening of fall semester. The first issue of the student newspaper for the 1956–57 academic year featured photographs of Dr. Wenger and the new student body president, senior Charles E. "Chuck" Hester of Greensboro. The October issue of *The Collegiate* also contained a photograph of the newly completed classroom building accompanied by an article proclaiming that a different atmosphere prevailed at ACC with four new buildings opening for the first time. The two structures described as "real gone" were the administration building, which was air-conditioned, and the classroom building, which was designed to accommodate 1,500 students but provided actual seating space for 850. The enlarged campus seemed appropriate for AC College's new status as a successful, fully accredited institution.[7]

The college's eighth president, a native of Aberdeen, Idaho, held a B.A. degree from Bethel College in Newton, Kansas, and a B.D. and honorary L.L.D. from Texas Christian University. During World War II, Wenger had served as a chaplain with United States Army combat units in Austria, Germany, Belgium, and Luxembourg. He later became director of special promotions and

A college institution, "Tweetie" Etheridge in his restaurant. Inlay is one of Tweetie's advertisements in the Pine Knot. *1967* Pine Knot.

religious activities at TCU and served as pastor of Disciples churches in Pennsylvania and Texas. He and his wife, the former Doris Kellenbarger of Newton, Kansas, were the parents of three boys, Arthur Frank, aged nine; Jon Michael, six; and Mark Randolph, 3. The family had lived in Wilson earlier when Wenger served as assistant to President D. Ray Lindley from 1950–52.[8]

While the Wenger family settled into their new home on West Vance Street in the autumn of 1956, ACC students attended class and socialized at Tweetie's, a favorite college hangout across Lee Street from Harper Hall, opened in 1947 by Norman "Tweetie" Etheridge, class of 1937. Etheridge became a legendary figure on campus during the 1950s. Students filled the booths and bar stools for morning coffee, lunch, and late evening snacks; to finish homework assignments; and to catch up on campus gossip. Professors and administrators also frequented the booths, discussing academic concerns, evaluating the most recent production of Stage and Script, or discussing Bulldog basketball with colleagues and students over coffee or a soda. Sarah Bain Ward recalled that Harper Hall women, restricted to the dorm after dinner, looked forward each evening to their thirty-minute "Tweetie Break," a campus tradition of the 1950s and 1960s. It was not uncommon for students to list "Homecoming, Bohunkus, and Tweetie" among their most enduring memories of college life. Etheridge's outgoing personality, love of people, and intimate knowledge of nearly every student endeared him to the college community. *The Rocky Mount Evening Telegram* in the autumn of 1956 described Tweetie's as an essential part of college life. Etheridge's willingness to listen to students' problems and dispense advice enabled him to fill "a position at Atlantic Christian College as important as that of any official on campus." Years later, President James B. Hemby Jr. called Etheridge "the Tony Tilley of his day," comparing Tweetie to the college's popular director of food services of the late twentieth and early twenty-first centuries.[9]

Conversations at Tweetie's during the early fall semester of 1956 undoubtedly focused on the status of a new student union, which college leaders occasionally mentioned and students had anticipated more eagerly than any structure since completion of the gymnasium in 1934. On Friday morning, 2 November, President Wenger cut a ribbon, officially opening the school's first student union. Designed by art professor Russell Arnold and featuring modern furniture donated by the alumni association, the union occupied a large part of the refurbished basement of Hardy Dining Hall. Students reacted positively to the brightly painted union, which featured bridge tables and chairs, a television, and, the most popular attraction, a soda fountain. Naming their new union the "Bohunk," students considered it one of the most attractive places on campus. The college invited Tweetie Etheridge to manage the soda shop area of the union and left the decision of hiring student help to his discretion. Sliding doors separated the student union from new offices for the dean of women and the dean of men. The relocation of the college bookstore and the post office to the area made the Hardy basement one of the busiest sites on campus. Joe Hardegree, coeditor of *The Collegiate*, pointed out that the building now provided students with all their needs, adding that a freshman boy allegedly spent an entire week in Hardy Hall, emerging only three hours each day to attend classes.[10]

The growth and changing status of the Greek organizations produced the greatest change in social life at ACC during the 1950s. Having first appeared on the campus in 1925 with the organization of Phi Kappa Alpha and Sigma Alpha, fraternities and sororities had gradually replaced the literary societies as centers of student activity during the 1940s. By 1957–58, two additional fraternities, Phi Delta Gamma and Sigma Rho Phi, had been added, along with four sororities—Delta Sigma, Omega Chi, Phi Sigma Tau, and Sigma Tau Chi. Of the eight early Greek organizations, only Sigma Phi Epsilon and Alpha Sigma Phi remain on the campus in the twenty-first century. Although critics insisted that fraternities were cliquish and undemocratic and undermined the spirit of campus unity, supporters of the Greek organizations won the argument. They answered that sororities and fraternities created enthusiasm and provided opportunities for competition, which encouraged individuals and groups to develop important skills.[11]

Prior to the spring of 1958, all of ACC's sororities and fraternities remained local organizations that had not attempted to attain national affiliation. Between March 1958, when trustees permitted Greeks to join national groups, and February 1959, all four fraternities formed national affiliations. Phi Kappa Alpha became the first to go national, becoming a part of Delta Sigma Phi in March 1958. The following month, Sigma Rho Phi became Sigma Phi Epsilon, and Sigma Alpha joined Alpha Sigma Phi. Finally, in January 1959, Phi Delta Gamma, the remaining ACC fraternity, became nationally affiliated with Sigma Phi. In November 1959, ACC was represented for the first time at a meeting of the National Interfraternity Council held in New York City. Sigma Phi Epsilon member Bob Collins, fraternity-sorority editor of *The Collegiate* and a junior from Miami, Florida, wrote in February 1959 that national affiliation brought an increased spirit of rivalry between the Greek organizations which was demonstrated in intramural competition. He noted that nationalization also heightened a determination to enhance each chapter's image, resulting in movement into new houses and the creation of large signs for front yards. By the spring of 1959, all ACC fraternities had their own houses. Among sororities, which had not become nationally affiliated, only Phi Sigma Tau had a house.[12]

Greek events received increased coverage in *The Collegiate* and *Pine Knot* during the 1950s and 1960s, including rush and pledge activities, stag parties, beach trips, intramural athletic rankings, and service projects. Omega Chi sorority and Sigma Phi Epsilon fraternity were winners of what was, apparently, the college's first Greek sing in the autumn of 1961. Most importantly, fraternities and sororities sponsored a variety of popular dances, including the informal annual Harvest Dance, given by Sigma Tau Chi; the Top Hat Dance, a semiformal affair held each fall by Phi Sigma Tau; and the Ring Dance, a semiformal event sponsored by Omega Chi each January. The interfraternity council sponsored larger dances, frequently featuring expensive, big-name bands and orchestras such as the Glenn Miller Band directed by Ray McKinley which played at the Wilson Recreation Center in November 1960. The bands of Woody Herman and Tommy Dorsey also played at homecoming and at large fraternity, sorority, and class-sponsored dances.[13]

The Christmas Dance, December 1951. 1952 Pine Knot.

The interfraternity council replaced the Panhellenic council as the governing body of ACC's Greek organizations in 1959. In February 1959, the college newspaper noted that Greeks held most of the top offices on campus, including the four top offices of the Cooperative Association and the office of president of each class except the freshman class. In addition, the presidency of the Golden Knot Honor Society and the editorship of *The Collegiate* were both held by James Bishop, a senior from Philadelphia and president of Sigma Phi Epsilon. An editor of the college newspaper for the 1959–60 academic year argued that a grasp for power by Greek organizations endangered the unity which had traditionally characterized Atlantic Christian College. The writer, who was not identified, judged the Greeks' goal of creating "a completely autonomous system of fraternity and sorority" governance, without any interference from the faculty or staff, to be short-sighted, divisive, and detrimental to the overall well-being of the college. The coeditors of *The Collegiate* of 1959–60 were senior religion majors Robert "Tarzan" Collins, a member of Sigma Phi Epsilon, and Ralph Messick, vice-president of Campus Christian Association.[14]

While the Greek chapters experienced dramatic growth upon the ACC campus during the 1950s and early 1960s, other clubs also thrived. Stage and

Script, Golden Knot Honor Society, band and chorus, Student National Education Association, science club, young Democrats club, and young Republicans club all continued to be active. Relatively new organizations included the accounting club, the business club, Sigma Pi Alpha (an honorary language fraternity), the English club, Circle K, the political science club, the physical education club, and the weight-lifting club.[15]

While unable to match the dramatic growth of fraternities and sororities, the discipline most involved with serious study of the ancient Greeks maintained its steady influence upon the college. Religious studies and activities remained central to the college's educational and cultural mission. Presidents of the school continued to be ordained Disciples ministers and maintained active associations with Christian churches. D. Ray Lindley in 1950 was the first president who did not hold faculty rank or teach religion classes. James Moudy, the second highest administrator as academic dean, held a dual appointment as professor of religion during the administrations of Lindley, White, and Wenger. When Moudy left to become dean of the graduate school at TCU, effective 1 February 1957, Randall B. Cutlip, dean of student life became dean of the college. Cutlip's appointment marked the first time that neither the president nor the dean of the college held faculty rank. Neither Cutlip nor Millard Burt, who followed Cutlip, in 1958, held divinity degrees although both were graduates of Disciples colleges. The main reason the chief academic officer became a full-time administrator was likely the college's tremendous enrollment growth. Between 1956 and 1959, regular student enrollment increased from 683 to 1,219 students. With the opening of fall term in 1960, the student body grew to 1,400 students, as the increase topped 100 percent.[16]

The *North Carolina Christian* reported that the college expected to enroll seventy-three students in 1957 who planned careers in full-time religious service, an increase of 16 percent above the previous year. Forty-eight of the religion majors were Disciples, an increase of 41 percent above the 1955–56 academic year. Allan R. Sharp, acting chairman of the department of religion and philosophy, reported that student preachers served churches throughout eastern North Carolina during the 1956–57 academic year, ministering to thirty-seven congregations in seventeen counties. Also, during the summer of 1957, thirty-one ACC graduates and thirteen members of the faculty and staff, including President Wenger, served sixty-five Christian churches, 51 percent of Disciples churches in the state. Wenger commented that the college felt privileged to serve area churches, both to assist congregations without pastors and to provide vacation time for ministers. The religion and philosophy department also established an annual two-day Christian Vocations Conference on the campus in order to demonstrate available church-related service opportunities to Disciples of high school age. The department's goal was to enroll 100 full-time Christian Service students by 1960. While that goal was not reached, in the autumn of 1960 the number of religion majors increased to seventy-nine, forty-two of whom were Disciples. Editors of *The Collegiate* lauded the college's commitment to attract and educate church leaders of the future.[17]

In addition to serving Disciples churches and religion majors, ACC continued to offer an impressive array of religious organizations and programs for the student body. Main goals of the Student Christian Association (SCA) included reminding the campus of God's presence through chapel programs and serving as sponsor of Religious Emphasis Week. The latter event, a complete week devoted to religious activities, brought notable speakers to the campus and provided sermons, discussion groups, and other programs focusing on such themes as "Fulfilling the Christian Dream" and "The Master Among Us." The Campus Christian Association, which replaced the SCA, brought alumnus and former missionary C. Manly Morton to the college as featured speaker for Religious Emphasis Week in the autumn of 1958.[18]

The most controversial Religious Emphasis Week, occurring 17–21 April 1961, apparently was also the most memorable. In publicizing the event, the campus newspaper noted that attendance was mandatory for morning chapel sessions, Monday–Friday, and urged students to attend evening activities which promised to blend dramatic, musical, and artistic interpretation with discussion group sessions. The Campus Christian Association cabinet had adopted "God is Dead" as its theme with the goal of stimulating the college community to examine the thesis that God was dead because modern society excluded Him from its institutions and individuals closed Him out of their hearts. The event featured Dr. Robert W. Funk, a thirty-five-year-old Indiana native, Disciples preacher, and professor of New Testament at the Theological School of Drew University in Madison, New Jersey. Funk held degrees from Butler and Vanderbilt Universities and had taught at TCU and Harvard Divinity School. His lectures blended modern scholarship from a variety of disciplines in presenting a contemporary view of Christianity. The impact of Religious Emphasis Week of April 1961 apparently succeeded in stimulating moderates and liberals but alarmed conservatives. Three issues of *The Collegiate* devoted extended coverage to the controversial sessions, providing the assertion that the result of the week's impact was "to throw the campus into a mild state of shock." The newspaper's editorials and surveys argued that the event had resulted in causing negative publicity beyond the campus but had provided a valuable experience on the campus itself.[19]

Campus Christian Association represented an intent to spread the Christian faith throughout the campus. Every student on campus was automatically a member of CCA and each religious denomination was represented on the cabinet, which was elected by the student body. CCA sometimes cooperated with other groups in presenting programs, including a venture with the science department to produce "What About This Monkey Business," an interdisciplinary discussion of evolution. Presented at the Alpha Sigma Phi fraternity house, J. P. Tyndall, science department chairman, was the featured speaker for the event. CCA also joined Stage and Script to organize and produce dramatic presentations prior to the Christmas holidays. Two additional campus religious organizations, Christian Service Workshop and Campus Ministerial Association, typically appealed to and served religion majors preparing for careers as ministers or directors of religious education.[20]

Examination of religious affiliations among the 1,198 students entering Barton College's sixtieth year in the autumn of 1961 showed Baptists leading with 370 students, Methodists second with 244, and Disciples third with 208 students. Ninety Presbyterians and seventy-four Free Will Baptists completed the top five religious sects represented on campus. The ecumenical nature of the school encouraged Baptist students to form their own denominational club, a Baptist Student Union, which met initially at Wilson's First Baptist Church in November 1959. Presbyterian students, with encouragement from CCA, followed the Baptists' lead by announcing plans to organize their own fellowship in November 1960.[21]

Although the number of graduates from the department of religion and philosophy remained consistent during the late 1950s and early 1960s, graduates in other disciplines surged ahead. Business and accounting majors rose to second place, following education graduates of 1960, 1961, and 1962. Within those three classes, education graduates numbered 163; business administration and accounting majors totaled 103; physical education, 54; science, 46; history, 41; and religion, 38. Expanding professional opportunities in education, business, and recreation fields continued to change patterns in college and university programs. Religion, which had led literary and music majors in numbers of ACC graduates during the early twentieth century, held sixth place in the early 1960s, slightly ahead of math and English graduates. These figures are based on the listing of majors among graduating seniors in the college yearbooks for 1960, 1961, and 1962.[22]

Additional areas of the college that felt the changing impact of economic and political forces included presidential inaugurations and commencement events. The keynote speaker at Arthur Daniel Wenger's inauguration, 3 May 1957, was Luther H. Hodges, governor of North Carolina. In addition to representatives from various colleges, universities, and professional organizations, important guests included John D. Larkins, chairman of the executive committee of the state Democratic Party and later associate justice of the North Carolina Supreme Court. Dr. Harlie L. Smith, president of the board of higher education of the Christian Church, issued the presidential charge to Dr. Wenger. Thomas J. Hackney, chairman of the board of trustees, presided over the luncheon, and Millard Burt, president of the alumni association, presided over the inaugural ceremony.[23]

Wenger presided over commencement on 2 June 1957, the first of many graduations to be held on the terrace of the new classroom building. The college president also preached the baccalaureate sermon at the First Christian Church. Dr. William A. Archie, dean of Wake Forest College, delivered the commencement address. In addition to conferring degrees upon ninety-nine seniors, the college honored former President D. Ray Lindley with the honorary degree of Doctor of Laws.[24]

Graduates in the class of 1957 included John Marley, a social science and physical education major, and Billy Widgeon, a math and physical education major. For the past four years, they had played prominent roles in determining the college's basketball fortunes. A second championship to match the one of 1954–55 did not happen, but the 1955-56 team compiled an overall record of 19–7 and 12–4 in the conference, good enough for second place. The team extended its home court winning streak to thirty-two games and Marley's forty-seven points against Western Carolina was the highest individual mark in the state that season. The 1956–57 year brought a lower, but still respectable, 16–10 overall record and a fourth place finish in the conference with a 10–6 mark. Particularly satisfying to Bulldog fans were the three basketball victories over the East Carolina Pirates to retain possession of the Bohunk. Widgeon and Marley later were inducted into the Barton College Athletic Hall of Fame. Jack McComas' 1957–58 team looked forward to playing home games in Wilson's new Recreation Center, and the coach would later join players from his 1955 championship team in the college's Athletic Hall of Fame.[25]

Between 1955 and 1961 the college added three new sports, bringing the number of teams competing in intercollegiate athletics to six. Track joined basketball, baseball, and tennis in April 1956, and golf and cross-country were both added in September 1957. While the teams usually struggled to compete in the North State Conference, the cross-country team managed to go undefeated in its initial season, partly a result of coach Gordon E. "Sam" Coker's wise decision not to overschedule. In an event that local sports writers described as providing great thrills for Bulldog fans, ACC's initial cross-country team made its debut with a 25–30 victory over the favored harriers of East Carolina. Students watching the race at Wilson's Recreation Park cheered as the Bulldog runners captured three of the first five places in their only match of the 1957 season. The college also expanded the size of its athletic fields in December 1957 with the purchase of the Corbett Tract. Measuring some 388 feet by 361 feet, the field was located behind a row of houses facing Corbett Avenue and along Gold Park Road.[26]

Milton Adams served as business manager and director of athletics during the period of expansion before Ed Cloyd assumed the latter post in the autumn of 1961. Cloyd oversaw a program that included coaches McComas and Coker, as well as Frank Montgomery, assistant in basketball and baseball, and tennis coach Ronald Hyatt. Competing for a spot on the Bulldog's 1962 and 1963 tennis squads was junior Edwin Thomas Parham Jr., a physical education and English major from Robbins, who was also a member of the basketball team from 1960–63. Parham, who referred to himself as "a duffer" in tennis, listened and learned from Cloyd, Hyatt, McComas, and other ACC coaches. Returning as a faculty member and coach in 1964, Parham led his alma mater to national prominence in tennis during the 1970s and 1980s. Parham's Bulldog teams competed successfully in several National Association of Intercollegiate Athletics tennis tournaments. The former ACC athlete, teacher, and coach became a member of the college's Athletic Hall of Fame in 1986.[27]

Although weight lifting never became an official sport, ACC may have had the greatest one-man team in the nation in 1959. After winning a regional contest at Georgia Tech, senior Joe Addison Grantham of Smithfield received an invitation to compete in the 1959 National Intercollegiate Weight Lifting Championships at Pittsburg. He approached Milton Adams about financial aid to travel to Pittsburg. Adams was astounded to learn that Grantham had traveled to Atlanta at his own expense and won the match. Although the college had no budget for weight lifting, Grantham received $40 toward expenses. Later, when Adams asked how he had fared in national competition, Grantham replied "I didn't do so well. I finished second. A boy from the University of Bridgeport beat me." Struggling for words, Adams managed to stammer, "You mean you finished second in a national meet?" Competing against the top collegiate

Golf coach Ed Cloyd and director of athletics Milton Adams. 1961 Pine Knot.

weight lifters in America, the ACC senior actually won two of the three events of the match. He finished second only because the eventual champion had lifted more weight in the first event, beating Joe Grantham by a total of ten pounds. Grantham remained undiscouraged. Traveling to Greensboro in late April 1959, again at his own expense, Joe was named top individual performer among thirty-five athletes at the Carolinas and Virginia regional Amateur Athletic Union (AAU) weight lifting match. Grantham's feats likely inspired the formation of the college's first weight-lifting club during the following year. Articles in the student newspaper stated that weight lifting and body building, two gymnastic-related sports enjoying dramatic growth nationally, had become popular at the college. In 1960–61, an ACC club attracted fifteen members, elected officers, and made arrangements with the city of Wilson to use weight-lifting facilities at the recreation center. After graduating in 1959, Grantham returned to his alma mater as a member of the army to speak to the weight-lifting club in November 1960. The Johnston County native ranks among the college's great athletes. While stationed at Fort Carson, Colorado, in 1960, Grantham continued competition, earning rankings of fifth, third, second, and first in the four national contests that he entered. As one of the nation's best weight lifters, he considered trying out for the 1964 Olympic Games. In May 1959, *The Collegiate* stated, "They're interested in weight lifting at Atlantic

Christian College. They have to be. For $40 they picked up the top one-man weight lifting team in the country."[28]

The college's intramural program contained many gifted athletes who did not participate in intercollegiate sports. The department of physical education cooperated with the men's intramural council and the women's recreational association in directing the intramural program. Team sports for men included basketball, soccer, touch football, and volleyball. The four fraternities and a team composed of dormitory residents and day students competed for the men's intramural championship. Individual competition existed in badminton, clock golf, horseshoes, table tennis, tennis, and wrestling. Women competed individually in badminton, clock golf, table tennis, and volleyball. Team sports included basketball, softball, and tennis. An award was presented to the most outstanding woman athlete on awards day, and college publications publicized intramural results, including team standings, on a regular basis.[29]

Partisan politics practically became a team sport at the college during the late 1950s and early 1960s when controversial issues and national figures such as Truman, Eisenhower, Goldwater, Kennedy, and Nixon prompted serious campus debate. The increasing impact of the mass media made those who reached adulthood during "Eisenhower's America" better informed on national and world politics than earlier generations had been. Much more than their fathers and mothers, they became vulnerable to and enlightened by political propaganda. On 17 October 1955, political science professor Robert Capps led a small group of students in organizing the Young Democrats Club (YDC), the first formal partisan political group on campus. A student newspaper editorial welcomed the arrival of the YDC and remarked that discussions and debates on political issues could promote good citizenship. Led by president Gene Spruill, a Wilson sophomore, with Dr. Capps as advisor, the YDC adopted a constitution and hosted its first speaker, Nash County Congressman Harold D. Cooley.[30]

Republicans became active during the fall semester of 1956, hoping to help reelect Eisenhower, who was finishing his first term as President. Rossville, Illinois, junior Jay Prillaman, a feature writer for *The Collegiate*, had organized an "unofficial Young Republicans Club" with Professor Holsworth as advisor. Young Democrats supported Illinois governor, Adlai Stevenson, running for a second time after losing to Ike in 1952. In a YDC poll of the student body shortly before election day, a majority of students selected Stevenson as their choice for President by a total of 195–146, but also indicated by a vote of

227–77 their belief that Ike would win. In the vice-presidential race, voters rejected incumbent Republican Richard Nixon by a large margin, 221–80. In a question regarding draft laws, students favored the continued use of the draft by 220–85.[31]

The presidential campaign of 1960 between Richard Nixon and John F. Kennedy was the first political race to stimulate substantial numbers of college students to become active in national elections. During the summer of 1960, three members of ACC's student government executive board—president David Smith of Greenville, South Carolina, secretary Zarelda Walston of Farmville, and treasurer Bette Pomfrey of Wilson—attended the national Conference of Student Body Presidents in Minneapolis. A straw vote among the delegates gave Nixon the victory over Kennedy by a margin of 58.8 percent to 35.2 percent. The 1960 race also afforded ACC students a chance to meet a former president. As election day approached, Harry Truman visited Wilson on behalf of the Kennedy–Johnson ticket. Approximately 200 special guests, including Governor Luther Hodges and gubernatorial candidate Terry Sanford, were expected to accompany Truman to Fleming Stadium on Friday, 14 October, for a 1:00 PM speech. College officials urged students to attend and announced that midday classes would not meet so that students and faculty might hear Truman's speech.[32]

Truman's visit served to increase the campus partisanship that the approaching election had already stimulated. The former President's famous "give 'em hell style" prompted a Young Republican Club leader and coeditor of *The Collegiate* to write that Truman had displayed his "sordid colors . . . [and was] outwardly crude, if not utterly uncouth." The writer also described the Kennedy–Johnson ticket as socialistic. The local GOP response was to bring Senator Barry Goldwater, conservative Arizona Republican, to Wilson to campaign for the Nixon–Lodge ticket. Campus politicking peaked with a separate rally by each club in a colorfully decorated gymnasium within a week of the election. A two-day poll of the student body on 4–5 November resulted in Kennedy's defeating Nixon, 375–209; Johnson topping Lodge, 372–210; and Terry Sanford defeating Robert L. Gavin in the governor's race, 354–228.[33]

The fact that the 1960 election was then the closest presidential race in modern American history seemed to galvanize students. The YDC and YRC both remained active throughout 1961, inviting outside speakers and involving faculty members in their programs. Partisan activities also led to faculty presentations at scholarly forums on the meaning of liberalism and conservatism. On 16 November 1961, at the invitation of the Campus Awareness

Committee led by Jim VanCamp, a political science major from Jacksonville and a member of the class of 1962, William Troutman, professor of political science, spoke on the topic "What is a Liberal?" Identifying himself as a liberal, Troutman paid tribute to another well-known liberal on campus, C. H. Hamlin, who attended the lecture. A few days later, Dan McFarland, professor of history, addressed the issue of "Conservatism in Politics." *The Collegiate* stated that the speakers presented informative sessions on the topics and praised VanCamp and CAC for sponsoring the events.[34]

Few issues separating conservatives and liberals in the late twentieth century have proven as divisive as that of racial justice. At the time of the Supreme Court's 17 May 1954 ruling that the Jim Crow system of racial segregation was unconstitutional, young adults of college age in and beyond the South struggled with racial prejudices inherited from previous generations. When the high court announced its decision in *Brown v. Board of Education*, white Southern leaders, including governors, sought ways to evade the law and preserve segregation. On the Atlantic Christian College campus, with the exception of one salient letter to the editor in the student newspaper of 1 June 1954, little public reaction followed the Brown decision. Written by Jack Hamilton, a senior religion major from Waycross, Georgia, the letter argued that, based on morality, Christian principles, and the rule of law as based upon the fourteenth amendment to the Constitution, the Court had no choice but to strike down racial segregation. Photography editor of the *Pine Knot* and a member of *The Collegiate* staff, Hamilton praised the courage of the justices in rendering the decision. He wrote that "Skin color is a very relative thing and is an altogether unsatisfactory basis for judging an individual or a group of people. Yet segregation on this very superficial basis results in second-class citizenship, second-class education, second-class employment opportunities." While acknowledging that opposition to the decision was certain to follow, Hamilton predicted that Christian principles would prevail and the Court's verdict would stand.[35]

The ending of the academic year soon after the Brown decision announcement and the campus-wide excitement over what proved to be a championship basketball season were factors that may have delayed further public discussion of racial segregation. When a new season brought a chance for the reigning champions to defend their crown in the autumn of 1955, an intriguing event placed ACC leaders, trustees, and administrators in an unexpected and vexing predicament. The season's second basketball game was a home contest scheduled for 25 November against Pikeville Junior College of Pikeville, Kentucky. On 10 November, the ACC athletic director received a letter from

A packed house in Wilson Gym during the 1951–52 season. 1952 Pine Knot

Pikeville inquiring whether the Kentucky team's one black ballplayer would be allowed to participate. The charter of Atlantic Christian College was quite specific on that point, proclaiming that the school was "for the education and instruction of the youth of both sexes of the white race." Based on the wording of the charter and the knowledge that the present board of trustees favored keeping the college segregated, the administrative council decided that the black player would not be allowed to participate. Pikeville officials responded that they understood ACC's position and indicated that the black youth would not accompany the team. When the Pikeville contingent appeared in Wilson, however, the black student was with the team. The school's coach explained that other teams on the scheduled road trip had agreed to his participation. The young man stayed with and ate with the Pikeville team but was not permitted to play. Although the outcome of the game, an ACC victory by the score of 120–70, would not likely have been changed by one player's performance, larger issues remained. A student from one college had been humiliated, and students of both schools had been offended by a policy they considered unfair.[36]

In a letter to the editor in the December issue of *The Collegiate*, Joseph Hardegree Jr., a religion and English major from Charleston, South Carolina, explained the dilemma faced by college officials in a balanced assessment of the issue. A member of the junior class, Hardegree opposed the decision to prevent the African American student, who was not identified by name, from playing with his team. Although he disagreed with the decision and shared the embarrassment felt by a group of faculty and students, Hardegree did not fault the college officials, whose actions were limited by terms of the charter. His letter was an indictment of a society that accepted intolerance and rejected Christian principles and human dignity.

> The issue involved is more than whether a Negro ballplayer should play on the court of the Atlantic Christian College gymnasium. It goes down to the very core of our Southern heritage. A majority of the people who direct the destiny of Atlantic Christian College believe that segregation should be kept on this campus for as long as possible. They stand behind the rusting shield of custom even though it represents a doctrine of intolerance that is the direct antithesis of the teachings of Jesus Christ.
>
> Perhaps some day the people will heed the voice of the students. Perhaps they will look beyond their noses and see the world of 1955 and not the one of Reconstruction days. Perhaps some day we will be one people, under God, living harmoniously with one another.[37]

The next issue of *The Collegiate* carried a front-page photograph of another black youth receiving a very different reception upon his visit to ACC two months later. At the invitation of the Student Christian Association, Kenneth Henry, a senior at Jarvis Christian College in Texas, was welcomed as the featured speaker at ACC's chapel assembly. Described as "an outstanding student leader" with a national reputation, Henry also spoke to individual classes on campus. The student newspaper commented that "Mr. Henry has given the students much to think about." An article written by leaders of the SCA appeared in the February issue of *The Collegiate* praising Henry's inspirational talks.[38]

Interestingly, African Americans also attended ACC basketball games in Wilson during the 1950s. *Pine Knot* photographs show young black men watching the Bulldog team play at the Wilson Recreation Center during the 1956–57 season. Nevertheless, most letters to the editor appearing in student newspaper issues in 1956 supported trustee efforts to continue upholding the traditional policy of segregation. One letter suggested that the presence of black students would create social pressures at the school that could lead to interracial dating and marriage. The issue of racial justice received less publicity on campus in the following months but did not disappear. One of three student-produced one-act plays presented by Stage and Script in the spring of 1960 dealt with racial discrimination. Written by Carl W. Metts, a senior English major from Richlands, "The Cotton Still Grows" was praised in the student newspaper. In critiquing the three dramatic productions, Dr. Hartsock wrote that Metts's play dealt with "a racial theme in a way that impressed the audience as serious, poetic, and thoughtful." She added that students and faculty should feel a sense of pride in all three student productions.[39]

As John F. Kennedy called for a "new frontier" in his successful campaign for the presidency in the autumn of 1960, ACC's student government leaders brought the controversy over racial segregation back into local headlines. The executive committee of the Student Cooperative Association approved travel funds to send senior student body leaders David Smith and Zarelda Walston to attend the annual convention of the National Student Congress in Minneapolis in August 1960. By a 90 percent vote, the NSC delegates adopted a resolution supporting peaceful sit-in demonstrations as a means of attaining desegregation. The ACC delegates, who had voted with the majority, now found themselves carrying the politically sensitive resolution back to North Carolina, where, during the previous February, students from a Greensboro college had first used the tactic of sit-ins to demonstrate opposition to racial segregation.[40]

When the SGA executive committee met in October, Smith and Walston presented the desegregation resolution. Following much discussion, the group approved the national resolution and decided that the vote would "stand as the voice and decision of the students of Atlantic Christian unless officially protested by the student body." If no protest occurred, the committee members would write letters to local public restaurants and businesses suggesting that such facilities be desegregated. The document also specified the committee's decision to write letters of encouragement to peaceful participants of sit-in demonstrations whose actions had prompted their arrest. Letters would be written on behalf of the student body one week following the executive committee's action. The measure passed without opposition, one member abstaining.[41]

An editorial appearing in the issue of *The Collegiate* that reported the board's decision was a warning of events to come. The editorial praised the courage of the SGA leaders without endorsing the resolution. An article by student government leaders in the following edition affirmed the vote and explained the committee's position. The article also argued that state laws that were "destructive of human dignity" should be stricken from the books because they violated the fourteenth amendment of the Constitution. However, located immediately above the article was a large headline reading "Sit-In Resolution Is Opposed." An accompanying article stated that almost twice the required number of signatures necessary for calling a campus-wide vote on the desegregation issue had been secured.[42]

Headlines appearing two weeks later were more emphatic: "505 Oppose Sit-In Move; Faculty Group Disagrees." At a special assembly the previous week students had rejected the resolution by a vote of 505–132. Members of the faculty decided against participating in the assembly vote in order to let the students reach their own decision. In a separate vote the faculty had favored the desegregation resolution by "a slim margin." Professor Hartsock stated that a "personal resolution" would be posted on campus, inviting students and faculty to sign their names if they desired to take a stand in support of desegregation. Letters and editorials in the 18 November issue of *The Collegiate* referred to "the religious battle existing on campus" and the "hullabaloo over desegregation." The paper noted that the issue so dominated the atmosphere of the college that students delayed departures for weekend visits home, professors lingered after class for additional discussion, and students pounded card tables in the Bohunk while making their points.[43]

While occasional letters and editorials continued to appear through February 1961, including a letter from President Wenger explaining the steps necessary for changing the college's segregation policy, the controversy had, for the time being, run its course on campus. The student newspaper appearing immediately after Thanksgiving break contained a single letter from a concerned student struggling against prejudice in an effort to form his own views on the vexing problem of racial justice. For the moment, however, civil rights issues took a back seat to routine concerns which college students typically faced—the approach of spring registration, campus parking problems, selection of a *Pine Knot* Queen, and, most immediately, the opening of basketball season.[44]

Spring semester 1961 coincided with the early months of John F. Kennedy's presidential administration. Initially, the new chief executive moved cautiously in dealing with civil rights, choosing to focus upon other issues. Kennedy's youth, style, and bold challenge for Americans to consider what they could do for their country held special appeal for the nation's youth. In March 1961, students followed news of the establishment of the Peace Corps with considerable interest and became enthralled with America's competition with the Soviet Union in the race to conquer space. Barely a week after television viewers marveled as astronaut Alan Shepard rocketed into space aboard *Freedom 7*, newspaper coeditor Horace Alton Lee Jr., a senior religion and English major from Raleigh, wrote in the 12 May issue of *The Collegiate* of his excitement upon viewing the epic space flight. Lee expressed exuberance at the thought of living in an age of "unlimited possibilities" and raised the rhetorical question, "What does lie beyond?"[45]

For Alton Lee and 192 other seniors, immediately beyond lay graduation day on 28 May. Commencement afforded an appropriate ending for an eventful final semester at the college. Kennedy's inauguration had preceded a campus-wide controversy over the appropriateness of the "God is Dead" theme of Religious Emphasis Week, followed by argument over the issue of segregation at the college. Graduation exercises included the awarding of honorary degrees to two outstanding former graduates. Elizabeth House Hughey of Raleigh, cum laude graduate of the class of 1936, who served as librarian of the State of North Carolina and as president of the North Carolina Library Association, received the Doctor of Literature degree. Joshua Ernest Paschall of Wilson, class of 1918, president of Branch Banking and Trust Company and member of the board of trustees, was awarded the Doctor of Laws degree. For Arthur D. Wenger, commencement meant the completion of five years' service as president of the college and promised time for regrouping before beginning preparations for another academic year. The arrival of September 1961 would mark the opening of Atlantic Christian College's sixtieth year.[46]

THIRTEEN

A Display of Fire and Flower Power

AS ARTHUR D. WENGER began his sixth year as president in September 1961, he could hardly have been more pleased with the status of Atlantic Christian College than were other friends and supporters of the school. As ACC's eighth president, Wenger had already served the third longest term as chief executive in the institution's history. Upon completion of the 1961–62 academic year, his tenure not only would double that of the last two presidents combined but would provide a stability of leadership welcomed by the college community. Student enrollment had grown by more than 100 percent during Wenger's first five years, increasing from 683 to 1,400 regular-term students. The growth pattern verified the view that the college's reputation continued to improve among high school graduates and their parents. The faculty had also increased in size, from thirty-seven to fifty-one full-time instructors and from seventeen to twenty-four part-time teachers. Faculty members who had served lengthy terms at the college included Gene Purvis, Warren Tait, and Kenneth St. John in education; Doris Capps in psychology; Ben Bardin, Harry Swain, and Ashton Wiggs in business; John Dunn and Bob Frazier in mathematics; Mildred Hartsock, Edna Johnston, Dorothy Eagles, and Ruby Shackleford in English; C. H. Hamlin and Bob Capps in social sciences; Esther Long and Hugh B. Johnston Jr. in modern languages; Bob Hollar and J. P. Tyndall in science; Vere Rogers, Allan Sharp, and Gene Purcell in religion; Ed Brown and Russell Arnold in art; and Ed Cloyd in physical education.[1]

While the college's growth owed much to projects begun by previous presidents, including the construction of new buildings and Southern Association accreditation, Wenger continued the momentum and began programs of his own. Requested by the president in early 1959 to chart a future growth plan to accommodate the enrollment surge, trustees responded by authorizing construction of a new dormitory for men. In October 1961, the board approved the largest monetary campaign in the school's history, a fifteen-year, $3.5 million drive to provide funds (in three five-year phases) for land acquisition, new buildings, endowment, and faculty salaries. Thomas J. Hackney Jr. headed the statewide campaign, assisted by S. M. Cozart, K. D. Kennedy Sr., and John D. Palmer.[2]

The college newspaper noted that the Wenger family had little difficulty readjusting to the local community upon their return from Texas, quoting Mrs. Wenger's remark that Wilson was "the friendliest town I have ever lived in." During the homecoming of 1961, the Wengers invited trustees and the college community to tour ACC's new president's house on Wilshire Boulevard, the only house that the college has ever built. Constructed from Kinsey Hall bricks and nestled beneath towering pines, the spacious residence afforded both adequate space for entertaining guests of the college and comfortable living quarters for the president's family. Doris Wenger used the new facility to enhance the school's social events while establishing a reputation as a meticulous and gracious hostess to trustees, faculty, students, and friends of the college. Ann Cloyd led a drive to organize the college women at a meeting of faculty wives and female members of the faculty and staff in Harper Hall parlor in February 1955, approximately six months before the Wenger family returned to Wilson. Utilizing members of the Faculty Woman's Club and selected students and children of faculty-staff members, Mrs. Wenger hosted formal receptions that became leading social occasions each year.[3]

President Wenger's dedication to ACC and his positive relationship with students, faculty, and staff brought recognition from several sources. The Raleigh *News and Observer* designated him "Tarheel of the Week" in 1960, and members of the college community honored him with a surprise "President's Day" in 1961. The president's self-confidence and versatility led to his debut as an actor with Stage and Script in the spring of 1962, further endearing him to students and faculty. Wenger performed the title role of Civil War figure John Brown in the March 1962 dramatic presentation of "John Brown's Body," directed by Doris Holsworth. Students also noted that their president seemed to enjoy participating in spring carnival activities sponsored by the Greek organizations. Dedicating the 1963 *Pine Knot* in Wenger's honor, the editors singled out "kindness, friendliness, understanding, and Christian leadership" among the significant qualities that Dr. Wenger brought to the college.[4]

While the Wenger family ended its fifth year as ACC's first family, newly inaugurated President John F. Kennedy struggled to define the goals of his administration regarding issues on foreign affairs and racial justice. Kennedy's bold

President Arthur D. Wenger, 1956–77. 1961 Pine Knot.

inauguration day challenge that Americans ask "what you can do for your country" held significant appeal for many citizens, especially among college-age youths. The Peace Corps became the most attractive New Frontier program on college campuses, promising to bring pragmatic solutions and America's democratic ideas to poor nations of the Third World. Beginning in September 1961 and continuing throughout the decade, *The Collegiate* carried news of Peace Corps activities and opportunities for service. Among the Peace Corps' first recruits from ACC was Doris Campbell Holsworth, a fifteen-year veteran of the faculty. During the spring of 1962, the college newspaper announced that Professor Holsworth planned to retire at the end of the spring semester and would teach overseas as a Peace Corps volunteer. The veteran drama director remained popular as she finished her career at ACC. *The Collegiate* of 4 May carried a photograph of Holsworth accepting congratulations from the editor of the yearbook following the announcement that the 1962 *Pine Knot* had been dedicated in honor of the "Duchess."[5]

After leaving the college in June, Holsworth served as a teacher at a girls' school in India. The 30 November 1962 issue of *The Collegiate* printed a letter addressed to friends at Atlantic Christian College in which Holsworth described her teaching experiences at Isabella Thoburn College in Lucknow, India. She expected that her overseas job would end prematurely because of fears of an impending Chinese invasion of India and stated that she planned to return to Wilson. Former ACC student Rex B. Jarrell Jr., class of 1960, joined the Peace Corps after serving in the United States Navy. A photograph in an April 1963 issue of the college newspaper showed Jarrell teaching a biology class at the Teacher Training College in Sierra Leone, Africa. The Durham native had taught science and coached various sports at the school for more than a year. Peace Corps volunteer service continued to interest ACC students during the late twentieth century, nearly four decades after President Kennedy's assassination.[6]

The campus newspaper's coverage of national and international news improved dramatically during the 1960s. The attraction of a youthful and charismatic American President and a growing awareness of the perils which confronted the United States in the role of military and economic superpower helped raise the quality of feature articles and letters appearing in *The Collegiate* in the autumn of 1962. The impact of the Cuban missile crisis in October stirred conscientious staff writers Jerry Arthur Ridling, religion and philosophy major from Memphis, Tennessee, class of 1963, and Dwight Wagner of Salisburg, Maryland, class of 1967, to provide a continuous news analysis under "News and Views" from 19 October 1962 to 18 May 1967. In December 1963, Wagner wrote that Kennedy's assassination demonstrated the necessity of bringing greater understanding of the threat posed by tyranny, hatred, and terrorism in a complex world of constant and violent change. Wagner considered Kennedy's death a warning that America must strengthen her vigilance and improve the education of her citizens.[7]

The 1960s was a decade of political polarization and national disruption which sparked student rebellions on college campuses throughout America. Emotions stirred by a growing civil rights struggle and an increasingly unpopular war in southeast Asia were intensified by the increased use of marijuana and hard drugs. The nation's youth turned away from mainstream activities to form a counterculture of peace vigils and demonstrations which produced serious disturbances in higher education from Cornell and Columbia University on the east coast to Berkeley and Southern California on the west coast. The conservative South, including North Carolina, Wilson, and Atlantic Christian College, which had been bypassed earlier, did not escape the impact of radical movements during the 1960s.

Regarding lackadaisical student behavior of the 1950s and 1960s, Sarah Bain Ward quoted Mildred Hartsock's remark that what ACC's bored and apathetic students really needed were "a few good five-cent sins." Except for occasional raucous behavior at basketball games and rare instances of drinking disturbances, petty theft, and vandalism, student conduct during the first six decades of Barton College's history could be accurately described as restrained and comparatively orderly, basically in accordance with the sort of behavior that one would expect to find on a small church-related campus. The conflicting attitudes and values of the 1960s, however, challenged and threatened to change the placid, behaviorally correct image of the school. An editorial in *The Collegiate* of May 1960 indicated dissatisfaction with ACC's campus governance system, arguing that students had too little power and implying that the policies of the administration and trustees were frequently in conflict with the best interests of the students. President Wenger's letter of reply suggested that, in his view, the problem appeared to be a case of poor communication rather than one of unreasonable limitations on student power. The students were unconvinced and in April 1965 succeeded in changing the form of campus government from a cooperative association of students and faculty, established in 1936, to a true student government association. They amended the constitution to remove faculty as voting members of the executive board. Under the new structure the dean of students and one faculty representative chosen by faculty vote served as advisors to the executive board.[8]

College regulations that students continued to find oppressive included those pertaining to required chapel and to gender inequities regarding female students. Chapel attendance was mandatory on Tuesday and Thursday mornings. Although the administration recorded attendance, students sometimes handed in signed attendance slips for friends. Some students also turned in their own slips and exited via the back door without remaining for the assembly program. A student poll on mandatory chapel during spring semester 1966 resulted in an inconclusive response. Some students who considered the assembly programs beneficial also voted against compulsory attendance. In the fall of 1967, the administration changed the policy to require mandatory attendance at convocations each Tuesday. The college agreed to provide advance description of programs at the beginning of each semester. Students who cut four or more convocations would be subject to suspension from school. Editors of *The Collegiate* remained firmly opposed to any required attendance at speeches, concerts, lectures, religious services, and other events. Student editors

Fire and Flower Power

deemed a refined policy, issued in February 1968, which promised more interesting programs and specified what would be an acceptable excused absence, a step forward but still unsatisfactory. The newspaper did support a new provision that reserved the 11:00 AM hour on Thursdays for voluntary class or club meetings rather than a required assembly.[9]

While female students continued to face strict policies regarding study hours and were required to sign in and out of the dormitory, the college did begin allowing freshmen women to ride in automobiles while dating after the Thanksgiving holidays in 1959. In December 1961 the administration also rescinded the ban upon a new dance called the Twist which it had invoked at the beginning of the fall semester. The editor of *The Collegiate* remarked that the newspaper staff, realizing that other church-related schools were not as tolerant of dancing as ACC was, had exercised patience in allowing college officials time to reconsider the ill-conceived ban rather than starting a protest campaign. Interestingly, both Tweetie and Professor Hartsock determined that the Twist and other new dances were offensive and vulgar enough to warrant making their views public in the campus newspaper. Commenting upon dancing that he had observed during fall semester 1964, Tweetie expressed shock at the "animalistic contortions . . . more suitable for a group of sex-deprived maniacs than for our high level college students." Speaking to student government leaders the following spring, Hartsock objected to the "blare of unbelievable noise" and charged that some new dances were "imitative of the sexual act and . . . repulsive to those who watch it." Students paid little heed to criticism raised by their elders regarding what constituted acceptable behavior on the dance floor. Establishing a "Peppermint Lounge" and "temple of twist," they continued to dance the night away. Professor Hartsock also demonstrated persistence in responding to student criticism of Dean of Men Robert Bennett's actions in stopping students from dancing at a concert in the gymnasium during homecoming 1967. The fiery English professor pointed out that the event was scheduled as a concert, a student dance was also held that weekend, and that dancing damaged the gymnasium floor. Replying to objections that the dean called upon the help of a police officer in monitoring the crowd, she answered that the officer had been hired for such a purpose. Referring to a tall and obviously drunk male whose rude behavior had caused concern among female chaperones, Hartsock wrote "I think I could handle a six-foot inebriate. But then I was a Girl Scout with twenty merit badges."[10]

Surging enrollment numbers brought relief for some females who had grown tired of dormitory restrictions. In November 1965, trustees revised regulations to permit males and females aged twenty-one and older who could not obtain college housing to petition the dean of men or women for permission to make their own housing arrangements. The change marked the first time that females were allowed to live off campus. In an April 1967 issue of *The Collegiate*, Sam McPhail, senior religion major, president of Campus Christian Fellowship (CCF), and a Who's Who selection, focused his sarcastic wit on ACC's educational double standard. He regarded the restrictive policy as a show of disrespect for female students by leaders of the college. The writer suggested that administrators feared that female students would travel "down the highway of sin." He suggested installing electronic eyes near classroom doorways which would automatically measure the hemline of entering co-eds for "the protection of male faculty members."[11]

Clashes between students and the administration sometimes occurred over such generally mundane matters as the quality, quantity, and distribution of food. On Thursday evening, 3 December 1964, approximately 200 students staged a demonstration protesting the "general food service" at the ACC cafeteria. Prior to that event, some forty to fifty students had registered dissatisfaction with the meal by dumping their "hickory smoked hamburger steaks" onto the tops of tables in the dining hall. Approximately 100 students left their cafeteria trays on the tables along with notes charging that the dining hall offered unsatisfactory service and the food served was "100 per cent dog food." A disturbance at Hackney Dormitory about midnight that evening ended quickly after officials contacted the Wilson police department. *The Collegiate* supported student concerns about the food service but suggested that channels existed through which issues could be resolved without disrupting campus services and pointed out that students were responsible for some dining hall problems, such as breaking into line. President Wenger met with approximately 400 students on Friday morning to discuss the situation. The executive board of the SGA appointed a special committee to study the problem and suggest a solution by the middle of spring semester. The 13 April 1967 issue of *The Collegiate* announced that ACC had entered into a contract with ARA-Slater Food Service to begin service on campus beginning with the first summer term.[12]

Dr. Wenger sometimes struggled to control his emotions in dealing with cases of student misconduct, particularly when the offenses disturbed the community beyond the campus. During the spring semester of 1966, the dean of students received a letter from officials at Fike High School protesting incidents of smoking and rude conduct by ACC students at a concert featuring

Martha Reeves and the Vandellas. Although no damage had occurred to the auditorium, the letter stated that college students had strewn cigarette butts on the floor of the lobby and implied that they were also responsible for leaving "a wheelbarrow of whiskey bottles and beer cans" in the school parking lot. In the future, college students would not be allowed in the Fike auditorium without an official request from the dean of students, the dean of the college, or the president. Editorials in the campus newspaper commented that rude behavior had undermined efforts to establish good will between the college and community.[13]

On Wednesday, 30 March 1966, the beginning of Greek week on the college campus, Dr. Wenger received a call about 11:30 PM from Wilson police captain A. J. Hayes regarding a boisterous group of students disturbing residents near the ACC campus by loud singing and shouting. What started out as a serenade of co-eds had turned into a potentially volatile situation when an estimated 65 to 100 male students, having marched along streets adjacent to the campus to the front of Harper Hall, refused to settle down and began shouting vulgarities at policemen attempting to disperse the crowd. Captain Hayes called President Wenger, who mistakenly went first to Hackney Hall, where he also discovered students being loud and vulgar. After attempts to ease the situation were generally ignored, he calmed the students by threatening them with expulsion from school should they continue the disruption. Wenger was also disappointed to find residents shouting out the windows of the other dormitories. Upon joining Chief Hayes and Robert Washer, dean of men, Wenger witnessed a number of women leaning out the windows of Harper Hall making "catcalls" and other noises. The disturbance finally ended about 12:30 AM. Student letters in the next issue of *The Collegiate* berated college officials and the Wilson police for interrupting the students' "good clean fun" and criticized *The Wilson Daily Times* for biased reporting of the incident. The letters also accused Wenger of referring to students as "hoods" and "damned baboons," when they had only been exercising "student freedom."[14]

The college president was not amused. In a carefully worded letter to the students carried on the front page of the 21 April 1966 issue of *The Collegiate*, Wenger addressed incidents of student conduct at Fike as well as along Deans Street and in front of Harper Hall during Greek week. Admitting that he had used comments in the heat of anger and disappointment which might have been worded differently, Wenger stated that he was willing to engage in discussion and negotiation upon almost any issue; however, common decency was not among them. He also stated that the executive committee of the board of trustees was quite concerned about recent student misconduct. Mildred Hartsock apparently kept quiet publicly during the rude and vulgar behavior and police-baiting of March 1966. In December, however, shocked by what she considered brashness from a religion major, she reached for her pen. The student had criticized two of Dr. Wenger's assembly speeches, something Hartsock had also done. However, in expressing his boredom at listening to the president read the college constitution, the student referred to the speaker as "Art Wenger." If he were her son, Hartsock stated, she would "invite him to the proverbial woodshed and proceed to knock his teeth down his throat." While she objected to criticism of a man who was trying his best to strengthen the college, what she really wanted to emphasize was "courtesy and civilized behavior on the part of the very young." She ended her remarks by requesting that students refrain from any future food throwing while people in India were starving.[15]

While judged as radical behavior by some at staid Atlantic Christian College, the Greek week embarrassment of spring 1966 was quite modest by national standards. America's involvement in the Vietnam War and the growing civil rights movement were events that energized and polarized college communities as never before. Antiwar and civil rights activists found college campuses fertile ground for organizing protest groups. By 1965 student antiwar protesters cursed Lyndon Johnson, carried Vietcong flags, and attempted to block troop trains at locations including Berkeley, California. In the conservative Midwest, police arrested 114 students at the University of Kansas at a sit-in opposing the war and racial discrimination. In October 1962, three days before an American-Russian standoff over Cuban missile sites threatened to trigger a nuclear war, columnist Jerry Ridling wrote about the military conflict in South Vietnam in *The Collegiate*. As more American servicemen were drafted and President Johnson escalated the war by bombing North Vietnam, student reaction increased in Wilson and across the country. The student newspaper of 28 October 1965 reported that the President had directed the justice department to investigate rumored Communist infiltration of antiwar and antidraft demonstrations. Dwight Wagner argued that many protesters lacked sufficient understanding of the issues and suggested that the most radical antiwar and antidraft groups, including Students for a Democratic Society (SDS), had been infiltrated by Communists. Radical activist Allard Lowenstein, a graduate of the University of North Carolina and a founder of SDS, accepted a Cooperative Association invitation in April 1964 to address a required ACC assembly meeting on racial discord in South Africa. Apparently, the controversial North Carolina

State social science professor made no attempt to recruit student protesters during his visit, and student editors criticized his speech for being overly partisan and bordering on sensationalism.[16]

An increase in radical group activity made the year 1968 a time of controversy and confrontation on the ACC campus and throughout the nation. The Wilson campus had begun to take on a more radical tone, beginning in January 1967, with the establishment of an ACC chapter of the Young Americans for Freedom (YAF). The ultraconservative group, formed in Connecticut in 1960, held demonstrations in support of American prosecution of the Vietnam War and against the Test Ban Treaty of 1963. The local YAF chapter elected officers, wrote a constitution, and named Professor Hugh B. Johnston Jr. as advisor. The ACC Young Republican Club (YRC), when filing its own constitution with the SGA, announced that the organization had not been, and had no desire to be, affiliated with YAF. Senior Sam McPhail wrote in the student newspaper in February 1968 that the YAF was one of the fastest growing political organizations nationally. Pointing out the group's reputation for intolerance and a tendency to take over YRC groups on other campuses, McPhail ended his column with a quote from eighteenth-century English writer Samuel Johnson that "Patriotism is the last refuge of a scoundrel." Not to be outdone, the vice-chairman of the YAF responded to McPhail's article by quoting from Thomas Jefferson and Edmund Burke in defending the conservative political group. Two members of the school's YAF joined like-minded students from Duke and NC State in a Raleigh demonstration against IBM over the company's sale of computers to Communist bloc countries.[17]

Mainstream political groups also remained active. The Young Republicans brought conservative political scientist John East to the campus and furnished officers to serve the state YRC. The Young Democrats welcomed Indiana Senator Birch Bayh to campus and sent delegates to the national YDC convention. It was the nonpartisan Campus Awareness Committee, however, which sponsored the most controversial event of 1968 and provoked an unwelcome intrusion of McCarthyism upon the Wilson campus. Retired Air Force Lt. Col. Wilbur G. Outlaw—a native of Ellenton, South Carolina, class of 1940, and state coordinator of the John Birch Society—addressed an assembly meeting in support of a petition asking Congress to cut off all trade with countries of the Communist bloc. He also advocated bombing Russian ships in North Vietnamese harbors and implied that nuclear weapons might be the answer to ending the war in Vietnam.[18]

Outlaw also brought to the campus controversial John Birch literature, which insinuated that one of the college's most revered professors had engaged in un-American activities while advancing the Communist Party's goal of world domination. The Collegiate issue of 25 April 1968 provided an explanation of the problem in a scathing editorial condemning an ACC classroom incident in which a professor reportedly had referred to a colleague as a "communist." The newspaper suggested that "it is not the accused whom students should shun, but rather the accuser." In the same issue Professor Tom Marshall expressed outrage at the rumored character assassination in "An Open Letter of Dismay." The 9 May issue of The Collegiate identified Professor Hamlin as the faculty member whose name had been smeared and charged Wilbur Outlaw with being one of the parties responsible for the attack.[19]

The newspaper labeled the smear campaign as a blemish upon the reputation of the college, denounced the executive board of the SGA for failing to support a resolution supporting Hamlin, and apologized that The Collegiate staff had not taken prompt action to help clear up confusion regarding the issue. Introduced by junior Kay Antone, the resolution labeled the accusations against the social science professor absurd and praised Hamlin as "an upright and moral individual who has consistently supported his principles of peace and love for his fellow man." The same issue of the newspaper also printed an open letter to Col. Wilbur Outlaw of Fayetteville, North Carolina, from Professor Hugh B. Johnston Jr., attempting to end the controversy on campus. Addressing Outlaw as "Dear Bill," Johnston denied any role in compiling or distributing the pamphlet, although some of his ACC colleagues "erroneously believe" him to have been a participant. Johnston added that although he had disagreed with some of Hamlin's views, he doubted that the professor had ever been a "conscious or active supporter of Communism."[20]

According to the John Birch philosophy, Hamlin should be labeled "pink," an unwitting tool of the Communist conspiracy and in the same category as countless Americans, including former President Eisenhower. Ike's brother Milton, a college professor, was in the group's more dangerous "red" category, the designation for individuals who knowingly supplied aid to the Communists. The radical right-wing group may have been reacting to Hamlin's joining with faculty of colleges and universities across the state to support students who faced jail terms for refusing to obey the newly amended Selective Service Laws. An earlier edition of The Collegiate reported that three members of the ACC faculty/staff had signed "A Statement in Support of Students Conscientiously Refusing Military Service." In addition to Hamlin, Gerald Harris,

T. J. Hackney Sr., board chairman 1935–65. The Collegiate, December 1964.

associate professor of religion, and Virginia Ann Shenk, assistant librarian and instructor, had signed the document.[21]

Most faculty activities of the decade were not as controversial as signing a statement opposing the draft. In December 1964, the college chapter of the American Association of University Professors (AAUP) honored Thomas J. Hackney Sr. at a dinner attended by the Hackney family, the executive committee of the board of trustees, and ACC faculty members. The honoree had announced his decision to give up the post of board chairman the previous month, following thirty consecutive years at the helm. Gene Purvis, AAUP president, presided over the festivities, which included presenting Hackney with a certificate of appreciation on behalf of the faculty. The college string ensemble provided dinner music, and Mildred Hartsock was the featured speaker. Praising the college's record of progress under Hackney's guidance, Hartsock turned to her favorite literary scholar for an appropriate theme: "A character in one of Shakespeare's plays asked the question: What's in a name?

Those who know the developing history of Atlantic Christian College might answer a goodly segment of that history is in a name. The name Hackney, is memorialized in one of our buildings, but far more significantly memorialized in a long tradition of family service to the institution." [22]

Tom Hackney's father, George, a trustee from 1902 to 1948, also served as board chairman for twenty-four years from 1907 to 1931. Thomas J. Hackney Sr. served as a trustee from 1932 to 1965 and was chairman from 1935 to 1965. Thomas J. Hackney Jr. joined the board in 1957, served as chairman from 1966 to 1985, and remained a trustee in 2001. Members of the Hackney family helped lead Barton College throughout the school's first 100 years of service and chaired the board for nearly three-quarters of a century. Other members of the Hackney family have been ACC students and served as benefactors and trustees. In 1902, Mrs. Orpah Hackney, widow of Willis Napoleon Hackney and mother of George Hackney Sr., provided a gift of real estate that became the college's initial endowment. Willis N. Hackney, a cousin of Tom Hackney Sr., became one of the school's most enthusiastic and generous supporters. The Hackney family's lengthy record of leadership and continuous service to Barton College may be unmatched by a single family in the history of any college or university in North Carolina.[23]

During the decade of the 1960s, leadership provided by the Hackneys and Arthur D. Wenger enabled ACC to realize significant growth in enrollment and facilities. Enrollment between 1960 and 1970 increased from 1,400 regular students to 1,544. The 1960s was the most active construction decade in college history. Five buildings were dedicated during homecoming festivities in November 1966, including the classroom building named in honor of benefactor J. W. Hines. In addition to Hines Hall and Wilson Gymnasium, the college dedicated the Roma Hackney Music Building, completed in 1963 and named for Mrs. Willis N. Hackney. Case Art Building, completed in 1966, was named in honor of Perry Case, who served as professor and administrator between 1916 and 1960. The latter building houses a classroom, offices, studios, and the Barton Art Museum, including the Lula E. Rackley Gallery and the Virginia Graves Gallery. Hilley Hall is a residence hall named in honor of Howard S. Hilley, who served the college from 1920–49 as professor of religion and ancient and modern languages, academic dean, and its fifth president. The new student center, later named in honor of C. H. Hamlin, and the men's residence hall, named for John Mayo Waters, were completed in 1968. Waters served as professor and business manager of the college.[24]

The new structures enabled the college to provide adequate student housing and maintain suitable classroom and office space for the departments of art, music, and physical education. Home basketball games no longer had to be played away from campus in area high schools or at the Wilson Recreation Center. The new student center included room for a modern, spacious cafeteria with large kitchen, a campus post office and bookstore, student affairs offices, interview rooms for placement service, an ample lounge and recreation area, and a soda shop. The capital campaign, begun in 1963 with a goal of $3.5 million, provided construction funds that were supplemented by government grants and loans. The student union alone cost $700,000, plus $25,000 contributed by dedicated alumni for furnishings. Major benefactors included Willis Hackney, who contributed $100,000 to the campaign in 1963.[25]

In addition to providing space to meet the varied needs of a steadily growing school, the new facilities helped ACC meet accreditation standards required by the National Council for Accreditation of Teacher Education (NCATE) and to secure reaccreditation by the Southern Association of Colleges and Schools (SACS). ACC's teacher education program had met the standards of the North Carolina Department of Public Instruction (SDPI) for many years. During fall semester 1963, the school began a self-study that culminated with visitations by teams from both NCATE and SDPI in February and March 1965. SDPI approved reaccreditation in December 1965, and NCATE awarded initial accreditation in October 1966. The latter event meant that graduates of the college's teacher education program were recognized as meeting national standards by accrediting agencies throughout America. ACC received SACS reaccreditation, pertaining to all of its programs, in December 1967.[26]

The college continued to realize academic achievement in all departments and programs during the 1960s. Graduating seniors were named to Who's Who and received prestigious scholarships and internships for graduate work at such colleges and universities as Appalachian State College, Converse School of Music, Duke University, East Carolina College, University of Miami, University of North Carolina, Richmond Professional Institute, Vanderbilt University, and Yale University. In 1968, D. Jerry White, senior English major from Pendleton, Indiana, became ACC's first Woodrow Wilson National Fellowship winner, gaining a graduate scholarship and recognition as one of the best future college teacher prospects in the United States and Canada.[27]

Talented students, faculty, and friends of the college also continued to support Stage and Script, as the dramatics club celebrated its fiftieth anniversary with a 10–12 May 1967 presentation of Shakespeare's romantic comedy *Love's*

Labour's Lost, under the trees on center campus. Directed by ACC graduate and assistant professor of English and drama Cecil Willis, the play was the culmination of the college's fifth annual North Carolina Shakespeare Festival. In addition to a dramatic production, the festival typically included programs of Shakespearean music and lectures by well-known Shakespearean scholars including Louis B. Wright of the Folger Shakespeare Library. In a critique of the production in the school newspaper, English professor William McGill praised the event as "another in a long line of fine presentations by talented, determined, and hardworking students, and . . . delightful entertainment."[28]

The English and art departments joined forces to create *Crucible*, a new publication at the college during fall semester 1964. First announced in the 16 October 1964 issue of *The Collegiate*, coeditors Russell Arnold and Mildred Hartsock indicated that the magazine would feature quality work submitted by students, faculty, alumni, and contributors from the community at large. Of particular interest were short stories, poems, essays, reviews, plays, musical compositions, drawings, architectural drawings, paintings, photography, and photography of sculpture. Funding of the magazine would come from contributions and sales. The first issue, scheduled for publication in December 1964, was made possible by money from the Doris Holsworth Memorial Fund. An art auction on 10 December 1964 raised $650 for the *Crucible*. Although only 150 magazines were sold by mid-December, the editors remained optimistic. In January 1965, Arnold and Hartsock proclaimed the new literary and art magazine a success. Most of the contributors to the first issue of *Crucible* were students, faculty, and alumni of the college. The second issue, appearing in May 1965, included student and faculty contributions and also featured a portfolio of artwork by nationally known illustrator Leon Bellin. Literary pieces included poems and short stories by various authors and an article by Canadian composer Charles Jones. In the 1970s, art professor Tom Marshall and Jim Hemby, professor of English, succeeded Arnold and Hartsock as editors of *Crucible*. In the year 2000, with Professor Terry Grimes as editor, *Crucible* celebrated its thirty-sixth year as the third oldest literary publication in North Carolina. The magazine continues to present high-quality art and literature from well-known artists and writers and from individuals publishing for the first time.[29]

Crucible remained in the planning stages in the early 1960s when the struggle for racial justice in America inspired ACC students to begin writing letters and editorials for *The Collegiate* supporting the admission of black students. In the autumn of 1962, Jerry Ridling's letter to the editor questioned whether a

Christian college that thought of itself as being somewhat liberal intended to be the last school in the state to enroll black students. Pointing out that North Carolina was the home of one of the nation's largest groups of Negro Disciples, Ridling suggested that opening the school's doors to black students would help strengthen the denomination that supported the college. Jesse L. Maghan, assistant editor of *The Collegiate*, supporting Ridling's position, quoted from the ACC *Catalog* regarding the college's commitment to Christian education and spiritual insight. A junior from Arlington, Virginia, Maghan commented on recent civil rights victories, including James Meredith's success in desegregating the University of Mississippi, an event that sparked a riot resulting in the deaths of two people.[30]

The student newspaper increased its coverage of civil rights news during 1962–63, including a report about Harvey Gantt's becoming the first black student at Clemson University. Of even greater news for the college was *The Collegiate*'s May 1963 report that a resolution passed by the North Carolina Christian Church Convention urged trustees to amend the college charter to allow the enrollment of all races. Jesse Maghan applauded the Disciples of Christ resolution as a "Noble Incentive" and expressed hope that trustees would approve the request. A poll of the student body, taken in May by *The Collegiate*, revealed that students generally favored the admission of black students. While positive responses outnumbered negative replies, many students assumed a noncommittal position on the issue, and some made flippant remarks such as the comment from an eastern North Carolina co-ed that admitting blacks should "help our basketball team." As the approaching commencement of 1963 brought thoughts of a summer break, Maghan's editorial warned that increasing black disillusionment with nonviolence as a means of gaining racial justice threatened to turn the civil rights movement toward violent tactics. Ridling's "News and Views" used sarcasm in awarding "honors" to those who had made significant contributions during the year. He conferred "The I Wish You Were Somewhere Else Award" upon all of the Greek organizations, gave the "Muckraker of the Year Award" to himself, and bestowed "The Little Black Boy Award" upon the board of trustees. Ridling also warned that the motto of *The Collegiate* in 1963–64 would be "Digs up the dirt like a Bulldozer."[31]

Supporting the growing student view to accept applicants regardless of race, in October 1963 the faculty voted 54–8 in favor of accepting qualified black students. The trustees also responded positively. In March 1964, the board adopted a resolution that supported amending the college's charter to permit the enrollment of nonwhite students. The trustees' action was subject to approval by the North Carolina Disciples of Christ. At its meeting in Washington, North Carolina, 25 April 1964, the North Carolina Christian Church Convention approved the trustee's resolution "to allow the admission of qualified members of all races" without opposition. Headlines in *The Collegiate* of 1 May 1964 announced "AC College Will Integrate," accompanied by an article expressing President Wenger's satisfaction that the trustees and church had resolved the difficult issue.[32]

Despite the appearance of occasional letters in the school newspaper from individuals opposing racial integration, most students apparently considered the matter resolved. During the autumn of 1964, comments appearing in *The Collegiate* regarding racial issues focused on incidents at other colleges and universities in the North and South. Columbia University had ordered that all fraternities and sororities adopt a pledge of nondiscrimination. Black student enrollment remained slow at predominately white Southern colleges, and the University of Alabama had acted over strong student objection to ban famed musician Louis Armstrong from appearing on campus.[33]

The peaceful accord on the Wilson campus was broken by the discovery that the February 1965 trustees' meeting had produced a resolution forbidding the college to recruit black athletes. The faculty demonstrated its disapproval of the recent development by adopting its own resolution, which protested the trustees' new policy. Student response ranged from a newspaper cartoon depicting a tall black basketball player accompanied by the caption, "All American American—But Not At ACC," to charges that the latest policy was "the most ridiculous ruling ever made by ACC's Board of Trustees." A student referendum in support of recruiting black athletes held in March recorded a vote of 445 in favor and 161 opposed, with 107 listing no opinion on the matter.[34]

When placed in perspective, trustees' reluctance to change the college's traditional discriminatory policies regarding nonwhite students is not difficult to understand. Intimidated by emotion-charged campaigns throughout much of the country by such radical right-wing groups as the John Birch Society and the Ku Klux Klan, conservative state and local leaders strongly resisted attempts to desegregate social and educational institutions. It was not unusual to find a Klan rally in virtually any area of the state during the 1960s. The grounds of the governor's mansion became the scene of cross-burnings in the summers of 1964 and 1966. Wilson County Klan activities made statewide news in July and November 1964, involving the black Presbyterian Church of Elm City and an integrated Thanksgiving Day worship service at Wilson's

Freshman Doris Greene and senior Barbara W. Singletary. 1967 Pine Knot.

First Baptist Church. Reports from the Federal Bureau of Investigation and the House Un-American Activities Committee labeled North Carolina as the number one Klan state in the country during 1964–66. Despite such pressure, college trustees again dealt with the controversy, voting in May 1965 to revise their earlier policy and permit the institution to recruit nonwhite students.[35]

The first black students to enroll at Atlantic Christian College entered during fall semester 1966. The 1967 *Pine Knot* pictures three African American students among a student body of 1,475, including Barbara W. Singletary, a senior from Winston-Salem who was apparently the first black graduate of ACC. Thelma Brown, a junior from New Bern, and Doris Greene, a freshman from Trenton, were also enrolled in 1966–67. Ross Albert, Paul Crouch, and Gene Purcell, members of the faculty during the 1960s recalled Greene as the first black student, apparently because of her active participation in campus activities, including Stage and Script, chorus, and United Campus Christian Fellowship (UCCF). *The Collegiate* described Greene's dignified portrayal of the princess of France in *Love's Labour's Lost*. Paul Crouch directed Greene in *Six Characters in Search of an Author*, in which she played "Madame Pace," in November 1967; in *The Little Foxes*, as "Adie," in October 1968; and in *The American Dream*, in December 1968. Greene won the drama award for contributions to Stage and Script in 1968 and was selected for "Who's Who" as one of fifteen seniors in 1970.[36]

Head coach Ira Norfolk and assistant Tom Parham likely anticipated the impact that talented black athletes could make upon a future basketball team. Meanwhile, the 1967–68 basketball team, led by All Carolinas Conference play-

Stage and Script cast members with director Cecil Willis. 1967 Pine Knot.

ers Larry Jones, a Mount Olive senior, and Ed Carraway, a junior from Maury, achieved a record of 10–6 and fourth place in the conference race. Carraway led the team in scoring with 21.6 points per game and established an ACC record with a total of 541 points for the season. Jones added 14.3 points and led the team with 12 rebounds per game. Juniors Clyde Stallsmith from Meadville, Pennsylvania, Bobby Gilmore from Sanford, and Bob Covington from Rockingham each contributed double-figure scoring averages.[37]

Carraway, undersized and frequently underrated, was, in many ways, an appropriate representative of the competitive athletic teams fielded by Atlantic Christian College in the 1960s. Both he and the team worked diligently to compete against taller and more physical opponents. Even at small colleges, players standing no more than five feet, eleven inches rarely made significant contributions on the basketball court. Displaying savvy, talent, determination, and the ability to overcome injuries, Carraway joined Jones in leading the Bulldogs to a respectable overall 1967–68 record of 16–10. The most satisfying victories were an emotional 87–85 victory over Campbell and a remarkable upset of nationally ranked Guilford, both coming before appreciative home-court crowds in Wilson Gymnasium. Coach Ira Norfolk called the win over Guilford his most important victory since arriving at ACC in 1964.[38]

In May 1968, sports editor Billy Dixon predicted a brighter future for the college's basketball program. Under the headline "Go-Go With Conetoe," Dixon announced the signing of James Jones and Clifton Black, ACC's first black student athletes. The young men had starred in basketball at Conetoe High School in Edgecombe County where Jones had served as president of the student body, and both had finished near the top of their graduating class. Dixon, a sophomore English major and a graduate of Wilson's Fike High School, predicted that Jones and Black would complement the strong cast of returning players on the 1968–69 team and open the door to recruitment of other talented black athletes.[39]

Although Black and Jones contributed as freshmen, joining tri-captains Gilmore, Stallsmith, and Carraway, plus fellow seniors Covington and Larry Schwab of Portsmouth, Virginia, the team never seemed to reach its potential. Despite frequent periods of excellent individual play and occasional triumphs over highly regarded teams, the overall season record of 13–17 was disappointing. *The Collegiate* praised Carraway's impressive offensive performances against conference favorite Lenoir Rhyne, Appalachian, and other opponents, and the paper singled out as a high point of the season Carraway's stellar defensive play against star guard Eddie Biedenbach in a narrow 82–76 loss to North Carolina State. Barton College later honored the contributions of Gilmore, Stallsmith, and Carraway by inducting the three 1969 graduates into the school's Athletic Hall of Fame.[40]

Of the three athletes, Carraway, who grew up near Wilson as a Greene County resident, was familiar with Atlantic Christian College because of local news coverage by *The Wilson Daily Times*. Connections between Greene County and ACC extend to the early twentieth century, and graduates of the college have taught at Greene County Schools for decades. Former ACC athletes James "Babe" Harrell of Walstonburg, class of 1960, and James "Rabbit" Fulghum of Rock Ridge, class of 1961, coached Carraway's Greene Central teams to two state championship tournaments. Both men gained acclaim as baseball and basketball coaches, and Barton honored Fulghum with induction into the college's Athletic Hall of Fame in 1989. While Carraway was a student on the Wilson campus, other Greene Central graduates also represented ACC athletic teams, including Larry Barrow, class of 1970, basketball; Myra Price, 1972, cheerleading; and Robert Speight, 1972, baseball. In other campus activities, Myra Price was junior class vice-president; Mahlon Aycock, 1971, served as secretary of SGA; Elvyn Seymour, 1970, was sophomore class officer and 1969 homecoming queen; and Carolyn Mewborn was honored as most popular freshman girl at the dance of that name in December 1966. Greene Central graduates participated in other activities including chorus and vocal ensemble. The relationship between the college and the county assumed special significance in the 1960s and may be seen as an example of affiliations that served the college and numerous eastern North Carolina communities throughout the century.[41]

In 1967–68, twenty Greene County residents were included in Atlantic Christian College's 1,479-member student body. Although Greene's total only tied for thirteenth place among counties supplying students and contributed a mere 1.5 percent of the college's total, Greene Central High School graduates provided a significant contribution to ACC. During the following year, the number of enrollees from Greene County increased by 35 percent. In addition to Fulghum and Harrell, Greene Central teachers of the 1960s with ties to Atlantic Christian College included William R. Batchelor, class of 1962; Sam Bundy Jr., 1960; James R. McLawhorn, 1950; Judy Rose Bundy, 1965; and Joann Thomas Cobb, 1956. These alumni likely had an impact on the college's increased enrollment of Greene County students during the period.[42]

Using 1967–68 as point of reference, nine North Carolina counties and the state of Virginia furnished a majority of the students attending the college in the late 1960s, contributing 971 students and 65.7 percent of ACC's enrollment. The remaining one-third of the institution's enrollment came from fifty-seven counties, sixteen states, and five foreign countries, each sending fewer than twenty students. Males made up 52 percent of the student body, outnumbering females by 770 to 709. Baptists dominated churches represented with 487, followed by Methodists, 345; Disciples of Christ, 227; and Presbyterians, 132. The counties furnishing the majority of ACC students were Wilson, 334; Wayne, 101; Wake, 77; Nash, 76; Johnston, 75; Beaufort, 49; Pitt, 49; Edgecombe, 43; and Lenoir, 43. Virginia sent 114 students, followed by Pennsylvania, 11; New Jersey, 10; and Maryland, 9.[43]

Young men attending ACC in the late 1960s paid particular attention to news of changes in war-torn Vietnam as well as to the latest reports regarding the military draft. Three days before President Johnson announced that he would not be a candidate for reelection in 1968, an article in *The Collegiate* examined the political dispute regarding suggestions that draft boards withdraw the deferment status of male students who protested military recruiting on college campuses. The student newspaper of 28 March 1968 printed an article by the president of the National Student Association comparing the climate on American college campuses to "that of a ghetto before a summer riot." Lamenting the fact that ACC students were not more active politically, Jim Bussell, editor of *The Collegiate*, wrote a lengthy article portraying a mythical "Kingdom of Apathetica, Where All Noblemen Are Deaf and Subjects Are

Fire and Flower Power

Blind." An example of the political apathy on campus was that the assassination of Martin Luther King Jr. in April 1968 led to only one letter to the editor and an editorial copied from the *New York Times*.[44]

Johnson's withdrawal from the 1968 presidential race opened the way for one of America's most heated political races, featuring veterans Humphrey, Nixon, and Robert Kennedy, plus Eugene McCarthy and George C. Wallace, newcomers to national campaigns. Robert Kennedy's assassination in June was followed in August by Chicago Mayor Richard Daly's orchestrated policy of "police brutality" against demonstrators outside the Democratic Convention. At ACC during the autumn of 1968, except for an editorial criticizing the tactics used by the SDS at the Chicago convention and the local YDC's vow to support the Humphrey-Muskie ticket, *The Collegiate* made little mention of national politics. In mid-October the faculty held a public debate on the candidates and the issues. President Wenger served as moderator while Mildred Hartsock and William Paulsell supported the Humphrey-Muskie ticket and the Democratic Party platform. They were opposed by E. D. Winstead and Hugh B. Johnston Jr., who backed the Nixon-Agnew team and the Republican program. On 31 October, virtually the eve of the election, the college held mock presidential elections.[45]

Student radicalism and violence at colleges and universities during 1968 brought *The Collegiate* to contrast conditions at Columbia University with those at ACC, praising the existing respect for community on the Wilson campus and criticizing radical tactics at several schools across the country. However, the prevailing apathy at ACC may have furnished the reason for the local media's description of a "riot" on the local campus immediately after the national election. A 7 November headline in *The Collegiate* proclaimed "Riot Leaves None Injured." The "riot" described by reporter and photographer Ben Casey involved "a display of fire and flower power" in front of the student union which was witnessed by students headed to class on Wednesday morning following Tuesday's elections. Having received official permission, four campus hippies displayed antidraft posters that opposed the promilitary stance of materials brought to the campus by Marine recruiters. Confronted by a group of about fifty students, described as consumed by a "fear of Communism . . . [and] blind nationalism," the pacifists eventually sold their posters to students who promised to read their messages. The situation became confrontational when the hippies learned that their posters had been dumped into a trash can and were being burned in front of the student union. Although talk of physical force ensued, no blows were struck, and results of the "riot" were, apparently, limited to Casey's photographs which appeared on page one of the newspaper. In the reporter's judgment, neither side had won, and the "riot" was unlikely to have significant impact upon the student body. The writer apparently consoled himself with the thought that the confrontation meant that, at least for the time being, "apathy took a back seat" on the campus.[46]

Casey's evaluation of student body apathy appears to have been accurate. As the year 1968 ended, ACC students displayed little discernible interest in national or international events with one significant exception—Vietnam. As spring semester 1969 opened, anxiety continued to plague male students faced with the possibility of being drafted to fight an unpopular, escalating war in southeast Asia. Following the inauguration of a new American President committed to winning "peace with honor" in Vietnam, college-age Americans throughout the country wondered what the future would bring.

FOURTEEN

At the Still Point of the Turning World

THE YOUTH-DOMINATED Bohemian counterculture typically referred to as hippies or "flower children" maintained a small but vocal following at Barton College during the 1960s and 1970s. Faculty teaching at the college at the time maintain that true hippies on the campus numbered approximately a dozen students and never reached more than twenty individuals. However, hippies changed the nature of the student body by encouraging public opposition to the Vietnam War, openly challenging what were seen as unfair and archaic restrictions, and urging greater tolerance of ethnic diversity. Those who favored the goals of the counterculture contend that the movement helped to push American society in a more liberal and humane direction. Critics were shocked by the sexual freedom espoused by the Bohemians, offended by their unkempt, frequently dirty appearances, and disdainful of their loud, hard rock style of music.[1]

The issues identified with the "flower children" which conservative Americans tended to find most offensive were their open, illegal use of marijuana and hard drugs and their active role in encouraging draft-age males to ignore the law by refusing to participate in the Vietnam War. Surveys suggest that at least half the nation's college population of the late 1960s smoked marijuana and that a minority used such mind-altering drugs as LSD. At New York's Woodstock festival in August 1969, America's counterculture reached its peak when an estimated 400,000 young people gathered to celebrate their revolution against political and social institutions that they neither liked nor trusted. To conservatives who had experienced a surge of patriotism three weeks earlier during television coverage of Neil Armstrong's walk on the moon and been thrilled by the words "one giant leap for mankind," the profane sex and drug-dominated orgy at Woodstock represented a huge move in the wrong direction.[2]

During the late 1960s and the 1970s, the increasing availability of drugs on high school and college campuses prompted ACC officials to consider the problem's negative implications for their school. Concerned that "dangerous drugs and . . . narcotics" were already being used by some ACC students at locations away from the college, the executive board of the Student Government Association passed a resolution supporting the prohibition of hard drugs on campus. The Convocation Coordinating Council chose drug abuse as the theme for 1970–71 convocations, and the Campus Christian Association sponsored seminars at ACC and at Wilson's First Christian Church featuring former addicts warning against the use of hard drugs.[3]

A survey taken in the autumn of 1971 by the North Carolina State University student affairs office found that 35 percent of the students admitted to using marijuana; 11 percent had tried hallucinogenic drugs such as LSD; and 2 percent had used hard drugs including heroin. Some ACC students smoked marijuana on campus during the early 1970s, and, although no specific cases are recorded, reports indicate that heroin and cocaine were available. Headlines in *The Collegiate* of 21 October 1971 read "Female Student Is 'Busted' In Caldwell Dorm." Following an investigation and hearing, the college discipline committee composed of faculty, staff, and students found the freshman guilty of possession of marijuana and recommended her indefinite suspension from the college.[4]

Editorials and letters to the editor show that the student body was divided on the question of whether suspension was too severe a punishment for smoking marijuana. Articles appearing in both *The Collegiate* and *Pine Knot* indicate that smoking marijuana had become a routine event for some ACC students and that many who did not use the drug refused to condemn the practice. A poll taken by *The Collegiate* in December 1971 revealed that 77 percent (143 of 185 students who replied to the survey) indicated that they had tried marijuana, and 33 students stated that they used "pot" at least ten times per month. Eighty-four students replied negatively and forty-three positively to the question of whether they had ever tried hard drugs. Letters to the editor questioned the validity of the survey, pointing out that ACC's enrollment was nearly 1,800 students. An interesting article in *The Collegiate* quoted information printed by several newspapers from a study conducted by a Dr. Burke of the Smithsonian Institution suggesting that seven of the nation's early presidents, including Washington, Jefferson, Madison, and Jackson, had used marijuana and/or hashish. Although editors of *The Collegiate* had learned that no "Dr. Burke" worked at the Smithsonian, they suggested that evidence did exist to prove that early Americans had used mild drugs, including marijuana.[5]

Revealing articles by members of *The Collegiate* staff reported student use of alcohol and drugs during off-campus parties and summer vacations. A Bohemian-style Halloween party at a townhouse on Wilson's Vance Street was described in November 1973 as "a place for culture heroes to gather" and the "Happening" of the social year. Featuring exotic cross-dressing costumes, loud music, and substantial supplies of alcohol and other stimulants, the party, attended by an estimated 200–300 people, was judged as "all in all a very nasty affair, an exercise in poor taste, but of course everyone loved it." A summer backpacking adventure to Asheville and the Great Smoky Mountains National Park taken by another student was made more pleasurable by drinking peach brandy and smoking an occasional "joint."[6]

The hippie dress code, which included headbands, military-style clothing, and peace symbols, was partially adopted by a wide segment of college-age youth. ACC Greek organizations organized a colorful "Hippie Party" in 1970 and typically used peace symbols to adorn articles of clothing and sketches of hippies to make statements on posters and in cartoons. Hard rock music, a central component of the counterculture movement, became a fixture on college campuses, especially through the appearance of bands that specialized in that style of music. Rock groups that played in Wilson Gymnasium between 1969 and 1976—frequently to overflow crowds—included Bloodrock, Brownville Station, J. Geiles, Hydra Rocks, Atlanta Rhythm Section, Poco, Kool and the Gang, and K. C. and the Sunshine Band.[7]

The military draft and the Vietnam War were key issues polarizing college campuses during the late 1960s and early 1970s. Many students and faculty members had taken a wait-and-see approach following Nixon's election and inauguration in order to allow time for the new President to deal with those issues. On 15 October 1969, with Nixon's new "Vietnamization" policy seeming to have little effect upon ending the war, peace advocates staged a national Vietnam War Moratorium. ACC's Campus Awareness Committee joined the national effort, sponsoring events at a daylong moratorium held in front of the student union. Standing by a flag-draped coffin between 8:00 AM and 6:00 PM, participants read aloud from *The Congressional Record* the names of those killed in Vietnam to an estimated 200 students. Art professor Tom Marshall, an organizer of the moratorium, recalled that a brief confrontation erupted when opponents of the service threw fruit and vegetables at participants. Marshall was summoned to appear before Dean Lewis Swindell Jr. and Presi-

Students and faculty protest the Vietnam War at the student union fountain. 1974 Pine Knot.

dent Wenger to explain his reported absence from scheduled classes in order to take part in the moratorium. Wenger dismissed the case after Marshall presented his grade book and invited the administration to question any student enrolled in the classes in question. Later that evening, approximately 120 students attended a "funeral service" for the deceased, which included folk music and student and faculty remarks advocating peace and brotherhood.[8]

During the early 1970s, *The Collegiate*'s periodic updates regarding the military draft and the appearance of visiting speakers, including representatives of the National League of Families of Prisoners and Men Missing in Action, helped to keep student attention focused upon the war. Phi Mu and Sigma Sigma Sigma sororities joined the Campus Awareness Committee in fundraising, signature collecting, and letter-writing efforts aimed at convincing the North Vietnamese delegation attending the Paris Peace Conference that American prisoners of war should be humanely treated according to the Geneva Accords. Student volunteers also aided lobbying efforts on behalf of American MIAs in Vietnam. In November 1970, *The Collegiate* supported

North Carolina Governor Robert Scott's proclamation designating a Week of Concern For Prisoners of War and Men Missing in Action in Vietnam.[9]

In the spring of 1970, Nixon's action to widen the war by sending American troops into neutral Cambodia caused widespread disruptions among college and university students. On 5 May, Kent State University became a tragic, bloody scene when four students, two of whom were not engaged in the antiwar protest, were killed by young National Guardsmen. Massive protests swept the country, bringing violence and cancellation of classes and final examinations at numerous schools, including the University of North Carolina at Chapel Hill. At Atlantic Christian College, sophomore newspaper staff member Jim Abbott, a resident of Charlottesville, Virginia, responded to the Cambodian invasion and Kent State killings with a scathing denunciation of SGA leaders for failing to discuss a motion to denounce President Nixon for ignoring the advice of his cabinet and for not consulting Congress before he "single-handedly plunged America further into the ever widening Southeast Asian holocaust." Abbott charged that the student leaders chose to adopt a "carefree, nonchalant attitude," ignored the suffering and anguish of the "REAL world," and lacked "the moral courage necessary" to take a stand against unwise and destructive government policies. The same issue of *The Collegiate* carried a cartoon of a longhaired peace advocate who had lowered his "Get Out of Cambodia Now!" sign, with the caption reading, "On second thought, maybe it would be safer in Cambodia than at Kent State!"[10]

The next issue of the newspaper featured Abbott's interview with President Wenger regarding Kent State's implications for Atlantic Christian College. Commending the students for the peaceful and rational way in which they had dealt with sensitive and potentially volatile issues, Wenger agreed that there could be justification for temporarily closing an educational institution facing dire circumstances. He stated that small colleges sometimes benefited from a personal closeness seldom found on large university campuses and credited the "extensive reservoir of understanding and good will here on our campus" with helping ACC deal effectively with "some uprising of student emotions." The president added that he would ask that the National Guard be brought on the college campus "only as a last resort."[11]

Although Congress changed draft laws to end automatic exemptions for college students and extended the draft until the summer of 1973, the war was no longer a dominant issue on the college campus after controversial issues regarding Cambodia and Kent State peaked in the late spring of 1970. Increasing South Vietnamese corruption, including the siphoning of United States aid into black market operations, frustrated Americans and produced a realization that the South Vietnamese government was both corrupt and undemocratic. President Thieu's misuse of power to intimidate opposition candidates in the 1971 elections brought Jim Abbott, then editor of *The Collegiate*, to comment that both American lives and dollars were being wasted in the Vietnamese War.[12]

The Paris peace talks, return of POWs, and search for MIAs continued to be issues of discussion at the college, along with the controversial question of whether or not amnesty should be granted to those who had avoided the draft. Finally, the college community learned that the war was over. Newspaper editor Tim Corbett of Walstonburg, class of 1975, described the long-awaited moment: "At 10:15 PM, 23 January, four beautiful people, who had heard the announcement, headed for all corners of the campus to spread the news. . . . Within fifteen minutes the chapel was full of people—happy people! PTL. A hymn was sung rejoicingly, there was a reading on Peace, and finally a time of silent prayer, where each individual prayer could be heard by the good Lord Himself."[13]

ACC students of the 1970s wanted to dispel the myth that the typical college student was a pot-smoking, long-haired hippie. Most students were young adults "looking for some outlet to funnel their energy." Responding to polls taken by the student newspaper, students generally praised the members of the faculty and staff as well as the friendly atmosphere at the college. They were, however, critical of the lack of social life on the campus, especially on weekends when many students left. The writers suggested activities that they felt would improve the college: drinking, visitation, and co-ed dorms. Students expected trustees to take action on the issue of drinking at their 23 October 1969 meeting. A student life committee resolution called for permitting the consumption of wine and beer at scheduled college functions. The SGA had approved a similar motion that included fraternity houses and other off-campus sites. The two resolutions received a favorable vote of over 70 percent in a student body referendum. The trustees, however, referred the matter to an ad hoc committee, which, in early 1970, failed to resolve the issue when deliberations ended with a tie vote. Despite student protest, the impasse remained for the next two years.[14]

Undeterred and working through proper channels, students realized more success with their campaign for visitation rights. In the spring of 1969, the administrative council supported a limited visitation policy advocated by the student life committee. Beginning on the day after spring break, 8 April 1969, women were allowed to visit the lounge and television area of the men's residence halls, Hackney and Waters. During the following spring, the newly elected SGA executive board announced that the student life committee had approved a new visitation policy on a one-year trial basis to begin in the autumn of 1970. The policy allowed unchaperoned visitation by women students in fraternity houses during hours specified by the committee. Women who chose to participate would be required to have parental permission. The fact that freshman women were excluded from participating in the more liberal policy prompted an editorial in *The Collegiate* in September 1970 suggesting that "Freshmen Are Human, Too!!" While conceding that rules intended to help high school graduates adjust to college life might have been passed with good intentions, the author argued that the rule, which campused freshman women during weeknights, was unfair. The only place that freshman women could go after dinner on Sunday through Thursday evenings was the library. Subsequent letters and editorials also criticized the general lack of social opportunities at ACC. Noting that "Greeks are what's happening on the campus," the writers argued that students who were neither fraternity nor sorority members tended to be left without "meaningful social activities."[15]

As graduation drew near in late April 1972 with the drinking issue still unresolved, student leaders decided to employ more drastic measures by presenting a list of fourteen grievances to the administration. In addition to demanding the right to consume alcoholic beverages in dormitories, fraternity houses, and other off-campus sites, the grievances called for extended visitation time in men's dormitories and fraternity houses. One of the more interesting demands was "permission to go barefooted on campus." Student leaders warned that "certain actions will be taken" should the administration fail to take immediate action upon the proposals. The student life committee resolved the barefoot issue almost immediately, voting to "remove all restrictions on footwear." The situation reached a peak on 2 May when 400–500 students met with the administrative council for a frank discussion of campus restrictions. In a confrontational but orderly session, students informed the administration that drinking already existed in every dorm. They also suggested that since women were equal to men they should have equal rights. In *The Collegiate* of 5 May, editor Jim Abbott proclaimed, "Apathy Is Dead." A guest editorial in the same issue thanked the student life committee for supporting the students' campaign for additional rights. An earlier student life committee recommendation that visitation hours in fraternity houses and "bachelor apartments" be extended to match curfew hours had been opposed by the administrative council in 1971. Apparently, the council had approved another committee suggestion that "open house" in men's dorms be allowed on an experimental basis from 1:00–4:00 PM on four Sunday afternoons. Majority approval of the residents was required for a dorm to participate in the experiment.[16]

Aware that some dormitory residents freely ignored college regulations, the administration remained firm in its attempt to keep alcoholic beverages off the campus. In 1974, when the college discipline committee recommended that students be placed on probation rather than suspended in cases where the dean of men discovered beer in their rooms, Wenger asked for an explanation. The chairman, a faculty member, answered that the committee was willing to recommend suspension for repeat violators but did not agree that students who were neither disruptive nor deliberately flaunting alcoholic beverages should be sent home. The discipline committee was also convinced that the students' right to privacy within their rooms should be honored. Although the president pointedly stated his disagreement with the committee's position, he allowed the probation verdict to stand. Regulations ridiculed by editors of *The Collegiate* as "Senseless Rules" in February 1971 continued to be official policy. ACC's rule against alcoholic beverages not only applied to dormitories and fraternities but to student-occupied private apartments in Wilson. The editors asked, "Who plans to run into every apartment in town to run out ACC women at 11:00 PM?"[17]

Actually, running became fashionable on college campuses during the 1970s when the fad called "streaking" became part of America's social history. Headlines of a March 1974 issue of *The Collegiate* carried the headline "It's A Bird, It's A Plane, It's Superstreaker!" Leigh Taylor's front-page article posed the question: "What is streaking? Answer: A form of art where an individual or group runs 'au natural' past Peeping Toms." On Monday, 4 March 1974, the country's latest fad arrived in sedate Wilson. Shortly past 10:00 PM, "six figures became nude flashes. Running and yelling" down Deans Street as girls peered from Hilley Hall and New Dorm windows and a curious crowd assembled along the curb to watch the show. Twenty minutes later, "three new naked nomads . . . waved their arms and danced in the street. . . . One streaker tripped over his pants. Another . . . used his 10-speed to travel." By 11:45 PM, five total streaks had transpired, the largest involving about twenty runners. The latter group gathered at Tweetie's and ran "down the red brick path between Harper and Hilley to the fountain where they cooled their feet." The girls at New Dorm exclaimed, "'Oh my goodness?' The Hilley girls

Still Point of the Turning World   257

Streakers join liberated co-eds in frustrating Dean Ward. 1974 Pine Knot.

shouted, 'Go, Go, Go!' The crowd on the curb stammered, 'Great Caesar's Ghost!'"[18]

The daring revelers continued their brash merriment on the following evening, when "the streaks were few but the fannies flew." An estimated 105 streakers began their "mass masquerade" at Wilson Gym. A crowd of faculty and townspeople watched them "sail past Waters Dorm, Moye Science Building, Caldwell Dorm, and climaxing the tiring trauma at the old gym." The Wilson police broke up the revelry at midnight, and the streaking fad was apparently over at ACC for the duration. *The Collegiate* stated that "all streakers were notified that a penalty would be levied if any streaker was caught."[19]

Although all of the recorded streakers were males, the 1974 *Pine Knot* reminded the college community that females had played an important role. In addition to streaking on campus, "another 'first' . . . was broadcast from Charleston to Baltimore—'Windowing' was introduced to the national scene by several women on campus. For a further description of this new Streak technique, inquire with the ladies of Hilley." The statement refers to a daring group of co-eds who removed upper garments and leaned out dorm windows, brazenly exposing themselves to the night air and to the stunned crowd standing below. Prominently included in two of the *Pine Knot*'s five large photographs that captured the titillating and historic event for the ages, was an irate dean of women, stalking the darkened campus wrapped in an overcoat and carrying an enormous flashlight. Dean Ward's left hand is planted firmly on her hip while her right hand holds and points the huge beacon toward second and third story windows of the women's dorm. Witnesses remembered an obviously exasperated Miss Ward, shouting, "Stop that! You . . . get back in that window!" among other words of advice. Despite her best efforts, the evening did not belong to the dean.[20]

While likely not consoling to exasperated college officials, the following week's campus newspaper did put the streaking fad into perspective. A reprinted editorial from the Lexington, Virginia, newspaper, dated 6 March 1974, informed the university community that streaking at Washington and Lee actually dated to the early nineteenth century. A student had earned the nickname "Naked Crump," when, after being apprehended for running unclothed through the village on an early morning in 1804, the lad admitted his guilt. As a consequence, trustees had "set a precedent for which today's streakers may be grateful—his punishment was simply a reprimand." For those who felt "certain the world is speeding off to hell at the hands of the college generation" the paper added, William Crump later became a United States Congressman and ambassador to Chile.[21]

While students of both genders struggled to liberalize social regulations at ACC, individuals and government agencies were already at work suggesting changes which would cause the 1960s and 1970s to become a revolutionary era for women's rights. Founded in 1966, the National Organization for Women (NOW) included nearly 50,000 members by 1975. The National Women's Political Caucus began functioning in 1971, and *Ms.* magazine, started by Gloria Steinem in 1972, began spreading the news on feminist issues. The proportion of women working outside the home increased dramatically, and in 1972 Congress passed the Equal Rights Amendment (ERA) along to the states for ratification. The amendment stated that equal treatment under the law could not be denied on the basis of gender.[22]

While changes in restrictions regarding women came slowly to American college campuses, ACC co-eds read in their St. Valentine's Day 1974 issue of the student newspaper that events at Louisburg College suggested dramatic changes for female students. Writing under the headline "Commentary," Carroll Aldridge of Colonial Heights, Virginia, class of 1975, noted that the Department of Health, Education, and Welfare had notified the student government president at Louisburg College of a pending investigation of alleged discrimination against women regarding curfew hours. Aldridge stated that if the HEW investigation found that a college's policies discriminated against females, it would constitute a violation of Title IX of the Educational Amendment Act of 1972. The act stipulated that colleges could lose federal funding if its policies discriminated against females. HEW had cautioned Louisburg that the school's separate hours for women students might be discriminatory. Noting that "several students at ACC" had also complained to HEW, Aldridge found obvious pleasure in warning the "little Caesars" who ran the college that their rule of the campus was quickly coming to an end. An April article reported that separate curfew hours for women and sign-in cards had disappeared on the larger UNC campuses.[23]

The Collegiate of 5 September 1974 reported that the federal Office for Civil Rights within HEW had notified ACC 23 May that its policy of maintaining different dormitory regulations based on sex was a violation of Title IX. Regulations found to be discriminatory were: "1. Sign in and sign out requirements. 2. Curfew requirements. 3. Discriminatory action for lateness. 4. Nights out regulations. 5. Quiet hours rules. 6. Limitations on out of town trips. 7. Overnight visitation rules." The college was instructed to submit proposals regarding changes or implementations "to alleviate the differences based on sex" within thirty days. At the first convocation on 5 September 1974, President Wenger informed the college community about the steps the school was taking to satisfy federal law.[24]

On 30 October the board of trustees met to act on the administration's proposed steps to bring about compliance with HEW guidelines. Major changes included hiring student resident assistants for dormitories, locking resident halls at midnight each night, and using coded identification cards to gain entrance between midnight and 3:00 AM. Sign-in and out cards would be provided by all residence halls, but their use would be voluntary, and quiet hours would be in effect between 8:00 PM and 8:00 AM Sunday through Thursday. Visitation would be allowed in lounge areas of residence halls during hours when a receptionist was on duty, and women would have visitation rights at fraternity houses between the hours of 4:00 PM and midnight. Overnight guests might sign in and stay in dormitories on nights not preceding school days. Student resident assistants would be present on every dorm floor to help students and to hold weekly room inspections. Open house would be allowed in dormitories during weekends from 8:00 PM to midnight on Friday and Saturday, and from 1:00 PM to 6:00 PM on Sunday. The college stated that implementation of the new system would occur no later than the start of fall semester 1975. Total costs of suggested changes were estimated at almost $6,000.[25]

Another major step announced by the college was raising women's athletics from the intramural level to the intercollegiate competition stage. Just like the men's athletics programs, women's teams would function directly under the jurisdiction of the director of athletics. They would have the same insurance benefits and receive funding for travel, uniforms, and athletic scholarships. Staff writer Barry Morgan of Durham, class of 1975, welcomed the new system, stating it "should bring about more freedom for all of the students at Atlantic Christian College." He also reported an addition that was already benefiting the school. Athletics Director David Adkins had recruited Jack Lassiter of Southern Durham High School to assist with college athletics and to help build a sports medicine program on campus. The recipient of the college's first grant-in-aid scholarship for an athletic trainer in 1974, Lassiter brought six years of experience to his job of treating and preventing athletic injuries.[26]

Atlantic Christian College women athletes had competed for years on a club-level basis against North Carolina colleges in Sports Day events in Greensboro, Greenville, and Raleigh. Since the late 1960s, they had played regularly scheduled games against area schools. Calling themselves the "Puppies" and representing the ACC Women's Recreation Association (WRA), Coach Carol McKeel's "extramural" basketball team ended its 1969–70 season with a 5–5 record. Norma Jean Respass, class of 1971, starred on McKeel's basketball and volleyball teams of the late 1960s. Respass' skilled play and later success as an educator and coach brought her induction into Atlantic Christian College's Athletic Hall of Fame. Sandra Langley, class of 1974, was another WRA two-sport athlete who received Hall of Fame membership. Excelling in volleyball and basketball at ACC, after graduation the Edgecombe County native returned home where she won numerous honors as a teacher and became a successful basketball coach. Debbie Purvis, Bethel native and class of 1975, was yet another of McKeel's basketball and volleyball stars to merit Hall of Fame selection and attain a distinguished career in teaching and coaching. Returning to her native Pitt County, Purvis compiled phenomenal records while coaching volleyball, basketball, and softball. Coach McKeel joined her former players as a member of the college Athletic Hall of Fame in 2000.[27]

Coach Barbara Smith's WRA tennis team, playing in only its second season in the spring of 1970, faced a five-game schedule with only three returning players and a lack of team depth. With cheerleader Myra Price as one of the newcomers and the likely starter at the number six spot, the "Puppies" prepared for what sportswriter Billy Dixon of Wilson suggested "could make for a long, hot spring." Despite hard play and some fine individual performances, ACC's WRA basketball program also struggled to field a competitive team and to attract spectators to home games. The 1974–75 team, led by promising freshmen Susie Davis of Hopewell, Virginia, and Lorraine Riley of Nash

Joan Adams and Cathy Wall spark the Lady Bulldogs team of 1976–77. 1977 Pine Knot.

County almost broke even, finishing the season with six wins and seven losses.[28]

"We've come a long way, baby" was the song of choice for the women's volleyball and basketball teams as fall semester began in 1975. Sportswriter Leigh Taylor felt that the tune accurately described changes for the women's athletics program at the college. Freshmen Phyllis Parish of Wendell and Susan Cherry of Ahoskie joined returning veterans Joan Adams of Wilson, class of 1977, and Mary Beth Bottoms of Elizabeth City, class of 1976, in forming the nucleus of the women's tennis team, then known as the Bulldogs. Competing for the first time in the North Carolina Association of Intercollegiate Athletics for Women (NCAIAW), the team rebounded from a slow start with wins over UNC-Wilmington, Campbell, and Methodist College. ACC's volleyball team, led by

Susie Davis and Jackie Twisdale of Franklin, Virginia, defeated Chowan College and finished fourth in the conference tournament; the basketball team completed the regular season with a winning record of 10–4. During the 1976–77 season, Davis and freshman Kathy Wall earned All-District honors while leading the women's basketball team to a fine 12–6 regular season record.[29]

Despite excellent play by Joan Adams, the Bulldog women's tennis team struggled in 1977, ending the season near the bottom of the District II standings. A leader on both the basketball and tennis teams, Adams rarely lost a tennis match in four years of play, compiling a singles record of 67–14, while gaining wins over number one players at colleges that included North Carolina State, Campbell, and East Carolina. Adams won the Edward L. Cloyd Sr. Award as the senior athlete with the highest academic average and the Coggins Cup as the best all-around senior. She was also inducted into the ACC Athletic Hall of Fame and selected as an Academic All-American. Davis, class of 1979, was an Athletic Hall of Fame member who starred in volleyball and basketball, winning NCAIAW All-District honors three times and All-Carolinas Conference recognition twice. She is the college's only women's basketball player to score over 1,400 points and garner more than 1,400 rebounds. Kathy Wall, class of 1980 and Ellerbe native, was one of the school's great basketball players and holds the career scoring record with 1,727 total points. The Athletic Hall of Fame member was an All NCAIAW Division player four times, All-CIAC twice, and a cocaptain of ACC's 1980 Carolinas Conference championship team.[30]

In addition to increased funding, women's athletics benefited from conference membership, athletics scholarships, improved insurance coverage, services provided by an athletics director, and greater visibility through expanded coverage from local news media. Although women's athletic events still received less publicity than men's sports and attracted fewer spectators, women's gains during and after the mid-1970s were significant. Between 1972 and 1977, the college supported seven intercollegiate athletic teams for men. During the same period the women's teams played abbreviated schedules under the guidance and control of the Women's Recreation Association and the department of health and physical education. Between 1972 and 1975, the WRA sponsored basketball and tennis, adding volleyball in the autumn of 1975.[31]

During the two years immediately before Title IX implementation, 1972–74, the college newspaper's coverage for the seven intercollegiate men's athletic teams typically averaged three fourths of a page to one full page, while coverage of the two women's sports usually averaged less than one fourth of a page and was frequently excluded altogether. The 1974–75 year brought significant change. Women's athletic events were covered in virtually every edition of *The Collegiate* and typically occupied at least half as much space as men's sports. During the first two years of Title IX's impact, 1975 to 1977, the newspaper provided coverage of all three women's sports, but the coverage was sporadic and actually declined in quantity in comparison to that given the men's teams. The yearbook coverage of women's sports during the same period was far more equitable. If the two men's teams receiving the most coverage are compared with the coverage of women's basketball and tennis during 1972–75, and a third men's sport is included to match the addition of volleyball beginning in 1975, the coverage becomes nearly even. The visibility given to athletics through photographs in the official *Atlantic Christian College General Catalog* also reflects gender disparity. Photographs of men's sports appeared in four of five publications between 1976 and 1980 while only one catalog contained a photograph of women's intercollegiate athletics. Total photographs in the five catalogs were nine for male athletes and one for females.[32]

Women's basketball, volleyball, and tennis were headed by capable coaches McKeel and Smith, but the men's program boasted seven sports (six until 1972) to the three women's sports (two until 1975). Men's athletic teams also had an advantage through previous years of participation, and they usually controlled what meager finances were allotted for athletic scholarships. The provision listed in the ACC *General Catalog* that "Responsibility for developing policy for both men's and women's intercollegiate athletic programs is lodged in the College's Athletic Council" created part of the problem. Between 1969 and 1979, the Athletic Council typically consisted of eleven members, seven from the faculty-staff, two students, one trustee, and one alumnus. Although the student members typically included a male and a female, only 2 percent of the other members (2 of 96) who served during the ten-year period were females. Coach Mewborn (later McKeel) served in 1969–70, and Coach Smith served in 1976–77. By comparison, in the 2000–2001 academic year, Barton College sponsored six teams for men (baseball, basketball, cross-country, golf, soccer, and tennis) and six teams for women (basketball, cross-country, soccer, softball, tennis, and volleyball). The college offered grants-in-aid on a limited basis in each sport. Important change also occurred in the committee that recommended athletic policy. The Barton Athletics Committee in 2000–2001 had no trustees, alumni, or student members. The committee consisted of seven members of the faculty, four of whom were women.[33]

The 1970s were a successful period for several ACC athletic teams, marked by the performances of all-conference and all-district players and a coaching staff that ranks among the most gifted in the school's history. Clifton Black was named All-District 29 and the most outstanding athlete on campus in 1971. Coach Ben Pomeroy arrived at ACC as head basketball coach in 1972 and was joined by assistant coach Brian Chalk, a former Bulldog player. Allen Searson of Columbia, South Carolina, and Richard Battle of Rocky Mount were two of Pomeroy's players selected to the honorary All-Carolinas Conference team. When Pomeroy left the college to pursue other career options and devote more time to his family, praise for his positive impact upon the school came from all quarters.[34]

Edward L. Cloyd Jr., professor of education and senior member of the coaching staff, led his golf team to third place in the Carolinas Conference in 1972 and to back-to-back District 29 championships in 1974 and 1975. Leading the latter teams were Tom Barnes of Wilson, Carey Pittman of Scotland Neck, Butch O'Briant of Elm City, and Leigh Taylor. The team finished the 1975 season with a record of twelve wins and two defeats. The 1972 track team, led by John Liles of Raleigh and Danny Smith, placed second in the district and fourth in the Carolinas Conference. Liles, class of 1972, led the team for four years and became the first track star elected to Barton College's Athletic Hall of Fame. Teammate and classmate James Boykin Jr. of Wilson, in introducing Liles at the Hall of Fame banquet in 2000, called the honoree "the Jim Thorpe of the ACC track team."[35]

David Adkins arrived at the college in 1972 to coach soccer, the newest men's sport, and to serve as assistant professor and athletic director. Soccer soon attracted a large following and challenged basketball as the school's most popular sport. Fred Claridge and Steve Sellers, both from Falls Church, Virginia, were named to the All-Carolinas Conference team in 1974. Claridge was also a 1975 selection and was joined on the honorary team by Chuck Rierson of Greensboro and Chris Smallwood of Fairfax, Virginia. Adkins became District 29 Coach of the Year in 1976 after leading the Bulldogs to a school record season of eleven wins and five losses. Players on the All-District team included Chris Smallwood, David Smallwood, David Roughton of Virginia Beach, Mike Southard of Stokesdale, and Tony Barriteau of Wilson. The Smallwood brothers also won All-Carolinas Conference honors.[36]

The baseball and tennis teams appeared to justify sportswriter Russell Rawlings' evaluation of the overall quality of athletics in 1976–77 as "the finest ever in the history of Atlantic Christian College." The baseball team enjoyed a high district ranking, finishing with a record of 23–13 and advancing to the district playoffs. Centerfielder Robin Rose was named to the All-District 29 and All-Carolinas Conference teams, and Coach Larry Thompson became district Coach-of-the-Year. After the 1976 tennis team won a seventh straight district championship and earned yet another trip to the national tournament in Kansas City, Coach Tom Parham's overall record stood at 162 wins and 52 losses. Success continued in 1977 as Tom Morris won the singles crown and Pat Taylor became All-District for a record fourth time, and the two were joined on the All-District 29 team by teammates Brian Staub, Asad Niaz, Jay Aldridge, and Sam Modlin. Finishing the season with a record of 26–3, the best for any sport in ACC's history, the team ranked ninth nationally. Morris became the college's first athlete to win NAIA All-American honors as a singles player.[37]

Excellent teaching was as abundant in the classrooms as it was on the courts and playing fields of Atlantic Christian College during the decade of the 1970s. Shakespeare scholar Mildred Hartsock, prolific writer and gifted teacher, led a talented faculty, many of whom had been brought to ACC by President Wenger and Lewis Swindell Jr., dean of the college and professor of education. Religion and philosophy remained one of the strongest academic departments on campus despite the loss of Billy Tucker to Texas Christian University, where he later served as chancellor. In 1972–73, William Paulsell chaired the six-member department that included Roger Bullard, Gerald Harris, Dan Hensley, Eugene Purcell, and Allan Sharp. The group included faculty leaders, published scholars, distinguished preachers, community leaders, a future seminary dean, and a future seminary president. Chairman Russell Arnold led an art faculty of Ed Brown, Norbert Irvine, and Tom Marshall, each of whom brought distinction to the college through work displayed in galleries and museums around the country. Assistant professor of music William Duckworth's compositions gained national acclaim.[38]

Learning frequently took place outside traditional classroom settings such as poetry and short story contests and art festivals. In the spring terms of 1971 and 1972, the fourth and fifth Festivals of Contemporary Arts took place during five-day periods on the campus. ACC students and faculty members joined visiting artists in drama, art, and music lectures, discussions, and performances. Participants included the college chorus, the ACC band, and Stage and Script, along with Paul Crouch, director of drama, and music professors Ross Albert, James Cobb, and Andrew Preston. In 1972, *Crucible*'s second prize in poetry was awarded to Rebecca Jenkins Roughton, an ACC art graduate from Greensboro, who had won previous awards in art and poetry. Ruby Shackleford's creative writing students held a reading from *Rounding Off*, a volume of poems written by the class. Visiting speakers during the 1970s included social critic and futurist Alvin Toffler, author of *Future Shock*; South Carolina novelist and poet James Dickey; Atlanta civil rights leader Julian Bond; and Yale Shakespearean scholar Maynard Mack. In the spring semester of 1976, the English department sponsored a daylong workshop focused upon techniques for teaching Shakespeare in the high school classroom. Participants included Folger Shakespeare Library scholars, members of ACC's English faculty, and the college's early music ensemble directed by Ross Albert.[39]

Students and faculty also gained new insights through travel courses during the 1970s. Excursions included history and social sciences' trips to Monticello, Richmond, Philadelphia, and Washington, D.C., as well as the art department's annual New York museum tours and foreign travel in Canada and Europe. During the summer of 1971, Professor Gertrud Schatz chaperoned seven students on a successful trip to Germany that offered six semester hours of credit. Staying in hostels, which charged as little as $1.50 per night including meals, the group also visited Austria, Luxembourg, and Switzerland. In the summer of 1973, Schatz and her husband, Edward, took eighteen students to Europe to study economics and business or German history and culture. In 1975, political science professor Amrut Nakhre accepted an invitation from the International Peace Research Institute to travel to Oslo, Norway. In February 1976, he chaperoned students on a trip to Toronto, Canada, visiting Washington, D.C., and New York City en route.[40]

Not all faculty members were popular with students, and some gained reputations as boring and/or incompetent. Jim Abbott, editor of *The Collegiate*, phrased the problem bluntly in March 1972 in "What To Do With Faculty Duds." Abbott urged the SGA to conduct a faculty evaluation, "whether or not the faculty sanctions it." Receiving approval from the student life committee, the SGA held the evaluation in the spring of 1973. Some faculty expressed doubts about the idea, regarding the evaluation with skepticism and even hostility. "You're trying to get my job," one veteran faculty member accused the faculty advisor assisting with the evaluation. Unfortunately, after completing the survey, student enthusiasm waned at the idea of tabulating the results. When school reopened in the fall, students remembered the unfinished project. "Where are the results of the professor evaluation survey last spring?" questioned a guest editorial in *The Collegiate* of September 1973. Finally, in February 1974, new SGA president Andy Gay, a senior business major from Zebulon, announced the completion of the task and expressed general satisfaction with the project. He stated that the results of the survey, including "some 10,000 pages" of individual comments, would be filed in the SGA office and would be made available to members of the college community upon request. Copies went to department chairmen to share with faculty members desiring to learn from their students' opinions and improve instructional quality on the campus. Despite the problems that befell the project, the 1974 survey was the college's first campus-wide faculty evaluation and was initiated at SGA request.[41]

The beginning of the 1970s was especially significant for Atlantic Christian College because of the launching of the school's twelfth academic major, a baccalaureate degree nursing program. The board of trustees approved the venture in February 1970, following a two-year study led by Professor J. P. Tyndall and aided by college officials and representatives of medical boards and hospitals in Wilson and surrounding counties. In September, the school's first nursing majors joined chairman Laura W. Thigpen, professor Mary S. Steele, and adjunct professors Henry D. Haberyan Jr. and Robert P. Hadley in launching the new program. Tyndall, chairman of the ACC department of science, helped to guide the venture through its early stages. Following assurance from the National League for Nursing regarding the high probability of its granting national accreditation, the nursing program became the first offered by a private college in eastern North Carolina. Wilson physician Henry D. Haberyan, listed in the School of Nursing in the 1966–67 *General Catalog*, was apparently the college's first nursing faculty member. He was joined in 1967–68 by Dr. Robert P. Hadley. Dr. Thigpen, a native of Edgecombe County and the first chairman of the nursing department, held degrees from the University of North Carolina at Greensboro, Emory University, and the University of Pittsburgh. She had served in the United States Army Nursing Corps and directed nursing programs at Emory and at Wilson Memorial Hospital.[42]

Aided by college and regional medical support, the nursing program gained early accreditation from the North Carolina Board of Nursing and rapidly grew in size and prominence. In 1972–73, the college inaugurated a family nurse practitioner (FNP) program. By the time that the first nursing class graduated on 17 May 1974, there were 178 majors. Boasting eight full-time and two part-time faculty members, the department expected enrollment to exceed 225 majors during the following year. In September 1974, the college announced plans to build a Nursing Education Building containing approximately 14,700 square feet adjacent to Moye Science Hall at a cost of some $583,000. Funding for construction came from a federal grant of $302,152 and a Z. Smith Reynolds Foundation grant of $75,000. On 18 April 1975, the National League for Nursing granted accreditation to the ACC program to be retroactive for eight months prior to that date. At the time, the maximum number of 235 majors were enrolled, and the department planned to graduate about fifty nurses per year.[43]

A small but important project originated with a group of religion majors led by Steven Sprinkle, class of 1974, and guided by professor Gene Purcell. Students seeking an appropriate place to worship on the campus and often frustrated by Howard Chapel's lack of availability because of extensive use sought permission to build a meditation center on campus. Receiving encouragement from President Wenger and support from the student body, the group gained the trustees' approval in October 1973. The center would be a small, sturdy redwood structure of modular design located adjacent to Howard Chapel. After getting a cost estimate of $15,000 from the college's architect, the students formed a committee of laymen and Disciples leaders to raise funds and also elicited student promises to contribute much of the labor. In Sprinkle's words: "It is refreshing to be a part of a movement set in motion and sustained by the Spirit of Christ on the college campus, and A.C. students who are a part of the movement look forward to the day when our college will physically embody its claim to educate and nurture the spirits of its students as well as their minds."[44]

The Collegiate of 6 December 1973 contained a drawing of the meditation center and revealed that students, Disciples churches, individuals, and classes had contributed nearly $10,000 toward building costs. The college advanced the remaining $5,000 to the Campus Christian Association to enable construction to begin. Barry Morgan of Durham and Rob Coleman of Emporia, Virginia, members of the class of 1975, led efforts to raise money and organize labor on the campus. In May 1974, Sprinkle suggested "Still Point" as an appropriate name for the center. The name was taken from T. S. Eliot's poem *Four Quartets*, which reads "the light is still / At the still point of the turning world." *The Collegiate* of 16 January 1975 carried a photograph of the nearly completed building and revealed a new brick walkway leading to the entrance. Photographs in the 1974 *Pine Knot* showed students engaged in construction and fund-raising events on behalf of Still Point and depicted the center as "A DREAM COME TRUE."[45]

With Still Point completed in the early autumn of 1974, students began using the center for meditation and prayer. Guides from the admissions office proudly showed the center to prospective students and their parents, and Still

The Still Point. 1975 Pine Knot.

Point tours became a regular feature of orientation week. Unfortunately, a few people chose to violate the sanctity of Still Point by abusing the center. The deteriorating condition of Still Point prompted stern rebuke from senior staff writer Jamie Brame, a religion major from Eden, in *The Collegiate* of January 1976. Brame noted holes that had been knocked in the wall, damage to the carpet, and a broken door frame. Worse still was the desecration of the worship center caused by inappropriate student behavior. Referring to the usurpers as "desecrators of holy places," Brame asked for student body help in maintaining the sanctity of the center and warned that future offenders would find "a few of us turning into something other than loving mystics if we catch the meditation center being abused anymore."[46]

As Atlantic Christian College's seventy-fifth birthday approached during spring 1977, members of the college community reflected upon a lengthy list of recent accomplishments. Reaccreditation from NCATE in the fall of 1975 and the successful beginning of another SACS self-study in September 1976 indicated that the academic standing of the institution remained sound. Enrollment, which for 1972–73 had risen to 1,770 students with 1,599 listed as full-time, remained strong in 1976–77 with a total enrollment of 1,688 and 1,528 listed as full-time students. The necessity of modifying student record keeping and the school's commitment to continue graduating students adept in using current technology prompted installation of the first computers at the college, beginning with the registrar's office in spring 1972. Although construction on the campus had peaked during the previous decade, a new dormitory for women, completed in 1970, was followed by the meditation center in 1974, and the nursing education building in 1976. In addition, the new library neared completion in the spring of 1977. It was particularly satisfying that the college's fifteen-year fund-raising campaign, begun in 1962, showed promise of reaching its goal on schedule.[47]

Friends of the college also recalled significant recent losses, including deaths of earlier leaders and the demise of the neighborhood store that had become an ACC institution. A predawn fire dealt extensive damage to Tweetie's store and the adjacent College Beauty Salon on Sunday, 6 October 1974. Firefighters labored for hours to control the blaze, which was apparently caused by an electrical shortage in the roof of the building. Staff writer Randy Holloman noted that the little store had been a vital part of campus life for twenty-seven years, creating such customs as "Tweetie Hour" and "Tweetie Break." In a letter to the editor of *The Collegiate* of October 17, "Tweetie" Etheridge thanked the entire college community and especially "all the dear students" for offers of aid as well as multiple acts of kindness extended to his family. Although Etheridge considered restoring the popular site, the difficulties of meeting zoning restrictions and high estimated rebuilding costs ultimately brought an end to his dream. One of ACC's cherished institutions remained a charred shell until it was purchased and demolished by the college.[48]

An additional loss suffered by the institution in October 1974 was the death of Charles C. Ware at age eighty-eight in Jacksonville, Florida. Serving as curator, historian, and registrar of the school, Ware provided the institution with years of dedicated service crucial to the early success of the college. As founder and editor of *North Carolina Christian* between 1920–54, he tirelessly praised the virtues and chronicled the needs of the institution. Ware established the Carolina Discipliana Collection, a significant repository of manuscripts, documents, and histories related to the church in the Carolinas, whose ownership was shared by The Christian Church (Disciples of Christ) in North Carolina and Barton College. The author of twenty books, including *A History of Atlantic Christian College*, a biography of Barton Warren Stone, and a history of the Disciples of Christ in North Carolina, Ware was awarded an honorary doctor of divinity degree by the college in 1954.[49]

Ware's death was followed by that of the college's first male graduate, C. Manly Morton, who had entered the college on its opening day in 1902 and earned an A.B. degree in 1909. Morton died in Ft. Lauderdale, Florida, on 25 February 1976, two days prior to his ninety-second birthday. As a pioneer missionary and educator in Latin America, Morton had received honors from the Republic of Paraguay and the Commonwealth of Puerto Rico. The recipient of an honorary Doctor of Divinity degree from Atlantic Christian College in 1952, Morton was always a loyal friend and supporter, frequently visiting and speaking at his alma mater throughout his life. *The Collegiate* article reporting Morton's death praised the former missionary's friendly and generous spirit. Dr. Morton last visited the campus during homecoming festivities in the autumn of 1975, when he received the Alumnus of the Year Award.[50]

The greatest blow to ACC came on a quiet, overcast Saturday afternoon in February 1977 as the campus, the town of Wilson, and surrounding areas lay covered by a soft white blanket of snow, the result of a surprise storm. President Arthur D. Wenger was rushed from his home to Wilson Memorial Hospital following a heart attack. He was listed in fair to poor condition and expected to remain incapacitated for an extended period. Six days later, struck by a second attack as he remained in intensive care, Wenger spoke with family members and friends before dying on 25 February. The strength and vibrancy of the man had led to expectations of complete recovery; thus the college community was devastated by his sudden death. Tom Marshall, who had met with Wenger only a few hours prior to his hospitalization, expressed in a private letter the shock felt by many upon learning of Wenger's death. Marshall also found the weather on the day of the funeral, Sunday, February 27, to be very appropriate: "They buried him today. It thundered and rained and the sun shone, all at the same time. Symbolic . . . it was a lot like him, a booming voice, a forceful manner, great vision combined with a constant smile. Well, tomorrow we'll start to pick up the pieces and keep on moving ahead, but it'll never be the same."[51]

Following a memorial service for Dr. Wenger in Howard Chapel on Monday, 28 February, several members of the faculty lingered to talk briefly on the patio fronting Hines Hall. Turning to face the group, Roger Bullard stated, "Gentlemen, Atlantic Christian College as we have known her, is no more."

FIFTEEN

A Rich Lode in Our Own Backyard

ARTHUR D. WENGER'S sudden death stimulated talk of significant gains at Atlantic Christian College during a presidency that spanned twenty-one years. Wenger trailed only Howard S. Hilley in length of presidential tenure and was the only leader besides John J. Harper to die in office. In a special meeting honoring the ACC president in August 1976, Wilson Chamber of Commerce leader John Palmer drew comparisons between the college in 1956 when Wenger took the helm and the institution twenty years later. Palmer compared the recent "discovery" by the Wilson community of the college's true value to a man unexpectedly finding diamonds on his own property. Referring to the college as "a rich lode in our own backyard," Palmer noted that ACC had added ten new buildings and increased its estimated property value from $1.6 million to $7 million between 1956 and 1976. With completion of the new library then under construction, the value would increase to $8 million. While acknowledging that the financial stability of the college and other positive factors should not be attributed to Wenger alone, Palmer gave the president a "lion's share" of the credit. Years later, friends of the college and members of Wenger's immediate family recalled his modest nature and tendency to shift praise to others. Following Wenger's death, trustees acted quickly to establish a memorial fund in honor of the late president.[1]

Thomas J. Hackney Jr., chairman of the board of trustees, recalled his close relationship with the president and remembered traveling with Wenger to raise money for the college. Hackney praised the leadership, integrity, and public speaking skills of the former president. Faculty and students also lauded Wenger's virtues. Professor Gerald Harris, speaking at the memorial service on campus, stated that the president encouraged faculty members to express themselves freely and held no grudge against those who opposed the president's position. Milton Adams praised his former boss's love of the school, adding, "He was unquestionably Mr. Atlantic Christian College." Frederick Claridge, editor of *The Collegiate*, noted that Wenger impressed students with his concern and leadership. Claridge praised Wenger's role in supporting racial integration at the college and in persuading trustees to add a student representative to the board.[2]

Dennis Rogers, Raleigh *News and Observer* columnist and former ACC student, referred to Wenger as "the heartbeat of the school" and praised his devotion and leadership. Remembering the president's love of students, Rogers recalled a time when his own poor academic performance had prompted a summons to Wenger's office. Informing the young man that he was wasting his time, Wenger advised Rogers to drop out of school, join the army, gain maturity, and then try college again. Although angry with Wenger at the time, Rogers followed his advice carefully, adding that "I never had a chance to tell him thanks." The Raleigh writer suggested in his column that readers consider making a positive impact upon society by contributing to the Arthur D. Wenger Memorial Fund. The fund's rapid growth allowed the college to enroll the first two Wenger Scholars in the fall of 1980.[3]

With the exception of Milton Adams, James D. Daniell, Bethany R. Joyner, and Sarah Bain Ward, and a few senior members of the faculty, the college's administrative staff and faculty of 1977 had been hired during Wenger's tenure. They included Lewis H. Swindell Jr., dean of the college; Zeb Whitehurst III, dean of students; Milton Rogerson, director of publicity and special activities; David Cleveland, director of development; Dan Hensley, chaplain; Otis Coefield, library director; Harry Swain, director of summer school and college preparatory program; H. Larry McRacken, dean of men; David Adkins, athletic director; Bruce Tingle, director of placement; William E. Smith, director of alumni affairs; Lee Moore, superintendent of buildings and grounds; Harry A. "Al" Pridgen, assistant business manager; Marie Deans, director of financial aid; Judith Parrish, director of student center; Mary Frances Griffin, head nurse; Cleo Murray, bookstore manager; Jessie Daniel, assistant dean of women; and Rebecca Wiggins, executive housekeeper. These veteran administrators and members of their staff served ACC for years and helped to guide the college through a challenging period of leadership change. Catherine Gaylord, William Kent, Kathryn Lamm, Dick Bennett, Brenda Davidson, Ruth Dunn, and Melba Williams were others who rendered valuable service.[4]

Board chairman T. J. Hackney Jr. stated that an immediate search would begin for a permanent president and announced that Milton L. Adams had agreed to the trustees' request to serve as acting president. Widely respected

Milton and Sarah Loftin Adams. Scope, March–April 1981.

for his integrity and years of dedication to the college, the popular business manager had helped to make ACC one of the more financially stable private institutions in the state. In reporting the news of Adams' appointment, editors of *The Collegiate* noted that only twice during the past two decades had the school failed to finish a fiscal year with a balanced budget. The fact that many small colleges of the time faced serious economic difficulties made the achievement particularly impressive. Hackney also announced that Lewis Swindell would postpone retirement until a suitable replacement as academic dean could be hired. Respected throughout the region for his expertise in education, Swindell continued to be an active commissioner with the Southern Association of Colleges and Schools. His retirement from the college occurred 23 December 1977, when Kenneth St. John, former chairman of the education department, assumed the position of acting dean until the end of the 1977–78 academic year.[5]

A Rich Lode in Our Own Backyard 275

On 13 May 1977, Milton Adams presided at the college's seventy-fifth graduation as 355 seniors received degrees. The commencement speaker was Governor James Baxter Hunt Jr., a Wilson native who later served on the school's board of trustees. *The Collegiate* stated that Hunt's reputation as an education governor made him an especially appropriate commencement speaker since Atlantic Christian College led the state's private colleges in total number of public school teachers graduated. Barton College was the first school to award Governor Hunt an honorary degree. Both the governor and alumna Naomi Morris, North Carolina Court of Appeals judge and a college trustee, received honorary Doctor of Laws degrees. In December 1977, the annual faculty-staff Christmas dinner took on a different look when Milton and Sarah Adams broadened the event to include all full-time college employees. During a festive ceremony following the dinner, each member of the college family received a ham, turkey, or fruitcake, demonstrating the college's appreciation for their years of dedicated service.[6]

In September 1977, college publications announced that Dr. Harold C. Doster, president of Culver-Stockton College in Canton, Missouri, would become president of Atlantic Christian College 1 January 1978. Board chairman T. J. Hackney Jr. stated that the search committee was impressed with Doster's experience, enthusiasm, and proven abilities. A native of Mayfield, Ohio, the newly appointed president held an A.B. degree from Bethany College, a B.D. from Yale, and both M.A. and Ph.D. degrees from the University of Michigan. Doster had earned a reputation as a talented fund-raiser during his tenure at Culver-Stockton, where monetary giving tripled and the endowment fund had more than doubled. An ordained minister in the Disciples of Christ Church, Doster had held pastorates in Christian churches in Athens and Meighs counties, Ohio, and positions at Bethany College in West Virginia, Alice-Lloyd College in Kentucky, and Potomac State College in West Virginia prior to arriving at Culver-Stockton. Doster's wife, June Marken Doster, of Des Moines, Iowa, was a graduate of Iowa State University with a master's of religious education degree from Yale. Accompanying the Dosters to Wilson were their four children: Deborah, 17; Diana, 16; Donald, 13; and Denise, 8. The outgoing and energetic Doster family made positive impressions upon both the college and Wilson communities.[7]

Harold Doster was inaugurated as Atlantic Christian College's ninth president on Sunday, 8 October 1978, in a colorful event witnessed by an estimated crowd of 1,000 people, including representatives from seventy-five colleges, universities, and societies. T. J. Hackney Jr. presided over the ceremony,

President Harold Doster, 1978–83. 1979 Pine Knot.

which featured Governor James B. Hunt Jr., Congressman L. H. Fountain, and trustee vice-chairman Bruce Riley. After accepting a medallion and mace embedded with symbols representative of the college and crafted especially for the occasion, Doster announced seven major goals of his administration in his inaugural address. These were an endowment of at least $1 million for each 100 students enrolled, totaling approximately $15 million; current gifts to undergird the operating budget of $2 million; faculty compensation increased to the level of the average salaries of the state's public colleges and universities; a fund of approximately $5 million for land purchases, new buildings, remodeling, and equipment; an improved system of evaluating the quality of the college's educational system; a student life program that would facilitate leadership and learning; and the maintenance and enhancement of a community of scholars that would serve as a model of leadership for church-related liberal arts colleges. Doster concluded his address by stating that ACC had "a praise-worthy past, a promising present, and a challenging future."[8]

In addition to finding the administration busily planning inauguration events, students arriving for fall semester 1978 discovered other changes. Three new deans had arrived on campus, and a former dean now served in a new position. F. Mark Davis had become the new academic dean, Gordon Joyner was dean of students, and Alvah C. Monshower served as dean of men. Former dean of students Zeb Whitehurst had become the school's first director of college relations. An additional new position had been announced earlier—Milton Adams, who retained his post as business manager, had also been named the school's first vice-president.[9]

Mark Davis, a native of West Virginia, came to Wilson from Augsburg College in Minneapolis where he had served as associate dean and director of special programs. He held an A.B. degree from Bryan College in Dayton, Tennessee, an M.A. from the University of Tennessee, and a Ph.D. from Duke. Gordon L. Joyner, a native of Sims, arrived at ACC from Methodist College where he had served as dean of students. Joyner, who held a B.A. degree from Culver-Stockton College and a M.Ed. from Auburn, had completed a military career with the United States Air Force. Alvah Monshower, a native of Manhattan, Kansas, who was also a retired military officer, held a B.A. degree from the University of Maryland and an M.A. from East Carolina. Whitehurst, a native of Farmville, had earned a B.A. degree at Atlantic Christian College and a M.Ed. from the University of North Carolina at Chapel Hill. The popular former dean of students, who had served his alma mater since 1967, received praise for his dedication to students in the 1973 *Pine Knot* and was featured as one of the school's "Campus Celebrities" by *The Collegiate* staff in April 1978. The college honored Whitehurst with the alumni of the year award in 2000.[10]

Students greatly valued the counseling and friendship of other staff members, two of whom, Dan Hensley and Milton Rogerson, had each served the college for seventeen years. Hensley was chaplain and associate professor of religion and unofficially was master of ceremonies and auctioneer for a variety of campus causes and organizations. Milton Rogerson, director of public information and publications, served as the college's primary photographer and was advisor to student staffs of *The Collegiate* and the *Pine Knot*. In April 1977, the student newspaper publicly thanked Rogerson for his counsel and commitment, and the *Pine Knot* honored Rogerson and Hensley by dedicating a volume of the yearbook to each man in the 1970s. Although Bruce Tingle had been at ACC less than two years, *The Collegiate* staff of 1977–78 honored the director of placement as one of the "Campus Celebrities" because of his energy, enthusiasm, and dedication to the school. The ACC alumni associa-

Extracurricular activities, Greek Week games of 1979. 1979 Pine Knot.

tion honored registrar Bethany Rose Joyner, class of 1947, with an achievement award in April 1981. Joyner, whose thirty-seven-year tenure at the college was exceeded only by that of Dean Sarah Bain Ward, received her alma mater's alumni of the year award in 1992.[11]

Students of the 1970s and 1980s could choose to participate in extracurricular activities through more than thirty clubs or societies, in addition to intercollegiate athletics and the seven Greek organizations. Ranging from the accounting club to the Young Democrats Club, the organizations afforded opportunities for service, socializing, academic enrichment, and leadership training. Among the newer organizations on campus were the foreign language club, educators of the hearing impaired, sign language choir, student nurse organization, and sport parachute club. Two of the most active clubs were Circle K and Campus Christian Association. An affiliate of Kiwanis International, Circle K was formed at ACC in 1972 as a service club to the college and community. Active in conducting community-wide projects such as a bike-athon to raise funds for multiple sclerosis, the ACC Circle K Club won a state award in 1977 for its work with the local mental health center. The goal of

Campus Christian Association was "to provide opportunities for students to discover, question, and develop an awareness and understanding of the relevant involvement of faith in the life of the academic community and in the whole scope of human existence." CCA sponsored chapel services, concerts, discussions, coffeehouses featuring student talent, and religious retreats.[12]

Campus Christian Association's successful campaign to construct Still Point may also have helped to build the spirit of generosity which led to the creation of the Sprinkle Lecture Series in March 1981. Started by a $20,000 gift from Steve Sprinkle in honor of his father and uncle, the series continues to bring outstanding speakers to campus each March for the purpose of exploring "the relationship between theology and Christian preaching." Along with the E. G. Purcell Jr. Bible Conference and the Allan R. Sharp Religion in Life Lectures, the Sprinkle Lectures marked Barton College as a center offering a continuing and significant theological lecture series.[13]

Stage and Script, one of the college's oldest and most active student organizations, received a boost in the late 1970s when the college examined the feasibility of creating a major in drama. Associate professor of English and director of drama Paul Crouch agreed with an editorial in *The Collegiate* of September 1977 suggesting that ACC offer the new major and replied that efforts to add the program were already underway. Crouch also noted that before the addition could occur the board of trustees would have to feel confident that a drama major would attract enough additional students to justify hiring additional faculty. The opening of ACC Opera Theatre in the spring of 1978 helped to create new interest in theater by introducing a different type of dramatic production to the campus community. Crouch and music faculty members Ross Albert, Janie Bostick, and Robert Daniel led a group of students in a production of *Gianni Schicchi*, a comic opera by Puccini, in early February 1978. Stage and Script hired Blane Smith of Wilson to design the set. *The Collegiate* issue appearing the day before the opera opened revealed that efforts to bring performing arts sessions to the campus faced more problems than adding faculty and stimulating student interest. Photographs accompanying the front-page article depicted the deteriorated condition of Howard Chapel, the site of Stage and Script productions. Cracks in the walls, holes in the ceiling, missing windowpanes, poor security, and inadequate space clearly made the college landmark unsuitable for dramatic performances. The publicity given to the deteriorated state of the chapel prompted the college to repair the building prior to the opening of school in 1978.[14]

Favorable community reaction to the 1978 comic opera, followed by subsequent Stage and Script successes, helped convince the faculty, trustees, and new administration that a drama major could prove successful. When the fall semester of 1981 opened, courses for a drama program were in place and a second faculty member had been hired to help teach the major. Dennis McDowell joined the faculty as assistant professor of English and began working with Crouch to attract students and to build a successful program. By early September 1981, McDowell, who held a B.A. degree from Pfeiffer College and a M.F.A. in scene design and technical directing from the University of Georgia, was already attracting interest with his "very elaborate sets." McDowell built sets for *The Three Cuckolds,* a bawdy sixteenth-century Italian comedy directed by Crouch, and assisted with design and technical direction.[15]

Stage and Script productions continued to attract large, appreciative audiences and received positive reviews. Although sufficient numbers of students continued to appear for auditions, Crouch remarked that the cast for *The American Dame,* scheduled to open 18 November 1981, included only two drama majors. Consistently fine performances from such Stage and Script veterans as Jeff Batchelor, Beth Forbes, Patti Fahling, Bob Poole, and Sherrie Sisk brought good theater to the ACC campus. Sisk had studied drama at Governor's School while Batchelor and Poole worked summers with *The Lost Colony* staff. Fahling added a minor in drama to her social studies major, and Forbes's reputation as a performer was enhanced by winning the 1982 Miss Wilson crown as an ACC co-ed. An undertaking of particular interest by both Stage and Script and the music department was *Lizbeth,* an opera composed by alumnus Thomas R. Albert, class of 1970. The opera was based upon the life of Lizzie Borden, who was tried but not convicted in the notorious ax-murder trial in nineteenth-century Fall River, Massachusetts. Written by librettist Linde Herman, a colleague of Albert's at Shenandoah College and Conservatory of Music in Winchester, Virginia, the production opened in Howard Chapel in late February 1982. With Crouch as director, McDowell serving as set designer and lighting technician, and strong vocal and acting performances from the cast, *Lizbeth* was labeled "a smashing success."[16]

While successful dramatic and operatic productions brought culture and entertainment to ACC and the Wilson community, they did not attract enough students to save the drama major, which was discontinued following the spring semester of 1985. After McDowell left the faculty that same year, English and modern languages continued to offer a drama minor and a concentration in drama for teacher education majors. The drama major was resurrected as a theater major in 1996 under the direction of Robert D. Wagner.[17]

In addition to reviews and features on dramatic productions, the campus newspaper continued reporting news from beyond the campus. Of particular interest to students was President Carter's executive pardon of young men who had refused to fight in Vietnam and the dispute over capital punishment heightened by the execution of Gary Mark Gilmore. Editorials covered debates over the proposed Equal Rights Amendment and the "death with dignity" argument centered upon the tragic figure of Karen Ann Quinlan. Letters to the editor also revealed the depth of student concern over Iran's imprisonment of American soldiers and the landmark Supreme Court decision of *Roe v. Wade*.[18]

Campus politics dominated many issues of *The Collegiate* during the 1970s and 1980s. Coeditors Dale Adams of Four Oaks and Keith Bracknell of Wilson described SGA meetings as boring, tedious, and nonproductive. Exasperated by evidence of student apathy prior to elections of spring semester 1978, Bracknell wrote a caustic editorial entitled "Do Not Vote." During the following autumn, campus apathy may have contributed to one of the strangest events ever associated with ACC student government. *The Collegiate* of 16 November 1978 carried a photograph and headline proclaiming "Mystery Baffles Campus." The disappearance of the SGA president caused great concern for the college community. School officials confirmed that the young man had not communicated with his parents and that the police had been notified. Three weeks later, the college newspaper stated that no new clue had appeared regarding the student's disappearance, and the mystery continued. The college community heard nothing from the missing leader until the Christmas holiday when he contacted a relative in Rocky Mount. *The Collegiate* of 18 January 1979 reported that personal problems and school pressures had apparently caused the young man to leave ACC. Unnamed sources indicated that he was living and working in New York.[19]

Lisa Boykin, assistant editor of *The Collegiate*, noted that apathy continued to plague the campus in the early 1980s and expressed concern that Iran's release of the American hostages had left college students without unifying issues. Noting that "preppy is 'in' hippie is 'out,'" Boykin, a Wilson resident and class of 1984, argued that historians would likely record the 1980s as a decade without a cause. Although Boykin accurately described what journalists labeled the "me generation," some of her schoolmates and fellow newspaper staff members had discovered a riveting cause in politics and the law. Members of the class of 1982, Ralph Durham and Johnny Johnson from Wilson and Ernie Lee from New Bern, were energized by their involvement in party politics and reveled in the opportunity to offer constructive criticism of politicians and government actions through student newspaper editorials. As examples of civic-minded activists who had led college political clubs since the Kennedy-Nixon campaign of 1960, these writers attempted to stimulate and educate the college community. Their knowledgeable and well-written columns examined such ethical and legal issues as the death penalty, gun control, munitions sales to foreign nations, and the proliferation of nuclear weapons.[20]

As recipient of a prestigious North Carolina Legislative Internship for 1981, Ernie Lee was one of twenty students in a program offering twelve hours of college credit for two political science classes at North Carolina State University and an internship with the state House of Representatives. Much of the internship experience involved work with the House Committee on Redistricting, which modernized state political districts to conform with the 1980 census. Following graduation from ACC in 1982, Lee earned a degree from Campbell University Law School, gained admittance to the North Carolina state bar, and became an assistant district attorney in Onslow County. Ralph Durham also continued in the field of his major by entering graduate school in political science at UNC-Chapel Hill. After returning to Barton College as an interim instructor in 1998, Durham resumed work toward a Ph.D. in Chapel Hill.[21]

In 1982–83, English major Lisa Boykin, now editor of *The Collegiate*, continued writing editorials about apathy on the ACC campus. In April 1983, under the heading "Apathy Killing SGA," she complained that only 6 percent of the student body had voted in the spring election of student government officers (94 of 1,545.) She wrote, "today's student is lazy and spoiled . . . he never seems to have the time for activities like SGA. . . . He has no sense of loyalty or dedication. He cares about Number One, and that's it." In 2001, Lisa Boykin Batts continued to use her English major, critical point of view, and writing skills as Lifestyle Editor of *The Wilson Daily Times*. During the early 1980s, as a member of Boykin's college newspaper staff, Peter Purcell, native of Pikeville and member of the class of 1984, wrote critical editorials on President Reagan's tax increase and an analysis of the Supreme Court's 1982 ruling on abortion. After graduating from Barton with a major in chemistry, Purcell attended East Carolina University Medical School. In 1999 he became a clinical assistant professor of surgery at UNC-Chapel Hill, taught at UNC-Wilmington, and practiced medicine with Wilmington Health Associates and New Hanover Regional Medical Center. His father, Eugene Purcell Jr., was a religion professor, and Peter Purcell's other ties to Barton College include his mother, Betty, a 1988 graduate; stepbrother Eugene III, known as "Trip," a banker, novelist, and member of the class of 1979; and sister Bebe, who attended ACC before graduating from UNC-Greensboro in 1985.[22]

Much of the *The Collegiate*'s editorial page typically dealt with day-to-day student concerns, including the quality of cafeteria food and service, parking problems, campus security, and visitation policies. ARA Cafeteria Food Services transferred cafeteria director Steve Cummings from Lees-McCrae College in the fall of 1979 to improve the quality of ACC's dining hall service. Working with college officials and a student committee appointed by SGA, Cummings promised to improve sanitation and provide meals and a dining room atmosphere that would gain student approval. *The Collegiate*'s editorial page of 9 February 1981 quoted a Cummings claim that the ACC boarding fee of $375 per semester was a bargain in comparison with other colleges. The dining hall manager also boasted that the college's cafeteria was the best in the state. Student letters in the student newspaper agreed with Cummings' assessment, noting that there was "always a long line for seconds."[23]

By the late 1970s, increasing numbers of commuting students, combined with a loss of space to new buildings, produced a significant parking problem for the college. Following the paving and marking of the lot between Hackney and Waters residence halls, the administration levied a student parking fee of $15. The fee did not guarantee a parking space but provided what business manager Milton Adams called "a hunting license." Enlargement of the lot between Wenger and Harper relieved but failed to solve the parking problem. Occasionally, students greeted enforcement of parking regulations with enthusiasm. In late October 1981, city sanitation workers complained that a car left in the no-parking zone near the dumpsters behind Hamlin Student Center prevented trash removal. Unable to identify the vehicle's owner, Alvah Monshower, dean of men and the official charged with enforcing campus parking, had the car towed away. He later discovered that the automobile belonged to his boss, Gordon Joyner, dean of students, whose son had left the vehicle in a zone clearly marked "No Parking." Although somewhat chagrined at paying $25 to retrieve his car, Joyner handled the situation good-naturedly. Noting the irony in the fact that the new parking regulations were "Joyner's own policy," Monshower added that the towed vehicle was the first one of the semester. Twenty years later, as vice-president for administration and finance, Joyner recalled Monshower's gentle nature and devotion to helping students as well as the humor involved in the towing incident.[24]

Campus security became a focal point at the college following national news regarding violent assaults upon co-eds at state universities in Florida in January 1978. Newspaper editor Dale Adams reminded readers that a secure campus depended largely upon "safety from within," in other words, careful students. In the fall of 1979, the administration implemented a twenty-four-hour, unarmed safety patrol to guard against trespassing and vandalism. Eventually employing twenty students and several Pinkerton guards, the system featured improved communication, additional lighting for dark areas of the campus, and support from the Wilson police department.[25]

Students also experienced changes in college housing during the period between 1977 and 1983, including the closing of Caldwell Hall, extended visitation hours in residence halls, and the school's first co-ed dormitory. Student interest and administrative approval brought a new schedule of visitation hours in residence halls that voted to accept the policy in the autumn of 1978. Approved visitation hours included Friday and Saturday evenings until 1:00 AM and Sunday evenings until 10:00 PM. The closing of Caldwell dormitory became a factor in making Hackney ACC's first co-ed residence hall. Deterioration of Caldwell's masonry and wood structure forced the administration to heed the advice of architectural engineers and remove the structure from service as a residence hall. The oldest and one of the most picturesque buildings on campus, Caldwell suddenly faced an uncertain future. After college officials tried without success to find a way to save the landmark building, "Old Caldwell" was demolished in December 1982; some of her bricks were saved for use in constructing entrance gates to the college. Hackney, the only residence hall with corridors on the outside of the building, became a "dual-sex" or co-ed dorm in the autumn of 1982, largely as a way of solving the school's shifting housing needs. Originally, one floor housed women, and two floors housed men. As additional residence halls became co-ed dorms, the college followed the same pattern of housing men and women on different floors. At the beginning of the twenty-first century, only Wenger, which remained a women's residence hall, was not inhabited by members of both sexes.[26]

The new library constructed across Lee Street from Belk Hall opened during the summer of 1977 and was dedicated as the Willis N. Hackney Library on 5 November during homecoming weekend. Hackney Library contained 27,000 square feet of floor space and shelving for 160,000 volumes. Patrons of the library could choose carrels, tables, or lounge chairs for study. The old library building was renovated to house classrooms, admissions and administrative offices, and the Carolina Discipliana Collection. When the renovation was completed in spring semester 1979, the building became known as Hardy Center.[27]

An important component of the new Hackney Library was the Learning Resource Center administered by the department of English and modern languages. Initially under the direction of Tom MacLennan, assistant professor of English, the LRC provided help for students who needed to improve reading, writing, and study skills necessary for completing college-level assignments. Located on the library's second floor and open Monday through Friday, the center was staffed by trained peer tutors and volunteers. In 1983, the LRC was moved to the second floor of Hardy Center and expanded to offer tutoring in specific disciplines, including business, history, and nursing.[28]

More exotic learning opportunities could be experienced through travel offered by the college, including ski trips, museum tours, and foreign excursions. ACC offered ski trips carrying physical education credit to the French-Swiss Ski College in Boone for 1979 and 1982 and added Vermont as a ski-trip destination for winter 1981. New York City museums beckoned art students and the staff of *The Collegiate*. Foreign travel courses included "Theatre in Britain" with a focus on English theater and history. A visit to Stratford, including opportunities to see plays by Shakespeare and others, was a feature of the tour scheduled for December–January 1981–82. A tour of Mexico City, Cuernavaca, Acapulco, and other sites to study Mexican art, culture, history, and language was offered through a travel course scheduled in May 1983.[29]

The creation of a foreign language club and the opening of a language lab complemented the growing interest in foreign travel during the 1982–83 academic year. Club activities included foreign films, slide shows, food tasting visits to French, German, and Spanish restaurants, fund-raising projects, and trips abroad. The college installed a language lab in Hines 201 during the winter of 1982–83. Containing twenty individual stations and a master console, the lab was used for foreign language courses and was also available during certain hours for students and faculty desiring to listen to music or conversation tapes.[30]

National, regional, and state accrediting agency visits to the college attested to the continuing high quality of ACC's academic programs during the period 1977–80. The National Association of Schools of Music approved the college's bachelor of arts and bachelor of science degrees in music in November 1977. The Southern Association of Colleges and Schools approved ACC's overall academic standing for a ten-year period in January 1978. As a result of SACS recommendations, the college created a faculty research policy, adopted new faculty-staff bylaws that included a faculty senate, and began creation of new policies on promotion, tenure, and faculty development. In February 1980 a visiting team of educators representing the Council of Education of the Deaf recommended reaccrediting the hearing impaired program, which had offered a major leading to certification since 1969–70. Also, a team representing the North Carolina Department of Education visited the school in February 1980, resulting in reaccreditation of ACC's eleven teacher education programs for a five-year period.[31]

Between 1977 and 1980, Atlantic Christian College expanded several programs to improve advising and enhance the preparation of students planning professional careers in dentistry, law, medicine, medical technology, pharmacy, and veterinary medicine. In each program, the college offered specialized advising and courses designed to enable students to advance toward a professional career. An advisory committee composed of ACC faculty and local dentists, medical doctors, and veterinarians provided advisement and consultation. The college changed the medical technology major to provide a fourth year of study at ACC with support from the Wilson medical community, replacing a senior year of study at Bowman Gray Hospital in Winston-Salem.[32]

The use of computers for academic record keeping increased significantly following installation of the first computer in the spring of 1972. By 1980, the registrar's office operated an IBM S/34 online computer station with terminals in the business department, business office, and development office. The business department also used IBM S/3 computers for instruction purposes. The "Computer Age" actually arrived in force at ACC in the 1982–83 academic year. Utilizing federal funds provided under the Title III Act, the college provided fourteen Apple microcomputers primarily for support of business, math, and science majors and the Learning Resource Center. A computer laboratory in Hines Hall provided facilities for classroom instruction and individual computer use. In 1982–83, the college also began offering a computer science minor of eighteen hours as an interdisciplinary program jointly administered by the departments of business and mathematics. ACC added a major in computer information systems for one year in 1987–88 and resumed the major in 1999–2000. In the 1981–82 academic year, the school received federal funds under the Strengthening Developing Institutions Program (SDIP) of the Title III, Higher Education Act of 1965. The five-year grant provided funding for improving instruction, professional development, upgrading technology, information management, and enhancement of advising, counseling, and tutoring services.[33]

Nursing was one of many college programs aided by upgrading technology for classroom and laboratory instruction. In addition, the arrival of a new chairperson in 1977 forced the nursing program to adjust to a new leadership style for the third time since the start of the major in 1970. The college hired Ruby Barnes to replace the departing Lorna Thigpen in 1973. Dr. Barnes's credentials included degrees from Duke and UNC-Chapel Hill, as well as an Ed.D. from North Carolina State. She led the program prior to leaving in 1977 when Sue Hunter was hired to chair the department. Hunter, who held a doctorate from the University of Northern Colorado, sought to maintain existing strengths while resolving staffing problems and improving the retention rate of the nursing faculty. She also pushed the department to revise its curriculum and reduce the student turnover rate. The result was a stable program, which by 1981, rose from seventh place to first among the eleven baccalaureate nursing programs in the state. When President Doster reported the nursing program's impressive performance to the faculty-staff meeting, basketball coach Bill Robinette provided a touch of humor. One who rarely spoke out in the meeting, the coach rose to his feet and delivered a brief but inspirational pep talk, ending with a shout, "Hey! We're Number One." His wife, Susie, a popular member of the nursing faculty and usually the more outspoken of the two, quietly smiled and nodded in agreement. The nursing graduates had established a notable record. With a total of nearly 90 percent of the class passing the state examination, ACC led Duke, UNC-Chapel Hill, ECU, and seven others.[34]

The college also benefited academically from varied scholarly activities by the faculty. A sampling of faculty projects, including travel, forum participation, exhibitions, speaking engagements, and publications during 1977–83, demonstrated the diverse talents and interests of the academic side of the campus. English professor Ruby P. Shackleford, artist and published poet, participated in several poetry workshops and served as vice-president of the North Carolina Poetry Association. Economics professor Anand Jaggi participated in a seminar entitled "Utility Economics for Professors of Economics and Business Management" at Meredith College. Eugene Purcell Jr. participated in North Carolina Humanities Council programs, addressing topics on "The Dignity of Man" and "The Concept of Growth as a Human Problem" at sites including Fayetteville and the College of the Albemarle in Elizabeth City. Science professor Ho Keun Kim, a nuclear engineer, took part in a seminar on uses of solar energy at North Carolina Central University. Using a North Carolina Department of Commerce grant, Kim also worked on a solar energy project in Wilson. Norbert Irvine received invitations to exhibit his silkscreen prints at national arts festivals in Virginia, Ohio, and Pennsylvania. He was also elected to a two-year term as president of the North Carolina Art Education Association.[35]

Faculty members also published scholarly works and participated in global conferences. In 1978, William O. Paulsell published his second book, *Letters From a Hermit*. Amrut Nakhre traveled to Moscow in 1979 to participate in a discussion of Third World problems at the International Political Science Association World Congress. From Russia, he traveled to West Germany to present a scholarly paper at a meeting of the International Peace Research Association. In 1981, Richard Schneider, associate professor of English, published a comprehensive review of books on Henry David Thoreau in *The Emerson Society Quarterly*. Schneider received a National Humanities grant to study "New England Transcendentalism" in a 1983 seminar directed by renowned Thoreau scholar Walter Harding in Concord, Massachusetts. Roger Bullard, who ranks with Mildred Hartsock as the college's most prolific writers, translated ancient writings for *The Nag Hammadi Library*, published by Harper & Row in 1978. In 1981, Bullard completed work on *The Abingdon Dictionary of Living Religions*, edited with two other scholars.[36]

Much of the academic community also found time to support ACC intercollegiate sports, and the period 1977–83 was notable for its athletic success. Led by head coach David Adkins and assistant Mike Smith, Bulldog soccer enjoyed its first winning seasons in 1976 and 1977. In 1978, the team compiled a 12–4 record and won the school's first Carolinas Conference soccer championship. Willie Diamond, a freshman from Dunoon, Scotland, was conference player of the year, and Adkins won coach of the year honors. Diamond also became the school's first NAIA All-American selection in soccer. The 1979 team finished its season with a record of 14–4 and won its first District 26 soccer title. In 1980 as new head coach, Mike Smith won district coach of the year. In 1981, led by Sharhabil Humieda of Khartoum, Sudan, conference player of the year, ACC won both conference and district titles, ending the season with a national ranking of seventeenth. Smith's team captured its fourth consecutive district title in 1982 with a dramatic overtime victory over High Point.[37]

No athletic team in the conference or the district could match the success of Coach Tom Parham's ACC tennis program of the 1970s. Parham's team finished the 1977 season ranked tenth nationally. In 1978, led by All-American players Tom Morris of Columbia, South Carolina, and Roger Ossmin of Swe-

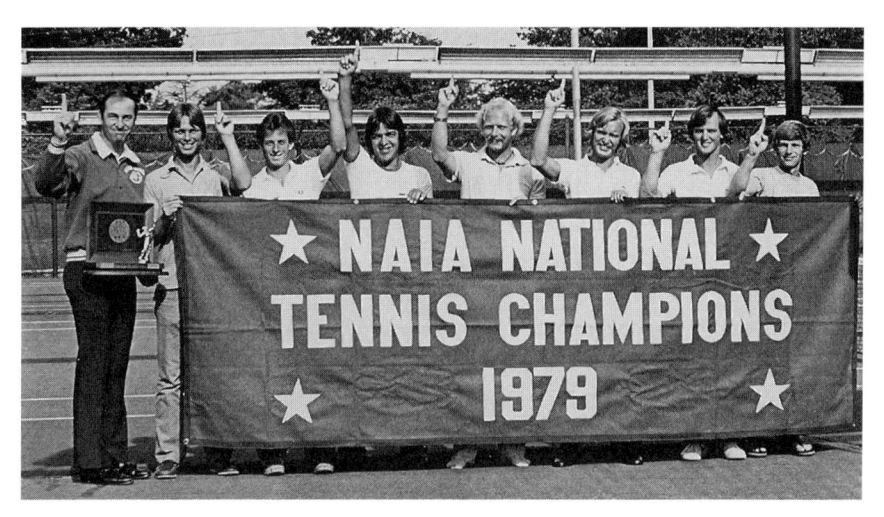

The 1979 national champions. From left—Coach Tom Parham, Jay Aldridge, Brian Staub, Andres Alvarez, Dan Attlerud, Soren Blomgren, Sam Modlin, and Tom Morris. Scope, June–July 1979.

den, the team finished second in the national tournament. In 1979, Parham entered his fifteenth season as tennis coach with a veteran team returning. After winning the school's tenth consecutive district championship, the trip to Kansas City and the national tournament seemed almost routine for the ACC squad. This time, led by the play of Morris and Andres Alverez, a junior from Cali, Colombia, the results were anything but routine. Both Morris and Alverez won All-American honors for a second time, and Parham gained his second national coach-of-the-year award. More importantly, the Bulldog tennis team reached the pinnacle of college athletic success by winning the national championship. The happy players celebrated their newly won status by throwing Coach Parham and President Doster, who had followed the team to the tournament, into the motel swimming pool.[38]

Other ACC teams of the era, while not matching the records of tennis or soccer, played competitively. The ACC volleyball team had its best season in 1981, establishing a record of 16–8 and finishing second in the District 26 tournament. Raleigh native Becky Pace, a sophomore, was named to the all-tournament team; and Suzanne George, a senior from Raleigh, was named all-tournament and all-conference for a second time. In 1979–80, after finishing third in regular season play, the women's basketball team won the CIAC tournament, the school's first conference title in basketball in twenty-five years. Cathy Wall and Tyra Boyd of Raleigh led Coach Carol McKeel's championship team. The 1982–83 squad was ranked eighteenth nationally and won a hard-fought 87–80 victory over Pembroke State University in the first game ever played between two nationally ranked teams in ACC's Wilson Gym. An appropriate addition to the college's athletic program was the opening of the Athletic Hall of Fame in the spring of 1983. Boyd came to Atlantic Christian College after starring at both Garner High School and Raleigh's Athens Drive High School and was inducted into the Athletic Hall of Fame in 1996. As a senior, Boyd broke the school's season scoring record and became Barton College's first basketball player and first female athlete to win All-American honors.[39]

Strong athletic performances lifted spirits on the campus during the late 1970s and early 1980s, but the loss of colleagues and teachers brought periods of sorrow. Losses mourned by the college community included Sam Modlin of Washington, North Carolina, and Victoria Louise Bazemore of Ahoskie, both killed in automobile accidents. Modlin, class of 1979, was a member of the national championship tennis team who returned to his alma mater as admissions counselor and recruiter in 1980 and died 29 October 1981. Bazemore, a junior mathematics major, died 29 November 1982. The college also mourned the deaths of Edward F. Bazzle, associate professor of business, and Ted C. Foy, assistant professor of English. Bazzle, a native of Bridgewater, Virginia, taught at the college from 1965 until his death on 10 March 1978. He was lauded by former students as an understanding professor and a loyal supporter of Phi Beta Lambda Business Fraternity. Foy, a native of Winston-Salem, was a popular Shakespearean scholar and advisor to Circle K Club. He suffered years of poor health before dying on 29 May 1979 at age thirty-four. The Ted C. Foy Scholarship Award is presented each year to an English major chosen by the department.[40]

The college community that mourned lost members in the late 1970s and early 1980s included a faculty, staff, and student body which, while overwhelmingly Caucasian, reflected greater ethnic diversity than ever before. Since the college did not maintain records of the institution's racial makeup, class yearbooks furnish the most reliable indication of ethnic change within the college community. After the college opened its doors to students of all races in the mid-1960s, black students began to enroll in significant numbers. Between 1967 and 1977, African Americans at Atlantic Christian College increased from zero faculty members, three students, and one graduating senior, to one faculty member, forty-five students, and six graduating seniors. Barbara Franklin Mills, RN, who joined the faculty as clinical assistant in nursing in 1975, became ACC's first black faculty member. In 1978, Joyce Bell McLeod, a graduate of the University of South Carolina and a clinical assistant in nursing, became the second black faculty member. Sanquinetti Cave's arrival to lead a new counseling program in 1982 added an African American to the staff. Serving as student development specialist and counselor, Cave held degrees from Fisk University and the University of South Carolina.[41]

As Doris Greene had demonstrated ten years earlier, black students effectively engaged in campus organizations and won coveted awards. ACC photographic records of 1976–77 show that twenty-two black students were among the 263 members of the freshman class, and one of the five class officers was African American. The campus Greek community, however, did not reflect racial integration. Finding themselves alienated from some segments of the campus social life, black students formed their own organizations. The first such group was the Afro-American Awareness Society, formed in 1974–75 to promote black culture. The group sponsored concerts, held banquets, supported ACC's gospel choir, built floats, nominated candidates for homecoming queen, participated in campus beautification projects, and collected food for "Hunger Emphasis Week." A second black organization, Sigma Gamma Nu, was established in 1975–76 by "young ladies who want[ed] to belong to an established group" and desired to develop character, leadership, and "sisterhood." Delta Sigma Theta, another black sorority, was founded in 1978. Alpha Kappa Alpha, America's first black sorority, and Alpha Phi Alpha, a black fraternity, indicated intent to establish charters on campus in 1982. Of these organizations, only the Afro-American Awareness Society survived, partially by its ability to retain official status as a college organization eligible for SGA funding. The fraternity and sororities lasted several years before disappearing from the official list of campus organizations. Although black sororities and fraternities continued to appear in the yearbooks, the 1995 college catalog listed only the gospel choir, and the 2001 catalog listed only the gospel choir and the Black Student Awareness Association.[42]

Many black students readily joined other clubs at the college, and many won recognition as student leaders. Mary Ballance of Aulander, Brenda Ford of Sims, Patricia Harris of Oxford, and Richard Battle were named to Who's Who in American Colleges and Universities. Winners of the coveted William Gear Spencer Sportsmanship Award included Richard Battle (1977), Lorenzo Jones of Cove City (1978), and Bob Peagues of Wilson (1980). Basketball star Kathy Wall of Ellerbe won the Kiwanis Award for Outstanding Female Athlete in 1980. Delores Williams of Washington, North Carolina, was first runner-up

Homecoming Queen 1980–81, Roberta "Bobbie" Edwards. 1981 Pine Knot.

in the 1976 homecoming queen contest and served as head cheerleader. Theresa McIntyre of Jamesville was vice-president of the 1980 senior class, and Sibyl Harris of Wendell was freshman class senator.[43]

In 1981, Roberta "Bobbie" Edwards, a junior from Camp LeJeune, became the college's first African American homecoming queen. Born in Honolulu as the daughter of a United States Marine Corps officer, Bobbie was also a member of the basketball team and secretary of the SGA. Edwards's escort at the homecoming dance, George Bell of New Bern, won the William Gear Spencer Award. Other black students were elected class officers and became leaders of campus clubs and organizations. Fifteen years after Barbara Ward Singletary became the college's first African American graduate, black students worked, studied, played, and worshiped on a campus with students from various ethnic backgrounds. The *Pine Knot* records thirty black students among 200

A Rich Lode in Our Own Backyard 293

members of the 1982 senior class. They later joined other members of the school's alumni in establishing productive careers. Perhaps some followed the example set by Mary Ballance, class of 1975, who combined a career with a sense of adventure and a desire to serve others by accepting a teaching job in Kenya. Other graduates of the class of 1982 also moved out of the state if not the country. Bobbie Edwards accepted challenges offered by missionary work with the Church of Christ in Florida. George Bell, a cum laude graduate, earned a M.B.A. degree at East Carolina University and was serving as a systems manager with Bank of America in Charlotte in 1999.[44]

On 16 May 1982, members of the most ethnically diverse graduating class of Barton's first eight decades celebrated the past, savored the present, and contemplated the future while awaiting the commencement address. The speaker, Governor James B. Hunt Jr., and students, trustees, members of the faculty and staff and assorted visitors in the large crowd seated at center campus appeared to savor the festive mood while lending support to graduating seniors and helping Atlantic Christian College celebrate a landmark eightieth commencement.

SIXTEEN

An Elegant Presence on Stately West Nash Street

CELEBRATION OF Atlantic Christian College's eightieth birthday began on Alumni Day, 3 April 1982, and continued with commencement events 16 May. An Alumni Day luncheon honoring distinguished graduates featured music by the ACC Jazz Band, followed by a baseball doubleheader. Alumni director Princie King Evans, class of 1972, presented alumni achievement awards to Dr. Selz Mayo, a native of Mesic and class of 1935, in the field of education; Dr. Elizabeth House Hughey Arline, Martin County native and class of 1936, in government service; Sam Ragan, Berea native and class of 1936, in journalism; and Dr. Robert Carr, Clinton native and class of 1938, in medicine. The recipient of the 1982 alumnus of the year award was former ACC acting president, dean, and professor, Cecil A. Jarman, class of 1928 and a native of Richlands.[1]

A cake cutting on center campus was the key feature of Founder's Day, held 1 May 1982, with Mrs. Charlotte Weyer of Kinston, a member of ACC's 1902 freshman class, cutting the birthday cake. Following the presentation of a one-act play by Stage and Script, the eightieth anniversary birthday ball was held in the student center. On the evening of 7 May, the Bulldog Club Drive steering committee heard President Doster describe plans for a proposed athletic, intramural, physical education, and recreation complex. The site of the planned complex was a thirty-acre tract of land purchased by the college near the campus. H. B. "Bud" Ruffin, chairman of the overall campaign, reported that the Bulldog Club had raised $253,000, 51 percent of its $500,000 goal. Others who spoke to the large crowd were Clyde Sullivan, class of 1951 and the honorary chairman of the drive, T. J. Hackney Jr., board chairman, and Edward L. Cloyd Jr., physical education department chairman. Vice-chairman Charles "Buddy" Bedgood introduced the evening's main attraction, University of North Carolina basketball coach Dean Smith. The legendary coach, who had mingled with the guests at a reception prior to the dinner, reminded the crowd of the college's importance to the community and urged support for the campaign.[2]

President Doster presided over commencement services with Dean F. Mark Davis presenting the graduating class. Receiving honorary degrees were William W. Shingleton, class of 1940 and professor of surgery at Duke University Medical Center, and Reverend David L. Alexander, pastor of Gordon Street Christian Church in Kinston. Senior class president Edie Dean of Raleigh spoke for the graduating class, which included nursing major Rebecca Hunt Hawley, daughter of the commencement speaker Governor James B. Hunt Jr. Governor Hunt paid tribute to ACC's achievements, which included graduating the top-ranking nursing class in the state and the positive reputation earned by the school's teacher education program. He noted that private higher education suffered nationally from "drastic cuts in federal aid in Washington." Promising that North Carolina would not reduce state aid to students, Hunt also urged graduates to follow the teachings of Christ in their lives by demonstrating compassion and charity for others. The governor ended his remarks by praising the graduating seniors for "representing the best we have in this state and this country."[3]

The president's annual report for 1981–82 noted that monetary gifts to the college in all areas had increased by more than $300,000 over the previous year. ACC had reached the two-thirds mark of Phase I (1980–83) of the goal established for a "Decade of Development," with 73 percent of the $4 million either paid or pledged. Doster sounded a cautionary note by stating that Title III funding had prevented important college programs from suffering budget cuts necessitated because of declining enrollment. A decline in new student enrollment over the previous year was only partially offset by an increase in the retention rate. The fiscal year ended with a budget surplus of about $15,000 in a year when total spending topped $7.5 million. Perhaps the worst news, although couched in positive terms, was the report on the college's endowment. Upon his arrival as president of ACC, Doster had indicated dissatisfaction with the institution's meager endowment. His 1982 report indicated that the endowment had risen above $2 million for the first time in the school's history. The figures of 31 May 1982, however, showed that the endowment had increased by only $73,460 over the previous year, a rate of increase which hardly could have pleased the president.[4]

In academic matters, Doster reported positive news, including the reaccreditation of the ACC nursing program for another eight years by the National League of Nursing and the growth of the satellite nursing program in

New Bern. The college had established and staffed a media center in Hackney Library, and enrollment in the adult and continuing education program for fall semester 1981 had grown to 185 students and 217 students for the spring of 1982. In addition, the college had strengthened the modern languages program by hiring two full-time teachers with Ph.D.s.[5]

The expansion of the campus by the purchase of the thirty-acre tract was a significant accomplishment in the school's history and a notable achievement of Doster's presidency. The acquisition increased the size of the campus from approximately eleven acres to more than forty acres. Located within half a mile of the main campus, the site was convenient for players and fans of Bulldog teams. Prior to the development of the new athletic complex, ACC had never hosted an intercollegiate baseball game, soccer match, or track meet on its own field. Beginning with the October–November 1978 issue of *Scope*, the Doster administration upgraded the college's bimonthly newsletter for parents, alumni, and other friends of the college. In addition to enlarging the size of *Scope* from an average of four pages to eight or more pages, the quality of the newsletter's pictures and articles was improved. Operating with a larger budget and capable staff, which included associate editor Jackie Harris, editor Milton Rogerson helped to enhance the college's image through a publication of impressive quality.[6]

While *Scope* and athletic facilities grew and improved, a stagnant economy and declining enrollments posed serious problems for private colleges. In 1982, twenty-four private colleges in North Carolina reported an average decline in admissions applications of over 13 percent. Doster's "State of the College" report to faculty and staff in September stated that ACC's health remained good but added that the school faced a period of "retrenchment." James B. Hemby Jr., who worked closely with Doster as college provost, remembered the 1982–83 year as a particularly stressful period. The decline in total enrollment resulted in sharp decreases of majors in several disciplines, prompting the administration to notify six members of the faculty-staff that they would not be rehired for the following year. In November 1982, *The Wilson Daily Times* reported that trustees had become concerned over declining morale and over a reported loss of confidence by the faculty in the administration. The article presented a six-page list of concerns which Professor Roger Bullard, faculty representative to the board had shared with Doster, board chairman T. J. Hackney Jr., and Judge Naomi Morris, chairman of the trustees' education committee. Labeled "the Bullard Letter" on campus, the document's actual title was "A Report on Faculty Morale at Atlantic Christian College."[7]

At Doster's request, editor Lisa Boykin interviewed the president in *The Collegiate*. Appearing in the same December issue was a letter from five students questioning the decision to fire the faculty members. Included also was a letter signed by T. J. Hackney Jr. dismissing unfounded rumors and reporting that the executive committee and Wilson trustees had indicated unanimous support for President Doster. In his interview with *The Collegiate*, Doster agreed that some faculty members likely experienced low morale. Stating his regrets that poor economic conditions and low enrollment had necessitated sending the letters, he assured that administrators had followed correct procedures in dealing with the sensitive matter. The president suggested that changes resulting from an unusually large recent turnover in the school's leadership positions had been a factor in producing an atmosphere of unrest and insecurity among faculty and staff. He also voiced confidence that existing problems would be resolved. An interview with Professor Bullard appeared in the student newspaper of 8 December. The professor stated that he had no reason to doubt the sincerity of the brief statements written by faculty members in response to his questions regarding faculty morale. Jim Hemby, who met regularly with the administrative council as provost, remembered that the controversy abated but did not disappear.[8]

Although the college community expected change to occur when Doster assumed the presidency in January 1978, few could have envisioned the extent of personnel change that developed. Within Doster's first four years, Milton Adams, Sarah Bain Ward, Zeb Whitehurst, Lewis Swindell Jr., Bill Paulsell, Gerald Harris, Bruce Tingle, Otis Coefield, and Kenneth St. John either retired or left the college to accept other positions. In addition to three new vice-presidents—Mark Davis, Ben Hobgood, and Dale Almond—new people filled the positions of dean of women, dean of men, director of athletics, library director, dean of students, provost, chaplain, director of deferred giving and church relations, director of alumni activities, director of food service, director of career planning and placement, director of the student center and Title III director with a 12-member staff. Mildred Hartsock, who retired earlier but continued to be active by serving on the board of trustees, died in December 1980. Although each of the departing faculty-staff members either retired or chose to leave for another job, such extensive personnel changes within a four-year period had a great impact upon the college.[9]

At the trustee meeting 25 February 1983, Doster informed the trustees of his decision to leave the college when his contract expired in May to pursue a different career in Christian higher education. Editor Hal Tarleton of *The Wil-*

son Daily Times reported that Doster had shared his decision with the executive committee of the board earlier and had agreed to that group's request that he remain with ACC for an additional six months to assist in implementing the new long-range plan and to pursue major gifts for the college. Board chairman T. J. Hackney Jr. announced that the trustees had accepted Doster's resignation with regret. On 1 March, Hackney met with the faculty, administration, staff, and SGA officers in Howard Chapel. Calling for unity and support while trustees led the search to find and hire a new president, he also lauded President Doster's numerous accomplishments, singling out the Undergraduate Fellowship Program, the development council, and the athletic and intramural complex for special praise.[10]

Established in 1980, the Undergraduate Fellows Program provided scholarships valued at up to $8,000 to qualifying students who enrolled at ACC and worked with mentors from among ACC's senior faculty. Acceptance into the Fellows Program required a minimum SAT score of 1,100, a ranking within the top 25 percent of one's graduating class, and demonstrated leadership potential. Led by a faculty coordinator, the Fellows Program provided special opportunities for student-faculty mentoring relationships, which included internships, research, and enhancement of leadership skills. In establishing the development council, Doster convinced prominent business leaders to join a capital campaign drive to raise $22 million during the decade of the 1980s. Of that sum, $15 million would go to increase the endowment. Robert E. Kirkland Jr., H. B. "Bud" Ruffin, and B. B. Plyler Jr. served as the council's first chairmen, helping to recruit and lead sixteen other business and civic leaders as division chairmen.[11]

Many members of the college and Wilson communities regretted seeing Dr. Doster leave. His affable nature and willingness to join students, faculty, and staff members in events ranging from Greek Week activities to the annual Turkey Day Race and cooking contests with faculty members made him a popular figure. The faculty also appreciated Doster's sensitivity and energy in establishing a faculty-staff house, located across Lee Street from Hardy Center, which the ACC Woman's Club had helped to furnish. An amusing encounter between Doster and free-spirited art professor Norbert Irvine exemplifies the president's congeniality and patience. Well known for wearing headbands and cowboy hats along with outrageous tee shirts and denim jeans to mask an Einsteinian appearance and gentle nature, Norbert Irvine appeared, unannounced, at the door of Doster's new office, a spacious, recently renovated room in the Hardy Center. Without uttering a word, the professor motioned with his fingers to beckon the startled president to step out from behind his desk. When Doster rose, stepping forward to approach Irvine, the latter walked past the puzzled president, settled comfortably into the empty chair, casually crossed his legs, and propped his feet up on the presidential desk. Smirking quietly for several moments, Irvine reached into his shirt pocket and tossed an envelope upon the desk, squarely in front of his bewildered boss. Doster pulled a letter from the opened envelope to discover that the return address listed the office of the governor of North Carolina. Much to his surprise, he read a note from Governor Hunt to Irvine congratulating him upon "your appointment as President of Atlantic Christian College." Norbert's deep-throated laughter spread across the office, and Doster smiled upon hearing the rest of the story. Irvine had indeed been elected president of the North Carolina Art Education Association. Someone in the governor's office had failed to read a news article carefully, and Norbert decided to make the most of his new status. [12]

In April 1983, trustees announced the appointment of college provost Jim Hemby as interim president, effective 1 June, and stated that a search committee to find a permanent president would be named by 22 April. The former English professor had gained administrative experience through participation in an American Council on Education Fellows Program (ACE), which allowed him to study all facets of ACC's administration and to work with President William C. Friday and the staff of the Consolidated University of North Carolina. Following Doster's recommendation, the trustees had named Hemby as "provost and professor of English," a post which he held from 1980–83. Working closely with Doster and the administrative staff, the provost was involved in planning and institutional advancement and in expanding the Undergraduate Fellows Program. Doster and Mark Davis recommended Hemby for the ACE fellowship. He had spent the 1979–80 academic year writing grant proposals; studying ACC's continuing education program; researching the advantages, disadvantages, and methodology of college merit reward and development systems; and examining the feasibility of a graduate program at the college.[13]

On 22 October 1983, the board of trustees appointed James B. Hemby Jr. the tenth president of Atlantic Christian College, the first alumnus selected to lead the school. After an exhaustive search which attracted some eighty applicants, Bruce Riley, Wilson trustee and chairman of the search committee, stated that Hemby had emerged as the candidate who "we felt was right to lead the institution." The Ayden native and 1955 graduate held a B.D. degree from Vanderbilt and a M.A. and Ph.D. from Texas Christian University.

President James B. Hemby Jr., 1983–, and family. From left, Scott, Jim, Joan, James, III, and Tom. Scope, Fall 1983.

Hemby served as chairman of the state competency test commission, director of the North Carolina writing project, and was president-elect of the North Carolina Literary and Historical Association. He had chaired the state Writers' Conference, and he had also been a member of the Wilson County board of education for over nine years. Mrs. Hemby, the former Joan Edwards of Wilson, was a 1957 graduate of ACC. The new first couple had three sons, James B. III, Scott Edwards, and Thomas Simmen. The president was an ordained Disciples of Christ minister, and the Hembys were members of Wilson's First Christian Church.[14]

The tenth president was inaugurated 14 April 1984 in a ceremony presided over by trustee chairman T. J. Hackney Jr. and featuring North Carolina Governor James B. Hunt Jr. and William C. Friday, president of the University of North Carolina. Bruce Riley, trustee vice-chairman, J. P. Tyndall, faculty representative, and Sarah Bain Ward, president of the alumni association, were other speakers who voiced greetings to the new president. Dr. Friday noted Hemby's period of service as an ACE fellow in the UNC office, spoke of his obvious dedication to Atlantic Christian College, and predicted that Hemby's strong character and penchant for hard work would guarantee success as a college president. Elizabeth "Libby" Mercer of Charlotte, president of the student government association, turned to appropriate words from the institution's past for her remarks. Quoting from Ware's *A History of Atlantic Christian College*, Mercer read from a May 1954 editorial in *The Collegiate*. Referring to President Travis White the editor had said, "He has a word for everyone he sees. Moreover far and wide across the state he has traveled . . . carrying with him the good will of the college, and boosting it always as he goes." After reading the quotation, Mercer revealed the 1954 student writer as Ayden junior James B. Hemby Jr. Dan Hensley, director of planned giving, read a special inauguration poem written by state poet laureate and ACC alumnus Sam Ragan.[15]

President Hemby's inaugural address recognized the importance of honoring the college's heritage while moving to meet future challenges. He stated that the school's major characteristics were a "compatible blend of the professional and liberal education and an individualized plan for the total development of each student." Hemby believed that the college provided experiences that helped to develop successful leaders. Priorities emphasized in a plan that the new president later labeled "A Design for Excellence" were accountability, sound budget management, and a firm commitment to the well-being of students.[16]

In addition to welcoming new leadership in the spring of 1984, Atlantic Christian College received a special gift of one of Wilson's architectural treasures. The Graves House, located on West Nash Street, was among the most significant contributions in the school's history. Considered one of the state's finest examples of Georgian Revival architecture, the house was given as a home for the college president by Thomas W. Graves, John Graves, and Elizabeth Graves Perkinson in memory of their parents, William W. and Gladys Wells Graves. Designed by prominent Greensboro architect Harry Barton and constructed in 1923, the Graves house provided facilities for entertaining alumni and friends near the main campus and gave the college an elegant presence on stately West Nash Street. The school planned to renovate the house using funds from the sale of the first president's house on Wilshire Boulevard.[17]

While periods of change typically follow the arrival of new presidents, for ACC the mid-1980s were years of exceptional transformation. The college added a new core curriculum, an innovative advising program, an honors program, an experiential education program, a May mini-term, and new majors in communications, American studies, and photography. The new gen-

The Graves House, the Barton College president's home, 800 West Nash Street. Photo by Keith Tew, 2001.

eral education core came about after faculty committees battled for nearly six years before compromising on such issues as hours required in the major, electives, foreign language requirements, and the difference between the bachelor of arts and bachelor of science degrees. President Doster appointed the initial committee after a March 1978 meeting with the faculty concerning curriculum revision. After failing to reach a consensus with the first committee, Dean Mark Davis and a second group of faculty received a positive vote from the faculty-staff assembly for a new general education core. The new core, instituted in 1985–86, required fewer specific courses, instead permitting students to choose from groups of courses in five perspectives. In humanities, fifteen semester hours were required; in social sciences, nine; in sports science, three; in natural sciences and mathematics, nine; and in fine arts, six hours. Students were also required to take two one-hour courses in the college success program (CSP). A change having the greatest impact upon entering freshmen was the requirement of proficiency examinations. Freshmen were required to take both writing and computational proficiency tests to determine their English and mathematics placement. Students receiving high scores on those tests could earn college credit by placing out of composition and algebra.[18]

Freshmen enrolling in the fall of 1985 also encountered a more effective advising program. A specially trained team of advisors guided freshmen students through their initial year at ACC and taught the college success program courses in both fall and spring semesters. The fall course, CSP 101, concerned becoming familiar with the campus and college life; academic, personal, and social adjustment; time management; building study skills; and stress management. CSP 102, taught during spring semester, emphasized decision making and career information. The program encouraged freshmen to examine various disciplines before declaring a major during their second semester. Barbara Andrews, assistant dean and director of advising, helped to prepare the new advising program during the 1984–85 academic year. Connie Swartzwelder, who became director of counseling in 1985 and later served as assistant to the dean and director of freshman advising, assumed the post of director of the college success program when Andrews left.[19]

Experiential programs also arrived in the autumn of 1985 under the office of continuing education, offering college credit for "learning that occurs in work-based experiences related to the major." Open to juniors and seniors making special application and maintaining a grade point average of at least 2.5, the program recognized the value of internships and the importance of the workplace as a laboratory experience within the college curriculum. Title III resources assisted in launching the program by providing an experiential programs director during the 1985–86 academic year. Kathryn Bottoms, who held an Ed.D. from North Carolina State University, served as the program director, and Clayton Sessoms, director of career planning and placement, supervised the program within the student affairs division of the college. The experiential programs approach to learning complemented the liberal studies degree which ACC began to offer in 1984. An interdisciplinary degree program designed for adult and continuing education students, liberal studies provided flexible tracks that fit the needs of individual students. The experiential education and the liberal studies programs continue to provide flexible learning opportunities as significant components of Barton College's Office of Lifelong Education in the twenty-first century.[20]

The college's extensive in-house scrutiny of courses, programs, degrees, and retention patterns during the 1980s convinced faculty and staff members that an honors program could help challenge accelerated students. In the fall of 1985, Dean Davis headed an honors council of five faculty members which provided guidance for a program charged with creating new opportunities for gifted students, encouraging innovative teaching and interdisciplinary courses, and improving the academic quality of the college. Entering freshmen with impressive secondary school records were invited to join one English and two history honors classes in 1985–86. Admittance to the honors program required the approval of the honors council and a minimum grade point average of 3.0. The council planned to have five honors classes available in English, history, religion, and science by 1986–87. At least nine honors courses were planned for 1988–89, and students would become eligible to graduate "with honors" by successful completion of eighteen semester hours of honors work. During the junior or senior year, students in the honors program were encouraged to take an independent study course in their major discipline that would serve as a "capstone" experience. Appointed by the president, the initial honors council included Mark Davis, Terry Grimes, Anand Jaggi, Murdina MacDonald and Jerry MacLean.[21]

The honors program seemed to fit perfectly with "Design For Excellence," the college's new capital campaign. President Hemby and campaign chairman T. J. Hackney Jr. officially launched the largest drive of its kind in ACC history, on 21 January 1986. Priorities included in the $5.5 million five-year campaign were the annual fund, endowed scholarships, an endowment to support excellence in teaching, and renovations to Howard Chapel and Moye Science Building. With trustees taking the lead, the campaign received early pledges exceeding $2 million, including a $1 million commitment from trustee Roger Page. A native of Wilson County, Page relocated to Winston-Salem where he operated businesses in real estate, oil drilling, and radio. Page's gift, among the largest single commitments ever made to the college, was to fund the Roger Page Foundation, which offered scholarships enabling outstanding students to attend ACC.[22]

New opportunities for academic enhancement in the 1980s included a May mini-term experience and the creation of new majors. Beginning in May 1984, a three-week mini-term provided students with options to earn credits through traditional courses as well as travel abroad. The English and modern languages department sponsored a travel course to London, Stratford, and the Lake District, focusing upon such great literary figures as Shakespeare, Dickens, Wordsworth, T. S. Eliot, and the Brontes. The increasing importance of communication and information technology led the college to offer a four-track interdisciplinary major in communications in the autumn of 1984. Administered within the department of English and modern languages, the four areas of focus were business communications, international communications, broadcast media, featuring radio and television, and print media, including journalism. A focus in film and video became a fifth option in the fall of 1985. The college hired Marc A. Krein as assistant professor of communications and director of the media center in the autumn of 1987. A native of Roswell, New

Mexico, Krein had taught communications courses and had worked in reporting, production, and direction at California, Washington, and Idaho radio and television stations. In November 1988, *The Collegiate* reported that the college had added a part-time instructor to teach introductory courses and help strengthen the communications programs.[23]

In the fall of 1986, the department of history and social sciences offered a major leading to both B.A. and B.S. degrees and a minor in American Studies. The interdisciplinary major provided courses in art, English, geography, history, music, political science, and religion. The most popular aspects of the major were the team-taught course in American material culture and the American studies practicum. Double listed as art and history, American material culture focused on study of the physical object as art and history. Highlights of the course, taught by art professor Chris Wilson and history professor Jerry MacLean, were field trips to historic sites, museums, house museums, and antiques collections. The American studies practicum, normally taken during the senior year, offered the option of a research paper or a practicum or internship with a museum or art gallery. A photography major, also begun in the fall of 1986 and offered through the art department, led to bachelor of fine arts and bachelor of science degrees. The new major expanded the dimension of art offerings and provided additional career opportunities for students.[24]

ACC graduates continued to gain acceptance and scholarships to prestigious graduate schools. Brad Almond, a history major from Wilson, class of 1987, graduated from the University of Alabama Law School and became a practicing attorney in Tuscaloosa. Science majors and undergraduate fellows Martin K. "Marty" Williams of Elizabeth City, biology, class of 1985, and Susan Maxwell of Moyock, chemistry, class of 1987, both earned medical degrees. Williams, president of Alpha Chi Honorary Society and assistant editor of *The Collegiate*, graduated from East Carolina University School of Medicine and married classmate Mary E. "Beth" Burton of Fayetteville, an undergraduate fellow, elementary education major, and business manager of *The Collegiate*. In 1999, the couple lived in Smithfield, where Reverend Burton-Williams, who earned a master's in divinity at Duke in 1988, served as minister of the First Christian Church. Dr. Williams, also active in the church, was associate clinical director at Goldsboro's Cherry Hospital and clinical assistant professor of medicine at East Carolina University's School of Medicine. The couple received alumni achievement awards from their alma mater in 1999.[25]

Susan Maxwell, an undergraduate fellow, academic All-American tennis player, and homecoming queen, earned Ph.D. and M.D. degrees from the University of Illinois. In 1999, Susan and her husband, classmate Archer "Art" Bane from Goldsboro, a business administration major and former Bulldog basketball player, lived in Winterville. Bane earned an M.A. degree at the University of Illinois and worked in pharmaceutical sales. Susan was a resident in obstetrics and gynecology at East Carolina University School of Medicine. In 1998, Dr. Susan Maxwell Bane was inducted into the Barton College Athletic Hall of Fame.[26]

Others from the class of 1987 accepted by graduate schools included Mary Ellen Goodwin at Wake Forest University school of business; Scott Edwards Hemby of Wilson, Emory University graduate school in psychology; Rodney William Morton of Elm City, North Carolina State University school of design; James Henry Trader III of Clarksburg, West Virginia, Lexington Theological Seminary, Lexington, Kentucky; and Amy Louise Wall of Elizabeth City, North Carolina State University school of engineering. Hemby received a Ph.D. from Wake Forest and serves as assistant professor of pharmacology at Emory University School of Medicine. Patsy Duke King, class of 1988, an Undergraduate Fellow and a political science major from Hollister, completed an internship in the office of the Wilson planning and zoning division which included a study of the residential neighborhood surrounding the main campus of the college. King earned a master's degree in regional planning at the University of North Carolina at Chapel Hill and serves as a regional planner with the Upper Coastal Plain Council of Governments in Rocky Mount.[27]

ACC students of the late 1980s witnessed the greatest changes to the physical appearance of the college campus since the building boom of the 1960s. Renovations were made to Hardy Alumni Hall, Hamlin Student Center, and Harper Hall. The Old Gym, demolished in February 1989, followed Caldwell Hall as the second building torn down in the 1980s. Although the gymnasium held fond memories for many people, its absence gave the campus a more open, aesthetically appealing look. In April 1984, director of alumni affairs Princie King Evans and the alumni council participated in a fund-raising drive to renovate Hardy Alumni Hall. The main room would be repainted and fitted with new carpet, drapes, and chandeliers at an estimated cost of $70,000. ARA Slater Foods, the school's food service provider, agreed to pay for enlarging the kitchen area in order to facilitate formal dinners. Alumni and friends of the college raised $90,127 for the project, which was completed in time for dedication services during homecoming weekend, Saturday, 2 November 1985. A ramp added to the west side of the front entrance made the building accessible to the handicapped. Ben Hobgood, vice-president for business and finance, served as general contractor for the renovation of both Hardy Alumni Hall and the Graves House in order to limit expenses.[28]

The administration announced plans to make even greater changes to the campus in 1987. Harper Hall would be closed at the end of spring semester 1987 to permit renovation of the first floor as administrative offices, while the second and third floors would continue to function as a residence hall. The most dramatic plan called for creating an entrance to the campus from Rountree Street. The entrance drive would begin with an arched brick entrance wall crowned by a white marble torch emphasizing the college motto, "They shall have the light of life." Continuing east past the wall, which would be built from bricks saved from Caldwell Hall, the entrance drive would follow a slight incline to a landscaped turning circle with three flagpoles and bordering on center campus. Harper Hall, the college's stately signature building, towered to the left, northeast of the cul-de-sac. The new entrance, which dramatically changed the face of ACC, was funded by the class of 1936. Members of the class conducted a yearlong campaign to raise $10,000 for their alma mater to celebrate and commemorate the fiftieth anniversary of their graduation. When the drive culminated at homecoming 1986, class members had passed their goal by some $3,000. The closing of Lee Street complemented the new entrance by physically uniting the campus and permitting the area between Hardy Center and Hackney Library to be bricked in a style similar to the refurbishing of Gold Street in the 1960s. The importance of Harper Hall was enhanced by the structure's imposing appearance, architectural significance, and legendary association with Sarah Bain Ward. The dean of women's determined effort to cultivate dignified and refined "Harper Hall Women" spanned three decades.[29]

The removal of four buildings along Rountree Street during the summer of 1987 preceded the paving and bricking of the entrance and driveway. An architectural drawing appearing in the Summer 1987 issue of *Scope* revealed the new configuration of the entrance to the college. After additional work, which included landscaping the turning circle, adding the torch, and affixing the name and founding date of the college, the entrance neared completion. The cover of the winter issue of *Scope* featured a beautiful color photograph of the new entrance and credited Wilson architect and alumnus Barry Lamm with donating work and time to design the entrance way. The electrical construction work was a donation of D/C Construction Company with Carl Pennington as president. Trustee K. D. Kennedy Sr., president of Electric Supply Company, donated the lighting fixtures. Georgia Brewer Campion presented the

Sarah Bain Ward, the original "Harper Hall Woman." Photo by Claude Anthony. Scope, December 1991.

new entranceway to ACC on behalf of the class of 1936 during homecoming weekend 1987, and President Hemby accepted the beautiful gift on behalf of the college.[30]

Further changes included an addition to Moye Science Hall, air-conditioning for Hackney Residence Hall, renovation of the snack bar in Hamlin Student Center, and carpet for Hines Hall. In addition, the college moved the writing center from the second floor of Hackney Library to the Riley House across the street from Hardy Center. With the exception of the science building, most of the work was completed by the opening of fall semester 1987. Additional improvements included new IBM computers for the computer lab on the first floor of Hines and for Hackney Library. Also, the department of English, modern languages, and communications opened a new word-processing room, equipped with twenty-five new IBM computers, on the second floor of Hines.[31]

Students returning for fall semester 1987 were pleased to discover the new snack bar nearing completion. The grand opening of the new facility was held in Hamlin Student Center on 23 September. Christened "Bully's," a name associated with the "Bulldogs," the snack bar was designed by architect Barry Lamm, class of 1958, to resemble an English pub. The new facility provided seating for approximately 100 people and featured a stereo sound system, televisions behind the bar, and facilities to accommodate entertainers. Guitarist Mike Bowen provided music for the grand opening, and Tony Tilley, popular food services director and campus gadfly, poured "mocktails" for thirsty students. Advertising "Good Food—Great Selection—Terrific atmosphere," the new snack bar offered onion rings, "Wings of Fire," nachos with cheese dip, french fries, soup, "Bully Salads," burgers, subs, pizza, "Sandwich Fixin's," and soft drinks.[32]

Most changes to the campus during the 1980s were funded by the $5.5 million "Design for Excellence" campaign headed by trustee Thomas J. Hackney Jr. Hackney led the board from 1966 to 1985, when he resigned as chairman but remained a trustee. Recognizing Hackney's contributions, the school awarded him an honorary Doctor of Laws degree in 1978 and joined the Fund for Higher Education in presenting "The Flame of Truth Award" to Hackney in December 1982. Proceeds from the award dinner funded the Thomas J. Hackney Jr. Undergraduate Fellowship and the Thomas J. Hackney Jr. Endowment Fund for a foreign exchange program for ACC students and faculty members. At the college's eighty-fourth annual commencement 4 May 1986, President Hemby presented the Presidential Award to Tom Hackney Jr. for his "unusual and distinguished service to the college." Hackney became the first person to receive the highest honor that the college bestows.[33]

Under the leadership of Hackney, Hemby, and the steering committee, the "Campaign For Excellence" became the most successful fund-raising drive in Atlantic Christian College history. The winter 1988 issue of *Scope* announced that the drive had exceeded its goal by $500,000 with gifts and pledges totaling more than $6 million. Dale Almond, vice-president for institutional advancement, noted that 55 percent of the total contributors, (over 1,600 of more than 3,000) were ACC alumni. At a "Campaign Victory Celebration" 18 November 1988, Hackney and Hemby were joined by board of trustees chairman Walter L. Brown Jr. of Raleigh, senior minister Dr. Hubert W. Westbrook of Kinston's Gordon Street Christian Church, and featured speaker Dr. William C. Friday in paying tribute to campaign supporters. In the only individual presentation of the evening, President Hemby honored Roger and Doris Page with the

T. J. Hackney Jr., chairman of the board 1966–85. Scope, Winter 1988.

"Distinguished Philanthropic Presentation." Walter Brown expressed pleasure in the generosity of the trustees, noting that board members had contributed 37 percent of the original $5.5 million goal. Hackney summarized the gratitude of the steering committee and evaluated the drive's significance to ACC. Commenting that the success of the campaign "underscored the confidence that all of us have in the institution and its leadership," Hackney predicted, "The success of this campaign provides a building block for securing the future of the college."[34]

Friends charting the school's accomplishments during the last decades of the twentieth century applauded academic achievements gained by the college. The nursing graduates, who ranked at or near the top among North Carolina's baccalaureate degree programs, were a continuous source of pride. ACC's senior nursing classes led the twelve North Carolina college and university programs in percentage of graduates passing the state examination in

1981, 1985, 1986, and 1992. The 1987 and 1996 classes earned passing marks of 100 percent. Since 1977, nursing graduates of Atlantic Christian/Barton College frequently ranked within the top four schools offering baccalaureate nursing programs.[35]

ACC students preparing for careers in business occupations also excelled during the same period. Phi Beta Lambda business organization captured nine awards at the state leadership conference in March 1985. Seniors Paul Blake III of Wilson and Veronica Wood of Erwin won top honors and competed at the national conference in Houston, Texas. At a state conference in Charlotte in November 1989, ACC delegates, representing the largest chapter in North Carolina, won eleven awards. In the summer of 1996, Jeff Hawley and Rhonda Hawley of Wilson teamed with Anthony Rawls of Zebulon to place first in the business decision-making category at the national leadership conference in Washington, D.C. Advised by Teresa Parker, Kay Mitchell, and Ron Eggers, the ACC chapter competed with 3,000 delegates representing thirty-two states. When celebrating its fortieth birthday in January 2001, Barton's Phi Beta Lambda chapter remained the largest in the state with a membership of 125 students.[36]

The opening of a writing center at the beginning of fall semester 1986 was another step taken to improve academic performance. Located on the second floor of Hackney Library and directed by English professor Rebecca Smith, the writing center replaced the learning resources center and offered tutorial assistance for students desiring to improve writing skills. After being relocated twice, the center finally gained a permanent home in February 2000 when the college officially opened the Sam and Marjorie Ragan Writing Center on a site beside Hackney Library and bordering Bruce Riley Plaza. The new writing center contains offices for the director and a visiting scholar, a seminar room, and eight writing centers. The Ragan Center provides an appropriate forum for a variety of learning opportunities, including lectures, seminars, poetry readings, and other programs open to the college community and the general public.[37]

Positive evaluations of the school's academic programs came after visitations by the Southern Association of Colleges and Schools in both 1988 and 1998. *The Collegiate* reported that ACC had passed the 1988 SACS reaccreditation exam "with Flying Colors." Dean Mark Davis, who worked with the steering committee and chairman Robert C. Frazier, stated that the school had passed with very few recommended changes, a situation that he termed as "enviable" in comparison to recent SACS visits to other colleges. A good report also came from the 1998 NCATE visitation team that evaluated the teacher education program. David Dolman, dean of the school of education, announced that NCATE had praised the college's record of graduating outstanding young teachers.[38]

Atlantic Christian College led all private colleges and universities in numbers of teachers provided to North Carolina public schools. In 1988 President Hemby stated that the college took pride in its "distinguished tradition of educating teachers" and would continue to offer a program which ranked among the best in the state. The teacher education program was led by committed faculty members such as Gene Purvis, Warren Tait, Olivia Philyaw Tyndall, Doris Capps, David Webb, Greg Hastings, Neil Lowell, and David Dolman. ACC graduates in education accrued honors throughout North Carolina and beyond. Former teacher and principal Aaron Fussell, native of Rose Hill and a former superintendent of Wake County Schools and member of the state General Assembly, received an alumni achievement award in government and education from his alma mater in 1987. Howard Chapin, class of 1947 and a former star athlete from Kinston, was another successful educator/legislator alumnus. Upon returning to his alma mater as convocation speaker in the autumn of 1986, Chapin voiced a "sense of pride" in being an ACC graduate. His wife, Mary Alice Beasley Chapin, a graduate in education in 1948, taught in public schools and community colleges.[39]

Other notable ACC graduates included former student government president Howard Blake of Fairfield, who received a Great Teacher Award from Temple University in 1990. Following graduation in 1959, Blake earned a Ph.D. degree and taught future generations of teachers. Memphis, Tennessee, chemistry teacher Diane Moore Jernigan, a native of Rock Ridge and class of 1964, won a Presidential Award for Science and Math Teaching from the National Science Foundation in 1987. The teacher education program at the turn of the century continues to produce outstanding teachers. Jackie Strum Ennis, assistant professor of education and class of 1981, considered her 2001 student teachers to be the best senior class that she has taught.[40]

Bulldog athletic programs also excelled, earning a 1983–84 ranking of fourteenth nationally among NAIA schools. Three Bulldog teams earned top twenty rankings: men's tennis ranked first; women's tennis, fifteenth; and golf, nineteenth. The 1983 soccer team coached by Mike Smith and led by All-American Sharhabil Humieda of Omdurman, Sudan, won a fifth consecutive district title. In October 1995, Humieda joined his former coaches David Adkins and Mike Smith as a member of the Barton College Athletic Hall of

An Elegant Presence 313

The 1984 national champions. From left—Coach Parham, Krister Eriksson, Jagadish Gowda, Johan Samuelsson, Stefan Vanemo, Thomas Linne, and John Malpas. Scope, *Summer 1984.*

Fame. The 1984 baseball team, led by veteran coach Jack Sanford, captured a conference title and finished second in the district tournament. Wilson junior John Williams led Coach Cloyd's golf team to its high NAIA ranking in 1984.[41]

The 1985–86 Bulldog basketball team, coached by Gary Edwards and led by cocaptains Vincent Dooms and Rick Melendez, won the Carolinas Conference regular season crown and the NAIA District 26 title. The appearance of a new "mascot," a student wearing a bulldog costume, helped the cheerleaders build enthusiasm in the community and brought an outpouring of support from the student body. Edwards' team won a second consecutive regular season title and district championship in 1986–87. The team won another trip to the NAIA national tournament in Kansas City and compiled a final record of 25–9.[42]

After finishing in fourth place nationally the previous year, Parham's tennis team returned to Kansas in 1984 for a thirteenth time and won the school's second national title. Unlike 1979, when ACC finished alone atop the standings, the school shared the 1984 title with Southwest Missouri Baptist College. The Bulldogs enjoyed a banner season en route to the championship, adding ACC's thirteenth district and tenth conference titles. Led by All-Americans Thomas Linne, Johan Samuelsson, and Stefan Vanemo, the 1984 team finished the college's twentieth consecutive winning season with a record of 14–4. Parham left ACC to become assistant athletic director and men's tennis coach at Elon College in 1985. The popular professor had become the most successful coach in Atlantic Christian College history, and his reputation reached legendary status among tennis followers. Parham took fourteen Bulldog teams to the national tournament and gained induction into the college's Athletic Hall of Fame in 1986.[43]

Coach Barbara Smith's women's tennis team competed in the NAIA championships for the first time in 1983, finishing the season ranked fifteenth nationally. In 1985, Smith's team finished second in the conference as sophomores Annika Andborn and Susan Maxwell and freshman Sonali Mukerjee of Calcutta, India, made all-conference. In the fall of 1986, Sheila Milne arrived from Cheltenham, England, and helped lead Coach Jerry Cooper's team to an 18–3 season, conference and district championships, and an eighth place national ranking. Milne was named all-conference and all-district during each of her four years and became the school's only three-time All-American. Ranking as high as eighth nationally, Milne compiled an overall singles record of 124–15 and a record of 14–5 at the highest level of NAIA tennis competition. She graduated magna cum laude in business administration in 1990 and garnered Academic All-American honors twice. Following graduation, Milne remained at the college as an admissions counselor and adviser to international students and became coordinator of advising and retention prior to assuming the position of college registrar in 1999. She was inducted into the Barton Athletic Hall of Fame 20 October 2000.[44]

In 1984, Coach Carol McKeel's women's basketball team finished second in the conference as center Gloria Burks, a former Wilson Beddingfield star, set a single game scoring record of forty points on her way to national rankings in scoring and rebounding, plus designation as an All-American. The 1988 Lady Bulldogs of Coach Mark Tobin were led by senior center Rhonda Bynum from Woodbridge, Virginia, who was named all-conference, all-district, and All-American.[45]

The success of ACC athletic teams during the last quarter of the twentieth century received assistance from an unlikely source, professor of history Walter W. Anderson Jr. An affable Virginia scholar with a Ph.D. from Scotland's St. Andrews University, Anderson served as coordinator of the international student program and worked closely with Parham, Smith, and other coaches to provide financial aid funds to enable international scholar-athletes to attend Barton. The effort succeeded in bringing many foreign students to Wilson, some of whom brought acclaim to the college through success on the courts and playing fields, particularly in tennis. Some also gained individual distinction by earning all-conference, all-district, and All-American honors.[46]

The arrival of increasing numbers of foreign players, in addition to globalizing the tennis and soccer teams, changed the nature of the college in other important aspects. The new venture added a noticeable ethnic and international diversity to the campus, provided experience in working with foreign students, and served as a preliminary stage leading to internationalization of all of Barton's academic programs during the next decade.

SEVENTEEN

A Touch Of Class for Barton

AN INNOVATIVE STRATEGY to internationalize the college became a prominent issue at the initial faculty-staff assembly in the autumn of 1988. President Hemby suggested that the college begin immediately to internationalize every facet of the institution. His plan proposed that each year the school emphasize a nation that exerted strong economic impact upon North Carolina. Realizing that adoption of the proposal would change the mission of the college, members of the assembly requested more information before endorsing the plan. They inquired about estimated costs of the proposal, asked why the academic community had not been consulted earlier, and raised questions regarding implementation and governance of the program. Following further discussion of the issue, the assembly accepted the president's suggestion and approved the concept of a global focus for the college.[1]

In an interview with editor Sonya Epps in *The Collegiate* of 3 November 1988, Hemby described "International Focus" as a plan "to provide an arena for the free exchange of global ideas in a community of learners committed to service" without changing the liberal arts emphasis of the college. Goals of the program included having 200 students from countries with businesses in North Carolina attending the college by 1992. Students, faculty, and staff would be encouraged to travel to foreign countries and to spend a semester abroad. Hemby explained that traditional Barton students and international students would benefit from a mutual exchange of ideas and learn from each other. British citizen Sheila Milne, class of 1990, became the college's first international recruiter.[2]

Barton College's "International Focus" program emphasized a different country each year, beginning with the United Kingdom in 1988–89. "Focus on Britain" was the theme of the first international week held on the campus 27–31 March 1989. Events included a cricket match at the athletic complex, a

"British Afternoon Tea" in Harper Hall parlor, a dart tournament in Bully's, a concert of Irish, Welsh, and English folk songs performed by the ACC chorus, and exhibits displayed throughout the campus. President Hemby formally opened the event with a flag-raising ceremony, accompanied by music provided by the Beddingfield High School band. Highlights of the week included a slide-lecture presentation on "English Decorative Arts as Collected by Eastern North Carolinians" by art professor J. Chris Wilson and a forum entitled "Northern Ireland: Challenge and Prospects," led by sociology professors from UNC-Chapel Hill. The featured event, on 30 March, was a traditional British dinner and remarks by a representative of the British Foreign Service and consul general in Atlanta.[3]

The college's second international week, in March 1990, focused upon France and featured a "Tour de Wilson" bicycle race sanctioned by the United States Cycling Federation. The week included concerts by a French pianist and composer, a fashion show, a dinner of French cuisine, and a keynote speech by the consul general and senior French trade commissioner. The highlight of projects honoring Japan, the third "Global Focus" nation, was a Japanese teahouse garden created by art professor Edward C. Brown. The beautifully crafted garden, exhibited throughout the year in Case Art Gallery, represented an estimated 2,000 hours of work by Brown, other faculty, and students. Built with careful attention to detail and authenticity, the garden evoked a restful, contemplative mood that conveyed an air of "hallowed ground." The college distributed a commemorative poster of a Milton Rogerson photograph of the teahouse printed by Jerry O'Boyle.[4]

The college community reacted positively to the Global Focus program. Responding to a question regarding the program's value to students, Pearly de Leon, Raleigh resident and class of 1992, remarked that she felt "more well-rounded" and had greater awareness of other countries. Gretchen Zhender, class of 1995 from Virginia Beach, answered that she had become more sensitive to the views of other people. Although the college did not meet the goal of enrolling 200 international students, Global Focus contributed to increased foreign travel among faculty and students and encouraged members of the ACC community to study abroad. Barton students who spent at least a semester studying abroad in 1993–94 included Wes Johnson, a senior religion and philosophy major from Catharpin, Virginia, who attended Franklin College in Lugano, Switzerland, a school sharing an exchange agreement with Barton. Students also studied at universities in Israel and Scotland. Art majors Ben Bridgers of Zebulon, class of 1995, and Paula Frances Miller of Wilson, class of

Global Focus—The Japanese teahouse garden in Case Art Gallery. Photo by Milton Rogerson. Scope, March 1991.

1996, spent the fall semester of 1995 in Cortona, Italy, where both finished at the top of their class in a prestigious international art program sponsored by the University of Georgia.[5]

In conjunction with Global Focus, the Jefferson Pilot faculty member of the year award, established in 1988, provided cash stipends for foreign travel and study. Beginning in 1991–92, two recipients were named each year, and by the autumn of 2000, twenty-two faculty members had received travel funds through this award.

Faculty and staff also received grants and sabbaticals to study and teach in foreign exchange programs. In 1990, President Hemby received a Fulbright grant, which he utilized to study international higher education and to establish exchange programs. He visited Germany and the Netherlands in 1990 and Korea and Japan in 1992, where he formed educational agreements with "sister institutions." The J. Chris Wilson family traveled in September 1994 to Nagoya, Japan, where the Barton professor taught classes in art appreciation and art and literature at Aichi Shukutoku University, one of Barton's new sister institutions. Wilson painted, exhibited his art at the Nagoya International Center, and traveled extensively before returning to North Carolina in January 1995. The Japanese university later participated in the exchange by sending two students to study in Wilson. During the fall semester of 1999, Professor Amrut Nakhre received a sabbatical to travel and conduct research in India. The focus of Nakhre's study was recent nuclear proliferation trends in India and Pakistan.[6]

Creating opportunities for foreign travel was among the factors that convinced the college to add a January term beginning with the 1994–95 academic year. The cost of the three-week term was factored into regular tuition, and enrollment in at least two January terms was a requirement for graduation. Led by director Terry Grimes, professor of English and dean of the college of arts and sciences, January term encouraged innovative learning experiences, and international travel courses proved to be highlights of the special session. Travel classes involving faculty and students included Comparative Study of Social Work and Social Welfare (Great Britain); The Land of the Maya (Mexico); Adventures in Religious History and Art (Italy); People, Culture, and Religion (China); Art and Theater (England); and Tropical Reef Ecology (Belize). Courses sponsored by the department of religion and philosophy included trips to Israel (1998) and Ireland (2001). Joe Jones, professor of religion and philosophy, utilized Barton's television station to present programs on ethnic diversity issues and global travel experiences of members of the college community. Jones served as host of "Faculty Forum," a monthly presentation on Wilson Educational Television, WEDT, Channel 16.[7]

While administrators, faculty, and staff worked to make Global Focus an effective part of Barton's academic programs, the board of trustees wrestled with another important issue—changing the name of the institution. While seeking to broaden ACC's base for recruiting students during the 1960s and 1970s, the admissions staff discovered that the school's name had become a significant problem for recruiters, particularly at out-of-state high schools and junior colleges. Increasing misuse of the word "Christian" to promote conservative agendas had caused mainstream Americans to identify the term with fundamentalist Bible colleges and right-wing groups that opposed the intellectually open and nonsectarian approach to education offered at Atlantic Christian College. As a result, high school graduates, knowing nothing else about the college, frequently took one look at the name on recruitment brochures and dismissed the school "as a fundamentalist, anti-intellectual institution."[8]

In January 1990, rumors of a pending name change prompted *The Collegiate* to poll a few students regarding whether the name should be changed. Another question asked was, "If a change is made, what new name should be chosen?" Student opinion was divided on changing the name, and new names suggested included Atlantic Global College and International College of North Carolina. In an early February issue of the student newspaper, staff member Bryant Camp interviewed President Hemby on the issue. Hemby reported that the trustees intended to discuss the matter at the next executive committee meeting of the board and added that changing the name had been a topic of conversation for fifty years. The president also said that the proposal did not call for a change in the school's relationship with the Christian Church.[9]

At their 26 February 1990 meeting, the trustees unanimously voted to change the name of the college and appointed a committee to study the issue and suggest a new name. *The Collegiate* quoted an unidentified spokesman for the college as saying that the new name "will more accurately define ACC's purpose and mission and help the public understand it as an excellent liberal arts college." President Hemby called a special meeting of the college community to explain the board's decision and sent memos to graduates of the class of 1991 offering the option of a diploma featuring the new name or Atlantic Christian College. After hearing the president's remarks and discussing the issue with members of the admissions staff, some students, including senior Candace Skinner of Havelock, editor of *The Collegiate*, junior Amy Jones of Richmond, Virginia, and freshman Becky Howard of Zebulon indicated support for the name change.[10]

The committee charged with recommending a new name included three trustees, an alumnus, a faculty member, a student, and the college president. During several meetings, the group discussed hundreds of names, including ancient, symbolic, foreign, and biblical terms. The names of famous Americans, including educators, politicians, persons who had served at ACC, and others, received scrutiny. On 29 August 1990, the board unanimously approved the committee's recommendation and set 6 September as the date to announce officially the new name. Fall convocation, held outside on center campus, attracted some 1,500 students, trustees, faculty, staff, and friends. Dr. William E. Tucker, chancellor of Texas Christian University and class of 1953, delivered the principal address. That event was followed by a "Celebration of Naming," featuring an unveiling of the school's new name, Barton College. Board chairman Walter L. Brown Jr. and SGA president Gareth Hosford removed the cover from the name, and President Hemby explained the action taken by the

Announcing a new name for the college at fall convocation, September 1990. From left, board chairman Brown, SGA president Hosford, and President Hemby. Scope, December 1990.

board. Alumni association president William R. Batchelor, class of 1962 and a member of the name-change committee, discussed the difficulty of finding the right name for his alma mater in the December 1990 issue of *Scope*. After months of research and discussion, the committee and the board settled upon the first name of Barton Stone. Barton W. Stone, 1772–1844, was one of the principal founders of the Christian Church, Disciples of Christ, a renowned Disciples preacher, and a respected educator.[11]

Some alumni, students, faculty, staff, and other friends of the school were dismayed at the choice and struggled to accept the new name. While exceptions existed, members of the faculty and staff typically supported the decision to change the school's name and accepted Barton as a positive choice. Although physical education instructor and basketball coach Wendee Saintsing had been at the college only three years, she seemed to voice the sentiment held by many faculty and staff members. Saintsing remarked that she supported the new name as appropriate for the school and thought that the change would be an asset in recruiting students. The trustees' bold move did not please everyone; after eighty-eight years as Atlantic Christian College, the original name stirred fond memories and a heartfelt reverence among some alumni.[12]

While the new name received most of the headlines, numerous other changes occurred at Atlantic Christian/Barton College during the 1980s and 1990s, including the creation of new majors, a large fund-raising campaign, and important technology upgrades. Working with sociology professor Robert Capps, Dan Shingleton, class of 1963 and assistant professor of sociology, urged the administration to add an accredited social work program to the curriculum in 1972. While the department of history and social sciences added a social work concentration to its academic offerings two years later, a major in the discipline was not offered until 1990. Following the acceptance of a proposal from Shingleton and department chairman Jerry MacLean in 1988, the college hired Susan E. Rentle, an experienced program director and teacher with a master's degree in social work, to build an accredited program. Barton added a third faculty member with a master's in social work in 1990, completed the required candidacy period, and in October 1996 received national accreditation from the Council of Social Work Education (CSWE). Rentle served as director and dean of the social work program until 2000. The dream of Capps and Shingleton finally became a reality when Barton's first bachelor of social work (BSW) students graduated in 1995. In the autumn of 2000, the Council of Social Work Education reaccredited Barton's program for a full eight years and commended the college in eight specific areas of strength. In 2001, Barton's social work program claimed approximately seventy-five majors, and the Hamlin Society, the student social work organization, contained thirty-five members.[13]

A criminal justice major, also organized by Dan Shingleton, gained the approval of the board in February 1997. After forming an agreement with Wilson Technical Community College to cooperate in supporting the program, Barton became the only college in North Carolina offering a major in criminal justice with law enforcement certification. Majors in criminal justice took a sixteen-week Coastal Plain law enforcement training program during the senior year. In 1998, Barton's school of social work added a full-time faculty member with a master's degree in criminal justice to teach and direct the program. Two years later, operating within the school of behavioral sciences led by Dean Richard Groskin, the program had thirty-eight majors.[14]

Academic scholarship funds increased markedly in the late 1980s and early 1990s. In 1991 a total of $1,050,000 from the estate of Sarah Condon Rogers established the Will and Sarah Condon Rogers Memorial Scholarship fund. The scholarships provided two thirds of the cost of tuition, room, board, fees, and books. The July 1991 *Scope* announced that the Rogers scholarship fund, one of the largest cash gifts from a family or individual in the college's history, would go to students in eastern North Carolina. Additional scholarships were established in honor of Mamie Jennings Lucas and George C. Stronach Jr. Ann Jennings Goodwin funded the former grant to honor her aunt, who had recently celebrated her 104th birthday. The grant honoring Mr. Stronach was given by Mrs. George C. Stronach Jr., Samuel C. Stronach, and trustee George T. Stronach III. A major gift in 1998 created the Barker-Ferguson Scholarships for students attending Barton College from Vance and Granville counties. Eddie and Debra Ferguson of Oxford established the scholarships in honor of their parents. Eddie Ferguson, class of 1977, served as president of the college alumni council, and Mrs. Ferguson's sister, Sheila Barker Wiggins, was a 1975 graduate.[15]

The January 1997 *Scope* noted that Barton's academic programs, which had remained firmly based upon a liberal arts foundation for ninety-five years, were increasingly delivered by rapidly changing technology. Nontraditional materials including satellite dishes and web-servers were utilized within classrooms and the library to prepare students for challenges of the twenty-first century. A satellite dish added to the Hackney Library roof in 1991 enabled Barton to subscribe to Satellite Communications for Learning (SCOLA). Based in Omaha, Nebraska, the network provided colleges and universities with twenty-four-hour international programming. In 1994, the installation of a satellite dish on the roof of Roma Hackney Music Building accommodated Barton's newly added television station. The college also installed an underground fiber-optic network to provide information highway access to residence hall rooms, faculty and administrative offices, and some classrooms. Students, faculty, and staff could access the college library LINC system via any web browser. Barton LINC offered such services as access to the library online catalog, connection to other databases, access to other libraries, and connection to subject-related internet sites. On 20 April 1998, Barton added North Carolina Libraries for Virtual Education (NCLIVE), which provided access to electronic information and print resources in libraries statewide.[16]

During the fall semester of 1999, the college provided 125 computer stations across the campus. Additional equipment included presentation panels consisting of portable computer equipment, software for classroom use, and cable television connections in every residence hall room. Effective utilization of a sophisticated communications networking system also prompted the college to enlarge its staff of trained communications personnel. The 2001 *Barton College Catalog* listed offices of administrative computing and information technology. The college web page listed two directors, one assistant director, and four network support specialists.[17]

The increasing cost of providing essential technology and meeting the needs of existing and anticipated academic programs were factors which caused the college to launch a $10 million capital campaign in the fall of 1992. Campaign goals included strengthening academic programs, endowing scholarships and faculty chairs, constructing and maintaining facilities, and providing funds to cover operating and maintenance costs. Addressing a gathering of trustees, friends, and faculty-staff members in front of Hardy Alumni Hall on Saturday morning, 12 September, trustee chairman Darwin McCaffity, K. D. Kennedy Jr., and President Hemby formally opened "The Campaign for Barton College: Enriching the Tradition." As chairman of the steering committee, Kennedy reported that pledges covering more than half of the goal had already been received, including a $2.2 million commitment from trustees. Kennedy himself set the pace for the campaign with a $1 million pledge from his family. Generous early commitments also came from Edna Earle Boykin, college trustee; BB&T, announced by bank CEO and college trustee John A. Allison IV; and Standard Commercial Corporation of Wilson, announced by president Marvin Coghill. Additional major pledges came from First Union Bank, Centura Bank, the Merck Foundation, trustee Gerald Quinn, and *The Wilson Daily Times*. The newspaper's pledge was made by publisher Morgan Dickerman, class of 1979, whose sisters, Alice Adams, Sarah Evans, and Margaret Dempsey had also attended the college.[18]

While Barton raised money and upgraded technology in preparation for the twenty-first century, concern over declining enrollment prompted an unusual move by the administration. The results produced major restructuring of academic programs and a dramatic change in the on-campus governance system of the college. On 24 February 1996, trustees unanimously approved a strategic plan as outlined by a presidential task force. The announced goal of the plan was strengthening recruitment and retention. A second goal was reduction of personnel; nine faculty-staff positions would be eliminated within a year, mostly through attrition. The new plan, which was revealed to the faculty-staff assembly on the afternoon before the trustee meeting, called for sweeping changes in the academic core, for placing academic departments within five schools, for acceptance of a prepared students' bill of rights, and for changing the college's internal governance structure.[19]

The required hours in the liberal arts core would be reduced from the previous total of forty-eight to fifty-six semester hours to forty-two to fifty-two, depending on varying requirements in different academic majors. Reductions would occur in the natural science and math disciplines, cutting required hours from eleven to seven and humanities hours from fifteen to twelve. In order to add more flexibility to core requirements and reduce personnel, courses formerly required in history, literature, and religion would become optional. All core courses would meet five days a week for half a semester (seven weeks). A feature article in *The Collegiate* of 29 February described the strategic plan and included praise from President Hemby and Dean Davis regarding innovative aspects of the program. The newspaper also reported that the five schools, including arts and sciences, behavioral sciences, business, education, and nursing, had been selected according to popularity or current enrollment figures. The task force consisted of the college president and seven members of the faculty-staff.[20]

A special feature on the strategic plan, carried by *The Wilson Daily Times* on 22 June 1996, reported that the nature and implementation of the changes mandated by the task force report had sharply divided the college community and had "motivated some faculty to quietly rebel against changes they consider a de-emphasis from academic rigor and a de-emphasis of the college's traditional religious ties." President Hemby lauded the work of the committee and dismissed criticism that the new program required less academic rigor. However, editor Hal Tarleton's inclusion of quoted remarks from faculty and former faculty members indicated the serious nature of the split within the academic community. Professor of chemistry J. William Kilgore stated that academic rigor had been compromised in a number of areas, including laboratory science courses. He also argued that the new core ignored or minimized the value of history, literature, religion, and philosophy, disciplines which he labeled "essential to the liberal arts tradition." Former religion and philosophy professor Eugene Purcell Jr. accused the strategic plan of breaking long-standing traditions, including the required course in religion. He also criticized the elimination of faculty governance over the curriculum.[21]

President Hemby emphasized that administrative and trustee action had been prompted by "a need for urgency" in meeting the challenges of a changing environment in higher education. A year later in a second feature by *The Wilson Daily Times,* Hemby stated that, although too little time had elapsed for a true evaluation, he considered the preliminary results positive. He also noted that retention rates had risen by 6 percent over the previous year. Laura Hyatt, assistant professor and chair of the department of psychology, voiced support for the new academic core. The newspaper also included remarks by a

The Kennedy Recreation and Intramural Center (KRIC), dedicated 7 February 1997 in honor of the families of K.D. Kennedy Sr. and K. D. Kennedy Jr. Chairman of the board K. D. Kennedy Jr., 1997– . Photo by Keith Tew. Scope, December 1992.

Barton student who supported the new curriculum because of the wider range of options.[22]

Although in-house fighting can be brutal within academic communities, a sense of commitment to the college and strong professional standards kept faculty and staff focused upon the greater objectives of providing quality teaching and services to Barton students. They also devoted firm support to the largest capital campaign in school history as "Enriching the Tradition" results began to make a difference on the campus. Changes to facilities included construction of a recreation and intramural center, renovation of Moye Science Hall, and enhancement of Hackney Library. The recreation center featured an indoor swimming pool, a weight and fitness center, and an auxiliary gymnasium. On 5 December 1995, Kennedy, McCaffity, and C. H. "Buddy" Bedgood, fund-raising chairman for the recreation and intramural center, led a "Just Add Water" thematic start of the facility. Officially opened on 7 February 1997, the Kennedy Recreation and Intramural Center (KRIC) was attached to Wilson Gymnasium near the intersection of Woodard Street and Atlantic Christian College Drive. The weight and fitness center of the $2.35 million state-of-the-art facility added a much-needed training area for Barton athletic teams. The site became a popular exercise arena for all members of the college community desiring to swim, tone muscles on the exercise machines, walk on the indoor track, or play basketball. An unidentified member of the student volunteer group known as the "A-Team" was quoted by *The Collegiate* as stating that the KRIC was her favorite site to show to prospective students and parents on campus tours because the facility provided "a touch of class" for Barton.[23]

An additional touch of class was provided by the new twelve-court tennis complex built by the college beside the intramural field off Corbett Avenue. Wilson attorney Turner Bunn III led steering committee efforts to raise $275,000 for the complex, which was to be built on the site of the existing five-court facility. Committee members, consisting of local civic leaders and tennis enthusiasts, offered naming rights to each of the twelve courts for contributions of at least $15,000. Courts were named for Cinny Bunn, S. M. "Zeke" Cozart, Dan and Paula Michalak and family, the John L. Benson and Thomas J. Rhodes families, Hubert and Inza Walston, Ed Cloyd, Tom Parham, L. Vincent Lowe, the H. H. Walston Jr. family, Ed and Helen Brown, J. Marshall Tetterton, and the Rotary Club of Greater Wilson. The new tennis complex, designed by Coach Tom Morris, was among the finest in the conference and rapidly became a popular site for college matches, conference tournaments, Wilson Tennis Foundation matches, and high school tournaments.[24]

The new tennis complex and the Kennedy Recreation and Intramural Center arrived at an appropriate time. Barton College entered a new era in athletics in 1995 with membership in the National Collegiate Athletic Association, Division II, and in a new conference, the Carolinas-Virginia Athletic Conference (CVAC). Gary Hall, athletic director and men's soccer coach, stated that a key reason for the change to NCAA affiliation was to equalize scholarship allocations between men's and women's sports while maintaining associations with schools where traditional relationships existed. Barton joined Anderson, Belmont Abbey, Coker, Erskine, Lees-McRae, Limestone, Longwood, Mount Olive, Pfeiffer, Queens, and St. Andrews in the CVAC. Barton would compete intercollegiately in a total of ten sports: basketball, soccer, and tennis for men and women, baseball and golf for men, and softball and volleyball for women. In both the 1996–97 and 2000–2001 seasons, Bulldog teams proved to be competitive in their new affiliations, finishing second in the race for the Joby Hawn Cup given annually to the school with the best overall winning record in the CVAC. In the 1996–97 season, Coach Ron Lievense led the men's basketball team to a place in the NCAA II tournament, and the volleyball team finished second in the conference with a 23–5 season record. Both tennis teams had good seasons, with the men leading the conference race with a record of 10–0, and the women finishing second, with a 9–1 record. The men's soccer team finished near the middle of the conference standings and helped Coach Hall reach a personal landmark in winning his one hundredth game. Equally significant, improved facilities and the new athletic affiliations were likely factors in convincing scholar-athletes such as outstanding tennis player Dominic LaFlamme of Quebec, Canada, and soccer star Todd Bailes, of Manassas, Virginia, to select Barton College.[25]

While Bulldog teams utilized the new athletic facilities, trustees and supporters continued the major fund-raising drive. The capital campaign passed the $8 million mark in late February 1995 and topped $10.4 million by the end of June 1996. Following record-breaking total receipts of over $2 million for the fiscal year, Dale Almond, vice-president for institutional advancement, chose the milestone as a suitable time to announce his retirement. Russell Rawlings became the new director of development, Kathy Daughety assumed the post of director of public relations, and Greg Abeyounis became assistant director of admissions.[26]

On 30 November 1997, the most successful fund-raising campaign in the college's history ended, as "Enriching the Tradition" raised a total of $12.57 million. Monies raised to support the campaign's three main components included $4.27 million for endowment, $5.8 million for facilities enhancement, and $2.5 million for college operations. Other improvements included the establishment of the Sara Lynn Kennedy Recording Studio in the music building and renovations to Hines Hall. Endowment monies included $1 million for two faculty chairs and over $100,000 to strengthen faculty development. Facilities enhancement funds provided for the construction of the Kennedy Recreation and Intramural Center (KRIC), completed the automation of Hackney Library, and provided a $1.2 million renovation of Moye Science Hall. While publicly thanking the drive's numerous supporters, Chairman K. D. Kennedy Jr. referred to the campaign as one of the "most rewarding experiences" of his life. He remarked that the success of the campaign had given him a "strong sense of assurance that Barton College and Wilson will continue to grow and prosper."[27]

The endowed faculty chairs, funded by the K. D. Kennedy family in the school of business and by Dr. Bill and Mrs. Jeanne Jordan in the department of English and modern languages, served as significant steps toward enhancing Barton's academic programs. In the fall of 2000, John J. Bethune, professor and dean of the school of business, became the first faculty member to

Chairmen of the board of trustees. From left: Walter L. Brown Jr., 1986–90; William D. Schubert, 1990–92; Darwin McCaffity, 1992–97. Scope, Spring 1986; December 1990; December 1991.

hold the K. D. Kennedy Business Chair. The appointment of a recipient of the Elizabeth "Bep" Jordan English Chair remained to be named, and interest from the endowment would bring visiting scholars to the campus until the position was filled.[28]

Kennedy's strong commitment to the college was further demonstrated when he became the eleventh chairman of the school's board of trustees in 1997. When T. J. Hackney Jr. stepped down as chairman in 1985, the trustees established a five-year tenure policy for the chairman. Walter L. Brown Jr. of Raleigh served as leader of the board during 1986–90, followed by William D. Schubert of Valdese from 1990–92. Both men were veteran members of the board and effective chairmen. Darwin McCaffity of Raleigh became the first graduate of the college to lead the trustees in 1992. Dr. McCaffity, class of 1949, had received an alumni achievement award from his alma mater in 1983 and was named alumnus of the year in 1991. His wife, Margaret Brown McCaffity, class of 1952, was honored with the same award in 1996.[29]

Barton College observed its ninety-fifth birthday the year that Kennedy assumed leadership of the board. The new chairman and the college president suggested that trustees consider the institution's one hundredth birthday as an appropriate time for launching another capital campaign. In the spring of 2001, the board announced the official opening of "The Centennial Campaign of Barton College," a $21 million fund-raising drive. The campaign steering committee, led by chairman George C. "Chuck" Finklea Jr., class of 1978, set goals of $7 million for scholarships; $6 million for a performing arts center; $2 million each for endowed faculty chairs, international travel, and a school of education; $800,000 for property acquisition; $600,000 for a bell tower; $500,000 for the Ragan Writing Center; and $100,000 for the tennis complex. When the campaign was officially announced to the public, in February 2000, pledges of $12.25 million already had been secured, mainly through commitments from trustees.[30]

Ronald Fautz arrived in March 2000 as vice-president for institutional advancement and became a member of the centennial campaign. Fautz, who graduated from North Dakota University, assumed responsibility over fundraising and management of the capital campaign. Greg Abeyounis became director of development in April 2000, and Laura Miller, a West Virginia native who had joined the institutional advancement division in September 1999, served as director of alumni affairs. An earlier administrative change also occurred in the division of academic affairs. Vernon Lindquist, a native of Maine with a Ph.D. from the University of New Brunswick, Canada, assumed the position of vice-president of academic affairs, 1 July 1997. On 24 May 1998, Lindquist, who came to Wilson from Notre Dame College, in Manchester, New Hampshire, delivered Barton College's commencement address.[31]

In 1999, President Hemby appointed a committee to plan Barton's centennial celebration. Chaired by Dr. Hemby, the committee included Kathy Daughety, Laura Miller, Russell Rawlings, Rebecca Smith, Keith Tew, and Jerry MacLean. The first scheduled event involved restoration of Founders' Day, 1 May 2000, with a ceremony honoring educator Joseph Kinsey, a founder of Barton College. Members of the Kinsey family participated in commemorating the first building on campus by unveiling a plaque at the site of Old Kinsey Hall. A second Founders' Day in 2001 honored the Hackney family with a luncheon and skit in Hamlin Student Center. The centennial committee scheduled a third Founders' Day and formed plans for other events which would culminate in November 2002, with a celebration of the school's one hundredth birthday.[32]

On 20 May 2001, James B. Hemby Jr. presided over Barton College's ninety-ninth commencement on a campus vastly different from that of the original fledgling institution. Led by President James C. Coggins in 1902–03, Atlantic Christian College consisted of a single building on a campus of less than six acres. During the first academic year, a total of 218 students, representing ten states, enrolled in courses offered in ten schools or disciplines. The college conferred B.S., A.B., and B.D. degrees, mostly in ministerial studies, English, and classical studies. The full-time faculty of eight members, which included President Coggins, taught Bible and religious studies, ancient and modern languages, art, music, expression, oratory, mathematics, and natural science. Music, ministerial studies, and languages made up the most popular areas of study. Headed by Dr. Hemby, the school's tenth president, Barton College in 2001 claimed twenty-one buildings on a seventy-acre campus. Barton's total enrollment of 1,202 students represented twenty-nine states and eighteen countries. The college offered B.A., B.S., B.F.A., B.L.S., B.S.N., and B.S.W. degrees in a total of twenty-nine majors or disciplines and twenty-three minors located in five schools. A full-time faculty of sixty-eight members taught courses ranging from art, chemistry, English, history, mathematics, and religion and philosophy, to athletic training, business administration, computer information systems, criminal justice, education of the deaf and hard of hearing, environmental science, gerontology, Hispanic studies, nursing, social work, and theater. The most popular majors were business and accounting, education, and nursing.[33]

In the spring of 2001, President Hemby discussed future retirement plans and expressed a sense of satisfaction with changes during his tenure. Adopting a new name for the college, increasing the size of the campus, establishing campus-wide computer and internet access, adding new academic majors, and implementing Global Focus were some of the accomplishments of Hemby's administration. He was especially pleased by his record of consistently increasing faculty and staff salaries despite periods of slow economic growth, of reducing the teaching load from fifteen to twelve semester hours, of introducing sabbatical leaves for faculty, and of providing rewards for teaching excellence. Yet, his greatest achievement came in the area of fund-raising. Presiding over the three largest capital campaigns in the college's history, Hemby secured funds to modernize the campus and raise Barton's endowment from under $2 million to over $22 million.[34]

The president also emphasized the importance of his wife's role in accomplishing goals that they had established together. Early in Hemby's tenure, Joan Edwards Hemby, class of 1957 and the only alumna to serve as first lady of Barton College, gave up her career as director of a Wilson County reading program to support efforts to improve her alma mater. Specific goals included effectively using the campus and the Graves House to involve trustees and the local community in the life of the college and making Barton more active in the cultural life of Wilson. The Barton–Wilson Symphony and the Friends of the Barton College Library were town-gown groups that the Hembys helped to organize and actively support. The symphony and the Friends of the Library, along with Barton Theatre, the Victor Small Lecture Series, the Elizabeth Jordan Lecture Series, and the Barton Museum (which included the Lula E. Rackley Gallery and the Virginia Thompson Graves Gallery), significantly increased Barton's role in the cultural life of Wilson and the Coastal Plain area.[35]

The Hembys carefully maintained the architectural integrity of the Graves House while utilizing the attractive and spacious home to entertain guests and enhance the image of the college. In an interview with college historians in December 1996, Dr. Hemby listed image building and the high quality and firm commitment of trustees among the positive aspects of his presidency. He also was proud of the increased ratio of Ph.D. degrees on the faculty and a consistent record of balanced budgets. Those accomplishments were among factors that prompted the board, in 1999, to convince the president to delay plans to retire.[36]

As the college held its ninety-ninth commencement, on 20 May 2001, returning alumni undoubtedly joined members of the faculty and staff in anticipating the coming academic year and the college's hundredth birthday celebration. The approach of the centennial year prompted friends of Barton throughout the country to recall the institution's rich legacy as they reminisced about their own experiences on the campus. Older alumni and members of the faculty and staff likely remembered stories about how the founders and early presidents of the college, frequently at great personal sacrifice, struggled to recruit students during the formative years of the institution. They also would have heard that the Christian Church–Disciples of Christ had been crucial in providing encouragement and guidance as well as spiritual and economical support. Through the years, the venerable old school had experienced difficulty in balancing the annual budgets and survived hard times, especially during the Great Depression, which threatened to close the college's doors. Two world wars and the Korean War forced the institution to witness its students, faculty, and staff members leave the school to serve their country as soldiers, nurses, chaplains, and defense workers. In addition, the college community had faced controversy and social pressure while adopting new policies to guarantee fair and equal treatment regardless of race or gender. An unpopular and prolonged war in Vietnam had divided the campus and required sacrifices from former students and staff members engaged in military service. More recently, leaders of the college had worked creatively and diligently to maintain the school's competitive position while explaining the rationale for renaming the institution. Meeting and conquering adversity frequently helped to unify and strengthen the college community, as it did when returning veterans brought greater maturity and a new sense of confidence to the campus. Atlantic Christian-Barton College had met these many challenges while educating successful ministers, teachers, and school administrators; talented artists, musicians, and actors; productive scientists, nurses, and social workers; and successful businessmen, political figures, and military leaders. The college also had provided solid undergraduate foundations for doctors, lawyers, educators, and others choosing to earn graduate degrees before embarking upon professional careers.

The Centennial Campaign of Barton College had received pledges to cover approximately 60 percent of its $21 million goal by commencement day 2001. Campaign leaders considered the critical needs of the twenty-first century as they coordinated efforts to raise money to build new structures, including an alumni bell tower and a performing arts center with a first-rate teaching theater. Additional endowment funds for scholarships, international travel, faculty chairs, and the Ragan Writing Center would help equip future graduates for exciting and rewarding careers. Drawing strength from the school's rich legacy and encouragement and support from talented and committed trustees, faculty, and staff, the college continued to receive respect, devotion, and generous monetary pledges from alumni and friends, some of whom traced family ties to the college spanning nearly 100 years. The strength of that commitment evoked feelings of both confidence and humility within members of the college community as they prepared to help Barton prepare for another century of distinguished service.

EPILOGUE

Prior to writing the centennial history of Barton College, I had the opportunity to observe the last thirty years of the institution's life through the perceptions of a "college family," who attended picnics and dinners, supported dramatic presentations and athletic events, joined Easter egg hunts, and participated in festive parties at Halloween and Christmas. An additional advantage came with "seeing" the school through the eyes of a "Barton faculty brat." Born in Chapel Hill, the Fike High School senior wanted to go to Carolina but was persuaded by her mom to try Barton for at least one year. She would live on campus, enjoying freedom from parental restrictions and allowing ample time and opportunity to become engaged fully in the activities of college life.

Bobby White's personal appearance at Fike's awards day to announce Barton College scholarship winners pleased the recipients and helped Laura accept the idea of joining the 1988 freshman class as an undergraduate fellow. Helping her move into Wenger residence hall was a bittersweet experience for her parents, but the enthusiasm and helpful spirit shown by Big Sisters eager to take her "under their wing" reassured us. To put it bluntly, Laura hit the campus running and never stopped. She and the college seemed to be made for each other. Dawn-Marie Singleton and other caring co-eds made her feel at home from the beginning.

The great respect that I already held for my colleagues on the faculty-staff was enhanced by Laura's positive perceptions. Mildred Hartsock's contention that students could get an education at Barton equal to that provided anywhere was true. In 2001, recalling her experiences with Barton's professors almost ten years earlier, Laura remembered few classes that she had not valued. Courses and teachers that she had found to be especially rewarding were science with Tom Brugh and Doug Graham, art with Tom Marshall, geography with Harlow Head, sociology with Dan Shingleton, and religion with Roger Bullard.

While students of the 1980s and 1990s experienced many stimulating academic challenges at the college, it was the "Barton bunch" that "blew them away." Responding by e-mail in the spring of 2001 to the question of what had made the college seem a special place to them, alumni who graduated between 1990 and 1994 shared memories of personal experiences at Barton. All comments were quite positive and singled out individual members of the administrative staff who had been important in helping students shape their lives. Five staff members were mentioned by name and were referred to collectively as "the 'Barton bunch'" or "gang." The gang included Russell Rawlings, special assistant for public relations; Bobby White, vice-president for enrollment services; Morgan Daughety, chaplain; Tony Tilley, director of food services; and Kim Watson, director of student activities. Others mentioned were Gary Hall, director of athletics; Tom Morris, tennis coach; and Kathy Daughety, associate director of admissions. These staff members shared a love of people, a willingness to listen, and a strong commitment to the college. Six of the eight staff members were Barton graduates. Laura summed up their value to the school: "All colleges have dorms and dining halls, libraries and lecture halls. It was the 'Barton bunch' that made this small liberal arts campus memorable, real and lively. It's truly a special place that lures back its own graduates like Russell Rawlings, Bobby White, Morgan Daughety and Tom Morris to nurture tomorrow's generation. That talent plus folks with mega-watt energy like Kim Watson and Tony Tilley creates a learning environment that's as comfortable and easy-going as home."[1]

The alumni communication came from Tammy Ayscue, Pearly de Leon, Scott Ginn, Martha Hutchinson, Charray Johnson, Pat O'Boyle, and Dawn-Marie Singleton. Their e-mail mentioned Morgan Daughety's kindness, sage advice, and "genuine concern." Russell and Bobby were friendly good-old-boy types, loaded with "home-grown anecdotes, tall tales and colorful zingers [that] could make you chuckle until your sides hurt." Tony's irreverent, boisterous nature, "peppery speech and saucy attitude," and a loud and chiding personality that spared neither campus custodians nor the college president made eating in the cafeteria a happening. Kathy Daughety's gentle disposition and strong commitment to the college made her popular with students, and Kim Watson was recalled as a caring person with an uninhibited nature and assertive personality. Tom Morris and Gary Hall were fine coaches who emphasized the importance of academics and fairness while building competitive teams. Laura and her teammates developed athletically and grew as people while playing intercollegiate tennis on teams coached by Tom and Carol Morris. Called "Mr. Coach" and "Mrs. Coach" by the players, the popular couple also taught good sports-

manship and ethical behavior. Arguably, this versatile and talented staff was as effective and as important to the success of Barton College as any staff in the school's history.[2]

The rapidity of response to questions about campus life and the graduates' deep appreciation for what the college meant to them as students and continues to mean to them as young adults must be gratifying to those who love Barton College. Although some of the faculty-staff members mentioned have since moved on to other careers, the acts of kindness, sharing of spiritual guidance, and friendships formed on the campus linger as legacies of the college. When alumni, former faculty-staff members, and others who love the venerable institution gather with the current college community to celebrate the hundreth birthday of Atlantic Christian College-Barton College in November 2002, they will share memories and reflect upon that legacy—a common core of beliefs and values that provides strength and guidance. The legacy that they share is described in the college motto and found in the biblical passage of John 8:12— Habebunt Lumen Vitae—*"They shall have the light of life."*

APPENDIX A

Alumnus of the Year Award

Norman ("Tweetie") Etheridge '37 (1968)
Naomi E. Morris '43 (1969)
H. Leman Barnhill '26 (1970)
J. P. Tyndall '45 (1971)
J. E. Paschall '18 (1972)
William E. Tucker '53 (1973)
Larry A. High '41 (1974)
Milton L. Adams '37 and Madeline Tripp '38 (1975)
C. Manley Morton '09 (1976)
Paul C. Southard '26 (1977)
Howard E. Blake '43 (1978)
Robert M. Clark Jr. '49 (1979)
Sarah Bain Ward '38 (1980)
William W. Shingleton '40 (1981)
Cecil A. Jarman '28 (1982)
Jack D. Brinson '33 (1983)
Ray G. Silverthorne '40 (1984)
Johnnie C. Baker '63 (1985)
Georgia Brewer Campion '36 (1986)
James D. Daniell '48 (1987)
Clayton D. Weeks '41 (1988)
James B. Hemby Jr. '55 (1989)
Samuel T. Ragan '36 (1990)
Darwin W. McCaffity '49 (1991)
Bethany Rose Joyner '47 (1992)
Joseph Q. Holliday '42 (1993)
Gilbert D. Davis Jr. '46 (1994)
A. C. Dawson '37 (1995)
Margaret Brown McCaffity '52 (1996)
John F. Lee '82 (1997)
Stephen V. Sprinkle '74 (1998)
Rebecca Lennon Crowder '65 (1999)
Zeb M. Whitehurst III '55 (2000)
Virginia "Gina" Allen McCuen '65 (2001)

APPENDIX B

Alumni Achievement Award

1980
Robert L. Denny '38
Lawrence A. Moye '20
E. Thomas Parham '63

1981
Milton L. Adams '37
George Max Barber '57
Samuel M. Jones '16
Bethany Rose Joyner '47

1982
Elizabeth House Arline '36
Robert E. Carr '38
Selz C. Mayo '35
Samuel T. Ragan '36

1983
Gilbert D. Davis Jr. '46
Henry C. Hilliard '56
Darwin W. McCaffity '49
A. J. Walston '58

1984
Sarah Loftin Adams '36
David C. Hardison '49
Joseph Q. Holliday '42
Harriet S. Plyler '11

1985
Onnie R. Cockrell Jr. '38
Dewitt C. Daughtry '35
Hazel Gunter Sorrell '37
Woodrow B. Sugg '39

1986
John Thurman Denning '36
Griffith A. Hamlin '39
Myra Joyner Mitchiner '36
Red William Wiegmann '30

1987
Eva Mae Whitley Brothers '34
Aaron E. Fussell Sr. '46
Harold W. Hardison '46
Richard L. Harrison Jr. '68
Lill C. Tomlinson '15

1988
Johnas F. Hockaday Jr. '51
G. Howard Phillips '50
Gerald H. Quinn '59

1989
G. Barry Lamm '58
Ambrose N. Manning '43
Kaoru Nonaka '57
Margarette D. Silverthorne '28

Appendix B: Alumni Achievement Award

1990
Don E. Lee Jr. '59
Kenneth R. Thornton '64
Mary Brewer Walters '36

1991
Kenneth Hill Brinson '59
Nan Mattox Cheek '54
James Edwin Rogers Sr. '39
Phillip H. Warren '71

1992
Robert Van Andrews '73
William Cole Andrews '73
William Ruffin Batchelor '62

1993
Gilbert Douglas Ferrell '54
Samuel Franklin Freeman Jr. '33
Edward Daniel Shingleton '63

1994
Thomas G. Aycock '69
C. E. Maurice Belanger '64
A. Franklyn Brooks Jr. '61
James V. Creasy '41

1995
Robert L. "Bobby" Dunn Jr. '60
Vivian M. Hamilton '56
Rick R. Stewart '68

1996
Ellis Williamson '40
Dennis R. Sherrod '79

1997
Donald W. Cameron '65
Thomas Edward Brown III '73

1998
William H. Vaughan Jr. '68
Katherine A. Vaughan '71
Edward Earl "Eddie" Summerlin '69
George C. "Chuck" Finklea Jr. '78

1999
Walter B. Jones '67
Donna J. Simms '76
Mary Elizabeth Burton-Williams '85
Martin K. Williams '85

2000
Miriam "Mickey" Moore Dunn '47
William Preston Nixon Jr. '64

APPENDIX C

Coggins Cup Recipients

Mabel Lynch	1920	Ada Kathryn Coor	1945
Christian Whitley	1921	Willie L. Parker	1946
Della Winstead	1922	Margaret Taylor	1947
Annie Elizabeth Etheridge	1923	Mary Ellen Jones	1948
Ruth Skinner	1924	Elizabeth Ann Leach	1949
Ruth Skinner	1925	James Walton Coley	1950
James T. Lawson	1926	W. J. "Bill" Waters	1951
C. M. Banks	1927	Marshall Long	1952
Margarette Silverthorn	1928	June Holton	1953
Virginia Payne	1929	William E. "Bill" Tucker	1953
Bill Wiegmann	1930	Peggy Mae Shackleford	1954
Meeda Weaver	1931	James B. Hemby Jr.	1955
Clara Bass	1932	Mamie Davis	1956
Sue Todd	1933	Charles E. Hester	1957
Jessie Wethington	1934	Sylvia A. Widgeon	1958
B. Eugene Taylor	1935	James Warren Bishop	1959
Bill Cunningham	1936	George Ralph Messick	1960
Milton Adams	1937	Vivian Zarelda Walston	1961
Sarah Bain Ward	1938	Margaret Lee Walker	1962
G. A. Hamlin	1939	Roland Hatten Hodges	1963
Selma Arner	1940	Cesar Emile Maurie Belange	1964
Mary E. Ward	1941	Jane Lindsay Osgood	1965
Joe Holliday	1942	Kathleen Traylor Sink	1966
Celia N. Crawley	1943	Dwight Lowry Wagner	1967
Katherine Lewis	1944	Donald Jerry White	1968

Appendix C: Coggins Cup Recipients 343

Benjamin Earl Casey	1969	Elizabeth Rose Mercer	1985
Robert Willian Koelling Jr.	1970	Sharon Aycock Burt	1986
Joseph Charles Jeffcoat	1971	Susan Marie Maxwell	1987
Jeannette Adele Norfolk	1972	Patsy D. King	1988
John Nixon McDaniel	1973	Sonya Epps	1989
Steven Venable Sprinkle	1974	Susan Dillard Clayton	1990
Patricia Aileen Parish	1975	Fawn Rogene Powers	1991
Ellen Bowen	1976	Laura Elizabeth MacLean	1992
Joan Adams	1977	Richard E. Cuddington Jr.	1993
Dale Adams	1978	William L. Perry Jr.	1994
Marcia Karen Page	1979	Peter Alan Carter	1995
Robert Carl Frazier Jr.	1980	Jeffrey Shane Bass	1996
Sandra Beitler	1981	Amanda Martin Ross	1997
Bobby C. Gardner	1982	Heather Karen Loyd	1998
Mary K. Tinnea	1983	Thomas Dean Goebel	1999
Lisa H. Boykin	1984	April Noelle Deigert	2000
Peter N. Purcell	1984	Richard Casey Prince	2001

APPENDIX D

Hilley Cup Recipients

Kathryn D. Butt	1957	Cheryl Faye Hollar	1980
Sylvia A. Widgeon	1958	Rose Marie Rand	1981
Anna L. Lovelace	1959	Juanita Fay Gryder	1982
Peggy Louise Keene	1960	Mary K. Tinnea	1983
Bobetta S. Persons	1961	Peter N. Purcell	1984
Betty Lou McLamb	1961	Jennifer Gail Black	1985
Joseph Bruce Baker	1962	Lynda Owen	1985
Linda Salter Busby	1963	Donna McLean Gibbons	1986
Fred Stanley Ayscue	1964	Mary Ellen Goodwin	1987
Jane Lindsay Osgood	1965	Kimberly Lane Hancock	1987
Kathleen Traylor Sink	1966	Jennifer Lynne Creech	1988
Gertrude B. Anderson	1967	Wilma P. Pittman	1989
Marvin Ray Joyner	1968	Lisa Ann Oliver	1990
Elaine Barnes Bailey	1969	Diana Hilliard	1991
Catherine Jane Arrington	1970	Richard S. Ziegler	1991
William Richard Dixon IV	1971	Danny Ray Ellis	1992
Jeanette Adele Norfolk	1972	Bobbie Lynn Lequire	1993
Susan Tyndall Williams	1973	Terrie Pearce Davis	1994
Pamela Anne Cobb	1974	Jennifer Leigh Starret	1995
Catheirne Ritko McDonald	1975	Jeffrey Shane Bass	1996
Judy Wall Poland	1976	Bracey Nicole Pearson	1997
Deborah Griffin	1977	Heather Karen Loyd	1998
Jeannette Gambrell	1977	Thomas Dean Goebel	1999
Janie Jones Sowers	1978	Silvia Joy Bailie	2000
Rebecca Godwin Smith	1979	Hrvoje Knezovic	2001

APPENDIX E

Jefferson-Pilot Faculty Members of the Year

Coleman C. Markham	1988
Sue M. Robinette	1989
Thomas E. Marshall III	1990
David M. Dolman	1991
Katherine H. James and J. William Kilgore	1992
Claudia L. Duncan and Douglas A. Graham	1993
Terrence L. Grimes and H. T. Stanton Jr.	1994
Harlow Z. Head and Carol H. Ruwe	1995
Ronald E. Eggers and Susan E. Rentle	1996
Sharon Montano and E. Daniel Shingleton	1997
Evelyn "Pet" Pruden and Murali K. Ranganathan	1998
Joe F. Jones III and Rebecca G. Smith	1999
Zhixiong Cai and Jane M. Kolunie	2000
Barbara F. Mize and Robert D. Wagner	2001

APPENDIX F

All-America Selections

ALL-AMERICANS

Alvarez, Andres, tennis, two times
Blacutt, Oscar, tennis
Boyd, Tyra, basketball
Burks, Gloria, basketball
Bynum, Rhonda, basketball
Cooper, Ben, tennis
Diamond, Willie, soccer
Edmonds, Karen, basketball
Evans, Alex, tennis
Grisewood, D. J., soccer
Humieda, Sharhabil, soccer
Irani, Zubin, tennis, two times
LaFlamme, Dominic, tennis
Linne, Thomas, tennis, two times
Milne, Sheila, tennis, three times
Morris, Tom, tennis, two times
Mulay, Sandeep, tennis
Nayar, Vishal, tennis
O'Boyle, Patrick, soccer
O'Neal, Jody, baseball
Ossmin, Roger, tennis
Phillips, Danny, tennis
Radford, Stacey, soccer
Samuelsson, Johan, tennis, two times
Sturen, John, tennis, two times
Thompson, Danny, tennis
Vanemo, Stefan, tennis

ACADEMIC ALL-AMERICANS

Adams, Joan, tennis, basketball
Andborn, Annika, tennis
Cuddington Jr., Richard, basketball
Godwin, Douglas, baseball
Hamm, Drew, soccer
Hosford, Gareth, tennis
Kay, Jon, soccer
LaFlamme, Dominic, tennis
MacLean, Laura, tennis
Maxwell, Susan, tennis
Milne, Sheila, tennis
Mulay, Sandeep, tennis
Newall, Kenny, soccer
O'Boyle, Patrick, soccer
O'Brien, Craig, tennis
Parker, Kimberly, tennis
Scott, Patricia, softball
Simpson, Joseph, golf

APPENDIX G

Athletic Hall of Fame

Adams, Milton, 1937, 11-1-85, Wilson, Athletic Director

Adkins, David, 1964, 10-23-92, Greenville, Soccer Coach

Aldridge, Jay, 1979, 10-21-94, Shreveport, LA, tennis

Allsbrook, Jack, 1951, 10-22-93, Rocky Mount, basketball

Atkinson, William R. "Bobby," 1961, 11-6-87, basketball, baseball, track

Bane, Susan Maxwell, 1987, 10-23-98, Winterville, tennis

Bell, H. F. "Buster," 1933, 4-14-83, Wilson, football, baseball, basketball

Bird, M. J. "Red," Wilson, 4-14-83, Coach, Athletic Director

Black, Cliff, 1972, 10-26-84, Conetoe, basketball

Boykin, Matthew, Honorary, 4-4-83

Broughton, Harmon W. "Red," 1940, 10-24-97, Garner, basketball

Carraway, Ed, 1969, 10-1-8, Greene County, basketball

Chapin, Howard, 1947, 11-4-83, Kinston, basketball, baseball

Clark, Jay, 1952, 11-1-85, Wilson, baseball, basketball, football

Cloyd, Edward L., Jr., 10-26-84, Wilson, Golf Coach

Cockrell, Onnie, 1938, 10-6-90, Wilson, baseball, basketball, track

Colombo, Vince, 1947, 11-1-85, Brockton, MA, basketball, baseball

Cunningham, H. H., 1936, 4-14-83, Owenington, KY, basketball, baseball, tennis

Davis, Henry "Hank," 1949, 10-6-90, Wilson, basketball, baseball, football

Dawson, A. C., Jr., 1937, 11-4-83, Jacksonville, tennis, baseball, basketball

Diamond, Willie, 1983, 10-19-96, Scotland, soccer

Dunn, Bobby, 1960, 10-5-91, Edgecombe County, basketball, tennis

Eatman, John, 1965, 10-5-91, Wilson, tennis

Eriksson, Krister, 1985, 10-22-99, Sweden, tennis

Eure, Bruce, 1913, 10-31-86, Spring Hope, baseball

Ferrell, Gilbert, 1954, 10-6-90, Wilson, basketball, baseball, football

Flowers, Bennett, 1953, 11-6-87, Wilson, basketball, football

Fulghum, James "Rabbit," 1961, 10-7-89, Rock Ridge, baseball, basketball

Fulghum, Monroe, 1929, 4-14-83, Wilson, football

Fulp, Gordon, 1967, 10-20-95, Jacksonville, golf

Gilmore, Bobby, 1969, 10-23-92, Robbins, basketball, tennis, track

Glazer, Paul, 1950, 11-4-83, Chelsea, football, basketball, baseball

Godwin, William Troy, 1947, 10-3-98, Dunn, basketball, baseball

Hackney, Willis N., 4-14-83, Wilson, Honorary

Hedlum, Annika Andborn, 1987, 10-24-97, Sweden, tennis

Helmer, Harry, 1950, 4-14-83, Goldsboro, baseball, football

Holder, Rebecca Pace, 1984, 10-21-94, Franklinton, basketball

Holliday, Joe, 1942, 10-6-90, Jamesville, tennis

Humieda, Sharhabil, 1984, 10-20-95, Sudan, soccer

Jones, Joan Adams, 1977, 10-7-89, Wilson, tennis, basketball

Jones, Larry, 1968, 10-23-92, Mt. Olive, basketball

Keel, Debbie Purvis, 1975, 10-22-99, Bethel, basketball, volleyball

Knox, Dick, 1961, 10-5-91, Indianapolis, IN, basketball, track

Langley, Sandra, 1974, 10-23-92, Edgecombe County, basketball, volleyball

Lassiter, Marion, 1942, 10-23-98, Conway, basketball, baseball

Liggon, Charles "Ned," 1950, 4-14-83, Wilson, football

Marley, John, 1957, 10-31-86, Franklinton, basketball

McCaskill, Thomas "Sparky," 1950, 10-24-97, Greenville, baseball, football

McComas, Jack E., 11-6-87, Raleigh, Basketball Coach

Morris, Tom, 1979, 10-7-89, Columbia, SC, tennis

Munn, A. Randolph "Ranny," 1929, 10-31-86, Deep Run, basketball, football, tennis

Myers, Susan Davis, 1979, 10-5-91, Hopewell, VA, basketball, tennis

Norfolk, Ira, 10-22-99, Baltimore, MD, Basketball Coach

Parham, Tom, 1963, 11-31-86, Robbins, Tennis Coach

Percise, Ronald, 1956, 11-1-85, Goldsboro, basketball, baseball

Phillips, Danny, 1973, 10-1-88, Goldsboro, tennis

Powell, Tyra Boyd, 1983, 10-19-96, Garner, basketball

Rand, Kenneth "Kenny" T., Jr., 1971, 11-31-86, Raleigh, tennis

Respass, Norman, 1971, 10-1-88, Long Acre Community (Beaufort Co.), basketball, volleyball

Sharp, Allan, 10-22-93, Wilson, Honorary

Smith, Ed, 1947, 10-26-84, Micro, baseball, basketball

Smith, Mike, 1975, 10-21-94, Wilson, Soccer Coach

Stallsmith, Clyde, 1969, 10-22-99, Meadsville, PA, basketball

Tart, Bobby, 1951, 10-19-96, Dunn, basketball, baseball

Appendix G: Athletic Hall of Fame

Thompson, Louis D. "Danny," 1972, 11-6-87, Rocky Mount, tennis

Thorne, J. D., 1949, 10-26-84, Elm City, baseball

Traylor, Kermit, 1933, 4-4-83, Newell, AL, basketball

Wall, Cathy, 1980, 10-22-93, Pinehurst, basketball

Widgeon, Billy, 1957, 11-4-83, Newport, basketball

Wiggins, William A., 1950, 4-14-83, Wilson, football

Wilkins, Danny, 1976, 10-24-97, Raleigh, soccer

Williams, Jerry, 1956, 11-1-85, Fuquay-Varina, basketball, baseball

APPENDIX H

Barton College Board of Trustees

CHAIRMEN

John J. Harper, 1902–1903
J. Boyd Jones, 1904–1905
Curtis W. Howard, 1906
George Hackney, 1907–1931
N. J. Rouse, 1932–1935
Thomas J. Hackney Sr., 1935–1965

Thomas J. Hackney Jr., 1966–1985
Walter L. Brown Jr., 1986–1990
William D. Schubert, 1990–1992
Darwin McCaffity, 1992–1997
K. D. Kennedy Jr., 1997–

TRUSTEES EMERITI 2001

Jack D. Brinson

K. D. Kennedy Sr.

Adams, Billy, 1984–1987, Smithfield
Adams, George H., 1955–1987, Wilson
Alexander, David L., 1967–1970, Wilmington
Alexander, Raymond L., 1959–1962, Washington
Allison, John A., 1987–1993, Wilson
Andrews, C. Howard, 1965–, Rocky Mount
Ange, A. W., 1943–1963, Winterville
Arnold, D. W., 1902–1904, Farmville
Artis, Amos, 1974–1977, Goldsboro
Asker, John, 1927–1949, Raleigh
Bagby, Richard, 1930–1936, Washington
Baker, Johnnie, 1985–1991, Wrightsville Beach

Barnhill, H. L., 1958–1992, Williamston
Basnight, J. S., 1902–1919, New Bern
Bell, J. H., 1904, Tarboro
Best, Carlton E., 1982–1985, Pfafftown
Black, James W. A., 1984–1987, Winterville
Bows, Albert J., 1964–1967, Atlanta, GA
Boykin, Edna Earle, 1981–, Wilson
Braxton, H. Galt, 1923–1974, Kinston
Brinson, Jack D., 1947–1987, Arapahoe
Brinson, Zeb E., 1953–1970, Tarboro
Brown, T. Ed, 1955–1981, Wilson
Brown, Walter L., Jr., 1977–, Raleigh
Browning, John, 1981–1984, Rocky Mount

Appendix H: Barton College Board of Trustees

Brunson, W. H., 1921–1950, Charleston, SC
Bussell, James H., 1987–1993, Williamston
Campion, Georgia B., 1988–, Durham
Cannon, C. C., 1921–1959, Ayden
Chapman, L. J., 1914–1936, Grifton
Coan, G. W., Jr., 1932–1936, Winston-Salem
Cole, Eric D., 1998–, Jamestown
Combs, Catherine P., 2001–, Rocky Mount
Cooper, Sully, 1922–1923, Dunn
Cory, A. E., 1926–1927, Kinston
Cowell, John W., 1935–1970, Bayboro
Cox, Z. B. T., 1956–1959, Farmville
Cozart, S. M., 1959–, Wilson
Cozart, Thomas A., 1994–, Wilson
Cunningham, A. B., 1906–1907, Grifton
Cuthrell, George F., 1928–1930, Raleigh
Davis, D. W., 1905, Washington
Davis, Warren A., 1921–1924, Washington
Deans, J. B., 1904–1917, Wilson
DeMar, Gregg A., 1995–, Stamford, CT
Denlinger, Ann, 1995–1998, Durham
Dunn, Robert L., Jr., 1994–, Wilson
Eagles, C. S., 1921–1958, Saratoga
Eagles, Sidney S., Jr., 1990–, Raleigh
Edwards, E. Merle, 1981–1988, Kinston
Edwards, Tommy, 1988–, Greenville
Emory, Frank E., 1977–, Wilson
Farish, Hayes, 1920–1922, Belhaven
Farmer, W. W., 1904–1905, Wilson
Ferguson, Jack E., 1996–, Oxford
Finklea, George C., Jr., 1994–, Wilson
Forbes, Vance T., Sr., 1970–1997, Wilson
Forbes, Vance T., Jr., 1994–1999, Wilson
Freeman, S. F., 1905–1916, Washington
Gardner, G. T., 1920–1928, Grifton
Glenn, W. B., 1974–1979, Wilson
Goff, John F., 1954–1955, Ayden
Graves, Thomas W., Jr., 2000–, Raleigh
Gregory, J. M., Jr., 1970–1979, Wilson
Griffin, A. T., 1904–1910, Goldsboro
Griffin, Janie D., 1970–, Wilson
Griffin, Patrick C., 1986–, Washington
Groover, H. H., Jr., 1972–1975, Greensboro
Hackney, George, Sr., 1902–1948, Wilson
Hackney, George, Jr., 1915, Wilson
Hackney, Robert H., Jr., 1990–1999, New York
Hackney, T. J., Sr., 1932–1965, Wilson
Hackney, T. J., Jr., 1957–, Wilson
Hadden, W. J., Jr., 1968–1971, Greenville
Haney, H. Glenn, 1949–1952, Greenville
Hardy, Clarence L., 1926–1949, Maury
Harper, Clarence P., 1934–1942, Selma
Harper, J. J., 1902–1904, Smithfield
Hartsock, Mildred E., 1975–1980, Wilson
Hillyer, E. C., 1924–1929, Raleigh
Hines, J. W., 1902–1928, Rocky Mount
Hodges, F. R., 1904–1915, Institute
Holliday, Joseph Q., 1986–1988, Raleigh
Holliday, McD, 1909–1912, Dunn
Hooker, W. E., 1921–1939, Greenville
Horne, Rexford L, 1995–, Wilson
Howard, C. W., 1904–1932, Kinston
Howard, Curtis W., 1935–1967, Kinston
Howard, Phyllis P., 1999–, Raleigh
Hufford, Robert G., 1964–1967, Greenville
Hunt, James B., Jr., 1988–1991, Wilson
Jarman, Robert E., 1953–1955, Greensboro
Johnson, William P., 1975–1983, Goshen, IN
Jones, J. Benhow, 1943–1957, Winston-Salem
Jones, J. Boyd, 1904–1905, Wilson

Jones, Phil, 1997–2000, Ayden
Jones, R. H., 1904, Winston-Salem
Jones, Robert, 1960–1963, Charlotte
Jones, S. M., 1944–1948, New Bern
Jordan, William R., 1998–, Fayetteville
Keel, R. V., 1940, Greenville
Kennedy, K. D., Sr., 1968–1989, Wilson
Kennedy, K. D., Jr., 1989–, Raleigh
Kennedy, W. L., 1958–1967, Newton Grove
Kinsey, Joseph, 1902, Wilson
Kirkland, B. B., 1923–1934, Columbia, SC
Kirkland, R. E., 1980–1983, Wilson
Kiser, Claude, 1918–1938, Greensboro
Lamm, W. T., Jr., 1968–1989, Wilson
Lang, W. M., 1911–1914, Farmville
Langston, Ira, W., 1954, New York
Latham, J. F., 1939–1947, Bath
Law, Thomas L., 1970–1994, Raleigh
Ledford, John B., 2001–, Washington
Lee, John F., 1989–, Wilson
Leggett, B. Frank, 1979–1982, Dunn
Lilley, Arthur D., 1985–1987, New Bern
Loftin, G. F., 1937–1955, Kinston
Long, W. Ray, 1994–, Raleigh
Lowe, L. Vincent, Jr., 1984–1990, Wilson
MacAfee, C. O., Jr., 1951–1957, Macon, GA
MacDonald, Claude R., 1969–1974, Williamston
Manning, W. C., 1916–1936, Williamston
Mashburn, C. B., 1922–1946, Charlotte
Matthews, Frank P., 1989–1992, Smithfield
McCaffity, Darwin W., 1980–, Raleigh
McQuade, John, 2000–, Wilson
Melton, B. H., 1902–1904, Wilson
Melvin, J. L., 1977–1980, Goldsboro

Messick, E. R., 1925–1927, Winston-Salem
Messick, Ralph G., 1975–1978, Wilson
Mewborn, S. G., 1911–1923, Wilson
Morris, Naomi E., 1971–1983, Raleigh
Moye, A. J., 1904–1927, Farmville
Moye, E. A., 1902–1914, Greenville
Moye, Florence C., 1990–, Maury
Moye, Frances D., 1998–, Farmville
Moye, Lawrence A., 1950–1984, Maury
Nurney, C. F., 1905–1916, Wilson
Page, Roger F., 1982–, Bermuda Run
Palmer, John, 1982–1991, Wilson
Parker, W. L., 1951–1953, Greensboro
Paschall, J. E., 1948–1977, Wilson
Peel, Elbert S., 1937–1970, Williamston
Peel, Paul H., 1992–2000, Rocky Mount
Perry, Ely J., Sr., 1950–1968, Kinston
Perry, Ely J., Jr., 1969–1996, Kinston
Peterson, M. W., 1967–1968, Charlotte
Proctor, John, 1948–1974, Greenville
Proctor, W. E., 1924–1926, Grimesland
Quinn, Gerald H., 1986–, Warsaw
Rawls, C. H., 1925–1947, Raleigh
Richardson, J. C., 1917–1929, Garnett
Richardson, S. W., 1928–1948, Wilson
Ridenhour, Norman, 1981–1990, Greensboro
Riley, Bruce W., 1961–1988, Wilson
Roberson, S. L., 1948–1955, Robersonville
Roberson, Sherwood L., 1957–1960, Robersonville
Roberson, W. R., Jr., 1951–1954, Washington
Robinson, N. J., 1948, Raleigh
Roebuck, E. Leon, 1931–1972, Washington
Rogers, David C., 1965–1969, Columbia, SC
Rouse, Charles, 1950–1987, Raleigh
Rouse, N. J., 1905–1934, Kinston

Appendix H: Barton College Board of Trustees

Rouse, Robert H., 1935–1936, Kinston
Ruffin, Harvey B., Jr., 1982–, Wilson
Saunders, P. D., 1955–1961, Charleston, SC
Schubert, William D., 1964–1992, Valdese
Seburn, W. H., 1939–1942, Greensboro
Sellers, Eric W., 1997–, Selma
Shackleford, A. D., 1939–1962, Wilson
Sharpe, Dave, 1998–, Macclesfield
Shore, I. C., 1928–1939, Winston-Salem
Silverthorne, Ray G., 1970–1991, Washington
Smith, Aubrey, 1985–1993, Elizabethtown
Sosebe, J. W., 1951–1956, Columbia, SC
Southard, Paul C., 1954–1982, Stokesdale
Stanford, W. Elmo, 1972–1981, Greensboro
Stephenson, Russell L., Jr., 1999–, Raleigh
Stewart, Carl, 1960–1979, Winston-Salem
Strobhar, A. D., 1940–1942, Savannah, GA
Stronach, George, III, 1981–1996, Wilson
Stuart, J. E., 1920–1924, Wilson
Stubbs, E. W., 1916–1925, Belhaven
Sullivan, Clyde, 1980–1985, Southern Pines
Swords, Otis L., Jr., 1969–1972, Charlotte
Tart, L. A., 1929–1965, Dunn
Taylor, S. B., 1904–1928, Catherine Lake
Taylor, J. Fred, 1905–1925, Kinston
Tetterton, J. Marshall, 1986–1995, Rocky Mount
Thompson, Charles M., 1961–1964, Charleston
Thornton, James, 1958–1974, Fayetteville
Thornton, Kenneth R., 1986–1995, McLean, VA
Todd, M. C., 1943–1959, Wendell
Traylor, Kermit, 1957–1960, Winston-Salem
Turnage, H. W., 1930–1931, Albemarle
Turner, W. B., 1921–1933, Ellenton
Turnstall, K. R., 1902, Kinston
Tyer, Harold, 1955–1957, Bath
Van Camp, James R., 1984–1987, Southern Pines
Wake, J. Stuart, 1978–1981, Wilson
Ward, Sarah Bain, 1986–1989, Wilson
Ward, T. Boddie, 1951–1966, Wilson
Warren, Bowden G., 1954–1981, Newton Grove
Warren, John C., 1940–1953, Newton Grove
Waters, John M., 1920–1922, Arapahoe
Watson, R. P., Jr., 1967–1982, Wilson
Weaver, Glenn S., 1976–1979, Washington
Welsh, David L., 1986–1990, Wilson
Westbrook, W. "Buddy," 1988–1991, Kinston
White, William C., 1958–1961, Charleston, SC
Wiegmann, F. W., 1940–1943, Dunn
Williams, Beth Burton, 1999–, Smithfield
Williams, J. O. 1980–1983, Winston-Salem
Williams, J. Phillips, 1973–1976, Wilmington
Williams, T. Brown, 1951–1952, Dunn
Williford, C. Buren, 1994–1997, Wilson
Wilson, Charles H., 1986–1989, Eden
Wilson, W. G., 1904–1911, Wilson's Mills
Wimberly, E. J., 1955–1979, Columbia, SC
Woodard, Calvin, 1917–1919, Wilson
Woolard, W. H., 1932–1947, Greenville
Wooten, S. T., 1982–1985, Wilson
Worley, Bland W., 1968–1980, Winston-Salem
Wyndham, Neal, 1955–1958, Jacksonville
Youngblood, T. J., 1963–1966, Raleigh

APPENDIX I

Faculty and Administrative Officers, 1902–2001

PRESIDENTS, 1902–2001

Coggins, James C.	1902–1904	Moudy, James M., acting	1953
Harper, John J.	1904–1908	White, Travis A.	1953–1956
Caldwell, Jesse C.	1908–1916	Moudy, James M., acting	1956
Smith, Raymond A.	1916–1920	Wenger, Arthur D.	1956–1977
Hilley, Howard S.	1920–1949	Adams, Milton L., acting	1977
Jarman, Cecil A., acting	1949–1950	Doster, Harold C.	1978–1983
Lindley, D. Ray	1950–1953	Hemby, James B., Jr.	1983–

Abbitt, Margaret	1940–1941	Amlie, Thomas T.	1996
Abernathy, Betty S.	1960–1961	Amt, Carl	1972–1976
Abeyounis, Greg	1994–	Anderson, Bobby L.	1961–1964
Adams, Milton L.	1949–1981	Anderson, Elizabeth	1903–1910
Adkins, David C.	1972–1976	Anderson, Walter W., Jr.	1964–1992
Agard, Latonya	2000–	Andrews, Barbara C.	1981–1985
Aiken, Lewis R., Jr.	1958–1960	Anthony, John C.	1979–1985
Albert, Dawn H.	1974–1986	Anthony, T. L.	1927–1930
Albert, J. Ross	1964–1987	Arnberg, Christine	1902–1903
Alderman, Ruth M.	1902–1903	Arnold, D. W.	1902–1903
Aleksa, Linda C.	1987–1988	Arnold, Russell	1951–1974
Allen, Barbara A.	1980–1985	Ashworth, Louise	1923–1924
Allen, Mary	1983–1984	Aston, Margaret	1914–1915
Allen, R. Worden, Jr.	1960–1965	Avery, Frank W.	1980–1981
Almond, H. Dale	1979–1996	Aycock, Charles R.	1968–1973
Alvord, Elmira H.	1975–1976	Ayscue, Richard G., Jr.	1981–1982

Appendix I: Faculty and Administrative Officers, 1902–2001

Bagby, Mrs. Richard	1918–1919	Benton, Horace P.	1960–1965
Baggette, Elizabeth	1941–1943	Bergeron, Bernadette	1983–1984
Bailey, Edgar Lee	1947–1948	Bethune, John J.	2000–
Ballance, Priscilla D.	1972–1976	Bird, Mary L.	1962–1970
Barber, N. Lynn	1960–1961	Bird, Matthew J.	1944–1950
Barclay, John	1925–1926	Birnbaum, Vivian G.	1968–1976
Barden, James L.	1960–1964	Bissette, Allard C.	1992–
Bardin, Benjamin H.	1957–1979	Bissette, Vicky	1993–
Bardin, Sarah Z.	1959–1962	Black, Robert K.	1958–1959
Barham, E. L.	1910–1917	Blackburn, Casey, L.	1933–1935
Barham, Mrs. E. L.	1910–1917	Blackwell, Robin	1999–2000
Barker, Marshall J.	1975–1976	Blake, Eugenia Q.	1959–1960
Barnes, Doris	1981–1997	Blauvelt, Robert O.	1925–1926
Barnes, Eugene	1955	Blythe, Carl S.	1948–1949
Barnes, Rebecca	1949–1950	Blythe, Mrs. Carl S.	1948–1949
Barnes, Ruby G.	1973–1977	Boettcher, Janet	1980–1983
Basinger, Mark A.	2000–	Boineau, Ernestine	1947–1950
Basu, Manjusri	1996–1997	Boles, Janet T.	1951–1964
Batts, Holly	1996–1997		1966–1967
Batts, Paula H.	1997–1999	Boles, William B.	1954–1955
Baxter, Polly H.	1969–1971	Bonner, Katie S.	1910–1912
Baxter, Susanna	1997–2000	Bookout, R. Ernice	1989–1990
Bazzle, Edward F.	1965–1978	Bostick, Dorothy J.	1969–
Beach, Laura J.	1922–1924	Bottoms, G. Kathryn	1985–1986
Beaman, B. Sue	1978–1997	Bowen, Clint	1999–
Beaman, Stephen L.	1976–1977	Bowles, George	1997–1999
Beckerdite, Fred W.	1969–1971	Bowles, J. D.	1907–1908
Beeler, Edward E.	1960–1961	Bowman, Bulow W.	1959–1963
Bell, George E.	1923–1924	Bowman, Kerith M.	1999–2000
Benedict, Ruth H.	1972–1974	Bowmer, Nina A.	1965–1966
Bengtson, Neal M.	1996–	Boyer, Harold N.	1977–1978
Bennett, K. Dick	1969–1980	Boyette, Gretchen B.	1968–1985
Bennett, Robert E.	1963–1969	Boyette, Michelle	1998–1999
Bennett, Rolla James	1945–1947	Boykin, Edna E.	1959–1966
Bennett, Ronald	1996	Boykin, J. Robert, III	1976–1980

Boyle, Helen	1980–1984	Burnett, Carol H.	1977–1979
Brabec, Leonard B.	1918–1919	Burrus, Patricia	1994–
Bradshaw, Bertha	1951–1953	Burt, Millard P.	1953–1956
Bradshaw, J. Clinton	1951–1955		1958–1963
Brame, Mary H.	1959–1960	Buss, Harriet W.	1978–1980
Brandon, Helen G.	1947–1948	Cadden, Shane	1999–2000
Brandt, James L.	1957–1958	Cai, Zhixiong	1991–
Brauff, Frances	1950–1951	Cain, Harry I.	1977–1978
Brayboy, Shannon	1997–1999	Caldwell, Jesse Cobb	1907–1916
Brewer, Georgia	1939–1942	Caldwell, Mary S.	1915–1916
Bridgers, John F.	1967–1980	Caldwell, Martha E.	1977–1979
Briley, William C.	1965–1983	Callahan, Janice R.	1977
Britt, Anthony	1988–1999	Callery, Kathleen	1983–1984
Broadwater, Jeff	1992–1995	Calvin, Lisa M.	1997–1999
Brothers, Marie Powers	1919–1920	Campbell, Clinton P.	1949–1950
Broussard, Sherry M.	1977–1979	Campbell, Joseph L.	1956–1974
Brown, C. Lynn	1950–1956	Cannaday, Ada Lee	1927–1930
Brown, E. Edward	1964–1969	Cannon, Virginia Dickens	1957–1964
Brown, Edward C.	1959–1995	Capps, Doris F.	1956–1993
Brown, Minnie E.	1906–1907	Capps, Robert G.	1954–1988
Brown, Robin	2000–	Carpenter, May F.	1903–1904
Brownfield, Kathryn G.	1988–1995	Carr, Noel C.	1948–1956
Browning, H. D., Jr.	1945–1946	Carrasco, Candide	1978–1981
	1955–1956	Carson, B. G.	1926–1929
	1964–1967	Carter, Jennie Lee	1916–1917
Brugh, Thomas H.	1977–	Carter, Margaret S.	1993–1995
Bryan, Frank R.	1984–1987	Case, S. Perry	1916–1926
Bryant, Eloise	1935–1938		1936–1960
Bublic, John M.	2000–	Case, Mrs. Perry	1918–1921
Bullard, Roger A.	1965–1994		1925–1926
Bullock, Ann	1956–1959	Casey, Benjamin E.	1971–1976
Bullock, R. D., Jr.	1933–1934	Castelli, Perry A.	1998–2001
Bumgarner, Stan	1977–1978	Castelli, Vivian	2000–2001
Bunting, Blanche	1972–1975	Cate, Ann Griffin	1967–1969
Burley, Marvin M., Jr.	1970–1978	Cauley, Lisa W.	1993–
	1979–1982	Cave, Sanquinetti	1982–1984

Chalk, Bryan L.	1975–1980	Crenshaw, Margaret G.	1961–1963
Chandler, Jane	1981–1983	Cress, Faye	1982–1984
Chappell, S. G.	1936–1943	Croom, Judson H.	1978–1980
	1952–1959	Crossingham, Chase	1993–1996
Charles, Gladys	1932–1945	Crouch, Paul H.	1967–1995
Chen, Rong–Yaw	1965–1966	Crutchfield, William J.	1949–1951
Clark, James A.	1994–	Culbreath, Eva L.	1942–1944
Clark, Mary R.	1962–1965	Cummings, Michael M.	1983–1992
Clay, Lida Pearl	1916–1918	Cummings. Steve	1982–1984
Clay, Lura Newby	1916–1917	Cunningham, May	1905–1906
Clayton, Susan	1953–1955	Cunningham, Robin	1980–1983
Cobb, James V.	1956–1972	Currey, Alida G.	1966–1967
Coefield, Otis W.	1964–1982	Curtis, Bruce R.	1982–1986
Coggin, Bill	1982–1983	Curtis, Kader R.	1945–1946
Coggins, James Caswell	1902–1904	Custer, Paul F., III	1999–2000
Coggins, Mrs. James	1902–1903	Cutlip, Randall B.	1953–1958
Coker, Gordon E.	1956–1963	Dale, Timothy C.	1978–1980
Cole, Glenn G.	1902–1904	Dalton, Bruce A.	1978–1979
Cole, Henry C.	1967–1972	Daniel, Jessie M.	1958–1980
Collins, Francis M.	1969–1973	Daniel, Robert M.	1972–1976
Collins, Karen Thorsen	1983–1984	Daniell, James D.	1955–1987
Constantine, Gus A.	1955–1960	Daniels, Katherine L.	1986–1987
Cooper, Jerry D.	1967–1968	Danielson, Janet M.	1962–1964
	1969–1991	Daughety, G. Keith	1992–1999
Corbett, Justine	1982–1989	Daughety, Kathy	1987–
Corbett, Rena	2001–	Daughety, Morgan	1987–
Corbin, Irma L.	1982–1995	Daughtry, Frances	1982–1986
Corbin, James B.	1969–1975	Davidson, Amy	1996–1998
Coyle, Nancy H.	1980–1982	Davidson, Brenda D.	1970–1982
Crapps, Ken	1987–1988		1990–
Craver, Eric	1992–1995	Davis, Dave A.	1993–1996
Creach, Jerome F. D.	1994–2000	Davis, Elizabeth A.	1963–1964
Creech, Frank	1981–1983	Davis, Essie	1956–1961
Creekmore, Judith Carolyn	1964–1966	Davis, F. Mark	1978–1997
Cregger, Ronald M.	1994–1998	Davis, James R., Jr.	1972–1973
Crenshaw, Jimmy L.	1964–1965	Davis, Jerry W.	1975–1976

Dean, Brenda G.	1988–1990	Eagles, J. C., Jr.	1936–1942
Dean, Rebecca L.	1973–1977	Eason, Frances R.	1972–1976
Deans, Marie E.	1968–1989	Edelbrock, Elbert	1965–1966
Deese, Janis A.	1977–1978	Edmonston, Martha L.	1928–1941
De Garzon, Laurel	1983–1986	Edmundson, Robert M.	1991–
DeLage, Joseph O., Jr.	1960–1961	Edwards, Gary P.	1984 1987
Delp, Robert W.	1963–1968	Edwards, Roberta	1983–1985
Demchick, Paul H.	1990–	Edwards, William P.	1965–1967
DeMent, Russell D.	1967–1978	Egbert, James D.	1983–1988
Denton, Amy	1996–	Eggers, Ronald E.	1978–
Deratt, Allan	1952–1953	Eicher, C. Franklin	1943–1948
Derick, Robert G.	1947–1948	Eicher, Eva	1936–1948
Derick, Mrs. Robert G.	1947–1948	Eliason, Nancy B.	1942–1944
Dickerman, John M.	1956–1961	Elliott, Vida	1957–1966
Dietz, John F.	1980–1981	Ellis, Bridgett	1989–1992
Dillard, Hughes	1978–1996	Ellis, Jo Ann	1966–1968
Dixon, Buford W.	1964–1965	Ellis, S. Dee	1998–2000
Doherty, Kathleen T.	1997–1998	Emory, Frank E.	1971–1979
Dolman, Ann	2001–	English, Sondra K.	2000–
Dolman, David M.	1987–	Ennis, Jackie S.	1995–
Doster, Harold C.	1978–1983	Eskridge, T. J.	1952–1954
Dowell, Juliana	1977–1986	Esplugas, Celia	1982–1985
Doyle, Poplin	2001–	Evans, Elva E.	1970–1978
Druckenmiller, Elizabeth W.	1942–1944	Evans, Guyla C.	1984–1992
Duckworth, William E.	1966–1973	Evans, Princie K.	1982–1984
Dulaney, Peggy E.	1975–1977	Evaul, Thomas W., Jr.	1955–1956
Duncan, Claudia L.	1989–	Everhart, Duane D.	1998–2000
Dungan, D. R.	1903	Ewell, Louise H.	1976–1977
Dunlap, T. R.	1909–1911	Faithful, Mark F.	1986–1993
Dunlap, Mrs. T. R.	1909–1911	Falor, Craig H.	1979–1984
Dunn, John W.	1951–1991	Farmer, C. M.	1911–1914
Dunn, Miriam M.	1956–1958	Farmer, Mrs. C. M.	1911–1913
Dunn, Robert L., Jr.	1967–1971	Fautz, Ronald A.	2000–
Dunn, Ruth	1962–1984	Featherstone, Gene	1959–1962
Eagles, Dorothy D.	1947–1972	Fecho, Susan C.	1997–

Appendix I: Faculty and Administrative Officers, 1902–2001

Feith, David A.	1984–1987	Garrett, Charles	1984–1987
Ferencik, Bernie	1990–1994	Gattis, Sarah B.	1962–1990
Ferguson, Benn J.	1917–1919	Gaylord, Catherine S.	1969–1984
Ferriter, Steve	1999–	Gibson, Brenda D.	1989–1992
Fern, Gilbert H.	1912–1914	Gifford, Suzanne	1999–
Fern, Mrs. Gilbert H.	1912–1913	Giles, Rebecca W.	1979–1982
Fields, Wilbert O., Jr.	1976–1979	Gillette, Burt	1976–1977
Finch, Pearl L.	1972–1980	Glasgow, William A.	1968–1971
Fitzgerald, Jim	1998–1999	Glendenning, Marguerite	1953–1955
Fleming, Ola I.	1939–1956		1956–1957
Flowers, Celia S.	1982–1983	Glover, Annie Morris	1950–1951
Flowers, John M., Jr.	1952–1954	Goebel, Donald W., Jr.	1987–1988
Flowers, Rosabelle	1952–1953	Goff, F. Keith	1988–1991
Flynn, Lenora W.	1994–1998	Gold, John D., Jr.	1967–1968
Folmsbee, Grant O.	1966–1981	Gordon, E. E.	1907–1908
Fontaine, John W.	1935–1950	Gordon, Mark	1999–
Ford, Elizabeth	1911–1914	Goss, Lance	1999–
Foust, Gladys	1920–1921	Graff, Paul W.	1941–1942
Fox, E. L.	1925–1926	Graham, Douglas A.	1968–2000
Foy, Ted C.	1971–1979	Grau, Joshua M.	1999–2000
Francis, L. Denise	1991–1993	Gray, Adele J.	1978–1988
Frank, Elliot	1978–1979	Gray, Irene T.	1955–1981
Frazier, Robert C., Sr.	1959–1997	Gray, Susan G.	1956–1958
Frazier, Yvonne D.	1993–1997		1969–1975
French, Ruth E.	1928–1930	Gray, Walter	1956–1960
Fukuchi, Michael S.	1981–	Grayson, Anna Beatrice	1908–1910
Fulghum, James E.	1952–1955	Green, H. C.	1948–1949
	1956–1960	Green, Peter J.	2000–
Fulling, Richard W.	1987–	Greene, John F.	1979–1980
Fulton, Harriet	1944–1947	Gregory, Albert M.	1948–1950
Funderburk, Earl C.	1972–1976	Gregory, Shirley	1988–
Garber, Garl E.	1993–1995	Griffin, Mary F.	1957–1984
Garner, C. Leon	1947–1948	Griffin, Pauline Helen	1916–1918
Garner, Mrs. H.W.	1909	Griffin, Richard W., III	1949–1950
	1916–1920	Grim, Ethel McD.	1917–1925

Grim, Fred F.	1917–1943	Harmon, Steve	2000–
Grimes, Ira B.	1904–1908	Harnar, Frank E.	1915–1916
Grimes, Terrence L.	1971–	Harper, Frances F.	1904–1940
Grizzle, Rebecca	2000	Harper, John James	1903
Groff, Natalie	1997–1999		1904–1908
Groner, Miriam	1940–1941	Harper, Kenneth L.	1991–1993
Grooms, Duane	1991–1993	Harper, Myrtie L.	1907–1939
	2000–	Harper, Wilmer M.	1972–1973
Groskin, Richard B.	2000–	Harrell, Irene	1958–1964
Grossnickle, Betty D.	1976	Harrell, Janice F.	1979–1982
Grove, Eugene F.	1941–1942	Harrell, Rosanne W.	1997–
Guerrant, W. U.	1908–1909	Harrington, Marjorie L.	1995–2001
Guilfoyle, Philip	1995–1999	Harris, Jackie M.	1985–1992
Gurganus, Josephus	1909–1910	Harris, O. Gerald	1966–1982
Gurgone, James	1982–1988	Harris, Stephanie	1996–1998
Gwaltney, O. Elwood	1980–1981	Harris, Winfred R.	1948–1953
Gwaltney, Sally J.	1977–1981	Harrison, R. Woody, Jr.	1973–1977
Haberyan, Henry D.	1966–1979	Harrison, William N.	1960–1962
Hackney, John	1996–	Harriss, Jean Abbitt	1944–1954
Hackney, John N., Jr.	1956–1958	Hartsock, Mildred E.	1940–1973
Hadley, Robert P.	1968–1979	Hastings, Gregory A.	1981–1991
	1980–1983	Haynes, Laureen L.	1942–1944
Haladay, Diana J.	1973–1974	Head, Harlow Z.	1974–
Hale, W.R.	1942–1943	Helms, Milton	1997–2000
Hall, Doris B.	1962–1964	Hemby, James B., Jr.	1959–1962
Hall, Gary	1989–		1965–1983
Hamlin, C. H.	1925–1976	Hendrick, James P.	1950–1951
Hamlin, Griffith A.	1948–1950	Henkle, Joan	1983–1987
Hanchrow, J. H.	1973–1980	Hensley, Daniel J.	1961–1995
Hancock, John A.	1989–1997	Herndon, Nan M.	1957–1958
Handorf, Howard	1994–1998		1966–1969
Harbaum, Darrell	1957–1961	Herring, William A.	1938–1946
Hardison, Dail	1986–1987	Hervey, Chris R.	1996–1997
Hare, Barbara	1961–1963	Hewitt, Lura M.	1978–1984
Harley, Ann	1991–1994	Hill, Charlotte	1931–1937
Harlow, Linda	1982–1985	Hilley, Howard Stevens	1919–1949

Appendix I: Faculty and Administrative Officers, 1902–2001

Hilley, Maggie T.	1919–1920
Hinegardner, W. S.	1923–1924
Hines, Larry L.	1993–1994
Hinnant, Patricia	1972–1974
Hinshaw, Donald G.	1959–1964
Hinton, Nannelle Paulk	1931–1934
Hiss, Patricia H.	1967–1973
Hobgood, Ben C.	1981–1991
Hodam, Cecil	1927–1928
Hodges, Catherine Taylor	1938–1939
Hodges, Filo A.	1929–1948
Hodges, Mrs. Filo A.	1938–1948
Hodges, Roland H., Jr.	1963–1966
Hodgson, Richard C.	1965–1966
Hoffman, Albert R.	1949–1955
Hoffman, Mrs. Albert R.	1951–1955
Holcomb, Patricia	1979–1983
Holden, Dorothy H.	1946–1948
Holland, Amanda	1998–2000
Hollar, Robert P.	1954–1981
Holloman, Richard	1997–2000
Holloway, Edward B.	1962–
Holsapple, Cortell K.	1926–1935
Holsworth, Doris Campbell	1947–1962
Hooks, Edgar W., Jr.	1959–1960
Hope, Robert C.	1959–1962
Hopkins, Marbry B.	1996–1998
Horie, Donna	1976–1977
Horton, Donna	1950–1952
Houff, Suzanne G.	1997–2000
Hough, J. M.	1940–1945
House, Virginia	1951–1958
Howard, Anna L.	1902–1908
Howard, Lee J.	1951–1958
Howell, W. R.	1903–1904
Hudson, O. Jane	1979–1981
Hudson, William E.	1981–1984
Hufty, Frank R.	1928–1930
Hughes, Nina	1944–1946
Humphrey, Amanda	1997–
Humphrey, Inez Faith	1914–1915
Hunter, Sue E.	1977–1986
Hutto, Danny	1975–1977
Hyatt, Laura	1993–1999
Hyatt, Ronald W.	1961–1962
Inabinett, Thomas P.	1949–1953
Irvine, Norbert W.	1967–1985
Issette, Stephanie	1978–1987
Jaggi, Anand P.	1971–2000
James, Katherine H.	1979–
James, Lydia E.	1954–1955
	1960–1961
Janoscrat, Agnes J.	1977–1979
Jarman, Cecil Albert	1935–1955
Jauss, David P.	1984–1987
Jeffries, Catherine W.	1964–1989
Jenkins, Margaret	1953–1954
Jenkins, Sadie	1935–1940
Jennings, Pauline	1907–1909
Jensen, Robert E.	1967–1969
Jernigan, James	1989–1992
Johns, Robin F.	1990–1999
Johnson, Alan H.	1982–1985
Johnson, Janie O.	1958–1973
Johnson, Mary	1947–1948
Johnson, Virginia W.	1972–1975
Johnston, Edna L.	1953–1983
Johnston, Hugh B., Jr.	1953–1984
Johnstone, Peter	2001–
Jolly, Geraldine V.	1988–1996
Jones, Bobby F.	1968–1974
Jones, Jean P.	1977–1980

Jones, Joe	1986–	Laffiteau, Dorothy E.	1975–1976
Jones, Mabel	1907–1909	Lafond, Jo Carol	1988–1993
Jones, Pauline	1960–1962	Lamb, Marvin L.	1973–1977
Jones-Grooms, Rebecca	2001–	Lamb, Thomas	1989–1991
Jordan, Elizabeth H.	1960–1964	Lambert, E. Helen	1919–1921
	1968–1969	Lamm, A. Kathryn	1952–
Joyner, Bethany R.	1947–1992	Landing, Miriam	1980–1998
Joyner, Gordon L.	1978–	Lane, Alan	1990–
Kalmbach, Frank	1964–1965	Langley, Emily	1936–1937
Kaplan, Ralph	1989–1994	Langley, Tassie R.	1966–1977
Kastner, Meredith V.	1983–1984	Langston, Myrtle	1917–1918
Kearney, Carolyn J.	1919–1921	Lappin, W. C.	1917–1919
Keel, Nell M.	1908–1910	Lappin, W. O.	1914–1919
Kelly, John W.	1966–1968	Lappin, Mrs. W. O.	1915–1918
Kennerly, Susan M.	1986–1989	Larsen, Phama M.	1989–1993
Kent, John B.	1914–1915	Larson, Eric D.	1988–1990
Kent, William T.	1976–1977	Larson, Kim	1993–
Kilgore, J. William	1974–1996	Lascell, Ann F.	1967–1968
Kilpatrick, Christopher	1992–1996	Latham, Mildred B.	1968–1976
Kim, Ho Keun	1966–1983	Lawhon, Joel	1952–1954
King, Betty	1982–1983	Ledbetter, Gorman W.	1956–1960
King, Deborah H.	1999–	Lee, Cyrus F.	1946–1962
Kinney, Carmen A.	1994–1996	Lee, Darlene R.	1975–1976
Kirby, Susan A.	1979	Lee, Paul N.	1992–2000
Kline, Donald S.	1986–1988	Lee, Richard	2001–
Knight, Cathy	1974–1977	Lehman, Betsy B.	1980–1982
Koesy, Shelden F.	1965–1967	Lehman, Ethel L.	1935–1939
Kolunie, Jane M.	1990–	Lenard, Mary J.	1997–
Kori, Abdullah	1902–1903	Lewis, Charlotte S.	1981–1986
Kornegay, Jane	1990–1995	Lewis, Deanna M.	1970–1971
Krein, Marc A.	1985–1992	Lewis, Georgia K.	1972–1976
Krise, Carrie Lee	1916–1917	Lievense, Ron	1996–
Krise, Nellie Mae	1916–1919	Lindley, D. Ray	1950–1953
Kruger, Mary Ann	1989–1998	Lindquist, Vernon R.	1997–
Kupsco, Elizabeth A.	1991–1993	Lineberger, Fred L.	1947–1949
Kurtts, Stephanie A.	1999–2000	Little, John R.	1992–1994

Appendix I: Faculty and Administrative Officers, 1902–2001 363

Livingston, Cora Lynn	1916–1917	Massengill, Bessie	1939–1942
Locklair, Ernest J.	1984–1987	Massey, Christine W.	1985–
Long, Esther L.	1944–1967	Massey, Lynda	1986–1987
Lowe, Carrie	2001–	Matheny, Paul D.	1990–1991
Lowe, Marvin E.	1939–1940	Mattox, W. T.	1921–1926
Lowell, Neil F.	1981–1988	Mattox, Mrs. W. T.	1924–1925
	1992–1993	Maudie, Joyce	1993–1996
Lozier, Gilmour G.	1968–1970	May, Roger D., II	1995–1999
Lucas, Claudia	1945–1949	Maye, Rodney	1992–1993
Lucas, Mamie J.	1910–1912	Mayes, Frank	1978–1984
	1925–1934	McAdams, R. M.	1970–1979
Luke, Ray	1950–1951	McAlister, Gary D.	1983–1990
Lutz, Edwin J.	1976–1977	McBride, Charles	1991–1992
Lynch, Mabel	1920–1921	McCain, Sadie M.	1960–1962
Lynn, Justine	1941–1942	McCann, Katherine	1997–1999
MacDonald, Murdina D.	1983–2000	McClive, Vera H.	1977–1986
MacLean, W. Jerry	1970–	McComas, James E.	1951–1964
MacLennan, Thomas G.	1979–1984	McDaniel, Katrina W.	1994–
Magill, John W.	1960–1963	McDonald, Agnes	1981–1985
Mallison, Dallas	1933–1936	McDonald, Kathleen M.	1979–1980
Mannen, Jerry A.	1965–1966	McDowell, Dennis L.	1981–1984
Manning, Courtney	1999–	McEwen, Joseph L.	1923–1924
Manning, Lucy	1902–1903	McFarland, Daniel M.	1957–1963
Mansell, Judith A.	1996–	McFarland, Irene McC.	1957–1958
Markham, Coleman C.	1981–	McFarlane, Earl J.	1955–1961
Marrs, Suzanne W.	1967–1969	McGarvey, Frances	1914–1916
Marshall, David F.	1972–1980	McGill, William M.	1963–1984
Marshall, June E.	1993–1997	McGirt, Roger M.	1925–1928
Marshall, S. Elaine	1986–	McIver, Sally M.	1962–1964
Marshall, Thomas E., III	1964–1996	McKeel, Carole M.	1967–1988
Martin, Austin G.	1916–1918	McLean, Effie F.	1962–1963
Martin, Brenda T.	1988–2000	McLeod, Joyce A. B.	1977–1978
Martin, Judith	1982–1983	McManus, Shonra	1994–
Martin, M. Adele	1902–1903	McNeil, Cheryl	1982–1983
Martin, W. S.	1916–1918	McPherson, Judy B.	1991–1995
Martinez, Purificacion	1994–1995	McRacken, Herbert L.	1976–1978

Meadows, Alfred C.	1918–1920	Moore, Nina M.	1944–1945
Meadows, Thomas B.	1948–1949	Moore, Richard H.	1985–1996
Meeks, Tim	1990–1992	Moore, Robert L.	1961–1989
Mercer, Gordon E., Jr.	1963–1965	Morey, Megan	1992–1993
Mercer, Karen M.	1980–1982	Morgan, Annie Laurie	1943–1944
Mercer, Margaret Bryan	1936 1939	Morgan, Mrs. Hilliard F.	1942–1943
	1942–1943	Morgan, Raymond E.	1937–1941
Meskey, Joseph T.	1990–1995	Morin, Denise	1992–1996
Meyer, Louis B.	1963–1971	Morris, Louise	1957–1958
Michels, Connie M.	1976–1980	Morris, Naomi	1956–1963
Middleton, Janice A.	1942–1944	Morris, Tom	1994–1998
Miele, Sandra D.	1979–1986	Morriss, Robert F.	1966–1967
Miele, William D.	1979–1990	Morrow, Robert O.	1956–1958
Miller, Betty	1968–1969	Moss, Nancy	1946–1947
Miller, Harold E.	1955–1957	Moudy, James Mattox	1953–1957
Miller, Laura	2000–	Mountney, Joyce L.	1982–1983
Miller, Raymond R.	1946–1951	Moye, Fannie	1918–1921
Miller, Troy H., Jr.	1977–1983	Muilberger, Albert E.	1909–1915
Mills, Barbara F.	1975–1977	Mullen, Malcolm P.	1959–1961
Milne, Sheila	1990–	Mullis, Joe W.	1983–1987
Mink, Joanna	1987–1990	Murray, Cleo	1971–1991
Minton, Mrs. V. B.	1902–1903	Murray, Lessie Lee	1948–1952
Mitchell, Jennifer A.	1999–	Muskovin, Marie	1989–1992
Mitchell, Kay A.	1986–1998	Mutchler, Christy H.	1995–1998
Mize, Barbara	1982–	Nadelman, Martin H.	1972–1975
Mizell, W. Henderson	1906–1907	Nakhre, Amrut	1972–2000
Molineux, Allen W.	1977–1988	Nance, Jennifer	2001–
Monk, Pearl Fay	1912–1914	Neff, Lori	1990–1994
Monshower, Alvah C.	1978–1987	Neff, Sheryl L.	1996–
Montano, Sharon	1985–	Neimeyer, Bruce	1990–1991
Montgomery, Kent	1976–1978	New, James A.	1981–1986
Montgomery, Louise A.	1913–1914	Newton, F. Brian	1994–2000
Moore, Mrs. Allen R.	1922–1930	Newton, Margaret	1960–1974
Moore, Ann F.	1915–1918	Newton, Margaret R.	1945–1947
Moore, Clarice L.	1966–1989	Nicholls, Peggy	1955
Moore, Harris C.	1946–1949	Nichols, Elizabeth T.	1982–1983

Appendix I: Faculty and Administrative Officers, 1902–2001

Niles, Carl E.	1950–1951	Petway, C. Briggs, Jr.	1989–1994
Nisbet, Susan S.	1977–1982	Petway, Renita J.	1985–1998
Noer, Amy J.	1996–1997	Pfohl, James C., Jr.	1962–1969
Norfolk, Ira P.	1964–1972	Pfohl, Tina	1976–1977
Nowell, Frances E.	1968–1984	Phillips, Debbie	1995–
O'Boyle, Linda	1984–1989	Phillips, William E., Jr.	1956–1959
	1995–	Pickard, Phyllis B.	1976–1979
O'Connor, Elizabeth B.	1998–	Pilley, Claude F., Jr.	1952–1953
O'Connor, Michael L.	1994–1996	Ping–Robbins, Nancy R.	1990–1995
Odom, J. T., Jr.	1959–1960	Piner, Rexford E.	1967–1968
O'Donoghue, Jennifer	2001–	Plyler, B. B., Jr.	1951–1954
Oehler, Susan E.	1973–1974	Pomeroy, Benjamin B.	1972–1977
Oertling, John T.	1974–1975	Pope, Sarah A.	2000–
O'Neal, Neal	1961–1965	Powell, Bobby	1983–1987
Orcutt, David S.	1972–1974	Powell, Jean	1984–1989
Parham, E. Thomas	1964–1984	Powers, James W.	1976–1977
Parker, Teresa C.	1978–	Poythress, Daryl	1992–1993
Parker, Walter R., Jr.	1971–1995	Preston, Andrew C.	1967–1969
Parrilla, Osvaldo	1999–		1970–1987
Parrish, Judith M.	1970–1998	Preston, Lamarr H.	1977–1983
Patterson, Clinton E.	1973–1976	Pridgen, Harry A.	1965–1988
Patterson, William C.	1970–1980	Pridgen, Randal	1988–
Paulsell, William O.	1962–1981	Pritchard, Selma	1968–1971
Payne, Virginia C.	1979–1982	Privette, April C.	1975–1976
Pearce, Fred M.	1923–1924	Privette, Don H.	1959–1961
Pearce, Virginia L.	1972–1976	Pruden, Evelyn S.	1974–
Peele, Agnes L.	1920–1947	Purcell, Eugene G., Jr.	1957–1984
Peery, William Wallace	1934–1935	Purser, Jimmie M.	1974–1976
Pennington, Patti	1982–1986	Purvis, Gene A.	1961–1988
Periconi, Frances O'C.	1972–1975	Purvis, Rae	2001–
Perkins, Robert	1954–1955	Rabil, Lillian Therese	1956–1957
Perry, Louise Belle	1905–1909	Rakow, Charles W.	1960–1996
Perry, Patricia B.	1994–1999	Ramsay, William T.	1956–1960
Perry–Brandon, Patricia	1994–	Rand, William R.	1965–1971
Petersen, Bruce W.	1965–1967	Ranganathan, Murali K.	1991–
Peterson, Mark	2001–	Raphael, Janice	1976–1980

Name	Years
Rawlings, Russell T.	1984–1987
	1990–1999
Ray, Eliza Jane	1970–1976
Raynor, Mickey G.	1956–1959
Reece, John M.	1965–1979
Reed, Joy F.	1977–1982
Reitmeyer, Jennifer A.	1984–1998
Rentle, Susan E.	1988–
Reynolds, Charles E.	1986–1988
Reynolds, Katherine L.	1944–1951
Reynolds, Robert K.	1949–1951
Rich, John	1958–1961
Rich, Tara C.	1986–1989
	1999–
Richardson, Rahkiya	1999–
Riddle, Walter L.	1966–1968
Rider, Edward	1953–1956
Riley, Jo M.	1956–1959
Rivers, Nancy J.	2000–
Roberson, Mamie	1908–1913
Roberts, William	1957–1959
Robinette, Sue M.	1978–1993
Robinette, William D.	1977–1983
Roebuck, Russell	1940–1941
Roeder, Lucile F. L.	1972–1974
Rogers, Joseph M.	1970–1972
Rogers, Vere H.	1955–1964
Rogerson, James F.	1974–1977
Rogerson, Milton	1961–1990
Rose, A. D.	1935–1938
Rose, Glenn P.	1995–1999
Rose, Shelley	1987–1988
Ross, Julia	1914–1933
Ross, Mildred D.	1927–1974
Rouse, Bessie E.	1902–1903
Routh, Donna C.	1992–1998
Rowe, Louise	1968–1969
Ruhsenberger, Henrietta M.	1924–1927
Russell, Anne	1989–1992
Russell, Sharri I.	1989–1992
Ruwe, Carol H.	1986–
Sadler, S. Lee	1916 1923
Saintsing, Wendy	1987–
Salmon, Kathleen L.	1906–1915
Sammon, Margaret	1955–1956
Sanderson, J. Ormand, Jr.	1958–1959
Sanford, John D.	1966–1984
Sarvey, Sharon I.	1988–1994
Sasser, Thelma P.	1974–1975
Saunders, Ruth C.	1959–1961
Schatz, Edward R.	1969–1974
Schatz, Gertrud K.	1969–1978
Scherer, Wallace B.	1949–1951
Schneider, Richard J.	1973–1980
Schockey, Luther Reic	1902–1903
Scott, John B.	1955–1956
Scriven, Karen	1990–2000
Scudder, John R., Jr.	1956–1967
Scudder, Mary C.	1956–1967
Sen, Promila C.	1976–1977
Sessoms, Barbara R.	1982–1984
Sessoms, Clayton	1982–1994
Settle, Harriet Clay	1911–1915
Sexauer, Mira	1977
Shackleford, Ruby P.	1946–1947
	1962–1979
Sharp, Allan R.	1953–1991
Sharp, Glyn H.	1953–1955
Sharpe, P. Dave	1986–1987
Sharpe, W. H. D., Jr.	1934–1935
Shelton, William A.	1975–1976
Shenk, Virginia A.	1964–1968

Appendix I: Faculty and Administrative Officers, 1902–2001

Sherrod, Dennis R.	1979–1988	Solomons, Anne	1958–1963
Shindler, Jennie O.	1912–1916	Spangler, Robert F.	1947–1949
Shingleton, E. Daniel	1970–	Speier, Ronald P.	2000
Shookley, J. Watson	1926–1929	Speight, Estelle	1963–1968
Shoptaugh, J. A.	1902–1903	Speight, Louise	1955–1956
Sieber, Charlotte	1981–1987	Sprinkle, Stephen V.	1983–1989
Simmons, Sandra L.	1975–1978	Sproles, Charles B.	1975–1982
Sinclair, Lida	1936–1937	St. John, Kenneth D.	1962–1977
Singletary, Alyce	1982–1984		1978
Singleton, Mary	1982–1983	Stagg, Ella M.	1941–1943
Sisk, Jessie P.	1973–1977	Stair, John W.	1959–1960
Skillman, Virginia C.	1962–1963	Stair, Nellie C.	1959–1960
Slade, Victor	1996–1997	Stalhut, Leslie	2001–
Small, John	1999–	Stallings, Ed. T.	1920
Smalley, Madeline	1939–1943		1929–1951
Smith, Barbara B.	1963–1987	Stancill, Miriam	1911–1913
Smith, Bruce B.	1967–1968	Stanislaw, Edythe W.	1967–1969
Smith, Ella H.	1910–1921	Stanton, Henry T.	1976–2000
Smith, Ella M.	1904–1905	Stapleton, Hazel S.	1960–1961
Smith, Guy	1946–1947	Stark, Lloyd W.	1945–1950
Smith, Ivy M.	1916–1927	Starr, Elma	1925–1926
Smith, Jerry A.	1979–1985	Steele, Annette	1924–1926
Smith, Laurence C.	1950–1953	Steele, Mary R. S.	1970–1973
Smith, Lou	1982–1992	Steinbeck, Rachel	1964–1967
Smith, Raymond Abner	1905–1906	Stell, Samuel C.	1960–1961
	1916–1920	Stelljes, Jack R.	1970–1972
Smith, Rebecca G.	1986–	Stephenson, C. D.	1902–1903
Smith, Robert E.	1939–1942	Stevenson, George N.	1914–1915
Smith, Ruth S.	1964–1968	Stewart, Marletta D.	1977–1988
Smith, William E.	1970–1978	Stoddard, Carla E.	1999–
Snow, Betsy L.	1978–1982	Stokes, Ruth B.	1973–1974
Snow, Susan V.	2000–	Stoll, Mrs. H. M.	1927–1928
Snyder, Eleanor G.	1935–1941	Stone, Raymond A.	1956–1959
Sobolik, Kelly	1994–1995	Stork, Kurt	1996–
Solomon, Gretchen	1990–1992	Stough, Mary F.	1968–1978
		Strachan, Jean H.	1943–1944

Street, Jutta	1999–	Thompson, Ernest L.	1969–1980
Streeter, Montrose	2000–	Thompson, Kathy M.	1975–
Strickland, Johnnie D.	1962–1964	Thompson, Pat	1981–1987
Strickland, Mary E.	1991–1996	Thunberg, Frances	1982–2000
Stringfield, Margaret J.	1902–1903		2001
Struthers, Webster	1992–	Tilley, Tony G.	1987–
Stuart, Annabel G.	1955–1956	Tingle, Bruce B.	1976–1979
Stutts, Lora	1992–1994		1987–1997
Suhr, Jung Karp	1968–1972	Tobin, Mark E.	1986–1989
Sumerel, Marie B.	1992–1994	Tomlinson, Lill C.	1917–1921
Sutherland, Walter M.	1970–1971		1930–1931
Sutter, Robert F.	1967–1969	Tomlinson, Rachel	1902–1903
Sutton, Mrs. S.	1905–1906	Tomlinson, Rebecca	1951–1957
Swain, George Harry	1953–1989	Treadwell, Candice S.	1980–1983
Swain, Myrtle T.	1954–1965	Treanor, Laura J.	1989–1994
Swarthout, G. Eastman	1910–1912	Troutman, William F.	1956–1962
Swarthout, Mary D.	1904–1912	Tucker, Garland S., III	1974–1976
Swartzwelder, Constance M.	1985–1997	Tucker, William E.	1959–1966
Swindell, Lewis H., Jr.	1963–1977	Turk, Gayla C.	1986–1998
Swords, Irby R.	1974–1976	Turley, Anthony	1986–1987
Tait, Warren R.	1956–1985	Tweddale, Ed. R.	1926–1927
Tanner, Paul	1950–1951	Tweddale, Mrs. Ed. R.	1926–1927
Taylor, Ella K.	1946–1951	Tyer, Annie L.	1912–1913
Taylor, G. Thomas	1962–1965	Tyndall, Jesse Parker	1949–1990
Taylor, Mary K.	1966–1968	Tyndall, John W.	1902–1903
Taylor, Raymond M.	1963–1964	Tyndall, Margaret H.	1970–1977
Taylor, Rebekah L.	1977–1982	Tyndall, Olivia P.	1971–1993
Teets, Louis E.	1967–1969	Tyndall, Rosa	1958–1966
Tessnear, Eddie S.	1975–1990	Tyson, Ada L.	1902–1903
Tetterton, Nancy	1995–1997	Tyson, Linda	1993–
Tew, Keith	1990–	Uzzle, Meta G.	1905–1910
Thigpen, Lorna W.	1970–1973	Van Boxel, Ann M.	1995–1998
Thomas, Albert S.	1978–1981	Van Roekel, Delva L.	1988–1990
Thomas, Karen	1983–1986	Vanguri, Pradeep R.	2000–
Thomas, Karen W.	1976–1980	Vester, Agnes Peele	1973–1977
Thompson, Bruce W.	1984–1987	Vick, Susan Frances	1947–1948

Appendix I: Faculty and Administrative Officers, 1902–2001

Villanova, Geri	1987–1990	Whelan, Raymond E.	1986–2000
Wachs, W. Ronald	1968–1983	Wheeless, W. Kent	1992–
Wade, Timothy	1983–1987	Whitaker, Pamela P.	1979–1980
Wagner, Elizabeth Cleland	1938–1940	White, Bobby D.	1983–1998
Wagner, Robert D.	1995–	White, Travis Alden	1953–1956
Walker, Ersie Caroline	1909–1910	Whitehurst, Garnett B.	1982–1990
Wall, Cathy	1982–1983	Whitehurst, Virginia A.	1988–1998
Wallace, James G.	1968–1973	Whitehurst, Willard T.	1965–1966
Wallace, William	1996–	Whitehurst, Zebulon M., III	1967–1980
Walston, Gerald D.	1963–1965	Whitfield, Carrie L.	1961–1972
Walters, Marc	1999–	Whitfield, Lee	1908–1909
Walters, John R.	1960–1962	Whitley, Eva Mae	1942–1944
Ward, Lee	1990–1991	Whitley, John L.	1968–1970
Ward, Sarah Bain	1944–1980	Whitlock, Larry D.	1964–1971
Ware, Charles C.	1915–1926	Whitney, Clarence F.	1916–1918
Warren, D. L.	1960–1963	Wiggins, Donna M.	1975
Washer, Robert J.	1964–1968	Wiggins, Rebecca	1966–1980
Waters, Carole S.	1997–1999	Wiggs, Ashton P.	1959–1990
Waters, John Mayo	1927–1968	Wiggs, Deems N.	1958–1979
Watkins, Maud Memory	1917–1918	Wilkinson, Bessie	1906–1907
Watkins, Patricia	1995–1996	Wilkinson, Todd	1988–1995
Watson, Kim	1984–1998		2000–
Webb, David	1987–2000	Willard, George S.	1952–1976
Webb, David M.	1973–1981	Williams, Frances B.	1975–1980
Webster, Jane S.	2000–	Williams, George A.	1921–1925
Weems, John E.	1955–1959	Williams, Leonard J.	1989–1991
Weinstein, Lawrence	1990	Williams, Maureen	2000–2001
Welch, Byron	1957–1958	Williams, Melba	1974–1990
Welch, Martha H.	1983–	Williams, Norma M.	1975–
Wells, Ella A.	1949–1956	Williams, Todd	1989–1996
Wenger, Arthur D.	1950–1952	Willis, Cecil R.	1962–1967
	1956–1977	Wills, Camilla Louise	1944–1950
West, Lynne N.	1954–1965	Wilson, Glenn F.	1981–1985
West, R. Fred	1950–1953	Wilson, John C.	1974–
Westbrook, Betty L.	1992–	Wilson, Mary H.	1938–1961
Westmoreland, Roger	1957–1963	Wilson, Patricia Casey	1982–1986

Wilson, Rebecca S.	1974–1976	Woodard, Katherine M.	1978–1980
Wilson, Robert P.	1956–1962	Woodard, Varina	1925–1926
Winstead, Elton D.	1962–1977	Woodard, Walker W.	1959–1973
Winstead, Janet	1957–1968	Woodward, Jeannette	1982–1988
Winstead, Laura B.	1959–1960	Woolverton, James A.	1968–1974
Winston, Karen L.	1977–1978	Wooten, William Isler	1920–1921
Winterrowd, Gretchen	1926–1927	Worcester, Martha L.	1972–1974
Wisdom, Stanley L., Jr.	1971–1975	Workman, John H.	1941–1945
Witherington, Philip D.	1966–1996	Yavorski, Elizabeth E.	1930–1941
Wolff, Bonita	1916–1919	Yerby, Karen	1980–1982
Wood, Charlotte	1984–1986	Yionoulis, Mary N.	1942–1949
Wood, Sheryl	1981–1984		1956–1957
Woodard, David W.	1977–1979	Zachry, Jeannette	1904–1907
Woodard, Frances P.	1957–1962	Zavada, Betty	1993–1994
	1964–1967	Zipf, Robert E.	1980–1989
Woodard, Jo Anne	1989–1997	Zombo, Steven M.	2000–

APPENDIX J

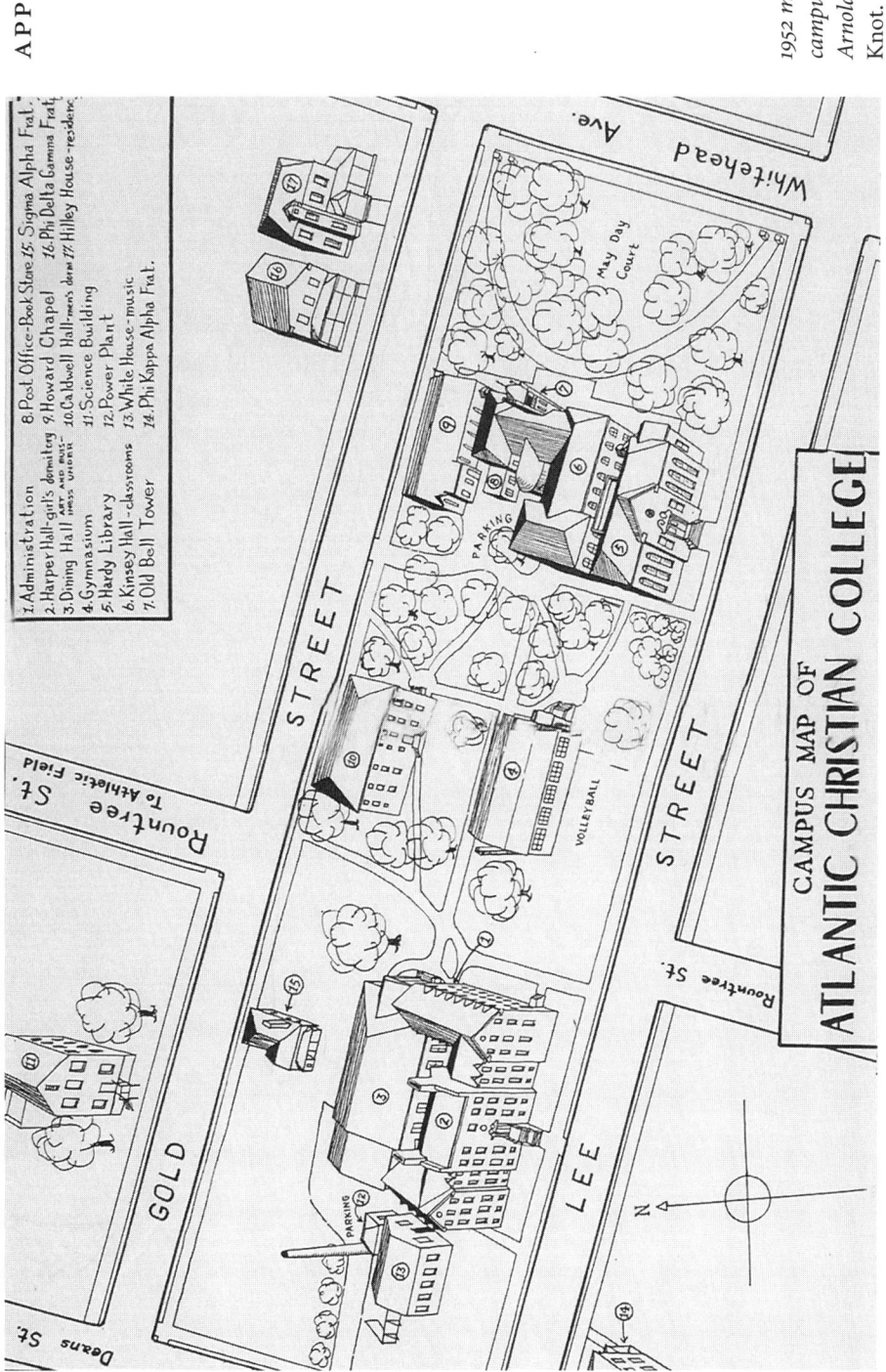

1952 map of campus by Russell Arnold. 1953 Pine Knot.

1. Administration
2. Harper Hall–girl's dormitory
3. Dining Hall art and music mess urorm
4. Gymnasium
5. Hardy Library
6. Kinsey Hall–classrooms
7. Old Bell Tower
8. Post Office–Book Store
9. Howard Chapel
10. Caldwell Hall–men's dorm
11. Science Building
12. Power Plant
13. White House–music
14. Phi Kappa Alpha Frat.
15. Sigma Alpha Frat.
16. Phi Delta Gamma Frat.
17. Hilley House–residence

CAMPUS MAP OF
ATLANTIC CHRISTIAN COLLEGE

Notes

Abbreviations

    ACC   *A History of Atlantic Christian College* by Charles C. Ware
    Cat   *Catalog* (Atlantic Christian College/Barton College general catalog)
    Coll   *Collegiate* (Atlantic Christian College/Barton College newspaper)
    NCC *North Carolina Christian*
    PK   *Pine Knot*
    Rad   *Radiant*
    TWT *The Watch Tower*
    WDT *The Wilson Daily Times*

Notes to Chapter 1

1. Daniels, *Tar Heel Editor*, 55–74.
2. Sudor, "One Hundred Year History of Ayden Christian Church (Disciples of Christ) 1893–1993," 6–10.
3. Ware, *ACC*, 60–61. Cummins, *The Disciples Colleges*, xiv, 2–3. Walter Anderson served as curator of the Carolina Discipliana Collection in 2001 and is a former Barton College history professor. Anderson, "A Church Historian Looks at the Closing of Carolina Christian College," 7.
4. Ware, *ACC*, 32–33.
5. Ware, *ACC*, 32–33.
6. Ware, *ACC*, 32–33, 64. Sudor, 16.
7. *Cat*, 1902–03, 23–24.
8. *Cat*, 1902–03, 4.
9. Ware, *ACC*, 74. *TWT*, 7 February 1902, 1. *The Watch Tower* is a publication of the Christian Church Disciples of Christ and should not be confused with the Jehovah's Witnesses tract of the same title.
10. Ware, *ACC*, 73–75. *Cat*, 1903, 4. *TWT*, 7 February 1902, 1.
11. Ware, *ACC*, 83. *TWT*, 24 January 1902, 1.

12. Ware, *ACC*, 83–84.
13. *TWT*, 7 February 1902, 1; 28 March 1902, 2.
14. *TWT*, 11 July 1902, 1. *Cat*, 1902–03, 24.
15. *TWT*, 3 January 1902, 3; 28 March 1902, 3; 11 July 1902, 1; 18 July 1902, 5.
16. Ware, *ACC*, 77.
17. Ware, *ACC*, 72, 77.
18. *Cat*, 1902–03, 26–27, 36.
19. McKinney, "Journal of Journeys: Down Memory Lane, 1888–1987," 18–19.
20. Ware, *ACC*, 76.
21. Ware, *ACC*, 76–78. *WDT*, 9 May 1902, 6.
22. *Cat*, 1902–03, 26.
23. *Cat*, 1902–03, 26, 31.
24. Ware, *ACC*, 78–79. *TWT*, 18 April 1902, 2; 29 May 1903, 2.
25. *TWT*, 29 May 1903, 2.
26. *Cat*, 1902–03, 24. *PK*, 1910, 7, 11, 58, 113.
27. *PK*, 1910, 6–9. *Cat*, 1902–1903, 1, 24.
28. *Cat*, 1902–03, 1; 1904–05, 2. *Rad*, January 1909, ix; June 1910, cover.
29. Ware, *ACC*, 87.
30. Ware, *ACC*, 85–86.
31. *TWT*, 3 January 1902, 3; 24 January 1902, 1.
32. *TWT*, 21 June 1901, 3.
33. Ware, *ACC*, 84–88.
34. *TWT*, 10 July 1903, 1.

Notes to Chapter 2

1. *The Elm City Elevator*, 28 March 1902.
2. "Bicycle," *World Book Encyclopedia*, 227. *WDT*, 22 August 1998, 18A. *The Elm City Elevator*, 28 March 1902. *Cat*, 1906–07, 40–41. *PK*, 1910, 58, 111.
3. *Cat*, 1904–05, 37–38.
4. *PK*, 1910, 8. Ware, *ACC*, 87.
5. Ware, *ACC*, 84, 87.
6. Ware, *ACC*, 87. *TWT*, 22 January 1904, 1; 18 March 1904, 3.
7. Ware, *ACC*, 89–90.
8. Ware, *ACC*, 88. *Cat*, 1904–05, 7.
9. Ware, *ACC*, 90. *TWT*, 20 May 1904, 5. *Cat*, 1904–05, 6.
10. *PK*, 1910, 8. Ware, *ACC*, 86–87.
11. Ware, *ACC*, 91. *TWT*, 24 June 1904, 4.
12. As quoted in *TWT*, 17 June 1904, 4.
13. Ware, *ACC*, 92–93. Annie Harper Chamblee interview, 11 January 1995.
14. *Rad*, February 1908, 13–14.
15. Ware, *ACC*, 93–94. *TWT*, 15 January 1883.

16. Sarah Bain Ward interview, 17 June 1993.

17. *Cat*, 1904–05, 7–8. Ware, *ACC*, 92. *TWT*, 15 April 1904; 27 January 1905.

18. Ware, *ACC*, 94. *TWT*, 17 March 1905, 8.

19. *TWT*, 30 June 1905, 6–8.

20. *TWT*, 27 January 1905, 9; 12 May 1905, 7, 10.

21. Ware, *ACC*, 43, 95–96. *TWT*, 18 April 1906, 4. *Cat*, 1904–05, 6.

22. Ware, *ACC*, 96. *Cat*, 1906–07, 6.

23. *Cat*, 1906–07, 41–42.

24. *Cat*, 1906–07, 31.

25. *Cat*, 1906–07, 31. *Rad*, April 1908, 37–39; November 1908, 32, 42–44; May 1909, 48–49. *PK*, 1910, 97–107; 1940, 37–60; 1942, 43–67. Wright, *Transylvania: Tutor to the West*, 294.

26. *TWT*, 20 January 1906, 18; 4 August 1906, 20.

27. *The Carolina Evangel*, 14 March 1907; 4 April 1907, as quoted in Ware, *ACC*, 97.

28. *PK*, 1910, 9–10.

29. *Rad*, April 1908, 1–2. *PK*, 1910, 9–10.

30. *Rad*, April 1908, 1–3. *PK*, 1910, 29, 85, 87, 103.

31. Ware, *ACC*, 100–101. *The Carolina Evangel*, 1 August 1907, as quoted in Ware, *ACC*, 100.

32. *PK*, 1910, 10.

33. *Rad*, February 1908, 8, 47–49.

Notes to Chapter 3

1. *Cat*, 1907–08, June 1908, 9, 41–45. *The Carolina Evangel*, 6 February 1908.

2. *Cat*, 1910, 9–10.

3. Selected school statistics, 1900, 1920, quoted in William J. Cooper Jr. and Thomas E. Terrill, *The American South: A History*, 562; *Cat*, 1911, 44–45. *PK*, 1910, 36–37.

4. *PK*, 1910, 12.

5. *PK*, 1910, 8–12. *Rad*, February 1908, 9–18; April 1908, 1–3.

6. *Rad*, April 1908, 29.

7. *Rad*, June 1908, 15–17, 19. *PK*, 1910, 31–35; 1913, 17–19; 1916, 36–37.

8. *Rad*, April 1908, 4–6, 12.

9. *Rad*, January 1911, 71–72; February 1912, 63, 78.

10. *Rad*, November 1908, 25–29; January 1909, 1, 13–16; May 1909, 21–26; June 1911, 177–184.

11. Boyer, et al., *The Enduring Vision*, 290.

12. *Rad*, May 1909, 28–29; April 1911, 159, 174.

13. *Rad*, June 1910, 160–164. *PK*, 1910, 31.

14. *Rad*, November 1910, 35–37, 109; January 1911, 65–67.

15. *Rad*, June 1911, 188–196. Boyer, *The Enduring Vision*, 679.

16. *Rad*, April 1908, 7–8; January 1911, 75–78.
17. *Rad*, June 1911, 204.
18. *Rad*, May 1909, 14–19; June 1911, 201–214.
19. *Rad*, May 1909, business advertisements; November 1908, 33–34.
20. *Rad*, June 1910, 130–135.
21. *Rad*, June 1910, 130–135; April 1908, 29. *PK*, 1910, 3.
22. *Rad*, June 1910, 175.
23. *Rad*, June 1910, 174–175. Daniels, *Tar Heel Editor*, 260.
24. *Rad*, January 1909, 35; June, 1910, 174–175, 190–191.
25. *Rad*, November 1910, 42; January 1911, 107.
26. *Rad*, April 1908, 34–35; November 1908, 39–41; May 1909, 53–54; January 1911, 64, 94, 104–105; June 1911, 224.
27. *Rad*, April 1908, 33.
28. *Rad*, May 1909, 32–33. *PK*, 1910, 48, 98, 109.
29. *Rad*, January 1909, 6–9; May 1909, 55–61; June 1910, 137–148. *PK*, 1910, 140; 1913, no page number.
30. *Rad*, November 1911, 22.

Notes to Chapter 4

1. See www.marie.com/asp/history.asp?action=process
2. Mamie Jennings Lucas interview, 27 May 1992.
3. Mamie Jennings Lucus interview, 27 May 1992.
4. Mamie Jennings Lucas interview, 27 May 1992.
5. Mamie Jennings Lucas interview, 27 May 1992.
6. *PK*, 1913, no page number. Ware, *ACC*, 105–106. *Rad*, November 1915, 21–22.
7. Ware, *ACC*, 103. Cummins, *The Disciples Colleges*, 83.
8. Ware, *ACC*, 107.
9. Ware, *ACC*, 103–104. *Proceedings of the North Carolina Christian Missionary Convention*, Ayden, 30 October–2 November 1911, 8.
10. Ware, *ACC*, 106. *Proceedings of the North Carolina Christian Missionary Convention*, Asheville, N.C., 3–6 November 1913, 11. *TWT*, 27 August 1914, 2; 10 November 1915, 2; 23 February 1916, 5–6; 8 March 1916, 6. *Rad*, March 1916, 94–96.
11. *Rad*, February 1912, 45. Ware, *ACC*, 107.
12. Ware, *ACC*, 107–108. *Rad*, February 1912, 45.
13. *Rad*, February 1912, 45; April 1912, 105.
14. *Rad*, June 1912, 161.
15. *Rad*, November 1912, 38; February 1913, 81.
16. *Proceedings of the North Carolina Christian Missionary Convention*, 2–5 November 1914.
17. *TWT*, 27 August 1914, 2. Ware, *ACC*, 111. *Rad*, December 1914, 40–41. See the Ministerial Association picture in *PK*, 1913, no page number.

18. *North Carolina Christian Missionary Convention, Minutes,* 18–21 November 1912 and 2–5 November 1914.

19. Mamie Jennings Lucas interview, 27 May 1992. *Rad,* November 1912, 43; November 1913, 23–24.

20. Ware, *ACC,* 97, 102, 105. *Rad,* February 1915, 97, 102–103.

21. *Rad,* March 1916, 103. Ware, *ACC,* 97, 102, 105, 107.

22. *TWT,* 5 May 1916, 6; 24 May 1916, 6.

23. *Rad,* November 1915, 58–69.

24. *Rad,* November 1912, 43–45; December 1914, 39–40.

25. *Rad,* February 1913, 80; March 1916, 102.

26. *Rad,* February 1914, 92–93.

27. *PK,* 1913, no page number. *Rad,* April 1913, 141.

28. *Rad,* April 1914, 144; November 1915, 37. *Cat,* 1997–98, 33. B. B. Plyler Jr. conversation, 14 January 1999.

29. *Rad,* December 1914, 53; April 1915, 107–110, 131–132. *TWT,* 24 February 1915, 4. Ware, *ACC,* 126.

30. *The Carolina Evangel,* 10 September 1913, 1. *Rad,* November 1915, 29–31. The 1916 yearbook contradicts some of those claims, advertising the last three grades of high school among the five major areas of the curriculum and placing the library holdings at "more than two thousand volumes." *PK,* 1916, 134, Ads. 2.

31. *The Carolina Evangel,* 15 October 1913, 1. Ware, *ACC,* 109–110.

32. *PK,* 1913, no page number; 1916, 17–23. *Cat,* 1909–10, 4–5; 1913–14, 4.

33. Ware, *ACC,* 109. Mamie Jennings Lucas interview, 27 May 1992.

34. *PK,* 1910, 18; 1916, 62.

35. *Rad,* 1916, 94–96. Ware, *ACC,* 114–115.

36. *Cat,* 1911–12, 53; 1912–13, 59; 1913–14, 66; 1914–15, 64; 1915–16, 72. *Rad,* March 1916, 94–99. Ware, *ACC,* 114. Mamie Jennings Lucas interview, 27 May 1992.

37. *PK,* 1916, 6–9. *Rad,* March 1916, 94.

Notes to Chapter 5

1. *Rad,* March 1916, 94–97.

2. Lemmon, *North Carolina's Role,* 1–2.

3. *Rad,* March 1916, 77. Lemmon, *North Carolina's Role,* 6–12.

4. *Cat,* 1916, 5. The next three *College Catalogs* listed him, respectively, as "President and Professor of Education," "President," and "President and Professor of Education and Biblical Literature." *Cat,* 1917, 7; 1918, 7; 1919, 7.

5. Ware, *ACC,* 111, 115, 119.

6. *TWT,* 19 April 1916, 4; 9 May 1916, 1. In 1916, Outlaw, who had attended but not yet graduated from *ACC,* served as editor of the *South Carolina Christian.* Ware, *ACC,* 119–121.

7. *TWT,* 7 June 1916, 4–6.

8. *TWT,* 9 April 1919, 1–2; 23 April 1919, 7. Ware, *ACC,* 120–121.

9. Lemmon, *North Carolina's Role,* 3, 6, 14–18. Paschal, *History,* vol. 3, 86–89. Ware, *ACC,* 123–124. *Rad,* March 1918, 87–89; *Cat,* 1917–18, 101.

10. Lemmon, *North Carolina's Role,* 39. *Rad,* November 1917, 9–20; December 1917, 62; March 1918, 78. *Cat,* 1916–17, 9; 1917–18, 10, 113.

11. *Rad,* November 1917, 19–20; December 1917, 61.

12. *TWT,* 21 August 1918, 1. *Cat,* 1920–21, 83.

13. *PK,* 1920, 43; 1921, no page number. Lemmon, *North Carolina's Role,* 41. *TWT,* 21 August 1918, 1. Ware, *ACC,* 124. *Cat,* 1918–19, 102–107.

14. *Rad,* December 1917, 48–49.

15. *Cat,* 1921, 83. *Rad,* December 1917, 59–61; March 1918, 77–80, 95–104; May 1920, 95.

16. Ware, *ACC,* 124. *TWT,* 21 August 1918, 1. *Rad,* September 1919, 34–35; Alumni Issue, June 1920, 95. Lemmon, *North Carolina's Role,* 66–67.

17. *Rad,* March 1918, 79–89. Ware, *ACC,* 112.

18. Paschal, *History,* vol. 3, 95. Powell, *North Carolina Through Four Centuries,* 460. *PK,* 1920, 39–43; 1921, no page number.

19. *Cat,* 1916, 5. The Men and Millions Movement had been established by the national Christian Church (Disciples of Christ) for the purpose of raising a total of $7 million. Within seven years the canvas had exceeded that goal. Atlantic Christian College's participation in that campaign was led by Caldwell, Smith, and Ware. Ware, *ACC,* 121–127.

20. *PK,* 1920, 53. *Cat,* 1918–19, 16–17. Ware, *ACC,* 123–124. Wilson County Register of Deeds, vol. 111, 536.

21. Ware, *ACC,* 124. *NCC,* February 1920, 2.

22. *Rad,* November 1917, 18. *PK,* 1916, 46, 53; 1921, no page number.

23. *TWT,* 21 February 1917, 2. *Rad,* March 1917, 17–18.

24. *Rad,* March 1917, 17–18. *Cat,* 1917–18, 10.

25. *Rad,* January 1920, 78–80. *PK,* 1920, 48.

26. *PK,* 1920, 13–19, 69.

27. *TWT,* 9 April 1919, 1–2; 23 April 1919, 7.

28. *TWT,* 6 August 1919, 2.

29. *NCC,* February 1920, 1.

30. *TWT,* 10 March 1920, 1–7.

31. *TWT,* 23 June 1920, 1–3.

32. *TWT,* 23 June 1920, 1–3.

33. *NCC,* April 1920, 2, 9. *TWT,* 21 April 1920, 1–2, 5; 5 May 1920, 2; 19 May 1920, 6; 23 June 1920, 6.

34. Murray, *Red Scare, 1919–1920,* 150–151.

35. Wright, *Transylvania: Tutor to the West,* 336–343. Murray, *Red Scare,* 169–170.

36. *NCC,* March 1920, 9; April 1920, 9. *Rad,* March 1917, 2; January 1920, 89; June

1920, 159–160. North Carolina Christian Missionary Committee, *Minutes of the 73rd Session,* November 1917, 5–6. *Cat,* 1918–1919, 6.

37. *Rad,* June 1920, 174–175, advertisement page. *PK,* 1920, 39–41.

38. *Rad,* June 1920, 124, 140, 159–160.

39. *Rad,* June 1920, 155–160, 175. *PK,* 1920, 98.

Notes to Chapter 6

1. Levinson and Christensen, *Encyclopedia of World Sport,* vol. 1, 91, 94. Coulter, *College Life in the Old South,* 348. Paschal, *History,* vol. 2, 35. Henderson, *The Campus of the First State University,* 248. Harville, *Sports in North Carolina,* 220.

2. *Cat,* 1906–07, 6–7. *Rad,* April 1908, 37, 41; January 1909, 41–42; May 1909, 44–45.

3. *Rad,* November 1908, 1, 35–36. Players mentioned by Guerrant included pitcher J. J. Lane and/or left fielder Rosser Lane; J. J. Walker; and first baseman Lamar Winstead. *PK,* 1910, 114, 115. *Cat,* 1909–1910, 42–45.

4. *Rad,* November 1908, 27, 43–44; May 1909, 44–46.

5. Harville, *Sports in North Carolina,* 165. Daniels, *Tar Heel Editor,* 66.

6. Hearn's later career included a successful period as baseball coach at the University of North Carolina at Chapel Hill. Mamie Jennings Lucas interview, 27 May 1992. *Rad,* February 1912, 73; June 1912, 164; November 1912, 39–40; April 1913, 139.

7. Paschal, *History,* vol. 2, 320.

8. Roosevelt used the word "mucker" to refer to low-level, unsportsmanlike play. He is credited with coining the term "muckraking" to describe the new exposé journalism of the early twentieth century. Levinson and Christensen, *Encyclopedia of World Sport,* vol. 1, 340; Lucas and Smith, *Saga of American Sport,* 242–243. *Rad,* January 1909, 36–38; November 1911, 35.

9. *Rad,* November 1911, 35.

10. Levinson and Christensen, *Encyclopedia of World Sport,* vol. 1, 100. Kelley, *Yale: A History,* 303.

11. Johnson, *A History of Meredith College,* 126–127.

12. *Cat,* 1912, 9. *Rad,* November 1912, 40; November 1913, 28, 34.

13. *Rad,* December 1914, 56–58. *TWT,* 22 March 1916, 6.

14. *Rad,* March 1917, 33–34; November 1917, 28–29. *PK,* 1916, 22, 130–131; 1920, 95, 98; 1921, no page number.

15. *Cat,* 1913, 11–12. *Rad,* May 1913, 209–210; November 1913, 28.

16. Lucas and Smith, *Saga of American Sport,* 221–222. *PK,* 1913, no page number. *Rad,* November 1912, 39; May 1913, 210; November 1913, 28. *Cat,* 1913, 5–7, 11–12. Letters from M. A. Bishop to G. S. Alderman, 8 and 21 November 1913. Ashley Futrell Sr. interview, 25 January 1998.

17. *Rad,* December 1914, 56, 59; February 1915, 103; September 1919, 30. *PK,* 1913, no page number.

18. *Rad,* December 1916, 22–23. Warren Curtis Lappin, apparently the son of faculty

members W. O. and Cora Lappin, attended high school and college at ACC and also served as instructor in violin from 1917 to 1919.

19. *Rad*, May 1918, 131–132. *Cat*, 1918, 43.

20. *Rad*, May 1918, 131–133; September 1919, 27; January 1920, 64; June 1920, 158. *PK*, 1920, 80–81, 93–99.

21. Levinson and Christensen, *Encyclopedia of World Sport*, vol. 3, 1017–1020. Kelley, *Yale: A History*, 303. Henderson, *The Campus of the First State University*, 251–253. *TWT*, 22 March 1916, 108. *Rad*, April 1908, 41; November 1908, 43; November 1911, 37–38; November 1912, 40. *PK*, 1910, 116–117.

22. *Rad*, November 1917, 28–29; May 1918, 131–133; June 1920, 165–166. *PK*, 1920, 98–99; 1921, no page number.

23. *Rad*, November 1908, 35–36; January 1909, 36–38.

24. *Rad*, November 1911, 35; November 1912, 39–40.

25. *PK*, 1920, 98.

26. *PK*, 1921, no page number.

27. *PK*, 1921, no page number. *Rad*, December 1920, 38–39. Lewis, "The History," 2.

28. *Rad*, December 1920, 38–39. Lewis, "The History," 2.

29. *Rad*, December 1920, 38–39. *PK*, 1921, no page number. Lewis, "The History," 2.

30. Marion Brinson also was active in the fellowship club, the wranglers, the dramatic club, the boys' glee club, Phi Epsilon Tau, and the student council. *PK*, 1921, no page number; 1923, 28, 46, 92–101; 1924, 23, 56, 64, 67, 114–120. The 1926 *Pine Knot* listed eight students from Arapahoe, including senior Mae Reel, junior Cecil Reel, and sophomore Kate Brinson. *PK*, 1926, 23, 44, 50–51, 59–63. Within the next two years, six more students from Arapahoe enrolled at ACC. *PK*, 1928, 25, 50–53, 63.

31. Lewis, "The History," 3–6.

32. *Rad*, December 1920, 39. *PK*, 1920, 134–137; 1921, no page number; 1923, 111–112; 1924, 128–129; 1925, 104–105; 1926, 84, 99–100.

33. *PK*, 1923, 96–97; 1924, 114–115.

34. Lewis, "The History," 7–8. *PK*, 1924, 117. Lenoir College mentioned here is Lenoir Rhyne.

35. *PK*, 1924, 117; 1926, 114–115.

36. Lewis, "The History," 9–10.

37. Lewis, "The History," 10–11. Paschal, *History*, vol. 3, 112, 116.

38. *Rad*, April 1911, 156–158; 1920, 23, 38–39. *PK*, 1921, no page number; 1923, 28, 31.

39. *PK*, 1926, 113; 1928, 70–81. Lewis, "The History," 12–14.

40. *Coll*, 1929, 26. Lewis, "The History," 12–16.

41. *Coll*, 1931, 32; Lewis, "The History," 17. *PK*, 1928, 74, 77.

42. *PK*, 1928, 69–87; 1929, 26.

43. *PK*, 1928, 69–87. *Rad*, June 1920, 158, 165–166.

Notes to Chapter 7

1. *NCC,* May 1920, 4.

2. *NCC,* May 1920, 4. *Rad,* June 1920, 140, 160. *Cat,* 1918–19, 9–10; 1919–20, 3; 1920–21, 6. Ware, *ACC,* 130–131.

3. *Rad,* June 1920, 160. Ware, *ACC,* 130–131.

4. Onnie Cockrell interview, 14 December 1999; Milton Adams and Sarah Loftin Adams interview, 15 December 1999; Mamie Jennings Lucas interview, 27 May 1992. *PK,* 1920, 13; 1921, no page number; 1923, 16; 1925, 12, 81; 1928, 10–11; 1938, 10. Ware, *ACC,* 238.

5. Ware, *ACC,* 131. *Rad,* June 1920, 127–128.

6. *Rad,* June 1920, 127–128. *NCC,* February 1920, 6. *PK,* 1924, 19. *Cat,* 1920–21, 84–88.

7. *NCC,* May 1920, 13.

8. Ware, *ACC,* 126–129.

9. *Rad,* June 1920, 155–157. *PK,* 1921, no page number.

10. *PK,* 1921, no page number. *NCC,* June 1921, 6; September 1922, 6; April 1925, 6.

11. *News and Observer* article quoted in Ware, *ACC,* 132–133. *NCC,* June 1922, 6; February 1923, 1; April 1923, 6.

12. Ware, *ACC,* 132–133. *PK,* 1928, 25–38. *Cat,* 1928, 64–68.

13. *PK,* 1921, no page number. *NCC,* July 1925, 6; August 1925, 5; June 1926, 6; July 1926, 6; September 1926, 6.

14. Ware, *ACC,* 241.

15. *NCC,* July 1924, 2; October 1925, 13. E. M. Barnes and Odell Barnes interview, 1989.

16. *Cat,* 1916, 6; 1918, 10; 1924, 5, 7. *PK,* 1923, 19, 29; 1924, 100; 1925, 14, 15; 1926, 16, 18; 2000, 8. *NCC,* March 1923, 6; October 1923, 8.

17. *PK,* 1926, 17. *Cat,* 2000, 8, 124.

18. *PK,* 1921, no page number; 1928, 12. *NCC,* July 1926, 6; October 1927, 6, 10; February 1928, 6. Ware, *ACC,* 133–134.

19. *NCC,* January 1928, 6; February 1928, 6; October 1928, 10; November 1928, 6; February 1929, 6; May 1929, 6; November 1929, 6. *Cat,* 1925, 5.

20. *NCC,* April 1930, 6.

21. Boyer, *The Enduring Vision,* 682.

22. *NCC,* November and December 1921, 7; February 1922, 6.

23. *PK,* 1925, 4–5. *NCC,* May 1923, 6.

24. *NCC,* November and December 1921, 7; November 1922, 6; May 1924, 5; January 1926, 6; November 1926, 6; October 1927, 10; November 1927, 6; December 1927, 6; April 1928, 6; May 1928, 6; November 1928, 6; December 1928, 6; November 1929, 6; April 1930, 6. *PK,* 1925, 17, 127; 1926, 21.

25. *NCC,* June 1927, 6; April 1928, 6.

26. *NCC*, April 1927, 6; June 1927, 6–7.

27. *NCC*, June 1927, 6–7. *PK*, 1925, 53; 1926, 59, 64.

28. *PK*, 1924, 19.

29. *Cat*, 1923, 7; 1924, 7; 1925, 6. *PK*, 1924, 50, 56, 57; 1925, 32–35; 1926, 22–28.

30. *PK*, 1923, 27–34, 65–80; 1924, 75–90; 1925, 59–71; 1926, 70–78, 82–87; 1928, 107–130. *Cat*, 1916, 6.

31. *PK*, 1921, no page number; 1923, 9, 42, 117; 1924, 6, 130; 1925, 6A, 29, 109, 110; 1926, 31, 99, 102, 103; 1928, 16, 40, 48, 88, 121; 1930, 5, 28. Franklin, "The 20th Century, Where Were You?"

32. *PK*, 1925, 6.

33. *PK*, 1916, advertisements, 12, 13; 1920, 149, 151, 158, 163, 165; 1921, no page number; 1923, 153, 156; 1924, 164; 1925, 138; 1926, 135; 1928, 156; 1929, 29, 34. *NCC*, June 1928, 5; November 1928, 3; October 1929, 5.

34. A graduate of the class of 1924, Jefferson combined academic accomplishments and athletic and musical skills with his editorship of the *Pine Knot*. *PK*, 1923, 45; 1924, 14–15, 25, 30–31.

35. Raulen, editor of the annual and a 1925 graduate, was active in drama, music, art, and debating. Quinerly was class poet and president of the Hesperian Society and the YWCA. *PK*, 1925, 22, 112; 1926, 20, 26, 79–80.

36. Ware, *ACC*, 145. *NCC*, November 1925, 2.

37. *NCC*, January 1926, 6; February 1926, 6; March 1926, 5; April 1926, 1, 6; May 1926, 6–7; June 1926, 5. The requests called for gifts of $19,600 by 30 June 1926.

38. The Disciples newspaper of July 1923 reported total pledges at $185,821.50, including 1,697 pledges from 146 churches. Of those, only 331 had been paid in full; 714 had paid in part; 98 had covered part or all of their pledge by personal note; and 554 had paid nothing. Ware, *ACC*, 129–130; *NCC*, July 1923, 1.

39. Ware, *ACC*, 130–135. *NCC*, October 1927, 7; September 1929, 1; December 1929, 4–5. In December 1929, despite announcements that pledges had reached $320,000, the campaign remained approximately $60,000 short of the $200,000 needed by 1 January 1930 to gain a $100,000 challenge made by a potential benefactor.

40. Ware, *ACC*, 134–145. *NCC*, January 1923, 1; February 1923, 6; April 1923, 1; February 1927, 2; October 1927, 7; September 1929, 4. *PK*, 1923, 2–3; 1928, 6–7.

41. *NCC*, March 1928, 6; April 1928, 6; May 1928, 6.

42. *NCC*, October 1928, 10; December 1928, 5–6. Ware, *ACC*, 85, 231–232. *Cat*, 1996–1997, 7–8.

43. *NCC*, October 1928, 10; December 1928, 5. *The Wilson Daily News*, as quoted in *NCC*, December 1928, 5–6.

44. Nault, *World Book of America's Presidents: Portraits of the Presidents*, 180–181.

Notes to Chapter 8

1. *NCC*, December 1929, 4. *The Collegiate*, 1929 yearbook, 26–27. *The Collegiate* temporarily replaced *Pine Knot* as the name of the college yearbook between 1929 and

1934, creating confusion because the student newspaper, started in 1927, also bore the title *The Collegiate.*

2. *NCC,* January 1930, 6. *The Collegiate,* 1929 yearbook, 18.

3. *NCC,* February 1930, 6.

4. *NCC,* April 1930, 6; May 1930, 2.

5. *NCC,* June 1930, 6; June 1931, 6; June 1932, 5; June 1933, 6. Ware, *ACC,* 155.

6. *NCC,* May 1930, 6; November 1930, 6; December 1930, 6. The *News and Observer,* 21 February 1931, as quoted in *NCC,* March 1931, 6. *NCC,* May 1931, 6. *The Collegiate,* 1931 yearbook, 10, 15, 21, 28, 31.

7. *NCC,* December 1930, 6; May 1931, 6; February 1934, 6. *The Collegiate,* 1931 yearbook, 9. *Cat,* 1930–31, 5.

8. *NCC,* October, 1930, 10.

9. *NCC,* February 1931, 5. For the Wilson church, the comparisons between 1931 and the previous year were: membership, 511 and 547; pledges, 195 and 265; and total amounts pledged, $5,798.84 and $6,893.64. *NCC,* November 1930, 4; May 1931, 4; October 1931, 12; December 1931, 4.

10. *NCC,* November 1931, 3, 8; March 1932, 2.

11. *NCC,* June 1931, 7.

12. Sarah Bain Ward interview, 17 June 1993. *Coll,* 17 September 1937, 2.

13. Onnie Cockrell interview, 14 December 1999. *PK,* 1938, 15, 17. Sarah Bain Ward interview, 17 June 1993. Letter from junior Sue Todd to "Dear Margaret," apparently a cousin and high school senior, who was considering attending ACC. *NCC,* June 1933, 6.

14. Ashley Futrell Sr. interview, 25 January 1998.

15. *NCC,* April 1932, 6.

16. *NCC,* May 1932, 6; October 1932, 5; November 1932, 6; May 1933, 6. *The Collegiate,* 1933 yearbook, 9.

17. *The Collegiate,* 1931 yearbook, 19, 32; 1933 yearbook, 10, 13, 15, 21–23, 28, 31, 34, 37. *NCC,* June 1933, 6. *Cat,* 2000, 18, 162. *Scope,* Winter 2000, 5. Ware, *ACC,* 231–232.

18. *The Collegiate,* 1934 yearbook, 18, 32. *NCC,* June 1933, 6; June 1934, 6. *Cat,* 2000, 36.

19. *NCC,* December 1932, 5; October 1933, 6; November 1933, 6; May 1934, 6; October 1934, 5. The alumni secretary recorded three ACC alumni serving as high school principals in Wilson County, three in Pitt, and two in Lenoir. *Coll,* 18 April 1934, 5.

20. *NCC,* April 1930, 6; November 1930, 6; April 1931, 6; July 1931, 6; April 1932. The student newspaper known as *The Collegiate* was established in 1927.

21. *NCC,* April 1933, 6.

22. *NCC,* June 1933, 7; December 1933, 6; January 1934, 6. Mallison, whose home was later listed as Pantego, had joined the faculty in 1933. The college paid his salary, and the alumni association paid expenses related to alumni affairs. *NCC,* January 1935, 5. *Cat,* 1932–33, 6; 1933–34, 7; *Coll,* 15 December 1933, 1.

23. *NCC,* September 1932, 5; May 1933, 6; October 1933, 5; October 1934, 5. Interview

of Dixie Barnes Edmundson, class of 1935, Ruby Barnes Brown, 1939, and Melissa Edmundson, 1999, 4 June 1996.

24. *NCC,* November 1934, 6. Painted in school colors and carrying the college name, the school bus is pictured in 1939 and 1941 issues of the yearbook. *PK,* 1939, 65; 1941, 37.

25. Sarah Loftin Adams conversation, 24 February 2000. *The Collegiate,* 1933 yearbook, 20, 33, 37; 1934 yearbook, 22, 26–32, 35–38, 41–44. *Coll,* 17 March, 1934, 1–4; *PK,* 1935, no page number; 1936, no page number; 1937, no page number. Hill taught physical education.

26. *The Collegiate,* 1934 yearbook, 1, 22, 26–31, 42–44; 1935, no page number; 1936 yearbook, no page number; 1937 yearbook, no page number. Atlantic Christian College Athletic Hall of Fame Program, 1 November 1985.

27. *Coll,* 17 March 1934, 1. *PK,* 1937, no page number. Dawson gave up only five runs in sixteen innings at Guilford, with the Quakers winning the first game of the doubleheader 4–2. *Coll,* 18 May 1934, 3. Atlantic Christian College Athletic Hall of Fame Program, 4 November 1983.

28. *PK,* 1938, 15, 53–57. Barton College Athletic Hall of Fame Program, 6 October 1990.

29. *Coll,* 18 November 1933, 1, 4, 5. Charlie Ware was the son of C. C. Ware. Milton Adams interview, 13 March 1992.

30. *Coll,* 15 December 1933, 1, 3.

31. *NCC,* August–September 1933, 8. *Coll,* 15 December 1933, 6; 20 January 1934, 1, 3; 15 February 1934, 1, 3; 17 March 1934, 3.

32. *Coll,* 15 December 1934, 1, 4.

33. *Coll,* 15 December 1934, 1; *PK,* 1935, no page number; 1936, no page number. The 1935–36 ACC boxing team tied the NC State varsity team and defeated Louisburg, Guilford, and the NC State "B" team. Ware, *ACC,* 156.

34. Clarence L. Hardy served as trustee between 1926 and 1949. Ware, *ACC,* 156–157, 183–194, 231. *Cat,* 2000, 8.

35. *Coll,* 17 September 1937, 1.

36. *Pine Knot* of 1935, Ragan's junior year, lists his hometown as Willow Springs. *PK,* 1935, no page number; 1936, no page number. *Scope,* Winter 2000, 5.

37. Sarah Bain Ward interviews, 17 June 1993 and 24 June 1995. *PK,* 1938, 12, 19, 44–45. *Scope,* Winter 2000, 5.

38. Serving under the Executive Council, the dormitory councils each contained ten to eleven members. *PK,* 1937, no page number; 1938, 44–45. *Coll,* 15 December 1933, 1, 4.

39. *Coll,* 15 December 1934, 1, 3.

40. Interestingly, *College Catalogs* for the 1930s do not mention the existence of an honor code although college newspapers beginning in 1934 insist that the campus did have an honor system. *Coll,* 15 December 1934, 1, 3; 16 May 1938, 4; 17 November 1938, 2; 15 December 1938, 1; 19 January 1939, 2; 17 February 1939, 1.

41. *Coll,* 15 December 1933, 1.

42. *Coll,* 15 December 1933, 1, 3.

43. *Coll,* 15 February 1934, 2.

44. The ACC musicians who played for the dancers, Gladys Charles of Grifton, class of 1935, and Russell Roebuck of Williamson, class of 1937, apparently had traveled to Greenville to support the team. Both served as pianists for the Alethian Society. *Coll,* 15 February 1934, 2. *The Collegiate,* 1934 yearbook, 42; 1935 yearbook, no page number; 1937 yearbook, no page number. *Cat,* 1934, 6, 55.

45. *Coll,* 20 January 1934, 2, 4.

46. *NCC,* May 1932, 6; May 1934, 6. *Coll,* 20 April 1935, 1–3; 18 May 1935, 1–3; 21 February 1938, 1, 6; 23 April 1938, 1–2; May 16, 1938, 1. Dixie Barnes Edmundson, Ruby Barnes Brown, and Melissa Edmundson interview, 4 June 1996. Sarah Bain Ward interview, 24 June 1995. *PK,* 1935, no page number.

47. *The Coll,* 17 September 1937, 1. *Cat,* 1934–35, 50. Ware, *ACC,* 157, 231.

48. *Coll,* 17 September 1937, 1.

49. *Coll,* 17 September 1937, 1.

50. Mamie Jennings Lucas interview, 27 May 1992; Sarah Bain Ward interview, 17 June 1993 and 24 June 1995; Milton and Sarah Adams interview, 17 June 1997; Dixie Barnes Edmundson and Ruby Barnes Brown interview, 4 June 1996.

Notes to Chapter 9

1. *Cat,* 1932–33, 57; 1937–38, 68. *Coll,* 17 September 1937, 1. *WDT,* 20 February 1937, 5. Sarah Bain Ward interview, 17 June 1993. John M. Waters served as J. J. Harper Professor of Bible and Religious Education and Perry Case as professor of philosophy in 1936–37. *Cat,* 1936–37, 7.

2. *Coll,* 17 September 1937, 3; 16 October 1937, 3–4; 21 February 1938, 2–6; 16 May 1938, 2–6.

3. *Coll,* 14 May 1937, 2–4; 17 September 1937, 3–4; 16 October 1937, 3–4; 21 February 1938, 2–6; 23 April 1938, 2–4; 16 May 1938, 2–4. *PK,* 1938, 65–75.

4. *Coll,* 21 February 1938, 1, 6.

5. *Cat,* 1938, 63. *Coll,* 21 February 1938, 2, 4. *PK,* 1939, 23, 57.

6. *Coll,* 15 May 1939, 1, 3. The bucket's name was also spelled Bo-Hunk-Us and Bohunkus.

7. *WDT,* 10 January 1939, 3. *Coll,* 23 May 1939, 1–3; 22 September 1939, 3. Yavorski, the son of Elizabeth E. Yavorski, instructor in music, apparently left school after his junior year. He is not listed as editor of the school annual or as a member of the senior class of 1940. *PK,* 1940, 10, 22, 38.

8. *WDT,* 2 February 1938, 3; 10 December 1938, 3; 15 December 1939, 7; 16 January, 1940, 2. *PK,* 1937, no page number; 1938, 58; 1939, 56; 1940; 65. *Coll,* 16 October 1937, 3; 15 December 1938, 2–4; 13 January 1939, 3; 16 October 1937, 3. The length of ACC's undefeated boxing string was controversial. *The Wilson Daily Times* account is two years,

while *The Collegiate* mentions the 1940 loss as "the first setback in four years of campaigning." *WDT,* 16 January 1940, 2. *Coll,* 22 January 1940, 3.

9. *WDT,* 3 January 1939, 2.

10. *Coll,* 23 April 1938, 1, 4; 15 December 1938, 1; 19 January 1939, 1; 15 March 1939, 1. *PK,* 1939, 17, 62; 1940, 38; 1941, 18, 38, 49–54. *Cat,* 1939, 59–63.

11. Charles H. Hamlin interview, 9 June 1976; Sarah Bain Ward interview, 17 June 1993; Milton Adams interview, 13 March 1992.

12. Charles H. Hamlin interview, 9 June 1976.

13. E. M. Barnes interview, June 1987. *NCC,* February 1937, 5.

14. *Coll,* 21 February 1938, 1; 15 March 1939, 2. Griffith Hamlin was president of the 1938–39 ministerial club, treasurer of his senior class, a member of The Golden Knot Honor Society, and a member of the Glee Club. *PK,* 1939, 13, 17, 43–47.

15. *Coll,* 21 February 1938, 1.

16. *Coll,* 16 May 1938, 1.

17. *Coll,* 17 February 1939, 1, 4; 15 March 1939, 1; 16 January 1941, 1. *Cat,* 1940–41, 7.

18. *PK,* 1916, no page number; 1923, 135; 1924, 146. Ware, *ACC,* 173. Dixie Barnes Edmundson and Ruby Barnes Brown interview, 4 June 1996; Milton and Sarah Adams interview, 16 June 2000; Sarah Bain Ward interview, 17 June 1993. *Coll,* 18 May 1935, 1; 15 February 1943, 1.

19. Elizabeth Hilley High interview, 6 July 2000.

20. *The Torchlight,* February 1945, 3, 12–13. *Cat,* 1945, 55. *The Torchlight* replaced both *The Collegiate* and *Pine Knot* during 1944 and 1945. *PK,* 1948, 110.

21. Charles H. Hamlin interview, 2 September 1976. *PK,* 1967, 52, 62.

22. *WDT,* 2 March 1932, 4. *Coll,* 18 November 1933, 1. Elizabeth Hilley High interview, 6 July 2000.

23. *Coll,* 20 April 1935, 4; 24 February 1937, 1, 4. Charles H. Hamlin interview, 2 September 1976.

24. *Coll,* 20 April 1935, 1; 18 May 1935, 2. *The Wilson Daily Times* reported that the practice of college and university students voting to take a definite stand on certain policies of government had begun at Oxford University around 1934, when students there had shocked conservative Britons by declaring that "under no consideration would they fight for King and Country." *WDT,* 28 April 1936, 5.

25. *Coll,* 24 February 1937, 1, 4; 14 May 1937, 1. *WDT,* 23 April 1937, 4. *NCC,* May 1937, 5.

26. *Coll,* 15 March 1939, 1, 4. Charles H. Hamlin, *Educators Present Arms, the Use of the Schools and Colleges as Agents of War Propaganda, 1914–1919,* 1939, 47.

27. *WDT,* 21 March 1939, 4. *Coll,* 17 April 1939, 1, 4.

28. *Coll,* 17 April 1939, 1–2; 23 May 1939, 1, 4. *Cat,* 1937–38, 63; 1938–39, 59–68. *PK,* 1939, 22, 35; 1940, 19, 48.

29. *Coll,* 22 September 1939, 1–4; 20 October 1939, 1–4.

30. *Coll,* 22 September 1939, 1; 20 October 1939, 1.

31. *Coll,* 15 November 1939, 3; 21 November 1939, 1, 4.

32. *Coll,* 21 November 1939, 1, 4. *WDT,* 4 November 1939, 4, 7. *Cat,* 1936–37, 10; 1999–2000, 9. C. W. Howard served on the board of trustees from 1904 to 1932. Ware, *ACC,* 232.

33. *Coll,* 22 January 1940, 1. Sarah Bain Ward interview, 17 June 1993.

34. *Coll,* 16 May 1940, 1. *WDT,* 27 May 1940, 4; 29 May 1940, 9. *NCC,* June 1940, 6.

35. *Coll,* 16 March 1940, 1–4; 23 April 1940,1–4; 16 May 1940, 1–4. Morris, *Encyclopedia of American History,* 364–365.

36. *NCC,* June 1940, 6; July 1940, 6.

37. *Coll,* 2 November 1940, 1–4; 18 November 1940, 1, 4.

38. Gardner, *Ava: My Story,* 7–25. *Coll,* 18 November 1940, 1. David Snipes was a freshman commercial studies major from Princeton. *Cat,* 1940–41, 67. *PK,* 1941, 14–15, 32, 34, 72–75.

39. *Coll,* 18 November 1940, 1–4. Byrd and Wiley were seniors in 1940–41, while Bullock was listed as a freshman. *Cat,* 1940–41, 59–68. *PK,* 1940, 32; 1941, 15, 20.

40. *Coll,* 18 November 1940, 3; 17 February 1941, 3. *WDT,* 9 December 1940, 2. "Bull" was likely sports editor Kirby Watson, a sophomore from Wilson. Hicks was a freshman from Easton, Pennsylvania. *PK,* 1940, 63; 1941, 9, 24, 30, 64–67; 1942, 19. *Cat,* 1939–40, 8, 62–64.

41. *NCC,* November 1940, 5; December 1940, 5.

42. *NCC,* December 1940, 5. *Coll,* 15 December 1938, 1; 19 January 1939, 1.

Notes to Chapter 10

1. *WDT,* 2 October 1940, 1. *Coll,* 17 February 1941, 1, 4; 15 March 1941, 2. *PK,* 1939, 16. *Cat,* 1940–41, 59–63.

2. *Coll,* 15 March 1941, 1. *WDT,* 4 March 1941, 4; 15 May 1941, 1–4.

3. *Coll,* 17 September 1941, 1, 4.

4. *Coll,* 17 September 1941, 3; 15 October 1941, 1. Gardner, 3.

5. *Coll,* 15 October 1941, 1; 15 January 1942, 1. *PK,* 1941, 74.

6. Gardner, *Ava: My Story,* 25, 156. *Cat,* 1976, 112. Relatives of Ava Gardner who have graduated from ACC/Barton College include: Ethel Thorne Boswell '48, James Daniel Thorne '49, John Julius Thorne '50, Blessin Thorne Vick '59, Rachel Thorne '77, Patrick Dave Sharpe '85, Jerri Thorne Moore '85, and Elizabeth Grantham McBroom '91. Blessin Thorne Vick conversation, 24 August 2000. *Barton College Alumni Directory,* 1999, 22, 110, 130, 138, 174, 194. (Subsequent citings will say *Alumni Directory.*)

7. *Coll,* 15 December 1941, 1, 4.

8. *Coll,* 15 January 1942, 1, 4; 18 February 1942, 1, 4. *NCC,* January 1942, 6. Ware, *ACC,* 176. *Cat,* 1937, 59.

9. *Coll,* 18 March, 1942, 1, 2; 18 April 1942, 1; 15 May 1942, 1.

10. Coll, 18 November 1940, 3; 18 February 1942, 1; 30 September 1942, 1, 4; 15 May 1943, 4. *Cat,* 1937, 59; 1941, 65. Ware, *ACC,* 176–178.

11. *Coll*, 15 January 1943, 1; 15 February 1943, 1; 15 March 1943, 1; 15 April 1943, 1–6; 15 May 1943, 2, 4.

12. *Coll*, 15 April 1943, 1. 15 May 1943, 3, 4. Roebuck graduated in 1937, Walters belonged to the class of 1941, and Blake was a member of the class of 1943. *Cat* 1937, 60; 1941, 60; 1943, 55–60.

13. *Coll*, 15 December 1942, 2, 4; 15 February 1943, 2, 4. *Cat*, 1943, 58.

14. *Coll*, 30 September 1942, 1. *Cat*, 1935, 57; 1937, 59–62. Ware, *ACC*, 177. *PK*, 1938, 14.

15. *Coll*, 30 September 1942; 15 October 1942, 4; December 1942, 4; 15 April 1943, 1; 15 May 1943, 1.

16. *Coll*, 16 November 1942, 4; 15 December 1942, 3; 15 January 1943, 1, 3; 15 April 1943, 4; 15 May 1943, 3. *WDT*, 11 December 1942, 2.

17. *NCC*, January 1942, 6. February 1943, 6. *Coll*, 15 May 1942, 1; 15 March 1943, 1; April 1943, 1.

18. *Coll*, April 1943, 1–5: 15 May 1943, 2.

19. *Coll*, 15 December 1942, 2; 15 February 1943, 2; 15 May 1943, 1, 2.

20. *WDT*, 17 December 1943, 4. *NCC*, November 1943, 6; January 1945, 6. *Cat*. 1937–1941, 68; 1942, 69; 1943, 64; 1944, 60; 1945, 60. *The Torchlight*, Fall Issue 1943, 3, 6. *The Collegiate* resumed publication in 1946 and the *Pine Knot* in 1947. *Coll*, 9 November 1946; *PK*, 1947, 5.

21. *NCC*, June 1943, 6; December 1943, 6; September 1944, 6; March 1945, 6; July 1945, 6.

22. Ware, *ACC*, 177–178. *The Torchlight*, December 1943, 9; November 1944, 7; December 1944, 2; March 1945, 5; *PK*, 1940, 22, 44, 53. *Cat*, 1940, 60; 1942, 63; 1977, 118. *Alumni Directory*, 1999, 214, 217.

23. *NCC*, September 1945, 6; October 1945, 7; February 1946, 6; July 1946, 6; September 1946, 6; September 1947, 6. *WDT*, 9 January 1946, 1. Totals for regular enrollment and total enrollment from 1946 to 1948 were: 1946, 336 and 404; 1947, 499 and 670; 1948, 588 and 805. *Cat*, 1945, 60; 1946, 62; 1947, 62; 1948, 65; 1949, 68.

24. *WDT*, 29 April 1946, 5: 25 March 1947, 2; 22 August 1947, 9. *Coll*, 15 February 1949, 1. *NCC*, December 1946, 6. Photographs show that the "White House" was located on the space between where Harper and Hilley Halls stand today. *PK*, 1949, 4.

25. *WDT*, 30 May 1945, 2; 25 January 1946, 2; 20 February 1946, 6; 5 April 1946, 2; 24 April 1946, 2; 9 May 1946, 6; 11 May 1946, 2; 20 May 1946, 2. 12 December 1946, 10; 11 February 1947, 6; 13 February 1947, 10; 19 February 1947, 6. Interestingly, the 1947 *Pine Knot*, erroneously pictures the 1946 baseball team without mentioning the 1947 team. *PK*, 1947, 76.

26. *WDT*, 21 February 1946, 4; 23 September 1946, 2; 12 November 1946, 8. *NCC*, September 1946, 6; November 1946, 6; December 1946, 6. *PK*, 1947, 75.

27. WDT, 9 May 1947, 8; 16 October 1948, 6. *Coll*, 25 November 1947, 3: 17 December 1947, 3; 24 March 1948, 3; 15 December 1948, 3. *NCC*, January 1948, 6; October 1948, 6; November 1948, 6; December 1948, 6. *PK*, 1948, 107. Ware, *ACC*, 184–185.

28. *Coll*, 25 November 1947, 3; 15 December 1948, 3; 22 February 1951, 3; 15 October 1951, 3. *Cat*, 1948, 56–59; 1949, 58, 60. *PK*, 1949, 94; 1951, 81.

29. *Athletic Hall of Fame Programs*, 1983–2000.

30. *Coll*, 15 November 1948, 3. *WDT*, 20 February 1946, 6; 12 November 1946, 8. *NCC*, February 1946, 5; November 1946, 6.

31. *Coll*, 15 February 1949, 3.

32. *PK*, 1948, 1–3, 31, 60–61, 69, 101–106, 113.

33. *PK*, 1948, 32–34, 43, 101–106. Each contestant was sponsored by a campus organization. *Coll*, 25 November 1947, 1. Sarah Bain Ward interview, 27 November 1984.

34. *The Torchlight*, Fall Issue 1944, 6. *Coll*, 22 May 1947, 2–4; 24 March 1948; 15 December 1948, 1; 15 February 1949, 1. Sarah Bain Ward interview, 27 November 1984. *Cat*, 1944–45, 6.

35. *Coll*, 22 April 1948, 1–2.

36. *Coll*, 30 October 1947, 2, 4; 25 November 1947, 1, 2; 15 October 1948, 1. Sarah Bain Ward interview, 17 June 1993. Milton and Sarah Adams conversation, 11 August 2000.

37. *PK*, 1941, 8; 1943, 11; 1947, 12. *Coll*, 15 November 1948, 2.

38. Dixie Barnes Edmundson and Ruby Barnes Brown interview, 4 June 1996. Sarah Bain Ward interview, 17 June 1993. *Coll*, 22 May 1947, 2; 15 February 1949, 1.

39. *WDT*, 3 July 1947, 1; 7 July 1947, 1. *NCC*, July 1947, 1; September 1947, 6. *ACC*, 185–186.

40. *NCC*, June 1948, 2. *Cat*, 1932–33, 5; 1933–34, 5; 1934–35, 5; 1948, 6. Ware, *ACC*, 231–232.

41. *WDT*, 16 April 1949, 1. *NCC*, May 1949, 2. Ware, *ACC*, 186.

Notes to Chapter 11

1. *NCC*, May 1949, 2. Ware, *ACC*, 186–187.

2. *NCC*, May 1949, 2. Ware, *ACC*, 187. Mamie Jennings Lucas, 27 May 1992, Sarah Bain Ward, 17 June 1993, and James B. Hemby Jr. interviews, 19 December 1996; and Elizabeth Hilley High interview, 6 July 2000.

3. *NCC*, June 1926, 6; June 1948, 1; June 1949, 6. *Coll*, 28 October 1949, 1. *Cat*, 1940, 6–7; 1945, 6–7.

4. *PK*, 1950, 19. Waters Hall, a residence hall completed in 1968, is named in honor of John Mayo Waters, an ACC graduate, who served the college as endowment secretary, business manager, and professor of religion between 1927–1955. *Cat*, 2000–2001, 9–10. Ware, *ACC*, 241. Photographs in the *Pine Knot* of 1948 capture scenes of students enjoying a snow holiday. *PK*, 1948, 111.

5. *Scope*, January–February, 1981, 12. *The Torchlight*, Fall 1944, 6, 8; November 1944, 8. Sarah Bain Ward interview, 17 June 1993.

6. *The Torchlight*, November 1944, 9. *PK*, 1949, 8–12; 1956, 9. *Cat*, 1950, 6–9; 1952, 8; 1953, 6–8; 1955, 6–8; 1985, 133–142.

7. *NCC*, July 1948, 4; December 1948, 2–3. *Coll*, 23 February 1950, 1.

8. *Coll*, 31 March 1950, 1. *NCC*, July 1948, 4; February 1950, 2.

9. *Coll*, 31 March 1950, 2. *NCC*, June 1951, 6.

10. *Coll*, 15 February 1949, 2; 20 March 1951, 2; May 1952, 2. *PK*, 1949, 17. Paul Crouch interview, 15 June 1995. Griffith Hamlin was actually a member of the class of 1939. *Alumni Directory*, 1999, 84.

11. Sarah Bain Ward interviews, 27 November 1984 and 24 June 1995. Bob Hollar taught science at ACC from 1954–1981. *Cat*, 1981, 109. *The Torchlight*, May 1945, 6. Herb Jeffries managed Belk's of Wilson and married Kay W. Jeffries, class of 1962, who later taught physical education at ACC. *Alumni Directory*, 1999, 104. *Cat*, 1985, 139. Ware, *ACC*, 237.

12. *Coll*, 31 October 1950, 1. *PK*, 1951, 3–4. The 1951 *Pine Knot* contains several photographs of the inauguration ceremonies. *PK*, 1951, 3, 4, 91.

13. *PK*, 1951, 3–14. *Coll*, 29 January 1947, 1; 15 February 1949, 2.

14. *PK*, 1951, 2, 12, 67; 1952, 49; 1953, no page number; 1954, 34–35; 1955, 34–35. *Cat*, 1948, 8. *Coll*, 30 October 1947, 1; 31 October 1950, 1; 22 February 1951, 1; April 1951, 1; 15 November 1951, 1; December 1952, 5; February 1953, 1; 6 April 1953, 3; October 1953, 1; November 1953, 1; January 1954, 1; 2 March 1954, 1; 1 June 1954, 2.

15. *Coll*, October 1953, 1; November 1953, 1–4; January 1954, 1; 2 March 1954, 1; 1 June 1954, 2. *PK*, 1955, 34–35, 60, 62.

16. *Coll*, November 1953, 1, 3. *Cat*, 2000, 45. Paul Crouch interview, 15 June 1995.

17. *Coll*, October 1953, 1; January 1954, 1; 2 March 1954, 1. *PK*, 1955, 22–23, 34–35, 62. James B. Hemby Jr. interview. *Cat*, 1960, 8; 1962, 8; 1966, 9; 1973, 111; 1979, 108.

18. *Coll*, April 1951, 1; May 1951, 1; 15 October 1951, 1; November 1952, 7.

19. *Coll*, December 1952, 1.

20. *Coll*, February 1953, 2. Ware, *ACC*, 198.

21. *Coll*, May 1952, 6–7. Ware, *ACC*, 192–193. *NCC*, April 1952, 6. Braxton served on the board from 1923–1974. Barton College *Fact Book*, 1998–1999, 16. *The Wilson Daily Times* and the *North Carolina Christian* incorrectly reported that the honorary degrees presented by Lindley were the college's first. President Coggins had conferred nine honorary degrees, three in 1903 and six in 1904. *WDT*, 4 May 1952, 1–2; 16 September 1952, 1, 8. *NCC*, March 1952, 6. Ware, *ACC*, 192.

22. *PK*, 1953, no page number. *Cat*, 1952, 2–6; 1953, 4–6. *NCC*, October 1952, 6. *Coll*, March 1953, 3. Perry Case stepped down as dean, registrar, and professor of religion at the end of the fall semester of 1952. Moudy became dean and professor of religion. *The Collegiate* of March 1954 reported that trustees had honored Case with the title of dean emeritus. *Coll*, 2 March 1954, 1.

23. *Coll*, March 1953, 2. Ware, *ACC*, 200–201. *PK*, 1953, no page number.

24. *Coll*, May 1953, 3. Ware, *ACC*, 201–202. *PK*, 1953, no page number.

25. *Coll*, May 1952, 6: May 1953, 4. *NCC*, June 1951, 6. Ware, *ACC*, 92–199, 231–233.

26. James B. Hemby Jr. interview, 19 December 1996. *Coll*, October 1953, 5; 6 April

1954, 1; 8 May 1954, 1–3. *WDT,* 24 April 1954, 1–2. Ware, *ACC,* 203. *NCC,* November 1949, 6; December 1949, 6.

27. *Coll,* March 1954, 1; 6 April 1954, 5. *Cat,* 1954, 73. *PK,* 1954, 100.

28. *Coll,* November 1952, 4–5; October 1953, 4; November 1953, 4; December 1953, 4–5; October 1953, 4.

29. *Coll,* 31 October 1950, 3; 15 October 1951, 3; 1 February 1952. The two victories came against Ft. Bragg at Fayetteville on 27 November and against Westinghouse Apprentice School of Pittsburg, Pennsylvania, to close the season on 20 February. *Coll,* 18 December 1951, 4–5; March 1952, 4; May 1952, 3.

30. *Coll,* March 1952; May 1952, 4. McComas, a gifted baseball player himself, played third base during the summer and managed the Wilson Tobs team of the Coastal Plains League. He led the league with twenty-five home runs in 1952. *PK,* 1953, no page number.

31. *Coll,* March 1953, 5; December 1953, 4; 2 March 1954, 5. *Cat,* 1984–85, 10.

32. *PK,* 1954, 111–119.

33. *Coll,* 6 April 1953, 6; 6 April 1954, 2. *Cat,* 1953, 5, 57–70; 1954, 7–8, 71–72. *PK,* 1953, no page number.

34. *Coll,* March 1953, 5; December 1953, 5; 8 October, 1954, 5; 19 November, 1954, 7; 12 April, 1955, 6; 20 May, 1955, 8; September 1955, 3; November 1955, 4. *Cat,* 1952, 6; 1957, 9; 1979, 113; 1983, 137. *PK,* 1952, 11, 77; 1953, no page number; 1954, 107–109, 120–121.

35. *Coll,* 8 October 1954, 5; 19 November 1954, 7.

36. *Coll,* 8 October 1954, 1, 5.

37. *Coll,* 19 November 1954, 1. *PK,* 1955, 14, 92, 109, 130–131. *Cat,* 1955, 74.

38. *Coll,* 12 April 1955, 5. North State Conference Tournament Official Program, 1955. *PK,* 1955, 106–117.

39. *Coll,* 19 November 1954, 7; 15 December 1954, 8; 18 February 1955, 5; 10 March 1955, 1, 4; 12 April 1955, 5; 20 May 1955, 9. *PK,* 1955, 106–117, 138–139. North State Conference Tournament Official Program, 1955. ACC set North State Conference tournament records for total points, 108, and foul shots converted, in defeating Lenoir Rhyne 108–85. The Bulldogs made fifty-four of sixty foul shots attempted. *WDT,* 28 February 1955, 6; 1 March 1955, 6; 3 March 1955, 11. Kim Buchanan, a 6'5" forward and Raleigh native, played three seasons at North Carolina State before joining the army. Recruited by Coach McComas following his discharge, Buchanan enrolled at ACC for spring semester 1955.

40. *Cat,* 1952, 72; 1955, 76; 1958, 55–56. *Coll,* 12 April 1955, 1.

41. *Coll,* 6 April 1955, 3. *PK,* 1954, 11, 12; 1956, 18; 1957, 16; 1958, 19; 1959, 15.

42. *Coll,* October 1953, 3; December 1953, 7; 8 May 1954, 1; 8 October 1954, 1; 20 May 1955, 6; *Cat,* 1938, 59; 1954, 7. *NCC,* November 1950, 6.

43. *Coll,* 20 May 1955, 5.

44. *Coll,* 8 May 1954, 5; 8 October 1954, 2; 12 April 1955, 3, 6; 20 May 1955, 1. *Cat,* 1955,

8. Edward Rider, a graduate of the University of California, was assistant professor on the faculty between 1953–56. *Coll,* October 1953, 6. *Cat,* 1953, 8; 1955, 8.

45. *Coll,* 20 May 1955, 1, 5.

46. *Coll,* 20 May 1955, 1, 5. *Cat,* 1954, 71.

Notes to Chapter 12

1. Counting special students, 683 students enrolled for regular semester classes. Evening school and summer school enrollees brought the total head count to 1,045. *Cat,* 1956–57, 82.

2. *Coll,* September 1955, 1; December 1955, 3. *WDT,* 2 December 1955, 1.

3. *WDT,* 2 December 1955, 2. *NCC,* December 1955, 6.

4. *Coll,* May 1956, 1. *NCC,* May 1956, 6.

5. *Coll,* April 1956, 1; May 1956, 1. *NCC,* June 1956, 6.

6. *NCC,* July 1956, 6. *Coll,* 4 May 2000, 1, 8.

7. *Coll,* 1 October 1956, 1. *Cat.* 1957, 75. *PK,* 1957, 20, 66.

8. *Coll,* 1 October 1956, 1, 4. *NCC,* July 1950, 6; September 1952, 6; September 1956, 6. *Cat,* 1952, 5.

9. *Coll,* May 1951, 4. Sarah Bain Ward interview, 17 June 1994. Conversation with James B. Hemby Jr., 28 September 2000. Connor Jones's article in *The Evening Telegram* appeared in *The Collegiate* in October 1956. *Coll,* 17 October 1956, 1, 4.

10. *Coll,* 16 November 1956, 1–2.

11. *Coll,* 6 February 1959, 3. *PK,* 1958, 108–115. *Cat,* 2000–01, 39.

12. *Coll,* 26 September 1958, 4; 6 February 1959, 3; 4 December 1959, 2. *PK,* 1959, 43, 111, 118–131.

13. *Coll,* 18 October 1957, 4; 21 November 1958, 1, 4; 27 February 1959, 3; 6 March 1959, 3; 13 March 1959, 3; 17 April 1959, 4; 20 November 1959, 4; 8 January 1960, 4; 15 April 1960, 4; 13 May 1960, 6; 28 October 1960, 1; 27 October 1961, 4. *PK,* 1960, no page number; 1961, 104–120, 124–135; 1962, 102–133.

14. *Coll,* 27 February 1959, 3; 13 March 1959; 4 December 1959, 2. *PK,* 1958, 94–107; 1959, 19, 141; 1960, no page number.

15. *Coll,* October 1955, 3; November 1955, 1–2; 2 November 1956, 1; 10 October 1958, 4; 21 October 1960, 4; 28 October 1960, 3; 4 November 1960, 3; 18 November 1960, 6. *PK,* 1959, 103–107, 113–114; 1961, 97–100.

16. *Cat,* 1952–53, 6; 1953–54, 6–7; 1955–56, 6–7; 1956–57, 6–7; 1959–60, 89; 1960–61, 91. *Coll,* 18 January 1957, 1. *NCC,* January 1957, 8. Cutlip was a graduate of Bethany College, and Burt earned the A.B. degree at ACC. *Cat,* 1957–58, 7; 1958–59, 7.

17. *NCC,* December 1956, 6; June 1957, 6; September 1957, 6. *Coll,* 4 March 1960, 2; 14 October 1960, 4.

18. *PK,* 1957, 24–26; 1958, 92–93, 103; 1961, 92–93. *Coll,* 26 September 1958, 1, 4; 26 February 1960, 1.

19. *Coll*, 14 April 1961, 1, 2; 21 April 1961, 1–2; 28 April 1961, 1–2, 4.

20. *Coll*, 7 November 1958, 2; 11 December 1959, 2. *PK*, 1959, 100–101.

21. There is an unexplained difference of 92 students between the *North Carolina Christian* figure of 1,198 and the college *Catalog's* listing of 1,290 enrollees for 1961–62. *NCC*, October 1961, 6. *Cat*, 1961–62, 91. *Coll*, 4 December 1959, 3; 11 December 1959, 4; 29 April 1960, 4; 4 November 1960, 3.

22. *PK*, 1960, no page number; 1961, 48–71; 1962, 37–58.

23. *Coll*, 2 May 1957, 1; 27 May 1957, 1, 3. *NCC*, May 1957, 6.

24. *Coll*, 27 May 1957, 1.

25. *PK*, 1956, 135–137; 1957, no page number. *Coll*, 22 March 1957, 3; 18 October 1957, 3; 16 January 1958, 3.

26. *Coll*, April 1956, 3; 4 October 1957, 3; 2 December 1957, 1, 3. *PK*, 1958, 133; 1961, 144.

27. *PK*, 1953, no page number; 1954, 11; 1960, no page number; 1961, 135–139; 1962, 143–150; 1963, 57, 140–146. *Cat*, 1979, 116.

28. *PK*, 1958, 47. *Coll*, 1 May 1959, 3; 2 December 1960, 1; 22 September 1961, 1; 3 November 1961, 2. *Coll*.

29. *Coll*, 1 May 1959, 2. *Cat*, 1961, 27. *PK*, 134–138; 1959, 78–79; 1960, no page number; 1961, 147; 162, 148–150.

30. *Coll*, October 1955, 3; November 1955, 1–2.

31. *Coll*, October 1955, 3; November 1955, 1–2, 6; 17 October 1956, 2–3; 16 November 1956, 1, 4. *PK*, 1956, 48, 85; 1957, 84.

32. *Coll*, 23 September 1960, 1; 14 October 1960, 1. *PK*, 1961, 63–68, 94.

33. *Coll*, 21 October 1960, 1–2; 4 November 1960, 1–2. *PK*, 1961, 65.

34. *Coll*, 21 October 1960, 3; 3 May 1961, 1; 29 September 1961, 1; 27 October 1961, 3; 3 November 1961, 1; 17 November 1961, 3; 1 December 1961, 1; 8 December 1961, 1, 4; 12 January 1962; 16 March 1962. *PK*, 1962, 55.

35. *Coll*, 1 June 1954, 4, 6. *PK*, 1954, 32–37, 65.

36. *Coll*, December 1955, 2. *PK*, 1956, 137.

37. *Coll*, December 1955, 2, 6. *PK*, 1956, 40–41, 92; 1957, 28–29, 64.

38. *Coll*, December 1955, 6; February 1956, 1–2; 1957, 121. *PK*, 1956, 137.

39. *PK*, 1957, 121. *Coll*, 2 November 1956, 2, 4; 4 March 1960, 2.

40. *Coll*, 13 May 1960, 5; 28 October 1990, 1.

41. *Coll*, 28 October 1960, 1.

42. *Coll*, 28 October 1960, 2; 4 November 1960, 1.

43. *Coll*, 18 November 1960, 1, 5; 9 December 1960, 1; 3 February 1961, 2.

44. *Coll*, 2 December 1960, 1–2; 3 February 1901, 2.

45. *Coll*, 12 May 1961, 2. PK, 1961, 59.

46. *Coll*, 5 May 1961, 1, 3.

Notes to Chapter 13

1. *Coll*, 22 September 1961, 3. *Cat*, 1956–57, 7–9, 82; 1957–58, 73; 1958–59, 75; 1959–60, 89; 1960–61, 9–12, 91; 1980–81, 105–114.

2. *Coll*, 13 March 1958, 1; 9 January 1959, 1; 3 November 1961, 1, 3; 1 February 1963, 1.

3. *Coll*, 18 February 1957, 1; 9 October 1959, 4–5; 3 February 1961, 3. Sarah Bain Ward, Mildred Hartsock, Ola Fleming, and Mrs. James Moudy helped Cloyd organize the new club. *Coll*, 18 February 1955, 7.

4. *Coll*, 8 January 1960; 17 February 1961, 1; 2 February 1962, 1, 4; 9 February 1962, 1; 17 May 1963, 1, 4; 13 April 1967, 4. *PK*, 1963, 6.

5. *Coll*, 29 September 1961 2; 20 October 1962, 1; 13 April 1962, 1; 4 May 1962, 1; 30 November 1962, 2; 5 April 1963, 4; 29 April 1965, 3; 5 May 1966, 2; 25 April 1968, 4. *PK*, 1962, 4–5, 50, 93, 101.

6. *Coll*, 30 November 1962, 2; 5 April 1963, 4. *PK*, 1960, no page number. Jarrell was a retired teacher living in Durham in 1999. *Alumni Directory*, 1999, 104.

7. *Coll*, 19 October 1962, 2; 2 November 1962; 16 November 1962, 2; 11 January 1963; 8 February 1963, 2; 22 February 1963, 2; 20 December 1963, 2; 28 February 1964, 2; 2 October 1964, 2; 18 May 1967, 2. Ridling was president of CCF and a member of the Golden Knot Honorary Society. *PK*, 1963, 60. Wagner was SGA president and editor of *The Collegiate*. *PK*, 1966, no page number; 1967, 118–120, 178, 185.

8. Sarah Bain Ward interview, 24 June 1995. *Coll*, 6 May 1960, 2; 13 May 1960, 2; 29 April 1965, 1, 4; 6 May 1965, 2. *Cat*, 1963–64, 33; 1964–65, 33. *PK*, 1965, 19; 1966, no page number.

9. *Coll*, 27 September 1963, 2; 17 February 1966; 5 May 1966, 1, 4; 2 November 1967, 2. 15 February 1968, 1, 3; 22 February 1968, 1, 2.

10. *Coll*, 9 October 1959, 5; 1 December 1961, 2; 9 October 1964, 2; 6 May 1965, 1; 17 November 1967, 2; 7 December 1967, 2. *PK*, 1962, 120–121, 127; 1963, 83; 1968, 190.

11. *Coll*, 4 November 1965, 1; 6 April 1967, 2. *PK*, 1967, 49, 128, 174, 184. In 1999, Sam E. McPhail served as pastor of Belmont United Methodist Church in Roanoke, Virginia. *Alumni Directory*, 1999, 133.

12. *Coll*, 11 December 1964, 1, 2, 4; 21 January 1965, 2; 13 April 1967, 1.

13. *Coll*, 3 March 1966, 2.

14. *Coll*, 31 March 1966, 1, 2, 6. *PK*, 1966, no page number.

15. *Coll*, 21 April 1966, 1; 8 December 1966, 2; 15 December 1966, 2.

16. O'Neill, *Coming Apart, An Informal History of America in the 1960's*, 144, 285. *Coll*, 19 October 1962, 2; 31 January 1964, 2; 17 April 1964, 1, 3; 24 April 1964, 2; 8 May 1964, 2; 4 December 1962, 2; 11 February 1965, 2, 4; 18 February 1965, 2; 28 October 1965, 2; 6 January 1966, 2. Link, *William Friday, Power, Purpose and American Higher Education*, 111.

17. *Coll*, 12 January 1967, 2, 3, 4; 2 February 1967, 2; 16 February 1967, 2, 4; 2 May 1968, 1.

18. *Coll,* 22 February 1968, 1, 4; 29 February 1968, 1, 3; 7 March 1968, 1; 21 March 1968, 2; 28 March 1968, 1. Wilbur Gerald Outlaw served as president of the drama club, vice-president of YMCA, and chaplain of Phi Delta Gamma fraternity. *PK,* 1940, 20. *Cat,* 1937–38, 63; 1939–40, 59.

19. *Coll,* 25 April 1968, 2; 2 May 1968, 2; 9 May 1968, 1, 2, 3.

20. *Coll,* 9 May 1968, 1; *PK,* 1967, 150; 1968, 125: 1969, 203. Antone, a member of the class of 1969, was an officer of Sigma Sigma Sigma and secretary of her freshman class. Kay Antone Mitchell returned to her alma mater as a member of the business department faculty in 1986.

21. *Coll,* 25 April 1968, 5. *PK,* 1967, 136; 1968, 171, 173–174. *Cat,* 1967–68, 84, 86.

22. *NCC,* November 1964, 6. *Coll,* 13 November 1964, 1, 3; 11 December 1964, 1, 4.

23. Daniel, *Hackney, The History of a Company,* 3–4. *Barton College Fact Book,* 1998–99, 11–18. Ware, *ACC,* 85, 231. Thomas J. Hackney Jr., interview, 19 June 1997.

24. *NCC,* June 1966, 8. *Cat,* 1960–61, 91; 1968–69, 93. *Coll,* 23 February 1963, 2; 14 January 1964, 4; 31 January 1964, 1; 22 September 1966, 1; 14 November 1966, 1; 16 October 1969, 1. *NCC,* November 1966, 15. *Cat,* 2000–01, 5, 9.

25. *Coll,* 11 January 1968, 1, 4; 21 March 1968, 1; 25 April 1968, 1. *NCC,* June 1966, 8.

26. *Coll,* 25 October 1963 1; 5 March 1965, 1, 4; 16 December 1965, 1; 27 October 1966, 1; 7 December 1967, 1. *NCC,* November 1966, 15.

27. *Coll,* 15 November 1963, 1; 23 September 1965, 3; 8 December 1966, 1; 9 March 1967, 1; 6 April 1967, 1; 22 February 1968, 4; 2 May 1968, 1. *PK,* 1966, no page number; 1967, 165; 1968, 164.

28. *PK,* 1967, 34–35, 62–63. *Coll,* 4 May 1967, 1; 11 May 1967, 1, 4; 18 May 1967, 1. *Cat,* 1966–67, 10–12.

29. *Coll,* 16 October 1964, 1; 20 November 1964, 1; 17 December 1964, 1; 21 January 1965, 3. Terry Grimes conversation, 27 October 2000. Doris Holsworth died in February 1964. *Coll,* 14 February 1964, 1.

30. *Coll,* 26 September 1962, 2; 5 October 1962, 2.

31. *Coll,* 26 October 1962, 2; 11 January 1963, 2; 8 February 1963, 2; 3 May 1963, 2; 17 May 1963, 1, 4. *NCC,* May 1963, 9.

32. *Coll,* 18 October 1963, 1; 8 November 1963, 1; 6 March 1964, 1; 1 May 1964, 1. *NCC,* May 1964, 7. The faculty poll was conducted by the ACC Central Committee of Instruction, which consisted of the dean of the college and departmental chairmen. *Cat,* 1963–64, 12.

33. *Coll,* 2 October 1964, 3; 23 October 1964, 5; 21 January 1965, 4.

34. *Coll,* 25 February 1965, 1–3; 5 March 1965, 2; 18 March 1965, 1.

35. *Coll,* 23 September 1965, 2. Raleigh *News and Observer,* 15 July 1964; 15 August 1964; 29 November 1964; 20 October 1965; 24 October 1965; 11 July 1966, 24. Greenville *Daily Reflector,* 28 September 1964. Wendell W. Smiley, "The North Carolina Press Views the Ku Klux Klan From 1964 Through 1966," 78–79, 90.

36. *PK,* 1967, 52, 62, 151, 159, 177; 1968, 83, 198; 1969, 85, 198; 1970, 104; 164. *Alumni Di-*

rectory, 1999, 30, 176. *Coll*, 18 May 1967, 1; 26 October 1967, 4; 9 November 1967, 4; 17 November 1967, 1; 10 October 1968, 1; 17 October 1968, 1; 12 December 1968, 1. *Cat*, 1966–67, 99. Ross Albert, Paul Crouch, and Gene Purcell conversations, 22–24 May 2000.

37. *Coll*, 30 September 1965, 3; 19 October 1967, 3; 2 November 1969, 3; 7 December 1967, 1, 3; 22 February 1968, 5; 29 February 1968, 3.

38. *Coll*, 10 February 1966, 3; 8 February 1968, 3; 15 February 1968, 3; 22 February 1968, 5.

39. *Coll*, 9 May 1968, 3; 16 May 1968, 3.

40. *PK*, 1968, 101; *Coll*, 21 November 1968, 3; 12 December 1968, 3; 9 January 1969; 6 February 1969, 3; 13 February 1969, 3; 6 March 1969, 4. The Hall of Fame induction dates were Carraway, 1988; Gilmore, 1992; and Stallsmith, 1999.

41. *PK*, 1967, 52–54, 86, 93, 95, 113, 152, 155; 1968, 80–81, 153, 197–198, 200; 1969, 121, 188, 200, 214; 1970, 169; 1971, 76, 119, 161, 168. *Coll*, 22 October 1966, 4; 8 December 1966, 1; 2 February 1967, 3; 12 December 1967, 3; 26 September 1968, 3; 31 October 1968, 1; 14 November 1968, 1.

42. *Coll*, 5 October 1967, 1, 3.

43. *Coll*, 5 October 1967, 1, 3. *NCC*, October 1968, 5.

44. Rosenberg and Rosenberg, *In Our Times, America Since World War II*, 176–177. *Coll*, 22 February 1968, 3; 28 March 1968, 2; 25 April 1968, 2.

45. *Coll*, 26 September 1968, 2; 10 October 1968, 1, 2; 31 October 1968, 1, 2.

46. *Coll*, 7 November 1968, 1–2. Casey, a native of Wilson and class of 1969, later joined the college as director of financial aid and admission counselor. *PK*, 1968, 205; 1969, 105, 204. *Cat*, 1975, 111.

Notes to Chapter 14

1. Boyer, *The Enduring Vision*, 872–874. Thomas E. Marshall III conversation, 1 December 2000.

2. Boyer, *The Enduring Vision*, 873. Moss, *Moving On, The American People Since 1945*, 200.

3. *Coll*, 6 November 1969, 2; 13 November 1969, 2, 4; 24 September 1970, 1; 19 November 1970, 1; 10 December 1970, 2.

4. *Coll*, 21 October 1971, 1; 28 October 1971, 1; 4 November 1971, 1. Thomas E. Marshall III conversation, 1 December 2000.

5. *Coll*, 28 October 1971, 2, 3; 8 November 1973; 18 November 1971, 1; 9 December 1971, 1; 16 December 1971, 2.

6. *Coll*, 8 November 1972, 2; 9 September 1976, 3; 16 September 1976, 3; 23 September 1976, 3.

7. *PK*, 1969, 6–7; 1970, 122; 1971, 25; 1973, 50–51; 70–71; 1974, 22, 118–119; 1975, 66–67, 70–73. *Coll*, 30 September 1976, 1; 14 October 1976, 1.

8. *Coll*, 23 October 1969, 1. Thomas Marshall III conversation, 1 December 2000.

PK, 1970, 30–31. Participants in the evening moratorium service included Wilmington senior Al Cooke, president of the CAC and a member of the track team, Chaplain Dan Hensley, and religion professors Gerald Harris and Gene Purcell. *PK,* 1970, 163, 172.

9. *Coll,* 30 October 1969, 1, 4; 11 December 1969, 1, 4; 7 May 1970, 1; 12 November 1970, 2; 30 September 1971, 1. *PK,* 1972, 90, 100.

10. *Coll,* 7 May 1970, 2. *PK,* 1972, 114–115, 191, 209.

11. *Coll,* 14 May 1970, 1.

12. *Coll,* 30 September 1971, 1; 7 October 1971, 2.

13. *Coll,* 1 February 1973, 2. *PK,* 1975, 227.

14. *Coll,* 18 September 1969, 2; 25 September 1969, 2; 9 October 1969, 2; 16 October 1969, 2, 4; 23 October 1969, 1, 4; 30 October 1969, 2; 5 February 1970, 2; 1 February 1973, 2. *PK,* 1970, 102–103, 171, 175. The student life committee consisted of the dean of students, the dean of women, seven faculty members, and four students. *Cat,* 1970, 93, 100.

15. *Coll,* 13 March 1969, 1; 23 April 1970, 1; 24 September 1970, 2; 1 October 1970, 4; 8 October 1970, 1–2. *Cat,* 1969, 89, 91. The administrative council consisted of the president, dean of the college, business manager, director of development, director of admissions, and dean of students. *Cat,* 1970, 93, 99.

16. *Coll,* 18 February 1971, 1; 25 February 1971, 2; 28 April 1972, 1; 5 May 1972, 1–2, 4.

17. Arthur D. Wenger conversation, spring semester 1974. In 1973–74, the discipline committee consisted of the dean of students, three faculty members, one of whom served as chairman, the SGA president, and two additional students. *Cat,* 1974, 116. *Coll,* 25 February 1971, 2.

18. *Coll,* 14 March 1974, 1. Deans Street was renamed Atlantic Christian College Drive.

19. *Coll,* 14 March 1974, 1, 2.

20. *PK,* 1974, 128–129.

21. *PK,* 1974, 128–129. *Coll,* 21 March 1974, 2.

22. ERA died in 1982, three states short of the three-fourths required for ratification. Boyer, *The Enduring Vision,* 897–899.

23. *Coll,* 14 February 1974, 2; 25 April 1974, 2.

24. *Coll,* 5 September 1974, 1; 12 September 1974, 1.

25. *Coll,* 31 October 1974, 1, 3.

26. *Coll,* 30 January 1975, 1; 6 February 1975, 1.

27. *Coll,* 12 February 1970, 3; 19 March 1970, 3. Respass became the first female member of the college's Hall of Fame in 1988. Langley was honored with induction in 1992, and Debbie Purvis Keel became a member in 1999.

28. *Coll,* 9 April 1970, 3; 13 February 1975, 4; 15 January 1976, 4; 22 January 1976, 4; 3 March 1977, 4. *PK,* 1970, 146; 1975, 124–127.

29. *Coll,* 9 October 1975, 6; 16 October 1975, 4; 30 October 1975, 6. *PK,* 1975, 236; 1976, 114–121.

30. *Coll,* 3 March 1977, 4; 31 March 1977, 4; 7 April 1977, 4; 21 April 1977, 4. Barton

Athletic Hall of Fame Program, 20 October 2000. Joan Adams Jones was inducted into the college's Athletic Hall of Fame in 1989, followed by Susan Davis Myers, in 1991, and Cathy Wall, in 1993.

31. *Cat*, 1973, 19–20; 1977, 17–21.

32. In the two years between 1972–74, the seven men's athletic programs received approximately nine times the coverage devoted to the women's two sports programs in *Pine Knot*. In the 1975 yearbook, the coverage of men's athletics declined to about four times that of women's sports. For the following two years, with volleyball added to women's sports, the advantage dropped to slightly over two times in favor of the men. If the two most favored men's sports are used instead of seven to match the two women's sports between 1972–75 and three between 1975–77, the coverage becomes more equitable. For 1972–73, men's sports received approximately four times that of women's coverage; by 1976–77, the advantage had decreased to one and a half times. Athletics photos, narrative, and schedules are from the 1973–77 editions of *Pine Knot*. *Cat*, 1976; 1977; 1978; 1979; 1980.

33. In 1969–70, the council consisted of only seven members; all were faculty-staff members, and four were coaches. Beginning in 1970, the council added two students, and, in 1973, added one alumnus and one trustee. In 1976 the size of the council was reduced to ten members, six of whom were faculty-staff. Traditionally, three of the faculty-staff representatives have been coaches or noncoaching members of the department of health and physical education. *Cat*, 1969 to 1979; 2000–01, 24, 40. The 2000 athletics committee contained three males and four females, one of whom chaired the committee. Of the two coaches who served, one was a male who was also athletic director; the second, a female, served as assistant athletic director. Other members included the vice-president for institutional advancement; the chair of the department of physical education and sport studies, a female; and three additional faculty members, two of whom were female. *Cat*, 2000, 162–168.

34. *Cat*, 1976, 112–119. *Coll*, 4 March 1971, 3; 13 May 1971, 1; 14 April 1972, 4; 21 March 1974, 4; 28 March 1974, 1; 17 March 1977, 4. *PK*, 1977, 192.

35. *Coll*, 1 May 1969, 3; 23 April 1970, 3; 24 September 1970, 3; 12 May 1972, 4; 21 March 1974, 4; 17 April 1975, 4; 24 April 1975, 4; 17 March 1977, 4; 24 March 1977. *PK*, 1972, 192, 196, 210, 214; 1974, 136–137; 1975, 136–137; 1976, 132–133. *Cat*, 1976, 119; 1982, 126. Barton Athletic Hall of Fame Program, 20 October 2000.

36. *Coll*, 14 April 1972, 2; 11 November 1976; 9 December 1976. *PK*, 1975, 112–117, 206–207; 1976, 103–107, 179–180; 1977, 106–109; 1978, 84–89, 173.

37. *Coll*, 1 April 1976, 4; 29 April 1976, 6; 1 September 1977, 4. *PK*, 1977, 122–125.

38. *PK*, 1973, 176, 178. *Coll*, 15 October 1970, 1, 4; 14 October 1971, 2; 5 May 1972, 1; 18 January 1973, 1; 8 February 1973; 22 March 1973, 1; 18 April 1973, 1; 8 November 1973, 1; 13 December 1973, 1; 24 January 1974, 1; 26 September 1974, 1. *Cat*, 1972, 97–98.

39. *Coll*, 12 March 1970, 1; 25 March 1971, 4; 17 March 1972, 4; 21 April 1972, 1; 8 March 1973, 1; 26 September 1974, 1; 12 February 1976, 1; 1 April 1976, 1.

40. *Coll*, 16 December 1971, 3; 11 October 1973, 1, 6; 13 March 1975, 1; 10 April 1975, 1; 19 February 1976, 1.

41. *Coll*, 3 March 1972, 2; 27 September 1973, 2; 21 February 1974, 1. *PK*, 1974, 220.

42. *Coll*, 5 February 1970, 1; 19 March 1970, 1; 1 October 1970. *Cat*, 1967, 9; 1968, 84; 1969, 84. 1971, 32, 95–101. *PK*, 1972, 155.

43. The initial graduating class contained twenty-six seniors. *Coll*, 28 September 1972, 3; 8 February 1973, 1; 21 March 1974, 1, 3; 2 May 1974, 1; 5 September 1974, 1, 4; 2 May 1975, 1. *PK*, 1973, 66–67, 177; 1975, 190–195.

44. *Coll*, 11 October 1973, 1; 6 December 1973, 1.

45. *Coll*, 6 December 1973, 1. The name "Still Point" also came from Father William Johnston's *The Still Point of the Turning World*, an anthology of prose, poetry, and photographs regarding the life of Christ. *Coll*, 2 May 1974, 2; 16 January 1975, 5. *PK*, 1973, 120–121; 1974, 144–145; 1975, 10–11.

46. *Coll*, 22 January 1976, 2–3.

47. *Coll*, 21 April 1972; 2 November 1972, 1; 23 October 1975, 3; 23 September 1976, 1; 30 September 1976, 1; 4 November 1976, 1. *Cat*, 1971, 108. The final stage of the college's Fulfillment Fund drive had raised $2,112,250 of the $2,730,000 capital improvements goal by late October 1975. *Coll*, 16 October 1975, 3.

48. *Coll*, 10 October 1974, 1; 17 October 1974, 2; 23 January 1975, 3.

49. *NCC*, January 1974, 1. *Coll*, 7 February 1974, 1.

50. *NCC*, March 1976, 3. *Coll*, 6 November 1975, 1; 11 March 1976, 4.

51. *Coll*, 24 February 1977, 1; 3 March 1977, 1. Joyner and Wenger, "Dr. Arthur D. Wenger." Thomas E. Marshall III, unsent letter to "Dear Mom and Dad," Sunday, 26 February 1977. Copy in Barton College archives. Dan Hensley Jr., J. Stuart Wake, and Alex Mooty officiated at the funeral services held at Wilson's First Christian Church, at 3:00 PM, Sunday, 27 February. Burial followed in Maplewood Cemetery in Wilson.

Notes to Chapter 15

1. *Coll*, 14 October 1976, 1; 3 March 1977, 1; 17 March 1977, 1. *Scope*, March 1977, 1. Joyner and Wenger, "Arthur D. Wenger." Doris K. Wenger interview, 12 December 2000.

2. Thomas J. Hackney Jr. interview, 19 June 1997. Joyner and Wenger, "Arthur D. Wenger." *Coll*, 3 March 1977, 2.

3. Dennis Rogers, "Art Wenger Put His Mark on Atlantic Christian," Raleigh *News and Observer*, 4 April 1977. *Scope*, October–November, 1979, 7.

4. *Cat*, 1977, 110–111.

5. *Coll*, 17 March 1977, 1; 19 January 1978, 1; 23 February 1978, 1, 5; 24 August 1978, 1. *Scope*, April 1977, 4; September 1978, 2; January 1978, 4.

6. *Scope*, May 1977, 1; June 1977, 1, 4. Jim Hunt received a second honorary degree from his alma mater, North Carolina State University, on 14 May, one day later. Hunt was a member of the ACC board of trustees from 1988–1991. Judge Morris served

much of her 1971–1983 term as chair of the board's education committee. *Coll*, 28 April 1977, 1. *Barton College Fact Book*, 1998–99, 11, 13.

7. *Scope*, September 1977, 1, 4; January 1978, 1–2. *Coll*, 1 September 1977, 1. Doster officially assumed his new position on Monday, 2 January 1978.

8. *NCC*, October 1978, 1. *Scope*, September 1978, 1, 4; October–November, 1978, 1–3, 8. *Coll*, 14 September 1978, 5; 12 October 1978, 1, 5, 9.

9. *Coll*, 19 January 1978, 1; 24 August 1978, 1. *Scope*, January 1978, 1.

10. *Scope*, March 1978, 1, 4; September 1978, 2, 3; December 1978–January 1979, 1. *Coll*, 27 April 1978, 1; 24 August 1978, 1. *PK*, 1973, 6–7. *Cat*, 1978, 116; 1980, 105.

11. *Coll*, 7 April 1977, 2; 16 February 1978, 1; 14 April 1981, 3. *PK*, 1971, 6–7; 1972, 4–5. *Cat*, 1979, 110. *Coll*, 6 September 1979, 1.

12. *Coll*, 24 March 1977, 1; 31 August 1978, 1, 6; 1 September 1980, 6–7; 2 September 1981, 1; 30 September 1981, 5; 16 September 1982, 5; 11 November 1982, 4; *Cat*, 1981, 25. *PK*, 1974, 144–145; 1977, 83; 1980, 68–109; 1981, 75–76.

13. *PK*, 1974, 144–145. *Coll*, 23 February 1981, 3; 30 March 1981, 6. The Sprinkle, Purcell, and Sharp biblical study sessions are planned and implemented by the college's department of religion and philosophy. *Cat*, 2001, 40.

14. *Coll*, 8 September 1977, 2; 15 September 1977, 2; 26 January 1978, 1; 2 February 1978, 1–3. *Scope*, February 1978, 1.

15. *Coll*, 26 August 1981, 7; 9 September 1981, 7; 30 September 1981, 1; 21 October 1981, 4. *Cat*, 1982, 124.

16. *Coll*, 3 February 1982, 7; 10 February 1982, 4–5; 3 March 1982, 3.

17. *Cat*, 1984, 141; 1985, 77; 1986, 81, 153–154; 1997, 90–91, 168.

18. Coll, 20 January 1977, 2; 3 February 1977, 2; 10 February 1977, 3, 4; 17 February 1977, 2; 31 March 1977, 1, 3; 3 December 1979, 2; 10 December 1979, 2, 5; 10 February 1982, 2; 11 November 1982, 2.

19. *Scope*, May 1977, 4. *Coll*, 16 February 1978, 2; 16 March 1978, 2; 16 November 1978, 1, 2; 18 January 1979, 1.

20. *Coll*, 21 October 1981, 2. *PK*, 1982, 179–180.

21. *Coll*, 12 December 1980, 4; March 16, 1981, 1.

22. *Coll*, 10 February 1982, 2; 2 September 1982, 2; 21 April 1983, 2. *Scope*, September 1998, 2–3. *Alumni Directory*, 160.

23. *Coll*, 1 February 1979, 1, 6; 17 September 1979, 5; 4 February 1980, 1, 4; 9 February 1981, 1; 27 January 1982, 2. *Cat*, 1982, 13.

24. *Coll*, 8 September 1977, 2, 3; 30 August 1979, 1, 6; 28 October 1981, 4; 30 September 1982. Gordon Joyner conversation, 12 January 2001.

25. *Scope*, Fall 1982, 9. *Coll*, 26 January 1978, 2; 14 September 1978, 2; 28 September 1978, 2; 22 February 1979, 6; 26 April 1979, 2; 16 June 1980, 4; 16 September 1981, 3. *PK*, 1978, 64, 172.

26. *Coll*, 9 November 1978, 1; 7 December 1978, 1; 24 February 1982, 1; 16 September 1982, 1. *Coll*, 11 November 1982, 1. Gordon Joyner conversation, 12 January 2001.

27. Willis N. Hackney, one of ACC's most generous benefactors, donated $200,000 toward building the library. *Scope,* September 1977, 2–3; December 1977, 1, 4. *Coll,* 1 September 1977, 1; 8 September 1977, 3; 10 November 1977, 1. 9 November 1978, 1; 8 February 1979, 1.

28. *Coll,* Orientation Issue, Summer 1981, 7; 26 August 1981, 1; 21 October 1981, 1; 16 March 1983, 1, 2.

29. *Coll,* 18 January 1979, 1; 4 November 1981, 10; 18 November 1981, 4, 5; 8 August 1981, 2; 2 September 1981, 1; 31 March 1983, 2; 21 April 1983, 4.

30. *Coll,* 16 September 1982, 5; 27 January 1983, 1, 3.

31. *Coll,* 8 December 1977, 1; 19 January 1978, 2; 4 February 1980, 5; 3 March 1980, 1. *Cat,* 1968–69, 39–42; 1979–80, 43, 46–47. *Scope,* December 1979–January 1980, 3.

32. *Cat,* 1981–82, 73, 103–114, 128. *Coll,* 16 November 1978, 1, 6; 24 September 1979, 5; 22 September 1980, 7; 30 October 1980, 8.

33. *Scope,* Fall 1982, 5. *Coll,* 21 April 1972, 3; 6 April 1978, 2–4; 1 September 1980, 3; 30 September 1982, 1, 3. *Cat,* 1982–83, 52, 58–59; 1983–84, 60, 66–67; 1986–87, 74; 1987–88, 63, 71–73; 1988–89, 64–65, 72, 73; 1998–99, 130–131; 1999–2000, 134–135, 138–139.

34. *Coll,* 8 February 1973, 1; 13 September 1973, 1; 15 September 1977, 3; 1982 Orientation Issue, 5. Cat, 1978, 120. The nursing graduates scored 88.9 percent, with thirty-two of thirty-six students passing the exam. The previous year's graduating class of nurses, class of 1980, had finshed third in the state with 85.7 percent passing the examination. *Coll,* 16 September 1981, 1. *Scope,* number 190, Bulldog Issue, 1981, 1.

35. *Coll,* 28 April 1977, 1; 8 February 1979, 8; 7 December 1978, 1, 7; 3 December 1979, 7; 5 May 1983, 7. *Scope,* December 1978–January 1979, 10.

36. *Coll,* 16 March 1978, 1; 26 April 1979, 6; 24 September 1979, 4; 30 March 1981, 3; 18 November 1981, 1; 5 May 1983, 7. *Cat,* 1980–81, 112.

37. The 1976 and 1977 teams finished at 11–5 and 9–4–4, respectively. *PK,* 1977, 106. *Coll,* 3 November 1977, 4. *Scope,* December 1978–January 1979, 3, 6–7. *Coll,* 7 December 1978, 3; 12 November 1979, 3, 4; 17 November 1980, 1, 4; 2 December 1981, 7; 11 November 1982, 11.

38. *WDT,* 2 June 1979, 1, 3, 14; 4 June 1979, 1, 2, 14. Parham's teams placed sixth nationally in 1971, fifth in 1972, tenth in 1973, ninth in 1975, fifteenth in 1976, tenth in 1977, second in 1978, and first in 1979. *Coll,* 30 August 1979, 3, 6. *PK,* 1976, 170; 1977, 122–125; 1980, 60–63. *Coll,* 24 August 1978, 3, 10; 24 August 1979, 3; 30 August 1979, 3, 6, 8. *Scope,* December 1978–January 1979, 8–9; June–July 1979, 1–2.

39. *PK,* 1977, 132–135. *Coll,* 28 April 1980, 1, 3; 4 November 1981, 11; 10 February 1983, 8; 21 April 1983, 8. *Scope,* Spring 1983, 18.

40. *Coll,* 16 March 1978, 1; 30 August 1979, 1; 18 November 1981, 2, 6; 2 December 1982, 1. *Scope,* June–July 1979, 1–2, 7; October–November 1979, 7. *PK,* 1980, 208–209.

41. *PK,* 1977, 166–203, 219; 1978, 202; 1982, 141. *Cat,* 1976, 117; 1978, 121; 1983, 124. *Scope,* Fall 1982, inside front cover.

42. *PK,* 1967, 52, 62, 151; 1968, 83, 198; 1976, 24–29, 32, 76, 84–85; 1977, 82, 89, 183; 1979,

83; 1980, 70, 74, 100–101, 181; 1981, 71, 104–105; 1982, 71, 81, 97–98, 101. *Coll*, 8 September 1977, 1. *Cat*, 1975, 16; 1976, 18–19; 1986, 29–30; 1990, 36–37; 1995, 35; 2000–01, 39.

43. *PK*, 1975, 100–109, 219, 225, 228; 1976, 24, 94, 207; 1977, 204, 210–211; 1978, 183, 212; 1979, 184; 1980, 123, 126, 151, 155, 178, 181, 183, 186–187.

44. *PK*, 1979, 171; 1980, 159; 1981, 50–55, 88–90, 134, 137, 152, 159, 167, 173–174, 212–213; 1982, 69, 86, 165–166, 175–183. *Coll*, 17 April 1975, 1. *Alumni Directory*, 1999, 7, 17. The college listed 267 graduating seniors for 1982. *Scope*, eightieth anniversary issue, 1982, 2.

Notes to Chapter 16

1. *Scope*, Commencement Issue, 1982, 15–18.

2. Ruffin reported gifts to the campaign from Belk-Tyler Stores of Wilson, through Herbert M. Jeffries Jr. and from John Bolt. *PK*, 1982, 64–65. *Scope*, Commencement Issue, 1982, cover, 9–14, 21–22. Following the purchase of the thirty-acre tract, official groundbreaking ceremonies occurred on 1 May 1979. The tract bordered Tilghman Road, Kincaid Avenue, and Grove Street. An architectural drawing of the proposed complex, including planned playing fields for softball, baseball, soccer, and tennis, was printed in *Scope*, Bulldog Issue, 1981, cover, 7–9. *Coll*, 1 March 1973, 1.

3. Shingleton also received the college's alumnus of the year award in 1981. *Scope*, Commencement Issue, 1982, 1–8.

4. *Scope*, Winter 1982–83, 5–13.

5. *Scope*, Winter 1982–83, 5–13.

6. *Scope*, October–November 1978, 1–8; June–July 1979, 1–12; Bulldog Issue, 1981, 7–8; Summer 1985.

7. Doster, "Presidential Precis," 20 September 1982, 1–5. "Precis" was President Doster's weekly newsletter, which went to the faculty and staff between July 1982 and May 1983. *WDT*, 20 November 1982. James B. Hemby Jr. interview, 19 December 1996. A copy of Bullard's report on faculty morale at the college is on file in Barton College archives.

8. *Coll*, 2 December 1982, 1–3; 8 December 1982, 1, 3. James B. Hemby Jr. interview, 19 December 1996.

9. *Coll*, 19 January 1978, 1; 23 February 1978, 1, 5; 24 August 1978, 1; 17 April 1979, 5; 6 September 1979, 1; 30 March 1980, 4; 1 September 1980, 1; 8 December 1980, 1, 6; 30 March 1981, 7. *Cat*, 1982, 117-128. *Cat*, 1979, 109. *Scope*, April–May 1979, 7; Commencement Issue, 25.

10. *Coll*, 3 March 1983, 1, 4.

11. *WDT*, 26 February 1983, 1. *Coll*, 3 March 1983, 1, 4. The capital campaign targeted $15 million for endowment, including scholarships, professorships, the library, and other priority needs; $5 million for facilities (which included remodeling Hardy and Belk Halls), a fine arts auditorium, land acquisition, an indoor swimming pool, an additional gymnasium, dormitory upkeep, renovation of Caldwell Hall, energy conser-

vation, and campus beautification; and $2 million for salary increases, financial aid, utilities, athletics, maintenance, and faculty-staff development. *Scope*, February–March 1979, 4, 8; February–March 1980, 9; Number 190, 1981, 2.

12. *Coll*, 28 April 1977, 1. *PK*, 1981, 122. Sarah and Milton Adams conversation, 31 January 2001.

13. *Cat*, 1980, 109; 1981, 109; 1982, 122; 1983, 128. *Coll*, 6 September 1979, 1; 21 April 1983, 1. *Scope*, August–September 1980, 21. Hemby's official title was acting president and professor of English. *Cat*, 1984, 139.

14. *Coll*, 2 September 1983, 2; 27 October 1983, 1. *Scope*, Fall 1983, cover, 1.

15. *Coll*, 26 April 1984, 1. Other inauguration speakers were Dean Mark Davis; trustee John Palmer; Wilson mayor Ralph El Ramey; Roy L. Champion, chairman of the Wilson County board of commissioners; Dr. Duane Cummings, president of the division of higher education of the Christian Church (Disciples of Christ); and Reverend Bernard C. Meese, regional minister of the Disciples of Christ in North Carolina. *Scope*, Summer 1984, cover, 1–4, 7; Fall 1987, 6. Ware, *ACC*, 221.

16. *Scope*, Summer 1984, 3–4.

17. The Graves house was officially deeded to the college 26 March 1984, and the keys were presented 17 April 1984. *Coll*, 26 April 1984, 1. *Scope*, Summer 1984, 5.

18. *Coll*, 16 March 1978, 1, 7; 28 February 1985, 1. *Cat*, 1986, 40–43; 1986–87, 42–46.

19. *Scope*, Winter 1984, 3. *Cat*, 1986, 44, 148; 1987, 158; 1989, 160. *Coll*, 30 August 1984, 4.

20. *Coll*, 28 February 1985, 1. *Cat*, 1984, 42; 1986, 44–45, 51–52, 148; 2001, 65–67, 163.

21. *Coll*, 16 January 1986, 4; 2 October 1986, 7; 15 October 1987, 1. *Cat*, 1987, 41. *Scope*, Spring 1986, 9. The college discontinued the honors program in 1996. *Cat*, 1996, 60–61; 1997, 175.

22. Specific priorities of the "Design For Excellence" fund-raising drive were annual fund $1.5 million; endowed scholarships, $1.29 million; endowment for excellence in teaching, $1 million; science building renovation, $750,000; computer literacy, $400,000; memorial opportunities, $345,000; and campaign administration, $215,000. *Coll*, 30 January 1986, 1. *Scope*, Fall 1985, cover, 1. *PK*, 1986, 181.

23. *Cat*, 1984, 62, 77–78, 83; 1985, 62, 77–83; 1986, 81–88. *Coll*, 1 March 1984, 3; 3 November 1988, 4. *Scope*, Winter 1987, 20.

24. *Coll*, 2 February 1984, 6; 3 October 1985, 5; 30 January 1986, 4; 17 September 1987, 1. *Cat*, 1988, 52–55, 103–106. *Scope*, Summer 1987, 11–12. The college retained the minor but dropped the major in American studies in 1996 because the school's accreditation status required a full-time faculty member with a graduate degree in the discipline. *Cat*, 1996, 130; 1997, 102; 2001, 103.

25. *Alumni Directory*, 4, 33, 213. *PK*, 1985, 24–25, 63–64, 191, 195; 1987, 61, 92, *Scope*, Spring 1984, 9. *Coll*, 21 March 1985, 5.

26. *Scope*, Summer 1986, 24; Winter 2000, 19. *PK*, 1987, 61, 173, 177. *Alumni Directory*, 10.

27. *Scope,* Summer 1987, 6; Winter 1987, 14–15. *Coll,* 3 December 1987, 1. *PK,* 1986, 70; 1987, 61, 72, 164, 168.

28. *Coll,* 26 April 1984, 1; 19 September 1985, 4; 14 November 1985, 3; 18 February 1988, 1; 23 February 1989, 1. *Scope,* Winter 1988–89, 13. By the spring of 1986, the college had received more than $100,000 for renovations to Hardy Alumni Hall. *Scope,* Spring 1986, 20.

29. *Coll,* 15 January 1987, 1; 19 March 1987, 1, 2. *Scope,* Summer 1987, 10–11. The Wilson City Council voted officially to close Lee Street in late December 1986.

30. *Scope,* Summer 1987, 10–11; Winter 1987, 2–3. *Coll,* 1 October 1987, 3. *Cat,* 1987, 170.

31. *Coll,* 26 February 1987, 2; 3 September 1987, 1; 17 September 1987.

32. *Scope,* Winter 1987, 8. *Coll,* 1 October 1987, 1, 3. Lamm also donated his time and talent in designing "Bully's."

33. Previous winners of the Flame of Truth Award included Frank Borman, former astronaut; William M. Batten, chief executive officer of the New York Stock Exchange; and Reverend Theodore M. Hesburgh, former president of Notre Dame University. *Scope,* Winter 1982–83, 1-3; Summer 1986, 3.

34. *Scope,* Winter 1988, 1–3.

35. *Coll,* 16 September 1981, 1; Orientation Issue, 1982, 5; 28 February 1985, 5; 19 September 1985, 8; 18 September 1986, 2; 3 September 1987, 1; 29 August 1996, 1–2. *Scope,* Fall 1985, 17. The college ranked among the top one-third of the state's nursing progams during nine of twenty-four years. List of ACC/Barton College ranking on state nursing examinations 1977–2000 furnished by Barton school of nursing. Evelyn Pruden, e-mail, 15 March 2001.

36. *Coll,* 18 April 1985, 4; 7 December 1989, 3. *Cat,* 1985, 29–30. *PK,* 1985, 80, 185; 1989, 90; 1990, 83, 171. *Alumni Directory,* 21, 107. Rhonda Hawley and Anthony Rawls are 1996 graduates, while Jeff Hawley graduated in 1997. *Scope,* January 1997, 17. Teresa Parker conversation, 1 March 2001.

37. *Coll,* 18 September 1986, 4; 8 December 1988, 3; 31 October 1998, 1, 8; 2 March 2000, Insert 1–4. *Cat,* 1989, 11.

38. F. Mark Davis interview, 29 July 1998. *Coll,* 23 February 1989, 3. *Cat,* 1989, 160. *Scope,* September 1998, 10.

39. *Scope,* Summer 1988, 8. *Cat,* 1988, 76–90; 1993, 106; 1998, 133; 2001, 45. Each year the department faculty selects a rising senior education major to receive the Gene A. Purvis most exemplary student award. Fussell was a 1946 cum laude graduate in social studies education. The Chapins established the Mary Alice and Howard B. Chapin Education Scholarship in 1987–88. The scholarship is awarded to students demonstrating strong academic and leadership ability who plan to teach in North Carolina. *Scope,* Summer 1985, 24; Winter 1986–87, 9–10; Winter 1987–88, 3–4, 14. *Alumni Directory,* 38. *PK,* 1947, 19, 34, 75–77.

40. *Scope,* Spring 1988, 11; Summer 1990, 25; September 1998, 10. Jackie S. Ennis conversation, 1 March 2001.

41. *Coll,* 10 November 1983, 8; *Coll,* 26 April 1984, 8. *Scope,* Summer 1984, 26; Fall 1984, 10–11; March 1996, 10–11. *PK,* 1984, 96, 165.

42. *Coll,* 14 November 1985, 1, 6; 13 February 1986, 6; 20 March 1986, 8. *Scope,* Winter 1982–83, 25; Fall 1984, 11; Summer 1987, 16–17. *PK,* 1986, 25, 150–157, 172; 1988, 184; 1989, 105, 189. Players on the 1985–86 team were Art Bane, Lowell Bockert, Ed Boone, Doren Chapman, Greg Nance, Rick Henry, Gilbert Rucker, Keith Seegers, Craig Stewart, Arnold Vinson, and Ashby White. *Scope,* Spring 1986, cover, 10–11. The 1986–87 team featured Bane, Bockert, Boone, Chapman, Dooms, Henry, Hobbs, Melendez, Seegers, Stewart, White, Kevin Borden, Brent Grinnel, Kevin Hobbs, Rucker, Darryl Turner, and Vinson. *PK,* 1987, 114–117.

43. *Coll,* 18 April 1985, 8; 28 April 1988, 10; Orientation Issue, Fall 1988, 6. *Scope,* Summer 1983, 20–21; Fall 1984, cover, 1, 10; Summer 1985, 22; Summer 1990, 17. *PK,* 1984, 102. Athletic Hall of Fame Program, 1986.

44. *Coll,* 10 November 1983, 7; 19 January 1984, 8; 26 April 1984, 8; 18 April 1985, 8. *PK,* 1984, 103; 1985, 157; 1987, 128–129, 154; 1988, 130–131, 167. *Alumni Directory,* 122.

45. *Coll,* 16 February 1984, 8; 1 March 1984, 8. *PK,* 1984, 98; 1987, 118–119; 1988, 118–119. *Scope,* Fall 1984, 10; Fall 1987, 33.

46. *PK,* 1984, 187. *Cat,* 1984, 136.

Notes to Chapter 17

1. *Coll,* 6 October 1988, 2; 3 November 1988, 1.

2. *Coll,* 3 November 1988, 1; 21 September 1989, 1. *Scope,* April 1992, 8–9.

3. *Scope,* Spring 1989, 6–11. *Coll,* 9 February 1989, 11; Orientation 1989, 1.

4. *Coll,* 22 February 1990, 1; 29 March 1990, 11; 4 October 1990, 5; 7 February 1991. Edward C. Brown interview, 13 June 1995. *Scope,* Summer 1990, 6–10; December 1990, 6–7; March 1991, cover; July 1991, 8–9. Others who contributed to the poster were Ed Brown, Thomas Marshall III, Jackie Harris, and Keith Tew. O'Boyle, a resident of Matthews and the father of art major Pat O'Boyle, published the poster for the college at cost.

5. *Coll,* 3 October 1991, 2; 13 October 1994, 1, 3. *PK,* 1991, 139. *Scope,* October 1995, 10–11; March 1996, cover, 5–6; Winter 1999–2000, 8–10. *Alumni Directory,* 39.

6. *Scope,* Winter 2000, 8. J. Chris Wilson, e-mail, 20 March 2001. Harlow Z. Head conversation, 26 March 2001. *WDT,* 30 June 1990, 1–2A.

7. *Scope,* September 1994, 13. *Coll,* 25 February 1993, 1, 3; 29 April 1993, 3; 3 March 1994, 1; 12 September 1996, 3; 26 February 1998, 1; 4 March 1999, 1, 8; 5 October 1999, 3; 11 November 1999, Global Focus insert, 1–8. *Cat,* 2001, 65.

8. Jack Claiborne, *The Charlotte Observer,* 13 March 1990.

9. *Coll,* 26 January 1990, 2; 8 February 1990, 1. *The Collegiate* article of 1990 indicated that college leaders had discussed changing the school's name for only fifteen years. Hemby later stated that fifty was the number he had communicated to the newspaper. James B. Hemby Jr. conversation, 19 March 2001.

10. *Coll,* 22 February 1990, 2; 15 March 1990, 1; 29 March 1990, 2. *Scope,* December 1990, 2–5. *PK,* 1990, 86, 97, 121.

11. William R. Batchelor, conversation, 21 October 2000. Members of the committee in addition to Batchelor were trustees Georgia B. Campion, Darwin McCaffity, Marshall Tetterton, and Hubert Westbrook; student representative Hosford; faculty representative Coleman Markham; and President Hemby. *Scope,* December 1990, 2–5. Annual Convocation and Celebration of Naming Program, 6 September 1990. *Coll,* 20 September 1990, 1, 3, 5. Hosford, class of 1991, was a native of Linden, South Africa, and a member of the tennis team. *PK,* 1989, 118, 171.

12. *Coll,* 20 September 1990, 2–5; 15 March 1990, 1; 19 September 1991, 11; 18 December 1991, 2; 30 January 1992, 3.

13. The social work concentration was offered between 1974 and 1990. *Cat,* 1975, 94; 1991, 133–142. *Coll,* 24 October 1996, 1. *Scope,* Winter 1988–89, 12; January 1997, 5. Shingleton was the recipient of an alumni achievement award in education and social work from his alma mater in 1993. *Scope,* September 1993, 6; January 1998, 8; September 1998, 8. Dr. Dean Pierce, chair, commission on accreditation, CSWE, to President James B. Hemby Jr., 30 November 2000. Archives Susan Rentle, e-mail, 6 March 2001.

14. *Cat,* 1998, 148–150; 1999, 155–158, 166; 2001, 166. *Scope,* June 1997, 16–17. Richard Groskin, e-mail, 6 March 2001. Groskin served as associate professor of criminal justice and dean of the school of behavioral sciences.

15. *Scope,* Winter 1989–90, 11, 13; Summer 1990, 12; July 1991, 15; September 1998, 15. At least half of the Rogers grants are awarded to students from Wilson and Greene Counties with the remaining half available to residents from throughout eastern North Carolina. The Mamie Jennings Lucas scholarship is granted to a student majoring in the department of English, modern languages, and communications. The George C. Stronach scholarship is awarded at the discretion of the financial aid office to supplement academic scholarships.

16. *Scope,* December 1991; January 1997, 2–3; September 1998, 10–11.

17. *Coll,* 17 February 1994, 3. *Scope,* March 1996, inside front cover. *Cat,* 2001, 164. The Barton College web page listed W. Kent Wheeless as director of administrative computing and Allard C. Bissette as director of information technology. Also listed were Clint Bowen as assistant director of information technology, two network user support specialists, and one audio-visual network support specialist. www.barton.edu.

18. *Coll,* 17 September 1992, 1; 1 October 1992, 3. Quinn, class of 1959, was a Warsaw businessman. *Scope,* December 1992, cover, 1–7; August 1993, 8–9.

19. *Coll,* 29 February 1996, 1, 7; 14 March 1996, 1.

20. *Coll,* 29 February 1996, 1, 7; 14 March 1996, 1.

21. *WDT,* 22 June 1996, 1A, 4–5A. Kilgore, who taught at the college for sixteen years, became professor emeritus of chemistry upon his retirement in 1996. Purcell retired as professor emeritus of religion and philosophy in 1984. *Cat,* 2001, 169.

22. *WDT,* 22 June 1996, 1A, 4–5A; 14 June 1997, 1A, 4A. *Scope,* January 1997, 2–3.

23. *Scope,* March 1996, 7, 13; June 1997, cover, 1–4. *Coll,* 6 February 1997, 1; 20 February 1997, 1, 8; 13 November 1997, 5. The "A-Team" assisted the admissions staff by welcoming prospective students and their parents.

24. *Scope,* April 1994, 5; January 1997, 2–4.

25. In 1998, Barton added cross-country for men and women. *Scope,* October 1995, 7–8; September 1998, 11. *Coll,* 24 October 1996; 20 February 1997, 6; 8 May 1997, 6–7. *WDT,* 26 April 2001, B1.

26. *Scope,* 29 August 1996, 4. *Cat,* 1996, 170–172; 1997, 162–164.

27. *Coll,* 4 December 1997, 1. *Scope,* January 1998, 12; September 1998, 12A.

28. *Scope,* June 1997, 1–4, 8. *Cat,* 2001, 165. "Bep" Jordan was an educator and Wilson civic leader who taught English literature at Atlantic Christian College.

29. *Barton College Fact Book,* 1999. Darwin W. McCaffity is a dentist in Wendell. Darwin W. McCaffity Jr. is also a graduate of the college, class of 1985. *Scope,* January 1997, 9.

30. *WDT,* 2 March 2001, 1A; 14 April 2001, 1C. Barton Centennial Campaign Case Book, 2001. *Coll,* 26 February 2001, 1; 12 March 2001, 1–2.

31. *Coll,* 24 April 1997, 1, 3; 4 May 2000, 3. *Scope,* January 1998, 13–15; Winter 1999–2000, 1.

32. *Coll,* 4 May 2000, 1, 8. Russell Rawlings was a member of the original centennial committee. Duane Grooms joined the committee in 2001.

33. Ware, *ACC,* 76–78. James B. Hemby Jr. conversation, 30 March 2001. Sheila Milne conversation, 25 May 2001. The twenty-one buildings include the President's Home or Graves House. Records of the Barton College registrar's office and the office of the vice-president for academic affairs. *Cat,* 2001, 8–10, 47, 69–70.

34. James B. Hemby Jr. conversations, 30 March 2001 and 25 May 2001.

35. James B. Hemby Jr. interview, 19 December 1996; conversation, 30 March 2001. Joan Edwards Hemby interview, 12 April 2001. *Coll,* 12 September 1996, 4; 10 October 1996, 3; 21 November 1996, 4; 5 May 1997, 3; 1 October 1998, 4; 4 March 1999, 4; 16 March 2000, 3. *Scope,* January 1997, 11.

36. James B. Hemby Jr. interview, 19 December 1996. Joan Edwards Hemby interview, 12 April 2001.

Notes to Epilogue

1. Laura MacLean, e-mail, 6 April 2001.

2. Tammy Ayscue Smith, Perlita "Pearly" de Leon, Scott Ginn, Martha Hutchinson Rucker, Charray Johnson, Patrick O'Boyle, and Dawn-Marie Singleton, e-mail, forwarded to the author by Laura MacLean. 6–9 April 2001.

Bibliography

Adams, Milton. Interview with author and Edward B. Holloway. 13 March 1992 and 15 December 1999.

Adams, Milton, and Sarah Adams. Conversations with author. 16 June 2000, 11 August 2000, 31 January. 2001.

Adams, Sarah Lofton. Interview with author and Edward B. Holloway. 15 December 1999. Conversation with author. 24 February 2000.

Albert, Ross. Conversations with author, Paul Crouch, and Eugene Purcell Jr. 22–24 May 2000.

Anderson, Walter. "A Church Historian Looks at the Closing of Carolina Christian College." *North Carolina Christian.* Summer 2000, 7.

Annual Convocation and Celebration of Naming Program. 6 September 1990. Barton College Archives.

Athletic Hall of Fame Banquet. 20 October 2000. Barton College Archives.

Athletic Hall of Fame Program, 1983–2000. Barton College Archives.

Barnes, E. M., and Odell Barnes. Interview with author during the filming of *Landmarks: A History of Wilson County,* 1989.

Barton Centennial Campaign Case Book, 2001. Barton College Archives.

Barton College Alumni Directory. White Plains, NY: Bernard C. Harris Publishing Company, Inc., 1999.

Barton College Fact Book, 1998–99. Office of the president, Barton College.

Batchelor, William R. Conversation with author. 21 October 2000.

"Bicycle." *World Book Encyclopedia.* 1973 edition.

Bishop, M. A. Letter to G. S. Alderman. 8 and 21 November 1913. James Y. Joyner Letters. Raleigh: North Carolina State Archives. Copy in Barton College Archives.

Boyer, Paul S., et al. *The Enduring Vision: A History of the American People.* 4th ed. Boston: Houghton Mifflin, 2000.

Brown, Edward C. Interview with author. 13 June 1995.

Brown, Ruby Barnes. Interview with author. 4 June 1996.

Bullard, Roger. Letter to Harold Doster, Thomas J. Hackney Jr., and Naomi Morris. 5 November 1982. Barton College Archives.

Chamblee, Annie Harper. Interview with Joan Edwards Hemby, Edward B. Holloway, and author. 11 January 1995.

Claiborne, Jack. *The Charlotte Observer*. 13 March 1990.

Cockrell, Annie, and Onnie Cockrell. Interview with author and Edward B. Holloway. 14 December 1999.

College Catalog. Atlantic Christian College/Barton College. 1902–01.

The Collegiate. Student newspaper. Atlantic Christian College/Barton College. 1927–2001.

The Collegiate. Yearbook. Atlantic Christian College. 1929–34.

Cooper, William J., and Thomas E. Terrill. *The American South: A History*. 2nd ed. New York: McGraw-Hill, 1996.

Coulter, E. Merton. *College Life in the Old South*. New York: MacMillan, 1928.

Crouch, Paul. Interview with author. 15 June 1995. Conversations with author, Ross Albert, and Eugene Purcell Jr. 22–24 May 2000.

Cummins, D. Duane. *The Disciples Colleges: A History*. St. Louis: CBP Press, 1987.

Daniel, J. Marshall. *Hackney, The History of a Company*. Wilson: Hackney Brothers Body Company, 1979.

Daniels, Josephus. *Tar Heel Editor*. Chapel Hill: University of North Carolina Press, 1939.

Davis, F. Mark. Interview with author. 29 July 1998.

Doster, Harold. "Presidential Precis." 20 September 1982. A publication of the Barton College president's office.

Edmundson, Dixie Barnes. Interview with author. 4 June 1996.

Edmundson, Melissa. Interview with author. 4 June 1996.

The Elm City Elevator. 3 January 1902 and 12 December 1902. Raleigh: North Carolina State Archives.

Ennis, Jackie. Conversation with author. 1 March 2001.

Franklin, Jon. "The 20th Century, Where Were You?" *News and Observer*. 31 December 1999.

Futrell, Ashley, Sr. Interview with author and Russell Rawlings. 25 January 1998.

Gardner, Ava. *Ava: My Story*. New York: Bantam Books, 1990.

Greenville Daily Reflector. 28 September 1964.

Grimes, Terry. Conversation with author. 27 October 2000.

Hackney, Thomas Jennings, Jr. Interview with author and Edward B. Holloway. 19 June 1997.

Hamlin, Charles H. *Educators Present Arms, the Use of the Schools and Colleges as Agents of War Propaganda, 1914-19*. Zebulon, NC: The Record Publishing Company, 1939.

Hamlin, Charles H. Interview with Walter Anderson, Ronald Wachs, and author. 2 September 1976.

Harville, Charlie. *Sports in North Carolina.* Norfolk: The Donning Company, 1977.

Head, Harlow. Conversation with author. 26 March 2001.

Hemby, James B., Jr. Interview with author and Edward B. Holloway. 19 December 1996. Conversations with author. 28 September 2000, 19 March 2001, and 25 May 2001.

Hemby, Joan Edwards. Interview with author. 12 April 2001.

Henderson, Archibald. *The Campus of the First State University.* Chapel Hill: University of North Carolina Press, 1949.

High, Elizabeth Hilley. Interview with author and Edward B. Holloway. 6 July 2000.

Johnson, Mary Lynch. *A History of Meredith College.* Raleigh: Edwards & Broughton, 1956.

Joyner, Bethany Rose, and Doris Kellenbarger Wenger. "Dr. Arthur D. Wenger, Eighth President of Atlantic Christian College, (1956–1977)." Barton College Archives.

Joyner, Gordon. Conversation with author. 12 January 2001.

Kelly, Brooks M. *Yale: A History.* New Haven: Yale University Press, 1974.

Langer, Willliam L. *Encyclopedia of World History.* 4th edition. Boston: Houghton Mifflin Company, 1968.

Lemmon, Sarah M. *North Carolina's Role in the First World War.* Raleigh: North Carolina Division of Archives and History, 1975.

Levinson, David, and Karen Christensen, eds. *Encyclopedia of World Sport.* 3 vols. Santa Barbara: ABC-CLIO, 1996.

Lewis, Milton H. "The History of Football at Atlantic Christian College." 1949. Barton College Archives.

Link, William A. *William Friday, Power, Purpose and American Higher Education.* Chapel Hill: University of North Carolina Press, 1995.

Lucas, John A., and Ronald A. Smith. *Saga of American Sport.* Philadelphia: Lea & Febiger, 1978.

Lucas, Mamie Jennings. Interview with author, Milton Adams, and Edward B. Holloway. 27 May 1992.

Marshall, Thomas E., III. Unsent letter to "Dear Dad and Mom." 26 February 1976. Copy in Barton College Archives.

Marshall, Thomas E., III. Interview with Edward B. Holloway and author. 5 June 1996. Conversation with author. 1 December 2000.

McKinney, Roberta Worthington. "Journal of Journeys: Down Memory Lane, 1888-1987." Original manuscript in possession of McKinney heirs; copy in Barton College Archives.

Milne, Sheila J. Conversation with author. 25 May 2001.

Morris, Richard B. *Encyclopedia of American History.* Rev. ed. New York: Harper & Row, 1965.

Moss, George D. *Moving On, The American People Since 1945.* Englewood Cliffs, NJ: Prentice Hall, 1994.

Murray, Robert K. *Red Scare: A Study of National Hysteria, 1914–1920.* New York: McGraw-Hill, 1964.

Nault, William H., ed. *World Book of America's Presidents: Portraits of the Presidents.* 2 vols. Chicago: World Book Encyclopedia, 1982.

News and Observer. Raleigh, North Carolina. 15 July 1964, 15 August 1964, 29 November 1964, 20 October 1965, 24 October 1965, 11 July 1966.

North Carolina Christian. Disciples of Christ monthly newspaper. 1920–2001.

North Carolina Christian Missionary Convention. Minutes. 8–21 November 1912 and 2–5 November 1914.

North Carolina Christian Missionary Committee. Minutes of the 73rd Session. November 1917.

North State Conference Tournament Official Program, 1955. Barton College Archives.

O'Neill, William L. *Coming Apart, An Informal History in the 1960's.* Chicago: Quadrangle Books, 1971.

Parker, Teresa. Conversation with author. 1 March 2001.

Paschal, George W. *History of Wake Forest College.* 3 vols. Raleigh: Edwards & Broughton, 1935–1943.

Pierce, Dean. Letter to James B. Hemby Jr. 30 November 2000. Barton College Archives.

Pine Knot, yearbook, Atlantic Christian College/Barton College, 1910–1994.

Plyler, B. B., Jr. Conversation with author. 14 January 1999.

Powell, William S. *North Carolina Through Four Centuries.* Chapel Hill: University of North Carolina Press, 1989.

Proceedings of the North Carolina Christian Missionary Convention. 30 October–2 November 1911, 3–6 November 1913, 2–5 November 1914.

Purcell, Eugene, Jr. Interview with Edward B. Holloway and author. 20 June 1995. Conversations with author, Ross Albert, and Paul Crouch. 22–24 May 2000.

The Radiant. Student quarterly magazine. Atlantic Christian College. 1908–20.

Rogers, Dennis. "Art Wenger Puts His Mark on Atlantic Christian College." *News and Observer.* 4 April 1977.

Rosenberg, Norman L., and Emily S. *In Our Times, America Since World War II.* 5th ed. Englewood Cliffs, N.J.: Prentice Hall, 1995.

Scope. College magazine. Atlantic Christian College/Barton College. 1978–2000.

Shackleford, Ruby Paschall. Interview with author. 21 January 2000.

Smiley, Wendell. "The North Carolina Press Views the Ku Klux Klan from 1964 through 1966." Greenville, North Carolina. Undated copies of newspaper articles in author's possession.

Sudor, Stephen. "One Hundred Year History of Ayden Christian Church (Disciples of Christ) 1893–1993." Barton College Archives.

Thigpen, Lula Hackney Ruffin "Hack." Interview with Edward B. Holloway and author. 2 June 1997.

The Torchlight. Student publication. Atlantic Christian College. 1943–47.

Bibliography

Tyndall, Jesse Paul. Interview with Edward B. Holloway and author. 23 January 1996 and 26 January 1996.

Vick, Blessin Thorne. Conversation with author. 24 August 2000.

Ward, Sarah Bain. Interview with Walter Anderson. 27 November 1984.

Ward, Sarah Bain. Interviews with author and Edward B. Holloway. 17 June 1993 and 24 June 1995.

Ware, Charles C. *A History of Atlantic Christian College.* Wilson, N.C.: Atlantic Christian College, 1956.

The Watch Tower. Christian Church, Disciples of Christ in North Carolina publication. October 1872–20 July 1927.

Wenger, Arthur D. Conversation with author. Spring, 1974.

Wenger, Doris K. Interview with author and Edward B. Holloway. 12 December 2000.

Wilson County Register of Deeds. Deed Book, Vol. 111, 536.

Wilson Daily Times, 28 April 1936–14 April 2001.

Wright, John D., Jr. *Transylvania: Tutor to the West.* Lexington, KY: Transylvania University Press, 1975.

www.barton.edu

www.marie.com/asp/history.asp?action=process

Index

Note: Page numbers followed by "f" indicate illustrations.

A-1 Club (cheerleaders), 97
A Club, 139
A-Team, 327, 407n 23
Abbott, Jim, 253–55, 266
Abeyounis, Greg, 328, 330
Academic All-Americans, 346
Accreditation
 of college, 205–6, 226, 269, 285–86, 311–12
 of nursing program, 267–68, 295
 of social work program, 322
 of teachers' program, 239, 312
The Acorn, 41
Adams, Alice, 324
Adams, Dale, 281, 284
Adams, Ivan, 182
Adams, J. H., 76, 77–78
Adams, Joan. *See* Jones, Joan Adams
Adams, Milton, 133, 134, 138, 187, 217f, 273, 274f
 as acting president, 273–75
 as athletic director, 216
 on Ava Gardner, 165
 on basketball team, 199
 on food service problems, 180
 leaving college, 297
 on parking problems, 283
 as vice-president, 277
 on weight lifting tournament, 216–17
 on Wenger, 272–73
Adams, Sarah Loftin, 132–33, 180, 274f, 275
Adams, William Dennis, 53

Addams, Jane, 113
Adkins, David, 260, 264, 273, 288, 312
Administrative officers, list of, 354–70
Advising program, 302–3
African Americans
 acceptance to college, 241–44, 243f, 290–93, 292f, 395n 32
 on athletic teams, 220–22, 243–45
 as basketball spectators, 222–23
 as college speakers, 152
 on college staff and faculty, 152–53, 290–91
 as Disciples of Christ members, 241
 organizations of, 291
Afro-American Awareness Society, 291
Albert, Ross, 243, 265, 266, 279
Albert, Thomas R., 280
Alcohol use, 251, 254–56
Alderman, Ruth, 9
Aldridge, Carroll, 258–59
Aldridge, Jay, 265, 289f
Alethian Society, 27, 55, 125, 131, 149
Alexander, David L., 295
All-America Selections, 346
Allan R. Sharp Religion in Life Lectures, 279
Allison, John A., IV, 324
Almond, Brad, 305
Almond, Dale, 297, 309, 328
Alpha Kappa Alpha sorority, 291
Alpha Phi Alpha fraternity, 291
Alpha Sigma Phi fraternity, 210, 214
Alumni Achievement Award, 340–41
Alumni Association, 114, 130

415

Alumni Honor Roll, 135
Alumnus of the Year Award, 339
Alvarez, Andres, 289, 289f
Ambulance, Wilson Sanitorium, 117
American Association of University Professors, 237
American Bankers Association, 38
American Bar Association, 38
American Council on Education Fellows Program, 299
American Cycle Company of New York City, 17
American Federation of Labor, 38
American Federation of Teachers, 38
American Legion Post, named for Robert Anderson, 70
American Red Cross, students involved in, during World War I, 66–67, 69
American Studies program, 305, 403n 24
Amerson, George "Red," 141
Andborn, Annika, 314
Anderson, James B., 90
Anderson, Miss (teacher), 9
Anderson, Robert B, 69–70
Anderson, Walter W., Jr., 27, 314
Andrews, Barbara, 303
Andrews, Eunice, 87
Anniversaries
 10th, 45
 25th, 113–14
 35th, 143
 50th, 193–94
 80th, 294–95, 402n 2
 95th, 329
Anthony, Marc, 100–101, 123
Anti-tobacco Club of Atlantic Christian College, 38
Antone, Kay. *See* Mitchell, Kay Antone
Applewhite, Jonathan, 2
ARA-Slater Food Service, 232, 306
Arabic (ship), 49–50
Arcade Beauty Shop, 146
Archie, William A., 215
Arline, Elizabeth House Hughey, 294
Armstrong, Louis, 242
Armstrong, Neil, 249
Arnberg, Christine, 10
Arnold, D. W., 4

Arnold, Russell, 187, 199, 209, 226, 240, 265
Art festivals, 265–66
Art museum, 238
Arthur D. Wenger Memorial Fund, 273
Athletic Association, 89, 98
Athletic Council, 263, 398n 33
Athletic Hall of Fame, 290, 347–49
Athletics, 82–102. *See also specific sports and teams*
 vs. academics, 89
 black athletes in, 242–45
 dangers of, 85–86
 facilities for, 296
 first director for, 98
 foreign students in, 314–15
 importance of, 101–2
 intramural, 134, 218
 newspaper coverage of, gender differences in, 262–63, 398n 32
 in 1983-1984, 312–15, 313f, 405n 42
 in 1950s, 197–201, 216–22, 217f
 in 1990s, 327–28, 407n 25
 non-student participation in, 85
 scholarships for, 147
 student fee for, 89
 Victorian attitude toward, 85
 women's. *See* Women's athletics
 after World War I, 93–94
 in World War I, 91
 after World War II, 174–77
 in World War II, 170
Athletics Committee, 263, 398n 33
Attlerud, Dan, 289f
Awards. *See also* Honorary degrees
 All-America Selections, 346
 Alumni Achievement Award, 340–41
 Alumnus of the Year, 339
 Athletic Hall of Fame, 290, 347–49
 Coggins Cup, 80
 Denny Cup, 114
 Duchess Trophy, 192
 Flame of Truth, 309, 404n 33
 Gene Purvis, 404n 39
 Hilley Cup, 80, 344
 Jefferson Pilot faculty member of the year, 318, 345
 Kiwanis Award For Outstanding Female Athlete, 291

Index 417

  most valuable player, 175
  Oettinger prize, 110
  Rotary Club cup, 114
  at twenty-fifth anniversary, 114
  William Gear Spencer Sportsmanship
    Award, 291
Aycock, Charles Brantley, 1
Aycock, Eunice, 115f
Aycock, Jack, 133
Aycock, Mahlon, 245
Ayscue, Tammy. *See* Smith, Tammy Ayscue
Azalea Festival, 202

Bagby, Richard, 52
Bailes, Todd, 328
Bailey, Marie, 91
Ballance, Mary, 291, 293
Bane, Archer "Art," 306, 405n 42
Bane, Susan Maxwell, 305–6, 314
Banks, Clem, 114
Banks, James B., 166, 167f
Banks, Neva, 131
Baptist Student Union, 214
Barclay, John, 108–10, 109f, 132
  at 1927 commencement, 114
  at 1940 commencement, 158
  at cornerstone ceremony, 121–22
  as football coach, 98
  at Frances Harper funeral, 158
  international focus of, 154
  interracial activities of, 151
  leaving Wilson, 164
  on North Carolina Commission on
    Interracial Cooperation, 152
  on peace, 155–56
  Thanksgiving address of, 123
Bardin, Ben, 226
Barham, E. L., 59
Barker-Ferguson Scholarships, 323
Barnes, Annie Morris, 202
Barnes, Dixie, 131, 384n 23
Barnes, Eugene, 177, 179, 189, 202
Barnes, Mrs. Jack, 125
Barnes, Ruby, 143, 287, 384n 23
Barnes, Tom, 264
Barnhill, Edna, 142
Barriteau, Tony, 264
Barrow, Larry, 245

Barton, Harry, 301
Barton—Wilson Symphony, 331
Barton Art Museum, 238
"Barton bunch or gang," 336
Barton Museum, 332
Barton Theatre, 331
Baseball
  in early 20th century, 84–85
  funding for, 98
  on high school level, 84
  in 1908, 82
  in 1909, 83–84, 84f
  in 1911, 86
  in 1912, 87
  in 1918, 90–91
  in 1946, 174, 388n 25
  in 1952, 198, 391n 30
  in 1954-1958, 215
  in 1970s, 264–65
  in 1984, 313
  plans for, 83
  support for, 86
Basketball
  black athletes in, 243–45
  at Charles L. Coon High School, 135
  funding for, 98
  in 1911, 86
  in 1912, 87
  in 1914, 87, 90
  in 1916-1917, 90
  in 1918, 91
  in 1920-1921, 94f
  in 1934, 140–41
  in 1935, 146
  in 1938-1939, 148–49
  in 1940-1941, 161–62
  in 1950s, 197–201, 201f, 220–23, 221f,
    391n 29
  in 1960s, 244–45
  in 1985-1986, 313, 405n 42
  in 1996-1997, 327
  origin of, 86
  women's, 82, 83, 86–89, 88f, 91, 98, 101,
    260–62, 261f, 289–90, 314
Basnight, J. S., 4
Batchelor, William R., 246, 280, 321
Batten, William M., 404n 33
Battle, Richard, 264, 291

Batts, Lisa Boykin, 281, 282, 297
Bayh, Birch, 235
Bazemore, Victoria Louise, 290
Bazzle, Edward F., 290
BB&T, 324
Beacham, Bill, 198
Beasley, Mary Alice, 178f, 179
Bedgood, Charles "Buddy," 294, 326
Belk Building, on site of early basketball court, 88
Belk-Tyler Stores, 402n 2
Bell, George, 292, 293
Bellin, Leon, 240
Ben Kori, Abdullah, 9
Benevolent Association, 79
Benevolent Homes of Disciples, 105
Bennett, Dick, 273
Bennett, Robert, 231
Benson, John L., 327
Bentonville Battleground, Harper homestead on, 22
Bert Clarence Hardy Dining Hall. *See* Hardy Dining Hall
Bethune, John J., 328–29
Bicycles, 17–18, 317
Biedenbach, Eddie, 245
Bill's Quick Lunch, 146
Bird, M. J. "Red," 174, 176
Bishop, James, 211
Bishop, M. A., 89
Bissette, Allard C., 406n 17
Bissette's Drug Store, 133, 146
Black, Clifton, 244–45, 264
Black Students Awareness Association, 291
Black Thursday (24 October 1919), 123
The Blackboard, 41
Blackburn, Casey L., 94–96
Blacks. *See* African-Americans; Racial issues
Blake, Howard E., 168, 312
Blake, Paul, III, 311
Blomgren, Soren, 289f
Blunk, James B., 193
Board of Trustees, 350–53
Bockert, Lowell, 405n 42
Bogart, Humphrey, 165
Bohunk student union, 209
Bohunkus/Bo-Hun-Kus trophy, 147–48, 147f, 156, 176, 215

Bolt, John, 402n 2
Bonclarken retreat, 132
Bond, Julian, 266
Boone, Ed, 405n 42
Borden, Kevin, 405n 42
Borman, Frank, 404n 33
Bostick, Janie, 279
Boswell, Anderson, 116
Boswell, Ethel Thorne, 387n 6
Boswell, Maude, 133
Bottoms, Kathryn, 303
Bottoms, Mary Beth, 261
Bowden, Basil, 157
Bowen, Carrie, 34
Bowen, Clint, 406n 17
Bowen, Maude, 53
Bowen, Mike, 309
Boxing, 136, 148, 149f, 385n 8
Boy Scouts of America, Hamlin recognition by, 150
Boyd, Tyra, 289–90
Boykin, Edna Earle, 324
Boykin, Edna Long. *See* Johnston, Edna
Boykin, James, Jr., 215, 264
Boykin, Lisa. *See* Batts, Lisa Boykin
Boys' Dormitory. *See* Caldwell Hall
Bracknell, Keith, 281
Bradley, Sidney, 114
Brame, Jamie, 269
Branch, Al, 90
Branch Bank, 165
Braxton, H. Galt, 121, 194, 390n 21
Brewer, Georgia, 132–33
Brewer, Mary, 132–33
Bridgers, Ben, 317–18
Briggs Hotel, 73, 180
Brinson, Elizabeth, 129
Brinson, Jack, 129
Brinson, Kate, 380n 30
Brinson, Lee E., 193
Brinson, Maria, 133
Brinson, Marion B., 80–81
  campus activities of, 96–97, 380n 30
  as cheerleader, 90
  on football team, 95, 96, 100
  on importance of athletics, 102
  as *The Pine Knot* athletics editor, 91
  as Sunday school superintendent, 72
  at twenty-fifth anniversary, 114

Index

Brinson, Zeb, 96, 100, 131
Brook, "Tiny," 56
Brooks, Madeline, 169
Broughton, Harmon W. "Red," 176
Brown, Ed, 226, 265, 317, 327, 405n 4
Brown, Helen, 327
Brown, Ruby Barnes, 143, 287, 384n 23
Brown, Thelma, 243
Brown, Walter L., Jr., 309–10, 320, 321f, 329, 329f
Brown v. Board of Education, 154, 220
Browning, Elizabeth Barrett, 37
Bruce Lamm Men's Shop, 134
Brugh, Tom, 335
Bruton, J. F., 2, 48
Bryan, Needham, 125
Bryan, William Jennings, 35
Bryant, Donahue, 142
Bryant, Esther, 115–16
Buchanan, Kim, 200, 391n 39
Buckner, George Walter, 195
Bullard, Roger, 265, 271, 288, 296, 297, 335
Bulldog Club Drive, 294
"Bulldogs." *See also specific sports*
　new name for, 197
　selection as athletic team name, 100
Bullock, Jackie, 161, 387n 39
Bundy, Judy Rose, 246
Bundy, Sam, Jr., 246
Bunn, Cinny, 327
Bunn, Turner, III, 327
Burke, Edmund, 235
Burks, Gloria, 314
Burt, Millard, 143, 202, 204, 212, 215
Burton, Mary E. "Beth," 305
Burton, Richard, 165
Bus service, 132, 132f, 199
Bussell, Jim, 246–47
Bynum, Rhonda, 314
Byrd, Charles M., 161, 387n 39
Byrd, Richard E., 155

C. H. Hamlin Student Center, 110
Caldwell, Elizabeth Settle, 28, 47, 50
Caldwell, Jesse Cobb, 51f
　academic strengthening by, 58
　African-Americans employed by, 152
　appearance of, 46
　appointment of, 31
　at baccalaureate of 1912, 50
　biography of, 28
　as "Bishop of the Carolinas," 49
　Caldwell Hall named for, 48
　called to presidency, 27–28, 30
　campus-town relations and, 52
　church growth efforts of, 49
　college indebtedness and, 47–48
　at commencement of 1910, 40
　contributions of, 63
　as dean, 28–29, 32
　on endowment fund-raising, 47–48, 51–52
　family of, 46–47
　Jennings on, 45–46
　Leighton on, 79
　in Men and Millions Movement, 378n 19
　multiple roles of, 59
　on Outlaw remarks on Smith's views, 65
　pilgrimage to Palestine, 49–50, 111
　preparatory program changes under, 58
　resignation of, 60–61
　salary of, 47
　as student literary supporter, 32
　at Valentine's Day of 1913, 55
　yearbook of 1916 dedicated to, 61
　yearbook poem mentioning, 59
Caldwell, Mary Settle, 28, 46–47, 50, 56, 60–61
Caldwell, Mildred, 47
Caldwell Hall, 55f, 143, 164
　closing of, 284
　naming of, 48
　renovation of, 195
　servicemen entertainment in, 171
　social events in, 54–55
　television for, 203
Camp, Bryant, 320
Campaign for Barton College: Enriching the Tradition, 324, 326, 328
"Campaign for Excellence," 309–10
Campion, Georgia Brewer, 307, 406n 11
Campus Awareness Committee, 219–20, 235
　Vietnam War opposition by, 251–52, 252f, 396n 8

Campus Christian Association, 213, 214, 278–79
    on drug use, 250
    on meditation center, 268
Campus Ministerial Association, 214
"Cannon Ball" and "Cannon Ball, Jr.", 153
Capps, Doris, 187, 226, 312
Capps, Robert, 187, 218, 226, 322
Carawan, Guy, 90
Carawan, Lottie, 125
Carawan, Roy, 90
Carlyle, Thomas, 39
Carolina Christian College, 1–2
Carolina Discipliana Collection, 22–23, 270, 285
"Carolina Enlargement Campaign," 71, 105–6
The Carolina Evangel, creation of, 27
Carolina Publishing Company, 77
Carolinas-Virginia Athletic Conference, 327
Carr, Robert, 142, 294
Carraway, Ed, 244–45, 396n 40
Carter, Jimmy, 281
Case, Everett, 197, 200
Case, Mable Catherine, 110, 114
Case, Perry, 68, 108, 110, 145, 158, 186, 194, 204, 238, 385n 1, 390n 22
Case Art Building, 110, 238
Casey, Ben, 247–48, 396n 46
Cave, Sanquinetti, 291
"The Centennial Campaign of Barton College," 329–30, 333, 407n 32
Central Lunch, 146
Centura Bank, 324
Century Club, 200
Chalk, Brian, 264
Chamber of Commerce Day, 202–3
Chamblee, Annie Harper, 374n 13
Champion, Roy L., 403n 15
Chapel. *See* Howard Chapel
Chapin, Howard, 167, 176, 312, 404n 39
Chapin, Mary Alice Beasley, 312, 404n 39
Chapman, Doren, 405n 42
Charles, Gladys, 137, 141, 385n44
Charles L. Coon High School, basketball at, 90, 135
Cheating problems, 139

Cheerleading, 90, 97
Cherry, Hugh, 127, 143
Cherry, Susan, 261
Cherry Hotel, 180, 189
Chestnutt, Willa, 56
Christian Endeavor, 8
Christian Service Workshop, 214
Christian Vocations Conference, 213
Christmas
    1929, 124
    1940, 162
    1977, 275
Church, Carl N., 192
Circle K, 278–79
Civil rights. *See* Racial issues
Civil War, Bentonville Battleground, 22
Claridge, Frederick, 264, 273
Clark, Bob, 181–82, 189
Clark, Jay, 197–98
Cleveland, David, 273
Cloyd, Ann, 199, 227, 394n 3
Cloyd, Edward L., Jr., 187, 199, 216, 217f, 226, 264, 294, 313, 327
Cloyd, Edward L., Sr., 262
Clubs, 211–12, 231, 278–79
Co-operative Association, 138–39
Coastal Plain law enforcement training program, 322
Cobb, James, 265
Cobb, Joann Thomas, 246
Cockrell, Onnie, 127, 134, 383n 13
Coefield, Otis, 273, 297
Coggins, James C., 330–31
    accepting presidency, 6
    fund-raising efforts of, 15
    on Harper as successor, 20
    honorary degrees granted by, 390n 21
    on male student accommodations, 12
    presidency offered to, 4–5, 5f
    problems faced by, 19
    resignation of, 19
    on Smith controversy, 76
    on status in July 1903, 16
    welcoming first student body, 7
Coggins Cup, 80, 342–43
Coghill, Marvin, 324
Coker, Gordon E. "Sam," 216
Cole, Glen G., 19, 76

Index

Coleman, Rob, 268
College Beauty Salon, 270
College Building. *See* Kinsey Hall
College Class Day (1927), 114
College success program, 302–3
The Collegiate
   demise of, 172
   foundation for, 44
   national recognition of, 156, 164
   yearbook vs. student paper, 382n 1
Collins, Robert "Tarzan," 210, 211
Colombo, Vincent, 167, 168, 174, 176
Commencements. *See* Graduations
Communications programs, 304–5, 323–24, 406n 17
Communism, accusations concerning, 235–37
Commuting students, 116–17, 131–32, 132f, 283
Computers, 308, 323–24, 406n 17
   first installation of, 270
   laboratory for, 286–87
   for record keeping, 286–87
Conference of Student Body Presidents, 218
Connor, Henry Groves, 2
Constructive State Work in South Carolina, fund-raising for, 105
Continuing education, 303
Convocation Coordinating Council, 250
Cooke, Al, 397n 8
Cooley, Harold D., 218
Coolidge, Calvin, 103
Coon, Charles L., 113, 120
Cooper, Jerry, 314
Corbett, Tim, 254
Corbett Tract, purchase of, 216
Core curriculum, 302, 324–25
Corey, Stephen A., 158
Cory, A. E., 121
Cotton, as payment method, 126
Council of Education of the Deaf, 286
Council of Social Work Education, 322
Covington, Bob, 244, 245
Coward, Gertrude Hooker, 14, 120
Cozart, S. M. "Zeke," 227, 327
Creasy, James V., Jr., 164
Criminal justice major, 322
Cross-country team, 215–16

Crouch, Paul, 190–92, 203, 243, 265, 279, 280
Crucible
   creation of, 240–41
   foundation for, 44
Crump, William, 258
Crumpler, G. Hinton "Crump," 82
Crumpler, Jo Ann, 202
Cuban missile crisis, 229
Cummings, Duane, 403n 15
Cummings, Steve, 283
Cuthrell, George F., 118, 121, 203
Cutlip, Randall B., 212

D. D. Club, 97
The Daily Times, 53
Daly, Richard, 247
Dancing
   before basketball game, 140–41
   classes for, 202
   opinions on, 139–42
   permission for, 179–80, 189
   sponsored by Greek organizations, 210
   Twist, 231
Daniel, Jessie, 273
Daniel, Robert, 279
Daniell, James D., 187, 273
Daniels, Jack, 147
Daniels, Josephus, 1, 120
   on baseball team, 84
   biography of, 40
   at commencement of 1910, 40–41
Darden High School
   Barclay visits to, 110
   glee club of, 151
Daughety, Kathy, 328, 330, 336
Daughety, Morgan, 336
Davidson, Brenda, 273
Davis, Christine Whitley, 131
Davis, Henry "Hank," 176
Davis, Lossie, 36–38, 39f
Davis, Mark, 277, 295, 297, 299, 302, 403n 15
   on accreditation, 311
   on honors council, 303–4
   on strategic plan, 325
Davis, Susan. *See* Myers, Susan Davis
Dawson, Amos C., Jr., 133–34, 203, 384n 27
de Leon, Perlita "Pearly," 317, 336, 407n 2
Dean, Edie, 295

Deans, Clyde, 169
Deans, Marie, 273
Deans, Mary Hunter, 87
Debating, 56, 131, 149–50
"Decade of Development," 295
Deems, Charles Force, 1
Defense Committee, 171
Delta Sigma Phi fraternity, 210
Delta Sigma sorority, 209
Delta Sigma Theta sorority, 291
Demosthenian Society, 27, 55–57
Dempsey, Margaret, 324
Denny Brothers Jewelers, 80
Denny Cup, 114
Denny's Credit Jewelers, 146
Depression, 123–56
Desegregation. See Racial issues
"A Design for Excellence," 301, 304, 309, 403n 22
Development council, 297, 203n 11
Diamond, Willie, 288
Dickerman, Morgan, 324
Dickey, James, 266
Dickinson, E. T., 117
Dick's Hot Dog Place, 146
Dining hall. See Hardy Dining Hall
Disciples Benevolent Association, 79
Disciples of Christ. See also North Carolina Christian Missionary Convention
  African-Americans in, 241
  Carolina Christian College, 1–2
  convention of 1907, 65
  convention of 1919, 71
  convention of 1925, 118
  critical time for, in early 20th century, 47–48
  Depression impact on, 126
  on desegregation, 241
  early support by, 6–7
  Inter-church Movement and, 77–78
  Kinsey Seminary, 1–4
  lack of financial support from, 61
  membership campaign for, 105
  membership growth in, 49
  missionaries of, 112–13
  officials of, in Lindley inauguration, 189–90
  Women's Board of Missions, 27

Disciples Yearbook (1897), 2
Dixie Tournament (debating), 150
Dixon, Billy, 244–45, 260
Dodo-Bio Club, 170
Dolman, David, 312
Dooms, Vincent, 313
Doris Holsworth Memorial Fund, 240
Dorsey, Tommy, 210
Doster, Deborah, 275
Doster, Denise, 275
Doster, Diana, 275
Doster, Donald, 275
Doster, Harold C., 276f
  on athletic complex, 294
  biography of, 275
  on curriculum revision, 302
  on "Decade of Development," 295
  development council and, 297, 203n 11
  expansion under, 296
  faculty retrenchment and, 296–97
  goals of, 276
  inauguration of, 275–76
  Irvine practical joke on, 298–99
  on nursing program, 287
  personnel changes under, 297
  "Precis" newsletter of, 402n 7
  resignation of, 297–98
  selection as president, 275
  on tennis team, 289
Doster, June Marken, 275
Drama, 280. See also Stage and Script; Theater
Drinking alcohol, 251, 254–56
Driver, Lalah, 131
Drug abuse, 229, 249–51
Duchess Trophy, 192
Duckworth, William, 265
Dudley, Harold J., 180
Duff, Howard, 165
Duke University, Oriental Seashore Summer School, 111
Dunn, John, 187, 199, 226
Dunn, Roy, 101
Dunn, Ruth, 273
Durham, Ralph, 281, 282

E. G. Purcell Jr. Bible Conference, 279
Eagles, Dorothy, 186, 226

Eagles, Kathleen, 169
East, John, 235
Eddy, Sherwood, 156
Edmonston, Martha, 125
Edmundson, Dixie Barnes, 131, 384n 23
Edmundson, Haywood, 2
Edmundson, John, 131–32
Edmundson, Melissa, 384n 23
Edward L. Cloyd Sr. Award, 262
Edwards, Gary, 313
Edwards, Joan. *See* Hemby, Joan E.
Edwards, Roberta "Bobbie," 292, 292f, 293
Eggers, Ron, 311
Eisenhower, Dwight D., 205, 218–19, 236
Eisenhower, Milton, 236
Elizabeth "Bep" Jordan English Chair, 329, 407n 28
Elizabeth Faye Brinson Memorial Scholarship, 129
Elizabeth Jordan Lecture Series, 331–32
Em-Jay Sporting Goods Company, 146
Emergency Peace Campaign, 155
Endowment
    Caldwell efforts on, 47–48, 51–52
    Hines gift for, 124–25
    in 1916, 70
    in 1982, 295
    in 1990s, 328
    student leader support of, 51–52
    Thomas J. Hackney, Jr., fund for, 309
Ennis, Jackie Strum, 312
Enriching the Tradition campaign, 324, 326, 328
Enrollment
    in 1902-1903, 7
    in 1903-1904, 18
    in 1904-1905, 24
    in 1905-1906, 25
    in 1908, 31
    in 1912, 51
    in 1915, 60
    in 1918-1921, 67–68, 104–5, 184
    in 1927-1928, 108
    in 1929, 129
    in 1932-1937, 131, 145
    in 1938, 172
    in 1939, 157
    in 1940-1945, 159, 172–73
    in 1945-1949, 173–74, 184, 388n 23
    in 1955, 202
    in 1956-1960, 212
    in 1960s, 226, 238, 246
    in 1970s, 269–70
    in 1981-1982, 295, 296
    in 2001, 331
Entrance to college, construction of, 307–8
Epps, Sonya, 316
Equal Rights Amendment, 258
Eriksson, Krister, 313f
Etheridge, Norman "Tweetie," 205, 208–9, 208f, 231, 256, 270
Eureka Plan, 137
Evans, Princie King, 294, 306
Evans, Sarah, 324
Evening college program, 195, 202

Faculty. *See also specific individuals*
    club for, 111
    endowed chairs, 328–29
    evaluation of, 266–67
    list of, 354–70
    payment of, 144, 206
    scholarly activities of, 287–88
Faculty Athletic Committee, 98
Faculty Cup (Coggins Cup), 80, 342–43
Faculty Woman's Club, 227, 298, 394n 3
Fahling, Patti, 280
Faison (janitor), 153
Farish, Hayes, 36, 69
Farm, purchase and sale of, 71–72, 72f, 117
Farmer, C. M., 89, 90
Farmer, J. B., 69–70
Farmer, Julia Estelle, 39–40, 39f
Farnell, Leland B., Jr., 163
Fautz, Ronald, 330
Federal Emergency Relief Administration grant, for gymnasium, 135
Federal Public Housing Authority, 174
Federal Works Agency, 174
Federation and Inter-church Movement, 77–79
The Fellowship, 125
Fellowships, Hackney funds for, 309
Feminism. *See* Women's rights
Ferguson, Debra, 323

Ferguson, Eddie, 323
Fern, Gilbert, 89
Ferrell, Gilbert, 197–98
Festivals of Contemporary Arts, 265–66
Finklea, George C. "Chuck," 329
First Union Bank, 324
Flame of Truth Award, 309, 404n 33
Fleming, Ola, 186, 394n 3
Flu epidemic of 1918, 70
Folger Shakespeare Library, 266
Food service. *See also* Hardy Dining Hall
  cafeteria service in, 180–81, 232
  dissatisfaction with, 180, 232, 283
  in Great Depression, 128
  student workers in, 137
  in Wilson restaurants, 146
Football
  brutality of, 85–86
  enthusiasm for, 86, 92–93
  funding for, 98
  importance of, 101–2
  in 1920-1921, 94–96, 96f
  in 1921-1922, 97
  in 1923-1926, 98–99
  in 1928, 101
  in 1929, 123
  in 1930, 101
  in 1946-1950, 174–76
  touch, 197
Forbes, Beth, 280
Ford, Brenda, 291
Ford, Henry, 112, 116
Ford Foundation grants, 206
Foreign language club, 285
Forum Techniques, 151
Founders' Day
  1927, 114
  1956, 207
  1982, 294
  2000, 330
  2001, 330
  2002, 330
Fountain, L. H., 276
Fox, James, 176
Foy, Ted, C., 290
Fraternities, 209–12
  Alpha Phi Alpha, 291
  Alpha Sigma Phi, 210, 214

Delta Sigma Phi, 210
  in intramural sports, 218
  Phi Delta Alpha, 162
  Phi Delta Gamma, 209, 210
  Phi Kappa Alpha, 116, 209, 210
  Sigma Alpha, 116, 209, 210
  Sigma Phi, 210
  Sigma Phi Epsilon, 210, 211
  Sigma Rho Phi, 209, 210
  women visitation rights in, 255, 397n 15
Frazier, Robert C., 194, 226, 311
Freeman, Samuel F., Jr., 129, 131, 206
French, Ruth, 111
Friday, William C., 299, 300, 309
Friends of the Barton College Library, 331
Fulghum, James "Rabbit," 199, 245
Fulghum, Monroe, 101, 114
Fund-raising. *See also* Endowment
  for bonded debt (1906), 27
  for Caldwell Holy Land trip, 49
  "Campaign for Excellence," 309–10
  for capital in 1992, 324
  "Carolina Enlargement Campaign," 105–6
  "The Centennial Campaign of Barton College," 329–30, 333, 407n 32
  "A Design for Excellence" program, 301, 304, 403n 22
  by Disciples of Christ, 105–6
  in early years, 14–15, 19
  Enriching the Tradition, 324, 326, 328
  for expansion in late 1920s, 119–20, 382n 38 & 39
  for expansion in 1960s, 226–27
  for Hardy Hall renovation, 306–7
  for Kinsey Hall furnishing (1902), 7
  for men's dormitory (1903), 12
  for student loans (1905), 25
  for student union, 239
  after World War I, 70–71
Funk, Robert W., 213
Fussell, Aaron, 312, 404n 39
Futrell, Ashley, Sr., 128

"G. I. Barracks," 174
Gable, Clark, 165

Gantt, Harvey, 241
Gardner, Ava, 160, 161f, 164–66, 387n 6
Garner, Claude, Jr., 166, 167f
Garner, Leon, 91
Garson, B. G., 111
Gavin, Robert L., 219
Gay, Andy, 266–67
Gaylord, Catherine, 273
Gender issues. *See also* Women's rights
   in athletics, 259–63, 261f, 327, 397n 27
      & 30, 398n 32
   in 1902, 10–12
   in 1960s, 230–32
General Assembly, sectarian school funding
   and, 2
George, H. H., 150
George, King of England, 125
George, Suzanne, 289
Gilmore, Bobby, 244–45, 396n 40
Gilmore, Gary Mark, 281
Ginn, Scott, 336, 407n 2
Girls' Athletic Association, 35
Glee club, 125
Glenn Miller Band, 210
Global Focus program, 316–19, 318f
Global issues. *See* International focus;
   Travel courses and programs
Godwin, Helen, 143
Godwin, Nona, 115f
Godwin, William Troy, 176
Goff, John, Jr., 182
Gold, Pleasant D., 2
Golden Knot Honor Society
   creation of, 139
   dance sponsored by, 180
   in World War II, 171–72
Goldwater, Barry, 218, 219
Golf team, 215–16, 264, 312
Goodwin, Ann Jennings, 323
Goodwin, Mary Ellen, 306
Gowda, Jagadish, 313f
Graduations
   1903, 15
   1905, 24
   1910, 39–40
   1911, 48
   1912, 50
   1920, 81
   1923, 113
   1927, 114
   1928, 108
   1930, 125
   1933, 131
   1940, 158
   1943, 168
   1950, 185
   1952, 193
   1953, 194–95
   1955, 203–4
   1956, 206
   1957, 215
   1961, 225
   1977, 275
   1982, 293, 294–95, 402n 2
   1986, 309
   2001, 15
Graham, Doug, 335
Graham, Frank P., 151
Grainger, Mrs., 162
Granger, Stewart, 165
Grant, Donald, 155
Grant, M. H., 94
Grant, Mrs. M. H., 94
Grant Six Motor Cars, 117
Grantham, Joe Addison, 216–18
Graves, Gladys Wells, 301
Graves, John, 301
Graves, Thomas W., 301
Graves, Virginia Thompson, 238, 332
Graves, William W., 301
Graves House, 301, 302f, 332, 403n 17
Great Depression, 123–56
Great War (World War I)
   college status during, 62–63, 66–70
   impact on athletics, 91
Greek organizations. *See also* Fraternities;
   Sororities
   on cheating, 139
   Greek week of 1966, 233–34
   "Hippie Party" of, 251
   power grasp by, 211
   racial segregation in, 291
Green, George D., 2
Greene, Doris, 243, 243f, 291
Greene, Sadie, 110, 114
Griffin, Lloyd, 204

Griffin, Mary Frances, 273
Grim, Ethel M., 75, 80, 108
Grim, Frederick F., 75–76, 80, 108
   on Carolina Enlargement Campaign, 106
   on financial needs, 81
   as summer school teacher, 110–11
Grimes, Terry, 240, 304, 319
Grinnel, Brent, 405n 42
Grooms, Duane, 407n 32
Groskin, Richard, 322, 406n 14
Guerrant, Will Upton, 82–83, 85, 89, 93, 379n 3
Guilford College, dancing at, 140
The Guilford Collegian, 41
Gurganus, Joseph T., 192–93
Gymnasium, 134–36, 136f
   dedication of, 238
   demolition of, 306
   renovation of, 197, 199

Haberyan, Henry D., Jr., 267
Hackney, Bess, 35, 53
Hackney, George H., 238
   on bond drive, 25
   college founding and, 2, 3f, 4
   daughter of, 53
   death of, 183
   honors for, 121
   mother of, 14, 238
Hackney, Lula, 53
Hackney, Orpah, 14, 238
Hackney, Roma, 121, 238, 323
Hackney, Thomas J., Jr., 294, 296, 310f, 329
   "Campaign for Excellence," 309–10
   on "A Design for Excellence," 304, 309
   at Doster inauguration, 275–76
   on Doster resignation, 298
   on Doster selection, 275
   on faculty retrenchment, 297
   Flame of Truth Award to, 309, 404n 33
   in fund-raising, 227
   at Hemby inauguration, 300
   on search for president, 273
   service of, 238
   on Swindell, 274
   on Wenger, 272
Hackney, Thomas J., Sr., 183, 215, 237f
   at Chamber of Commerce Day, 202–3

   dinner honoring, 237–38
   honorary degree for, 195
   service of, 238
Hackney, Willis Napoleon, 14, 174, 175f, 182, 238, 284–85, 401n 27
   building named for. *See* Willis N. Hackney Library
   student center donation from, 239
Hackney Brothers, 117
Hackney Brothers Body Company, 132
Hackney Hall, 121
   as co-ed dormitory, 284
   disturbance in, 232
   student disturbance before, 233
Hackney Library. *See* Willis N. Hackney Library
Hadge, Mary, 204
Hadley, Robert P., 267
Hall, Gary, 327, 328, 336
Hall of Fame, Athletic, 290, 347–49
Halloween celebrations, 54, 251
Hamilton, Jack, 220
Hamlin, Charles H., 154f, 164, 186, 226
   accused of communistic beliefs, 236
   description of, 110
   liberal views of, 220
   as Normal Thomas supporter, 155
   pacifist views of, 156
   on racial issues, 150–51, 153–54
   student center named for, 238
   as summer school teacher, 110–11
   tenure for, 195
Hamlin, Griffith, 139, 151, 189
Hamlin Society, 110, 322
Hamlin Student Center, 209, 238–39, 309
Hardegree, Joseph, Jr., 209, 222
Harding, Walter, 288
Harding, Warren G., 103, 112
Hardison, Fred, 125
Hardy, Bert Clarence, 137, 143
Hardy, Clarence Leonard, 136–37, 172
Hardy, Ruth, 53, 87
Hardy Alumni Hall, 137, 306–7
Hardy Center, 88, 285
Hardy Dining Hall, 137, 143
   dancing in, 180
   homecoming banquet in, 200
   Lindley inaugural luncheon in, 189–90

meal plans for, 180–81
student union in, 209
victory garden beside, 170
Hardy Library, completion of, 195
Harper, Annie, 116
Harper, Arrita Anderson Daniel, 22
Harper, Doris, 178f, 179
Harper, Frances F. "Miss Fannie," 23, 23f, 59
  on Christmas celebration, 124
  death of, 158
  describing snowy scene, 124
  on enrollment in Depression, 129
  in faculty club activities, 111
  on graduating class of 1933, 130
  on groundbreaking ceremony, 121
  inviting Helen Keller, 54
  loan fund named for, 158
  oak tree named for, 158
  portrait of, 158
  on radio programs, 125
  as teacher, 24, 76, 108
  at twenty-fifth anniversary, 114
Harper, John James, 3, 4, 15, 21f, 74
  biography of, 21–22
  call to presidency, 20–21
  death of, 29, 42, 272
  on ecumenical Christianity, 27
  first presidential year of, 24
  fund raising by, 25
  Leighton on, 79
  on Outlaw remarks on Smith's views, 64–65
  pastoral career of, 22–23
  sharing leadership with Caldwell, 28–29, 32
  on Smith, 62
Harper, Myrtle "Miss Myrtie," 23, 23f, 46
  as librarian, 58, 59, 76
  as math professor, 59, 108
  oak tree named for, 158
Harper Hall, 188
  completion of, 195
  dancing classes in, 202
  renovation of, 307
  student disturbance before, 233
  "The Harper Hall Woman," 138, 308f
Harrell, James "Babe," 245

Harriet Settle Plyler Memorial Scholarship, 56
Harris, Gerald, 236, 265, 272, 297, 397n 8
Harris, Jackie, 296, 405n 4
Harris, Patricia, 291
Harris, Sibyl, 292
Hartsock, Mildred, 185, 186f, 189, 226, 265, 288, 335
  assisting acting president, 186
  on basketball team, 199
  on *Crucible*, 240
  death of, 297
  on desegregation, 224
  in election debate, 247
  at Faculty Women's Club meeting, 394n 3
  at Hackney honor dinner, 237–38
  Hemby succeeding, 192
  on Metts play, 223
  on student apathy, 230
  student misconduct incidences and, 234
  tenure for, 195
  on Twist dancing, 231
  yearbook dedicated to, 190
Harvest Dance, 210
Harvey, N. T., 151
Hassell, Sylvester, 1
Hastings, Greg, 312
Hawkins, Bob, 101
Hawley, Jeff, 311, 404n 36
Hawley, Rebecca Hunt, 295
Hawley, Rhonda, 311, 404n 36
Hayes, A. J., 233
Hays, Brooks, 196
Head, Harlow, 335
Hearing impaired program, 286
Hearn, Bunn, 85
Helmer, Harry "Lefty," 175, 176
Hemby, James B., III, 300, 300f
Hemby, James B., Jr., 192, 300f, 308
  accomplishments of, 331–32
  biography of, 299–300
  Campaign for Barton College, 324
  "Campaign for Excellence," 309–10
  on Centennial Committee, 330
  on college name change, 320, 321f, 405n 9
  at commencement of 1986, 309

Hemby, James B., Jr., *continued*
  at commencement of 2001, 330
  as *Crucible* editor, 240
  "A Design for Excellence" program, 301, 304, 309, 403n 22
  on Etheridge, 209
  foreword by, ix–x
  at Founders' Day of 2000, 207
  Fulbright grant for, 318
  on Hilley, 185
  inauguration of, 300–301, 403n 15
  as interim president, 299
  in international week, 317
  on Lindley administration, 195
  as provost, 296, 297
  selection as president, 299
  on strategic plan, 325
  student writings of, 301
  on teacher education program, 312
  on White administration, 195
Hemby, Joan Edwards, 202, 300, 300f, 331
Hemby, Scott Edwards, 300, 300f, 306
Hemby, Thomas Simmen, 300, 300f
Henry, Kenneth, 222
Henry, Rick, 405n 42
Hensley, Dan, Jr., 265, 273, 277, 301, 397n 8, 399n 51
Herman, Linde, 280
Herman, Woody, 210
Herring, Doane, 121
Hesburgh, Theodore M., 404n 33
Hesperian Society, 27, 55, 56, 131, 149
Hester, Charles E. "Chuck," 207
Hicks, Johnny, 162, 387n 40
High, Elizabeth Hilley, 153–4, 386n 19
Higher Criticism controversy, 76
Hill, Charlotte, 132, 142
Hill, Clifford, 101
Hilley, Elizabeth. *See* High, Elizabeth Hilley
Hilley, Howard Stevens, 107f, 238
  accomplishments of, 184–85
  as acting president, 81, 103
  African-Americans employed by, 152
  announcing J. W. Hines gift, 124–25
  appointment as president, 106
  in automobile accident, 182–83
  baccalaureate sermons of
    1927, 114
    1930, 125
    1940, 158
  as baseball team manager, 91
  biography of, 103–4
  "Cannon Ball" nickname of, 153
  on cheating, 139
  on Christmas of 1940, 162
  at cornerstone laying, 121
  description of, 104
  enrollment goals of, 105
  Eureka Plan of, 137
  on expansion plans, 143
  at faculty club meeting, 111
  faculty quality concerns of, 108
  on food supplies, 128
  on football restoration, 174
  as Frances Harper funeral speaker, 158
  in Freshman Week of 1940, 159
  on full enrollment in 1933, 131
  fund-raising by, 106, 145
  on gymnasium, 135
  on Hackney family contributions, 121
  honorary degree for, 203
  honoring football team, 97
  international focus of, 154
  at Kiwanis Club meeting, 126
  on military service, 166
  on number of Disciple students, 106–7
  office in Caldwell Hall, 181
  opposed to dancing, 179
  in postwar era, 173–74
  preparatory program discontinued by, 108
  promoting school on radio, 128–29
  reflecting on ten years as president, 124
  relationship with students, 114–15
  resignation of, 183, 184
  on Ross loan service, 182
  on street closure, 190
  student aid strategies of, 127, 129, 132–33, 137, 143–44
  tenure of, 272
  on Thanksgiving celebration of 1940, 162
  at twenty-fifth anniversary, 114
  on veterans' facilities, 174
  Ware on, 104–5
  in World War II years, 170–72

Hilley, Howard Stevens, Jr., 167
Hilley, Maggie Tucker, 81, 103, 111
Hilley Cup, 80, 344
Hilley Hall, 238
Hines, J. W., 4, 14, 120, 121, 124–25, 238
Hines, Peter E., 23
Hines Hall
  computer lab in, 286
  dedication of, 238
  renovations to, 328
Hippie counterculture, 249–51, 254
Hiram College, Ohio, 48
Hitler, Adolph, speeches against, 156
Hobbs, Kevin, 405n 42
Hobgood, Ben, 297, 306–7
Hodges, Claire, 72, 87
Hodges, F. A., 141
Hodges, Luther H., 215, 219
Hoey, Clyde R., 151
Holiday celebrations, 54–55
Hollar, Robert P., 187, 189, 226, 390n 11
Holliday, Joe, 176
Holloman, Randy, 270
Holloway, Edward B., 166
Holmes, Sue Todd, 127f, 128–30, 383n 13
Holsapple, Cortell K., 111, 187
Holsworth, Doris Campbell "Duchess," 187, 190–92, 191f, 199
  directing Wenger in play, 227
  memorial fund for, 240
  as Peace Corps volunteer, 228–29
  as Young Republicans Club advisor, 218
Holton, R. C., 126
Holy Land, Caldwell trip to, 49–50, 111
Homecoming Festival
  1940, 162
  1954, 200
Honor code, 139, 384n 40
Honorary degrees
  1952, 193–95, 390n 21
  1955, 203
  1957, 215
  1961, 225
  1977, 275
  1982, 295
Honors graduates, 1930, 125
Honors program, 303–4, 403n 21

Hoover, Herbert, 103, 121, 125
Hosford, Gareth, 320, 321f, 406n 11
Hot Stove League, 83
Howard, Becky, 320
Howard, Curtis William, chapel named for. *See* Howard Chapel
Howard, Paul, 92
Howard Chapel, 159f, 182
  attendance requirements in, 230–31
  dedication of, 158
  deteriorated condition of, 279
  fiftieth anniversary convocation in, 194
  Lindley inauguration in, 189
  plans for, 145
  Stage and Script productions in, 191–92
  Still Point and, 268–69, 269f, 279, 399n 45
Hudson-Essex Motor Cars, 117
Hughes, Walter J., 151–52
Hughey, Elizabeth House, 225
Humieda, Sharhabil, 288, 312
Humphrey, Hubert, 247
Hunger Emphasis Week, 291
Hunt, James Baxter, Jr., 275, 276, 293, 295, 299, 300, 399n 6
Hunter, Naomi S., 153
Hunter, Sue, 287
Hussey, Moseley, 203
Hutchinson, Martha, 336
Hyatt, John, 125
Hyatt, Laura, 325–26
Hyatt, Ronald, 216

Inaugurations. *See specific presidents*
Influenza epidemic of 1918, 70
Information networks, 323. *See also* Computers
Inter-church Bulletin, 77
Inter-church Movement, 77–80
Inter-Class-Tug-of-War, 134
Inter-Collegiate Peace Contest, 56, 57
Interfraternity council, 211
International Club, 156
International focus, 111–12, 154, 316–19, 318f.
  See also Travel courses and programs
International Peace Research Institute, 266
International Red Cross, in World War I, 63
Internships, 303
Irvine, Norbert, 265, 288, 298–99

J. W. Hines Hall, 121
Jackson, George Marvin, 167–68
Jackson, Kathlyn "Kat," 70, 97
Jackson, Marvin, 166
Jaggi, Anand, 287, 304
January term, 319
Japanese teahouse garden, 317, 318f
Jarman, Cecil A., 143, 185, 186, 194, 294
Jarrell, Rex B., Jr., 229, 394n 6
Jefferson, C. Bonner, 117–18, 130
Jefferson, Milton, 95
Jefferson, Thomas, 235
Jefferson-Pilot Faculty Members of the Year, 318, 345
Jeffries, Herbert M., Jr., 189, 390n 11, 402n 2
Jeffries, Kay W., 390n 11
Jennings, Mamie. *See* Lucas, Mamie Jennings
Jernigan, Diane Moore, 312
Joby Hawn Cup, 327
John Birch Society, 235–36, 242
Johnson, Charray, 336, 407n 2
Johnson, Johnny, 281
Johnson, Lyndon, 219, 234, 246, 247
Johnson, Samuel, 235
Johnson, Wes, 317
Johnston, Edna, 187, 226
Johnston, Hugh B., Jr., 187, 226, 235, 236, 247
Johnston, Joseph E., 22
Johnston, W. G., 5, 6, 15
Joint Society, 114
Jones, Amy, 320
Jones, Charles, 240
Jones, J. Boyd, 20, 24
Jones, James, 244–45
Jones, Joan Adams, 261, 261f, 262, 398n 30
Jones, Joe, 319
Jones, Larry, 244
Jones, Lorenzo, 291
Jones, Mr. (contractor), 121
Jordan, Bill, 328
Jordan, Elizabeth "Bep," 329, 331–32, 407n 28
Jordan, Jeanne, 328
Joyner, Bethany Rose, 187, 273, 278
Joyner, Gordon L., 277, 283

K. D. Kennedy Business Chair, 329
Karl's Lunch, 146
Keel, Debbie Purvis, 260, 397n 27

Keller, Helen, 54
Kelly, Hugh, 149
Kendall, Charles, 152–53
Kendall, Myrtle, 153
Kennedy, John F., 218–19, 223, 224, 227–29
Kennedy, K. D., Jr., 324, 326, 326f, 328
Kennedy, K. D., Sr., 227, 326f, 307
Kennedy, Robert, 247
Kennedy, Sara Lynn, 328
Kennedy Recreation and Intramural Center, 326–28, 326f
Kent, William, 273
Kent State University confrontation, 253
Kilgore, J. William, 325, 406n 21
"Kilroy's Kennels, 174
Kim, Ho Keun, 287–88
King, Martin Luther, Jr., 247
King, Patsy Duke, 306
Kinsey, Joseph, 2–4, 15, 330
Kinsey Hall, 26f
  bricks from, for President's House construction, 227
  chapel attached to, 145
  on commemorative plate, 194
  construction on (1911), 48
  demolition of, 207
  description of, 6–7, 12–14, 13f
  dormitory life in, 75f
  Harper family living in, 23
  heating problems with, 19, 24
  Mamie Jennings arrival at, 46
  modernization of, 164
  peace bonfire before, 155
  refurbishing of, 15, 143
  residents of (1910), 11f
  servicemen entertainment in, 171
  town people reception hosted in, 52–53
Kinsey Seminary, 1–4, 183, 207
Kirkland, Robert E., Jr., 298
Kiwanis Club, 126, 202
  athletic award from, 291
  Circle K sponsored by, 278–79
  scholarship from, 114
Knott, Marsh, 127, 127f
Korean War, 192–93
Krein, Marc A., 304–5
Krise, Nell, 74, 75
Ku Klux Klan, 242–43

Index

LaBelle Beauty Shop, 146
Labor unions, student opinions on, 38–40
Lackey, Ruth, 87
Lafayette Escadrille, 63
LaFlamme, Dominic, 328
Lamm, Barry, 307, 309
Lamm, Kathryn, 187, 273
Lancaster, Burt, 165
Lane, J. J., 83, 379n 3
Lane, Judy, 200
Lane, Rosser, 83, 379n 3
Lang, Vernice, 91
Langley, Sandra, 260, 397n 27
Langston, Ira Wright, 131, 133, 196, 203
Langston, Sam, 129
Lappin, Cora A., 66, 69, 379n 18
Lappin, W. O., 68, 379n 18
Lappin, Warren Curtis, 68, 90, 379n 18
Larkins, John D., 215
Lassiter, Jack, 260
Lassiter, Marion, 162, 167
Latham, Josephus, 22
Latham, Thomas, 22
Lawson, James T., 102
Leach, Elizabeth Ann "Lib," 177, 178f, 179
Learning Resource Center, 285
Leder Brothers, 134
Lee, Mr. and Mrs. Don E., 206
Lee, Cyrus, 149, 150, 157
Lee, Ernie, 281, 282
Lee, Horace Alton, Jr., 225
Leighton, A. F., 79
Lemmon, Sarah M., 66
Lewis, Milton H., 95
Library. *See also* Willis N. Hackney Library
  Hardy, completion of, 195
  in 1913, 58, 377n 30
  as War Information Center, 69
Liegey, Irma, 155
Lievense, Ron, 327
Liggon, Charles "Ned," 176
Liles, John, 264
LINC system, 323
Lindley, Denton Ray, 188f, 212
  accomplishments of, 195
  on accreditation, 205
  baccalaureate sermon by, 193
  biography of, 187

evening program started by, 190
Hemby on, 195
honorary degree for, 215
inauguration of, 189–90
resignation of, 194
selection of, 187
Wenger assistant to, 208
Lindley, Gene, 187
Lindley, Maybon Marie Torrey, 187
Lindley, Neil, 187
Lindquist, Vernon, 330
Lingan, James Edmund, 55–56
Linkletter, Art, 45
Linne, Thomas, 313, 313f
Literary publications. *See The Pine Knot; The Radiant*
Literary societies, 26–27, 55–56, 116, 131, 149
Little, Bryce, 121
"Little Christians" football team, 94–96, 96f, 99
Little Five State Championship, for football, 101
Lively, Gerald, 67
Lodge, Henry Cabot, 219
Loftin, Sarah, 132–33, 180, 274f, 275
London Shop, 145
Long, Esther, 187, 195, 226
Lord, J. A., 28
Louisburg College, women's rights issues at, 258–59
Lowe, L. Vincent, 327
Lowell, Neil, 312
Lowenstein, Allard, 232
Lucas, Mamie Jennings, 47f
  arrival at college, 45–46, 59–60
  on baseball teams, 85
  Christmas pageant directed by, 124
  death of, 59
  as director of drama, 104, 116
  as director of expression, 59
  on faculty payments, 144
  on Hilley, 104, 185
  hosting faculty club, 111
  on Jessie Caldwell, 45, 46
  on Mary Settle Caldwell, 60–61
  play directed by, 114
  scholarship honoring, 323, 406n 15
Lucas, Silas, 2

Lucas, W. A., 111
Lucielle's Dress Shop, 145
Lula E. Rackley Gallery, 238, 332
Lynch, Mabel, 80–81

MacArthur, Douglas, 173
McBroom, Elizabeth Grantham, 387n 6
McCaffity, Darwin W., 324, 326, 329, 329f, 406n 11, 407n 29
McCaffity, Darwin W., Jr., 407n 29
McCaffity, Margaret Brown, 329
McCarthy, Eugene, 247
McCarthyism, 184, 235
McComas, Jack, 197–99, 215, 216, 391n 30 & 39
McDaniel, Mary, 153
MacDonald, Murdina, 304
McDowell, Dennis, 280
McFarland, Dan, 220
McGill, William, 240
McIntyre, Theresa, 292
Mack, Maynard, 266
McKeel, Carol. *See* Mewborn, Carol McKeel
McKinley, Ray, 210
McKinney, Horace, 170
McLawhorn, James R., 246
MacLean, Jerry, 304, 305, 322, 330
MacLean, Laura, 335, 336
MacLennan, Tom, 285
McLeod, Joyce Bell, 291
McPhail, Sam, 232, 235, 394n 11
McRacken, H. Larry, 273
Maghan, Jesse L., 241
Mallison, Dallas, 131, 383n 22
Malpas, John, 313f
Malvina Rountree Tract, purchase of, 71–72, 72f
Manning, James, 100
Manning, Jannie, 116
Map, of campus in 1952, 371f
March of Dimes, 176
Markham, Coleman, 406n 11
Marler, W. H., 76–77
Marley, John, 198, 200, 215
Marshall, Tom, 236, 240, 251–52, 265, 271, 335, 399n 51, 405n 4
Martin, Adele, 9

Mary Alice and Howard B. Chapin Education Scholarship, 404n 39
Mascot, for athletic teams, 100, 135–36, 147f, 153, 313
Matthews, Mary, 157, 203
Mattox, William Thomas, 66
Maxwell, Susan. *See* Bane, Susan Maxwell
May Day festivals
   1930s, 133, 142–43, 142f, 156
   1943, 169
Mayo, Selz, 294
Meade, Lucia Ames, 113
Meadows, Sollie, 91
Media center, 304–5
Meditation center (Still Point), 268–69, 269f, 279, 399n 45
Meese, Bernard C., 403n 15
Melendez, Rick, 313
Melton, B. H., 4–5, 15, 19
Men and Millions Movement, 70, 378n 19
Mercer, Elizabeth "Libby," 301
Merck Foundation, 324
Meredith, James, 241
Meredith College, athletics at, 86
Messick, Ralph, 211
Metts, Carl W., 223
Mewborn, Carol McKeel, 260, 263, 289, 314
Mewborn, Carolyn, 245
Michalak, Dan, 327
Michalak, Paula, 327
Mikan, George, 201
Miles, James E., 149
Miller, Laura, 330
Miller, Paula Frances, 317–18
Mills, Barbara Franklin, 290–91
Milne, Sheila, 314, 316
Mini-term experience, 302
Ministerial Association of Atlantic Christian College, 52
Misbehavior, in 1919, 73–75
Missionaries, visits from, 112–13
Mitchell, Elaine, 197
Mitchell, Kay Antone, 236, 311, 395n 20
Modlin, Sam, 265, 289f, 290
Mohorter, J. H., 78–79
Monk, Peal Fay, 87
Monshower, Alvah C., 277, 283
Montgomery, Frank, 216

Moore, Anna F., 66–67
Moore, Clement, 73
Moore, Jerri Thorne, 387n 6
Moore, Lee, 273
Moore, Macon, 115
Moore, Mary, 73–75
Mooty, Alex, 399n 51
Moratorium, Vietnam War, 251–52, 252f, 396n 8
Morehead Scholarship, 191
Morgan, Barry, 260, 268
Morgan, Ethel, 114
Morris, Carol, 336
Morris, Naomi, 275, 296, 399n 6
Morris, Tom, 265, 288–89, 289f, 327, 336
Morrison, Charles Clayton, 158
Morton, Clement Manly, 39f, 138
  death of, 271
  on financial problems in 1903-1904, 18–19
  on Harper-Caldwell contributions, 29
  honorary degree for, 194
  as literary publication editor, 34, 36, 43
  at missionary rally, 112
  as poet, 34
  preaching baccalaureate sermon of 1923, 113
  as Religious Emphasis Week speaker, 213
  tribute to, 112–13
Morton, Mrs. Clement Manly, 112
Morton, Rodney William, 306
Moses, Ray, 125
Motley, Daniel, 4, 15, 19
Mottern, Elmer, 156–57
Motto (Habebunt Lumen Vitae), 125, 337
Moudy, James, 194, 205–6, 212, 390n 22
Moudy, Mrs. James, 394n 3
Moye, Abram J., 25, 79, 143
Moye, E. A., 4
Moye, Lawrence A., 206
Moye, Moses T., 23, 116
Moye Science Hall, 267, 308
Muilberger, Albert, 53, 59
Mukerjee, Sonali, 314
Munn, Randolph, 101
Murray, Cleo, 273
Murray, Leslie L., 174, 176

Murray Hall, 174
Music
  department accreditation, 285
  extracurricular activities in, 116
  Festivals of Contemporary Arts, 265–66
  glee club, 125
  marching band, 202
  Opera Theatre, 279–80
  performances of, 53–54
  rock bands, 251
"Mutt," as team mascot, 100
Myers, Susan Davis, 260, 262, 398n 30

Nakhre, Amrut, 266, 288, 319
Name change, to Barton College, 319–21, 321f, 405n 9, 406n 11
Nance, Greg, 405n 42
Narron, Donnell, 168
Narron, Homer, 168
Narron, Jarley, 168
Narron, Talmadge, 168
National Association of Intercollegiate Athletics tournaments, 201, 216
National Association of Schools of Music, 285
National Collegiate Athletic Association, 38, 327
National Collegiate Playwriting Contest, 191
National Council for Accreditation of Teacher Education, 239, 312
National Council for Prevention of War, 113, 155
National Education Association, 38
National Forum, 151
National Interfraternity Council, 210
National League for Nursing, 267–68, 295
National League of Families of Prisoners and Men Missing in Action, 252
National Organization for Women, 258
National Student Association, 246
National Student Congress, 223
National Women's Political Caucus, 258
New Deal, gymnasium funding from, 135
New Frontier programs, 228
New Wilson Theatre, 146
Newbold, N. C., 150
Newborne, Hattie, 56

Niaz, Asad, 265
Nixon, Richard, 218–19, 247, 251, 253
Noble, Verdie, 36, 39f
Norfolk, Ira, 243, 244
North Carolina Art Education Association, 288, 299
North Carolina Association of Intercollegiate Athletics for Women, 261
North Carolina Board of Nursing, 267
North Carolina Christian, launching of, 77
North Carolina Christian Church Convention, on desegregation, 241–42
North Carolina Christian Ministers' Association, on Smith controversy, 65
North Carolina Christian Missionary Committee, 72
North Carolina Christian Missionary Convention
   Carolina Publishing Company, 77
   creation of, 22
   endowment request by, 52
   on new Disciples college, 3
North Carolina Commission on Interracial Cooperation, 150–52
North Carolina Department of Education, 108, 286
North Carolina Department of Public Instruction, 239
North Carolina Legislative Internship, 282
North Carolina Libraries for Virtual Education, 323
North Carolina Shakespeare Festival, 240
Nurney, Charles N., 14, 71
Nursing program, 267–68, 287, 401n 34
   accreditation of, 295
   success of, 310–11, 404n 35

Oakley, Annie Kate, 114
O'Boyle, Jerry, 317, 405n 4
O'Boyle, Patrick, 336, 405n 4, 407n 2
O'Briant, Butch, 264
Oettinger, Jonas, 2, 90
Oettinger prize, 110
Oettinger's, 145
Office of Lifelong Education, 303
Ogrodowski, Eugene, 149, 157
Old Kinsey. *See* Kinsey Hall
Old Maids' Club, 42f

Omega Chi sorority, 209, 210
Opera Theatre, 279–80
Oriental Seashore Summer School, 111
Osborne, Bill, 169, 171
Ossmin, Roger, 288
Outlaw, Cecil F., 42–43, 64–65, 76, 377n 6
Outlaw, Wilbur Gerald, 235–36, 395n 18

P. D. Gold Publishing Company, 53
Pace, Becky, 289
Page, Doris, 309–10
Page, Kirby, 156
Page, Roger, 304, 309–10
Palestine, Caldwell trip to, 49–50, 111
Palmer, John D., 227, 272, 403n 15
Panhellenic council, 211
Parham, Thomas, Jr., 216, 243, 265, 288–89, 289f, 313–14, 313f, 327
Paris Peace Conference, 252
Parish, Phyllis, 261
Parker, Teresa, 311
Parking problems, 283
Parrish, Judith, 273
Paschall, Joshua Ernest, 68–69, 114, 225
Patriotism
   in World War I, 66–69
   in World War II, 166
Paulsell, William O., 247, 265, 288, 297
Peace activities
   in Vietnam War era, 234, 237, 246, 249, 251–54, 252f, 396n 6
   before World War II, 155–56
Peace Corps, 224–25, 228–29
Peagues, Bob, 291
Pearce, F. M., 98
Peck, Gregory, 165
Peebles, Jim, 197, 198
Peele, Agnes, 131
Pennington, Carl, 307
Percise, Ronald, 198, 200
Perkinson, Elizabeth Graves, 301
Phi Beta Lambda business organization, 311
Phi Delta Alpha fraternity, 162
Phi Delta Gamma fraternity, 209, 210
Phi Kappa Alpha fraternity, 116, 209, 210
Phi Mu sorority, 252
Phi Sigma Tau sorority, 116, 209, 210

Index

Phillips, Mattie, 36
Phillips, Nettie Sue, 202
Pierce, Dean, 406n 13
Pikeville Junior College, basketball segregation issue and, 220–22
Pine Forest Apartments, 122f
The Pine Knot
   advertising in, 117
   cover of (1910), 33f
   dedicated to Hilley, 104
   demise of, 172
   early years of, 32–35
   initial issue of, 29
   queen of, 177, 178f, 179
Pippen, A. W., livery stable, 17
Pittman, Carey, 264
"Play Day," 199
Plyler, B. B., Jr., 298
Plyler, Harriet Settle, 53–54, 56, 57f
Polter, T. V., 90
Pomeroy, Ben, 264
Pomfrey, Bette, 218
Poole, Bob, 280
Poole, D. E., 125
Pope, Liston, 189
Power, Tyrone, 165
"Precis," 402n 7
Preparatory program, 31–32, 58, 108
Presidents, list of, 354
President's House
   on Nash Street, 301, 302f, 332, 403n 17
   on Wilshire Boulevard, 46, 227
Preston, Andrew, 265
Price, Myra, 245, 260
Pridgen, Harry A. "Al," 273
Prillaman, Jay, 218
"Prince" (college pony), 59–60, 60f
Proctor, Mary, 88
Proctor, Mrs. J. O., 14
Professors. *See* Faculty; *individual faculty members*
Progressive Movement, 35, 40
Prohibition movement, women involvement in, 36
Public schools, college relationship with, 113
Public Works Administration, gymnasium funding from, 135

"Puppies" athletic team, 260
Purcell, Bebe, 283
Purcell, Betty, 283
Purcell, Eugene, Jr., 226, 243, 265, 268, 279, 282, 287, 325, 397n 8
Purcell, Eugene "Trip," III, 283
Purcell, Peter, 282–83
Purvis, Debbie, 260, 397n 27
Purvis, Gene A., 226, 237, 312, 404n 39

Quinerly, Nannie Pearl, 115, 118
Quinlan, Karen Ann, 281
Quinn, Gerald, 324, 406n 18

Rabil, Ellis "Beau," 134
Racial issues
   in athletics, 220–23
   civil rights movement, 153–54, 229, 234, 241
   college desegregation, 241–44, 243f, 290–93, 292f, 395n 32
   community facility desegregation, 223–24
   Hamlin involved in, 150–51
   at North Carolina Commission on Interracial Cooperation convention, 151–52
   in Stage and Script presentations, 223
   in student newspaper, 240–41
   Supreme Court decisions on, 220
Rackley, Lula E., 238, 332
The Radiant
   early years of, 32–44
   exchange journal program of, 41
   first edition of, 22
   humor in, 41–42
   last issue of, 100
   staff of 1908, 33f
   success of, 32
Radio, 146
   first broadcast on, 125
   impact on global awareness, 112
   recruiting on, 128–29
   student and faculty enjoyment of, 125
Ragan, Marjorie, 44, 137
Ragan, Sam, 44, 137, 294, 301
Ragan Writing Center, 44, 137, 311
Ramey, Ralph El, 403n 15

Raulen, Charlie Grey, 118
Rawlings, Russell, 83, 264, 328, 330, 336, 407n 32
Rawls, Anthony, 311, 404n 36
Reagan, Ronald, 177, 178f, 179
"Red" (campus employee), 152
Red Cross, in World War I, 63, 66–67, 69
The Red Scare, 79–80
Red Seal Continental Motor Trucks, 117
Red's Barber Shop, 146
Reel, Archie, 96, 98, 100, 101
Reel, Cecil, 101, 380n 30
Reel, Mae, 116, 380n 30
Reeves, F. W., 118
Reeves, Martha, 233
Religious studies and activities
   lecture series, 279
   missionary visits, 112–13
   in 1950s, 212–13
   in 1970s, 265, 268
      Religious Emphasis Week, 213–14, 225
      Smith controversy and, 64–65, 76–79
Rentle, Susan E., 322
Respass, Elsie, 72
Respass, Norma Jean, 260, 397n 27
Rex Shoe Shop, 146
Reynolds, Z. Smith, 268
Rhodes, Thomas J., 327
Rider, Mrs. Edward, 203
Ridling, Jerry Arthur, 229, 240–41, 394n 7
Rierson, Chuck, 264
Riggan, C., 100, 101
Riley, Arthur, 91
Riley, Bruce, 276, 299, 300
Riley, Lorraine, 260–61
Ring Dance, 210
"Roaring Twenties," 103–22
Robinette, Bill, 287
Robinette, Susie, 287
Roe v. Wade, 281
Roebuck, Julian, 149
Roebuck, Russell, 141, 168, 385n 44
Roger Page Foundation, 304
Rogers, Dennis, 273
Rogers, Sarah Condon, 322–23, 406n 15
Rogers, Vere, 226
Rogerson, Milton, 273, 277, 296, 317
Roma Hackney Music Building, 121, 238, 323

Rooney, Mickey, 165
Roosevelt, Eleanor, 155, 166
Roosevelt, Franklin, 40, 131, 159
Roosevelt, Theodore, 1, 17, 85–86
Rose, Robin, 265
Ross, Mildred, 180–82, 181f, 187, 199, 200
Rotary Club, 114, 327
Roughton, David, 264
Roughton, Rebecca Jenkins, 265
Rountree, Robert Hart, 71
Rouse, N. J., 183
Rowland, C. H., Jr., 168
Rucker, Gilbert, 405n 42
Rucker, Martha Hutchinson, 407n 2
Ruffin, H. B. "Bud," 294, 298, 402n 2
Rules and regulations
   in 1902, 10–12
   in 1905, 25
   in 1950s, 188–89
   in 1960s, 230, 254–55
   in 1970s, 254–59
   in 1977-1983, 284
Russell, Maude, 72

S & M Pocket Billiards, 146
Sadie Hawkin's Day, 160, 169
Sadler, Magruder Ellis, 68, 164, 187, 193, 194
Sadler, S. Lee, 57–58
Safety patrol, 284
St. John, Kenneth, 226, 274, 297
St. Mary's, athletics at, 86–87
St. Mary's Muse, 41
Saintsing, Wendee, 321
Salmon, Kathleen, 59
Sam and Marjorie Ragan Writing Center, 44, 137, 311
Samuelsson, Johan, 313, 313f
Sanford, Jack, 313
Sanford, Terry, 219
Sanitary Cleaners, 146
Sara Lynn Kennedy Recording Studio, 328
Sasser, Margaret, 125
S.A.T.C. (Students' Army Training Corps), 68
Satellite Communications for Learning, 323
Schatz, Edward, 266
Schatz, Gertrude, 266
Schneider, Richard, 288

Index 437

Scholarships
  athletic, 147, 327
  for attracting new students, 110
  Barker-Ferguson, 323
  in Depression, 132
  Elizabeth Faye Brinson Memorial Scholarship, 129
  George C. Stronach, Jr., 323, 406n 15
  Harriet Settle Plyler Memorial Scholarship, 56
  Kiwanis Club, 114
  in late 1980s, 322–23, 406n 15
  Mamie Jennings Lucas, 323, 406n 15
  Mary Alice and Howard B. Chapin Education Scholarship, 404n 39
  Morehead Scholarship, 191
  Ted C. Foy Scholarship Award, 290
  Todd family, 130
  Undergraduate Fellows Program, 298, 299
  Will and Sarah Condon Rogers Memorial Scholarship, 322–23, 406n 15
Schubert, William D., 329, 329f
Schwab, Larry, 245
Scope, upgrading of, 296
Scott, Robert, 253
Searson, Allen, 264
Seburn, Harold, 203
Security, 284
Seegers, Keith, 405n 42
Segregation. *See* Racial issues
Selective Service laws, 236
Sellers, Steve, 264
Semi-Weekly Times, 53
Sessoms, Clayton, 303
Settle, E. E., 28
Settle, Harriet Clay, 53–54, 56, 57f
Settle, Horace, 56, 57, 82
Seymour, Elvyn, 245
Shackleford, Ruby P., 226, 265, 287
Shakespeare's works, 239–40, 266
Sharp, Allan R., 187, 212, 226, 265, 279
Sharpe, Patrick Dave, 387n 6
Shaw, Artie, 165
Shenk, Virginia Ann, 237
Shepard, Alan, 225
Sherman, William Tecumseh, 22
Sherwood, Robert E., 191
Shingleton, Dan, 322, 335, 406n 13

Shingleton, William W., 295
Shockey, Luther Reic, 9–10
Shoestring Players, 190–91
"Shortie" (campus employee), 152
Sigma Alpha fraternity, 116, 209, 210
Sigma Gamma Nu sorority, 291
Sigma Phi Epsilon fraternity, 210, 211
Sigma Phi fraternity, 210
Sigma Rho Phi fraternity, 209, 210
Sigma Sigma Sigma sorority, 252
Sigma Tau Chi sorority, 97, 116, 179, 209, 210
Silverthorne, Ray, 149, 150
Sinatra, Frank, 165
Singletary, Barbara Ward, 243, 243f, 292
Singleton, Dawn-Marie, 335, 336, 407n 2
Sisk, Sherrie, 280
Skinner, Candace, 320
Sloan, Norman, 198
Smallwood, Chris, 264
Smallwood, David, 264
Smith, Barbara, 260, 263, 314
Smith, Bill, 165
Smith, Blane, 279
Smith, Danny, 264
Smith, David, 218, 223
Smith, Dean, 294–95
Smith, Ed, 176
Smith, Grace, 62
Smith, Harlie L., 215
Smith, Ivy Mae, 74, 75, 116
Smith, Lawrence, 195
Smith, Mary Belle, 87
Smith, Mike, 288, 312
Smith, Raymond Abner, 24, 64f, 187
  biography of, 62
  concern over enrollment in 1917, 66
  controversy concerning, 64–65, 76–79
  on enrollment of 1918-1919, 67–68
  farm purchase under, 71–72, 72f, 117
  as gardener, 71, 72f
  inauguration of, 72–73
  legacy of, 80–81
  Leighton on, 79
  in Men and Millions Movement, 378n 19
  move to Texas Christian University, 80, 81
  post-war challenges to, 70–71
  responsibilities of, 63, 377n 4
  Sunday School establishment by, 72, 80

Smith, Rebecca, 311, 330
Smith, "Speedy," 199
Smith, Tammy Ayscue, 336, 407n 2
Smith, William E., 273
Snipes, David, 160
Soccer team, 264, 288, 312, 328
Social Darwinism, 43
Social work program, 322, 406n 13
Sororities, 209–12
   Alpha Kappa Alpha, 291
   Delta Sigma, 209
   Delta Sigma Theta, 291
   Omega Chi, 209, 210
   Phi Mu, 252
   Phi Sigma Tau, 116, 209, 210
   Sigma Gamma Nu, 291
   Sigma Sigma Sigma, 252
   Sigma Tau Chi, 97, 116, 179, 209, 210
Southard, Mike, 264
Southern Association of Colleges and Secondary Schools, 119, 205, 226, 239, 274, 285–86, 311
Spain, Agnes, 56, 91
Spanish flu epidemic of 1918, 70
Speight, Robert, 245
Spencer, William, 291, 292
Sports. See Athletics; *specific sports and teams*
Sports Day, 260
Sprinkle, Steve, 268, 279
Sprinkle Lecture Series, 279
Spruill, Gene, 218
Stage and Script, 244f
   activities of, 190–92, 191f, 279–80
   black students in, 243
   fiftieth anniversary of, 239–40
   vulgar language problems in, 191–92
   Wenger acting in, 227
Stallings, Ed, Jr., 53–54, 83
Stallsmith, Clyde, 244–45, 396n 40
Standard Commercial Corporation, 324
Starr, Annie, 87
Staub, Brian, 265, 289f
Steele, Mary S., 267
Stein, George, 132
Steinem, Gloria, 258
Stevenson, Adlai, 218
Stewart, Craig, 405n 42
Still Point, 268–69, 269f, 279, 399n 45

Stone, Barton W., 321
"Streaking" incidents, 256–58, 257f
Strengthening Developing Institutions, 286–87
Strickland, Ruth M., 169
Stronach, George, III, 7
Stronach, George C., Jr., 323, 406n 15
Stronach, Mrs. George C., Jr., 323
Stronach, Samuel C., 323
Student aid strategies, 127, 129, 132–33, 137, 143–44
Student center, 209, 238–39, 309
Student Christian Association, 213, 222
Student Cooperative Association, 223, 234
Student Government Association
   on drinking, 254
   on drug abuse, 250
   faculty evaluation survey of, 266–67
   on food service dissatisfaction, 232
   formation of, 230
   president disappearance and, 281
   Vietnam War position of, 253
   on visitation rights, 255
Student life committee, 254, 255, 397n 14
Student union facilities, 209, 238–39, 309
Students' Army Training Corps, 68
Students for Democratic Society, 232, 247
Suffrage, for women, 35, 38
Sullivan, Clyde, 294
Summer school, 110–11
Sunday school, 72, 80
Swain, George Harry, 187, 226, 273
Swain, Myrtle T., 187
Swartzwelder, Connie, 303
Swift Foot baseball team, 84
Swindell, Lewis, Jr., 251, 265, 273, 274, 297

T. G. Pettus Company, 117
Tait, Warren, 226, 312
Tanner, Mary Lee, 177
Tarleton, Hal, 297, 325
Taylor, Alva W., 113
Taylor, Charles E., 85
Taylor, Leigh, 256, 261, 264
Taylor, Pat, 265
Taylor, Robert, 165
Teacher(s), on college faculty. See Faculty; *individual teachers*

Index 439

Teacher education program
  accreditation of, 286, 312
  practice teaching in public schools, 113
  standards for, 107–8
  summer school for, 110–11
Teams. *See* Athletics; *specific sports and teams*
Ted C. Foy Scholarship Award, 290
Television, 203, 319, 323
Tennis, 83
  in 1996-1997, 327–28
  coeducational club for, 92
  courts for, 83, 91–92, 92f, 327
  in 1911, 86
  in 1912, 87
  in 1918, 90, 91
  in 1947, 175
  in 1954, 199
  in 1970s, 265, 288–89, 289f
  in 1980s, 312–15, 313f
  popularity of, 82, 91–92
  women's, 83, 91–92, 92f, 260–61, 262, 312, 314
Test Ban Treaty of 1963, 235
Tetterton, J. Marshall, 327, 406n 11
Tew, Keith, 330, 405n 4
Thanksgiving, of 1940, 162
Theater. *See also* Stage and Script
  extracurricular activities in, 116
Thieu, President, 254
Thigpen, Laura W., 267, 287
Thomas, Norman, 155
Thomas-Adkins, Inc..., 134
Thompson, Hilda, 152
Thompson, Larry, 265
Thorne, James Daniel, 176, 387n 6
Thorne, John Julius, 387n 6
Thorne, Rachel, 165, 387n 6
Tilley, Tony, 209, 309, 336
Tingle, Bruce, 273, 277, 297
Tingle, J. R., 77, 78
Titanic, 45, 50
Tobacco use, opposition to, 38
Tobin, Mark, 314
Todd, Mallie C., 130
Todd, Martha M., 130
Todd, Sue. *See* Holmes, Sue Todd
Toffler, Alvin, 266

Tomlinson, Bill, 198, 199
Tomlinson, Rebecca, 199
Top Hat Dance, 210
The Torchlight, formation of, 172
"Tour de Wilson" bicycle race, 317
Town-gown relationships, 52–53
Track team, 215, 264
Trader, James Henry, III, 306
Transylvania College, heresy trial at, 80
Travel courses and programs
  for faculty, 108, 317–19
  for students, 266, 285, 304, 316–19
Troutman, William, 220
Truman, Harry, 184, 218, 219
Trustees, Board of, 350–53
Tucker, William E., 194, 265, 320
Tunstall, K. R., 4
Turner, Darryl, 405n 42
Tuten, Ina Rivers, 142, 143
Tweddale, Edward R., 100
Tweetie's, 205, 208–9, 208f, 231, 256, 270
Twisdale, Jackie, 262
Tyndall, Jesse P., 187, 189, 194, 214, 226, 267, 300
Tyndall, Olivia Philyaw, 312
Tyson, Ada, 15–16

Undergraduate Fellows Program, 298, 299, 309
Unions, student opinions on, 38–40
United States Cycling Federation, 317

Valentine's Day celebrations, 54–55
VanCamp, Jim, 220
Vandellas, 233
Vanemo, Stefan, 313, 313f
The Vanity Shop, 145
VanKeuren, Evalyn May, 195
Vause, Joel E., 67–68, 90
Veterans, returning after World War II, 173–74, 177, 388n 23–25
Vick, Blessin Thorne, 387n 6
Victor Small Lecture Series, 7
Vietnam War, 229, 234, 235, 246, 247–48
  opposition to, 249, 251–54, 252f, 396n 6
Vinson, Arnold, 405n 42
Virginia Thompson Graves Gallery, 238, 332
Volleyball, 261–62, 289, 327

Von Zollars, Ely, 48
Voting rights, for women, 35, 38

Wagner, Dwight, 229, 234, 394n 7
Wagner, Robert D., 280
Waits, E. M., 50
Wake, J. Stuart, 399n 51
Wake Forest College, attitude toward athletics, 85, 86
Walker, D. C. "Pea Head," 99
Walker, James J., 82, 83
Walker, W. Graham, 27
Wall, Amy Louise, 306
Wall, Cathy, 261f, 262, 289, 291, 398n 30
Wallace, George, 247
Walsh, John T., 78
Walston, H. H., Jr., 327
Walston, Hubert, 327
Walston, Inza, 327
Walston, Zarelda, 218, 223
Walters, James D., 166, 167, 167f
War Defense Committee, 169
War Information Center, 69
War Plan Group, 166
Ward, Dean (chef), 185
Ward, George Roberson, 138
Ward, Sarah Bain, 273, 307, 308f
  on chapel-auditorium, 145
  on dancing, 179
  at Faculty Women's Club meeting, 394n 3
  on farm, 137–38
  on food service problems, 180
  in Golden Knot Honor Society, 139
  at Hemby inauguration, 300
  on Hilley, 185
  honorary degree for, 186
  on Kendall, 152–53
  leaving college, 297
  on May Day, 143
  at "Play Day" events, 199
  responsibilities of, 186
  rules and regulations and, 189
  on student apathy, 230
  tenure of, 278
  on "Tweetie Break," 208
  windowing incident and, 257–58

Ware, Charlie (son of Charles Crossfield Ware), 384n 29
Ware, Charles Crossfield, 78f, 132
  on Caldwell, 60
  on Carolina Christian College, 2
  as Carolina Enlargement Campaign director, 106
  college roles of, 108–9
  on construction expenses, 48
  death of, 270
  on departure of college supporters, 19
  as Disciples state secretary, 126
  on faculty retention, 48
  on fund-raising in 1920s, 119–20
  on Harper contributions, 22–23
  on Hilley's accomplishments, 184–85
  on Hilley's enrollment chart, 104–5
  honorary degree for, 203
  on honorary degrees, 58
  on Howard, 158
  on importance of educated ministry, 5
  on Inter-church Movement, 77–78
  in intramural sports, 134
  on Kendall, 152
  on kidnapping prank, 76
  on Korean War, 193
  in Men and Millions Movement, 378n 19
  on *North Carolina Christian*, 77
  on Nurney gift, 71
  quoted at Hemby inauguration, 301
  on Smith controversy, 64, 65, 77
  on World War II casualties, 173
Washer, Robert, 233
The Watch Tower, controversy over, 77–79
Waters, John Mayo, 114, 130, 145, 185, 194, 238, 385n 1, 389n 4
Watson, Clyde, 9–10, 12
Watson, Kim, 336
Watson, Kirby, 167, 387n 40
Weaver, C. C., 152
Webb, David, 312
Week of Concern for Prisoners of War and Men Missing in Action, 253
Weight lifting, 216–18
Wenger, Arthur D., 212, 228f
  biography of, 207–8
  death of, 271, 272, 399n 51

Index

dedicating student union, 209
on desegregation, 241
on drinking, 256, 308n 17
explaining draft options, 192
faculty under, 265
at five-years' service, 225, 226
on food service dissatisfaction, 232
inauguration of, 215
on Kent State incident, 253
on meditation center, 268
memorial fund for, 273
as moderator for election debate, 247
recognized at President's Day, 227
as religion instructor, 190
on segregation policy, 224
selection as president, 207
in Stage and Script productions, 227
student misconduct incidences and, 232–34
on student power, 230
on Title IX requirements, 259
tributes to, 272–73
on Vietnam War Moratorium, 252
Wenger, Arthur Frank, 208
Wenger, Doris Kellenbarger, 208, 227
Wenger, Jon Michael, 208
Wenger, Mark Randolph, 208
Wenger Hall, 284
Westbrook, Hubert W., 309, 406n 11
Weyer, Charlotte, 294
WGTM radio station, 146
Wheeless, W. Kent, 406n 17
White, Ashby, 405n 42
White, Bobby, 335, 336
White, D. Jerry, 239
White, Diana, 195
White, Ned, 195
White, Travis Alden, 196f, 301
　on accreditation, 205–6
　biography of, 195
　at Chamber of Commerce Day, 202–3
　Hemby on, 195
　honorary degrees awarded by, 203, 206
　inauguration of, 196, 202
　presenting Mildred Ross gold watch, 200
　priorities of, 196–97

　resignation of, 206
　selection as president, 194
White, Travis Alden, Jr., 195
"The White House," 174, 38n24
Whitehurst, Zeb, III, 192, 273, 277, 297
Whitley, R. B., 137
Whorton, Leamon, 90
Widgeon, Billy, 198, 200, 215
Wiegmann, F. W., 125, 195
Wiggins, Mittie, 116
Wiggins, Rebecca, 273
Wiggins, Sheila Barker, 323
Wiggs, Ashton, 192, 226
Wiley, Frank, 161, 387n 39
Will and Sarah Condon Rogers Memorial Scholarship, 322–23, 406n 15
William Gear Spencer Sportsmanship Award, 291, 292
Williams, A. F., 117
Williams, Delores, 291–92
Williams, Howard Y., 155
Williams, Jerry, 198, 200
Williams, John, 313
Williams, Martin K. "Marty," 305
Williams, Melba, 273
Williamson, Ellis W., 173
Willis, Cecil, 190–91, 240, 244f
Willis N. and Orpah Hackney Memorial Fund, 14
Willis N. Hackney Library, 121, 284–85, 401n 27
　media center in, 296
　satellite dish on, 323
　writing center in, 311
Wilson, J. Chris, 305, 317–19
Wilson, John D., 198
Wilson, Mary, 187
Wilson, Woodrow, 40, 45, 62, 66, 239
Wilson Chamber of Commerce, 272
Wilson Collegiate Institute, 1
Wilson Country Club, 179
Wilson County Public Schools, college relationship with, 113
The Wilson Daily Times, 324
Wilson Drug Company, 146
Wilson Educational Television, 319
Wilson Garden Club, 120–21

Wilson Hardware, 146
Wilson Junior Chamber of Commerce, 175
Wilson Sanitorium, 117
Wilson Smoke Shoppe, 146
Wilson Welfare Association, 162
Wimpy's, 146
Winder, Mary Ida, 155
Windham, Robert, 157
Windley, Hazel, 131
Windowing, 257–58
Winstead, Elton D., III, 173, 247
Winstead, Lamar, 83
Winstead, Robert Webb, 173
Woman's Peace Conference at Zurich, 113
Women
  organization for faculty and staff, 227, 394n 3
  in World War II service, 169
Women's Athletic Association, 199
Women's athletics
  basketball, 82, 83, 86–89, 88f, 91, 98, 101, 260–62, 261f, 289–90, 314
  intramural, 218
  in 1950s, 199
  in 1970s, 259–63, 261f, 397n 27 & 30, 398n 32
  tennis, 83, 91–92, 92f, 260–61, 262, 312, 314
  volleyball, 261–62
Women's Board of Missions, 27
Women's Christian Missionary Society, 126
Women's Recreation Association, 199, 260, 262
Women's rights
  in early 20th century, 35–38
  in 1970s, 258–59
Women's Rights Convention, Seneca Falls, New York (1848), 35
Wood, Veronica, 311
Woodard, Frederick A., 2
Woodard, Susie Gray, 91
Woodley, G. D., 91
Woodrow Wilson National Fellowship, 239
Woodstock festival, 249
Wooten, John K., 157
Work-based programs, 303

World affairs. See International focus; Travel courses and programs
World War I
  college status during, 62–63, 66–70
  impact on athletics, 91
World War II
  college adjustments after, 173–74, 177, 388n 23–25
  college status before, 154–64
  college status during, 163–73
Worthington, Roberta, 8–9
WPTF radio station, 125, 128–29
Wright, Louis B., 240
Wright, W. P. "Bill," 136
Wright brothers (Orville and Wilbur), 1
Writing Center, 44, 137, 311
Wyman, Jane, 177, 178f, 179

Yavorski, Elizabeth E., 125, 385n 7
Yavorski, John, 146–48, 157, 176, 385n 7
Yell Contest, 110
Yelverton, Collins, 141
Yeuell, Claris, 5–6
Young Americans for Freedom, 235
Young Democrats Club, 218, 235, 247
Young Men's Christian Association (YMCA)
  adopting war orphan, 163
  basketball origin in, 86
  inviting black glee clubs, 151
  Raleigh, basketball game at, 89–90
  in World War I, 68, 69
Young People's Society of Christian Endeavor, 8
Young Republicans Club, 218, 219, 235
Young Women's Christian Association (YWCA), 69
  adopting war orphan, 163
  Christmas activities of, 124
  inviting black glee clubs, 151

Z. Smith Reynolds Foundation grant, 268
Zackery, Miss (teacher), 9
Zhender, Gretchen, 317
Ziglar, Richard, 202